Praise for Political Ponerology

"I was most impressed with the combination of c
treatment of evil; depth in the search for and e...
or origins of different kinds of evil and of the systems that ge...
perpetuate evil, and breadth in the rich reach of ideas across many domains of knowledge. Together they combine to make fascinating, essential reading."

—Philip Zimbardo, Professor Emeritus of Psychology, Stanford University, and author of *The Lucifer Effect*

"There are only a few books that discuss the origin and nature of totalitarian pathocracies. How does pathological behavior become dominant in a society? Łobaczewski, who lived under communism, provides invaluable psychological analysis of what M. Scott Peck termed 'the people of the lie.' Read this valuable work and you'll better understand."

—Arthur Versluis, author of *The New Inquisitions* and *Conversations in Apocalyptic Times*

"Pathocracy is one of those hidden concepts that, once uncovered, suddenly helps to make sense of the world. It explains much of the chaos and suffering which has filled human history, and which still sadly afflicts the world today. For this, we owe Lobaczewski and his book *Political Ponerology* a massive debt."

—Steve Taylor, PhD, author of *DisConnected* and *The Fall*

"Andrew Lobaczewski's *Political Ponerology* is crucial reading for understanding, possibly, political theory's most important, but certainly its most neglected, explanation of modern governance dynamics: the shadowy role of clinical psychopaths in political life. If you want to get past the standard, bridled platitudes of conventional political science, to the real beating heart of human political life, this book is indispensable. Harrison Koehli's new edition even further enriches the book's contribution, fleshing out Lobaczewski's key ideas and arguments with cross-references to his elaborations in other works, not yet available in English. Additionally, Koehli's new footnotes constitute a catalogue of essential sources for anyone keen to follow the many avenues of exploration radiating out from Lobaczewski's rich and provocative political analysis."

—Michael McConkey, author of *The Managerial Class on Trial*

"If you don't know about criminal psychopathy as it relates to the political class, I wholeheartedly suggest you check out *Political Ponerology* by Andrew Lobaczewski."

—James Corbett, The Corbett Report

"This is an extraordinary book. I cannot judge the biological aspects of the tyrannical few who rule political and economic elites in the modern era, but intuitively I am convinced that it is a pathological condition. The analysis and prognosis offered in this book rang true and valid again and again when I thought about my own work, both with regards to 1948 and ... the history of the Israeli occupation."

—Ilan Pappé, Professor of History, University of Exeter, and author of *The Ethnic Cleansing of Palestine*

"I strongly recommend this book for anyone who is managing human or financial risk in this environment or is looking to create healthy change. ... The insights are deep and rich—they require focus and concentration. And the point comes home again and again: *Ignota nulla curatio morbi*—do not attempt to cure what you do not understand."

—Catherine Austin Fitts, president of Solari, Inc., and Assistant Secretary of Housing -in the first Bush Administration

"The book you hold in your hand may be the most important book you will ever read; in fact, it *will* be. ... This book is not just about macrosocial evil; it is also about everyday evil, because, in a very real sense, the two are inseparable. The long-term accumulation of everyday evil always and inevitably leads to grand systemic evil that destroys more innocent people than any other phenomenon on this planet."

—Laura Knight-Jadczyk, founder of Sott.net, and author of *From Paul to Mark: PaleoChristianity*

"[*Political Ponerology*] impressed me in lots of ways and provoked me to think more about the nature and origin of what we call 'evil.' The strongest part of the book is the analysis of how psychopaths gain power and of the behaviour of such societies. ... In all, a book I was pleased to have read and which I hope will continue to promote the study of how a certain kind of evil spreads. And especially in continuing to name as 'evil' things that many people are unable to see as such."

—Philip R. Davies, Professor Emeritus of Biblical Studies, University of Sheffield, and author of *Whose Bible Is It Anyway?*

"I think everyone should read this book because it provides the keys necessary for understanding events that we often can't comprehend. The book describes the origins of 'evil,' its true nature, and illustrates how it spreads throughout society."

—Silvia Cattori, freelance journalist

"*Political Ponerology* is an invaluable work that every human being striving to become conscious, should read, not only for its expose of the pathology of the individuals currently in control of the United States government, but also the light it may shed on individuals closer to home, some of whom may be friends, fellow-activists, business or civic leaders. The book's purpose is ... to cultivate discernment and buttress our trust of our innate intuition in order to navigate the daunting manifestations of evil that surround us in the twenty-first century."

—Carolyn Baker, psychotherapist, professor of history and psychology, and author of *Sacred Demise*

"[T]he subject of evil is long overdue to be studied in scientific terms rather than simply as an issue approached strictly in theological or moral terms (or, as is all too frequent currently, in political terms). ... Ultimately, only social science, with a strong dose of human biological science, will be able to study and treat this human characteristic. ... The author is ... probably correct that a field of enquiry called ponerology will be dependent on many fields of inquiry of both the scientific and humanistic persuasions to become a successful antidote to this perennial bane of human existence."

—Glenn R. Storey, Associate Professor of Classics and Anthropology, University of Iowa

POLITICAL PONEROLOGY

POLITICAL PONEROLOGY

The Science of Evil, Psychopathy, and the Origins of Totalitarianism

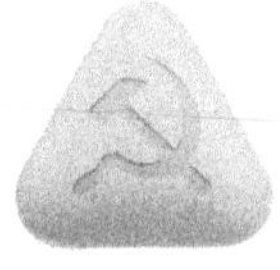

DR. ANDREW M. LOBACZEWSKI

Revised, Expanded Edition

Foreword by Michael Rectenwald
Edited by Harrison Koehli

Red Pill Press
2022

Red Pill Press
295 Scratch Branch Rd.
Otto, NC 28763, USA
www.redpillpress.com

Revised, expanded edition 2022

The original Polish text of Political Ponerology was written in 1984 and translated by Alexandra Chciuk-Celt, PhD, University of New York, NY, in 1985. The text was corrected by the author in 1998 and further grammatical and typographical corrections were made by the editors in 2006 and 2022. First published by Red Pill Press in 2006. Original English title: *Political Ponerology: A science on the nature of evil adjusted for political purposes.*

ISBN 978-1-7349074-5-2

CONTENTS

FOREWORD
by Michael Rectenwald

When I first encountered *Political Ponerology* by Andrew M. Łobaczewski, I had been struggling to understand just how authoritarian leftism had essentially taken over the United States of America. Ever since my encounters with the rabid social justice warriors as a Professor at New York University—as I recounted in my book *Springtime for Snowflakes*[1]—I began to note, with no little alarm, the authoritarian character of the contemporary left. Then the emergence of "woke" ideology and its metastasis from academia into the entire social body set me on a mission to understand the rise of totalitarianism—because I believed, and still do, that wokism is totalitarian.

I began with the Bolshevik revolution in Russia and continued by examining the exportation of Bolshevik variants to Eastern Europe and Asia. Communism was more interesting to me than Nazism and a much more neglected terrain in the U.S. academy. Further, it was more relevant in the current context. In attempting to research leftist political criminality, I was both amazed and enraged at how the academy had buried much of the history. For example, searches for the practices of "struggle sessions" and "autocritique," which were so prevalent during the Cultural Revolution in China, yielded next to nothing. These and related topics were either not treated or else simply disappeared. I suspected that a vast coverup had been undertaken.

Mind you, this area of study had never been my specialty. I had been an academic for almost thirty years. My work had been in the history of science and its intersections with culture in nineteenth-century Britain. I had latched onto a little-known development called "Secularism," founded by George Jacob Holyoake in 1851.[2] So, having relegated myself to this academic niche, I had quite a bit of catching up to do. Naturally, I foraged in *The Black Book of Communism*, a

[1] Rectenwald, Michael. *Springtime for Snowflakes: "Social Justice" and Its Postmodern Parentage: An Academic Memoir.* Nashville, TN: New English Review Press, 2018.

volume that is infamous among Western Marxists, and which, thanks to their blithe dismissal, was a book I'd never even bothered to open while a Marxist myself, let alone read. There was so much studying to do, including digging in the Stalinist Digital Archives, which were available to me as an official retiree from NYU. I also read the classic texts on totalitarianism and the literary accounts written by now famous but still too-neglected authors.

It wasn't until I read *Political Ponerology* that I had any means by which to understand the etiology of totalitarianism. Here was an author who made the bold claim that he'd uncovered "the general laws of the origin of evil." If true, this book was on par with Newton's *Principia* in the physical sciences, while being of greater practical importance. I was astonished to see the confidence and determination with which the author pursued this aim. And he approached this domain from the disciplinary perspective of psychology. Such an "individualist" methodology had been dismissed as mere "psychologism" in my own and many other humanities and social science fields. I wondered why Łobaczewski insisted on focusing on individual psychological disorders to understand the unfolding of "macrosocial evil." My assumption had always been that one needed to study political ideology and that political ideology explained nearly everything one needed to know about how and why totalitarian evil comes about.

As I first read through *Political Ponerology*, I started to become convinced that indeed a "mass formation"—a phrase recently introduced by dissidents and maligned by mainstream media in the context of covid propaganda—could begin with pathological individuals and spread throughout society, overtaking entire nations. Łobaczewski walks the reader through the process, from beginning to inglorious end. I recognized the patterns that Łobaczewski takes great pains to lay out. They matched the facts of historical totalitarianism. And I noted that these patterns hold today, down to the percentage of people that succumbs to totalitarian political ideology as well as the percentage that resists.

[2]See for example, Rectenwald, Michael. "Secularism and the Cultures of Nineteenth-Century Scientific Naturalism." *The British Journal for the History of Science* 46, no. 2 (2012): 231–54. https://doi.org/10.1017/s0007087412000738; Rectenwald, Michael. *Nineteenth-Century British Secularism: Science, Religion and Literature*. Palgrave Macmillan, 2016; Rectenwald, Michael. "Mid-Nineteenth-Century British Secularism and Its Contemporary Post-Secular Implications." Essay. In *Global Secularisms in a Post-Secular Age*, edited by Michael Rectenwald, Rochelle Almeida, and George Levine, 43–64. Boston, MA: De Gruyter, 2015.

Speaking of ideology, *Political Ponerology* explains a phenomenon that had vexed me. How did Communist ideologues manage to convince the masses that they undertook their crimes for "the workers," or "the people," or egalitarianism? But even more perplexing, how did the ideologues convince *themselves* that their crimes were for the good of the common man? Łobaczewski explains that totalitarian ideology operates on two levels; the terms of the original ideology are taken at face value by true believers, while the party insiders substitute secondary meanings for the same terms, and normal people are subjected to gaslighting. Only the cognoscenti, the psychopaths, know and understand the secondary meanings. They recognize that actions purportedly undertaken on behalf of "the workers" translate into the domination of the party and state on behalf of the psychopaths themselves. The truth is the opposite of what the party insiders claim to be the case, and they know it. *Political Ponerology* thus explains the origin of "doublespeak," which Orwell portrays so well. Coincidentally, Łobaczewski finished *Political Ponerology* in 1984.

Likewise, the book that lays before the reader is both an anomaly and a monumental achievement. It represents the inaugural volume in a new science—ponerology, or the science of evil. It explains the emergence and development of macrosocial evil thoroughly and with scientific precision.

Just how did this book come to be written and this scientific field discovered? Both were born in a living laboratory. Łobaczewski was not only one of the scientists developing its methods. He was also a subject in that laboratory. Łobaczewski came of age under Nazism with the German occupation of Poland and later lived under Communism. He became a psychologist, and given his clinical understanding of psychopathology, began to descry the psychopathological character of the Communist political system that had overtaken his homeland.

As I have mentioned, in *Political Ponerology*, Łobaczewski intervenes in this domain with a methodology—the methodological individualism and materialism of psychology—which had otherwise been thought inapplicable to it. He claims for this new science of ponerology the prospect of understanding, and more or less remedying, what is among the most pernicious developments in modern history and the source of untold suffering.

Łobaczewski argues that an adequate study of totalitarianism had hitherto been impossible because it had been undertaken in the wrong registers. It had been treated in terms of literature, ideology studies, history, religion, political science, and international politics, among other fields. One is reminded of the literary accounts and studies of the Soviet Union, the Eastern bloc, and Nazi Germany—of the classic works by Hannah Arendt, Aleksandr Solzhenitsyn, Václav Benda, Václav Havel, and many others. These had made indispensable contributions but had, owing to no fault of their own, necessarily failed to grasp the root of the problem, namely, the psychopathological dimension of the inception and development of "pathocracy," or rule by psychopaths.

The responses of normal human beings to the gross injustices and disfigurement of reality perpetrated by the ruling bodies had hitherto only been understood in terms of natural worldviews. Emotionality and moral judgments blinded victims to what beset them. The deficiencies in the approaches of scholars, as well as the moralism of laypersons, had left pathocracy essentially misapprehended and likewise left humanity without any effective defenses against it. Łobaczewski redresses these deficiencies and provides these defenses.

A crucial requirement for acquiring this knowledge is the introduction of a novel and appropriate taxonomy. Łobaczewski goes to great lengths to explain the necessity of taxonomy and to justify the introduction of objective, scientific terms, along with the concepts they convey. Every science that enters an unknown territory has had to do the same, the author reminds us. Łobaczewski rightly deems terminology essential to the task of the scientific endeavor at hand because it isolates and defines the elements and provides the tools for controlling them. "I had no choice," Łobaczewski writes, "but to resort to objective biological, psychological, and psychopathological terminology in order to bring into focus the true nature of the phenomenon..." I will leave to the editor and author himself the introduction of most of these terms along with their definitions, while noting only that the proper naming of pathocracy and its features is one of the author's major contributions. Such naming, he makes clear, provides the first best defense against its development and spread.

Sections of the book say so much that they may seem to convey mere generalities. But the reader must struggle to pay close attention as Łobaczewski discusses the normal psychological and psychosocial conditions of individuals and societies so that the emergence into power of pathological characters with their telling characteristics can be discerned, comprehended, and, if possible, prevented. These characteristics are discussed with penetrating insight and remarkable lucidity. As I did, the reader living under similar conditions will take note of patterns and will validate the author's findings by comparison to his or her own experience. He or she will thereby begin to find the defenses against the effects of pathocracy that the author promises. As Łobaczewski says, "[w]ith reference to phenomena of a ponerogenic nature, mere proper knowledge alone can begin healing individual humans and helping their minds regain harmony." Reading *Political Ponerology* thus constitutes an extended therapy session for those struggling to maintain their own sanity and humanity in the midst of insanity and inhumanity. It did for me.

For these and other reasons, the reader may find this book dizzying but also of the utmost importance. *Political Ponerology* is essential reading for concerned thinkers and all sufferers of past and present totalitarianism. It is especially crucial today, when leftist totalitarianism is once again on the rise, this time in the West, where it affects nearly every aspect of life, including especially the life of the mind.

Thus begins "an overall therapy of the world."

Michael Rectenwald, PhD
Pittsburgh, PA, February 27, 2022

Dr. Michael Rectenwald is the author of Thought Criminal *(2020);* Beyond Woke *(2020);* Google Archipelago *(2019);* Springtime for Snowflakes *(2018) and others. Michael is the Chief Academic Officer and co-founder of American Scholars, a pro-American education platform. He was a Professor of Liberal Studies and Global Liberal Studies at NYU from 2008 to 2019.*

EDITOR'S INTRODUCTION

> "Power is not a means, it is an end. One does not establish a dictatorship to safeguard a revolution; one makes the revolution in order to establish the dictatorship."
> —O'Brien, in George Orwell's *1984*

> "All governments suffer a recurring problem: Power attracts pathological personalities. It is not that power corrupts but that it is magnetic to the corruptible. Such people have a tendency to become drunk on violence, a condition to which they are quickly addicted."
> —Missionaria Protectiva, in Frank Herbert's *Chapterhouse: Dune*

> "I have always thought that in revolutions, especially democratic revolutions, madmen, not those so called by courtesy, but genuine madmen, have played a very considerable political part. One thing is certain, and that is that a condition of semi-madness is not unbecoming at such times, and often even leads to success."
> —Alexis de Tocqueville, in *Recollections on the French Revolution*

The year is 1951, just a few years after the imposition of communism in Poland and other Eastern and Central European nations. The place: the Gothic lecture hall at Jagiellonian University, Kraków.[1] Previously, students had heard lectures there by scholars like Roman Ingarden, a student of Husserl. But as the students herded into the hall that year to attend the recently introduced Marxist-Leninist indoctrination lectures, a strange man appeared at the lectern, informing them he was to be their new professor. This particular class of students—soon to graduate with degrees in psychology—were about to learn some important lessons about the nature of totalitarianism and psychopathology, though that certainly wasn't their "professor's" intention.

The man wasn't an actual professor, and it showed. He spoke nonsense unfitting for a university. The students immediately recognized this—or at least *most* of them did—and soon discovered that he had attended high school, but it was unclear if he had ever actually graduated. Whatever his education, this new "professor" treated the students with contempt and barely concealed hatred.

[1]Portions of this introduction first appeared on SOTT.net and in *The Postil Magazine*.

His tyrannical teaching style mirrored that of the communist party leadership—whom he had to thank for his new, "socially advanced" position.

The students' encounter with the new professor may not have succeeded in swaying many of them over to communism—communist indoctrination efforts were embarrassingly ineffective—but it *was* a crash course in the personalities and psychological processes at the heart of the communist system. The author of this book, Dr. Andrzej Łobaczewski (1921–2007),[2] was one of the students in that class, and he credits that professor as his first instructor in this brutal new reality. Without that professor, we probably might not have this book.

John Connelly has studied this stormy period in his book *Captive University: The Sovietization of East German, Czech, and Polish Higher Education, 1945–1956.* Regarding the template for this ideological takeover which had been established in the USSR, he writes:

> After universities had been emptied of enemies, they had to be filled with ostensible supporters: students from underprivileged social strata who would reward the regime with loyalty for upward social mobility. During the early breakthrough periods in Soviet history, preference was given to students of 'worker and peasant background.'[3]

The communists instituted a program of what we in the West call "affirmative action," actively seeking to enroll students from the "worker-peasant" class, the underprivileged who were numerically underrepresented in the education system. Remedial courses were set up to prepare such students for university. However, in the Czech lands, for instance, the Party had to enforce *downward* mobility on middle-class aspirants in order to make room for working-class students (a policy familiar to many Asian Americans today). While a success in many regards—worker students performed on par in many subjects, and excelled at others—in a reflection of affirmative action today, many of these students found themselves in over their heads, especially in technical fields, and dropped out at higher than average rates. Many suffered nervous breakdowns from the stress.[4] But this was communism, after all, and quotas must be met! So Polish and

[2]Anglicized as Andrew Lobaczewski.

[3]John Connelly, *Captive University: The Sovietization of East German, Czech, and Polish Higher Education, 1945–1956* (Chapel Hill, NC: University of North Carolina Press, 2000), p. 3.

East German functionaries solved this problem by simply lowering standards and graduating students early. Predictably, this gave students a sense of power: "at a January 1952 meeting of representatives of Poznań University with Vice-Minister of Education Krassowska, Rector Ajdukiewicz told the audience that there had been cases of 'improper behavior' among students who felt that the authorities 'have no choice but to graduate us, because otherwise they won't fulfill the plan.'"[5]

It wasn't just students who exploited the situation. In a section titled "Professors vs. Professors," Connelly describes what was perhaps "the most demoralizing experience" for faculty in those early years: the personal and professional attacks by some professors on their colleagues, leading to involuntary leave, early retirement, or dismissal. University administrations "voided the teaching qualifications of professors who had demonstrated a 'hostile attitude toward the People's Democratic regime'" and "voted to exclude fellow members who had been identified as politically untrustworthy."[6] Others used this new political climate to "settle old scores." In East Germany the "practice of voting against one's colleagues was also widespread"; sometimes professors voted to send a colleague to the state security services for ideologically incorrect remarks, in one case for remarks critical of "distinguished leaders of the working class."[7] The communist system depended on its ability to find examples of thoughtcrime, punish the offenders (whether guilty or not), and thus maintain a modicum of compliance and ideological consensus enforced by terror.

Flash forward to today, seventy years after Łobaczewski's experience of political indoctrination and the dawn of the politicization of higher education in Poland. Since at least 2016 an analogous process has been at work in universities across the Western world, though its seeds have been germinating for decades. The tortured logic of postmodernism and critical theory, "safe spaces," "microaggressions," "no-platforming," "trigger warnings," and the "cancellation" of dissi-

[4]For this phenomenon in American universities, see Heather Mac Donald, *The Diversity Delusion: How Race and Gender Pandering Corrupt the University and Undermine Our Culture* (New York: Griffin, 2018), pp. 53–61.

[5]Ibid., p. 275. One wonders if these students ever reached the obnoxious levels of entitlement displayed by those of Evergreen State College, Washington, in 2017.

[6]Ibid., p. 192.

[7]Ibid., p. 193.

dent voices are ubiquitous on college campuses.[8] (Jagiellonian University itself has not escaped the new indoctrination.[9]) Unfortunately, it's not just the universities. The current ideological virus—"social justice"—has since escaped the lab of the universities to mainstream culture: business, politics, church, education. Only this time, there was no government coercion necessary.

The fact is, social justice ideology, with roots in "gender theory," "critical race theory," and the ever-growing list of academically questionable "studies" departments, is a Trojan horse. On the surface level it promotes "diversity, equity, and inclusion" but enforces strict ideological conformity, inequality, and exclusion of those who disagree. If you have the temerity to dissent, you will be found guilty of "discrimination" (i.e., thoughtcrime) and of endangering the "safety" (i.e., hurting the feelings) of "historically marginalized groups" (regardless of what individuals from those groups might actually think). You will have proven yourself not diverse enough to be included, all in the name of equality. Its logic is Kafkaesque and its morality is Orwellian.

Łobaczewski, who died in 2007, warned about this over thirty years ago, diagnosing the psychopathological nature of totalitarianism in

[8]See ex-NYU Professor of Liberal Studies Michael Rectenwald's *Springtime for Snowflakes: "Social Justice" and Its Postmodern Parentage* (Nashville, TN: New English Review Press, 2018) for an account of his own cancellation and analysis of the ideology.

[9]In the summer of 2021, Polish conservative politician Ryszard Legutko, professor emeritus of philosophy at Jagiellonian, protested the creation and operation of a "Department of Security, Safety and Equal Treatment" at the school. Legutko correctly noted that "in the last few decades, universities have become a breeding ground for aggressive ideology—censorship, control of language and thought, intimidation of rebellious academics, various compulsory training sessions to raise awareness, disciplinary measures and dismissal from work," adding: "If we create a structure that is paid for and specially programmed to look for inequalities and discrimination, it is obvious that it will find them quite quickly to prove the reason for its existence, and sooner or later it will take steps that are taken at hundreds of other universities." All but two of the thirty-plus philosophy department faculty members then penned a response attacking Legutko for his "grotesque" "attacks." "The Students" (a nameless collective reminiscent of the ubiquitous but mostly imaginary "The People" of communist fame) joined in on the action, responding to Legutko's "discriminatory actions" and violation of others' "dignity," thus demonstrating the truth of his argument. The students, after all, were "raised in a spirit of tolerance and respect for others." As if that were relevant to Legutko's concerns.

all its forms, laying out how and why it develops, and proposing solutions in the hopes of preventing it from happening again. He had been hopeful that Poland would escape a repeat of the mass madness that led to the communist revolutions, hostile takeovers, and infiltrations of the twentieth century. He wasn't so hopeful for the United States. Unfortunately, his work remains obscure, and the window of opportunity in which it may have helped stave off disaster may already have passed. Whether or not that is the case, his book is needed now more than ever, and his ideas can help to make sense of the madness we see taking over the Western world today. But first, a brief history of how the book came to be is in order.

The History of Political Ponerology

In the years after the imposition of communism on the countries of Eastern and Central Europe in the late 1940s, a group of scientists—primarily Polish, Hungarian, and Czechoslovakian—secretly collaborated on a scientific study of the nature of totalitarianism. Blocked from meaningful contact with the West, their work remained secret both from the wider public in their own countries as well as from the outside scientific community.[10] Before his death in 2007, Łobaczewski was the last known living member of this group. This book contains the conclusions he formulated over his decades of experience living and working in communist Poland, and whatever other data he was able to gather from the other members of this group. An expert on psychopathy, he chose to christen their field of study "ponerology"—a synthesis of psychological, psychiatric, sociological,

[10]While many attempts to describe the nature of totalitarianism came out of the West in these and subsequent years (see references throughout the footnotes), none succeeded in describing the essence of the phenomenon. However, two psychological works from the period stand out as particularly important. First, American psychiatrist Hervey Cleckley's classic book *The Mask of Sanity* (first published in 1941, with subsequent editions in 1950, 1955, 1964, and 1976), while not touching on totalitarianism, was the first rigorous attempt to describe the psychopathic personality, which Łobaczewski argues is essential for understanding totalitarianism. Second, American psychologist Gustave Gilbert wrote *The Psychology of Dictatorship* (1950, never republished), an attempt to describe the nature and origins of Nazi totalitarianism based on his analysis of the Nuremberg defendants. Additionally, Harold D. Lasswell pioneered the field of political psychology with his 1930 book *Psychopathology and Politics.*

and historical studies on the nature and genesis of evil. Upon his request, two monks of the Benedictine Abbey in the historic Polish village of Tyniec provided the name. Derived from *poneros* in New Testament Greek, the word suggests an inborn evil with a corrupting influence, a fitting description of psychopathy and its social effects.

Practically all of what we know about this research comes from this book, though hints of it can be found elsewhere. Łobaczewski's sole contact with the other researchers was through Stefan Szuman (1889–1972), a retired professor who passed along anonymous research summaries to members of the group. The consequences for being discovered were severe; scientists faced arrest, torture, or even a fatal "accident at work," so a strict conspiracy of secrecy was essential. They safeguarded themselves and their work by adopting the mode of operation learned during the past decade of resistance to Nazi and Soviet occupation. This way, if any were arrested and tortured, they could not reveal the names and locations of their confederates.

In later interviews and writings, Łobaczewski only shared the names of two other Polish professors of the previous generation who were involved in some way in the early stages of this work—Stefan Błachowski (1889–1962) and Kazimierz Dąbrowski (1902–1980). Błachowski apparently died under suspicious circumstances; Łobaczewski speculated that the state police murdered him for his part in the research. Around this time, Dąbrowski emigrated and, unwilling to renounce his Polish citizenship in order to work in the United States, took a position at the University of Alberta in Canada, where he was able to retain dual citizenship. A close reading of Dąbrowski's published works in English shows the theoretical roots of what would eventually become ponerology.[11]

Like Łobaczewski, Dąbrowski considered psychopathy to be "the greatest obstacle in development of personality and social groups."[12] He warned: "The general inability to recognize the psychological type of such individuals causes immense suffering, mass terror, violent op-

[11]Unfortunately, only two of Dąbrowski's English-language books are currently in print. A digital archive containing scans of his entire body of work is available from https://www.positivedisintegration.com/. For an introduction to his life and work, see William Tillier, *Personality Development through Positive Disintegration: The Work of Kazimierz Dąbrowski* (Anna Maria, FL: Maurice Bassett, 2018).

[12]Translated by Elizabeth Mika in "Dąbrowski's Views on Authentic Mental Health," in Sal Mendaglio (ed.), *Dąbrowski's Theory of Positive Disintegration* (Scottsdale, AZ: Great Potential Press, 2008), pp. 139–53.

pression, genocide and the decay of civilization. ... As long as the suggestive [i.e., hypnotic, 'spellbinding'] power of the psychopath is not confronted with facts and with moral and practical consequences of his doctrine, entire social groups may succumb to his demagogic appeal."[13] In one of the first explicit mentions of political psychopathy, he remarked that the extreme of ambition and lust for power and financial gain "is particularly evident in criminal or political psychopathy."[14]

> Methods are developed for spreading dissension between groups (as in the maxim "*divide et impera*" [divide and rule]). Treason and deceit in politics are given justification and are presented as positive values. Principles of taking advantage of concrete situations are also developed. Political murder, execution of opponents, concentration camps and genocide are the product of political systems at the level of primary integration [i.e., psychopathy].[15]

In a passage decades before its time, Dąbrowski observed that less "successful" psychopaths are to be found in prisons, while successful ones are to be found in positions of power, i.e., "among political and military national leaders, labor union bosses, etc." (The concept of corporate or "successful" psychopathy only took off in the West in the last couple decades.) He cited Hitler and Stalin as two such examples of leaders characterized by this "affective retardation," both of whom showed a "lack of empathy, emotional cold-ness, unlimited ruthlessness and craving for power."[16]

Dąbrowski and Łobaczewski experienced this horror firsthand. In September 1939, the Nazis invaded Poland, after which they instituted a regime of terror that resulted in the deaths of an estimated six million Poles. As part of a larger goal of destroying all Polish cultural life, schools were closed and professors were arrested, sent to concentration camps, and some murdered.[17] Psychiatry was outlawed and, according to Jason Aronson of Harvard Medical School,

[13]Dąbrowski (with A. Kawczak and J. Sochanska), *The Dynamics of Concepts* (London: Gryf, 1973), pp. 40, 47. Łobaczewski calls this inability the "first criterion of ponerogenesis."

[14]Dąbrowski, *Multilevelness of Emotional and Instinctive Functions* (Lublin, Poland: Towarzystwo Naukowe KUL, 1996), p. 33.

[15]Ibid., p. 153.

[16]Dąbrowski (with A. Kawczak and M. Piechowski), *Mental Growth Through Positive Disintegration* (London: Gryf, 1970), pp. 29–30.

[17]The Soviet Union did the same. In the spring of 1940, the NKVD killed around 22,000 Polish military officers and intelligentsia in the Katyn massacre.

the Nazis murdered the majority of practicing psychiatrists. Only 38 survived out of approximately 400 alive before the invasion.[18] During this tumultuous time, Łobaczewski volunteered as a soldier for the Home Army, the underground Polish resistance organization, and his desire to study psychology grew.

The university that he would later attend, Jagiellonian, suffered greatly during the war years as part of a general program to exterminate the intellectual elite of the city of Kraków. On November 6, 1939, 138 professors and staff were arrested and sent to concentration camps.[19] They had been told that they were to attend a mandatory lecture on German plans for Polish education. Upon arrival, they were arrested in the lecture hall, along with everyone else present in the building. Thankfully, due to public protest, the majority were released a few months later. Despite the university having been looted and vandalized by the Nazis, survivors of the operation managed to form an underground university in 1942.[20] Regular lectures began again in 1945 and it was probably soon after that Łobaczewski began his studies at Jagiellonian under professor of psychiatry Eugeniusz Brzezicki, and met Stefan Szuman, a renowned psychologist who taught there. (As mentioned above, Szuman later acted as Łobaczewski's clearinghouse for secret data and research in later years.)

While Jagiellonian and the other Polish universities enjoyed a few years of freedom, this largely ended with the establishment of the Polish People's Republic in 1947 and the consolidation of power under Bolesław Bierut the year after. Poland became a satellite state of the Soviet Union, the Party took control of higher education, medical and psychiatric services were socialized, and clinical psychiatry was completely hollowed out. Thus the "Stalinization" of Polish education and research picked up where Hitler left off. Connelly writes:

> Perhaps because of the strength of the old professoriate there, the breaking down of universities went furthest in Poland. ... Restructuring shifted academic resources away from the humanities and social sciences. Previously,

[18]Preface to Dąbrowski, *Positive Disintegration* (Boston: Little, Brown, 1964), pp. ix–x.

[19]In total, 184 academics were arrested, the remainder from other universities. See https://en.wikipedia.org/wiki/Sonderaktion_Krakau and the Jagiellonian University website: https://www.uj.edu.pl/uniwersytet-z-collegium-medicum/historia.

[20]Błachowski, one of the two professors mentioned above, taught at one such underground university in Warsaw.

> one could study philosophy at any university in Poland, save the state university (UMCS) in Lublin. Now, studies in philosophy, psychology, or pedagogy were possible only in Warsaw.[21]

Łobaczewski's class was thus the last to be taught by the old psychology professors in Kraków, who were considered "ideologically incorrect" by the powers that be. As Łobaczewski tells it, it was only in their last year of schooling (1951), described above, that they fully felt the reach of the Party into university life. This experience of the inhuman "new reality" was to inspire the course of Łobaczewski's research for the rest of his life, just as the war had inspired his initial interest in psychology.

Łobaczewski grew up in a modest manor house in the Subcarpathian Province of Poland, "among old trees, dogs and horses." He practiced beekeeping and worked on the farm during summers, thus gaining some insights into hive psychology. After the war, he graduated from a mechanical high school and earned a living as a builder. During the three decades he spent living under communism after graduating, he worked in general and mental hospitals and as an industrial psychologist in the mining industry. While he was not allowed to pursue a career in academia, the intensified conditions of life in Poland provided ample opportunities to conduct his own research and to improve his skills in clinical diagnosis—skills he found essential for coming to terms with this new social reality. He was also able to give psychotherapy to those who suffered the most under such harsh rule.

Soon after the secret research project began in the late 1950s, the group tasked Łobaczewski with researching the various mental disorders contributing to the phenomenon. Originally, he only contributed a small part of the research, focusing mostly on psychopathy. The name of the person responsible for completing the final research synthesis was kept secret, but the work never saw the light of day. All of Łobaczewski's contacts became inoperative in the post-Stalin wave of repression in the early 1960s and he was left only with the data that had already come into his possession. All the rest was lost forever, whether burned or locked in some secret police archive.

Faced with this turn of events, he decided to finish the work on his own. Despite his efforts in secrecy, the political authorities came to suspect that he possessed "dangerous" knowledge. One Austrian

[21] Connelly, op. cit., pp. 60–61.

scientist with whom Łobaczewski had corresponded turned out to be an agent of the secret police, and Łobaczewski was arrested and tortured three times during this period. While working on the first draft of his book in 1968, the locals of the village in which he was working warned him of an imminent secret police raid. Łobaczewski had just enough time to burn the work in the central heating furnace before their arrival.[22] Years later, in 1977, the Roman correspondent for Radio Free Europe, to whom Łobaczewski had spoken about his work, denounced him to the Polish authorities.[23] Given the option of a fourth arrest or "voluntary" exile to the United States, Łobaczewski chose the latter and made his way to the USA. He left the country with practically nothing.

Upon arrival in New York City, the Polish security apparatus utilized their contacts in the city to block Łobaczewski's access to jobs in his field. In the case of scientists living abroad, the Polish secret police's *modus operandi* was to use dupes and "useful idiots" in the American Communist Party and related groups, suggesting certain courses of action to gullible members who then carried them out. Łobaczewski was thus forced to take a job doing manual labor, writing the final draft of his book in the early hours before work. Having lost most of the statistical data and case studies with his papers, he included only those he could remember and focused primarily on the observations and conclusions based on his and others' decades of study, as well as a study of literature written by victims of such regimes.

Once the book was completed in 1984 and a suitable translation made into English the following year, he was unable to get it published. The psychology editors told him it was "too political," and the political editors told him it was "too psychological." He enlisted the help of his compatriot, Zbigniew Brzezinski, who had just previously served as President Jimmy Carter's National Security Adviser and who initially praised the book and promised to help get it published. Unfortunately, after some time spent corresponding, Brzezinski became silent, responding only to the effect that it was a pity it hadn't

[22]Later, in Bulgaria, he attempted to send a second draft to a contact in the Vatican via a Polish-American tourist, but to his knowledge it was never delivered.

[23]Łobaczewski only learned the identity of his denouncer from the Polish Institute of National Remembrance in 2005. See the interview conducted Nov. 19, 2005: http://www.sott.net/article/159686-In-Memoriam-Andrzej-M-obaczewski.

worked out. In Łobaczewski's words, "he strangled the matter."[24] In the end, a small printing of copies for academics was the only result, and these failed to have any significant influence on academics or reviewers.[25]

Suffering from severely poor health, Łobaczewski returned to Poland in 1990, where he published another book[26] and transcribed the manuscript of *Political Ponerology* onto his computer. He eventually sent this copy to the editors of Red Pill Press, who published the book in 2006. His health once more failing, he died just over a year later, in November of 2007.

The Origins of Evil

The twentieth century was one of brutality on an industrial scale. Genocidal death squads, concentration and extermination camps, a bureaucracy of torture and terror, arrest and execution quotas, mass surveillance, Kafka-esque show trials and public executions, Orwellian propaganda as transparently absurd as it is mendacious—inhuman excesses of evil on a mass scale such as these often evoke a response such as the following: "How could a government do something like that to its own people?" Accounts of those who experienced the transition to such a system describe it like entering another world where left is right and right is wrong. Suddenly one's ideas about how the world works seem totally inadequate.

But it is not just evil on a mass scale. Relatively common crimes evoke a similar response on a daily basis. A con man scams an elderly woman with dementia, robbing her of her savings and leaving her destitute—in more extreme cases, he may even rape and murder her. A mother kills her only child and when interrogated, tells police, "What's the problem? I can always have another one." A serial killer hunts other humans, raping and mutilating them, before or after killing them, then goes home to his wife and child, who are none the wiser about his secret life. And we ask, "How could someone do something like that?"

[24]Ibid.

[25]During this time he also completed the first draft of a second book, *Logokracja* [Logocracy], which he would later substantially revise, and which was published in Polish in 2007, shortly before his death.

[26]*Chirurgia słowa* [Word Surgery], published in 1997.

Łobaczewski's thesis is as commonsense as it is novel: the answer to both questions is the same. The dynamics of evil and its genesis are similar no matter the scale—familial, social, or macrosocial. But we should first define evil—a word and concept many imprudently reject because of its alleged religious connotations. Psychologist Philip Zimbardo provides an adequate definition: "Evil consists in intentionally behaving in ways that harm, abuse, demean, dehumanize, or destroy innocent others—or using one's authority and systemic power to encourage and permit others to do so on your behalf."[27]

Answers to the second question—what explains *individual* acts of such evil?—tend to be split along the sides of nature vs. nurture. Many proponents of the latter have argued that all crime is socially constructed. Society made them do it—or their abusive parents—and nature had nothing to do with it. Change society, change consciousness, and you will eliminate crime. Others are convinced that criminals are simply bad seeds. Abusive childhoods or other environmental factors are irrelevant, cheap excuses for poor character.

The first question—what explains acts of *mass* evil, such as the Holocaust?—is what led Theodor Adorno and his colleagues to attempt to define the "authoritarian personality" after World War II. It led Stanley Milgram to conduct his famous experiments on obedience to authority in 1963. Its implications revealed themselves over the course of Philip Zimbardo's Stanford prison experiment in 1971. And it's the question behind Christopher Browning's book on German Reserve Police Battalion 101, "ordinary men" tasked with murdering Jews—men, women, and children—in occupied Poland during the war.[28] But the question answered by all these researchers could be better phrased as follows: "How could seemingly *ordinary people* turn into monsters?" That is, the question contains a hidden assumption that potentially blocks off other important explanations.

The results of all these studies suggest that, under certain conditions, ordinary people *can* and *do* commit atrocities. However, there is a wide gap between that important observation and the much broader conclusion that it is *only* or even *primarily* ordinary people

[27] Philip Zimbardo, *The Lucifer Effect: Understanding How Good People Turn Evil* (New York: Random House, 2008), p. 5.

[28] Christopher R. Browning, *Ordinary Men: Reserve Police Battalion 101 and the Final Solution in Poland* (New York: Harper Perennial, 2017), which also contains summaries of both Milgram and Zimbardo's work (Zimbardo also discusses Milgram on pp. 267–276 of *The Lucifer Effect*).

who commit acts of evil, or that their participation is the most significant contributor to the phenomenon as a whole. While it may describe how ordinary people are capable of such acts, it doesn't necessarily provide a comprehensive explanation. For one, it doesn't seem to integrate the results of the best answers to the *second* question, e.g., that the vast majority of serious crime is committed *by psychopaths.* In the nature vs. nurture debate, neither side is correct, or rather, *both* are. As Łobaczewski argues, in some cases biological factors alone strongly predispose toward evil (as in psychopathy); in others the combination of biological and environmental factors (e.g., brain damage, maternal neglect, and early childhood malnutrition).[29]

Take the Milgram experiment as an example. Some obvious questions are rarely given much thought. The test subjects take on the role of an ordinary cross-section of the population tasked with following criminal orders from an authority figure (in their case, to deliever potentially fatal shocks to what they believe are other volunteers). That much is easy to translate between real-life conditions and those artificially created in the lab. But it is the *experimenter*, who commands the test subject to (as far as the subject knows) murder another subject, who is arguably the most important variable to consider if we are to understand how the dynamic plays out in real life. After all, without him, none of those apparently lethal shocks would have been administered in the first place. The fact that he has to *play* the role in the first place should tell us something, because he ordinarily wouldn't do so in his everyday life. Otherwise we would have an epidemic of researchers routinely having test subjects murder other test subjects. The question isn't so much why ordinary people commit atrocities (though the answers to that question are informative), but *who gives the orders.* What real-life situation is being modeled in the lab, and what are its essential features?

Let's take a closer look at the results for a clue. The vast majority of test subjects were indeed willing to deliver a deadly electric shock on the orders of the experimenter under certain conditions (though compliance went down under different conditions, for instance, when another test subject refused). However, the devil is in the details. Milgram and Zimbardo's experiments demonstrated similar trends to those observed in the German police battalion records: a small

[29]See now Adrian Raine, *The Anatomy of Violence: The Biological Roots of Crime* (New York: Vintage, 2014).

minority (less than 20%) who *refuse* to kill, a much larger group of *reluctant* participants (who adapt themselves to the situation but might refrain from killing when not observed), and *a small nucleus of sadistic, enthusiastic killers.*[30] In Milgram's experiment, the majority who administered deadly shocks did so *reluctantly.*[31] Just as the experimenter wouldn't ordinarily order people to execute others for trivial reasons, the test subjects hadn't ordinarily been instructed to administer deadly shocks to others. The situation was *novel* and the vast majority only complied despite mounting inner tension. They were visibly uncomfortable, sweating, and emotionally overwrought. Many of the German reserve policemen described by Browning would vomit after committing atrocities, at least at first, and proceed to drink themselves into a stupor later. So in real life, who is most likely to take the role played by the *experimenter*, the ones deciding the policy and giving the orders? Do they tend to be "ordinary people," too? Or do humans tend to self-select according to other psychological criteria, like the small group of sadistic killers who discovered a new calling in life?

Again, Łobaczewski's answer is so commonsense as to be obvious in retrospect, yet rarely has it been stated with any degree of clarity. Ian Hughes summarizes this perspective in response to Zimbardo, who wrote that those who perpetrate evil and heroic deeds "are basically alike, in being just ordinary, average people." That may be true—when it comes to average people. However, Hughes writes:

[30]Browning, op. cit., pp. 168, 171–176. Even the reserve battalion was a special case and arguably composed of a more representative sample of "ordinary" Germans than a group like the SS with its own psychological selection mechanisms. For example, a study of 1,581 Nazi genocide perpetrators found that most either were long-term Nazis or had a pre-existing history of violent extremism. See Michael Mann, "Were the Perpetrators of Genocide 'Ordinary Men' or 'Real Nazis'? Results from Fifteen Hundred Biographies," *Holocaust and Genocide Studies* 14, no. 3 (2000). Commenting on the Nazi movement in Germany in the 1930s, Christopher Browning writes: "Apart from the activists, the vast majority of the general population did not clamor or press for anti-Semitic measures. ... Yet this majority was critical of the hooliganistic violence of party radicals toward the same German Jews whose legal persecution they approved" (op. cit., p. 200).

[31]Łobaczewski would call this type of obedience a "para-appropriate response," i.e., one that is appropriate or adaptive within certain parameters, but which becomes maladaptive or ponerogenic outside those parameters. See the subheading on the topic in Chapter IV.

> Modern psychology ... challenges the idea that we are all equally capable of violence and greed. While history clearly shows that ordinary people can, and do, participate in acts of atrocity, modern psychiatry is revealing that a small but significant minority have an innate and seemingly unalterable ability to treat others with brutality and disdain, of a different order to that of the majority.[32]

Pointing out that the tyrants of the twentieth century did not act alone, he adds:

> Instead, they were all part of a mass movement comprised of a small percentage of psychologically disordered individuals who were able to co-opt many psychologically normal people to their cause. A key to understanding the danger that people with dangerous personality disorders pose, therefore, is to understand how individual disorders become mass pathology.[33]

Humanity is complex, and an understanding of evil will require a sufficient understanding of this complexity. For example, humans vary on a number of traits. The current best model breaks down human personality into five traits which vary independently of each other: openness, conscientiousness, extraversion, agreeableness, and neuroticism. Conservatives tend to be higher in conscientiousness, and liberals are more likely to be higher in openness. Additionally, the "dark triad" model was developed to capture the traits most often associated with callous, malevolent individuals: narcissism, psychopathy, and Machiavellianism. The HEXACO model adds a sixth dimension to the big five, humility-honesty, which some argue may help capture the dark triad character traits. The dangerous personality disorders Hughes mentions, and those described by Łobaczewski in this book, may well fall under a model of this sort.[34]

Only when these individual traits are combined with group processes like negative selection (the process by which ordinary people of talent are removed from existing social hierarchies and replaced

[32]Ian Hughes, *Disordered Minds: How Dangerous Personalities Are Destroying Democracy* (Winchester, UK: Zero Books, 2018), p. 9.

[33]Ibid., p. 25.

[34]For example, low humility-honesty (e.g., low fairness and greed avoidance) combined with high conscientiousness (orderliness, perfectionism) may result in a diagnosis of obsessive-compulsive personality disorder; low h-h combined with high extraversion—histrionic personality disorder; with low extraversion and high neuroticism—avoidant personality disorder; with low extraversion and low neuroticism—schizoid personality disorder; with low agreeableness and low conscientiousness—antisocial personality disorder; with low agreeableness, low conscientiousness, and low neuroticism—psychopathy; etc.

by people with various personality disorders), and social processes like psychological induction (e.g., social contagion, mass hysteria, "spellbinding"), do we begin to approach that level of complexity.

This is the picture Łobaczewski provides, though greatly simplified. On the interpersonal level, personality-disordered individuals have a traumatizing effect on the psyches of others, especially their children, deforming their patterns of thought, feeling, and behavior, though the degree of deformation may vary according to the child's own personality traits. On the social level, such individuals can spellbind or mesmerize others with ideologies, mobilizing support by operationalizing grievances and amplifying ethnic and class divisions. The genesis of evil involves a complex web of causation including the diverse range of "ordinary" people responding within unordinary or extraordinary circumstances (which can include various social ills and conflicts) and the personality-disordered "Machiavellian" individuals exploiting and shaping those circumstances to their own advantage.

Finally, on the macrosocial level, an active nucleus of such individuals has a similar effect on *an entire population.* Such dynamics repeat, fractal-like, at all levels. A tyrant at the top is mirrored by tyrants at the bottom, enforcing pathological norms, punishing dissent, and rewarding those who best adapt to the new system. The majority only comply reluctantly, adapting to life at the cost of deformations to their own conscience.

Ponerology Today

In the opening of Chapter V of this book, Łobaczewski asks the reader to picture himself in a large, gothic university building: the lecture hall of Jagiellonian University mentioned above.[35] He thus places us, his readers, in his own place, to experience for ourselves what he experienced. He then proceeds to recount the experiences catalyzed by the "new professor," which would determine and inspire the rest of his personal and professional life, and ultimately, the conclusions contained in this book. His hope is that we will thus learn what he came to learn only after many years of suffering and effort,

[35] In the first edition, this section was placed at the beginning of Chapter I, since it provides such an engaging introduction to the themes and backstory to the book. For this edition I have moved it back to its original position in Chapter V, but new readers should feel free to skip ahead to read it if they so choose.

and possibly avoid a fate similar to that of all those who suffered under one of the worst tyrannies of human history ("communism")—a psychological immunization strategy he describes in Chapter IX.

It is an apt literary strategy, because within this recollection are all the essential features of his subject: the nature of that phenomenon most often called totalitarianism. Though he didn't know it at the time, his encounter with the new professor and the effect of that professor on a small percentage of the student body represented a microcosm of the phenomenon then metastasizing in Poland. This phenomenon would go on to characterize the communist nations for the next forty years.

The despotism of an entire empire played itself out in that lecture hall. The new professor played the role of petty tyrant, a Dolores Umbridge–type figure spewing ideological drivel with the self-certainty of a revolutionary zealot, ruling with an iron fist, and enforcing rules that violated all prior norms of common decency and scientific respectability. The reaction among most students was one of psychological shock. Social and emotional bonds were broken, and the class quickly became polarized along somewhat mysterious lines. Not *all* students were repulsed by the professor's personality, boorish behavior, and nonsensical ideas. Some 6% were swayed to his side, aping his manner, adopting his ideology, and turning on their former friends and colleagues. For some this was only temporary, but others joined the Party, becoming petty tyrants themselves. But only ever 6%. There was a natural limit to the number of recruits the professor could fish out of the student body.

The odd thing about this new division was that it replicated itself at every social level. Whether in the village or the city, among the rich or poor, religious or atheist, educated or not, the new division sliced straight through all prior social divisions. And for the next forty years, this 6% formed the core of the new leadership, as if they were individual iron filings attracted by the pull of some invisible magnet, the criteria for which bore no resemblance to those which had previously obtained, like talent, merit, experience, virtue, wealth, or birth.

Łobaczewski argues that communism was not just a "different" political or economic system, i.e., a one-party state with a command economy vs. liberal democracies with free markets. Those categories cannot adequately account for its inhuman brutality and mendacity. (Nor can they adequately explain the periods of madness that precede such systems coming into being.) Rather, he and his colleagues were convinced that communism represented a "macrosocial pathological phenomenon"—a social disease and a pathologically inverted social system. The Bolsheviks didn't just take over the Russian Empire; the revolution was not just a coup, as if one political party was violently kicked out and another moved in to take its place, one that just happened to have different policy objectives and plans for the empire. No, there was something fundamentally different about the Bolsheviks that distinguished them from other political groups, something in addition to, and *behind*, their ideology. In the decades following the revolution, the Soviets proceeded to completely destroy the existing social structure and replace it with something fundamentally new and different. For Łobaczewski, the only thing that came close to providing an adequate description of the nature of this phenomenon was the language of psychology, specifically in the field of psychopathology.

The radical restructuring of society during these years—helped along by violent purges at all levels—was in reality *an enforced psychological selection process.* In a normal and healthy society, social relations and status are governed by certain psychological criteria based in human nature, like talent, competence, and virtue. A computer programmer should be able to program. His boss should be competent. And people in positions of power and influence should have a degree of personal virtue and character. Those caught up in legitimate scandal—for corruption, breaches of basic morality, and criminal activity—lose their good standing in society. Those who grossly violate basic social norms are penalized—like psychopaths (who make up something like 20% of the American prison population). No society is perfect in this regard, but on the whole, this is how humanity *tends* to self-select, and the degree to which a society's individuals are well suited to their occupation and social position is a good measure of the health of said society. By necessity this society will be stratified. Some will always be richer than others, smarter, more talented, beautiful, or successful, and there will always be criteria (some more arbitrary than others) for inclusion in the higher classes.

The revolution and its artificial, top-down reproduction in satellite countries, as a great leveler, destroyed all this. It tore down the previous social strata and their foundations and replaced them with deviant psychological criteria. Like a criminal gang in which one must "prove oneself" by participation in violence and theft, the criteria for inclusion in the "new class," to use Milovan Djilas's phrase, were distinctly psychopathological. It should come as no surprise that a system that actively and explicitly promoted the absence of conscience came to be dominated by those without conscience. In fact, Łobaczewski's "new professor" wasn't just an uneducated Party hack. He was also a psychopath.

The science of psychopathy was still in its infancy at the time of the Russian Revolution in 1917, and the scientific works that would go on to shape the course of future research would only be published decades later in 1941.[36] Łobaczewski, lacking access to these and future developments from the West, came to similar conclusions about the subject independently, finding confirmation of his own thinking only after moving to New York. But he had been well prepared for a study of what was happening in the years to come. Jagiellonian at that time boasted a formidable psychology and psychiatry department—until the new political leadership ideologically neutered it (relevant textbooks were soon "memory-holed" and subdisciplines banned). No one educated from that point on had the necessary facts at their disposal, and the totalitarian nature of the new system meant that research not only couldn't be procured from abroad; it couldn't be shared *within* the country without the risk of arrest, torture, or death.

Psychopathy is a personality disorder characterized by a range of interpersonal-affective traits and antisocial behaviors. Psychopaths are manipulative and charming. They're also ruthless and completely self-centered. They don't feel emotion the way other people do. They feel no guilt, shame, or fear. They're the type of person to sell out their own mothers, all while convincingly assuring others of what great, loving sons they are. The most widely used assessment tool is Canadian psychologist Robert D. Hare's Psychopathy Checklist–Revised (PCL-R). Here are its items: glibness/superficial charm, grandiose sense of self-worth, pathological lying, conning/manipulative, lack of remorse or guilt, shallow affect, callous/lack of empathy,

[36]The basic concept had been around since the early 1800s ("moral insanity"), and was further developed in the early 1900s by researchers like Kraepelin and Schneider, but it wasn't until the late 1930s and early '40s (Henderson, Karpman, and Cleckley) that the focus turned from antisocial and immoral behaviors to core personality features. See Nicholas D. Thomson, *Understanding Psychopathy: The Biopsychosocial Perspective* (New York: Routledge, 2019), pp. 17–21.

failure to accept responsibility, need for stimulation, parasitic lifestyle, no realistic long-term goals, impulsivity, irresponsibility, poor behavioral controls, early behavioral problems, revoke conditional release, criminal versatility. Here is how Paul Babiak and Robert Hare describe them:

> Our point is that several abilities—skills, actually—make it difficult to see psychopaths for who they are. First, they have a talent for "reading people" and for sizing them up quickly. They identify a person's likes and dislikes, motives, needs, weak spots, and vulnerabilities. They know how to play on our emotions. We all have "buttons" that can be pushed, and psychopaths, more than most people, are always ready to push them ... Second, many psychopaths have excellent oral communication skills. They can jump right into a conversation without the social inhibitions that hamper most people. They make use of the fact that the content of a message is less important than its delivery. A confident, aggressive delivery style—larded with jargon, clichés, and flowery phrases—makes up for the lack of substance and sincerity in their interactions with others. This skill, coupled with the belief that they deserve whatever they can take, allows psychopaths to use effectively what they learn about a person against the person as they interact with him or her—they know what to say and how to say it to exert influence. Third, they are masters of managing the impressions of others; their insight into the psyche of others combined with a superficial—but convincing—verbal fluency allows them to change their personas skillfully as it suits the situation and their game plan. They have an ability to don many masks, change "who they are" depending upon the person with whom they are interacting, and make themselves appear likable to their intended victim.[37]

Making up an estimated 1% of the general population, researcher Kent Kiehl argues that the vast majority (over 90%) of adult male psychopaths are either in prison or otherwise caught up in the American criminal justice system, e.g., on parole or probation.[38] A substantial number of "successful" psychopaths (many of whom are criminals who just haven't yet been caught) can be found working for temp agencies.[39] Needless to say, they make for poor employees. However, the most gifted successful psychopaths—more intelligent and

---

[37]Paul Babiak and Robert D. Hare, *Snakes in Suits: Understanding and Surviving the Psychopaths in Your Office* (New York: Harper Business, 2019), pp. 49–50.

[38]Kent A. Kiehl and Morris B. Hoffman, "The Criminal Psychopath: History, Neuroscience, Treatment, and Economics," *Jurimetrics* 51 (2011): 355–397.

[39]In a study on temp-agency workers, Raine found that up to one out of three were psychopathic. Just under half had never been convicted for crimes they admitted to committing. These "successful" psychopaths showed greater than average executive functioning compared to the poor functioning of the unsuccessful, among other physiological differences (see Raine, op. cit., pp. 120–28).

less impulsive than those found in prison or temp agencies—may con their way into positions of influence and prestige (though, as with the gifted generally, they will be outnumbered by their more mediocre counterparts). Hare, the world's leading expert on psychopathy, once remarked that if he didn't study psychopaths in prison, he would do so at the stock exchange. Psychopaths may in fact be *over*represented in such places, "on the assumption that psychopathic entrepreneurs and risk-takers tend to gravitate toward financial watering-holes, particularly those that are enormously lucrative and poorly regulated."[40] Conning comes naturally to psychopaths: even experts with years of experience interacting with them are regularly fooled. Cleckley called this expertise in impression management a "mask of sanity" (the title of his classic book on the subject).

In communism, by contrast, Łobaczewski found this reality reversed. Practically *all* of society's psychopaths integrated into the new system; the proportion approached 100%. It was *their* presence and influence that was responsible for alien, brutal, and anti-human nature of the totalitarian regime, their methods, and the surreal quality of the new system, shaping its motivations, goals, and practices. Imagine a system of government where all of these individuals—career criminals, irresponsible freeloaders, incompetent egotists, and savvy, intelligent manipulators—find themselves in positions of influence within every social institution: at all levels of government, the military, federal and local police, the courts, education, business, factories, homeowners' associations, youth groups. This process, which took place over decades in the USSR, was artificially reproduced in Eastern Europe over the course of about a decade after WWII (though nowhere near as successfully, for reasons Łobaczewski gives in Chapter V).

One of the primary questions ponerology seeks to answer is what gives totalitarianism its defining "flavor," in all its varieties. Though Nazi Germany, the USSR, Mao's China, and Pol Pot's Cambodia all had important and sometimes profound differences, the similarities were significant enough that political scientists have tended to classify

Researchers hypothesize that IQ, socioeconomic status, parenting style, and executive brain function may contribute to the severity of the disorder, as measured by antisocial behavior.

[40] "The Wall Street Ten Percenters" (May 20, 2012), http://www.hare.org/comments/comment2.html. On corporate psychopathy, see Babiak and Hare, *Snakes in Suits* (2019).

them all as "totalitarian." But one can't escape the feeling that the classic studies of totalitarianism are missing something important, that they haven't delved deeply enough into the heart of the matter. It is like trying to focus on an object that remains forever in your peripheral vision—you know it is there, but can't quite make out the details. Just as a personal encounter with a psychopath can leave one bewildered, terrorized, and demoralized (and broke)—especially when one does not know what exactly one has just experienced—so too does an encounter with psychopathy on the macrosocial level.

Psychopaths see and experience the world differently. They think the world owes them something—or everything—and they have zero qualms about using any and all means necessary to get what they want and keep it, whether terror, torture, murder, or extermination. If conditions don't permit those means, they're happy to stand over the ruins of your reputation or your career. It's a dog-eat-dog world, the law of the jungle, survival of the fittest, and they're the fittest (in their eyes). The type of world they dream about is the one where they're in charge, not "normies" with their naïve morality, religion, tradition, and virtue. Those are for suckers. They want "freedom," "liberation," "equality," "utopia," but not in a form any reasonable normal person would imagine. They want the freedom to do what they do without going to prison or getting lynched in the street.

In the last century, political psychopaths used convenient ideologies like communism, fascism, and Islamism to achieve absolute power in multiple countries—ideologies with wide appeal and enough public support to carry them to the top, often unbeknownst to the naïve true believers caught up in the madness and clearing the way for them. (When the time comes, it is the true believers' turn to be purged.) Social justice is just such an ideology. This is why it is a Trojan horse. To their critics, ideologies are bad enough on the surface, as they are simplistic, destructive, and often just plain wrong. But it's worse than even these critics imagine. Such ideologies are the means by which social structures are completely destroyed and replaced by pathological caricatures.

The best contemporary book on totalitarianism comes not out of any political science department, but from a religious studies professor and expert on mysticism and gnosticism: Arthur Versluis's *The New Inquisitions: Heretic-Hunting and the Intellectual Origins of Modern Totalitarianism.* Versluis identifies the pattern common not only to the twentieth-century totalitarianisms, but also to the

Spanish Inquisition and the French Revolution, tracking a common intellectual lineage connecting past forms to present ones in the process. Highlighting the importance of ideology to all these regimes, he calls them examples of *ideocracy*: "rule based on enforcement of ideology through an apparatus of centralized state terror."[41] As readers will see in these pages, Łobaczewski would certainly agree with the importance of this dimension. However, Versluis gets even closer to the crux of the matter by remarking on the ideo*pathological* nature of these systems ("pathological insistence on a rigid ideology that results in many victims").[42] Łobaczewski's name for this system brings its nature as a macrosocial disease to the fore: *pathocracy* (rule by the diseased).

Professor Zbigniew Janowski makes a similar observation in his *Homo Americanus: The Rise of Totalitarian Democracy in America*, published in 2021:

> In so far as large-scale pathological behavior is characteristic of totalitarian regimes, it is because totalitarianism not only allows pathologies to develop

[41] Arthur Versluis, *The New Inquisitions: Heretic-Hunting and the Intellectual Origins of Modern Totalitarianism* (New York: Oxford University Press, 2006), p. 141. Versluis was one of the few to identify the inquisitional and totalitarian features of the George W. Bush administrations' war-on-terror policies (ch. 13, "The American State of Exception"). Similarly, liberal feminist author Naomi Wolf argued in her 2007 book *The End of America: Letter of Warning to a Young Patriot* that the ten steps through which all violent dictatorships progress were put into place to some degree during the Bush years: 1) invoke an external and internal threat, 2) establish secret prisons, 3) develop a paramilitary force, 4) surveil ordinary citizens, 5) infiltrate citizens' groups, 6) arbitrarily detain and release citizens, 7) target key individuals, 8) restrict the press, 9) cast criticism as "espionage" and dissent as "treason," 10) subvert the rule of law. Taking a somewhat different approach, political theorist Sheldon S. Wolin, in his book *Democracy Incorporated: Managed Democracy and the Specter of Inverted Totalitarianism* (2010), contrasted "classical totalitarianism," in which revolutionary forces led by a charismatic leader seek to overthrow a decaying political system, to "inverted totalitarianism," which finds anonymity in the corporate state. "Inverted totalitarianism" gives lip service to democratic ideals while actively working to subvert them, for example by promoting the illusion of free elections when lobbyists are the ones who influence legislation. It allows a degree of dissent, as long as it remains ineffectual, maintaining control without recourse to the cruder forms of oppression characteristic of classical regimes. Instead it uses technology, mass communication, and economic forces to promote and sustain its ideology. However, as these forms of control falter, controls must be tightened and the system will come to resemble "classical totalitarianism" more closely.

[42] Versluis, op. cit., p. 152.

> and flourish to an extent that would be considered pathological in what we call free societies, but because totalitarianism is itself pathological.[43]

While Łobaczewski's description of this social disease and the role of psychopathy is groundbreaking and essential for understanding totalitarianism, another feature of his work is even more important for Western society to understand at this time: *how* pathocracy develops in the first place. Łobaczewski's own initiation into the mysteries of pathocracy was unwittingly facilitated by the "new professor." As he writes:

> He spoke with zeal, but there was nothing scientific about it: he failed to distinguish between scientific concepts and popular beliefs. He treated such borderline notions as though they were wisdom that could not be doubted. For ninety minutes each week, he flooded us with naive, presumptuous paralogistics and a pathological view of world and human affairs. We were treated with contempt and poorly controlled hatred. Since scoffing and making jokes could entail dreadful consequences, we had to listen attentively and with the utmost gravity.

Describing the students who fell under the sway of the new professor, he writes: "They gave the impression of possessing some secret knowledge ... We had to be careful of what we said to them." Unfortunately, these descriptions are not far off from what is experienced today by students across the Western world, at all levels of education. The ideology of "social justice" has moved from the unscientific fringes of the academy into the mainstream: corporations, media, entertainment, politics, the military.[44] "Diversity, equity, and inclusion" are current ideological buzzwords of the day.[45]

---

[43] Zbigniew Janowski, *Homo Americanus: The Rise of Totalitarian Democracy in America* (South Bend, IN: St. Augustine's Press, 2021), pp. 200–201. Whiles Janowski sees a tension between a purely scientific explanation for the perpetrators of large-scale evil and a morality-based judgment based on conscience, favoring the latter, Łobaczewski argues for an explanation that takes into account both: the existence of fundamentally abnormal individuals whose conscience is stunted from a very early age, and the possibility for individuals and systems to hinder the development of the moral sense in others.

[44] For a concise summary of the extent to which this "revolution" has been successful, and how it came to be so, see N. S. Lyons's "No, the Revolution Isn't Over," theupheaval.substack.com (Jan. 18, 2022).

[45] See the entries for each in Lindsay's *Translations from the Wokish: A Plain-Language Encyclopedia of Social Justice Terminology* on *New Discourses*: https://newdiscourses.com/translations-from-the-wokish/. The "Environmental,

Something is happening in the Western world—something eerily familiar to the processes described in this book and the events which took their course in the twentieth century, from the Russian Revolution of 1917 to Mao's Cultural Revolution in the late 1960s. While seeds of this process can be traced back to weaknesses and contradictions inherent in the philosophies that form the bedrock of our current sociopolitical systems, the intellectual lineage of the current social justice ideology tracks back to the postmodernism and critical theory/New Left of the 1960s and 1970s. In 2018, Professor Michael Rectenwald described this ideology as "practical" or "applied" postmodernism:

> [Social justice's] beliefs, practices, values, and techniques bear the unmistakable birthmarks of postmodernism—although one must know what to look for. For this reason, and because social justice is having such a real-world impact, I call contemporary social justice "practical postmodernism," or "applied postmodern theory." These phrases should strike reasonable readers familiar with postmodernism as oxymoronic. How could such an obscure, anti-pragmatic, and nearly indescribable set of propositions as postmodern theory ever be applied or made practical?, they rightly ask. By being put into practice, I answer. Contemporary social justice is the very impractical "practical" application of postmodern theory to everyday life.[46]

Helen Pluckrose and James Lindsay later described these ideological "mutations" as follows:

> [T]hese ideas mutated, solidified, and were made politically actionable in a set of new Theories that emerged in the late 1980s and 1990s ["applied postmodernism"]. ... [B]eginning around 2010, [the second evolution of these ideas] asserted the absolute truth of the postmodern principles and themes ["reified postmodernism"]. ... This change occurred when scholars and activists combined the existing Theories and Studies into a simple, dogmatic methodology, best known simply as "Social Justice scholarship."[47]

Social, and Governance" (ESG) index for rating corporations is a similar corporate tool for ideological control. See Rectenwald, "The Woke Hegemony: The ESG Index and The Woke Cartels" (*Lotus Eaters*, Feb. 23, 2022).

[46]Rectenwald, *Springtime for Snowflakes*, p. xiii.

[47]Helen Pluckrose and James Lindsay, *Cynical Theories: How Activist Scholarship Made Everything about Race, Gender, and Identity – and Why This Harms Everybody* (Durham, NC: Pitchstone, 2020), p. 17. See also Douglas Murray, *The Madness of Crowds: Gender, Race and Identity* (London: Bloomsbury Continuum, 2021); and Stephen Baskerville, *The New Politics of Sex: The Sexual Revolution, Civil Liberties, and the Growth of Governmental Power* (Kettering, OH: Angelico Press, 2017).

Eastern Europeans living in or visiting the United States or Canada experience a troubling sense of déjà vu. Łobaczewski writes about the social climate of the USA during the 1980s: "Grey-haired Europeans living in the U.S. today are struck by the similarity between these phenomena and the ones dominating Europe at the times of their youth [i.e., pre-WWI]." But whereas Europeans in the 1980s saw conditions in America as similar to turn-of-the-century Europe, today they see America as increasingly totalitarian and resembling life under communist ideology. In his book *Live Not by Lies: A Manual for Christian Dissidents*, journalist Rod Dreher writes: "I spoke with many men and women who had once lived under communism. I asked them ... Did they also think that life in America is drifting toward some sort of totalitarianism? They all said *yes*—often emphatically."[48] The same can be said for Chinese immigrants.[49]

Two conservative Polish philosophers have written challenging but important books on the subject. Professor Ryszard Legutko's 2016 book *The Demon in Democracy: Totalitarian Temptations in Free Societies* (originally written in 2012) was one of the first to identify these tendencies in democratic countries. His first inkling came on a visit to the U.S. during the '70s upon witnessing the "extraordinary meekness and empathy toward communism" among several liberal-democratic friends. These thoughts were renewed in the wake of 1989, when Polish anticommunists were seen as a threat to liberal democracy; and further in the '90s through his experience working in the European Parliament—"a stifling atmosphere typical of a political monopoly."[50] Zbigniew Janowski, in his already-mentioned *Homo Americanus*, writes:

> Only few Americans seem to understand that we, here in the United States, are living in a totalitarian reality, or one that is quickly approaching it. Any visitor from a country formerly behind the totalitarian Iron Curtain quickly notices that the lack of freedom in today's America is, in many respects, greater than what he had experienced under socialism ... the behavior of

[48] Rod Dreher, *Live Not by Lies: A Manual for Christian Dissidents* (New York: Sentinel, 2020), p. xi.

[49] See, for example, Xiao Li, "America's Cultural Revolution Is Just Like Mao's," *UnHerd* (Jul. 6, 2020), and Wenyuan Wu, "Mao's Red Guards and America's Justice Warriors," *Minding the Campus* (Oct. 4, 2021). See also the interviews with Lily Tang Williams at https://www.youtube.com/channel/UCDPh5TTtWO5PBxJadJbGN_Q.

[50] Ryszard Legutko, *The Demon in Democracy: Totalitarian Temptations in Free Societies* (New York: Encounter Books, 2018), pp. 1, 4.

> today's Americans is painfully reminiscent of the old Homo Sovieticus, and even more of the Chinese man of the period of the Cultural Revolution.[51]

And on the current political climate, Dreher writes:

> In the West today, we are living under decadent, pre-totalitarian conditions. Social atomization, widespread loneliness, the rise of ideology, widespread loss of faith in institutions, and other factors leave society vulnerable to the totalitarian temptation to which both Russia and Germany succumbed in the previous century.[52]

Over the last few years, similar observations about the increasingly totalitarian nature of Western (particularly North American) politics and culture have come from all parts of the political spectrum, including sociologist Mathieu Bock-Côté, professor of international relations Angelo Codevilla, political scientist Wayne Cristaudo, humanities professor Paul Gottfried, political scientist Gordon M. Hahn, mathematician James Lindsay, liberal scholar Michael Rectenwald, Arthur Versluis, and feminist author Naomi Wolf.[53]

Now in 2022, in addition to social justice, the global response to the COVID-19 crisis has seen a troubling rise of authoritarian measures more or less worldwide, many willingly accepted by populations.[54] This headline captures the mentality: "We need Big Brother to defeat this virus" (*The Times*, Apr. 20, 2020). Naturally, critics of the (often blatantly illegal) totalitarian power grabs and policies are labeled "racist," "misogynist," and just downright bad people.

---

[51] Janowski, op. cit., pp. 1, 12.

[52] Dreher, op cit., p. 93.

[53] See the bibliography for relevant articles and books by these authors.

[54] See for example, Robert F. Kennedy Jr.'s talk, "Pandemic and the Road to Totalitarianism," Ron Paul Institute (Oct. 8, 2021), and his book, *The Real Anthony Fauci: Bill Gates, Big Pharma, and the Global War on Democracy and Public Health* (New York: Skyhorse, 2021); John G. West's "The Rise of Totalitarian Science, 2022 Edition," *Evolution News and Science Today* (Jan. 31, 2022); psychoanalyst Norman Doidge's four-part article "Needle Points: Why So Many Are Hesitant to Get the COVID Vaccines, and What We Can Do about It," *Tablet* (Oct. 27, 2021); Michael Rectenwald's article "Living in the Age of Covid: 'The Power of the Powerless'" (*The Mises Institute*, Aug. 18, 2021), which draws connections between the bureaucratic "post-totalitarianism" of late-stage communism and what he sees as the specter of a "covid post-totalitarianism," with reference to Václav Havel's classic 1978 essay, "The Power of the Powerless"; and Rectenwald's novel, *Thought Criminal* (Nashville, TN: New English Review Press, 2020).

Whether our future more resembles Huxley's *Brave New World* (a hedonistic, technocratic "soft" totalitarianism, in which people fully accept their slavery, with practically no dissent) or Orwell's *1984* (brutally oppressive, "a boot stamping on a human face—forever"), or some combination of the two, remains to be seen. Our gulags may simply be "social credit house arrest."[55] Or it may be the case that Huxley must necessarily transform into Orwell. Reading Łobaczewski suggests the latter—unless a society's social structure, norms, religion, traditions, and institutions are strong enough to repel the assault. Unfortunately, one look at the state of such things in the West doesn't leave much room for hope.

Book Summary

The book can be divided into introductory and foundational material (Chapters I–IV), followed by the application of that material to the phenomenon of pathocracy and specific areas of interest (V–VIII), and solutions and conclusions in the final two chapters (IX–X). After a short introductory chapter, Chapter II introduces the basic psychological concepts that will serve as background for the phenomena described in subsequent chapters (especially Chapter IV). These concepts include short overviews of Łobaczewski's understanding of individual and group psychology, the shortcomings of common understandings of each, and key features of human nature that are relevant to his subject matter, e.g., psychological functions like associative memory, general and emotional intelligence, the natural variability of these capacities and individual talents, socio-professional adjustment (the degree to which one's occupation makes use of one's talents), and the phenomenon of social hysteria (a measure of the degree to which any given society is subject to emotional contagion, cognitive errors, and loss of common sense).

The features of human nature elucidated in this chapter are important for several reasons. First, as human universals, they must be taken into account when drafting and implementing policies affecting individuals or groups of any size, as well as when dealing with issues of individual psychology in social interactions. When they are ignored or denied, interpersonal problems arise, policies fail, and negative consequences result. (According to Łobaczewski, all modern political

[55] https://twitter.com/ConceptualJames/status/1425136353369546753.

systems are founded on such flawed understandings to one degree or another, thus creating openings for the potential development of various types of macrosocial illness.) Second, they are the features affected or deformed in the various types of psychopathology described in Chapter IV. As such, effective human interactions and policies must not only take into account human nature, but also characteristic *deviations* from that nature. Third, these features are exploited by individuals whose cognitive-emotional makeup is deformed whether by nature or the environment, or both. Thus, knowledge of these basics can serve as protective means against dangerous personalities, as well as a guide to which courses of action have the most promising prospects for success. Finally, human nature and its variations are what determine the shape and structure of any given society, as well as the outlines of basic human morality. To the degree that certain features are ignored (for instance, when talent ceases to be a criterion for social position in any given field), the social structure will be unhealthy. By contrast, the fullest possible understanding and expression of human nature results in a healthy, creative social structure.

Chapter III describes the cycle of social hysteria (or the "hysteroidal cycle"). While secular cycles have been the object of historical, economic, and sociological study for generations, Łobaczewski stresses the importance of the psychological aspects of such cycles of growth and decline. Following the work of one of his professors, E. Brzezicki, Łobaczewski observes that the tail ends of such cycles are characterized by endemics of social hysteria which facilitate the possible emergence of pathological social structures such as the type described in Chapter V, which he calls pathocracy. At the time of writing, Łobaczewski predicted that the United States was at risk of passing through such a process some decades in the future (i.e., in the 2000s or 2010s). His predictions closely match those of researchers like Peter Turchin, whose work is described further in the footnotes.

Chapter IV then introduces the main concepts and processes of ponerology which are operative at all levels (i.e., from interpersonal and familial interactions up to the macrosocial level of national politics). The most central of these include the "psychopathological factors" commonly known as personality disorders in modern psychiatry. While the Western approach is almost exclusively descriptive (categorizing disorders by clusters of symptoms or traits), Łobaczewski classifies these factors based on their causes, distinguishing between two main etiologies: inherited and acquired (i.e., nature *and* nurture). He refers to the former as "psychopathies." These are disorders of personality, i.e., basic personality traits, rooted in abnormal development of what he calls the emotional-instinctive substratum. The most important such disorder in ponerology and the phenomenon of pathocracy is psychopathy (which Łobaczewski refers to as "essential psychopathy"). Other personality disorders of note include schizoid, avoidant (or "asthenic"), and obsessive compulsive (or "anankastic").

He breaks down the "acquired" disorders into two further etiological pathways: the result of organic brain damage (particularly in infancy) and the personality-deforming effects of certain types of parental influence (i.e., when the mother, father, or both suffer from one of the relevant disorders). The *former* he refers to as "characteropathies" (following Tadeusz Bilikiewicz), and includes the results of damage to the frontal lobes (producing effects similar to those seen in borderline and antisocial personality disorders), paranoid personality disorder, and the deadening of one's emotional responses common to various other types of brain damage (e.g., from certain drugs and infections). The *latter* (i.e., parental influences) he elsewhere refers to as "sociopathies." He argues, for instance, that paranoid personality disorder can result from either organic brain damage, or the functional effect of being raised by such an individual. Thus he identifies three distinct pathways for the development of personality disorder: genetic (psychopathy), organic (characteropathy), and social (sociopathy).

This view is resonant with, though not identical to, the current "psychobiosocial" approach to psychopathology, which argues such disorders should be understood in terms of various risk factors of distinct but overlapping types: genetic predispositions, personality traits, brain damage and dysfunction, and various social/environmental influences. According to this model, there may be environmental contributors to the disorders Łobaczewski understands as purely inherited, and biological predispositions behind those he understands as purely acquired.

He then describes further ponerological concepts, such as ponerogenic associations (groups where personality-disordered individuals are grossly over-represented, such as criminal gangs and corrupt social and political movements), dissociative or "conversive" thinking (cognitive errors), egotism (narcissism, self-importance, and the unwillingness to consider other viewpoints), "reversive blockades" ("big lies"), paramoralisms (the means by which normal moral impulses are inverted), para-appropriate instinctive responses (normally adaptive responses to situations which become maladaptive in certain conditions, e.g., when dealing with psychopathology), "spellbinders" (political agitators), ideologies (which most often include inherent flaws based on their misunderstanding or oversimplification of human nature), the ponerization process (by which groups are progressively overcome by pathological factors), etc. All of these phenomena and dynamics are rooted in the deformation or exploitation of the features of human nature already described in Chapter II.

Chapter V contains his main object of inquiry and centerpiece of the book: the nature and development of pathocracy. Dispensing with economic, political, and social explanations of totalitarianism as chronically missing the point, he presents the psychopathological roots of the main features of such social systems. Each factor described in Chapter IV contributes in its own characteristic fashion to the phenomenon described in this chapter. For instance, Łobaczewski argues that schizoids, characteropaths, and sociopaths contribute most to the early stages of pathocracy (shizoids as ideological theorists and utopian revolutionaries, characteropaths and sociopaths as ideological spellbinders, political agitators, and early administrators). Over time, psychopathic individuals gain supremacy, forming a pathological political network, at which point characteropaths and schizoids are relegated to the sidelines. While the schizoid and characteropathic phases of pathocracy are characterized by social upheaval and mass atrocities (e.g., the Russian Revolution, Civil War, and Great Terror), the psychopathic phase is relatively more stable and less violent, increasingly characterized by a dissimulative or duplicitous "mask of sanity" akin to the psychopath's (e.g., the final forty-odd years of the Soviet Union). Controls on the normal human population are more targeted, with particular attention placed on preventing exposure of the essential psychopathological features of pathocracy. This includes academic bans on certain subject matter and practices, e.g., the study of psychopathy, and necessitates limiting scientific collaboration with researchers from non-pathocratic countries, where academic freedom allows for such research. Thus, the essential diagnosis of the problem is prevented.

Łobaczewski then describes the function of ideology under pathocracy, as the mask by which its psychopathic nature is cloaked; the imperialistic expansion of pathocracy as necessitated by its parasitic nature; and the means by which pathocracy can be imposed. Pathocracy can take a primary form, in which ponerization occurs within either the existing ruling elites "above," or homegrown revolutionary forces "below" (or both), or secondary forms, when an existing pathocratic nation conquers another and imposes pathocracy by force, or "artificially infects" it via psychological, political, and revolutionary warfare.

Chapter VI describes the experience of normal people under pathocratic rule. One of the main features of pathocracy is the sharp division of society along psychobiological lines. The previous social order is destroyed and the personality-disordered segment of the population becomes the new ruling class. This eventually has the effect of creating a strong bond of solidarity among the common population, in opposition to the pathological rulership. Łobaczewski calls this the emergence of a "society of normal people," who create parallel institutions and understandings by which they learn to navigate the Kafka-esque reality in which they find themselves. He focuses on three key features: the adaptations normal people have to make in order to survive (which nevertheless have distorting effects on personality development), the development of a common language (the counterpart to the pathological doublespeak used by the pathocratic elite), and the psychological immunity or resistance developed as a result of long exposure to pathocracy. This "natural immunity" is the key to Łobaczewski's proffered treatment and prevention measures to the macrosocial disease of pathocracy. When an individual has suffered under the traumatic influence of a personality-disordered parent, family member, partner, boss, or co-worker, simply learning about the nature of such a person has a remarkable healing effect. Learning the nature of pathocracy has a similar healing effect. Thus, Łobaczewski suggests that the most effective healing measure is education. Those living under pathocracy gain an understanding that strengthens their immunity and gives them clarity of understanding; those who have not experienced pathocracy for themselves gain a kind of substitute "artificial immunity" that, while not as strong, can act as a preventive measure against susceptibility to the development of pathocracy.

Chapter VII focuses on the state of psychology and psychiatry under pathocracy (e.g., censorship, and the abuse of psychiatry as a means of repressing political dissidents). Chapter VIII deals with issues of religion. Pathocracy can take either a secular form (in which case it persecutes religion harshly), or a religious form, in which case it perverts religious institutions to create an Inquisition-like theocracy. Łobaczewski argues that religions may contain pathological material from their inception or acquire them over time, and that such material must be identified as such in order to prevent religious ponerogenesis. Religious institutions, for Łobaczewski, form the primary societal means of defense against ponerogenesis. When a primary pathocracy emerges autonomously, it indicates that the local religion has failed to prevent it.

Chapter IX presents Łobaczewski's recommendations for healing pathocracy and preventing its emergence. This includes concepts introduced in Chapter VI, including the healing power of truth, the importance of forgiveness in preventing new cycles of ponerogenesis, what approach to take with pathocratic ideologies, artificial immunization, and some specific policy recommendations such as laws barring psychopaths from leadership positions. He concludes in Chapter X with his vision of the future, which includes the main subject of his subsequent book, *Logokracja* [Logocracy], his vision of a state system founded on natural law and which incorporates a ponerological understanding.

A Note on the New Edition

As many have discovered since it was first published in 2006, reading Łobaczewski's *Political Ponerology* for the first time can be daunting—but equally rewarding. When I first dove into its pages fifteen years ago, some passages left me mystified, though others gave the distinct impression that a hole in my perception of reality had been finally filled. I have returned to the book countless times in the intervening years, always discovering some new insight. And it has only been in preparing this new edition that I realized how much of my reading and research over the years have been guided by Łobaczewski's book. I hope to have put it to good use.

Łobaczewski never planned to write this book. Another scientist was supposed to synthesize the work of others, but he fell off the map—probably into a secret police prison, or worse—and eventually so did all the others. As the only remaining member of this underground network, Łobaczewski took up the task to the best of his ability, finally completing it in exile after several run-ins with the authorities.

With this new edition I find myself in a somewhat similar position, though not nearly as dangerous. I am by no means an expert in any of the subjects under discussion here, but I have an interest in most of them and at the present time there doesn't seem to be anyone else to do the job. I hope that changes. When *Ponerology* was first written, then published, psychopathy remained a relatively obscure concept for many, and ponerology a barely glimpsed intuition in the minds of perhaps only a few. That hasn't changed much, but with dozens of recent books on psychopathy, TV specials and documentaries, and a small but growing collection of works moving in a distinctly ponerological direction, the necessary awareness of these topics is slowly entering the public consciousness.[56]

In addition to the works on totalitarianism cited above, a handful of important books have been published since 2006 that deserve to be mentioned (many of which will be cited repeatedly in the footnotes), including a steady output of works directly relevant to the "pathopolitical" aspects of ponerology. The year after Łobaczewski's book was first published saw the release of American engineer Barbara Oakley's book, *Evil Genes: Why Rome Fell, Hitler Rose, Enron Failed, and My Sister Stole My Mother's Boyfriend* (Prometheus Books, 2007). Oakley independently not only made the connection between totalitarianism and certain personality disorders and brain dysfunctions; she also identified the stable network of such individuals that makes up the totalitarian system, among other insights.[57]

In the same year, psychologist Philip Zimbardo finally published his book on the Stanford prison experiment, *The Lucifer Effect: Understanding How Good People Turn Evil* (Random House, 2007), which includes his thoughts on the experiment's wider social and political implications. While Zimbardo downplays the importance of individual character traits, and his work has received criticism as to

[56] I have done my small part to promote the book, writing numerous articles on the subject, appearing on several radio shows and podcasts, as well as hosting my own podcasts.

[57] See her description of "stable sinister systems" in *Evil Genes*, pp. 271–80, 336–337. As she writes: "Machiavellians can build tightly interlocked systems that keep naysayers in check and allow themselves to remain in control" (p. 278). Dark triad researchers have also begun studying the links to politics. See Blais and Pruysers, "The Power of the Dark Side: Personality, the Dark Triad, and Political Ambition" (2017); Peterson and Palmer, "The Dark Triad and Nascent Political Ambition" (2019); Chen et al., "The Dark Side of Politics: Participation and the Dark Triad" (2021).

the study's methodology and the conclusions to be drawn from it, his focus on the situational factors that can influence ordinary people to commit atrocities is an important aspect of ponerology, as described above.[58]

Seven years after that, psychopathy expert Adrian Raine published his own magnum opus, *The Anatomy of Violence: The Biological Roots of Crime* (Vintage, 2014), an important survey of the current state of research on the factors contributing to antisocial behavior, including strongly heritable disorders like psychopathy, various brain-damaging influences in the womb, childhood, and adulthood, and the known interventions for treatment and prevention. (A number of important works on psychopathy were also published, identified in the notes and bibliography.)

In 2018, one of the first works to directly cite *Political Ponerology* appeared: Irish physicist and psychoanalyst Ian Hughes's *Disordered Minds: How Dangerous Personalities Are Destroying Democracy* (Zero Books, 2018). Chapters 2 and 3 contain ponerological case studies of Stalin, Mao, Hitler, Pol Pot, and their respective ponerogenic networks.[59] The most recent overview of the psychological profiling of world leaders is neurobiologist and science writer Dean A. Haycock's *Tyrannical Minds: Psychological Profiling, Narcissism, and Dictatorship* (Pegasus Books, 2019). (Psychiatrist Jerrold M. Post, an analyst and profiler for the CIA from 1965 to 1986 whose work is featured in the book, wrote several of his own books and papers on the topic.)

In 2020 mathematician James Lindsay of "Grievance Studies Affair" fame published an essay inspired by *Ponerology* titled "Psychopathy and the Origins of Totalitarianism" (*New Discourses*, Dec. 25, 2020). In 2021, Joshua Slocum launched his "Disaffected" podcast, devoted to elucidating the "Cluster B dynamics" (i.e., narcissistic, border-

[58] His analysis skews toward systemic and situational factors, downplaying the active and inspirational role of those for whom personality and character *do* play the primary role. For example, Zimbardo acknowledges his own role in creating the "system" and inspiring the climate in which his "guards" came to abuse their "prisoners" (p. 329), but he does not extrapolate this to real-world applications. See the critique of Zimbardo's interpretations work in Oakley, op. cit., pp. 303–304.

[59] Hughes summarizes key ponerology concepts on pp. 25–30, which he uses to frame for his case studies (see also the references on pp. 34, 51, 67, 103, 125). One of the first to extensively review *Ponerology* was "Howard" at SystemsThinker.com (http://www.systemsthinker.com/interests/ponerology/).

line, histrionic, and antisocial) among the "social justice" left and in politics in general. Also in 2021, freelance scholar and educator Dr. Michael McConkey launched *The Circulation of Elites* substack,[60] devoted to exploring "the intersection of biopolitics, pathocracy, and the Italian school of political realism."[61]

As *Political Ponerology* reaches more readers, I hope it will produce a new generation of ponerologists who can take Łobaczewski's insights and expand, correct, and refine them. The processes he describes are currently taking place once again under new ideological masks, and there's no guarantee they can be stopped—at least not before things get a lot worse. But one thing is certain: an awareness of the concepts in this book can at least mitigate the effects for individuals. And if that happens to enough people, it will facilitate rebuilding the ties that make for a "society of normal man."

For the first-time reader, and those returning to *Ponerology* to mine its depths once more, I have provided notes with up-to-date research, relevant quotations from other sources, and other explanatory material. To the degree that I have been able, I have attempted to write the notes I wish I had had fifteen years ago. In many cases it is difficult to fully grasp some of Łobaczewski's generalities without

---

[60] See, for example, "Politics, Psychopathy, Pathocracy" (Oct. 24, 2021, https://thecirculationofelites.substack.com/p/politics-psychopathy-pathocracy) and "Psychopaths and the Managerial Class" (Nov. 17, 2021, https://thecirculationofelites.substack.com/p/psychopaths-and-the-managerial-class). See also his book, *The Managerial Class on Trial* (Vancouver, BC: Biological Realist Publications, 2021).

[61] Brief mention should also be made to chapter 8 ("Sociopathy at the Institutional Level: Corporations and Governments") of Martha Stout's *Outsmarting the Sociopath Next Door: How to Protect Yourself against a Ruthless Manipulator* (New York: Harmony Books, 2020), as well as her previous book, *The Paranoia Switch: How Terror Rewires Our Brains and Reshapes Our Behavior—and How We Can Reclaim Our Courage* (New York: FSG, 2007).

English psychologist Steve Taylor discusses Łobaczewski's concept of pathocracy in his 2021 papers, "Toward a Utopian Society: From Disconnection and Disorder to Empathy and Harmony," *Journal of Humanistic Psychology* (Jun. 2021), and "The Problem of Pathocracy," *The Psychologist* 34 (Nov. 2021).

Clinical psychologist Mattias Desmet's work on mass formation (with reference to Gusave le Bon's *The Crowd* [1895]) is also worth checking out, as it pertains to the transition from mass hystericization to totalitarianism, or pathocracy. (See his interviews with Dan Astin-Gregory [https://youtu.be/uLDpZ8daIVM] and Aubrey Marcus [https://youtu.be/IqPJiM5Ir3A]) His forthcoming book, *The Psychology of Totalitarianism* (Chelsea Green, in press), promises to deal with the subject in greater detail.

a basic familiarity with the specifics. And of course, as he points out, it is almost impossible to grasp the reality of life under pathocracy without having lived it. That's why I have tried my best to listen to those who know.

Łobaczewski's few original footnotes are prefaced by "*Author's note*" to distinguish them from my own, which are marked "—Ed." To aid in the notes' readability, the first time a source is quoted I have included only the author, title, and year of publication. Subsequent mentions use a shortened form of the title. Full publication details can be found in the bibliography.[62]

I have also checked the English translation against the 2006 Polish edition (*PPP*) which Łobaczewski prepared in 1997. Where *PPP* contains additional material not present in the English translation, I have integrated it into the text or included it in the notes prefaced by "*Author's note (1997)*" (in the latter case, most often that material which was clearly written in 1997). I have also included in the notes short excerpts from Łobaczewski's 2000 Polish booklet *Ponerologia* (a revised and expanded version of material mostly found in Chapter IV) and his 2007 Polish book *Logokracja*, which include details that expand on what he writes here. I have updated the translation in places where its meaning is at odds with the Polish, a word or phrase has been mistranslated, or the meaning was otherwise obscure. Some uncommon word choices have been changed to more familiar synonyms, e.g., "nescience" to "ignorance," "variegated" to "varied" or "diverse," "imaginings" to "notions," etc. I have also included appendices with new translations of some material unique to *PPP* (its preface and a number of paragraphs on democracy from the final chapter), as well as a short section included in *Ponerologia* in which he responds to a priest's reaction to ponerology.

My thanks go to Aneta Wolanska for assisting in translating new material and checking portions of the original translation. Iza Rosca checked the entire text against the original Polish and provided helpful comments, criticisms, and additional sources for the Introduction and notes, as well as further corrections to the English translation. Dr. Gabriela Segura provided relevant sources on medical matters. Lucien Koch and Michael Rectenwald read and commented upon the text, and Michael graciously agreed to write the foreword. Damian

[62] I have also added section subheadings for the sections under "The Human Individual" in Chapter II.

Assels designed the cover, and Sergey Kopeyko was essential in formatting the book for print.

Through my show *MindMatters* I have had the opportunity to speak with several of the researchers cited in the notes of this book, and whose work I greatly value (though sometimes our analyses may be at odds): Joseph Àzize, John Buchanan, Nicholas Capaldi, James Carpenter, Tom Costello, Rod Dreher, Zbigniew Janowski, Ryszard Legutko, Michael Rectenwald, George K. Simon, Joshua Slocum, Richard B. Spence, and Arthur Versluis. I would like to extend my thanks and appreciation to them and my cohosts, Elan Martin, Adam Daniels, and Corey Schink. Participants in the Rectenwald Reading & Writing Treehouse read drafts of chapters and the introduction, offering helpful feedback and suggestions, as well as encouragement.

It was Łobaczewski's wish to see this book made widely available, and that wouldn't be possible without all of his readers, past and future, whom I also thank. In this regard, the biggest thanks must go to Laura Knight-Jadczyk, the editor of the first edition of this book, without whom it would never have been published. It was her research page on psychopathy, with conclusions strikingly similar to many of Łobaczewski's, which initially caught his attention, prompting him to send a copy of his manuscript.[63]

And finally, thanks must to go Andrzej Łobaczewski himself, for descending into hell in order to return wiser, kinder, and armed with the knowledge necessary to stave off disaster. Whether we put it to use is up to us.

Harrison Koehli
Editor, Red Pill Press

[63]See, for example, volume 7 of her Wave series of books, *Almost Human: The Metaphysics of Evil* (2nd edition, Otto, NC: Red Pill Press, 2021), which features extensive discussions of John Nash and Ira Einhorn, and the implications of psychopathy on the politics and economics of evil. I have retained or adapted a number of her and Henry See's footnotes from the first edition. Her original foreword to the first edition of the book is now available for free on redpillpress.com.

PREFACE TO THE ORIGINAL MANUSCRIPT

In presenting my honored readers with this volume, which I generally worked on during the early hours before leaving to make a difficult living, I would first like to apologize for the defects which are the result of anomalous circumstances. I readily admit that these lacunae should be filled, time-consuming as that may be, because the facts on which this book are based are urgently needed; through no fault of the author's, these data have come too late.

The reader is entitled to an explanation of the long history and circumstances under which this work was compiled, not just of the content itself. This is, in fact, the third manuscript I have created on this same subject. I threw the first manuscript into a central-heating furnace, having been warned just in time about an official search, which took place minutes later. I sent the second draft to a Church dignitary at the Vatican by means of an American tourist and was absolutely unable to obtain any kind of information about the fate of the parcel once it was left with him.

This long history of subject-matter elaboration made work on the third version even more laborious. Prior paragraphs and former phrases from one or both of the first drafts haunt the writer's mind and make proper planning of the content more difficult.

The two lost drafts were written in very convoluted language for the benefit of specialists with the necessary background, particularly in the field of psychopathology. The irretrievable disappearance of the second version also meant the loss of the overwhelming majority of statistical data and facts which would have been so valuable and conclusive for specialists in the field. Several analyses of individual cases were also lost.

The present version contains only such statistical data that had been memorized due to frequent use, or that could be reconstructed with satisfactory precision. I also added those data, particularly the more accessible ones from the field of psychopathology, which I considered essential in presenting this subject to readers with a good general education, and especially to representatives of the social and political sciences and to politicians. I also nurse the hope that this work may reach a wider audience and make available some useful scientific data which may serve as a basis for comprehension of the contemporary world and its history. It may also make it easier for readers to understand themselves, their neighbors, and other nations of the world.

Who produced the knowledge and performed the work summarized within the pages of this book? It was a joint endeavor not only consisting of my efforts, but also representing the results of many researchers, some of them not known to the author. The situational genesis of this book makes it virtually impossible to separate the accomplishments and give proper credit to every individual for his or her efforts.

I worked in Poland far away from active political and cultural centers for many years. That is where I undertook a series of detailed tests and observations which were to be combined with the resulting generalizations of various other experimenters in order to produce an overall introduction for an understanding of the macrosocial phenomenon surrounding us. The name of the person who was expected to produce the final synthesis was a secret, as was understandable and necessary given the time and the situation. I would very occasionally receive anonymous summaries of the results of tests made by other researchers in Poland and Hungary; a few data were published, as they raised no suspicions that a specialized work was being compiled, and these data could still be located today.

The expected synthesis of this research did not occur. All of my contacts became inoperative as a result of the wave of post-Stalin repression and secret arrests of researchers in the early sixties. The remaining scientific data in my possession were very incomplete, albeit priceless in value. It took many years of lonely work to weld these fragments into a coherent whole, filling the lacunae with my own experience and research.

My research on essential psychopathy and its exceptional role in the macrosocial phenomenon was conducted concurrently with, or shortly after, that of others. Their conclusions reached me later and confirmed my own. The most characteristic item in my work is the general concept for a new scientific discipline named "ponerology." The reader will also find other fragments of information based on my own research. I also effected an overall synthesis to the best of my ability.

As the author of the final work, I hereby express my deep respect for all those who initiated the research and continued to conduct it at the risk of their careers, health, and lives. I pay homage to those who paid the price through suffering or death. May this work constitute some compensation for their sacrifices, regardless of where they may be today. Times more conducive to an understanding of this material may recall their names, both those which I never knew and those I have since forgotten.

New York, NY, August 1984

PREFACE TO THE FIRST EDITION

Twenty years have passed since the writing of this book. I became a very old man. One day, my computer put me in contact with the scientists of the Quantum Future Group who convinced me that the time had matured for my book to become useful and to serve the future of humanity. They took the trouble of publishing it.

The passing of these last twenty years has been fraught with political events. Our world has changed in essential ways due to the natural laws of the phenomenon described in this book. Knowledge has increased dramatically thanks to the efforts of the people of good will. Nonetheless, our world is not yet restored to good health; and the remainders of the great disease are still active. The illness has reappeared connected to another ideology. The laws of the genesis of evil are working in millions of individual cases of individuals and families. The political phenomena threatening peace are confronted by military force. The small-scale events are condemned or restrained by the word of moral science. The result is that great efforts of the past, undertaken without the support of objective natural knowledge about the very nature of evil, have been insufficient and dangerous. All these efforts have been made without taking into account that great maxim of medicine that serves as a motto in this book: *Ignoti nulla est curatio morbi.*[1] The end of communist subjugation has come at a high price, and those nations that now think they are free will soon find they are paying still.

The question must be asked: why was this work, produced by eminent researchers and the author for just this purpose—to prevent the spread of the disease of macrosocial evil—not able to perform its function? This is a long story. I had been recognized as the bearer of this "dangerous" science in Austria by a "friendly" physician who then was revealed to be an agent of communist secret services. All the Red nodes and networks in New York were mobilized to organize a counteraction against the information contained in this book being

[1] *Author's note*: There is no treatment for a disease we do not understand. Symptoms may be temporarily alleviated, but the disease remains and symptoms will return. [Literally: "There is no cure for an unknown disease." —Ed.]

made publicly and widely available. It was terrible to learn that the overt system of suppression I had so recently escaped was just as prevalent, though more covert, in the United States. It was demoralizing to see how the system of conscious and unconscious pawns worked; to watch people who trusted their conscious "friends"—unknown to them as communist agents—and performed the insinuated activities against me with such patriotic zeal. As a result of these activities, I was refused any assistance, and to survive, I had to take work as a laborer when already of an age to retire. My health collapsed and two years were lost. I learned also that I was not the first such emissary who had come to America bringing similar knowledge; I was rather the third one—the other two had been similarly dealt with.

In spite of all these circumstances, I persevered and the book was finally written in 1984 and carefully translated into English. It was esteemed by those who read it as being "very informative," but it was not published. For the psychological editors it was "too political"; for political editors, it contained too much psychology and psychopathology. In some cases, the "editorial deadline was already closed." Gradually, it became clear that the book did not pass the "insider's" inspections.

The time for this book's major political value is not over; its scientific essence remains permanently valuable and inspirational. It may serve a great purpose in coming times, when properly adjusted and expanded. Further investigations in these areas may yield a new understanding of human problems that have plagued humanity for millennia. Ponerology may buttress the centuries-old moral sciences by a modern naturalistic approach. Thus this work may contribute to progress toward a universal peace. That is the reason that I labored to retype on my computer the whole already-fading manuscript after twenty years. No essential changes have been introduced, and it is presented as it was written in New York all those many years ago. So let it remain as a document of a very dangerous work of eminent scientists and myself, undertaken in dark and tragic times under impossible conditions—still a piece of good science.

The author's desire is to place this work in the hands of those who are capable of taking this burden over and progressing with the theoretical research in ponerology, enrich it with detailed data to replace that which has been lost, and put it in praxis for various valuable purposes it may serve—for the good of all peoples and nations.

I am thankful to Madame Laura Knight-Jadczyk and Professor Arkadiusz Jadczyk, and their friends, for their heartfelt encouragement, understanding, and their labor in bringing my old work to be published.

Andrew M. Łobaczewski
Rzeszów, Poland, December 2005

CHAPTER I
INTRODUCTION

Hopefully my readers will forgive me for recounting here a youthful reminiscence that will lead us directly into the subject. My uncle, a very lonely man, would visit our house periodically. He had survived the great Soviet Revolution in the depths of Russia, where he had been shipped out by the tsarist police. For over a year he wandered from Siberia to Poland. Whenever he met with an armed group during his travels, he quickly tried to determine which ideology they represented—White or Red—and thereupon skillfully pretended to profess it. Had his ruse been unsuccessful, he would have had his head blown off as a suspected enemy sympathizer. It was safest to have a gun and belong to a gang. So he would wander and war alongside either group, usually only until he found an opportunity to desert westward toward his native Poland, a country which had just regained its freedom. Along the way he witnessed rape, senseless murder, and cannibalism.

When he finally reached his beloved homeland again, he managed to finish his long-interrupted law studies, to become a decent person, and to achieve a responsible position. However, he was never able to liberate himself from his nightmarish memories. Women were frightened by his stories of the bad old days and he thought it would make no sense to bring a new life into an uncertain future. Thus, he never started a family. Perhaps he would have been unable to relate to his loved ones properly.

This uncle of mine would recapture his past by telling the children in my family stories about what he had seen, experienced, and taken part in; our young imaginations were unable to come to terms with any of it. Nightmarish terror shuddered in our bones. We would think of questions: why did people lose all their humanity, what was the reason for all this? Some sort of apprehensive premonition choked its way into our young minds; unfortunately, it was to come true in the future.

***

If a collection were to be made of all those books which describe the horrors of wars, the cruelties of revolutions, and the bloody deeds of political leaders and their systems, many readers would avoid such a library. Ancient works would be placed alongside books by contemporary historians and reporters. The documentary treatises on Soviet and German extermination and concentration camps, and of the extermination of the Jewish nation, furnish approximate statistical data and describe the well-organized "labor" of the destruction of human life, using a properly calm language, and providing a concrete basis for the acknowledgement of the nature of evil.

Foremost among these books would be those written by witnesses to criminal insanity such as Arthur Koestler's *Darkness at Noon*, from prewar Soviet life; *Smoke over Birkenau*, the personal memories of Seweryna Szmaglewska from the Auschwitz German concentration camp for women; *A World Apart*, the Soviet memoirs of Gustaw Herling-Grudziński; and the Solzhenitsyn volumes turgid with human suffering.[1] The autobiography of Rudolf Höss, the commander of camps in Auschwitz and Birkenau, is a classic example of how an intelligent psychopathic individual with a deficit of human emotion thinks and feels.[2]

The collection would include works on the philosophy of history discussing the social and moral aspects of the genesis of evil, but they would also use the half-mysterious laws of history to partly justify the blood-stained solutions. However, an alert reader would be able to detect a certain degree of evolution in the authors' attitudes, from an ancient affirmation of primitive enslavement and murder of

[1]Arthur Koestler, *Darkness at Noon* (1941); Seweryna Szmaglewska, *Smoke over Birkenau* (1947); Gustaw Herling, *A World Apart: Imprisonment in a Soviet Labor Camp During World War II* (1951); Aleksandr Solzhenitsyn, *The Gulag Archipelago: An Experiment in Literary Investigation* (1973). For a modern history of the Gulag utilizing documentation made public after the fall of the Soviet Union, see Oleg V. Khlevniuk, The History of the Gulag: From Collectivization to the Great Terror (2013). —Ed.

[2]Rudolf Höss, *Death Dealer: The Memoirs of the SS Kommandant at Auschwitz* (1992 [1959]). Nuremberg prison psychologist Gustave M. Gilbert diagnosed Höss with schizoid personality (see Chapter IV of this book). See also the revealing interviews with Stalin-era Polish officials in Teresa Torańska's *"Them": Stalin's Polish Puppets* (1987), as well as Gilbert's *Nuremberg Diary* (1947) and psychiatrist Leon Goldensohn's *The Nuremberg Interviews: An American Psychiatrist's Conversations with the Defendants and Witnesses* (2004). —Ed.

vanquished peoples, to the present-day moralizing condemnation of such methods of behavior.

Such a library would nevertheless be missing a single work offering a sufficient explanation of the causes and processes whereby such historical dramas originate, of how and why human frailties and ambitions degenerate into bloodthirsty madness. Upon reading the present volume, the reader will realize that writing such a book was scientifically impossible until recently.[3]

The old questions would remain unanswered: what made this happen? Does everyone carry the seeds of crime within, or is it only some of us? No matter how faithful and psychologically true, no literary description of events, such as those narrated by the above-mentioned authors, can answer these questions, nor can they fully explain the origins of evil. They are thus incapable of furnishing sufficiently effective principles for counteracting evil. The best literary description of a disease cannot produce an understanding of its essential etiology,[4] and thus furnishes no principles for treatment. In the same way, such descriptions of historical tragedies are unable to elaborate effective measures for counteracting the genesis, existence, or spread of evil.

In using natural language[5] to circumscribe psychological, social, and moral concepts which cannot properly be described within its sphere of utility, we produce a sort of surrogate comprehension leading to a nagging suspicion of helplessness. Our natural system of concepts and notions—formed through our instinctual responses, innate emotionality, and environmental and cultural transmission—is not equipped with the necessary factual content to permit reasoned comprehension of the quality of the factors (particularly the psychological ones) which were active before the birth of, and during, such inhumanly cruel times.

[3]Several previous attempts, now considered classics, are worth mentioning, including F. A. Hayek, *The Road to Serfdom* (1944); Karl Popper, *The Open Society and Its Enemies* (1945); Gustave Gilbert, *Psychology of Dictatorship* (1950); and Hannah Arendt, *The Origins of Totalitarianism* (1951). More recently, Jordan B. Peterson's *Maps of Meaning: The Architecture of Belief* (1999) was inspired by many of the same questions; and Arthur Versluis's *The New Inquisitions: Heretic-Hunting and the Intellectual Origins of Modern Totalitarianism* (2006) traces the philosophical and archetypal forebears of twentieth-century totalitarianism. —Ed.

[4]The cause(s) or manner of causation of a disease or condition. —Ed.

[5]The ordinary, everyday speech of conversation, novels, newspapers, etc., which Łobaczewski distinguishes from the more precise, specialized language such as is necessary for use in various scientific fields (see *Ponerologia*, p. 12). —Ed.

We must nevertheless point out that the authors of such literary descriptions sensed that their language was insufficient and therefore attempted to infuse their words with the proper scope of precision, almost as though they foresaw that someone—at some point in time—might use their works in order to explain what cannot be explained, not even in the best literary language. Had these writers not been so precise and descriptive in their language, this author would have been unable to use their works for his own scientific purposes.

Such literature inspires dread and, in hedonistic societies, a tendency to escape into ignorance or naive doctrines. Some people even feel contempt for people who are suffering. The influence of such books can thus be partially harmful; we should counteract that influence by indicating what the authors had to leave out because our ordinary world of concepts and notions cannot contain it.

The reader will therefore find herein no bloodcurdling descriptions of criminal behavior or human suffering. It is not the author's job to present a graphic account of material already adduced by people who saw and suffered more than he did, and whose literary talents are greater. Introducing such descriptions into this work would run counter to its purpose: it would not only focus attention on some events to the exclusion of many others, but would also distract the mind from the real heart of the matter, namely, *the general laws of the origin of evil.*

In tracking the behavioral mechanisms of the genesis of evil, one must keep both abhorrence and fear under control, submit to a passion for scientific epistemology, and develop the calm outlook needed in natural history. Nevertheless, we must not lose sight of where the processes of ponerogenesis[6] can lead and what threat they can pose to us in the future.

This book therefore aims to take the reader by the hand into a world beyond the concepts and notions he has relied on to describe his world since childhood, and trusted perhaps too egotistically, because his parents, surroundings, and the community of his country used concepts similar to his own. Thereafter, we must show him an appropriate selection from the world of natural concepts which are the fruit of recent scientific thinking and which will allow him an understanding of what has remained indefinable in his everyday system of concepts.

[6]The genesis of evil. See Glossary. —Ed.

However, this tour of another reality will not be a psychological experiment conducted upon readers' minds for the sole purpose of exposing the weak points and gaps in their natural worldview, or perhaps just to de-egotize their attitudes.[7] Rather, it is an urgent necessity due to our contemporary world's pressing problems, which we can delay only temporarily and ignore only at our peril. For when we realize that we cannot possibly distinguish the path to nuclear catastrophe from the path to creative dedication unless we step beyond this world of natural egotism[8] and familiar concepts, then we will also realize that the path was chosen for us by powerful forces, against which our nostalgia for homey, familiar human concepts can be no match. We must step beyond this world of natural and literary concepts for our own good and for the good of our loved ones.

The social sciences have already elaborated their own conventional language which mediates between the ordinary man's view and a fully objective naturalistic view. It is useful to scientists in terms of communication and cooperation, but it is still not the kind of conceptual structure which can fully take into account the biological, psychological, and pathological premises at issue in the second and fourth chapters of this book.[9] In the social sciences, this eliminates critical standards and puts ethics on ice;[10] in the political sciences, it leads to an underrated evaluation of the psychological factors that significantly shape social and political situations.[11]

This social-science language left the author and other investigators feeling helpless and scientifically stranded early in our research on the mysterious nature of this inhuman historical phenomenon which engulfed our nation, and still fires his attempts to reach an objective understanding of it. Ultimately, I had no choice but to resort to objective biological, psychological, and psychopathological terminology

[7]For more on the natural worldview and the natural language with which humans express it, see the discussion under the heading "Objective Language" in Chapter II. —Ed.

[8]That is, the natural tendency to place an excessive or exaggerated value on one's own opinions and judgments, which are most often not formed on sound reasoning and evidence. Discussed in more depth in Chapter IV under the heading "Ponerogenic Phenomena and Processes." —Ed.

[9]See Lasswell, *Psychopathology and Politics*, pp. 38–43. —Ed.

[10]For example, according to social constructionism, crime is purely a product of social forces, which tends to downplay or even eliminate the role of the individual. —Ed.

[11]See Lasswell, *Psychopathology and Politics*, p. 45. —Ed.

in order to bring into focus the true nature of the phenomenon—the heart of the matter—and if contact with its true nature was not to be lost to the already fashionable doctrinarism[12] of the time.

The nature of the phenomena under investigation as well as the needs of readers, particularly those unfamiliar with psychopathology, dictate a descriptive approach which must first introduce the data and concepts necessary for further comprehension of psychologically and morally pathological phenomena. We shall thus begin with aspects of human personality, intentionally formulated in such a way as to coincide largely with the experience of a practicing psychologist, passing then to selected questions of societal psychology. In the "Ponerology" chapter, we shall familiarize ourselves with how evil is born with regard to each social scale, emphasizing the actual role of some psychopathological phenomena in the process of ponerogenesis. Thus, the transition from natural language to the necessary objective language of naturalistic and psychological science—supported by some statistical data—will take place gradually, though it may be somewhat irksome for readers.

Ponerology reveals itself to be a new branch of science born out of historical need and the most recent accomplishments of medicine and psychology. In the light of objective naturalistic language, it studies the causal components and processes of the genesis of evil, regardless of the latter's social scope. When we attempt to analyze these ponerogenic processes which have given rise to human injustice—armed with proper knowledge, particularly in the area of psychopathology—we always meet with the effects of pathological factors whose carriers are people characterized by some degree of various psychological deviations or defects.

Moral evil and psychobiological evil are, in effect, interlinked via so many causal relationships and mutual influences that they can only be separated by means of analysis and abstraction. However, the ability to distinguish them *qualitatively* can help us to avoid a moralizing interpretation of the pathological factors.[13] This error in understanding social and moral affairs, to which we are all prone, poisons the human mind in an insidious way.[14] Ponerology therefore provides us with some much-needed mental hygiene.

[12]The tendency to think solely in categories of, and to invoke, a doctrine, theory, or ideology in all circumstances regardless of practicality or suitability. —Ed.

[13]See the subsection on this topic under "Ponerogenic Phenomena and Processes" in Chapter IV. —Ed.

The ponerogenesis of *macrosocial phenomena* (large-scale evil), which constitutes the most important object of this book, appears to be subject to the same laws of nature that operate within human questions on an individual or small-group level. The role of persons with various psychological defects and anomalies of a clinically low level appears to be a perennial characteristic of such phenomena. In the macrosocial phenomenon we shall later call "pathocracy," a certain hereditary anomaly isolated as "essential psychopathy" is catalytically and causatively essential for the genesis and survival of large-scale social evil.

Our natural human worldview actually creates a barrier to our understanding of such questions; thus, it is necessary to be familiar with psychopathological phenomena, such as those encountered in this field, in order to breach that barrier.[15] May then the readers please forgive the author's occasional lapses along this innovative path and fearlessly follow his lead, familiarizing themselves rather systematically with the data adduced in the first few chapters. Thus, we shall be able to accept the truths provided in later chapters without reflex protests on the part of our natural egotism.

Specialists familiar with psychopathology will find the road less novel. They will, however, notice some differences in interpreting several well-known phenomena, resulting in part from the anomalous conditions under which the research was done, but mostly from the *more intensive penetration* needed to achieve the primary purpose. That is why this aspect of our work contains certain theoretical values useful for psychopathology. Hopefully, non-specialists will depend upon the author's long experience in distinguishing individual psychological anomalies found among people and factored into the process of the genesis of evil.

---

[14]See also Chapter IX, "Therapy for the World." American professor of biology and neurology Robert Sapolsky makes a similar argument in chapter 16 of his book, *Behave: The Biology of Humans at Our Best and Worst* (2017), pp. 580–613. —Ed.

[15]See, e.g., Martha Stout, *The Sociopath Next Door: The Ruthless Versus the Rest of Us* (2005). As psychologist Jordan B. Peterson writes in his book *12 Rules for Life: An Antidote to Chaos* (2018), p. 24: "Naive, harmless people usually guide their perceptions and actions with a few simple axioms: people are basically good; no one really wants to hurt anyone else; the threat (and, certainly, the use) of force, physical or otherwise, is wrong. These axioms collapse, or worse, in the presence of individuals who are genuinely malevolent." —Ed.

Considerable moral, intellectual, and practical advantages can be gleaned from an understanding of the ponerogenic processes thanks to the naturalistic objectivity required. The long-term heritage of ethical questions is thereby not destroyed; quite the contrary, it is *reinforced*, since modern scientific methods confirm the basic values of moral teachings. However, ponerology forces some corrections upon many details.

Understanding the nature of macrosocial pathological phenomena permits us to find a healthy attitude and perspective toward them, thus protecting our minds from being poisoned by their diseased contents and the influence of their propaganda. The unceasing counter-propaganda resorted to by some countries retaining a normal human system could easily be superseded by straightforward information of a scientific and popular-scientific nature. For we can only conquer this huge, contagious social cancer—and overcome the threat of its reappearance due to the emergence of some new suggestive ideology—if we comprehend its essence and its etiological causes. This would eliminate the mystery of this phenomenon as its primary survival asset. *Ignoti nulla est curatio morbi!*

Such an understanding of the nature of the phenomenon leads to the logical conclusion that the measures for healing and reordering the world today should be completely different from the ones heretofore used for solving international conflicts. Solutions to such conflicts should function more like modern antibiotics, or, even better, psychotherapy properly handled, rather than old-style weapons such as clubs, swords, tanks, or nuclear missiles.

With reference to phenomena of a ponerogenic nature, mere proper knowledge alone can begin healing individual humans and helping their minds regain harmony. Toward the end of this book, we shall be discussing how to use this knowledge in order to arrive at the correct political decisions and apply it to an overall therapy of the world.

CHAPTER II
SOME INDISPENSABLE CONCEPTS

Three principal heterogeneous items coincided in order to form our European civilization: Greek philosophy, Roman imperial and legal civilization, and Christianity, consolidated by time and the efforts of later generations. The culture, or cognitive/spiritual heritage, thus born was internally incoherent; the philosophically young language of concepts—barely detached from natural human concepts, or overly attached to the needs of law and materialism—turned out to be too rigid to comprehend aspects of psychological and spiritual life.

Such a state of affairs had negative repercussions upon our ability to comprehend reality, especially that reality which concerns humanity and society. Europeans became unwilling to study reality (subordinating intellect to facts), instead tending to impose upon nature their own extrinsic ideological schemes, not completely coherent and often subjective. Not until modern times, thanks to great developments in the hard sciences, which study facts by their very nature, as well as the apperception of the philosophical heritage of other cultures, could we help clarify our world of concepts and permit its own homogenization.

It is surprising to observe what an autonomous tribe the culture of the ancient Greeks represented. Even in those days, a civilization could hardly develop in isolation, without being affected by older cultures in particular. However, even with that consideration, Greece was relatively isolated, culturally speaking. This was probably due to the era of decay the archaeologists refer to as the "dark age," which occurred in those Mediterranean areas between 1100 and 750 B.C., and also due to the alienation and belligerence of the arriving tribes.[1]

[1]The Greek city states were also geographically isolated. The tendency to cultural isolation is exemplified in Plato's *Laws*. Historian Russell Gmirkin writes: "The dangers of travel and cultural intermixture were discussed at Plato, *Laws* 12.949e-951e. A conscious program of cultural isolation, modeled on that of Sparta, helped to ensure that outside information and knowledge of other customs would not foster dissatisfaction and a desire for change.

The Greeks developed a wealth of mythological imagery reflecting the country's and its people's direct contact with nature, as well as their experiences of life and war. These conditions saw the birth of a literary tradition, and later of philosophical reflections searching for generalities about human experience, essential contents, and criteria of rightness and moral values. The Greek heritage is fascinating due to its richness and individuality, but above all due to its primeval nature. Our civilization, however, would have been better served if the Greeks had made more ample use of the achievements, traditions, and reflections of other civilizations.

Rome was too vital and practical to reflect profoundly upon the Greek thoughts it had appropriated. In this imperial civilization, administrative needs and juridical developments imposed practical priorities. For the Romans, the role of philosophy was more didactic, helping to develop the thinking process which would later be utilized for the discharge of administrative functions and the exercise of policy. The Greek reflective influence softened Roman customs, which had a salutary effect on the development of the empire.

However, for any imperial civilization, the complex problems of human nature are seen as troublesome factors complicating the legal regulations of public affairs and administrative functions. This begets a tendency to dismiss such matters of a more subtle nature and to develop a concept of human personality simplified enough to serve the purposes of law and administration. Roman citizens could thus achieve their goals and develop their personal attitudes within the framework set by fate and legal principles, which determined an individual's situation based on premises having little to do with their actual psychological properties. The spiritual life of people lacking the rights of citizenship was not an appropriate subject of deeper studies. Thus, psychological understanding remained barren, a condition which always produces moral decline at both the individual and public levels.

Plato consciously designed his laws limiting cultural contacts with peoples from other nations so as not to be as crudely hostile to foreigners as those of Sparta ... Unlike Sparta's xenophobic laws that had given their country an evil reputation, Plato allowed delegations to travel abroad to Greek festivals and similar reciprocal visits from foreigners, but regulated in such a manner as to prevent positive views of foreign cultures to infiltrate the *polis*" (*Plato and the Creation of the Hebrew Bible* [2017], pp. 280–281) —Ed.

Christianity, inheriting the values of Judaism, had stronger ties with the ancient cultures of the Asiatic continent, including their theological, moral, and psychological reflections. This was of course a dynamic factor rendering it more attractive, but it was not the most important one. Observing and understanding the transformations faith caused in human personalities created a school of psychological thought and art on the part of the early believers. This new relationship to another person, i.e., one's neighbor, characterized by understanding, forgiveness, and love, opened the door to a psychological cognition which, often supported by charismatic phenomena, bore abundant fruit during the first three centuries after Christ.[2]

An observer at the time might have expected Christianity to help develop the art of human understanding to a higher level than the older cultures and religions of the sages. Thus one might have hoped that such knowledge would protect future generations from the dangers of speculative thought divorced from that profound psychological reality which can only be comprehended through sincere respect for another human being.

History, however, has not confirmed such hopes. The symptoms of decay in sensitivity and psychological comprehension, as well as the Roman imperial tendency to impose extrinsic patterns upon human beings, can be observed as early as the end of the fourth century A.D.[3] During later eras, Christianity passed through all those difficulties which result from insufficient psychological understanding of human

---

[2]On the nature of these personality transformations among the earliest Christians, see Timothy Ashworth, *Paul's Necessary Sin: The Experience of Liberation* (2016), and Troels Engberg-Pedersen, *Paul and the Stoics* (2000). In *Logokracja* (p. 70), Łobaczewski cites Clement of Alexandria (ca. 150–215), who was influenced by the Alexandrian gnostic Basilides. See Arthur Versluis, *The Mystical State: Politics, Gnosis, and Emergent Cultures* (2011), pp. 17–18. —Ed.

[3]Emperor Theodosius (347–395) established Nicene Christianity as the official state religion in 380 A.D., after which pagan worship was forbidden and all other Christian sects declared heretical. In 385 A.D., Priscillian was the first Christian to be executed by the Church for heresy. Versluis argues that the ideological background to this trend extends to the antiheretical writings of Irenaeus in the late second century and Tertullian (the "father of Latin Christianity") in the early third century, whose writings absorbed and repurposed Roman legal tradition. See Versluis, *New Inquisitions*, pp. 4–6, 52–59, and *Mystical State*, pp. 91–92 (on simplistic, extrinsic doctrines that "quickly become grotesque ... and produce totalizing centralized bureaucratic apparatuses" built on compulsion and coercion). —Ed.

nature, and then passed through a severe illness. Exhaustive studies on the historical reasons for this suppression of the development of human cognition in our civilization would be an extremely useful endeavor in modern times, when we are on the way to correcting this effect.

First of all, Christianity adapted the Greek heritage of philosophical thought and language to its purposes. This made it possible to develop its own philosophy, but the primitive and materialistic traits of that language imposed certain limits. This also hampered communication between Christianity and other religious cultures for many centuries.

Christ's message expanded along the seacoast and beaten paths of the Roman empire's transportation lines, within the imperial civilization, but only through bloody persecutions and ultimate compromises with Rome's power and law. The Christian Church appropriated Roman organizational forms and adapted to existing social institutions. As a result of this unavoidable process of adaptation, Christianity inherited Roman habits of legal thinking, including its schemes for simplifying the human personality and its indifference to human nature and its variety.[4]

Three heterogeneous systems were thus linked together so permanently that later centuries forgot just how strange they actually were to each other. However, time, compromise, and the effort of further reflection did not eliminate the internal inconsistencies, and Roman influence divested Christianity of too much of its original psychological knowledge. (It seems that in this domain, Rome triumphed over even the Greatest Psychologist.) Christian tribes developing under different cultural conditions created forms so diverse that maintaining unity turned out to be an historical impossibility.

Thus was born a civilization hampered by a serious deficiency in an area which both can and does play the creative role of fostering

[4]Professor of Roman law Pascal Pichonnaz writes that "apart from Latin ... law is the only contribution to the Western world that comes solely from Rome" (Pauchard, "How Ancient Rome Influenced European Law" [2013]). On the Christian adoption of Roman legalistic thinking and the bureaucratic centralization of power in the period between Tertullian and Augustine, see Versluis, *New Inquisitions*, pp. 4–6. Christianity was now to be "deployed as the basis of a judicial system" in which one seeks "to impose one's own understanding upon others," in contrast to a "negative politics," in which "one concentrates on the beam in one's own eye, not on the mote in someone else's" (*Mystical State*, p. 23). —Ed.

human connection and understanding, and which is supposed to protect societies from various kinds of evil which arise from a lack of that understanding. This civilization developed formulations in the area of law, whether national, civil, criminal, or finally canon, which were conceived for invented and simplified beings—the philosophical "cardboard cut-outs" of humanity.[5] These formulations gave short shrift to the total contents of the human personality and the great psychological differences between individual members of the species *Homo sapiens* which have been hidden behind social organization structures and economic divisions. For many centuries, any understanding of certain psychological anomalies found among some individuals was out of the question, even though these anomalies cause disaster on every social scale.[6]

We ourselves have painfully experienced the consequences of the fact that our civilization was insufficiently resistant to evil, which originates beyond the easily accessible areas of human consciousness and takes advantage of the enormous gap between doctrinaire or legal thought and psychological reality. In a civilization deficient in psychological knowledge, hyperactive individuals driven by an inner angst caused by a feeling of being different easily find a ready echo in other people's insufficiently developed consciousness. Such individuals dream of imposing their power and their different experiential manner upon their environment and their society. Unfortunately, in a psychologically ignorant society, their dreams to impose on societies their own, different way of experiencing and conceptualizing, and then, their power, still stand a chance of being accomplished.

Psychology

Specialized psychological knowledge lay dormant in European culture for centuries. At the end of the seventeenth century, philosophers

[5] See William B. Ewald, "The Roman Foundations of European Law" (1994). —Ed.

[6] *Author's note (1997):* It is only nowadays that we are dealing with the reverse process, which must take its time. Our civilization, and with it Christianity, is becoming saturated with biological and psychological knowledge. In the midst of many difficulties, this aforementioned deficit is gradually being compensated for. However, contradictions—real and Leibnizian—and unnecessary fears remain. Therefore, this venture requires work, courage, and confidence.

intuited the existence of the subconscious,[7] and they gradually developed a wealth of knowledge in this area. But it was not until the 1870s that this tempestuous search culminated in specific research into the hidden truth about human nature. This was a secular movement based on biological and medical progress carried out mainly by physicians; thus its inquiries originated in the material sphere.[8] Such an approach to human personality was always going to prove to be one-sided, however, as it attempted to rediscover knowledge that had previously been studied from the spiritual perspective.[9] From the very outset, many researchers had a vision of the great future role of this science for the good of peace and order. People like Ivan Pavlov,[10] C. G. Jung,[11] and others soon noticed this one-sidedness

[7]In *Logokracja*, Łobaczewski cites Ralph Cudworth (1617–1688), English Anglican clergyman, theologian, philosopher, and one of the "Cambridge Platonists." In *The True Intellectual System of the Universe*, "Cudworth ascribes dreams, and all other operations of what we call the unconscious mind to Plastic Nature [the link between divine mind and matter] manifest in the human mind. Included in these, Cudworth holds, are the most basic projection of order onto our perceptions, so that we can be capable of logical deliberation." See Charles M. Richards, "Ralph Cudworth (1617–1688)" (n.d.). —Ed.

[8]Wilhelm Wundt (1832–1920), German physiologist and philosopher, is considered the father of experimental psychology. In 1879 he was the first to open a lab devoted exclusively to psychology. Wundt was strongly influenced by the seventeenth-century philosopher Leibniz's theoretical psychology. Leibniz's distinction between "unnoticed" and "perceived" sensory impressions later influenced thinking about the unconscious. (Leibniz himself had been influenced by Cudworth.) See Jochen Fahrenberg, "The Influence of Gottfried Wilhelm Leibniz on the Psychology, Philosophy, and Ethics of Wilhelm Wundt" (2016). —Ed.

[9]See, for example, Glenn McCullough, "Jacob Boehme and the Spiritual Roots of Psychodynamic Psychotherapy: Dreams, Ecstasy, and Wisdom" (2019). Böhme was a seventeenth-century German Lutheran theologian and mystic. See also the work of modern mystics like G. I. Gurdjieff and J. G. Bennett: Joseph Azize, *Gurdjieff: Mysticism, Contemplation, and Exercises* (2020); Russell Schreiber, *Gurdjieff's Transformational Psychology: The Art of Compassionate Self-Study* (2013); J. G. Bennett, *A Spiritual Psychology* (1999). —Ed.

[10]Ivan Pavlov (1849–1936), Russian physiologist famous for his work on classical conditioning. For the definitive biography of Pavlov, see Daniel P. Todes, *Ivan Pavlov: A Russian Life in Science* (2014). While the USSR turned Pavlov into a symbol of Soviet science—even persecuting physiologists in the name of "protecting Pavlov's heritage"—Pavlov himself he was a lifelong critic, writing, for instance: "We have lived and are living under an unrelenting regime of terror and violence. ... Most of all, I see the resemblance of our life to that of ancient Asian despotisms. Spare the homeland and us." And in a 1934 letter to the Minister of Health of the RSFSR, G. N. Kaminsky: "Unfortunately, I

and attempted to reach a synthesis.[12] Pavlov, however, was not allowed to state his convictions in public.[13]

Psychology is the only science wherein the human mind studies itself, the observer and the observed belong to the same species, and in an act of introspection they become the same person. It is thus easy for subjective error to steal into the reasoning process of the thinking person's commonly used notions and individual habits. Error then often bites its own tail in a vicious circle, or emotions come into play, thus giving rise to problems due to the lack of distance between observer and observed, a difficulty unknown in other disciplines.

Some people, such as the behaviorists, attempted to avoid the above error at all costs. In the process, they impoverished the cognitive contents to such an extent that there was very little matter left. However, they produced a very profitable discipline of thought.[14] Progress was very often elaborated by persons simultaneously driven by internal anxieties and searching for a method of ordering their own

---

feel in relation to your revolution almost directly opposite to you. It disturbs me very much ... Many years of terror and the unrestrained willfulness of the authorities are turning our Asian nature into a shamefully slave-like one. And how much good can you do with slaves? Pyramids? Yes; but not general true human happiness." ("Ivan Pavlov," Russian Wikipedia, translated). —Ed.

[11] Carl Gustav Jung (1875–1961), Swiss psychiatrist and psychoanalyst. He is best known for his idea of the collective unconscious, his work on religion, myth, and archetypes, and for conceptualizing introversion and extraversion, still in use today as part of various personality theories and models, including the Big Five. —Ed.

[12] For example, William James (1842–1910), the father of American psychology, who pioneered the psychology of religion in his work *The Varieties of Religious Experience* (1902). —Ed.

[13] While Pavlov was a scientific materialist and atheist, he saw religion as a biologically based human instinct serving a psychological function and was a firm believer in freedom of religion. Soviet propaganda used his atheism to justify anti-religion policies, which he strongly opposed. See George Windholz, "Pavlov's Religious Orientation" (1986). —Ed.

[14] Preceded by Pavlov's work on conditioning, American behaviorists John B. Watson (1878–1958) and B. F. Skinner (1904–1990) focused on observable, testable facts (reinforcement, punishment, stimuli, responses, etc.) over subjective experience. The behaviorist theory of cognition posited a strict correlation between external stimulus and behavioral response, thus negating the reality of any meaningful internal experience like volition, a sense of "self," or mental causation. For a psychologist like Kazimierz Dąbrowski, by contrast, the higher the brain function (deliberate actions, creativity), the lesser the role played by external stimuli. See Dąbrowski et al., *Mental Growth Through Positive Disintegration* (1970), pp. 101–103. —Ed.

personalities via the road of knowledge and self-knowledge. If these anxieties were caused by a defective upbringing, then overcoming these difficulties gave rise to excellent discoveries. However, if the cause for such anxieties rested *within human nature*, it resulted in a permanent tendency to deform the understanding of psychological phenomena, and consequently also of moral phenomena. Within this science, progress is unfortunately very contingent upon the individual values and nature of its practitioners. It is also dependent upon the social climate. Wherever a society has become enslaved to others or to the rule of its own overly privileged class, psychology is the first discipline to suffer from censorship and incursions on the part of an administrative body which starts claiming the last word as to what represents scientific truth.[15]

Thanks to the work of outstanding pathfinders and the development of demanding methodological principles, however, the scientific discipline exists and continues to develop in spite of all these difficulties; it is useful for the life of society. Many researchers fill in the gaps of this science with detailed data which function as a corrective to the subjectivity and vagueness of famous pioneers. The childhood ailments of any new discipline persist, including a lack of general order and synthesis, as does the tendency to splinter into individual schools, expounding upon certain theoretical and practical achievements, at the cost of limiting themselves in other areas.

At the same time, however, experience gradually grows and findings of a practical nature are gleaned in connection with activity undertaken for the good of people who need help. The direct observations furnished by the everyday work of therapists in the field are more instrumental in forming scientific comprehension and developing the language of contemporary psychology than any academic experiments or deliberations undertaken in a laboratory. After all, life itself provides diverse conditions, whether comfortable or tragic, which subject human individuals to experiments no scientist in any laboratory would ever undertake. This very volume is a result of such inhuman experimentation upon entire nations.

Experience teaches a psychologist's mind how to track the psychological course of another person's life quickly and effectively, discovering the causes that conditioned the development of his personality and behavior. Our minds can thus also reconstruct those factors which

[15]See Chapter VII. —Ed.

influenced him, although he himself may be unaware of them. In doing this, we do not, as a rule, use the natural structure of concepts, often referred to as "common sense," relied upon by public opinion and many individuals. Rather, we use categories which are as objective as we can possibly achieve. Such a conceptual language, whose descriptions of psychological phenomena and their causal relations are independent of any common notions, has become an indispensable tool of practical activity. In practice, however, it usually turns into clinical slang rather than the distinguished scientific language it would behoove us to foster.

Objective Language

In the categories of psychological objectivity, cognition and thought are based on the same logical, epistemological, and methodological principles shown to be the best tool in many other areas of naturalistic studies. Exceptions to these rules have become a tradition for ourselves and for creatures similar to us, but they turn out to engender more error than usefulness. At the same time, however, consistent adherence to these principles, and rejection of additional *scientistic* limitations,[16] lead us toward the wide horizon from which it is possible to glimpse *supernatural* causality. Accepting the existence of such phenomena within the human personality becomes a necessity if our language of psychological concepts is to remain an objective structure and describe correctly the totality of the reality represented by man.[17]

[16] I.e., methodological naturalism, but without an excessive belief or trust in the power or completeness of scientific knowledge and its methods and assumptions (e.g., its materialism). —Ed.

[17] For example, intuition, insight, inspiration, and some forms of dreams. The idea of "supernatural causality" in cognition has roots in the psychology of F. W. H. Myers, whose work was admired by psychologists William James and Pierre Janet. Myers proposed a "filter" or "transmission" theory of consciousness to account for such phenomena as multiple, concurrent, dissociated streams of consciousness, automatisms, dreaming, hallucinogenic states, genius, memory, mystical experience, telepathy, mind-body correlations, etc. See Edward Kelly et al., *Irreducible Mind: Toward a Psychology for the 21st Century* (2007). See also James C. Carpenter, *First Sight: ESP and Parapsychology in Everyday Life* (2012); and John H. Buchanan and Christopher M. Aanstoos (eds.), *Rethinking Consciousness: Extraordinary Challenges for Contemporary Science* (2020); and Iain McGilchrist, *The Matter with Things: Our Brains, Our Delusions and the Unmaking of the World* (2021). —Ed.

In affirming his own personality, man has the tendency to repress from the field of his consciousness any associations indicating an external causative conditioning of his emotions, worldview, and behavior. Young people in particular want to believe they freely choose their intentions and decisions; at the same time, however, an experienced psychological analyst can track the causative conditions of these choices without much difficulty. Much of this conditioning is hidden within our childhood; the memories may be receding into the distance, but we carry the results of our early experiences around with us throughout our lives.

The better our understanding of the causality of the human personality, the stronger the impression that humanity is a part of nature and society, subject to dependencies we are ever better able to understand. Overcome by human nostalgia, we then wonder if there is really no room for a scope of freedom, for a *Purusha.*[18] The more progress we make in our art of understanding human causation, the better we are able to liberate the person who trusts us from the excessive effects of conditioning, which has unnecessarily constricted his freedom of proper comprehension and decision making. We are thus in a position to close ranks with our patient in a search for the best way out of his problems. If we succumb to the temptation of using the natural structure of psychological concepts for this purpose, our advice to him would sound similar to the many unproductive pronouncements he has already heard and that never quite manage to really help him to become free of his problem.

The natural psychological, societal, and moral worldview is a product of man's developmental process and family upbringing within a society, under the constant influence of innate traits.[19] Among these innate traits are mankind's phylogenetically determined instinctive foundations. No person can develop without being influenced by other people and their personalities, or by the values imbued by his civilization and his moral and religious traditions. That is why his natural human worldview can be neither sufficiently universal nor completely true. Differences among individuals and nations are the product of both inherited dispositions and the ontogenesis[20] of

[18]Literally "man" in Sanskrit, from the verb-root *pri*: to fill, make complete, bestow. Used in theosophy to express the "ideal man," spiritual self, cosmic being, divine essence. —Ed.

[19]It is simply "our human perception of reality" (*Ponerologia*, p. 13). —Ed.

[20]The development of an individual from the earliest stage to maturity. —Ed.

personalities.

It is thus significant that the main values of this natural human worldview indicate basic similarities in spite of great divergences in time, race, and civilization. This worldview quite obviously derives *from the nature of our species* and the natural experience of human societies which have achieved a certain necessary level of civilization. Refinements based on literary values or philosophical and moral reflections do show differences, but, generally speaking, they tend to bring together the natural conceptual languages of various civilizations and eras. People with a humanistic education may therefore get the impression that they have achieved mature wisdom on this path.[21] We shall also continue to respect the wisdom of that "common sense" derived from life experience and reflections thereon, although we recognize its deficits and inadequacies.

However, a conscientious psychologist must ask the following questions: Even if the natural worldview has been refined, does it mirror reality with sufficient reliability? Or does it only mirror *our species' perception*? To what extent can we depend upon it as a basis for decision making in the individual, societal, and political spheres of life?

Experience teaches us, first of all, that this natural worldview has permanent and characteristic tendencies to distort reality, as dictated by our instinctive and emotional features. Secondly, reality is often too complex and understanding it exceeds individual capabilities. Thirdly, our work exposes us to many phenomena which cannot be understood nor described by natural language alone. An objective scientific language able to analyze the essence of a phenomenon thus becomes an indispensable tool. (The situation thus becomes similar to that of many other fields of knowledge.) It has also shown itself to be similarly indispensable for an understanding of the questions presented within this book.

Now, having laid the groundwork, let us attempt a listing of the most important reality-deforming tendencies and other insufficiencies of the natural human worldview. First of all, it does not carry those biological and psychological data which have only been discovered by modern science; at the same time, it triggers an egotistical opposition against their acceptance. The emotional features which are a natural

[21] Łobaczewski calls this the "egotism of the natural worldview," discussed below. —Ed.

component of the human personality are never completely appropriate to the reality being experienced.[22] This results both from our instinct, our subconscious, and our common errors of upbringing. That is why the best traditions of philosophical and religious thought have counseled subduing the emotions in order to achieve a more accurate view of reality.[23]

The natural worldview is also characterized by a similar tendency to endow our opinions with moral judgment, often so negative as to represent outrage. This appeals to tendencies which are deeply rooted in human nature and societal customs.[24] We easily extrapolate this method of comprehension and judgment onto manifestations of improper human behavior, which are, in fact, caused by minor psychological deficiencies, or even a temporary medical condition.[25] Thus, any moralizing interpretation of minor psychopathological phenomena—which we are all prone to do—is erroneous and merely leads to an exceptional number of unfortunate consequences, which is why we shall repeatedly refer to it.

Another defect of the natural worldview is its lack of universality. In every society, a certain percentage of people have developed a

[22]Barbara Oakley writes in *Evil Genes: Why Rome Fell, Hitler Rose, Enron Failed, and My Sister Stole My Mother's Boyfriend* (2007), p. 192: "simply looking at the research results, one must conclude that people's first emotional responses about what's wrong, who is to blame, or how to proceed, particularly in relation to complex issues, must always—*always*—be considered suspect." See the section in which this quotation is found, "'Feel Good' Politics: How Machiavellians—and Altruists—Manipulate Emotions" (pp. 187–192). —Ed.

[23]See, for example, the modern resurgence of practical Roman Stoicism in works like William B. Irvine, *A Guide to the Good Life: The Ancient Art of Stoic Joy* (2009). —Ed.

[24]As Jonathan Haidt puts it in *The Righteous Mind: Why Good People Are Divided by Politics and Religion* (2013), p. xix: "human nature is not just intrinsically moral, it's also intrinsically moralistic, critical and judgmental." —Ed.

[25]For example, epilepsy used to be regarded as a mental illness, and before that, a sign of demonic possession (Sapolsky, *Behave*, pp. 605–610). Adrian Raine gives the example of a man who became pedophilic as a result of a brain tumor, but returned to normal with its removal (*The Anatomy of Violence: The Biological Roots of Crime* [2014], pp. 303–305, 324–328). See also Dvoskin et al., "A Brief History of the Criminalization of Mental Illness" (2019). More generally, when another individual behaves in a way that we deem to be bad, we tend to make a judgment of negative intent rather than seeking to understand the psychological and possibly physiological conditions that might be driving them and convincing them that they are behaving properly. This is known in social psychology as the fundamental attribution error. —Ed.

worldview a good deal different from that used by the majority. The causes of the aberrations are by no means qualitatively monolithic; we will be discussing them in greater detail in the fourth chapter.

Another essential deficiency of the natural worldview is its limited scope of applicability. Euclidean geometry would suffice for a technical reconstruction of our world and for a trip to the moon and the closest planets. We only need a geometry whose axioms are less natural if we reach inside of an atom or outside of our solar system. The average person does not encounter phenomena for which Euclidean geometry would be insufficient. However, sometime during his lifetime, virtually every person is faced with problems he must deal with. Since a comprehension of the factors actually at work is beyond the ken of his natural worldview, he generally relies on emotion: intuition and the pursuit of happiness.[26] Whenever we meet a person whose individual worldview developed under the influence of non-typical conditions, we tend to pass moral judgment upon him in the name of our more typical worldview. In short, whenever some unidentified psychopathological factor comes into play, the natural human worldview ceases to be applicable.[27]

Moving further, we often meet with sensible people endowed with a well-developed natural worldview as regards psychological, societal, and moral aspects, frequently refined via literary influences, religious deliberations, and philosophical reflections. Such persons have a pronounced tendency to overrate the value of their worldview, behaving as though it were an objective basis for judging other people. They do not take into account the fact that such a system of apprehending human matters can also be erroneous, since it is insufficiently objective. Let us call such an attitude the "egotism of the natural worldview." To date, it has been the least pernicious type of egotism, being merely an overestimation of that method of comprehension containing the eternal values of human experience.

Today, however, the world is being jeopardized by a phenomenon which cannot be understood nor described by means of such a natural conceptual language; this kind of egotism thus becomes a dangerous factor stifling the possibility of effective counteractive measures. Developing and popularizing the objective psychological worldview could

[26]In *Ponerologia* (p. 14) he adds a third factor: luck. —Ed

[27]Discussed further in the subsection "Para-appropriate responses" in Chapter IV. —Ed.

thus significantly expand the scope of dealing with evil, via sensible action and pinpointed countermeasures.[28]

Objective psychological language, based on mature philosophical criteria, must meet the requirements derived from its theoretical foundations, and meet the needs of individual and macrosocial practice. It should be evaluated fully on the basis of *biological realities* and constitute an extension of the analogous conceptual language elaborated by the older naturalistic sciences, particularly medicine. Its range of applicability should cover all those facts and phenomena conditioned upon cognizable biological factors for which this natural language has proved inadequate. It should, within this framework, allow sufficient understanding of the contents, and diverse causes, of the genesis of the above-mentioned deviant worldviews.

Elaborating such a conceptual language, being far beyond the individual scope of any scientist, is a step-by-step affair[29]; by means of the contribution of many researchers, it matures to the point when it can be organized under philosophical supervision in the light of above-mentioned foundations. Such a task would greatly contribute to the development of all biohumanistic and social sciences by liberating them from the limitations and erroneous tendencies imposed by the overly great influence of the natural language of psychological concepts, especially when combined with an excessive component of

[28]In his book *Homo Americanus: The Rise of Totalitarian Democracy in America* (2021), p. 221, Zbigniew Janowski writes: "Psychology has a paramount role to play in getting our society straight, provided it renounces the claims that make it sound like an ideological call to social action, and instead concerns itself with individual human beings ... The popularity of Jordan Peterson ... may be an indication that the *shadow man* may be once more rising. The question is: Will he survive in the hostile egalitarian-democratic environment?" —Ed.

[29]For example, American psychiatrist M. Scott Peck (1936–2005) describes his struggle pioneering the introduction of the concept of human evil into psychology (without moralistic judgment), and the resistance he encountered, in his book *People of the Lie: The Hope for Healing Human Evil* (1983). He credits his two mentors with making the first steps: social psychoanalyst Erich Fromm (1900–1980) and Jesuit priest Malachi Martin (1921–1999), citing their respective works, *The Heart of Man: Its Genius for Good and Evil* (1964) and *Hostage to the Devil* (1977). See also James L. Knoll, "The Recurrence of an Illusion: The Concept of 'Evil' in Forensic Psychiatry" (2008), who writes: "Interest in evil is growing. The psychological and psychiatric literature reflects steadily increasing attention to the concept of evil over the past two decades. ... While Simon cautions about the subjective moral judgment involved, Welner believes that 'defining evil is only the latest frontier where psychiatry ... will bring light out of darkness'." —Ed.

egotism.

Most of the questions dealt with in this book are beyond the scope of applicability of this natural language. The fifth chapter shall deal with a macrosocial phenomenon which has rendered our traditional social-scientific language completely deceptive. Understanding these phenomena thus requires a consistent break from the habits of that method of thinking and the use of the most objective system of concepts possible. For this purpose, it proves necessary to develop the contents, organize them, and familiarize the readers with them as well.

At the same time, an examination of the phenomena whose nature forced the use of such a system greatly contributes to enriching and perfecting it. While working on these matters, the author gradually accustomed himself to comprehending reality by means of this very method, a way of thinking which turned out to be both the most appropriate and the most economical in terms of time and effort. It also protects the mind from its own natural egotism and any excessive emotionalism.

In the course of the above-mentioned inquiries, each researcher went through his own period of crisis and frustration when it became evident that the concepts he had trusted thus far proved to be inapplicable. Ostensibly correct hypotheses formulated in the scientifically improved natural conceptual language adopted in the social sciences turned out to be completely unfounded in the light of facts and preliminary statistical calculations. At the same time, the elaboration of concepts better suited for reality under investigation became extremely complex; after all, the key to the question lies in a scientific area still in the process of development.

Surviving this period thus required an acceptance of and a respect for a feeling of ignorance truly worthy of a philosopher. Every science is born in an area uninhabited by popular notions. In this case, however, the procedure had to be exceptionally radical; we had to leave those notions behind and venture into any area indicated by systematic analysis of the facts we observed and experienced from within a full-blown condition of macrosocial evil, guided by the light of the requirements of scientific methodology. This had to be upheld in spite of the dangers and difficulties caused by extraordinary outside conditions and by our own human personalities.

Very few of the many people who started out on this road of scientific knowledge were able to arrive at the end, since they withdrew for various reasons connected to this period of frustration. They returned to the world of more familiar concepts. Some of them concentrated on a single question; succumbing to a kind of fascination regarding its scientific value, they delved into detailed inquiries. Their achievements may be present in this work, since they understood the general meaning of their work. Others gave up in the face of scientific problems, personal difficulties, or the fear of being discovered by the authorities, who are highly vigilant in such matters. Very few remained, and the postulated synthesis never came to fruition. This work is therefore its first attempt.

Perusing this book will therefore confront the reader with similar problems, albeit on a much smaller scale. A certain impression of injustice may be conveyed due to the need to leave behind a significant portion of our prior conceptualizations, the feeling that our natural worldview is inapplicable, and the expendability of some emotional entanglements. I therefore ask my readers to accept these disturbing feelings in the spirit of the love of knowledge and its redeeming values.

The above explanations have been crucial in order to render the language of this work more easily comprehensible to the readers. The author has attempted to approach the matters described herein in such a way as to avoid both losing touch with the world of objective concepts and becoming incomprehensible to anyone outside a narrow circle of specialists. We must thus beg the reader to pardon any slips along the tightrope between the two methods of thought. However, the author would not be an experienced psychologist if he could not predict that some readers will reject the scientific data adduced within this work, feeling that they constitute an attack upon the natural wisdom of their life-experience.

The Human Individual

When Auguste Comte[30] attempted to found the new science of sociology during the early nineteenth century, i.e., well before modern psychology was born, he was immediately confronted with the psychological problem of man, a mystery he could not solve. If he rejected the Catholic Church's oversimplifications of human nature,

[30]Comte (1798–1857), French philosopher of science, utopian socialist, and founder of positivism, adopted the term *sociologie* in 1838, believing positivist sociology would go on to become the centerpiece of the sciences. —Ed.

then nothing remained except traditional schemes for comprehending the personality, derived from well-known social relations. He thus had to avoid this problem, among others, if he wanted to create his new scientific branch under such conditions.

Therefore, he accepted the thesis that the family was the basic cell of society, something much easier to characterize and treat as an elementary model of societal relations. This could also be effected by means of a language of comprehensible concepts, without confronting problems which could truly not have been overcome at the time. Slightly later, J. S. Mill[31] pointed out the resulting deficiencies of psychological understanding and the role of the individual outside the family.

Only now is sociology successfully dealing with the difficulties which resulted, laboriously reinforcing the existing foundations of science by the achievements of psychology, a science which by its very nature treats the *individual* as the basic object of observation. This restructuring and acceptance of an objective psychological language will in time permit sociology to become a scientific discipline which can mirror social reality with sufficient objectivity and attention to detail in order to render it a basis for practical action. After all, it is man who is the basic unit of society, including the entire complexity of his human personality and the diversity of individuals.

In order to understand the functioning of an organism, medicine begins with cytology, which studies the diverse structures and functions of cells. If we want to understand the laws governing social life, we must similarly first understand the individual human being, his physiological and psychological nature, and fully accept the quality and scope of differences (particularly psychological ones) among the individuals who constitute two sexes, different families, associations, and social groups, as well as the complex structure of society itself.

[31] John Stuart Mill (1806–1873), English philosopher, political economist, and influential liberal thinker. He was an advocate of utilitarianism, the ethical theory systemized by his godfather Jeremy Bentham. See *John Stuart Mill: On Democracy, Freedom and Government & Other Selected Writings* (2019), edited by Zbigniew Janowski and Jacob Duggan. As Janowski writes: "[Mill] is to Liberalism what Marx and Engels are to Socialism, and if one wishes to understand the nature of today's liberal society, no one's writings are a better source to turn to" (p. xxxi). —Ed.

The instinctive substratum

The doctrinaire and propaganda-based Soviet system contains a characteristic built-in contradiction whose causes will be readily understandable toward the end of this book. Man's descent from the animals, bereft of any extraordinary events, is accepted there as the obvious basis for the materialistic worldview. At the same time, however, they suppress the fact that man has an instinctive substratum, i.e., something in common with the rest of the animal world. If faced with especially troublesome questions, they sometimes admit that man contains an insignificant survival of such phylogenetic heritage; however, they prevent the publication of any work studying this basic phenomenon of psychology.[32]

In order to understand humanity, however, we must gain a primary understanding of mankind's instinctive substratum[33] and appreciate its salient role in the development and life of individuals and societies. This role easily escapes our notice, since our human species' instinctive responses seem so self-evident and are so much taken for granted that it arouses insufficient interest. A psychologist, schooled in the observation and analysis of human beings, does not fully appreciate the role of this eternal phenomenon of nature until he has years of professional experience.

Man's instinctive substratum has a slightly different biological structure than that of animals. Energetically speaking, it has become less dynamic and more plastic, thereby giving up its job as the main dictator of behavior. It has become more receptive to the controls of reasoning, without, however, losing much of the rich specific contents of the human kind.

It is precisely this phylogenetically developed basis for our experience, and its emotional dynamism, that allows individuals to develop their feelings and social bonds, enabling us to intuit other people's psychological state and individual or social psychological reality.[34]

---

[32]See Chapter VII, "Psychology and Psychiatry under Pathocratic Rule." —Ed.

[33]The psychophysiological basis of humanity's emotional nature and personality development. For a treatment by one of Łobaczewski's contemporaries, see Kazimierz Dąbrowski, *Multilevelness of Emotional and Instinctive Functions* (1996). —Ed.

[34]For example, the ability to read social cues, as well as our intuition about social relations and hierarchies, our place within them, and the norms of navigating their complexities. Dean A. Haycock, in *Tyrannical Minds: Psychological Profiling, Narcissism, and Dictatorship* (2019), pp. 46, 236, describes what he

It is thus possible to perceive and understand human customs and moral values. From infancy, this substratum stimulates various activities aiming at the development of the mind's higher mental and emotional functions. In other words, *our instinct is our first tutor*, whom we carry inside all our lives. Proper child-rearing is thus not limited to teaching a young person to control the overly violent reactions of his instinctual emotionalism; it also ought to teach him to appreciate the wisdom of nature contained within and speaking through his instinctive endowment.

This substratum contains millions of years' worth of biopsychological development that was the product of species' life conditions, so it neither is nor can be a perfect creation. Our well-known weaknesses of human nature and errors in the natural perception and comprehension of reality have thus been conditioned on that phylogenetic level for millennia.[35]

This common human basis of our psychic life has made it possible for peoples throughout the centuries and civilizations to create concepts regarding human, social, and moral matters which share significant similarities.[36] Inter-epochal and interracial variations in this area are less striking than those differentiating persons whose instinctual human substratum is normal from those who are carriers of an instinctual biopsychological defect, though they are members of the same race and civilization.[37] It shall behoove us to return to this

calls "amateur profiling," i.e., our ability to "read people," to get an intuitive grasp on another's personality and experience, and to form impressions about their character, motivations, and psychological state. —Ed.

[35]See McGilchrist, *The Matter with Things*, esp. pt. 1 & pp. 679–684; Jaak Panksepp, *Affective Neuroscience: The Foundations of Human and Animal Emotions* (2004), and (with Lucy Biven), *The Archaeology of Mind: Neuroevolutionary Origins of Human Emotions* (2012); Stephen W. Porges, *The Polyvagal Theory: Neurophysiological Foundations of Emotions, Attachment, Communication, and Self-regulation* (2011). —Ed.

[36]Moral foundations theory posits six foundations characterizing humanity's basic moral judgments and motivations: Care/Harm, Fairness/Cheating, Loyalty/Betrayal, Authority/Subversion, Sanctity/Degradation, and Liberty/Oppression. Conservatives tend to value all five and liberals tend to value primarily harm and fairness (libertarians primarily value economic and lifestyle liberty). For a full discussion, see Haidt, *Righteous Mind* and Atari et al., "Morality Beyond the WEIRD: How the Nomological Network of Morality Varies Across Cultures" (2022), which finds Equality and Proportionality to be distinct foundations (as opposed to a single Fairness dimension). —Ed.

[37]For recent accounts of such deficits, with discoveries made in the intervening decades, see Raine, *Anatomy*, and Oakley, *Evil Genes*, esp. ch. 8. —Ed.

latter question repeatedly, since it has taken on a crucial importance for the problems dealt with in this book.

Man has lived in groups throughout his prehistory, so our species' instinctual substratum was shaped in this bond, thus conditioning our emotions as regards the meaning of existence. The need for an appropriate communal psychological structure, and a striving to achieve a worthy role within that structure, are encoded at this very level. In the final analysis, our self-preservation instinct is rivaled by another feeling: the good of society demands that we make sacrifices, sometimes even the supreme sacrifice. At the same time, however, it is worth pointing out that if we love a man, we love his human instinct above all.

Our zeal to control and fight anyone harmful to ourselves or our group is so primal in its near-reflex necessity as to leave no doubt that it is also encoded at the instinctual level. This is a result of the fact that retaliation was originally a necessity of life. Our instinct, however, does not differentiate between behavior motivated by simple human failure and behavior performed by individuals with pathological aberrations. Quite the contrary: we instinctively tend to judge the latter more severely, harkening to nature's striving to eliminate biologically or psychologically defective individuals.[38] Our tendency to such evil-generating error is thus conditioned at the instinctual level.[39]

It is also at this level that differences begin to occur between normal individuals, influencing the formation of their characters, worldviews, and attitudes. The primary differences are in the biopsychological dynamism of this substratum; differences of content are secondary. For some people the sthenic instinct[40] dominates their psychic life; for others, it easily relinquishes control to reason—sometimes too easily. It also appears that some people have a somewhat richer and more subtle instinctual endowment than others. Significant deficiencies in this heritage nevertheless occur in only a tiny percentage of the human population, and we perceive this to be qualitatively pathological.[41] We shall have to pay closer attention to such anomalies, since

[38]See the discussion on "natural eugenic processes" at the end of the section on "inherited deviations" in Chapter IV. —Ed.

[39]Similar views: Raine, *Anatomy*, p. 322; Sapolsky, *Behave*, pp. 609–10. —Ed.

[40]From *sthenia*: strong, vigorous, or active. The sthenic instinct is the impulsive, uninhibited tendencies associated with lack of emotional control. —Ed.

[41]What we today refer to as personality disorders. —Ed.

they participate in that pathogenesis of evil which we would like to understand more fully.

A more subtle structure of affect is built upon our instinctual substratum, thanks to constant cooperation from the latter as well as familial and societal child-rearing practices. With time, this structure becomes a more easily observable component of our personality, within which it plays an integrative role. The formation of this emotional structure is influenced by the personality of those closest to the child, who should remember that proper child-rearing requires the *self*-rearing (or self-education) of parents and caregivers. This higher affect is instrumental in linking us to society, which is why its correct development is a proper duty of pedagogues and constitutes one of the objects of a psychotherapist's efforts, if perceived to be abnormally formed. Both pedagogues and psychotherapists sometimes feel helpless if this process of formation was influenced by a defective instinctual substratum.

Psychological functions, structures, and differentiation

Thanks to memory, that phenomenon ever better described by psychology, but whose nature remains partly mysterious, man stores life experiences and purposely acquired knowledge. There are extensive individual variations in regard to this capacity, its quality, and its contents. A young person also looks at the world differently from an old man endowed with a good memory. People with a good memory and a great deal of knowledge have a greater tendency to reach for the written data of collective memory in order to supplement their own.

This collected material constitutes the subject matter of the second psychological process, namely association; our understanding of its characteristics is constantly improving, although we have not yet been able to shed sufficient light upon its nature. In spite of, or maybe thanks to, the valuable contributions to this question by psychologists and psychoanalysts,[42] it appears that achieving a satisfactory synthetic understanding of the associative processes will not

[42] *Author's note (1997):* And more recently by the holographic theory of memory and association. [The mathematics of holographic associative memory (HAM) were first developed in the late 1960s. Their potential application to human memory led Karl Pribram to develop holonomic brain theory, which posits quantum effects in the brain that create a consciousness field, and non-local memory storage and retrieval. See Karl Pribram, *Brain and Perception: Holon-*

be possible unless and until we humbly decide to cross the boundaries of purely naturalistic comprehension.[43]

Our reasoning faculties continue to develop throughout our entire active lives; thus, accurate judgmental abilities do not peak until our hair starts greying and the drive of instinct, emotion, and habit begins to abate. (The aptitudes of individuals in this domain show the greatest variation.) Our ability to think correctly is a collective product derived from the interaction between man and his environment, and from many generations' worth of creation and transmission. The environment may also have a destructive influence upon the development of our reasoning faculties. In a hysterical environment in particular, the human mind is contaminated by conversive thinking,[44] which is the most common anomaly in this process, and the influence of abnormal personalities on children can result in thinking anomalies persisting throughout the child's life. It is for this reason that the proper development of mind also requires periods of silence and solitary reflection on occasion.

Man has also developed a psychological function not found among animals. Only man can apprehend a certain quantity of material or abstract notions within his field of imagination and attention, inspecting them internally in order to effect further operations of the mind upon this material. This enables us to confront facts, effect constructive and technical operations, and predict future results. If the facts subjected to internal projection and inspection deal with man's own personality, man performs an act of introspection essential for monitoring the state of his personality and the meaning of his own behavior. This act of internal projection and inspection is the crown of our consciousness; it characterizes no species other than the human.

---

omy and the Structure of Figural Processing (1991), and more recently, *The Form Within: My Point of View* (2013). —Ed.]

[43]See, e.g., Alan Gauld's treatment of the subject in his chapter, "Memory," in Kelly et al., *Irreducible Mind*. See also Carpenter, *First Sight*, chs. 11 & 12; and Ross, *Trauma Model*, ch. 7, for memory in a clinical context. —Ed.

[44]I.e., dissociative thinking. In psychiatry, conversion disorders involve physical symptoms (e.g., paralysis or blindness) experienced by the patient but with no physical cause. Rather, they are rooted in emotional trauma, thus providing evidence of subconscious control of psychophysiological processes. The term comes from Freud's idea that anxiety is "converted" into physical symptoms. In dissociative or conversive thinking, correct premises or conclusions are subconsciously "converted" into incorrect ones, for example, as a defense mechanism against cognitive dissonance caused by certain uncomfortable truths. See the relevant section in Chapter IV and the Glossary entry. —Ed.

However, there is exceptionally wide divergence among individuals regarding the capacity for such mental acts. The efficiency of this mental function shows a somewhat low statistical correlation with general intelligence.[45]

Thus, if we speak of man's general intelligence, we must take into account both its internal structure and the individual differences occurring at every level of this structure. The substratum of our intelligence, after all, contains nature's instinctual heritage of wisdom and error, giving rise to basic intelligence[46] through the assimilation of life experience. Superimposed upon this construct, thanks to memory and associative capacity, is our ability to effect complex operations of thought, crowned by the act of internal projection, and to constantly improve their correctness. We are variously endowed with these capabilities, which make for an individual mosaic of gifts enriched with special talents.[47]

Basic intelligence grows from this instinctual substratum under the influence of a favorable environment and a readily accessible compendium of human experience; it is intertwined with higher affect, enabling us to understand others and to intuit their psychological state by means of a certain naive realism. This conditions the development of moral reason. This layer of our intelligence is widely distributed within society; the overwhelming majority of people have it, which is why we can so often admire the tact, the intuition of social relationships, and the sensible morality of people whose intellectual gifts are only average. This basic aptitude is also a necessary

[45] *Author's note (1997):* We also meet cases of damage to the frontal fields of the cerebral cortex, in whom this function is impaired. They develop pathological characters and through their actions cause extremely unfortunate results. Therefore, we will return to this issue in the chapter on ponerology.

[46] Also called emotional intelligence (*Logokracja*, p. 28), which comprises the ability to manage, understand, and perceive emotions (e.g., through the recognition of facial expressions), and to facilitate thought using emotion. Łobaczewski cites the Polish edition of Daniel Goleman's *Emotional Intelligence* (1997). See also Nicholas D. Thomson, *Understanding Psychopathy* (2019), p. 110–113; and McGilchrist, *The Matter with Things*, ch. 6. —Ed.

[47] In *Logokracja*, p. 32, Łobaczewski gives examples: "Some people are gifted with the ability to capture an unusually large amount of data in their field of attention. Others have a very capacious and durable memory. We know aesthetically sensitive people who have a talent for figurative reproduction or color composition; others are endowed with particularly good musical hearing, yet others have a talent for sensing and observing psychological phenomena." —Ed.

condition for good psychological work. However, we also see people with an outstanding intellect who lack these very natural values. As is the case with deficiencies in the instinctual substratum, the deficits of this basic structure of our intelligence frequently take on features we perceive as pathological.[48]

The distribution of human intellectual capacity within societies is completely different, and its amplitude has the greatest scope. Highly gifted people constitute a tiny percentage of each population, and those with the highest quotient of intelligence constitute only a few per thousand. In spite of this, however, the latter play such a significant role in collective life that any society attempting to prevent them from fulfilling their duty does so at its own peril. At the same time, individuals barely able to master simple arithmetic and the art of writing are, in the majority, normal people whose basic intelligence is often entirely adequate.

It is a universal law of nature that the higher a given species' psychological organization, the greater the psychological differences among individual units. Man is the most highly organized species; hence, these variations are the greatest. Both qualitatively and quantitatively, psychological differences occur in all structures of the human personality dealt with here, albeit in terms of necessary oversimplification. Profound psychological variations may strike some as an injustice of nature, but they are her right and have deep, creative meaning.

Nature's seeming injustice, alluded to above, is, in fact, a great gift of God and nature to humanity, enabling human societies to develop their complex societal structures and to be highly creative at both the individual and collective levels. Thanks to psychological differentiation, the creative potential of any society is many times higher than it could possibly be if our species were psychologically more homogeneous. Thanks to these variations, the societal structure implicit within can also develop. The fate of human societies—their dynamic development or decline—depends upon the proper adjustment of individuals within this structure and upon the manner in which diverse aptitudes are utilized.

---

[48]See, for example, Thomson, *Understanding Psychopathy*, esp. ch. 7, on environmental risk factors affecting the development of this "structure" of basic intelligence. —Ed.

Our experience teaches us that psychological differences among people are the cause of misunderstandings and problems. We can overcome these problems only if we accept psychological differences as a law of nature and appreciate their creative value. This would also enable us to gain an objective comprehension of man and human societies; unfortunately, it would also teach us that equality under the law is inequality under the law of nature.[49]

Supra-sensory reality

If we observe our human personality by consistently tracking psychological causation within, if we are able to exhaust the question to a sufficient degree, we shall come ever closer to phenomena whose biopsychological energy is very low, which begin to manifest themselves to us with a certain characteristic subtlety. We attempt to track our associations especially when we have exhausted the analytical tradition. At that time, we must admit to noticing something within us which is a result of supra-sensory causation. This path may be the most laborious of all, but it will nevertheless lead to the most "material" certainty regarding the existence of what all the sages and mystics have known. Attaining some small piece of truth via this path teaches us respect for the whole truth.[50]

If we thus wish to understand mankind—man as whole—without abandoning the laws of thought required by objective language, we are finally forced to accept this reality, which is within each of us, whether normal or not, whether we have accepted it because we have been brought up that way or have achieved it through faith, or whether we have rejected faith for reasons of materialism or science.[51] After

[49]See Janowski, *Homo Americanus*, ch. 9, "A New Opium of the Intellectuals: Plato's Trap and Mill's Liberalism." —Ed.

[50]That is, indications of the existence of something beyond the material universe. The English translation read "the preachings of faith." —Ed.

[51]See Chapter VIII. Kazimierz Dąbrowski, *Personality-shaping through Positive Disintegration* (2015), p. 26, writes: "The strength and universality of religious experience show that the internal attitude of man corresponds to a supersensual Being, transcendent as an object of these religious experiences and at the same time constituting a necessary condition for the very fact of the existence of this experience in our consciousness. ... In order to be able to receive and grasp the supersensual reality we may need special organs and functions, a kind of 'transcendental sense,' allowing us, through inner experience, to perceive the reality of the supersensual world." Dąbrowski describes these "subtle" emotional–cognitive processes dealing with suprasensory reality as "empirical

all, when we analyze negative psychological attitudes, we always discern an affirmation which has been repressed from the field of consciousness. As a consequence, the constant subconscious effort of denying concepts about existing things engenders a zeal to eliminate them in other people.

Trustfully opening our mind to perception of this reality is thus indispensable for someone whose duty is to understand other people in order to offer them good advice or psychotherapy, and is advisable for everyone else as well. Thanks to this, our mind is rendered free of internal tensions and stresses and can be liberated from its tendency to select and substitute information,[52] including those areas which are more easily accessible to naturalistic comprehension.

Personality disintegration and integration

The human personality is unstable by its very nature, and a lifelong evolutionary process is the normal state of affairs. Some political and religious systems advocate slowing down this process or achieving excessive stability in our personalities, attitudes, and beliefs, but these are unhealthy states from the point of view of psychology. If the evolution of a human personality or worldview becomes frozen long and deeply enough, the condition enters the realm of psychopathology. The process of personality transformation reveals its own creative meaning if it is consciously accepted as the natural course of things, which in turn allows for its rational control.[53]

Our personalities also pass through temporary destructive periods as a result of various life events, especially if we undergo suffering or meet with situations or circumstances which are at variance with

mysticism." See also Kelly and Grosso, "Mystical Experience," in Kelly et al., *Irreducible Mind.* —Ed.

[52]See note above on "conversive thinking." —Ed.

[53]Dąbrowski's theory of positive disintegration describes the various levels of emotional–intellectual development. According to Dąbrowski, most people live most of their lives at the level of *primary* integration (when personality development is "frozen," as Łobaczewski puts it), the lowest level of personality development, punctuated by disintegrations during major life changes or events. *Negative* disintegration results in psychosis or suicide while *positive* disintegration results in higher levels of emotional development, i.e., more empathic, understanding, insightful, and global in character. Lower levels, on the other hand, are more rigid, egocentric, short-sighted, narrow, and ruled primarily by biological and social determinants of thinking, feeling, and behavior. See https://www.positivedisintegration.com/levelIandII.htm. —Ed.

our prior experiences and notions. These so-called disintegrative stages are often unpleasant, although not necessarily so. A good dramatic work, for instance, enables us to experience a disintegrative state, simultaneously calming down the unpleasant components and furnishing creative ideas for a renewed reintegration of our own personalities. True theater therefore causes the condition known as catharsis.

A disintegrative state provokes us to mental efforts and explorations in attempts to overcome it in order to regain active homeostasis. Overcoming such states—in effect, correcting our errors and enriching our personalities—is a proper and creative process of reintegration, leading to a higher level of understanding and acceptance of the laws of life, to a better comprehension of self and others, and to a more highly developed sensitivity in interpersonal relationships. Our feelings also validate the successful achievement of a reintegrative state: the unpleasant conditions we have survived are endowed with meaning. Thus, the experience renders us better prepared to confront the next disintegrative situation.

If, however, we have proved unable to master the problems which occurred—because our reflexes were too quick to repress and substitute the uncomfortable material from our consciousness, because the situation was caused by an overly dramatic combination of events or we lacked the information necessary to understand it, or for some similar reason—then our personality undergoes regression and egotization,[54] which is not free of the sense of failure. The results are devolutionary; the person becomes more difficult to get along with. If we cannot overcome such a disintegrative state because the causative circumstances were long-lasting, overpowering, and accompanied by feelings of helplessness and danger, then our organism reacts with a neurotic condition.[55] This is because the psychological landscape is an integral part of the life of the organism.

***

[54]Dąbrowski writes: "Grave life experiences and stresses may facilitate the process, but in [the] case of very rigid integration, the disintegration which occurs under stress is temporary and is quickly followed by reintegration to the original level of primitive automatic functioning" (*Multilevelness*, p. 65). In other words, the individual is unable to achieve a higher personality integration and self-understanding, regressing back to his old state. This process is often accompanied by excuses and rationalizations, even when it is clear to others that he is not seeing things objectively. —Ed.

The diagram of the human personality presented herein, summarized and simplified for reasons of necessity, makes us aware of how complex human beings are in their psychological structure, their transformations and variations, and their mental and spiritual lives. If we wish to create social and political sciences whose descriptions of our reality would be capable of enabling us to rely on them in practice, we must accept this complexity and make certain that it is sufficiently respected. Any attempt to substitute this basic knowledge with the help of oversimplifying schemes leads to the loss of that indispensable convergence between our reasoning and the reality we are observing. It behooves us to reemphasize that using our natural language of psychological concepts for this purpose cannot be a substitute for objective premises.

Similarly, it is extremely difficult for a psychologist to believe in the value of any social or political ideology based on simplified or even naive psychological premises.[56] This applies to any ideology which attempts to grossly primitivize psychological reality,[57] whether it be one utilized by a totalitarian system or, unfortunately, by democracy as well.[58] People are different. Whatever is qualitatively different by nature and remains in a state of permanent evolution cannot be considered equal.[59]

***

The above-mentioned statements about human nature apply to normal people, with a few exceptions. However, each society on earth contains a certain percentage of individuals, a relatively small but

[55]No longer common in Western psychiatry, the term neurosis is roughly equivalent to what we now call anxiety and mood disorders (also obsessive-compulsive, dissociative, and stress-related disorders). For an in-depth look at these conditions as responses to trauma, see Colin Ross's book, *The Trauma Model.* According to Ross, "chronic childhood trauma is to psychiatry as germs are to general medicine" (p. 55). —Ed.

[56]Psychiatrist Norman Doidge writes: "Ideologies are substitutes for true knowledge, and ideologues are always dangerous when they come to power, because a simple-minded I-know-it-all approach is no match for the complexity of existence" (foreword to Peterson, *12 Rules*, p. xiv). —Ed.

[57]For example, economic and class schemes (*Logokracja*, p. 16) like *Homo economicus* or oppressor/oppressed divisions. —Ed.

[58]See Ryszard Legutko, *The Demon in Democracy: Totalitarian Temptations in Free Societies* (2016), esp. ch. iv. —Ed.

[59]See Zbigniew Janowski, "Against Equality of Opportunities" (2020). —Ed.

active minority, *who cannot be considered normal.* We emphasize that here we are dealing with qualitative, not statistical, abnormality. Outstandingly intelligent persons are statistically abnormal, but they can be quite normal members of society from the qualitative point of view.

There are ill people whose social role is insignificant. However, there are also those in whom mental deviations and anomalies of various qualities and severities can be diagnosed and whose negative social role is much greater. Many such people are driven by an inner angst caused by a sense of their own difference: they search for unconventional paths of action and adjustment to life with a characteristic hyperactivity. In some cases, such activity can be pioneering and creative, which ensures societal tolerance for some of these individuals. Some psychiatrists, especially Germans, have praised such people as embodying the principal inspiration for the development of civilization; this is a damagingly unilateral view of reality. Laymen in the field of psychopathology frequently gain the impression that such persons represent some extraordinary talents. This very science, however, explains that these individuals' hyperactivity and sense of being exceptional are derived from their drive to overcompensate for a feeling of some deficiency. The truth is that normal people are the richest of all.

The fourth chapter of this book contains a concise description of some of these anomalies, their causes and biological basis, selected in such a way as to facilitate comprehension of this work as a whole. Other data are distributed throughout many specialized works that will not be included here. However, we must consider that the overall shape of our knowledge in this area—which is so basic to our understanding of, and practical solutions to, many difficult problems of social life—is unsatisfactory. Many scientists treat this area of science as being peripheral; others consider it "thankless" because it easily leads to misunderstandings with other specialists. As a consequence, various concepts and various semantic conventions emerge that lead to ambiguity, and the totality of knowledge in this science is still characterized by an excessively *descriptive* nature. It was not until the late 1960s that research progressed. This book therefore encompasses efforts whose purpose was to bring to light the *causative* aspects of the descriptively known phenomena.

The pathological phenomena in question, usually of a lower severity which can be more easily concealed from environmental opinion, merge without much difficulty into the eternal process of the genesis of evil, which later affects individuals, families, and entire societies. Later in this book, we shall learn that these pathological factors become indispensable components in a synthesis which results in human suffering, and also that tracking their activities by means of scientific control and social consciousness may prove to be an effective weapon against evil.

For the above reasons, this scope of psychopathological knowledge represents an indispensable part of that objective language we have dealt with above. Ever-increasing accuracy in biological and psychological facts in this area is an essential precondition for an objective comprehension of many phenomena which become extremely onerous for societies and the political dramas we have witnessed, as well as for a modern solution to age-old problems. Biologists, physicians, and psychologists who have been struggling with these elusive and convoluted problems deserve assistance and encouragement from society, since their work will enable the future protection of people and nations from an evil whose causes we do not as yet sufficiently understand.

Society

Nature has fated man to be social, a state of affairs encoded on the instinctual level of our species early on, as described above. Our minds and personalities could not possibly develop without contact and interaction with an ever-widening circle of people. Our mind receives input from others, whether consciously or unconsciously, in regard to matters of emotional and mental life, tradition, and knowledge, first by means of resonant sensitivity, identification, and imitation, and then through the exchange of ideas and fixed messages ("common knowledge"). The material we obtain in these ways is then transformed by our psyche in order to create a new human personality, one we call "our own." However, our existence is contingent upon necessary links with those who lived before, those who presently make up our families and society, and those who shall exist in the future. Our existence only assumes meaning as a function of societal bonds; hedonistic isolation causes us to lose ourselves.

It is man's fate to actively cooperate in giving shape to the fate of society by two principal means: forming his individual and family life within it, and becoming active in the sum total of social affairs based on his sufficient comprehension thereof. This requires an individual to develop two somewhat overlapping areas of knowledge about things; his life depends on the quality of this development, as does his nation and humanity as a whole.

If, say, we observe a beehive with a painter's eye, we see what looks like a crowding throng of insects linked by their species-similarity. A beekeeper, however, tracks complicated laws encoded in every insect's instinct and in the collective instinct of the hive as well; this helps him understand how to cooperate with the laws of nature governing apiary society for the hive's benefit as well as his own. The beehive is a higher-order organism; no individual bee can exist without it, and thus it submits to the absolute nature of its laws.

If we observe the throngs of people crowding the streets of some great human metropolis, we see what looks like individuals driven by their own affairs and concerns, pursuing some crumb of happiness. However, such an oversimplification of reality causes us to disregard the laws of social life which existed long before the metropolis ever did, which are still present there, although somewhat impaired, and which will continue to exist long after huge cities are emptied of people and purpose. Loners in a crowd have a difficult time accepting that reality, which exists at the very least in potential form,[60] although they cannot perceive it directly.

In reality, accepting the laws of social life in all their complexity actually makes it easier to understand them, even if we find it difficult to comprehend them completely. Thanks to this acceptance and comprehension, or even just an instinctive intuition of such laws, an individual is able to reach his goals in harmony with them and to mature his personality in such activity. Thanks to sufficient intuition and comprehension of these conditions, a society is able to progress culturally and economically and to achieve political maturity.

The more we progress in this understanding, the more social doctrines strike us as primitive and psychologically naive, especially those based on the thoughts of thinkers living during the eighteenth and nineteenth centuries which were characterized by a dearth of psychological perception.[61] The suggestive nature of these doctrines derives

[60] As he describes below, the potential for a socio-psychological structure is inherent in the diversity of human individuals, and may be realized to greater or lesser degrees. —Ed.

from their oversimplification of reality, something easily adapted and used in political propaganda. These doctrines and ideologies show their basic faults, in regard to the understanding of human personalities and differences among people, all rather clearly if viewed in the light of our natural language of psychological concepts, and even more so in the light of objective language, in which case they must be invalidated using facts.

A psychologist's view of society and its natural laws, even if based only on professional experience, always places the human individual in the foreground; it then widens the perspective to include families, small groups, and finally societies and humanity as whole. We must then accept from the outset that an individual's fate is significantly dependent upon a combination of circumstances. When we gradually increase the scope of our observations, the picture gets clearer as causal relationships are added to it, and statistical data assume ever greater stability and credibility.

In order to describe the interdependence between someone's fate and personality, and the state of development of society, we must study the entire body of information collected in this area to date,

---

[61]For example, Marx and Engels in the nineteenth century, who were influenced by eighteenth-century philosophers like Jean Jacques Rousseau (French socialism) and Baron d'Holbach (French materialism). Foreshadowing the "social constructionism" of twentieth-century postmodern philosophy, Holbach and his followers believed that all individual and class differences, including crime, were the result of the social environment, not human nature. Holbach wrote that "everything conspires to render man vicious and criminal; the religion he has adopted, his government, his education, the examples set before him, irresistibly drive him on to evil." See Thomas Sowell, *Marxism: Philosophy and Economics* (2011), pp. 31–32.

Other nineteenth-century thinkers in this category include utilitarians like Bentham, Mill, and William Godwin; and social Darwinists like Thomas Malthus, Herbert Spencer, and Francis Galton. See Janowski's discussion of Mill in *Homo Americanus*, ch. 9; and Legutko's critique of Mill's reductionistic anthropology in the afterword to Janowski (ed.), *John Stuart Mill*, pp. 768–770. See also Steven Pinker's *The Blank Slate: The Modern Denial of Human Nature* (2002) for additional examples in philosophy, sociology, anthropology, and psychology. In contrast, Łobaczewski (*Logokracja*, pp. 16–17, 22) lists St. Augustine (354–430), Andrzej Frycz Modrzewski (1503–1572), and Baron Charles Louis de Montesquieu (1689–1755) among those who demonstrated a *talent* for grasping psychological realities, albeit with a natural psychological worldview, noting that Adam Smith (1723–1790) sought criteria for ethics in the knowledge of human nature. He also states that Thomas Aquinas (1225–1274) lacked such a talent for perceiving psychological realities. —Ed.

adding a new work written in objective language. Herein I shall adduce only a few examples of such reasoning in order to open the door to questions presented in later chapters.

The psychological worldview and structure of society

Throughout the ages and in various cultures, the best pedagogues have understood the importance of the scope of concepts describing psychological phenomena for the formation of a culture and a person's character. The quality and richness of concepts and terminology mastered by an individual and society, as well as the degree to which they approximate an objective worldview, condition the development of our moral and social attitudes.[62] The correctness of our understanding of self and others shapes the fundamental premises of our decisions and choices, be they mundane or important, in our private lives and social activities, as well as those concerning political affairs.

The level and quality of a given society's psychological worldview is also a condition of the realization of the full socio-psychological structure present as a potential in the psychological variety within our species. Only when we can understand a person in relation to his actual internal contents—his nature, problems, and talents—and not some substituted external label, can we help him along his path to proper adjustment to and self-realization in social life. This would be to his advantage and would also assist in the creation of a stable and creative structure of society. Supported by a proper sense and understanding of psychological qualities, such a structure would impart high social office to individuals possessing full psychological normality, sufficient talent, and specific preparation. The basic collective intelligence of the masses of people would then respect and support them. The only pending problems to be resolved would be those matters so difficult as to overwhelm the natural language of concepts, however enriched and qualitatively ennobled.

At the same time, however, there have always been "social pedagogues," less outstanding but more numerous, who have become

[62]See the section "Objective Language" above. See also Peterson, *Maps of Meaning*, on categorization of the known and unknown (pp. 32–89), and "natural categories," spontaneously generated groupings whose borders are fuzzy and overlap (pp. 95–96). If a society's psychological categories are deficient, so will be the range of concepts it is able to express, and thus also its understanding of reality and the choices it can make to negotiate that reality. —Ed.

spellbound by their own great ideas—which are sometimes true but often too narrowly conceived, emotionally conditioned, or containing the products of some hidden pathological thought. Such people have always resorted to pedagogical methods which would impoverish and deform the development of individuals' and societies' psychological worldview; they inflict permanent harm upon societies, depriving them of universally useful values. By acting in the name of a genuinely valuable idea, such pedagogues actually undermine the values they claim and open the door for ideologies of far less value.

At the same time, as we have already mentioned, each society contains a small but active minority of persons with various deviant worldviews, especially in the areas treated above, which are caused either by psychological anomalies, to be discussed below, or by the long-term influence of such anomalies upon their psyches, especially during childhood. Such people later exert a pernicious influence upon the formative process of the psychological worldview in society, whether by direct activity or by means of written or other transmission, especially if they engage in the service of some ideology or other.

Many causes which easily escape the notice of sociologists and political scientists can thus be broken down into either the development or involution of this factor, whose meaning for the life of society is as decisive as the quality of their language of psychological concepts.

Let us imagine that we want to analyze these processes: we would construct a sufficiently credible inventory method which would examine the contents and correctness of the area of worldview in question. After subjecting the appropriate representative groups to such testing, we would then obtain indicators of that particular society's ability to understand psychological phenomena and relationships within their country and other nations. This would simultaneously constitute the basic indicators of said society's talent for self-government and progress, as well as its ability to carry on a reasonable international policy. Such tests could provide an early warning system if such abilities were to deteriorate, in which case, it would be proper to make the appropriate efforts in the realm of social pedagogy.[63]

[63] In extreme cases, it might be proper for those countries evaluating the problem to take more direct corrective action, even to isolating the deteriorating country until the appropriate corrections are well under way, perhaps similar to the international divestment and boycott of the apartheid South African system during the 1980s. —Ed.

Let as adduce another example psychologically related to the above: the development of an adult human's gifts, skills, realistic thought, and natural psychological worldview will be optimal where the level and quality of his education and the demands of his professional practice correspond to his individual talents. Achieving such a position provides personal and material advantages to him, as well as moral satisfaction; society as a whole also reaps benefits at the same time. Such a person would then perceive it as social justice in relation to himself.

If various circumstances combine, including a given society's deficient psychological worldview, a person may be forced to exercise functions which do not make full use of his talents, often subject to a superior who is less capable than himself. When this happens, said person's productivity is no better, and often even worse, than that of a worker with satisfactory talents. Occasionally he has good ideas, but they are often unappreciated. He easily gets into conflicts with his superiors and frequently changes jobs. He easily learns a new job, which gives him a temporary opportunity to use his talents.

Such an individual then feels cheated and inundated by duties which prevent him from achieving self-realization. His thoughts wander from his duties into a world of fantasy, or into matters which are of greater interest to him; in his daydream world, he is what he should and deserves to be. As a result, he is more likely to have accidents. Such a person always knows if his social and occupational adjustment has taken a downward direction; at the same time, however, if he fails to develop a healthy critical faculty concerning the upper limits of his own talents, his daydreams may "fix on" an unfair world where "all you need is power." He would like to repair this world, and in his dreams he aims too high, reaching for positions that in reality require more than he is capable of. Revolutionary and radical ideas find fertile soil among such people in downward socio-occupational adjustments. It is in society's best interests to correct such conditions not only for better productivity, but to avoid tragedies.

On the other hand, those who achieve important posts because they belong to privileged social groups or organizations which have gained power[64] are subject to symptoms of *upward* socio-occupational

[64]In *Logokracja*, p. 33, Łobaczewski specifies economic, political, doctrinal, and racial privilege. Examples of such systems include plutocracies/oligarchies, hereditary aristocracies, one-party systems involving nepotism and affirmative action, theocracies, etc. —Ed.

adjustment when their talents and skills are not sufficient for their duties, especially the more difficult problems. Such persons then avoid the important but difficult and dedicate themselves to minor matters quite ostentatiously. A component of histrionics[65] gradually appears in their conduct and tests indicate that their correctness of reasoning deteriorates after only a few years' worth of such activities. In order to maintain their position, they begin to direct attacks against anyone with greater talent or skill or who criticizes them for their incompetence, removing them from appropriate posts and playing an active role in degrading their social and occupational adjustment. This, of course, engenders a feeling of injustice and can lead to the problems of the downwardly adjusted individual as described above. Upwardly adjusted people thus favor authoritarian governments which would protect their positions.[66] However, holding such positions and dealing with the struggles associated with them lead to permanent stresses that destroy their health. They suffer from so-called "diseases of civilization" and their bodies age faster. Psychologists may find explaining this to them to be a very troublesome duty.

Upward and downward social adjustments, as well as qualitatively improper ones, result in a waste of any society's basic capital, namely the talent pool of its members—the picture of a sick society.[67] This simultaneously leads to increasing dissatisfaction and tensions among individuals and social groups; any attempt to approach human talent and its productivity problematics as a purely private matter must therefore be considered dangerously naive. Development or involution in all areas of cultural, economic, and political life depend on the extent to which this talent pool is properly utilized. In the fi-

[65]Overly theatrical, emotional, attention-seeking behavior. —Ed.

[66]One-party totalitarian governments deliberately promote incompetent people for this very reason; see, for example, Yoram Gorlizki and Oleg Khlevniuk's description of Soviet "overpromotion" in *Substate Dictatorship: Networks, Loyalty, and Institutional Change in the Soviet Union* (2020), pp. 4, 43–45. In the case of communist Poland, the policy of "social advance" was designed to establish dependency and thus produce loyal party leaders. See Anne Applebaum, *Iron Curtain: The Crushing of Eastern Europe, 1944–1956* (2013), pp. 310–312, 391. —Ed.

[67]For a critique of institutionalized social maladjustment in the United States and its potential for disaster, see Heather Mac Donald's *The Diversity Delusion: How Race and Gender Pandering Corrupt the University and Undermine Our Culture* (2018). —Ed.

nal analysis, it also determines whether there will be *evolution* or *revolution.*

Technically speaking, it would be easier to construct appropriate methods that enable us to evaluate the correlations between individual talents and social adjustment in a given country, than to deal with the prior proposition of the development of psychological concepts. Conducting the proper tests would furnish us a valuable index that we might call "the social order indicator." The closer the figure to +1.0, the more likely the country in question would be to fulfill that basic precondition for social order and take the proper path in the direction of dynamic development. A low correlation would be an indication that social reform is needed. A near-zero or even negative correlation should be interpreted as a danger sign that revolution is imminent.[68]

The examples adduced above do not exhaust the question of causative factors influencing the creation of a social structure which would adequately correspond to the laws of nature and respect for tradition. Our species-instinct level has already encoded the intuition that the existence of society's socio-psychological structure, based on psychological variations, is necessary; it continues to develop alongside our basic intelligence, inspiring our healthy common sense. This explains why the most numerous part of populations, whose talents are near average, generally accepts its modest social position in any country as long as the position fulfills the indispensable requirements of proper social adjustment and guarantees decent living conditions.

In a healthy society, this average majority accepts and respects the social role of people whose talents and education are superior, as long as they occupy appropriate positions within the social structure. The same people, however, react with criticism and lose this respect whenever someone as average as themselves compensates for his deficiencies by flaunting an upwardly adjusted position.[69] The judgments

[68]Anthropologist Peter Turchin has developed a political stress index (PSI) that serves this purpose, combining three crisis indicators: declining living standards, increasing intra-elite competition (caused in part the production of too many aspiring elites), and a weakening state. See Peter Turchin and Sergey A. Nefedov, *Secular Cycles* (2009); also Lindsay, "Bourgeois Overproduction and the Problem of the Fake Elite" (2021). —Ed.

[69]Research on fairness in children suggests that people favor *fair*, not necessarily *equal*, distributions, and when these clash, prefer fair inequality over unfair equality. See Greg Lukianoff and Jonathan Haidt, *The Coddling of the American Mind: How Good Intentions and Bad Ideas Are Setting Up a Generation for Failure* (2019), pp. 218–19. —Ed.

pronounced by this sphere of average but sensible people can often be highly accurate,[70] which can and should be all the more remarkable if we take into account that said people could not possibly have had sufficient knowledge of many of the actual problems, be they scientific, technical, or economic. However, this phenomenon is comprehensible because basic intelligence functions within the framework of natural reason.[71]

An experienced politician can rarely assume that difficulties in the areas of economics, defense, or international policy will be fully understood by his constituency. However, he can and should assume that his own comprehension of human matters, and anything having to do with interpersonal relations within said structure, will find an echo in this same majority of his society's members. These facts partially justify the idea of democracy, especially if a particular country has historically had such a tradition, the social structure is well developed, and the level of education is adequate. Nevertheless, they do not represent psychological data sufficient to raise democracy to the level of a moral criterion in politics.[72]

The same politician should be conscious of the fact that society contains people who already carry the psychological results of socio-

---

[70]This tendency can be manipulated and exploited by modern public relations strategies and other forms of propaganda, allowing "upwardly adjusted" and psychologically abnormal public figures to portray themselves as competent and likeable. The opposite is also possible through character assassination. Public perception may also be manipulated through election fraud and false or misleading opinion polls, but all of these methods have their limits. —Ed.

[71]*Author's note (1997):* Unfortunately, under the conditions prevailing in Poland these universal values have been largely weakened and replaced by habits of pathological origin.

[72]*Author's note (1997):* If this structure has been largely destroyed and replaced by its pathological caricature, the implementation of democracy will undoubtedly encounter enormous difficulties and it may be necessary to resort to scientifically based means for its reconstruction. [Łobaczewski writes in *Logokracja*, p. 10: "A political system based on the opinion of the broad masses of society must, by default, be dominated by the natural psychological worldview with its deficits and naiveties, by human egoism, emotionalism, and by the shortsightedness of the average man. It remains always open to demagogic activity inspired from within or from without, and which exploits the fact of the existence of people of mediocre mind and character. Such a system has proved mostly incapable of defending itself against phenomena difficult to understand in terms of natural human reason due to the psychopathological component in their nature." See Appendix II, "On Democracy," as well as the works of Janowski and Legutko. —Ed.]

occupational maladjustment. Some of these individuals attempt to protect positions for which their skills are not commensurate, while others fight to be allowed to use their talents and seek appropriate self-realization in social life. Governing a country becomes increasingly difficult when such battles begin to eclipse other important needs. That is why the creation of a fair social structure continues to be a basic precondition for social order and the liberation of creative values. It also explains why the propriety and productivity of the structure-creation process constitute a criterion for a good political system.

Politicians should also be aware that in each society there are people whose basic intelligence, natural psychological worldview, and moral reasoning have developed improperly. Some of these persons contain the cause within themselves; others were subjected to psychologically abnormal people as children. Such individuals' comprehension of social and moral questions is different, both from the natural and from the objective viewpoint; they constitute a destructive factor for the development of society's psychological concepts, social structure, and interpersonal bonds.

At the same time, such people easily interpenetrate the social structure with a rapidly spreading, branched network of mutual pathological conspiracies poorly connected to the main social structure—its pathological underbelly. These people and their networks participate in the genesis of that evil which spares no nation.[73] This substructure gives birth to dreams of obtaining power and imposing its will upon society, as well as its mode of experiencing and conceptualizing. This dream has been realized many times in the history of the world, in various countries and cultures. It is for this reason that a significant portion of our consideration shall be devoted to an understanding of this age-old and dangerous source of problems.

Social divisions

Some countries with non-homogeneous populations manifest further factors which operate destructively upon the formation of a social structure and the permanent developmental processes of a society's

[73]See Roy Godson (ed.), *Menace to Society: Political-criminal Collaboration Around the World* (2003), with case studies of "political-criminal nexuses" in Colombia, Hong Kong, Taiwan, Italy, Mexico, Nigeria, Russia and Ukraine, and the U.S. See also Douglas Valentine, *The CIA as Organized Crime: How Illegal Operations Corrupt America and the World* (2017). —Ed.

psychological and moral worldview. Primarily among these are the racial, ethnic, and cultural differences existing in virtually every conquest-engendered nation. Memories of former sufferings and contempt for the vanquished continue to divide the population for centuries. It is possible to overcome these difficulties if understanding and goodwill prevail throughout several generations.

Differences in religious beliefs and the moral convictions related thereto continue to cause problems, albeit less dangerous than the above unless aggravated by some doctrine of intolerance or superiority of one faith above others. Doctrines that preach such superiority and instill in their followers a contempt for other people, or even a conviction that they do not quite belong to our species, are a source of considerable problems.[74] The creation of a social structure whose links are patriotic and supra-denominational has, after all, been demonstrated as possible.

All these difficulties become extremely destructive if a social or religious group, in keeping with its doctrine, demands that its members be accorded positions which are in fact upwardly adjusted in relation to these people's true talents. This erodes the social structure, resulting in the aforementioned sick society.

A just social structure woven of individually adjusted persons, i.e., creative and dynamic as a whole, can only take shape if this process is subjected to its natural laws rather than some conceptual doctrines.[75] It benefits society as a whole for each individual to be able to find his own way to self-realization with assistance from a society that understands these laws, individual interests, and the common good.

[74]See Chapter VIII. In a secular context, Hitler's brand of ethnonationalism applies. As he wrote in *Mein Kampf*: "[The folkish worldview] by no means believes in an equality of the races, but along with their difference it recognizes their higher or lesser value and feels itself obligated, through this knowledge, to promote the victory of the better and stronger, and demand the subordination of the inferior and weaker in accordance with the eternal will that dominates this universe" (quoted in Richard Weikart, *Hitler's Religion: The Twisted Beliefs that Drove the Third Reich* [2016], p. xx.) See Chapter XIII on religion for further examples. —Ed.

[75]Recall Łobaczewski's statement about "social pedagogues" above. This is one reason why planned economies and many social interventions fail despite ostensibly good intentions. —Ed.

Macropathy

One obstacle to the development of a society's psychological worldview, the building of a healthy societal structure, and the institution of proper forms for governing the nation, would appear to be the enormous populations and vast distances of giant countries.[76] It is just precisely these nations which give rise to the greatest ethnic and cultural variations. In a vast, spreading land containing hundreds of millions of people, individuals feel powerless to exert an effect upon matters of high politics and become inclined to retreat into the world of self-interest.[77] Individualized human cognition is then replaced by generalizations about different social or ethnic groups, and even slogans, which impairs the development of a psychological worldview. The individual can no longer rely on the support of a familiar homeland, its social structure, and tradition to provide stability, which robs him of the values necessary for psychological growth. The structure of society becomes lost in wide-open spaces. What remains are narrow, generally familial, links, as well as those of property, ethnicity, tribe, and personal matters. In such countries, the concept of what "society" means disappears.

At the same time, governing such a country creates its own unavoidable problems: giants suffer from what could be called permanent macropathy (gigantism, or giant sickness), since the principal authorities are far away from any individual or local matters.[78] The main symptom is the proliferation of laws and regulations required for administration; they may appear proper in the capital but are often meaningless in outlying districts or when applied to individual matters. Officials are forced to follow regulations blindly; the scope of using their human reason and differentiating real situations becomes very narrow indeed. Such behavioral procedures have an impact upon the society, which also starts to think in terms of regulations

[76] For example, Russia, China, the United States, and Brazil, all of which have a land area of over 8,000,000 square kilometers and populations in the hundreds of millions (over one billion in the case of China). —Ed.

[77] Globalization has arguably broadened the scope of this effect beyond the borders of any given nation. Alexander I. Yuriev writes: "Globalization is a planetary intellectual machine, which goes out of human control and performs a person's modification without their knowledge and understanding" ("About Psychology and Psychotherapy of the Times of Globalization" [2013]). —Ed.

[78] See the discussion of national gigantism and decentralization in Versluis, *Mystical State*, pp. 124–125. —Ed.

instead of practical and psychological reality. Legalistic morality supersedes natural morality.[79] The psychological worldview, which constitutes the basic factor in cultural development and activates social life, thus becomes involuted. Human relations become coldly impersonal, coarse, or brutal.

It thus behooves us to ask: Is good government possible? Are giant countries capable of sustaining social and cultural evolution? A case study of the largest countries in our world, with their differing political systems, seems to suggest this is not the case. It would appear, rather, that the best candidates for development are those countries whose populations number between ten and twenty million,[80] and where personal bonds among citizens, and between citizens and their authorities, still safeguard correct psychological differentiation and natural relationships. Overly large countries should be divided into smaller organisms enjoying considerable autonomy, especially as regards cultural and economic matters; they could afford their citizens a feeling of homeland within which their personalities could develop and mature.

If someone asked me what should be done to heal the United States of America, a country which manifests symptoms of macropathy, *inter alia*, I would advise subdividing that vast nation into thirteen states—just like the original ones, except correspondingly larger and with more natural boundaries.[81] Such states should then be given considerable autonomy in matters of administration, economics, the judiciary, and culture. That would afford citizens a feeling of homeland, albeit a smaller one, and liberate the motivations of local pa-

[79]In *Logokracja*, pp. 31, 19, Łobaczewski writes: "The traditional moral and legal doctrines of Europe assumed that man is a conscious and therefore responsible being. At the same time, the ability to understand the vast scope of causality operating in the human personality, as well as the fundamental role of the unconscious mental life have been neglected. ... in some democratic countries, in practice we have a situation where the law shapes morality and has become the basic measure of human relationships. This causes a moral devolution of society and life becomes burdensome and full of stress." —Ed.

[80]The Polish edition says 7–15 million. —Ed.

[81]Colin Woodard, in *American Nations: A History of the Eleven Rival Regional Cultures of North America* (2012), provides potential support for this idea. Woodard identifies twelve distinct geographical cultures in the United States (in order from most to least populous): Greater Appalachia, Yankeedom, the Deep South, the Midlands, El Norte, the Far West, New Netherland, the Left Coast, Tidewater, the Spanish Caribbean, New France, and Greater Polynesia. —Ed.

triotism and healthy competition among such states, as well as the development of psychological worldview and social structure. This would, in turn, facilitate solutions to other problems with a different origin.[82]

***

Society is not an organism subordinating every cell to the good of the whole; neither is it a colony of insects, where the collective instinct acts like a dictator. However, it should also avoid being a collection of egocentric individuals linked purely by economic interests and formal administrative and legal organizations. Rather, society is a socio-psychological structure woven of individuals whose psychological organization is the highest, and thus the most diverse. The significant scope of man's individual freedom derives from this state of affairs and subsists in an extremely complicated relationship with his manifold psychological dependencies and moral obligations with regard to this collective whole, from other individuals to humanity as a whole.

Isolating an individual's personal interest as if it were at war with collective interests is artificially reductive reasoning which radically oversimplifies actual conditions instead of tracking their complex nature. Asking questions based on such distinctions is logically defective, since they contain erroneous suggestions, and can therefore produce no real answers. In reality, many ostensibly contradictory interests, such as individual vs. collective or those of various social groups and substructures, could be reconciled if we could be guided by a sufficiently penetrating understanding of the good of man and society, and if we could overcome emotional attitudes as well as some more or less primitive and suggestive doctrines. Such reconciliation, however, requires transferring the human and social problems in question to a higher level of understanding and acceptance of the natural laws of life. At this level, even the most difficult problems turn out to have a solution, since they invariably derive from the same insidious operations of psychopathological phenomena. We shall deal with this question toward the end of this book.

[82] *Author's note (1997):* Similarly, when it comes to European unification it is vital to oppose the creation of a colossus state. A Europe of independent homelands is necessary to preserve our cultural traditions and their creative role, and for the meaningful spiritual development of our citizens.

A colony of insects, no matter how well-organized socially, is doomed to extinction whenever its collective instinct continues to operate according to the psychogenetic code, although the biological meaning has disappeared. If, for instance, a queen bee does not effect her nuptial flight in time because the weather has been particularly bad, she begins laying unfertilized eggs which will hatch nothing but drones. The bees continue to defend their queen, as required by their instinct; of course, when the worker bees die out the hive becomes extinct.

At that point, only a "higher authority" in the shape of a beekeeper can save such a hive. He must find and destroy the drone queen and insinuate a healthy, fertilized queen into the hive along with a few of her young workers. A net is required for a few days to protect such a queen and her providers from being stung by those bees loyal to the old queen. Then the hive instinct accepts the new one. The apiarist generally suffers a few painful stings in the process.

The following question derives from the above comparison: Can the human hive inhabiting our globe achieve sufficient comprehension of the macrosocial pathological phenomenon which human nature finds so dangerous, abhorrent, and fascinating at the same time, and find a way out? At present, our individual and collective instincts and our natural psychological and moral worldview cannot furnish all the answers upon which to base skillful counteractive measures.

Those fair-minded people who preach that all we have left is to trust in the Great Apiarist and a return to His commandments are glimpsing a general truth, but they also tend to trivialize empirical truths, especially the naturalistic ones. It is the latter which constitute a basis for comprehending macrosocial phenomena and targeted practical action. The laws of nature have made us very different from one another, and Providence has set us on different paths. Thanks to his individual characteristics, unique life-circumstances, and scientific effort, man may have achieved sufficient mastery of the art of objectively comprehending the phenomena of the above-mentioned type, but we must underscore that this could only occur because it was in accordance with the laws of nature and the will of God.

If societies and their wise people are able to accept this objective understanding of social and sociopathological phenomena, overcoming the emotionalism and egotism of the natural worldview for this purpose, they shall find a means of action based on an understanding of the etiology and essence of the phenomena—and their Achilles heel.

It will then become evident that a proper vaccine or treatment can be found for each of the diseases scourging the earth in the form of major or minor social epidemics.

Just as a sailor possessing an accurate nautical map enjoys greater freedom of course-selection and maneuvering amid islands and bays, a person endowed with a better comprehension of self, others, and the complex interdependencies of social life becomes more independent of the various circumstances of life and better able to overcome situations which are difficult to understand. At the same time, such improved knowledge makes an individual more liable to accept his duties toward society and to subordinate himself to the discipline which arises as a corollary. Better-informed societies also achieve internal order and criteria for collective efforts. This book is dedicated to reinforcing this knowledge by means of a naturalistic understanding of certain phenomena, something heretofore comprehended only by means of excessively moralistic categories of the natural worldview. In turn, a person who understands the nature of macrosocial pathology becomes immune to its spellbinding influence.

In the long run, a constantly improving grasp of the laws governing social life, and its atypical secluded recesses, will lead us to critically reflect upon the failings and deficiencies of those social doctrines expounded to date, which were based on an extremely primitive understanding of these laws and phenomena. Such critiques, as well as the process of learning how the laws of nature operate in former and existing social systems, will naturally lead to a greater reliance on a deeper understanding of said laws. A new idea is about to be born based upon this ever-deepening comprehension of natural laws, namely the building of a more perfect social and political system for nations.

Such a system would be better than any of its predecessors. Building it is possible and necessary, not just some vague futuristic vision. After all, a whole series of countries is now dominated by conditions which have destroyed the structural forms worked out by history and replaced them with social systems inimical to creative functioning, systems which can only survive by means of force. Introducing democracy in such countries is a path paved with errors and failures. We are thus confronted with a great construction project demanding wide-ranging and well-organized work. The earlier we undertake the job, the more time we will have to carry it out.

CHAPTER III
THE HYSTEROIDAL CYCLE

Ever since human societies and civilizations have been created on our globe, people have longed for happy times full of tranquility and justice, which would have allowed everyone to herd his sheep in peace, search for fertile valleys, plow the earth, dig for its treasures, or build houses and palaces. Man desires peace so as to enjoy the benefits accumulated by earlier generations and to proudly observe the growth of future ones he has begotten. Sipping wine or mead in the meantime would be nice. He would like to wander about, becoming familiar with other lands and people, or enjoy the star-studded sky of the south, the colors of nature, and the faces and costumes of women. He would also like to give free rein to his imagination and immortalize his name in works of art, whether sculptured in marble or eternalized in myth and poetry.

From time immemorial, then, man has dreamed of a life in which the measured effort of mind and muscle would be punctuated by well-deserved rest. Therefore, he strove to learn nature's laws so as to dominate her and take advantage of her gifts. Man enlisted the natural power of animals in order to make his dreams come true, and when this did not meet his needs, he turned to his own kind for this purpose, in part depriving other humans of their humanity simply because he was more powerful.

Dreams of a happy and peaceful life thus gave rise to force over others, a force which depraves the mind of its user. That is why man's dreams of happiness have not come true throughout history. This hedonistic view of "happiness" contains the seeds of misery, feeding the eternal cycle whereby good times give birth to bad times, which in turn cause the suffering and mental effort that produce experience, good sense, moderation, and a certain amount of psychological knowledge, all virtues which serve to rebuild more felicitous conditions of existence.[1]

---

[1]The list of twentieth-century scholars of historical cycles of war and revolution includes Russian Cosmist Alexander Chizhevsky in the 1920s, who influenced

During good times, people progressively lose sight of the need for profound reflection, introspection, knowledge of others, and an understanding of life's complicated laws. Is it worth pondering the properties of human nature and man's flawed personality, whether one's own or someone else's? Can we understand the creative meaning of suffering we have not undergone ourselves, instead of taking the easy way out and blaming the victim? Any excess mental effort seems like pointless labor if life's joys appear to be available for the taking. A clever, liberal, and merry individual is a good sport; a more farsighted person predicting dire results becomes a wet-blanket killjoy.[2]

Perception of the truth about the inner and outer reality of man, especially an understanding of the human personality and its values and shortcomings, ceases to be a virtue during the so-called "happy" times; thoughtful doubters are decried as meddlers who cannot leave well enough alone. This, in turn, leads to an impoverishment of psychological knowledge (the basis of moral values), the capacity of differentiating the properties of human nature and personality, and the ability to mold minds creatively. The qualities necessary to make rational decisions in individual and collective life disappear. Emotions begin to dominate over intellect, and the cult of the body increases. Is it not nicer to think more pleasing thoughts? The cult of power thus supplants those mental values so essential for maintaining law and order by peaceful means. A nation's enrichment or involution regarding its psychological worldview could be considered an indicator of whether its future will be good or bad.

Edward R. Dewey's work on economic cycles in the '40s; Pitirim A. Sorokin (sociological cycle theory) in the '30s; Quincy Wright and Arnold Toynbee in the '50s; and William Strauss and Neil Howe in the '90s (generational theory, presented in their book *The Fourth Turning: An American Prophecy – What the Cycles of History Tell Us About America's Next Rendezvous with Destiny* [1997]). The most recent and most scientific is Peter Turchin's structural-demographic theory (initially developed by sociologist Jack Goldstone) and the field of cliodynamics (from Clio, the muse of history). See, for example, Turchin's work on "imperiogenesis" and "imperiopathosis" in *War and Peace and War: The Rise and Fall of Empires* (2006). See Glossary entry "hysteroidal cycle" and further notes for additional discussion. —Ed.

[2] Jordan Peterson writes: "success makes us complacent. We forget to pay attention. We take what we have for granted. We turn a blind eye. We fail to notice that things are changing, or that corruption is taking root. And everything falls apart" (*12 Rules*, p. 156). —Ed.

During "good" times, the search for truth becomes uncomfortable because it reveals inconvenient facts. It is better to think about easier and more pleasant things. Unconscious elimination of data which are, or appear to be, inexpedient gradually turns into habit, and then becomes a custom accepted by society at large. However, any thought process based on such truncated information cannot possibly give rise to correct conclusions; it further leads to subconscious substitution of inconvenient premises by more convenient ones, thereby approaching the boundaries of psychopathology.[3]

Such contented periods—often rooted in some injustice to other people or nations[4]—start to strangle the capacity for individual and societal consciousness; subconscious factors take over a decisive role in life. Such a society, already infected by the hysteroidal state,[5] considers any perception of uncomfortable truth to be a sign of "ill-breeding." J. G. Herder's[6] iceberg is drowned in a sea of falsified unconsciousness; only the tip of the iceberg is visible above the waves of life. Catastrophe waits in the wings. In such times, the capacity for logical and disciplined thought, born of necessity during difficult times, begins to fade. When communities lose the capacity for psychological reason and moral criticism, the processes of the generation of evil are intensified at every social scale, whether individual or macrosocial, until they give rise to "bad" times.

We already know that every society contains a certain percentage of people carrying psychological deviations caused by various inherited

---

[3]See "Conversive thinking" in Chapter IV and the Glossary. —Ed.

[4]As Peter Turchin shows, eras of "good feelings" are often associated with successful wars of expansion as well as a "closing of the patriciate," i.e., homogenization of the elite. The U.S. has seen two such periods: the 1820s and the 1950s, which followed the War of 1812 and WWII, and were concurrent with the Indian Wars and the Korean War, respectively. See Turchin, *Ages of Discord: A Structural-Demographic Analysis of American History* (2016), pp. 106, 133–136, 180, 207. —Ed.

[5]That is, a state resembling hysteria: excessive, uncontrollable emotion (e.g., fear, panic), exaggerated excitability and suggestibility. (Łobaczewski describes the hysteroidal state in more detail below.) —Ed.

[6]Johann Gottfried Herder (1744–1803), German theologian and philosopher, had a teleological view of history and saw national cultures as organic beings, with their own phases of youth, maturity, and decline. He was also an early proponent of the theory of unconscious mental processes—thus the iceberg metaphor—in some ways anticipating depth psychology (e.g., Freud and Jung) and Daniel Wegner's more recent idea of the adaptive unconscious. See Timothy D. Wilson's *Strangers to Ourselves: Discovering the Adaptive Unconscious* (2004). —Ed.

or acquired factors which produce anomalies in feeling, thought, and character. Many such people attempt to impart meaning to their deviant lives by means of social hyperactivity.[7] They create their own myths and overcompensatory ideologies and have the tendency to egotistically insinuate them to others. Their goals and ideas, which result from their deviant manner of experiencing, easily hook into minds in which the sense and understanding of psychological realities has already started to deteriorate.

When a few generations' worth of "good-time" insouciance and increasing hysterics result in a societal deficit regarding psychological skill and moral criticism, this paves the way for pathological plotters, spellbinders, even more primitive impostors, and their organized systems of social and moral destruction to act and merge into the processes of the origination of evil.[8] They are essential factors in its synthesis. In the next chapter I shall attempt to persuade my readers that the participation of pathological factors, so underrated by the social sciences, is a common phenomenon in the processes of the origin of evil.

Those times which many people later recall as the "good old days" thus provide fertile soil for future tragedy because of the progressive devolution of moral, intellectual, and personality values which gives rise to Rasputin-like eras—times of deceit, bitterness, and lawlessness.

The above is a sketch of the causative understanding of reality which in no way contradicts a perception of the teleological sense of causality.[9] Bad times are not merely the result of hedonistic regression to the past; they have a historical purpose to fulfill. Suffering, effort, and mental activity during times of pervasive bitterness lead to a gradual, generally heightened, regeneration of lost values, which results in human progress. Unfortunately, we still lack a sufficiently exhaustive philosophical grasp of this interdependence of causality and teleology regarding events. It seems that prophets were more clear-sighted, in the light of the laws of creation, than philosophers such as E. S. Russell, R. B. Braithwaite, G. Sommerhoff, and others who pondered this question.[10]

[7]For example, various forms of social and political activism. —Ed.

[8]Oakley writes: "Machiavellians are *always* present in every system that relates to power. It's just that in times of troubles and in nontransparent systems, it's easier for them to reach the pinnacle" (*Evil Genes*, p. 335). —Ed.

[9]Teleology explains phenomena in terms of their end goal or purpose. —Ed.

[10]Edward Stuart Russell (1887–1954), Scottish philosopher and biologist and

When bad times arrive and people are overwhelmed by an excess of evil, they must gather all their physical and mental strength to fight for existence and protect human reason. The search for some way out of the difficulties and dangers rekindles long-buried powers of discretion. Such people have the initial tendency to rely on force in order to counteract the threat; they may, for instance, become "trigger-happy" or dependent upon armies. Slowly and laboriously, however, they discover the advantages conferred by mental effort: improved understanding of the psychological situation in particular, better differentiation of human characters and personalities, and, finally, comprehension of one's adversaries. During such times, virtues which former generations relegated to literary motifs regain their real and useful substance and become prized for their value. A wise person capable of furnishing sound advice is highly respected.

How astonishingly similar were the philosophies of Socrates and Confucius, those half-legendary thinkers who, albeit near-contemporaries, resided at opposite ends of the great continent. Both lived during evil, bloody times and adumbrated a method for conquering evil, especially regarding perception of the laws of life and knowledge of human nature.[11] They searched for criteria of moral values within human nature and considered knowledge and understanding to be virtues. Both men, however, heard the same wordless internal Voice warning those embarking upon important moral questions: "Socrates, do not do this." That is why their efforts and sacrifices constitute permanent assistance in the battle against evil.

---

author of *Form and Function* (1916). An opponent of mechanistic biology, Russell held teleological and holistic/organicist views of biology, as evident in the title of his 1945 work, *The Directiveness of Organic Activities*. Rupert Sheldrake has developed a similar line of thought in recent years, e.g., in *Morphic Resonance: The Nature of Formative Causation* (2009). See also McGilchrist, *The Matter with Things*, pp. 477–483 and ch. 27.

Richard Bevan Braithwaite (1900–1990), British philosopher of science and religion, with a focus on probability and statistics. His views on teleology can be found in *Scientific Explanation: A Study of the Function of Theory, Probability and Law in Science* (1953).

Gerd Sommerhoff (1915–2002), pioneer of theoretical neuroscience. He develops a non-teleological account of goal-directed behavior in *Analytical Biology* (1950). —Ed.

[11]Socrates (c. 470–399 B.C.), the founder of Western philosophy, lived through the Peloponnesian War. Confucius (551–479 B.C.), whose thought formed the basis of East Asian culture, lived through the fall of the Zhou dynasty. —Ed.

Difficult and laborious times give rise to values which finally conquer evil and produce better times. The succinct and accurate analysis of phenomena, made possible thanks to the conquest of the expendable emotions, conversive thinking, and egotism characterizing self-satisfied people, opens the door to causative behavior, particularly in the areas of philosophical, psychological, and moral reflection; this tips the scale to the advantage of goodness and order. If these values were totally incorporated into humankind's cultural heritage, they could sufficiently protect nations from the next era of "errors and distortions."[12] However, collective memory is impermanent and particularly liable to remove a philosopher and his work from his context, namely his time and place and the goals which he served.

Whenever an experienced person finds a moment of relative peace after a difficult and painful effort, his mind is free to reflect unencumbered by the expendable emotions and outdated attitudes of the past, but aided by the cognizance of bygone years. He thus comes closer to an objective understanding of phenomena and a view of actual causal relations, including those which cannot be understood within the framework of natural language. He thus meditates upon an ever-expanding circle of general laws while contemplating the meaning of those former events which separated periods of history. We reach for ancient precepts because we understand them better; they make it easier for us to understand both the genesis and the creative meaning of unhappy times.

These people try to pass such knowledge on to posterity, using a more natural language as a matter of course. Even then, however, they have a sense of the inadequacy of this language and feel anxious about whether this wisdom of theirs, acquired at the cost of the suffering and blood of many people, will reach the minds of future generations, brought up in happier times.

The cycle of happy, peaceful times favors a narrowing of the world-view and an increase in egotism; societies become subject to progressive hysteria and to that final stage, descriptively known to historians and more easily understood by psychopathologists, which finally produces times of despondency, violence, and confusion that have lasted for millennia and continue to do so.[13] The recession of mind and

---

[12]This was how communists typically explained away the brutal excesses and policy failures of prior leaders, i.e., as deviations not representative of "true" Marxism, which they now proclaimed to uphold. —Ed.

[13]Janowski writes: "When the number of paranoid people in any given society

personality which is a feature of ostensibly happy times varies from one nation to another; thus some countries manage to survive the results of such crises with minor losses, whereas other times it leads to revolution and the collapse of nations and empires.[14] Geopolitical factors have also played a decisive role.

The psychological features of such crises doubtless bear the stamp of the time and of the civilization in question, but one common denominator must have been an exacerbation of society's hysterical condition. This "highly contagious disease" or, better yet, *formative deficiency of character*, is a perennial sickness of societies, especially the privileged elites.[15] Individuals differ only in the severity of such symptoms. The existence of exaggerated individual cases, especially such characterized as clinical, is an offshoot of the level of social hysteria, quite frequently correlated with some additional causes such as carriers of minor lesions of brain tissue or hereditary features. Quantitatively and qualitatively, these individuals may serve to reveal these states' cyclical periods and to evaluate such times, as indicated in history's *Story of San Michele.*[16] From the perspective of historical times, it would be harder to examine the regression of the ability

---

reaches a high level, we can be pretty sure that we are sliding into large-scale paranoia, which can, and likely will, seek refuge under the umbrella of totalitarianism" (*Homo Americanus*, p. 214). See also Robert S. Robins and Jerrold M. Post, *Political Paranoia: The Psychopolitics of Hatred* (1997), pp. 42–67, on "mass paranoias" (or mass hysterias) and paranoid cultures. —Ed.

[14] See Turchin and Nefedov, *Secular Cycles*, which analyses Roman (Republican and Principate), French (Capetian and Valois), English (Plantagenet and Tudor-Stuart), and Russian (Muscovy and Romanov) cycles. —Ed.

[15] For a trenchant critique of the United States' bipartisan ruling class as an incompetent, crony-capitalist aristocracy of "professionals" (in government, finance, big business, media) with a self-proclaimed exclusive grip on "science" and overinflated sense of their own intellectual and social superiority, and whose policies produce pointless wars and massive debt, see Angelo M. Codevilla's *The Ruling Class: How They Corrupted America and What We Can Do about It* (2010). The current social hysteria of social justice is endemic among this "progressive" class, which Codevilla argues only ever have the support of up to one third of the American population. See also Michael McConkey, *The Managerial Class on Trial* (2021). —Ed.

[16] *The Story of San Michele* is an autobiographical work by Swedish physician and psychiatrist Axel Munthe (1857–1949). Its stories span a wide range of time and places, and range from interactions with celebrities of the time (like Jean-Martin Charcot, Louis Pasteur, and Henry James), mythological scenes, and conversation with animals (Munthe was known as "the modern St. Francis of Assisi"), to discussions on euthanasia, rabies research, and suicide. —Ed.

and correctness of reasoning or the intensity of "Austrian talk,"[17] although these approximate the crux of the matter better and more directly.

In spite of the above-mentioned qualitative differences, the duration of these time-cycles tends to be similar. If we assume that the extreme of European hysteria occurred around 1900 and returns not quite every two centuries, we find similar conditions.[18] For example, at the beginning of the eighteenth century, similar conditions could be observed in Western Europe, with France at the forefront. Such cyclical isochronicity[19] may embrace a civilization and cross into neighboring countries, but it would not swim oceans or penetrate into faraway and far different civilizations.[20]

When World War I broke out, young officers danced and sang on the streets of Vienna: "*Krieg, Krieg, Krieg! Es wird ein schoener Krieg.*"[21] While visiting Upper Austria in 1978, I decided to drop in on the local parson, who was in his seventies by then. When I told him about myself, I suddenly realized he thought I was lying and inventing pretty stories. He subjected my statements to psychological analysis based on this unassailable assumption, which he made clear to me. When I complained to an Austrian friend of mine about this, he was amused: "As a psychologist, you were extremely lucky to catch the survival of authentic Austrian talk ('*die oesterreichische*

[17] Defined two paragraphs below. —Ed.

[18] In *Ponerologia* (p. 58), Łobaczewski writes that he thinks the cycle is even shorter than that, "or perhaps variable and dependent on various historical circumstances." Such cycles of political instability in pre-industrial societies usually averaged around two to three centuries, largely determined by population growth (see Turchin and Nefedov, *Secular Cycles*). These cycles are not strictly periodic, but vary in length as a result of various systemic feedbacks and some random variables interacting dynamically. Industrial societies' cycles can thus be shorter in duration (largely due to the effects of immigration not present in pre-industrial societies). For example, the first American cycle (1780–1930) was 150 years. See Turchin, *Ages of Discord*, pp. 57, 244. Turchin also identifies a shorter 40–60-year cycle (roughly two generations) of political violence that operates within the larger cycle. —Ed.

[19] Cycles of equal lengths of time. —Ed.

[20] *Author's note (1997):* In Poland, Professor Eugeniusz Brzezicki from Krakow was an expert on hysteria and a researcher into these historical cycles. But as a result of the dehystericization of our society, this field of knowledge seems of little use to our contemporary psychologists and has therefore been neglected. [Eugeniusz Brzezicki (1890–1974), psychiatrist, neurologist, and head of the psychiatry department at Jagiellonian University. —Ed.]

[21] "War, war, war! Oh, what a beautiful war it will be." —Ed.

Rede'). We young ones would have been incapable of demonstrating it to you even if we wanted to simulate it."

In the European languages, "Austrian talk" has become the common descriptive term for paralogistic discourse.[22] Many people using this term nowadays are unaware of its origin. Within the context of maximum hysterical intensity in Europe at the time, the authentic article represented a typical product of conversive thinking: subconscious selection and substitution of data leading to chronic avoidance of the crux of the matter.[23] In the same manner, the reflex assumption that every speaker is lying is an indication of an hysterical anticulture of mendacity, within which telling the truth was considered a sign of ill breeding.

That era of hysteroidal regression gave birth to the Great War and the Great Revolution,[24] which extended into fascism, Hitlerism, and the tragedy of World War II. It also produced the macrosocial phenomenon whose deviant character became superimposed upon this cycle, screening and destroying its nature. Contemporary Europe is heading for[25] the opposite extreme of this historical sine curve. We could thus assume that the beginning of the next century will produce an era of better capability and correctness of reason, thus leading to many new values in all realms of human discovery and creativity. We can also foresee that realistic psychological understanding and spiritual enrichment will be features of this era.[26]

---

[22]Discourse that is out of touch with reality, involving illogical, fallacious, unwarranted premises and conclusions. See Glossary. —Ed.

[23]On the inability to make correct (even obvious) inferences, and its association with right hemisphere damage, see McGilchrist, *Matter with Things*, pp. 210–212. —Ed.

[24]World War I (1914–1918) and the Russian Revolution (1917–1923). The two revolutions of 1917 abolished tsarism in Russia and were followed by a massive civil war, which resulted in the victory of the Bolsheviks and the establishment of the Soviet Union. For the complex geopolitics of the time, see Gerry Docherty and Jim Macgregor, *Hidden History: The Secret Origins of the First World War* (2014); Jim Macgregor and Gerry Docherty, *Prolonging the Agony: How the Anglo-American Establishment Deliberately Extended WWI by Three-and-a-Half Years* (2018); Guido Giacomo Preparata, "Conjuring Lenin," in *Conjuring Hitler: How Britain and America Made the Third Reich* (2005), pp. 27–38; Richard B. Spence, *Wall Street and the Russian Revolution: 1905–1925* (2017); and Antony C. Sutton, *Wall Street and the Bolshevik Revolution: The Remarkable True Story of the American Capitalists Who Financed the Russian Communists* (2012 [1974]). —Ed.

[25]*Author's note (1997):* Now past.

[26]This assumes an unchanging two-century cycle. However, as pointed out above, societies are nonlinear dynamical systems, and modern cycles are shorter than

At the same time, North America, especially the USA, has reached a nadir for the first time in its short history. It is hard to judge whether we are observing the symptoms of incipient upward movement (i.e., dehystericization and recovery), although it seems likely.[27] Grey-haired Europeans living in the U.S. today are struck by the similarity between these phenomena and the ones dominating Europe at the times of their youth. The emotionalism dominating individual, collective, and political life, as well as the subconscious selection and substitution of data in reasoning, make communication difficult. They are impoverishing the development of a psychological worldview and leading to individual and national egotism. The mania for taking offense at the drop of a hat provokes constant retaliation, taking advantage of hyper-irritability and hypo-criticality on the part of others.[28] This can be considered analogous to the European dueling mania of those times. People fortunate enough to achieve a position higher than someone else are contemptuous of their supposed inferiors

historical ones. This suggests that Europe may also have entered an era of crisis rather than renewal, a possibility supported by Turchin's political stress index calculations for Western Europe. See Turchin et al., "The 2010 Structural-demographic Forecast for the 2010–2020 Decade: A Retrospective Assessment" (2020). —Ed.

[27] *Author's note (1997):* Written in New York, 1984. Currently, at the turn of the century, one can clearly see signs of recovery from this crisis. [The 1980s and early '90s in the USA saw several mass hysterias and social contagions, including the "satanic panic" with its allegations of widespread ritual abuse, recovered memory syndrome, a peak in serial killings, and epidemics of multiple personality disorder and eating disorders, primarily among girls and young women. See the discussion in Versluis, *New Inquisitions*, chs. 11 and 12. It was also the dawn of political correctness (see Janowski, *Homo Americanus*, p. 63), and the point at which elite overproduction began (Turchin, *Ages*, p. 234). Łobaczewski wrote his note four years before 9/11, which was followed by the 2008 financial crisis seven years later, the police shooting of Michael Brown in 2014 that inspired Black Lives Matter, the election of Donald J. Trump in 2016, the death of George Floyd in 2020 that inspired BLM and antifa riots, and the global COVID-19 crisis, all of which sparked or were products of widespread waves of social hysteria. See James Lindsay, "The Rise of the Woke Cultural Revolution" (2021), and Bagus et al., "COVID-19 and the Political Economy of Mass Hysteria" (2021). —Ed.]

[28] This tendency has intensified in the intervening years. Lukianoff and Haidt write of an "emerging morality of victimhood culture" in the U.S. characterized by "high sensitivity to slight," the tendency to resolve conflict by complaining to third parties, and cultivating "an image of being victims who deserve assistance" (*Coddling*, p. 210). See also Scott O. Lilienfeld, "Microaggressions: Strong Claims, Inadequate Evidence" (2017). —Ed.

in a way highly reminiscent of tsarist Russian customs. Turn-of-the-century Freudian psychology finds fertile soil in this country because of the similarity in social and psychological conditions.

America's psychological recession drags in its wake an impaired socio-occupational adjustment of this country's people, leading to a waste of human talent and an involution of societal structure. If we were to calculate this country's adjustment correlation index, as suggested in the prior chapter, it would probably be lower than the great majority of the free and civilized nations of this world, and possibly lower than some countries which have lost their freedom. A highly talented individual in the USA finds it ever more difficult to fight his way through to self-realization and a socially creative position. Universities, politics, and even some areas of business ever more frequently demonstrate a united front of relatively untalented persons. The word "overeducated" is heard more and more often. Such "overqualified" individuals finally hide out in some foundation laboratory where they are allowed to earn the Nobel Prize. In the meantime, the country as a whole—its administration and politics—suffers due to a deficit in the inspirational role of highly gifted individuals.[29]

As a result, America is stifling progress in all areas of life, from culture to technology and economics, not excluding political incompetence. When linked to other deficiencies, an egotist's incapability of understanding other people and nations leads to political error and the scapegoating of outsiders.[30] Slamming the brakes on the evolution of political structures and social institutions increases both administrative inertia and discontent on the part of its victims.

---

[29]On elite overproduction trends in the U.S., see Turchin, *Ages*, pp. 231–236. —Ed.

[30]As Codevilla writes: "America's best and brightest believe themselves qualified and duty-bound to direct the lives not only of Americans, but of foreigners as well" (*Ruling Class*, p. 22). George W. Bush's neoconservative administration's Global War on Terror and domestic Patriot Act created a groundwork easily exploited by totalitarians. (See Versluis, *New Inquisitions*, ch. 13; and Naomi Wolf, *The End of America: Letter of Warning to a Young Patriot* [2007].) The Barack Obama administrations followed suit, continuing Bush's wars and starting new ones. The weeks before and after President Joe Biden's inauguration saw widespread labeling of Trump supporters and Capitol Hill rioters as domestic terrorists, language that entered American political discourse during the Bush and Obama years. Critics of U.S. policy and media had already been labeled as "conspiracy theorists" and "terrorist sympathizers" if not actual terrorists. See Glenn Greenwald, "The New Domestic War on Terror Is Coming" (2021) and "The New Domestic War on Terror Has Already Begun—Even Without the New Laws Biden Wants" (2021). —Ed.

We should realize that the most dramatic social difficulties and tensions occur about a quarter of a century after the time of maximum hystericization and at least ten years after the first observable indications of having emerged from a psychological crisis, during the period of recovery. These difficulties can be regarded as sequelae—a delayed reaction to the crisis, since the process of psychological rehabilitation is still insufficiently developed. This can be dated to the beginning of the twenty-first century.[31] The time span for effective countermeasures is thus rather limited.

Therefore it appears that the United States is heading for a profound political crisis, comparable to those which have previously resulted from the circumstances described above. However, this vast country is so culturally diverse that it is enough to drive 50 miles to find oneself in a different social environment. For this reason what happens in one part of the country provokes a critical response in another. At the same time, the geopolitical situation of the country is very favorable. So shall we see what the future will bring?[32]

Is Europe entitled to look down on America for suffering from the same sickness the former has succumbed to several times in the past, with inhuman and tragic results? Is America's feeling of superiority toward Europe, derived from these past conditions and their resulting wars and revolutions, anything more than a harmless anachronism? It would be most useful if the European nations took advantage of their historical experience and more modern psychological knowledge so as to help America most effectively.

[31]Taking 1984 (when Łobaczewski wrote the book) as the peak of hystericization in North America puts this at 2009; taking 1997 (when he wrote the note above) as the first sign of recovery puts it at sometime after 2007. The financial crisis of 2007–2008 caused the biggest recession since the 1930s, since eclipsed by the COVID-19 recession of 2020. —Ed.

[32]In 2010 Peter Turchin predicted that "the next decade is likely to be a period of growing instability in the United States," a prediction that came true (*Ages of Discord*, p. 5). In 2016 he wrote: "As to the present, we live in times of intensifying structural-demographic pressures for instability. The PSI [political stress index] has not yet reached the same high level that triggered the Civil War of 1861–65. However, its explosive growth should be a matter of grave concern for all of us—our economic and political elites, as well as the general public. Will we be capable of taking collective action to avoid the worst of the impending demographic-structural crisis? I hope so" (*Ages of Discord*, p. 248). Turchin abandoned that hope in 2018 (see "The Ginkgo Model of Societal Crisis"). —Ed.

East Central Europe, now under Soviet domination,[33] is part of the European cycle, albeit somewhat delayed; the same applies to the Soviet empire, especially to the European portion. There, however, tracking these changes and isolating them from more dramatic phenomena eludes the possibilities of observation, even if it is only a matter of methodology. Even there, however, there is progressive growth in the grass-roots resistance of the regenerative power of healthy common sense, which will eventually lead to the emergence of a system based on better understanding of the laws of nature. In the meantime, this has already been partially accomplished. Year by year, the dominant system feels weaker vis-à-vis these organic transformations. May we add to this a phenomenon the West finds totally incomprehensible, and which shall be discussed in greater detail: namely, the growing specific, practical knowledge about the governing reality within countries whose regimes are similar. This facilitates individual resistance and a reconstruction of social links. Such processes shall, in the final analysis, produce a watershed situation, although it will probably not be a bloody counter-revolution.

***

The question suggests itself: Will the time ever come when this eternal cycle rendering the nations almost helpless can be conquered? Can countries permanently maintain their creative and critical activities at a consistently high level? Our era contains many exceptional moments; our contemporary Macbeth witches' cauldron holds not only poisonous ingredients, but also practical progress and understanding such as humanity has not seen in millennia.

Upbeat economists point out that humanity has gained a powerful slave in the form of electric energy and that war, conquest, and subjugation of other countries is becoming increasingly unprofitable. Unfortunately, as we shall see later in this work, nations can be pushed into economically irrational transformations and desires by other motives whose character is meta-economic. That is why overcoming these other causes and phenomena which give rise to evil is a difficult, albeit at least theoretically attainable, task. However, in order to master it, we must understand the nature and dynamics of said phenomena: an old principle of medicine that I will repeat again and again says: *Ignoti nulla est curatio morbi.*

---

[33] *Author's note*: At the time of writing, 1984.

One accomplishment of modern science contributing to the destruction of these eternal cycles is the development of communication systems which have linked our globe into one huge, interconnected system. The time cycles sketched herein used to run their course almost independently in various civilizations and on different continents. Their phases neither were, nor are, synchronized. We can assume that the American phase lags 80 years behind the European. When people, information, and news flow freely between countries and across oceans; when different social and psychological contents and opinions conditioned by unlike phases of said cycles, among other things, overflow all boundaries and information security systems;[34] all this will give rise to pressures which can change the causal dependencies herein.[35] A more plastic psychological situation thus emerges, which increases the possibilities for pinpointed action based on an understanding of the phenomena.

At the same time, in spite of many difficulties of a scientific, social, and political nature, we see the development of a new set of factors which may eventually contribute to the liberation of mankind from the effects of uncomprehended historical causation. The development

[34]For another view on mass-communication technology's effect on empires and cycles, see Turchin, *War and Peace and War*, ch. 14. —Ed.

[35]These remarks were prescient, given the rise of the Internet in the decades after they were written. However, while news and analysis can now be shared instantaneously worldwide, the Internet is also increasingly monitored, censored, and controlled, and domestic and global surveillance and collection of data are widespread. All major world powers engage in offensive and defensive cyberwarfare and employ "keyboard armies" to shape public opinion. Mass surveillance and collection of personal data are routine. Big tech censorship escalated sharply in the late 2010s and early 2020s. For the role of technology in the new totalitarianism, see Michael Rectenwald, *Google Archipelago: The Digital Gulag and the Simulation of Freedom* (2019), and Janowski, *Homo Americanus*, pp. 217–218. Already in 1920, Everett Dean Martin wrote in his book *The Behavior of Crowds: A Psychological Study*: "the leader in crowd-thinking *par excellence* is the daily newspaper. ... These great 'molders of public opinion,' reveal every characteristic of the vulgar mob orator. The character of the writing commonly has the standards and prejudices of the 'man in the street.' And lest this man's ego consciousness be offended by the sight of anything 'highbrow'—that is, anything indicating that there may be a superior intelligence or finer appreciation than his own—newspaper-democracy demands that everything more exalted than the level of the lowest cranial altitude be left out. The average result is a deluge of sensational scandal, class prejudice, and special pleading clumsily disguised with a saccharine smear of the cheapest moral platitude. Consequently, the thinking of most of us is carried on chiefly in the form of crowd-ideas" (pp. 45–46). —Ed.

of science, whose final goal is a better understanding of man and the laws of social life, will, in the long run, cause public opinion to accept essential knowledge about human nature and the development of the human personality, which will enable the harmful processes to be controlled.[36] Some forms of international cooperation and supervision will be needed for this.

The development of the human personality and its capacity for proper thinking and accurate comprehension of reality, unfortunately, demands overcoming comfortable laziness and applying the efforts of special scientific work under conditions quite different from those under which we have been raised, often accompanied by inconvenience and a certain amount of risk. Under such conditions, an egotistic personality—accustomed to a comfortably narrow environment, superficial thinking, and excessive emotionalism—begins to disintegrate, thus giving rise to intellectual and cognitive efforts and moral reflection which result in its positive evolution. The specially altered circumstances thus condition a transformation of the human personality which cannot be liberated artificially.

One example of such a program of experience is the American Peace Corps.[37] Young people travel to many poor, developing countries in order to live and work there, often under primitive conditions. They learn to understand other nations and customs, and their egotism decreases. Their worldview develops and becomes more realistic. They thus lose the characteristic defects of the modern American character. May God make the most gifted among them the president of this country some day.

---

[36]Provided this development of science is not suppressed or subordinated to ideology and/or power struggles, resulting in a scientistic dogmatism. See Chapter VII and, for example, *Against the Tide: A Critical Review by Scientists of How Physics and Astronomy Get Done* (2008), edited by Martín López Corredoira and Carlos Castro Perelman (thanks to Iza Rosca for suggesting this reference). Several trends in Western academic research and publishing are cause for concern, e.g., blocking publication of controversial research, succumbing to mob pressure to retract "politically incorrect" papers, scientific results falsified for corporate interests, and the so-called replication crisis. See McGilchrist, *The Matter with Things*, ch. 13 ("Institutional science and truth"). —Ed.

[37]The Peace Corps was set up in 1961 by President John F. Kennedy (1917–1963). In sixty years over 240,000 Americans (most with a college degree) have volunteered and served in 142 countries. The Corps was part of the early Kennedy administration's initiative to "curb the structural and ideological appeal of communism." See Dickey et al., "Russian Political Warfare: Origin, Evolution, and Application" (2015), pp. 88–89. —Ed.

In order to overcome something whose origin is shrouded in the mists of time immemorial, we often feel we must battle the ever-turning windmills of history. However, the end goal of such effort is the possibility that an objective understanding of human nature and its eternal weaknesses, plus the resulting transformation of societal psychology, may enable us effectively to counteract or prevent the destructive and tragic results sometime in the not too distant future—a vision that should be considered a real possibility, one already known to Ivan Pavlov.[38]

Our times are exceptional, and suffering now gives rise to better comprehension than it did centuries ago. This understanding and knowledge fit better into the total picture, since they are based on objective data. Such a view therefore becomes realistic, because people and problems mature in action. Such action should not be limited to theoretical contemplations, but rather, acquire organization and form.

In order to facilitate this, let us consider the selected questions and the draft of a new scientific discipline which would study evil, discovering its factors of genesis, insufficiently understood properties, and weak spots, thereby outlining new possibilities to counteract the origin of human suffering.

[38]Throughout his life, "the possibility of a Psychology that contributed to 'peace and order'" was an important foundation of Pavlov's quest (Daniel Todes, personal communication, Feb. 2021). See Todes, *Ivan Pavlov*, intro, chs. 21, 29, 49. —Ed

CHAPTER IV
PONEROLOGY

Ever since ancient times, philosophers and religious thinkers representing various attitudes in different cultures have been searching for the truth regarding moral values, attempting to find criteria for what is right and what constitutes good advice. They have described the virtues of human character and suggested how these may be acquired. They have created a heritage worthy of study, containing centuries of experience and reflection. While it is natural for their views and attitudes to differ, the similarity or complementary nature of the conclusions reached by famous ancient philosophers is striking, even though they worked in widely divergent times and places. It demonstrates that whatever is valuable is conditioned and caused by the laws of nature acting upon the personalities of both individual human beings and collective societies.

It is equally thought-provoking, however, to see how relatively little has been said about the opposite side of the coin: the nature, causes, and genesis of evil. These matters are usually cloaked behind the above-generalized conclusions with a certain amount of discretion, or have been too hastily personified.[1] Such a state of affairs can be partially ascribed to the social conditions and historical circumstances under which these thinkers worked; their *modus operandi* may have been dictated at least in part by personal fate, inherited traditions, or even prudery. After all, the virtues of justice, moderation, and truthfulness are the opposites of force, perversity, and mendacity, just as health is the opposite of illness. But there was another cru-

[1]As Todd Calder writes for the *Stanford Encyclopedia of Philosophy*: "Prior to World War II there was very little philosophical literature on the concept of evil in the narrow sense [i.e., 'the most morally despicable sorts of actions, characters, events']." Ancient philosophers dealt with evil in the broad sense (natural and moral evil), e.g., Manichaean dualism, or privation theories (lack of the Platonic form of goodness or virtue). Presumably Łobaczewski means that such matters have been too often dealt with in broad terms, too overly personalized (i.e., a moralizing interpretation), or personified (e.g., as the devil, the demiurge, "Ahriman," or even materiality itself). —Ed.

cial reason for this deficit. The factors that take an active part in the genesis of evil have only been identified recently, and nowadays scientific knowledge of them has begun to advance.

The character and genesis of evil thus remained hidden in discreet shadows, leaving it to literature to deal with the subject, which, though highly expressive, has never reached the primeval source of the phenomena. A certain cognitive space thus remained as an uninvestigated thicket of moral questions which resist understanding and philosophical generalizations. Present-day philosophers developing metaethics try to go further; as they slip and slide along the elastic space leading to an analysis of the language of ethics, they contribute toward eliminating the imperfections and habits of natural conceptual language.[2] However, penetrating this ever-mysterious nucleus is highly tempting to a scientist.

At the same time, active participants in social life and normal people searching for their way are significantly conditioned by their trust in certain authorities. However, eternal temptations such as trivializing insufficiently proven moral values or unjustly taking advantage of naive human respect for them find no adequate counterweight within a rational understanding of reality that could justify those values.[3] In such situations societies react intuitively, which may be the right response but sometimes proves to be inadequate.

If physicians behaved like ethicists, i.e., relegated relatively unaesthetic disease phenomena to the shadow of their personal experience

[2]In contrast to normative and applied ethics, metaethics deals with the conditions under which moral judgments can be considered true. See *Ponerologia*, ch. 1 ("Ethics and Ponerology"): "The validity of moral values, whose justification still relies on metaethical methods, is nevertheless proven by their negation. It is when we have disregarded the warnings of the sages and servants of God that unforeseen consequences arise, and the evil that builds up as a result harms other people and ourselves" (p. 9). Łobaczewski cites Tadeusz Styczeń's Polish work *Introduction to Ethics* (1995). Styczeń (1931–2010), who studied at Jagiellonian University in the early 1950s, was a Catholic priest, theologian, ethicist, and a close friend and student of Pope John Paul II. —Ed.

[3]Thus allowing radical ideologues to amplify these tendencies and exploit them. This can take the form of explicit disdain for traditional values, as in Critical Theory's rejection of all facets of Western civilization or Maoism's rejection of the "Four Olds" (Old Ideas, Old Culture, Old Habits, and Old Customs) of Chinese civilization; as well as the cynical exploitation of those moral values for political purposes, e.g., the pursuit of power under the guise of equality, social justice, liberation, etc. Systems and ideologies that assume all people are psychologically normal have no defenses against those who operate outside the bounds of those systems' norms and value hierarchies. —Ed.

because they were primarily interested in studying questions of physical and mental health, there would be no such thing as modern medicine. Even the roots of this science of health maintenance would be hidden in similar shadows. In spite of the fact that the theory of hygiene has been linked to medicine since its ancient beginnings, physicians were correct in their emphasis upon studying disease above all. They risked their own health and made sacrifices in order to discover the causes and biological properties of illnesses and, afterwards, to understand the pathodynamics of the courses of these illnesses. A comprehension of the nature of a disease, and the course it runs, after all, enables the proper curative means to be elaborated. "*Ignoti nulla est curatio morbi*," says the basic principle of this art.

While studying an organism's ability to fight off disease and become immune to known pathogens, scientists invented vaccination, which allows organisms to become resistant to an illness without passing through it in its full-blown manifestation. Thanks to this, medicine conquers and prevents phenomena which, in its scope of activity, are considered a type of evil.

The question thus arises: could some analogous *modus operandi* not be used to study the nature, causes, and genesis of other kinds of evil scourging human individuals, families, and societies—in spite of the fact that they appear even more insulting to our aesthetic and moral feelings than do diseases? Experience has taught the author that evil is similar to disease in nature, although possibly more complex and elusive to our understanding. Its genesis reveals many factors, pathological—especially psychopathological—in character, whose essence medicine and psychology have already studied, or whose understanding demands further investigation in these realms.

Parallel to the traditional approach, problems commonly perceived to be moral may also be treated on the basis of data provided by biology, medicine, and psychology, as factors of this kind are co-present in the question as a whole.[4] Experience teaches us that a comprehension of the essence and genesis of evil generally makes use of data from these areas. Philosophical reflection alone must then prove insufficient. Philosophical thought may have engendered all the scientific disciplines, but these did not mature until they became independent, based on detailed data and a relationship to other disciplines supplying such data.

[4]In addition to Sapolsky, *Behave*, pp. 580–613, see Raine, *Anatomy of Violence*, ch. 10 ("The Brain on Trial"), pp. 303–28. —Ed.

Encouraged by the often "coincidental" discovery of these naturalistic aspects of evil and its genesis, the author has imitated the methodology of medicine; a clinical psychologist and medical coworker by profession, he had such tendencies anyway. As is the case with physicians and disease, he took the risks of close contact with evil and suffered the consequences. His purpose was to ascertain the possibilities of understanding the nature of evil, its etiological factors, and to track its pathodynamics.

In the meantime, developments of biology, medicine, and psychology opened so many avenues that the above-mentioned behavior turned out to be not only feasible, but exceptionally fertile. Personal experience and the refined methods of clinical psychology permitted grasping phenomena with sufficient certainty and reaching ever more accurate conclusions.

A psychologist can gather many valuable observations, such as those used in this work, when he himself becomes the object of unjust treatment, as long as his intellectual curiosity overcomes his natural human feelings and reactions, or when he is forced to use his professional skills to save himself. The author never lacked for such opportunities in our homeland so full of violence and misery.

A major difficulty which had to be overcome based on my own investigations was insufficient data, especially in the area of the science of psychopathies.[5] This insufficiency was caused by neglect of these areas, theoretical difficulties facing researchers, and the unpopular nature of these problems, in addition to lack of access to existing works due to political censorship.[6] This work in general, and this chapter in particular, contain references to research conclusions the author was either prevented from publishing or unwilling to publish for reasons of personal safety. Sadly, it is lost now and age prevents

[5]"Psychopathies" are equivalent to what we now call "personality disorders"—stable, rigid personality structures characterized by pervasive emotional, cognitive, behavioral dysfunction impairing all areas of life (in the most severe cases). The use of the term in this sense goes back to Julius Koch's *Die Psychopathischen Minderwertigkeiten* [The Psychopathic Inferiorities] (1891), Kurt Schneider's 1923 book *Die Psychopathischen Persönlichkeiten* [The Psychopathic Personalities], and Pyotr Gannushkin's 1933 book [Manifestations of Psychopathies]. In his bibliography, Łobaczewski cites Antoni Kępiński (1918–1972), *Psychopatie* (1977), which details the following psychopathies: hysterical, psychasthenic, anankastic (obsessive), epileptoid (borderline), impulsive, paranoid, and sado-masochistic. —Ed.

[6]See Chapter VII. —Ed.

any attempts at recovery.[7] It is hoped that my descriptions, observations, and experience, here condensed from memory, will provide a platform for a new effort to produce the data needed to confirm again what was confirmed then.

Thus arose a new discipline; two monks, excellent Greek philologists, baptized it "PONEROLOGY" from the Greek *poneros* = evil. The process of the genesis of evil was called, correspondingly, "ponerogenesis." I hope that these modest beginnings will grow so as to enable us to overcome evil through an understanding of its nature, causes, and development.

***

From over 5,000 psychotic, neurotic, and healthy patients, the author selected 384 adults who behaved in a manner which had seriously hurt others. The type of harm they did to others varied greatly, from emotionally hurtful behavior and slander, physical and sexual abuse of a child, to physical injury and murder. They came from all circles of Polish society, but mostly from the large Silesian industrial center characterized by poor working conditions and substantial air pollution. They represented various moral, social, and political attitudes. Some 30 of them had been subjected to penal measures which were often excessively harsh. Once freed from jail or other penalty, some of these people attempted to readapt to social life, which made them tend to be sincere in speaking to me—the psychologist. Others had escaped punishment because they had hurt their fellows in a manner which does not qualify for judicial treatment under legal theory or practice. Some were protected by a political system which is in itself a ponerogenic derivate. The author had the further advantage of speaking to persons whose neuroses were caused by some abuse they had experienced.

All the above-mentioned people were given psychological tests and subjected to detailed anamnesis[8] so as to determine their overall mental skills, thereby either excluding or detecting possible brain tissue lesions, and evaluating them in relation to one another.[9] Other

[7] *Author's note (1997):* Confirmation of these results could later be found in some works published in the West.

[8] The case history of a medical patient as recalled by the patient. —Ed.

[9] *Author's note*: My basic test battery resembled more those used in Great Britain as opposed to the American versions. I used in addition two tests: one was an

methods were also used in accordance with the patient's actual needs in order to create a sufficiently accurate picture of their psychological condition and its causes. In most of these cases the author had access to the results of medical examinations and laboratory tests.

Analysis of their personalities and the genesis of their behavior revealed that only 14 to 16% of the 384 persons who had hurt others failed to exhibit any psychopathological factors which would have influenced their behavior. Regarding this statistic, it should be pointed out that a psychologist's failure to discover such factors does not prove their non-existence. In a significant part of this group of cases, the lack of proof was rather the result of insufficient interview facilities, imperfection of testing methods, and deficiency of skills on the part of the tester. Thus, natural reality appeared different in principle from everyday attitudes, which interpret evil in an overly moralizing way, and from juridical practices, which only in a small part of cases adjudicate a commutation of a sentence by taking the criminal's pathological characteristics into account.

We may often reason by means of the exclusionary hypothesis, e.g., pondering what would happen if the genesis of a particular wrongdoing did not have some pathological component. We then usually reach the conclusion that the deed would not have taken place, since the pathological factor either sealed its occurrence or became an indispensable component in its origin.

The hypothesis thus suggests itself that such factors are commonly active in the genesis of evil. The conviction that pathological factors generally participate in ponerogenic processes appears even more likely if we also take into account the conviction of many scholars in ethics that evil in this world represents a kind of web or continuum of mutual conditioning. Within this interlocking structure, one kind of evil feeds and opens doors for others regardless of any individual or doctrinal motivations.[10] It does not respect the boundaries of

---

old British performance test restandardized for clinical purposes. The other was completely elaborated by myself. Unfortunately, when I was expelled from Poland, it made it impossible for me to transfer any of my many results to other psychologists because I was deprived of all my research papers, in addition to almost everything else.

[10]See, for example, American psychologist Philip Zimbardo's *The Lucifer Effect: Understanding How Good People Turn Evil* (2008). Zimbardo argues for a "three-part analysis" that focuses on "the Person, the Situation, and the System," the latter of which he defines as consisting of "the agents and agencies whose ideology, values, and power create situations and dictate the roles and

individual cases, social groups, and nations. Since pathological factors are present within the synthesis of most instances of evil, they are also present throughout this continuum.

Further deliberations on the observations thus obtained considered only a selection of the above-mentioned number of cases, especially those which did not generate doubt by colliding with natural moral attitudes, and those which did not reveal practical difficulties for further analysis (such as absence of further contact with the patient). The statistical approach furnished only general guidelines. Intuitive penetration into each individual problem, and a similar synthesis of the whole, proved the most productive method in this area.

The role of pathological factors in a ponerogenic process can be played by any known, or not yet sufficiently researched, psychopathological phenomenon, and also by some pathological matters medical practice does not include within psychopathology. However, their activity in a ponerogenic process is dependent on features *other* than the obviousness or severity of the condition. Quite the contrary, the greatest ponerogenic activity is reached by pathological factors at an intensity which generally permits detection with the help of clinical methods, although they are *not yet considered pathological* by the opinion of the social environment.[11] Such a factor can then covertly limit the bearer's ability to control his conduct, or have an effect upon other persons, traumatizing their psyches, spellbinding them, causing children and adolescents' personalities to develop improperly, or inciting vindictive emotions or a lust for punishment. (A similar condition of an overt or clinical nature triggers critical thinking, which will lead to a reduction of its ponerogenic impact.)[12] A moral-

expectations for approved behaviors of actors within its spheres of influence" (pp. 445–446). —Ed.

[11]Such manifestations are called "subclinical" or "high-functioning" in modern parlance. Hervey Cleckley, in *The Mask of Sanity* (1988), pp. 188–221, first described "incomplete manifestations" of psychopathy—psychopathic individuals who are able to function as businessmen, politicians, and psychiatrists. Psychologists Paul Babiak and Robert Hare have published a book describing the havoc such individuals cause in the corporate environment titled *Snakes in Suits: Understanding and Surviving the Psychopaths in Your Office* (2019).The most useful model for measuring subclinical manifestations of "dark personalities" is currently the "Dark Tetrad" model, discussed in further notes. —Ed.

[12]"In the political sphere, blatantly delusional thinking is not the main concern. Such thinking is exceptional and evident to others. Far more dangerous is when the delusional thinking is borderline and consequently not easily recognized as the product of madness" (Robins & Post, *Political Paranoia*, p. 19). —Ed.

istic interpretation of the symptoms of such moderate conditions and the legacy of their actions impairs humankind's ability to see the causes of evil and to utilize common sense to combat it. This is why identifying such pathological factors and revealing their activities can so often stifle their ponerogenic functions.

In the process of the origin of evil, pathological factors can act from within an individual, who as a result commits a harmful act; such activity is relatively easily acknowledged by public opinion and the courts. Consideration is given much less frequently to how *outside influences* emitted by their carriers act upon individuals or groups. Such influences, however, play a substantial role in the overall genesis of evil.[13] In order for such influence to be active, the pathological characteristic in question must be interpreted in a moralistic manner, i.e., differently from its true nature. There are many possibilities for such activities; for the moment, let us indicate the most damaging.

Every person in the span of his life, particularly during childhood and youth, assimilates psychological material from others through mental resonance, identification, imitation, and other communicative means, thereupon transforming it to build his own personality and worldview. If such material is contaminated by pathological factors and deformities, personality development shall also be deformed. The product will be a person unable to understand correctly either himself and others, or normal human relations and morals. As a result of such influence, in his practice a psychologist encounters individuals to whom normal people, or those who were brought up normally, seem bizarre or foolish. As a result of such abnormal personality development such a person commits evil acts with a poor feeling of being faulty. Is he really at fault?

In ponerogenic processes, man's age-old, familiar moral weaknesses and deficiencies of intelligence, proper reasoning, and knowledge combine with the activity of various pathological factors to create a complex network of causation which frequently contains feedback relationships or closed causal structures.[14] Practically speaking, cause

[13]Zimbardo challenges "the traditional focus on the individual's inner nature, dispositions, personality traits, and character as the primary and often the sole target in understanding human failings," arguing instead that "most of us can undergo significant character transformations when we are caught up in the crucible of social forces" (*Lucifer Effect*, pp. vii, 211). —Ed.

[14]*Ponerologia* (p. 19) clarifies that such feedback systems "mutually condition one another or become locked into one another." —Ed.

and effect are often widely separated in time, which makes it more difficult to track the links. If our scope of observation is expansive enough, the ponerogenic processes are reminiscent of complex chemical synthesis, wherein modifying a single factor causes the entire process to change. Botanists are aware of the law of the minimum, wherein plant growth is limited by the component which is deficient in the soil. Similarly, eliminating (or at least limiting) the activity of one of the above-mentioned factors or deficiencies should cause a corresponding reduction in the entire process of the genesis of evil. This is what actually happens when, for example, a psychotherapist uses an appropriate explanation.

For instance, in the course of psychotherapy, we may inform a patient that in the genesis of his personality and behavior we find the results of influences from some person who revealed psychopathological characteristics. We thereby carry out an intervention that is painful for the patient, which demands we proceed with tact and skill. As a result of this interaction, however, the patient develops a kind of self-analysis which will liberate him from the results of these influences and enable him to develop some critical distance in dealing with other factors of a similar nature. Rehabilitation will depend on improving his ability to think critically and to understand himself and others. Thanks to this, he will be able to overcome his internal and interpersonal difficulties more easily and to avoid mistakes which hurt him and his immediate environment.

For centuries, moralists have taught us to develop ethical attitudes and human values, and sought the proper criteria for doing so. The greatest of them have emphasized the need to discover what is right, as well as respect for correct reasoning, whose value in this area is unquestionable. In spite of all their efforts, however, they have been unable to overcome the many kinds of evil that have scourged humanity for ages and that are presently taking on unheard-of proportions. By no means does a ponerologist wish to belittle the role of and respect for moral values and knowledge in this area; rather, he wants to buttress them with hitherto-underrated scientific knowledge in order to round out the picture as a whole and adapt it better to complex reality, thereby making more effective action possible in moral, psychological, social, and political practice.

This new discipline is thus primarily interested in the role of pathological factors in the origin of evil—the most scientifically neglected part of this complex causal system—especially since conscious control and monitoring of them on the scientific, social, and individual levels could effectively stifle or disarm these processes. Something which has been impossible for centuries is now feasible in practice thanks to progress in natural science. Methodological refinements are dependent upon the further progress of detailed research and upon the public conviction that doing so is valuable. Similar applications of these skills can serve other areas of life, especially psychotherapeutic treatment, crime prevention, or historical and sociological research. This work is focused on their use in political science.

Pathological Factors

Let us now attempt a concise description of some examples of those pathological factors which have proved to be the most active in ponerogenic processes. Selection of these examples resulted from the author's own experience, instead of exhaustive statistical tallies, and may thus differ from other specialists' evaluations. A small amount of statistical data concerning these phenomena has been borrowed from other works or are approximate evaluations elaborated under conditions which did not allow the entire front of research to be developed.

Mention should also be made of some historical figures, people whose pathological characteristics contributed to the process of the genesis of evil on a large social scale, imprinting their mark upon the fate of nations. It is not an easy task to establish diagnoses for people whose psychological anomalies and diseases died together with them. The results of such clinical analyses are open to question even by persons lacking knowledge or experience in this area, but only because the diagnosis of such conditions does not correspond to their historical or literary way of thought. While this is done on the basis of the legacy of natural and often moralizing language, I can only assert that I always based my findings on comparisons of data acquired through numerous observations I made by studying many similar patients with the help of the objective methods of contemporary clinical psychology. I took the critical approach herein as far as possible. Therefore, only the opinions of specialists elaborated using a similar method are fit consideration and further discussion.[15]

[15]"When it comes to ponerological theory, historical figures contribute less to its development than contemporary cases that can be carefully examined. This

Acquired Deviations

Among all the tissues of the body, brain tissue is very limited in its regenerative ability. If it is damaged and the lesion subsequently heals, a process of rehabilitation can take place whereby the neighboring healthy tissue takes over the function of the damaged portion. This substitution is never quite perfect; thus some deficits in the efficiency and correctness of psychological processes can be detected even in cases of very minor damage by using the appropriate tests. Specialists are aware of the diverse causes for the origin of such damage, including trauma and infections. We should point out here that the psychological results of such changes, as we can observe many years later, are more heavily dependent upon the *location* of the damage itself in the brain mass, whether on the surface or within, than they are upon the cause which brought them about.[16] The quality of these consequences also depends upon *when* they occurred in the person's lifetime and life conditions afterwards. The effects of perinatal or early infant brain injury have been shown to be more active as pathological factors of ponerogenesis than those of adult brain injury.[17]

---

is due to the fact that diagnosis based on secondhand reports, which are usually provided in the context of the natural worldview, presents well-known difficulties and is easily undermined; they do, however, provide a good means of conveying the concepts to readers and bringing a lecture to life. Such diagnosis also serves as a guide for historians and political scientists on how to interpret contemporary events in ponerological terms, which clarifies many complex issues" (*Ponerologia*, p. 19). See the discussion on profiling world leaders, including its inherent weaknesses, in Haycock's *Tyrannical Minds*, ch. 2. —Ed.

[16] "Prefrontal and associated subcortical areas of the brain [discussed below] appear to be very sensitive to a wide variety of substances and metabolic conditions. These conditions can result in increased irritability and impulsivity ... They are especially serious in individuals who show compromised cerebral function because of preexisting brain injury, or in people whose inhibitory controls are weak in general. Prefrontal lobes may be sensitive to these disorders because of their large demand for oxygen and other nutrients compared to other areas of the brain" (Golden et al., "Neuropsychological Correlates of Violence and Aggression: A Review of the Clinical Literature" [1996]). The prefrontal region of the brain normally acts to control and regulate the emotional feelings and reactions generated by deeper brain structures in the limbic system, which includes the hypothalamus, amygdala, and hippocampus. The limbic system plays an important part in regulation of human moods and emotions. —Ed.

[17] Children born very preterm (less than 32 weeks' gestation) and/or extremely low birth weight (less than 1 kg) are at increased risk for brain damage and

In societies with highly developed medical care, we find among the upper grades of elementary school (around ages 11 to 14, when tests can already be applied), that 5 to 7 percent of children have suffered brain tissue lesions which cause certain academic or behavioral difficulties. This percentage increases with age. Modern medical care (especially obstetrics) has contributed to a quantitative decrease in such phenomena, but in certain relatively uncivilized countries and during historical times, indications of difficulties caused by such changes are and have been more frequent.

Epilepsy and its many variations constitute the oldest known results of such lesions; it is observed in a relatively small segment of persons suffering such damage.[18] Researchers in these matters are more or less unanimous in believing that Julius Caesar, and then later Napoleon Bonaparte, had epileptic seizures.[19] Those were probably instances of vegetative epilepsy caused by lesions lying deep within the brain, near the vegetative centers.[20] This variety does not cause subsequent dementia. The extent to which these hidden ailments had negative effects upon their characters and historical decision-making, or played a ponerogenic role, can be the subject of a separate study and evaluation. In most cases, however, epilepsy is an *evident* ailment, which limits its role as a ponerogenic factor.

In a much larger segment of the bearers of brain tissue damage, the negative deformation of their characters grows in the course of time. It takes on diverse psychological pictures, depending upon

---

neurobehavioral impairments, including lower general intelligence, learning disability, and behavioral and emotional problems (Anderson et al., "Cognitive and Educational Deficits in Children Born Extremely Preterm" [2008]). Other birth complications negatively affecting the brain include hypoxia at birth, preeclampsia, maternal bleeding, and maternal infection (Raine, *Anatomy*, pp. 188–91). For the different brain regions associated with character disturbance and violence, see chapter 3 ("Murderous Minds") of Raine's book. —Ed.

[18] Brain structures commonly implicated in temporal lobe epilepsy include, among others, the amygdala and the hippocampus from the limbic system. "Detailed psychological and personality assessments of patients with epilepsy in the temporal lobe region of the brain suggests a high incidence of psychopathic-like behavior" (Kent Kiehl, "A Cognitive Neuroscience Perspective on Psychopathy: Evidence for Paralimbic System Dysfunction" [2006]). —Ed.

[19] A recent reappraisal of the existing evidence points to Julius Caesar suffering from a series of mini-strokes rather than epilepsy. See Francesco M. Galassi and Hutan Shirafian, *Julius Caesar's Disease: A New Diagnosis* (2017). —Ed.

[20] The autonomic centers of the midbrain or diencephalon (thalamus, hypothalamus, etc.). —Ed.

the properties and localization of these changes, their time of origin, and also the life conditions of the individual after their occurrence.[21] We will call such character disorders—*characteropathies.*[22] Some characteropathies play an outstanding role as pathological agents in the processes of the genesis of evil. Let us thus characterize their general ponerogenic effect, then select examples of their most active variants in this area.

Characteropathies reveal a certain similar quality, if the clinical picture is not obscured by the coexistence of other mental anomalies (usually inherited), which sometimes occurs in practice. Undamaged brain tissue retains our species' natural psychological properties. This is particularly evident in instinctive and affective responses, which are natural, albeit often violent and insufficiently controlled. The experiences, problems, and ideas of people with such anomalies grow in the medium of the normal human world to which they belong by nature. Thus their abnormal manner of experiencing, their thinking anomalies, and their egotistic aspirations find relatively easy entry into other people's minds and are perceived within the categories of the natural worldview and its moralizing tendencies.

Such behavior on the part of characteropathic personalities terrorizes and traumatizes the minds and feelings of normal people, gradually depriving them of the ability to use common sense. In spite of their resistance and critical reactions, normal people come to assimilate such psychological material and become used to the rigid habits of pathological thinking and experiencing. In young people, as a result, the personality suffers abnormal development leading to its malformation.[23] Characteropathies thus represent pathological,

[21] The "biosocial" model describes the interaction of biological and environmental risk factors. For example, individuals with both sets of risk factors can have rates of violence three times as high as those with just biological or social risk factors on their own. Social factors seem to act as triggers for already-existing biological factors. See Raine, *Anatomy*, pp. 185–91. For the biopsychosocial model, which adds psychological risk factors (e.g., temperament, personality, intelligence), see Thomson, *Understanding Psychopathy.* —Ed.

[22] *Author's note (1997):* This term was generally used by Professor T. Bilikiewicz to distinguish them from aberrations of hereditary origin. [Tadeusz Bilikiewicz (1901–1980) was a Polish psychiatrist and historian of medicine. Łobaczewski cites his textbook *Psychiatria* (1998). —Ed.]

[23] For an in-depth and highly readable descriptive and therapeutic account of these problems as they currently manifest in the United States, see clinical psychologist George K. Simon Jr.'s book *Character Disturbance: The Phenomenon of Our Age* (2011). —Ed.

ponerogenic factors which, by their covert activity, easily engender new phases in the eternal genesis of evil, opening the door to later activation of other factors which thereupon take over the main role, playing first fiddle in the satanic overture.[24]

A relatively well-documented example of such an influence of a characteropathic personality on a macrosocial scale is the last German emperor, Wilhelm II. He was subjected to brain trauma at birth. During and after his entire reign, his physical and psychological handicap was hidden from public knowledge. The motor abilities of the upper left portion of his body were handicapped. As a boy, he had difficulty learning grammar, geometry, and drawing, which constitute the typical triad of academic difficulties caused by minor brain lesions. He developed a personality with infantile features and insufficient control over his emotions, and also a somewhat paralogical way of thinking which easily sidestepped the heart of some important issues in the process of dodging problems.[25]

---

[24]Most contemporary books on the subject focus almost solely on the narcissism of individual leaders and the potential dangers they pose, e.g., titles such as Paul R. Lawrence's *Driven to Lead: Good, Bad, and Misguided Leadership* (2010), Jerrold M. Post's *Narcissism and Politics: Dreams of Glory* (2015), Bandy X. Lee's *The Dangerous Case of Donald Trump: 37 Psychiatrists and Mental Health Experts Assess a President* (2019), and John W. Dean and Bob Altemeyer's *Authoritarian Nightmare: Trump and His Followers* (2020). Such approaches either ignore or downplay factors such as ideological revolutionary movements, political warfare, and the ponerization of governmental institutions independent of any individual narcissistic leader (in addition to a focus on rightwing authoritarianism to the exclusion of leftwing authoritarianism). Ponerogenic nuclei can exist and operate relatively covertly, within intelligence agencies, corporations, financial institutions, or through a Gramscian "long march through the institutions" (family, education, media, religion, culture, and law), as is currently taking place in the West. See Mike Gonzalez, *The Plot to Change America: How Identity Politics is Dividing the Land of the Free* (2020), ch. 5, and Matthew Lohmeier, *Irresistible Revolution: Marxism's Goal of Conquest & the Unmaking of the American Military* (2021), pt. 2.

[25]Wilhelm II (1859–1941) was German Emperor and King of Prussia from 1888 to 1918. Łobaczewski cites the Polish biography by Frederyk Hartau, *Wilhelm II* (1992). "[D]espite efforts of his parents to give him a liberal education, the prince became imbued with religious mysticism, militarism, anti-semitism, the glorification of power politics. Some have claimed that his personality displayed elements of a narcissistic personality disorder. Bombastic, vain, insensitive, and possessed with grandiose notions of divine right rule, his personality traits paralleled those of the new Germany: strong, but off balance; vain, but insecure; intelligent, but narrow; self-centered yet longing for acceptance" (http://net.lib.byu.edu/estu/wwi/bio/w/willyii.html). —Ed.

Militaristic poses and a general's uniform overcompensated for his feelings of inferiority and effectively cloaked his shortcomings. Politically, his insufficient control of emotions and factors of personal rancor came into view. The old Iron Chancellor[26] had to go, that cunning and ruthless politician who had been loyal to the monarchy and had built up Prussian power. After all, he was too knowledgeable about the prince's defects and had worked against his coronation. A similar fate met other overly critical people, who were replaced by persons with lesser minds, more subservience, and, sometimes, discreet psychological deviations—negative selection took place.[27]

Since the common people are prone to identify with the emperor (and through the emperor, with a system of government), the characteropathic material emanating from the Kaiser resulted in many Germans being progressively deprived of their ability to use their common sense. A new generation grew up with psychological deformities regarding the feeling and understanding of moral, psychological, social, and political realities. It is extremely typical that in many German families having a member who was psychologically not quite normal, it became a matter of honor to hide this fact from public opinion, and even from the awareness of close friends and relatives (even at the cost of engaging in nefarious conduct). Large portions of German society ingested psychopathological material, together with that unrealistic way of thinking wherein slogans take on the power of arguments and inconvenient data are subjected to subconscious selection.

This occurred during a time when a wave of hysteria was growing throughout Europe, including a tendency for emotions to dominate and for human behavior to contain an element of histrionics. How individual sober thought can be terrorized by behavior colored with such material was evidenced particularly by women, who proved to be more zealous followers of the hysterical militaristic Prussian style

[26]Otto von Bismarck (1815–1898), Chancellor of the German Reich from 1817–1890. —Ed.

[27]For more examples of negative selection (or counterselection), see Oakley, *Evil Genes*, pp. 246, 275–276, 295–296. Łobaczewski expands on this in the Polish edition (p. 137), writing: "Abnormal individuals, especially psychopathic ones, adapt and advance more easily in such circumstances. ... Those who reject such governments and alliances on moral grounds, those with a normal psychological worldview, form a defiant opposition. ... Such a power must crack down on this opposition. People without remorse are needed to achieve this, which opens up avenues of advancement and privilege for them." —Ed.

than men. This progressively took over three empires and other countries on the mainland. To what extent did Wilhelm II contribute to this degeneration of common sense, along with two other emperors whose minds also were not attuned to the actual facts of history and government?[28] To what extent were they themselves influenced by an intensification of hysteria during their reigns? That would make an interesting topic of discussion among historians and ponerologists.

When international tensions increased and Archduke Ferdinand was assassinated in Sarajevo, neither the Kaiser nor any other governmental authority in his country were in possession of their reason. What came into play instead were Wilhelm's emotional attitude and the stereotypes of thought and action he inherited from the past. War broke out. General war plans that had been prepared earlier, and which had lost their relevance under the new conditions, unfolded more like military maneuvers. Even those historians familiar with the genesis and character of the Prussian state, including its tradition of subordination of the individual to the authority of king and emperor in the name of bloody expansionism, intuit that these situations contained some activity of an uncomprehended fatalism which eludes an analysis in terms of historical causality.[29]

Many thoughtful persons keep asking the same anxious question: how could the German nation have chosen for a Fuehrer a clownish psychopath who made no bones about his pathological vision of superman rule?[30] Under his leadership, Germany then unleashed a second criminal and politically absurd war. During the second half of this war, highly trained army officers honorably performed

---

[28]Tsar Nicholas II (1868–1918) of Russia, who reigned 1894–1917, and Franz Joseph I (1830–1916) of Austria-Hungary, who reigned 1848–1916. —Ed.

[29]If the West is currently passing through a similar hysteroidal state and into one of crisis (see Chapter III), the first twenty years of the current century make for an interesting comparison in terms of increasing social hysteria, overemotionalism leading to ill-planned and poorly executed wars, and negative selection within the staff of presidential administrations, bureaucracy, the military, corporations, not to mention pathological material being taught at all levels of education. —Ed.

[30]See Haycock, *Tyrannical Minds*, pp. 1–36, 238–241, for a recent psychological profile of Adolf Hitler (1889–1945). In his interview with SOTT.net, Łobaczewski remarked on the complex combination of psychopathologies in Hitler. See also Robert G. L. Waite's psychological biography, *The Psychopathic God: Adolf Hitler* (1993), originally published in 1977. More recent is Volker Ullrich's two-volume work with a focus on Hitler's personality: *Hitler: Ascent 1889–1939* (2017) and *Hitler: Downfall 1939–1945* (2020). —Ed.

inhuman orders, senseless from the political and military point of view, issued by a man whose psychological state corresponded to the routine criteria for being forcibly committed to a psychiatric hospital.

Any attempt to explain the things that occurred during the first half of our century by means of categories generally accepted in historical thought leaves behind a nagging feeling of inadequacy. Only a ponerological approach can compensate for this deficit in our comprehension, as it does justice to the role of various pathological factors in the genesis of evil at every social level.

The German nation, fed for a generation on pathologically altered psychological material, fell into a state comparable to what we see in certain individuals raised by persons who are both characteropathic and hysterical. Psychologists know from experience how often such people then let themselves commit acts which seriously hurt others. A psychotherapist needs a good deal of persistent work, skill, and prudence in order to enable such a person to regain his ability to comprehend psychological problems with more naturalistic realism and to utilize his healthy critical faculties in relation to his own behavior.

The Germans inflicted and suffered enormous damage and pain during World War I; they thus felt no substantial guilt and even thought that they were the ones who had been wronged. After all, they were behaving in accordance with their customary habit, without being aware of its pathological causes. After the war, the need for this state to be clothed in heroic garb in order to avoid bitter disintegration became all too common. A mysterious craving arose, as if the social organism had managed to become addicted to some drug. The hunger was for more pathologically modified psychological material, a phenomenon known to psychotherapeutic experience.[31] This hunger could only be satisfied by another similarly pathological personality and system of government. A characteropathic personality opened the door for leadership by a psychopathic individual. We shall return later in our deliberations to this pathological personality sequence, as it appears a general regularity in ponerogenic processes.

A ponerological approach facilitates our understanding of a person who succumbs to the influence of a characteropathic personality,

[31]McConkey terms this phenomenon "The Psychorium" (2021), "space of psychopathic mentality" which "effectively spellbinds the clinically normal people," the "the mass psychology that makes pathocracy possible." —Ed.

as well as comprehension of macrosocial phenomena caused by the contribution of such factors. Unfortunately, relatively few such individuals can be served by appropriate psychotherapy. All the more so, such behavior cannot yet be applied to nations too proudly defending their sovereignty. A theoretical question can be posed: what would happen if some internationally recognized institution announced publicly that certain leaders are mentally abnormal and their activities must inevitably lead to misfortune? We may consider the solution of such problems by means of the proper knowledge as a vision for the future.[32]

Paranoid characteropathy

It is characteristic of paranoid behavior for people to be capable of relatively correct reasoning and discussion as long as the conversation involves matters of—in their opinion—lesser importance. This stops abruptly when the partner's arguments begin to undermine their overvalued ideas, break down their long-held stereotypes of reasoning, or force them to accept a conclusion they had subconsciously rejected before. Such a stimulus unleashes upon the interlocutor a torrent of paralogical utterances, full of paramoralisms[33] and often insulting, but always containing some degree of suggestion.[34]

Utterances like these inspire aversion among cultivated and logical people, but they enslave less critical minds, e.g., people with other kinds of psychological deficiencies, people who have already been subject to the egotistical influence of individuals with character disorders, and, in particular, a large segment of the young. A proletarian may perceive this power to enslave to be a kind of victory over higher-class people and thus take the paranoid person's side. However, this is not the normal reaction among the common people, where perception of psychological reality occurs no less often than among the middle class.

[32] See Chapter X. —Ed.

[33] See Glossary and the subheading "Paramoralisms" later in this chapter, as well as the example about Lenin further below in this section. —Ed.

[34] Dąbrowski writes: "Paranoia is characterized by psychomotor excitability, rapidity of thinking, a great inclination to criticize others without self-criticism, and an intensified self-attention without feelings of self-consciousness and self-doubt. Paranoiacs present a very rigid integration with systematized delusions of persecution and grandeur, and egocentric excitability. They also reveal an inability to adapt to real situations that contributes to a narrow form of unilevel disintegration" (*Positive Disintegration* [2017], p. 12). —Ed.

In sum then, the response of accepting paranoid argumentation is more frequent in inverse proportion to the cultural maturity of the community in question, although it never approaches the majority. Nevertheless, paranoid individuals become aware of their enslaving influence through experience and attempt to take advantage of it in a pathologically egotistic manner.

We know today that the psychological mechanism of paranoid phenomena is twofold: one is caused by damage to the brain tissue,[35] the other is functional or behavioral and occurs less frequently. Within the above-mentioned process of rehabilitation, any brain tissue lesion causes a certain slackening of accurate thinking and, as a consequence, of the personality structure. Most typical are those cases caused by a prior infection in the diencephalon[36] by various pathological factors, less commonly by head trauma. This results in its permanently decreased tonal ability, and similarly of the tonus of inhibition in the brain cortex.[37] Particularly during sleepless nights, runaway thoughts give rise to a paranoid, distorted view of human reality, as well as to

[35]While some research associates traumatic brain injury with cases of paranoia (e.g., frontal and temporal lobe damage) and paranoid personality disorder (PPD), neither is generally understood in these terms. As one letter to a psychiatric journal says: "The available literature has been ambiguous with regard to the connection between organic brain factors and simple paranoid disorders in terms of pathophysiologic mechanisms and manifestations" (Søren Fryd Birkeland, "Paranoid Personality Disorder and Organic Brain Injury: A Case Report" [2013]). See also McGilchrist, The Matter with Things, pp. 140–141, on the link between right hemisphere damage and paranoid psychosis. —Ed.

[36]Located between the cerebral cortex and the midbrain, the diencephalon includes the thalamus and hypothalamus. Among other things, the hypothalamus functions as part of our basic "threat circuitry," as a relay station between regulatory and emotional areas of the brain. Persistent environmental stress or trauma damages the threat circuitry and increases its sensitivity and reactivity to threats, and can also affect the hormonal systems regulating this activity (James Blair et al., *The Psychopath: Emotion and the Brain* [2005], pp. 35–36, 96–109). Case reports of diencephalic lesions include euphoric, restless, and hyper-vigilant behavior; and excessive, uncontrollable, or incoherent talkativeness. It is often coupled with sexual disinhibition and sleep reduction. Paranoia, irritability, and aggression have been reported as well (Benke et al., "Mania Caused by a Diencephalic Lesion" [2002]). Affective dyscontrol, socially inappropriate behavior, and mood changes have been reported in some case studies of diencephalic lesions. Hyperactivity and a manic-like state have also been characteristic in some cases (Chung et al., "Behavioral Changes Caused by Diencephalic Lesion" [2009]). —Ed.

ideas which can be either gently naive or violently revolutionary. Let us call this kind *paranoid characteropathy.*[38]

In persons free of brain tissue lesions, such phenomena most frequently occur as a result of being reared by people with paranoid characteropathy, along with the psychological terror of their childhood.[39] Such psychological material is then assimilated, along with rigid stereotypes of abnormal experiencing. This makes it difficult for thought and worldview to develop normally, and the terror-blocked contents ("taboos") become transformed into permanent functional blocking[40] centers. Sometimes this gives the impression of participating in someone else's madness.[41]

Ivan Pavlov comprehended all types of paranoid states in a manner similar to this functional model without being aware of the basic and primary cause. He nevertheless provided a vivid description of paranoid characters and the above-mentioned ease with which paranoid individuals suddenly tear away from the discipline of facts and

[37]That is, reduced activity in the diencephalon and of inhibitory signals from the cortex, resulting in a heightened impulsivity and lessened ability to inhibit emotion. —Ed.

[38]Personality disorders today are primarily understood as maladaptive variants of common personality traits, i.e., the "Big Five" (openness, conscientiousness, extraversion, agreeableness, and neuroticism), with an underlying personality-disorder dimension—"a unitary dimensional construct with multiple phenotypes" (Newton-Howes et al., "Diagnostic Neglect: The Potential Impact of Losing a Separate Axis for Personality Disorder" [2015], p. 356). Paranoid personality disorder is associated with low agreeableness (mistrust, deception, aggression, tough-mindedness), high neuroticism (angry hostility), low extraversion (coldness, withdrawal, low positive emotion), and low openness (to actions and values) (Thomas A. Widiger and Paul T. Costa Jr., *Personality Disorders and the Five-Factor Model of Personality* [2013], p. 33). However, supporting Łobaczewski's categorization of paranoia as a "characteropathy" (character disturbance) rather than as a "psychopathy" (personality disorder), some argue that PPD is not a valid construct, as paranoid traits are common to many personality disorders (Mulder et al., "The Central Domains of Personality Pathology in Psychiatric Patients" [2011], p. 373). —Ed.

[39]Łobaczewski classifies such "functional" cases as "sociopathies" (*Ponerologia*, p. 28). Similarly, Colin Ross, who considers paranoia primarily a response to trauma, writes: "From a trauma-cognitive perspective, paranoid personality is caused by overgeneralization from childhood experience [e.g., being treated 'in a harsh, mean, inconsistent manner by his parents']" (*Trauma Model*, p. 185). —Ed.

[40]See the subheading "Conversive thinking" later in this chapter. —Ed.

[41]For example, "induced paranoia," where family members partially or wholly adopt the delusions of the patient. —Ed.

proper thought-processes.[42] Those readers of his work on the subject who are sufficiently familiar with Soviet conditions glean yet another historical meaning from his little book. Its intent appears obvious. The author dedicated his work—with no word of inscription, of course—to the chief model of a paranoid personality: the revolutionary leader Lenin, whom the scientist knew well.[43] As a good psychologist, Pavlov could predict that he would not be the object of revenge, since the paranoid mind will block out the relevant egocentric associations. He was thus able to die a natural death.

Lenin should nevertheless be included with the first and most characteristic kind of paranoid personality, i.e., most probably due to diencephalic brain damage, though a number of doubts arise as to the nature and location of these changes. Vasily Grossman[44] describes him as follows:

[42]See George Windholz, "Pavlov's Conceptualization of Paranoia Within the Theory of Higher Nervous Activity" (1996). For Pavlov paranoia was "characterized by the fact that a person is intellectually healthy in terms of logic and [understanding] of reality as are other people, sometimes even talented, but as soon as the matter concerns a particular theme, [this person] is mentally ill, failing to admit logic and reality" (p. 161). The nervous system's excitatory processes are stronger than the inhibitory ones, allowing weak stimuli to evoke strong reactions, e.g., reiterative, stereotyped, and permanent feelings, perceptions, and ideas. He concluded that it was rooted in heredity and provoked by taxing life experiences. —Ed.

[43]Windholz speculates that Pavlov had Stalin in mind: "Pavlov's article on paranoia was written in 1934 ... it is possible that he was reacting to the prevailing political situation in the Soviet Union. Pavlov made no secret of his opposition to the Soviet leadership. ... [V. M.] Molotov recalled that Pavlov would point to the portraits of Lenin and Stalin with the remark: 'Those are the ones who have ruined our lives!' It is possible that Pavlov was aware of the rumour that the psychiatrist V. M. Bekhterev, having examined I. V. Stalin in 1927, diagnosed Stalin as suffering from paranoia" ("Pavlov's Conceptualization," pp. 165–166). —Ed.

[44]Vasily Grossman (1905–1964), Ukrainian-Jewish journalist and author of the epic novel *Life and Fate*, the manuscript of which was confiscated and published for the first time in France in 1980 after being smuggled out of the USSR. The novel argues for a moral equivalence between Nazism and Soviet communism. The quotation is from his book *Everything Flows* (2009), pp. 170–171 (translated by Robert and Elizabeth Chandler). For a full biography of Lenin, see Hungarian journalist Victor Sebestyen's *Lenin: The Man, the Dictator, and the Master of Terror* (2017). —Ed.

In his personal relationships—when he gave someone help, when he stayed the night with friends or went out for a walk with them—Lenin was always polite, sensitive, and kind. Yet Lenin was always rude, harsh, and implacable toward his political opponents. He never admitted the least possibility that they might be even partially right, that he might be even partially wrong.	*Symptoms:* Asthenization.[45] Fixation, stereotypes, and transition to paralogisms. Pathological egotism.
"Venal ... lackey ... groveler ... hireling ... agent ... a Judas bought for thirty pieces of silver ..."—these were the words Lenin used of his opponents.	Paramoralisms.
It was never Lenin's aim, in a dispute, to win his opponent over to this own views. He did not even truly address his opponent; the people for whom his words were intended were the witnesses to the dispute. Lenin's aim was always to ridicule his opponent, to compromise him in the eyes of witnesses. These witnesses might be a few close friends, they might be an audience of a thousand conference delegates, or they might be the million readers of an article in a newspaper.	Spellbinding and consciousness of its effects. Lack of the self-criticism.

Although Lenin was not the mastermind of the Russian Revolution, his personality was a historically crucial pathological factor of ponerogenesis that paved the way for factors of a different, hereditary nature.

Frontal characteropathy

The frontal areas of the cerebral cortex (BA10 according to the Brodmann division)[46] are virtually present in no creature except man;

[45]The opposite of sthenia (strong instincts/emotions), asthenia is weakness of instincts. Psychasthenia use to be considered a nervous or mental fatigue characterized by low sensation threshold, malaise, irritability, and unstable moods. —Ed.

[46]The anterior prefrontal region of the brain, or prefrontal cortex. (Dysfunction in BA11 and 12, the orbitofrontal cortex, is associated with psychopathy—see further below.) The PFC is involved in executive functions such as "planning, attention, problem-solving, cognitive flexibility, working memory and error-monitoring, as well as decision-making and social cognition" (Thomson,

they are composed of the phylogenetically youngest nervous tissue. Their cytoarchitecture[47] is similar to the much older visual projection areas on the opposite pole of the brain.[48] This suggests some functional similarity. The author has found a relatively easy way to test this psychological function, which enables us to grasp a certain number of imaginary elements in our field of consciousness and subject them to internal contemplation. The capacity of this act of internal projection varies greatly from one person to another, though the correlation between this capacity and general intelligence is low. As described by researchers (Luria et al.), the functions of these areas—thought-process acceleration and coordination—seem to result from this basic function.[49]

Damage to this area occurs rather frequently at or near birth, especially in premature infants,[50] and less frequently later in life as a result of various causes (e.g., brain hemorrhaging or intoxication). The number of such perinatal brain tissue lesions has been significantly reduced due to improved medical care for pregnant women and newborns. The spectacular ponerogenic role which results from character disorders caused by this can thus be considered somewhat

---

Understanding, p. 79). For an overview of the latest research findings on prefrontal damage and its effect on character, see Raine, *Anatomy*, esp. ch. 5 ("Broken Brains"), and Oakley, *Evil Genes*, pp. 94–97. Early prefrontal damage commonly leads to impairment of executive function and behavioral control later in life, e.g., poor decision making and antisocial behavior, even when cognitive abilities are otherwise normal. The character changes resulting from damage to this region have been termed "pseudopsychopathy" and "acquired sociopathy" (see Raine, *Anatomy*, pp. 146, 255). —Ed.

[47] Cellular organization, the unique forms of which were used to establish the Brodmann areas. —Ed.

[48] The occipital lobe of the brain, which contains the primary visual cortex. —Ed.

[49] Aleksandr Luria (1902–1977) divided the human brain into three basic, interactively linked functional units. The first, located mainly in the brain stem, is responsible for regulating and maintaining arousal of the cortex. The second is responsible for encoding, processing, and storing information and encompasses the temporal, parietal, and occipital lobes. The third is located in the anterior region of the brain (the frontal lobes) and its functions include programming, regulating, and verifying human behavior. Within the third unit, the prefrontal cortex is considered by Luria as a superstructure that regulates or control mental activity and behavior. Łobaczewski cites a Polish edition of Luria's *Higher Cortical Dysfunction Due to Focal Brain Injury* (1967). —Ed.

[50] A comprehensive review paper highlights three major risk areas for early prefrontal damage: maltreatment, poverty, and preterm birth (Amanda S. Hodel, "Rapid Infant Prefrontal Cortex Development and Sensitivity to Early Environmental Experience" [2018]). —Ed.

characteristic of past generations and countries with deficient medical care.

Brain cortex damage in these areas selectively impairs the above-mentioned function without impairing memory, associative capacity, or, in particular, such instinct-based feelings and functions as, for instance, the ability to intuit a psychological situation. Such impairments do not demonstrably reduce the general intelligence of an individual. Children with such a defect are almost normal students; difficulties emerge suddenly in upper grades and affect principally these parts of the curriculum which place burden on the above function.

The pathological character of such people, generally containing a component of hysteria, develops through the years. The non-damaged psychological functions become overdeveloped to compensate, which means that instinctive and affective reactions predominate. Relatively vital people become belligerent, risk-happy, and brutal in both word and deed. Persons with an innate talent for intuiting psychological situations tend to take advantage of this gift in an egoistical and ruthless fashion.[51] In the thought process of such people, a short-cut develops which bypasses the handicapped function, thus leading from associations directly to words, deeds, and decisions which are not subject to any dissuasion.[52] Such individuals interpret their talent for intuiting situations and making split-second, oversimplified decisions as a sign of their superiority compared to normal people, who need to think for long time, experiencing self-doubt and conflicting motivations. For them, the fate of such inferior creatures is not worth dwelling on at length. The lack of insight into their own mental state and the dominance of primitive emotions lead to pathological vindictiveness.[53] They prove incapable of self-reflective withdrawal from a deluded course of action once it is taken.[54]

[51] Oakley speculates that borderlines' (see glossary) "hypersensitivity to the state of other people and their uncanny ability to read emotions" may be related to hyperactive amygdalae, just one of the brain dysfunctions associated with BPD (*Evil Genes*, p. 195). —Ed.

[52] A common feature of damage to the right dorsolateral prefrontal cortex. See McGilchrist, *The Matter with Things*, pp. 170–171. —Ed.

[53] On lack of self-insight and its association with right hemisphere dysfunction, see McGilchrist, *The Matter with Things*, pp. 150-–155. —Ed.

[54] See Oakley, *Evil Genes*, pp. 193–205. Most relevant here are antisocial and borderline personality disorders (as well as "borderpathy," British psychiatrists Nicholas Swift and Harpal Nandhra's term for individuals with a combination

Such "Stalinistic characters" traumatize and actively spellbind others, and their influence finds it exceptionally easy to bypass the controls of common sense. A large proportion of people tend to credit such individuals with special powers, thereby succumbing to the influence of their pathological egotism. If a parent manifests such a defect, no matter how minimal, all the children in the family evidence anomalies in personality development and require appropriate psychotherapy.[55]

The author studied an entire generation of educated adult siblings wherein the source of such influence was the eldest sister, who suffered perinatal damage of the frontal centers. From early childhood, her four younger brothers were exposed to and assimilated pathologically altered psychological material, including their sister's growing component of hysteria. They retained well into their sixties the deformities of personality and worldview, as well as the hysterical features thus caused, whose intensity diminished in proportion to the greater difference in age. Subconscious selection of information[56] made it impossible for these men to apprehend any critical comments regarding their sister's character, which they rejected with moral indignation; such comments were only capable of offending "family honor." The brothers accepted as real their sister's pathological delusions and complaints about her "bad" husband (who was actually a decent person) and her son, in whom she found a scapegoat to avenge her failures.[57] They thereby participated in a world of vengeful emotions, considering their sister a completely normal person and a model of virtue whom they were prepared to defend by the most unsavory

---

of both types of traits). Borderline personality disorder, bipolar disorder, and intermittent explosive disorder all show frontal cortex dysfunction and heightened reactive aggression (Blair et al., *The Psychopath*, p. 105). —Ed.

[55]For severe cases, see Christine Ann Lawson, *Understanding the Borderline Mother: Helping Her Children Transcend the Intense, Unpredictable, and Volatile Relationship* (2004). On covert as opposed to overt cases, see Stephanie Donaldson-Pressman and Robert M. Pressman, *The Narcissistic Family: Diagnosis and Treatment* (1997), a therapeutic model developed in response to a "puzzling and difficult patient population" (p. 1) whose parents were not alcoholic or overtly abusive, but who presented with similar psychological problems (e.g., PTSD, anxiety, depression, eating disorders, etc.). —Ed.

[56]See the subheading "Conversive thinking" later in this chapter. —Ed.

[57]In *Ponerologia* (pp. 29–30), Łobaczewski calls this "scapegoat syndrome," when one child is chosen as a substitute for the true cause of the mother's failures (i.e., her own character disturbance). It often accompanies an "ally complex" with her other children. —Ed.

methods, if need be, against any suggestion of her abnormality. They thought normal women were insipid and naive, good for nothing but sexual conquest. Not one among the brothers ever created a healthy family or developed even average life wisdom.

The character development of these men also included many other factors that were dependent upon the time and place in which they were reared, with a patriotic Polish father and German mother who obeyed contemporary custom by formally accepting her husband's nationality, but who still remained an advocate of the militarism and customary acceptance of the intensified hysteria which covered Europe at the turn of the century. That was the Europe of the three emperors: the splendor of three people with limited intelligence, two of whom revealed pathological traits.[58] The concept of "honor" sanctified triumph. Staring at someone too long was sufficient pretext for a duel. These brothers were thus raised to be valiant duelists covered with saber-scars; however, the slashes they inflicted upon their opponents were more frequent and much worse.

So when people with a humanistic education pondered the personalities of this family, they concluded that the causes for this formation should be sought in the contemporary time and customs. If, however, the sister had not suffered brain damage and the pathological factor had not existed (the exclusionary hypothesis), their personalities would have developed more normally even during those times. They would have become more critical and more amenable to humanistic and moral values and to acting with common sense. They would have founded better families and received more sensible advice from wives more wisely chosen. As for the evil they sowed too liberally during their lives, it either would not have existed at all, or else would have been reduced to a scope conditioned by more remote pathological factors.

Comparative analysis, based on a sufficiently large sample of examined individuals, also led the author to conclude that Iosif Vissarionovich Dzhugashvili, later known as Stalin, should be included in the list of this particular ponerogenic characteropathy, which probably developed against the backdrop of perinatal damage to his brain's prefrontal fields. Literature and news about him abounds in indications: brutal, spellbinding charisma; issuing of irrevocable, often

[58] At this time, Poland was partitioned between the Russian, Prussian, and Austro-Hungarian empires. —Ed.

infantile, decisions; inhuman ruthlessness; pathological vengefulness directed at anyone who got in his way; inability to provide any self-critical insight into his own mental state; and egotistical belief in his own genius on the part of a person whose mind was, in fact, only average.[59] This state explains as well his psychological dependence on a psychopath like Beria.[60] Some photographs reveal the typical deformation of his forehead which appears in people who suffered very early damage to the areas mentioned above. His daughter describes his typical irrevocable decisions as follows:

> Once he had cast out of his heart someone he had known a long time, once he had mentally relegated that someone to the ranks of his enemies, it was impossible to talk to him about that person any more. He was constitutionally incapable of the reversal that would turn a fancied enemy back into a friend. Any effort to persuade him to do so only made him furious. No one—not Redens nor Uncle Pavel nor Alexander Svanidze—could get anywhere when it came to that kind of thing. The only thing they accomplished by it was loss of access to my father and total forfeiture of his trust. When he saw each of them for the last time, it was as if he were parting with someone who was no longer a friend, with someone, in fact, who was already an enemy.[61]

We know the effect of being "thrown out of his heart," as it is documented by the history of those times.[62]

---

[59]Marian Wasilewski (in an interview prepared with Łobaczewski) also identifies Pol Pot (1925–1998) and Ayatollah Khomeini (1900–1989) as frontal characteropaths ("The Ponerology" [1984]). Mao Zedong (1893–1976) probably also falls under this category. See Jung Chang and Jon Halliday, *Mao: The Unknown Story* (2006), as well as Oakley, *Evil Genes*, pp. 216–252, who calls Mao the "perfect borderpath." Oakley highlights Mao's paranoia, charm, lack of empathy, sadism, poor "gut feelings" and inability to make commonsense decisions, emotional dysregulation, and "near mystical faith in his own role as leader." Mao was also conscious of his own manipulative spellbinding skills (e.g., "Getting upset is one of my weapons"; in a fight with his father, he once threatened to kill himself, saying later, "Old men like him didn't want to lose their sons. This is their weakness. I attacked at their weak point, and I won!"). See also Haycock, *Tyrannical Minds*, pp. 109–125. —Ed.

[60]Lavrentiy Beria (1899–1953), head of the Cheka (NKVD) secret police from 1938 to 1945, Deputy Chairman of the Council of Ministers from 1946 to 1953. After Stalin's death, he was arrested on charges of conspiracy, tried in secret, and executed by shooting. There is evidence Beria was a serial rapist, torturer, murderer, and pedophile. See Simon Montefiore, *Stalin: Court of the Red Tsar* (2005), pp. 506–508. The only full-length English biography of Beria is Amy Knight's *Beria: Stalin's First Lieutenant* (1993). —Ed.

[61]Svetlana Alliluyeva, *Twenty Letters to a Friend* (1967), p. 59. —Ed.

When we contemplate the scope of the evil Stalin helped to bring about, we should always take this most ponerogenic characteropathy into account and attribute the proper portion of the "blame" to it; unfortunately, it has not yet been sufficiently studied. We have to consider many other pathological deviations, as they played essential roles in this macrosocial phenomenon. Disregarding the pathological aspects of those recent, inhuman events and interpreting them in historical and moral terms leads to a sense of helplessness and leaves a huge cognitive gap. At the same time, it poisons people's minds and souls, which can open the door to the activity of further ponerogenic factors. Such reasoning should be thus regarded as not only scientifically insufficient but immoral as well. Therefore, a ponerological understanding of these times and people, as well as ensuring its widespread propagation, should be one of the building blocks on the path to lasting peace.

Drug- and disease-induced characteropathies

During the last few decades, medicine has begun using a series of drugs with serious side effects: they attack the nervous system, leaving permanent damage behind. These generally discreet handicaps gradually give rise to personality changes which are often very harmful socially. Streptomycin[63] proved a very dangerous drug; as a result, some countries have limited its use, whereas others have taken it off the list of drugs whose use is permitted.

The drugs used in treating cancers often attack the phylogenetically oldest brain tissue, the primary carrier of our instinctive substratum and basic feelings. Persons treated with such drugs progressively tend to lose their emotional color and their ability to intuit a psychological situation. They retain their intellectual functions but become praise-craving egocentrics, easily ruled by people who know how to take advantage of this. They become indifferent to other people's feelings

---

[62] See Haycock's profile in *Tyrannical Minds*, pp. 85–108. In addition to Montefiore's biography listed above, see his biography on Stalin's early years, *Young Stalin* (2008), as well as Russian historian Oleg V. Khlevniuk's *Stalin: New Biography of a Dictator* (2017), which utilizes previously unavailable primary sources. —Ed.

[63] An antibiotic used to treat tuberculosis and other bacterial infections which inhibits protein synthesis and damages cell membranes in susceptible microorganisms. Possible side effects include nerve damage that can result in dizziness and deafness. —Ed.

and the harm they are inflicting upon them; any criticism of their own person or behavior is repaid with a vengeance. Such a change of character in a person who until recently enjoyed respect on the part of his environment or community, which perseveres in human minds, becomes a pathological phenomenon causing often tragic results.

Was this the case with the Shah of Iran, who for years had been treated for cancer?[64] Again, diagnosing dead people is problematic, and the author lacks detailed data. However, this possibility should be accepted as a probability.[65] The genesis of that country's present tragedy also doubtless contains pathological factors which play ponerologically active roles.[66]

Results similar to the above in the psychological picture may be caused by bacterial toxins or viruses. When, on occasion, the mumps proceeds with a brain reaction, it leaves in its wake a discrete pallor or dullness of feelings and a slight decrease in mental efficiency.[67] Similar phenomena are witnessed after a difficult bout with diph-

---

[64]Shah Mohammad Reza Pahlavi (1919–1980), leader of Iran from 1941–1979, was diagnosed with chronic lymphocytic leukemia in 1974 and in addition to other drugs was given prednisone as part of his treatment, which can cause depression, confusion, and fatigue, among other side effects. Biographer Abbas Milani writes that as a result of his treatments, among other factors, the Shah "was beset with depression, indecision and paralysis, and his indecision led to the immobilisation of the entire system" (*The Shah* [2012], pp. 408–409). —Ed.

[65]*Author's note (1997):* The Polish soldiers who left the Soviet Union under the command of General Anders, after all, remembered a very different young Shah of Persia. [Władysław Anders, prominent member of the Polish government-in-exile in London. Arrested by the Soviets during WWII, Anders was released to fight the Germans, but he and his men (the "Anders Army") were eventually evacuated to Iran (along with tens of thousands of Polish refugees), Iraq, and Mandatory Palestine, passing under British command. Reza Shah ascended to the throne at this time, in 1941. —Ed.]

[66]That is, the Iranian Revolution of 1978–1979. See Mehdi Mozaffari, *Islamism: A New Totalitarianism* (2017), esp. ch. 4. —Ed.

[67]Patients who develop persistent complications after mumps central nervous system infection are presumed to have had brain inflammation (encephalitis), signs of which include the presence of seizures, pronounced changes in the level of consciousness, or focal neurological symptoms. Ataxia and behavioral changes can be seen in children during convalescence. Long-term morbidity is nowadays presumed to be rare (Hviid et al., "Mumps" [2008]). In a 1944 study, two-thirds of 371 people with mumps had abnormal spinal fluid showing signs of inflammation or infection. Mumps encephalitis can occur immediately or years later; progressive neurological problems can show up as many as 10 years after infection (Susan S. Weisberg, "Mumps" [2007]). —Ed.

theria.[68] Finally, when poliovirus attacks the brain, the higher the part of the anterior horns affected, the more severe the brain damage caused by the disease. People with leg paresis rarely manifest these effects, but those with paresis of the neck and/or shoulders must count themselves lucky if they do not. In addition to affective pallor, persons manifesting these effects usually evidence a tendency to avoid noticing other people's hardships, cognitive problems, and a certain indifference to truth. This is sometimes perceived as a kind of pathological indifference.[69]

We rather doubt that President F. D. Roosevelt manifested some of these latter features, since the poliovirus which attacked him when he was forty caused paresis to his legs.[70] After overcoming this, years of creative activity followed. However, it is possible that his naive attitude toward Soviet policy during his last term of office had a pathological component related to his deteriorating health.

Character anomalies developing as a result of brain tissue damage act as insidious ponerogenic factors. As a result of the above-described features, especially the one they share in common,[71] their influence easily bypasses the control of human reason and anchors in others' minds, traumatizing our psyches, impoverishing and deforming our thoughts and feelings, and limiting individuals' and societies' ability to use common sense and to discern psychological or moral situations. This opens the door to other pathological characters who

---

[68]Diphtheria bacteria secretes an exotoxin known to damage most types of body tissue, especially the heart and nervous system. Neurological complications usually hit 3 to 7 weeks after initial onset of illness (Susan S. Weisberg, "Diphtheria" [2007]). —Ed.

[69]See Oakley, *Evil Genes*, pp. 114–116, 326–327. Poliovirus regularly causes lesions in the hypothalamus and thalamus of the diencephalon (see paranoid characteropathy, above), as well as in the reticular formation (Mueller et al., "Poliovirus and Poliomyelitis: A Tale of Guts, Brains, and an Accidental Event" [2005]). Part of the reticular formation maintains attention and alertness. Some researchers hypothesize that psychopathy involves a core cognitive deficit in processing contextual clues and redirecting attention (Hamilton and Newman, "The Response Modulation Hypothesis," in Christopher J. Patrick [ed.], *Handbook of Psychopathy* [2018], pp. 80–93). —Ed.

[70]Franklin Delano Roosevelt (1882–1945), president of the U.S. from 1933–1945, contracted a paralytic illness in 1921 thought to be polio, though some doctors now believe his symptoms were more consistent with Guillain–Barré syndrome, an autoimmune neuropathy. —Ed.

[71]Presumably, dulled affect or "emotional pallor," which is "typical of patients with right hemisphere dysfunction" (McGilchrist, *The Matter with Things*, p. 197). —Ed.

most frequently carry some *inherited* psychological deviations, who then push the characteropathic individuals into the shadows and proceed with their ponerogenic work. That is why various types of characteropathy participate during the initial periods of the genesis of evil, both on the macrosocial scale and on the individual scale of human families.

An improved social system of the future should thus protect individuals and societies by preventing persons with the above deviations, or certain characteristics to be discussed below, from any societal functions wherein the fate of other people would depend upon their behavior. This of course applies primarily to top governmental positions. Such matters should decided by an appropriate institution composed of specialists with a reputation for their integrity and wisdom and with medical and psychological training. The features of brain tissue lesions and their characteropathic results are much easier to detect than certain inherited anomalies. Thus, stifling ponerogenic processes by removing these factors from the process of the synthesis of evil is effective during the early phases of such genesis, and much easier in practice.[72]

Inherited Deviations

Science already protects societies from the results of some physiological anomalies which are accompanied by certain psychological weaknesses. The tragic role played by hereditary hemophilia among European royalty is well known. In countries where the system of

[72]See Raine, *Anatomy*, ch. 7 ("A Recipe for Violence"), for a comprehensive account of the latest research on additional environmental and social risk factors that contribute to brain dysfunction and crime (e.g., nutritional deficiencies, sugar intake, and overexposure to heavy metals; abuse, neglect, poverty, overcrowding, and bad neighborhoods). When combined, biological and environmental risk factors lead to the worst outcomes, e.g., genetic predisposition *plus* birth complications *plus* maternal rejection. Chapter 9 ("Curing Crime") describes interventions known to mitigate violence, e.g., better nutrition starting in the womb and through childhood, reducing lead exposure, parenting skill education, omega-3 supplementation in prisons, meditation, etc. See also Suffren et al., "Prefrontal Cortex and Amygdala Anatomy in Youth with Persistent Levels of Harsh Parenting Practices and Subclinical Anxiety Symptoms over Time during Childhood" (2021), which found that harsh parenting practices (yelling, hitting, shaking) can affect the emotional, social, and brain development (prefrontal cortex and amygdala) of children in ways similar to those resulting from more serious forms of abuse. —Ed.

monarchy still survives, those responsible for such matters are anxious not to allow a carrier of such a gene to become king or queen. Any society exercising so much concern over individuals with blood-coagulation insufficiency would protest if a man afflicted with this anomaly were appointed to a high office bearing responsibility for many people. This behavioral model should be extended to many other inherited anomalies of a more psychological nature.

Daltonists, men with an impaired ability to distinguish red and green colors, are now barred from professions in which this could cause a catastrophe. We also know that this anomaly is often accompanied by a decrease in aesthetic experience, emotions, and the feeling of connection to a society of people who can see colors normally.[73] Industrial psychologists are thus cautious whether such a person should be entrusted with work requiring dependence upon man's autonomous sense of responsibility, as worker safety is contingent upon this sense.

It was discovered long ago that these two above-mentioned anomalies are inherited by means of recessive genes located in the X chromosome, and tracking their transmission through many generations does not meet with theoretical difficulties. Geneticists have similarly studied the inheritance of many other features of human organisms, and science in this area is progressing rapidly. However, they have paid scant attention to the anomalies interesting us here. Many features of human character have a hereditary basis in genes located in the same X chromosome, although it is not a rule. Something similar likely applies to the majority of the psychological anomalies to be discussed below, though this is certainly not true for them all.[74]

---

[73] For a review of the research, see Chan et al., "Subjects with Colour Vision Deficiency in the Community: What Do Primary Care Physicians Need to Know?" (2014). —Ed.

[74] "Genes on the X-chromosome not only influence general intelligence, but also have relatively specific effects on social cognition and emotional regulation. ... Differences in cognitive and social abilities between the sexes could be directly linked to the influence of X-chromosome genes" (David H. Skuse, "X-linked Genes and Mental Functioning" [2005]). While one discovery in 2008 by a team led by geneticist Dr. Jozef Gecz that duplicate genes on the X chromosome can produce excess protein leading to mental retardation, the most significant has been related to the chromosome's MAO-A gene. Around 34% of Caucasian males have a variation (the "warrior gene") resulting in low levels of the enzyme, and a tiny percentage produce none. Low levels have been associated with hypersensitivity to criticism, impulsive aggression, and antisocial personality disorder (see Raine, *Anatomy*, pp. 50–56, and Oakley,

Significant progress has recently been made in understanding a series of chromosomal anomalies resulting from defective division of the reproductive cells and their phenotypic psychological symptoms. This state of affairs enables us to initiate studies on their ponerogenic role and to introduce conclusions which are theoretically valuable, something which is already being done to some extent. In practice, however, the majority of chromosomal anomalies are not transferred to the next generation, so their carriers constitute a very small proportion of the population at large. Furthermore, on average most such people display a lower level of aptitude and lower participation in life activities, so their ponerological role is even smaller than their statistical distribution. Most problems are caused by the XYY karyotype which produces men who are tall, strong, and emotionally violent, with an inclination to collide with the law.[75] This has engendered research and discussion, but their role at the level studied herein is also very small.

Much more numerous are those psychological deviations which also play a correspondingly greater role as pathological factors involved in ponerogenic processes; they are most probably transmitted through normal heredity. However, this realm of genetics in particular is faced with manifold biological and psychological difficulties as far as recognizing these phenomena. People studying their psychopathology lack biological-marker criteria. Biologists lack clear psychological differentiation of such phenomena which would permit studies of heredity mechanics and some other properties.[76] However, this state of affairs is not an insurmountable obstacle if one appreciates the importance of this supposedly "politically" sensitive issue.

Evil Genes, pp. 80–82). Otherwise, molecular genetic research has not borne out Łobaczewski's prediction for the X chromosome's role in the disorders he mentions. —Ed.

[75]See Raine, *Anatomy*, pp. 47–51. XYY syndrome was first identified and reported in Buffalo, NY, in 1961. —Ed.

[76]Łobaczewski ascribes the reluctance to engage in such studies to "various kinds of psychological resistances and ideological beliefs" (*Ponerologia*, p. 35). The heritability and behavioral genetics of these disorders are now commonly studied. However, while the study of genetics has progressed in recent decades, individual genes for these disorders remain elusive, including for psychopathy. While researchers agree these disorders are highly heritable, many speak rather in terms of how nature and nurture "jointly influence the development" of traits and behaviors (Babiak and Hare, *Snakes in Suits*, p. 31)—the "biosocial" or "biopsychosocial" approach, discussed in further notes (see Raine, *Anatomy*, esp. pp. 242–72). —Ed.

At the time most of the observations on which this book is based were being made, much of the work of researchers in the latter half of the sixties that shed light upon many aspects of the matters discussed herein was either nonexistent or unavailable. Scientists studying the phenomena described below were hacking their way through a thicket of symptoms based on previous works and on their own efforts. An understanding of the essence of some of these hereditary anomalies—their biological properties and psychological manifestations—and their ponerogenic role proved a necessary precondition for reaching the primary goal, presented in the next chapter. Results were gleaned which served as a basis for further reasoning. For the sake of the overall picture, and because the approach elaborated also has a certain epistemic value, I decided to retain the methodology of description for such anomalies which emerged from my own work and from that of others at the time.[77] The results published later have been taken into account, as they proved to be consistent with those observations.

Numerous scientists during the above-mentioned fertile era, and some subsequent scientists, such as R. Jenkins, H. Cleckley, S. K. Ehrlich, K. C. Gray, H. C. Hutchison, F. K. Taylor, and others,[78] did cast more stereoscopic light upon the matter. As clinicians, they concentrated their attention upon the more demonstrative cases which play a lesser role in the processes of the genesis of evil, in accordance with the above-mentioned general rule of ponerology.[79] We therefore need to differentiate those analogous states which are less severe or contain less of a psychological deficit.[80] Equally valuable

[77]Problems with Western psychiatric diagnostic tools for personality disorders—the APA's *DSM-5* and the WHO's *ICD-10*—have long been recognized, including "arbitrary diagnostic thresholds, extensive overlap among categories, lack of evidence for 10 distinct categories, and insufficient clinical utility." See Bach and First, "Application of the ICD-11 Classification of Personality Disorders" (2018). —Ed.

[78]See the bibliography for specific citations. —Ed.

[79]That is, subclinical or high-functioning cases. —Ed.

[80]Researchers have found that the "dark" personalities in the "Dark Triad" model (narcissism, Machiavellianism, and psychopathy—the "Dark Tetrad" adds sadism) "value power, money, and social standing, and these values guide their career choices" (politicians score highest on narcissism, Machiavellians are more likely to choose business careers), though they are less likely to prove effective leaders. As Hare writes, "they will inevitably cause harm to their colleagues and employees, and, eventually, to their organization" (Babiak and Hare, *Snakes in Suits*, pp. 301–302). —Ed.

for ponerology would be inquiries concerning the biological nature of the phenomena under discussion which facilitate differentiation of their essence and analysis of their role as pathological factors in the genesis of evil.[81] Meanwhile, current knowledge in this field continues to be mostly a description of symptoms.[82]

Schizoidia

Schizoidia, or schizoidal psychopathy,[83] was isolated by the very first of the famous creators of modern psychiatry.[84] From the beginning, it was treated as a lighter form of the same hereditary burden which is the cause of susceptibility to schizophrenia. However, this latter connection, which could neither be confirmed nor denied with the help of statistical analysis, and the author's experience does not support its existence; no biological test was then found which would have been able to solve this dilemma. For practical reasons, we shall discuss schizoidia with no further reference to this traditional relationship.

Literature provides us with descriptions of several varieties of this anomaly, whose existence can be attributed either to changes in the genetic factor or to differences in other individual characteristics of a

[81] See Raine, *Anatomy*, and Thomson, *Understanding*, ch. 5. —Ed.

[82] This is the approach of the *Diagnostic and Statistical Manual of Mental Disorders* (*DSM-5*), published by the American Psychiatric Association. —Ed.

[83] Łobaczewski's description contains features of both schizoid and schizotypal personality disorders, both of which fall under the *ICD-11* "detachment" trait domain of personality disorder, characterized by interpersonal and emotional distance. There is also some overlap with Asperger syndrome and autism spectrum disorders in general. According to Raine, schizotypals are more likely to be violent and antisocial; they "have constricted affect—meaning that their emotions are blunted and reduced. ... They do not experience emotions in the same way that the rest of us do. [They] also have no close friends outside of their family members" (*Anatomy*, p. 235–36). On the overlap between psychopathy and schizotypal traits, see Raine, "Psychopathy, Schizoid Personality and Borderline/Schizotypal Personality Disorders" (1986). Other schizotypal features include: odd speech and eccentric behavior, suspiciousness, unusual perceptions, and magical thinking. On the wider implications of this worldview, see McGilchrist, *The Matter with Things*, ch. 9 ("What schizophrenia and autism can tell us"). —Ed.

[84] Emil Kraepelin (1856–1926), German psychiatrist, founder of modern scientific psychiatry, psychopharmacology, and psychiatric genetics. Kraepelin opposed Freud's conviction that psychiatric disorders are caused by psychological factors, arguing instead for the importance of biology and genetics. He pioneered the classification of mental disorders based on their common patterns of symptoms. —Ed.

non-pathological nature. The common feature of the varieties of this anomaly is a dull pallor of emotion and weakness of the feeling for psychological realities and situations—that essential component of basic intelligence. This can be attributed to an incomplete quality of the instinctive substratum, which operates with difficulty (as though sliding on sand-covered ice). Low emotional pressure enables them to develop efficient speculative reasoning, a kind of objectivity which is useful in non-humanistic spheres of activity like economics or for exploiting the emotionalism of others. However, their one-sidedness makes them prone to consider themselves intellectually superior to "ordinary" people who, in their opinion, are mainly guided by their emotions.

Carriers of this anomaly are hypersensitive and distrustful, but pay little attention to the feelings of others. They tend to assume extreme, moralizing positions, and are eager to retaliate for minor offenses. Sometimes they are eccentric and odd. Their poor sense of psychological situations and reality leads them to superimpose erroneous, pejorative interpretations upon other people's intentions. They easily become involved in activities which are ostensibly moral, but which actually inflict damage upon themselves and others. Their impoverished psychological worldview makes them typically pessimistic regarding human nature. We frequently find expressions of their characteristic attitudes in their statements and writings: "Human nature is so bad that order in human society can only be maintained by a strong power created by exceptionally rational minds in the name of some higher idea." Let us call this typical expression the "schizoidal declaration."[85]

Human nature does in fact tend to be "no good," especially when the schizoids embitter other people's lives as a result of their shortcomings, that is, or when schizoidal women are abandoned to loneliness.[86] Because of their shortcomings, they often become wrapped up in stressful situations that characteristically stifle their capac-

[85]See Glossary entry for examples of this cynical (often misanthropic) and authoritarianworldview, including Machiavelli, Hobbes, Pobedonostsev, Schmitt, and Marcuse. —Ed.

[86]A research project on academic feminism in this regard would be most fruitful (for reference, see Pluckrose and Lindsay, *Cynical Theories*, ch. 6), as well as the "incel" (involuntary celibacy) phenomenon. Elliott Rodger, the incel mass shooter who targeted women before killing himself in 2014, demonstrated schizoidal traits. —Ed.

ity for thought, sometimes so severely that they suffer a breakdown and fall into reactive psychotic states so similar in appearance to schizophrenia that they lead to misdiagnoses.[87] This was probably the reason a connection was made between such personalities and the tendency to this disease. Nowadays, however, such conditions are easily distinguished and treated with psychotherapy.

The quantitative frequency of this anomaly varies among races and nations. Estimates of this frequency range from negligible up to 3%: rare among Blacks, the highest among Jews.[88] In Poland it may be estimated as 0.7% of the population, in Europe 0.8%. My observations suggest this anomaly is autosomally hereditary.[89]

A schizoid's ponerological activity should be evaluated in two aspects. On a small social scale, such people cause their families trouble, easily turn into tools of intrigue in the hands of clever and unscrupu-

[87]See Robins and Post, *Political Paranoia*, p. 78. Possible examples include mathematician John Nash and school shooter James Holmes, both of whom were diagnosed with schizophrenia but who showed signs of schizoid personality or schizoaffective disorder. There is a strong genetic link between schizotypal personality disorder and schizophrenia (Kapfhammer, "The Concept of Schizoidia in Psychiatry: From Schizoidia to Schizotypy and Cluster A Personality Disorders" [2017]). —Ed.

[88]A 2008 American study (McGuire and Miranda, "Racial and Ethnic Disparities in Mental Health Care") found "lower or equal overall prevalence of mental disorders among minorities," with the exception of *higher* incidence of schizophrenia among Blacks, though "diagnostic problems may in part account for this difference." (Some argue that schizophrenia is a catchall diagnosis for depression among blacks.) In "A Family History Study of Schizophrenia Spectrum Disorders" (1994), psychiatrist Ann B. Goodman cites increased risk for schizophrenia and autism among Ashkenazi (Eastern European) Jews, hypothesizing that "increased prevalence of various rare autosomal recessive diseases among the Ashkenazim might contribute to the increased vulnerability." More recently, Israeli and American scientists discovered an Ashkenazi gene that predisposes for schizophrenia, schizoaffective disorder, and bipolar disorder, raising the chances of these disorders by 40% for carriers of the gene, compared to 15% in the general population (*Haaretz*, Nov. 26, 2013). See Lencz et al., "Genome-wide Association Study Implicates *NDST3* in Schizophrenia and Bipolar Disorder" (2013). —Ed.

[89]That is, from genes among the 22 chromosome pairs that are not sex chromosomes. (If the error is in a sex chromosome, the inheritance is said to be sex-linked.) In Great Britain, one recent study estimates schizoid personality disorder's prevalence at 0.8% (Coid et al., "Prevalence and Correlates of Personality Disorder in Great Britain" [2006]). While that study found a much lower prevalence of *schizotypal* (0.06%), a 2009 U.S. study found a prevalence of 3.9% for that variation (Pulay et al., "Prevalence, Correlates, Disability, and Comorbidity of DSM-IV Schizotypal Personality Disorder"). —Ed.

lous individuals, and generally do a poor job of raising children.[90] They affect their loved ones by provoking feelings of resignation and depression. Their tendency to see human reality in the doctrinaire, simplistic, "legalistic" manner they consider "proper" transforms their frequently good intentions into bad results.[91]

However, their ponerogenic role can have macrosocial implications if their attitude toward human reality and their tendency to invent great doctrines are put to paper and duplicated in large editions. Without recognizing the above-mentioned typical deficits, or even an openly schizoidal declaration, their readers do not realize what the authors' characters are really like; they assimilate the content of such works in a manner corresponding to their own natures. The minds of normal people tend toward a critically corrective interpretation due to the participation of their own richer psychological worldview. At the same time, many other readers will critically reject such works with moral protest but without being aware of the specific reason. People who are irritable and less reasonable, as well as being carriers of various psychological aberrations, fall under the spell of such works and their ponerogenic influence. This leads to a distinctive polarization of social opinions, inciting feelings of hostility. An analysis of the influence of Karl Marx's works easily reveals all the above-mentioned types of apperception and social reactions which engendered animosity between large groups of people. A typical lack of confidence in the positive aspects of human nature is noticeable in his entire body of work.[92]

When reading any of those disturbingly divisive works, let us ponder whether they contain any of these characteristic deficits, or even an openly formulated schizoidal declaration. Such a process will en-

[90]Many school shooters have schizoid, schizotypal, and avoidant (or asthenic) traits. See Ayim, "Personality Patterns of Students Who Make a Threat of Targeted School Violence" (2018). —Ed.

[91]In *Ponerologia* (p. 36), he adds: "They are prone to associate with other, similar people, forming organizations with clandestine goals inspired by their contemptuous attitude toward the normal person. They dream of power on every conceivable scale, but in doing so they open the way for other, more ruthless types of deviants." —Ed.

[92]See Sowell, *Marxism*, for a concise analysis of Marx and Engels's writings that identifies not only their implicit false assumptions, but also their inconsistencies and contradictions with other of Marx's *ad hoc* statements as well as with his own character and behavior. As Sowell observes, while Marxism is explicitly anti-authoritarian and humanistic, "his own personal style was dictatorial, manipulative, and intolerant" (p. 189). —Ed.

able us to gain a proper critical distance from the contents and make it easier to dig the valuable elements out of the fanatical doctrines contained therein. If this is done by two or more people who represent greatly divergent interpretations, their perceptions will come closer together, and the causes of dissent will dissipate. Let us make this attempt as a psychological experiment and for purposes of proper mental hygiene.

Essential psychopathy

Within the framework of the above assumptions, let us characterize another heredity-transmitted anomaly whose role in ponerogenic processes on any social scale appears exceptionally great. We should also underscore that the need to isolate this phenomenon and examine it in detail became evident to those researchers—including the author—who were interested in the macrosocial scale of the genesis of evil, because they witnessed it. I acknowledge my debt to Kazimierz Dąbrowski in doing this and calling this anomaly "essential psychopathy."[93]

Biologically speaking, the phenomenon seems similar to color blindness. It occurs with about ten times lower frequency as color blindness in men (slightly above 0.6%), but in both sexes.[94] Its severity also varies in scope from a level barely perceptible to an experienced observer to an obvious pathological deficiency. Like color blindness, this anomaly also appears to represent a deficit in stimulus transformation, albeit occurring not on the sensory but on the instinctive

[93]Kazimierz Dąbrowski (1902–1980), Polish psychologist, psychiatrist, and physician whose theory of positive disintegration is described in previous notes. He wrote: "The application of this concept [negative integration, or psychopathy] by the people responsible for education and politics could help in the early recognition of psychopaths and in preventing them from gaining positions of power and control over their countries" (*The Dynamics of Concepts* [1973], p. 40). —Ed.

[94]While 15–25% of prison inmates in the USA are psychopaths (fewer in Europe), the overall prevalence is estimated to be around 1.2%: 0.3–0.7% in women, 1–2% in men (Thomson, *Understanding Psychopathy*, p. 3). One study using the PCL:SV found a prevalence of 0.6% in Great Britain (Coid et al., "Prevalence and Correlates of Psychopathic Traits in the Household Population of Great Britain" [2009]). Another study on 203 corporate professionals found that 3.9% met the clinical threshold of psychopathy, though Hare cautions that this sample "cannot be generalized to the larger population of corporate managers and executives" (Babiak and Hare, *Snakes in Suits*, p. 216). —Ed.

level. Psychiatrists of the old school used to call such individuals "Daltonists of human feelings and socio-moral values."[95]

The psychological picture shows clear deficits among men only; among women it is generally toned down, as by the effect of a second normal allele.[96] This suggests that the anomaly is also inherited via the X chromosome,[97] but through a semidominant gene. However, the author was unable to confirm this by excluding inheritance from father to son, as this would require a broad research study.[98]

Analysis of the different experiential manner demonstrated by these individuals caused us to conclude that their instinctive substratum is defective, containing certain gaps and lacking the natural syntonic responses[99] commonly evidenced by members of the species *Homo sapiens.* Our species instinct is our first teacher; it stays with us

[95]Criminal psychologist Robert D. Hare describes psychopaths as having "a profound inability to experience empathy and the complete range of emotions, including fear. As a result, there is a reduction in the capacity for developing internal controls and conscience, and for making emotional 'connections' with others" (Babiak and Hare, *Snakes in Suits*, p. 32). —Ed.

[96]Alleles are gene variants. Since women have two X chromosomes, a healthy allele in one can compensate for an abnormality in the other (as in color blindness). While research suggests that the etiology of psychopathy is the same for boys and girls, "males and females generally differ in levels and manifestation of psychopathic traits ... [F]or a child to remain high on CU [callous-unemotional] traits into early adolescence, this is contingent on genetic factors for boys [78%] and environmental factors for girls [100%]" (Thomson, *Understanding*, pp. 64–65). —Ed.

[97]In "The Psycho Gene" (2010), Philip Hunter suggests two explanations for the observation that psychopathy affects more men than women: 1) genetic/neurological, "in particular if some of the relevant genes are linked to the X chromosome. Yet, this is speculative as few genes have been identified that contribute specifically to psychopathy, with most of the evidence for its heritability being statistical"; or 2) "It might be that women will, in many cases, fail to register on the Hare [PCL–R] because the more extreme traits [i.e., antisocial violence and impulsiveness] are cushioned by other female factors." It is also possible that some cases of female psychopathy are (mis)diagnosed as borderline personality disorder. See also Thomson, *Understanding*, pp. 57–73; Tiihonen et al., "Neurobiological Roots of Psychopathy" (2020); and Johanson et al., "A Systematic Literature Review of Neuroimaging of Psychopathic Traits" (2020). —Ed.

[98]Thomson writes: "parental antisocial behavior may influence the development of psychopathic traits, and in particular having a mother with a criminal conviction greatly impacted the interpersonal-affective features of psychopathy but not the impulsive-antisocial features. In contrast, having a father involved in the criminal justice system predicted both impulsive-antisocial psychopathic traits, as well as affective psychopathic traits" (*Understanding*, p. 134). —Ed.

everywhere throughout our lives. Upon this defective instinctive substratum, the deficits of higher feelings and the deformities and impoverishments in psychological, moral, and social concepts develop in correspondence with these gaps.[100]

Our natural world of concepts strikes such people as a nearly incomprehensible convention with no justification in their own psychological experience. They think our customs and principles of decency are a foreign system invented and imposed by someone else ("probably by priests"), foolish, onerous, sometimes even ridiculous. At the same time, however, they easily perceive the deficiencies and weaknesses of our natural language of psychological and moral concepts in a manner somewhat reminiscent of the attitude of a contemporary psychologist—except in caricature.

The average intelligence of essential psychopaths, especially if measured via commonly used tests, is somewhat lower than that of normal people, albeit similarly varied. However, this group does not contain instances of the highest intelligence, nor do we find technical or craftsmanship talents among them. The most gifted members of this kind may thus achieve accomplishments in those sciences which do not require a correct humanistic worldview or technical skills. (Academic decency is another matter, however.) Whenever we attempt to construct special tests to measure "life wisdom" or "socio-moral imagination," even if the difficulties of psychometric evaluation are taken into account, individuals of this type indicate a deficit disproportionate to their personal IQ.[101]

In spite of their deficiencies in normal psychological and moral knowledge, they develop and then have at their disposal a knowledge of their own, something lacked by people with a natural worldview.[102] They learn to recognize each other in a crowd as early as childhood,

---

[99]The "sympathetic" social and moral emotions that allow people to live in social harmony, facilitating emotional closeness, understanding, and cooperation. See Haidt's *Righteous Mind*, Daniel Goleman's books on emotional and social intelligence, as well as the works of Dąbrowski.—Ed.

[100]Psychopaths display a unique set of moral-foundations attitudes, showing less concern about harm to others, fairness, purity, and respect for authority, with no significant relationship for group loyalty (Thomson, *Understanding*, p. 113–114). —Ed.

[101]On psychopaths' general and emotional intelligence, see Thomson, *Understanding Psychopathy*, pp. 108-–111. While psychopathy's antisocial traits are associated with lower general intelligence, its interpersonal/affective traits are associated with higher *verbal* intelligence. —Ed.

and they develop an awareness of the existence of other individuals similar to them.[103] They also become conscious of being different from the world of those other people surrounding them.[104] They view us from a certain distance, like a parallel species. Natural human reactions—which often fail to elicit interest from normal people because they are considered self-evident—strike essential psychopaths as strange and therefore interesting, even comical. They therefore observe us, deriving conclusions, forming their own different world of concepts. They become experts in our weaknesses and sometimes effect heartless experiments.[105] The suffering and injustice they cause inspire no guilt within them, since these are a direct result of their emotional "otherness" and apply only to "those" people they perceive to be not quite conspecific.[106] A normal person with a natural worldview can neither fully conceive nor properly evaluate the existence of this world of different concepts, or he interprets it through a moralistic lens.

A researcher into such phenomena can glean similar deviant knowledge through long-term studies of the personalities of such people. He can then use it—not without some difficulty—as if it was a learned foreign language, which makes it easy to recognize this anomaly. As we shall see below, a similar practical skill becomes rather widespread in nations afflicted by that macrosocial pathological phenomenon wherein this very anomaly plays the inspiring role.[107] After all, a

---

[102] Later referred to as psychopaths' "special psychological knowledge." —Ed.

[103] Possibly supporting this is the fact that children with psychopathic traits "tend to have more delinquent peers" (Thomson, *Understanding*, p. 134). For anecdotal accounts from self-described psychopaths, see "Can psychopaths recognize other psychopaths?" on *Quora*. Haycock comments on the tendency of pathological leaders to express admiration for each other, e.g., Stalin admired Hitler's treatment of his political opponents, Hitler admired Stalin's capabilities, and both Saddam Hussein and Idi Amin expressed admiration for Hitler and Stalin (*Tyrannical Minds*, p. 246). —Ed.

[104] As one psychopath told research psychologist Kent A. Kiehl: "I've always known I was different. ... I've read a lot about psychopathy since I interviewed with you last time. I read the list of symptoms, and I can see that I have almost all of them" (Kiehl, *The Psychopath Whisperer: The Science of Those Without Conscience* [2015], p. 256). —Ed.

[105] "They observe us and learn to exploit our weaknesses for their own selfish ends" (*Ponerologia*, p. 38). On this psychopathic cunning and manipulation, or Machiavellianism, see Oakley, *Evil Genes*, pp. 42, 189, 281. —Ed.

[106] Of the same species. —Ed.

[107] Above, Łobaczewski lists Beria and Bormann as examples of political psychopaths. Elsewhere, he suggests that Leon Trotsky (1879–1940) was an essen-

normal person can learn to speak their conceptual language, but the psychopath is never able to incorporate the worldview of a normal person, although they often pretend to do so all their lives.

The result of their efforts is only a role they play and a mask behind which they hide their deviant reality. Another self-delusion and role they often play, albeit containing a grain of truth,[108] would be the psychopath's brilliant mind or psychological genius; some of them actually believe in this and attempt to insinuate this belief to others.[109] In speaking of the mask of psychological normality worn by such individuals (and by similar deviants to a lesser extent), we should mention the book *The Mask of Sanity* by Hervey Cleckley, who made this very phenomenon the crux of his reflections. A fragment:

> Let us remember that his typical behavior defeats what appear to be his own aims. Is it not he himself who is most deeply deceived by his apparent normality? Although he deliberately cheats others and is quite conscious of his lies, he appears unable to distinguish adequately between his own pseudointentions, pseudoremorse, pseudolove, etc., and the genuine responses of a normal person. His monumental lack of insight indicates how little he appreciates the nature of his disorder. When others fail to accept immediately his "word of honor as a gentleman," his amazement, I believe, is often genuine. His subjective experience is so bleached of deep emotion that he is invincibly ignorant of what life means to others.
>
> His awareness of hypocrisy's opposite is so insubstantially theoretical that it becomes questionable if what we chiefly mean by hypocrisy should be attributed to him. Having no major value himself, can he be said to realize adequately the nature and quality of the outrages his conduct inflicts upon others? A young child who has no impressive memory of severe pain may have been told by his mother it is wrong to cut off the dog's tail. Knowing it is wrong he may proceed with the operation. We need not totally absolve him of responsibility if we say he realizes less what he did than an adult who, in full appreciation of physical agony, so uses a knife. Can a person experience the deeper levels of sorrow without considerable knowledge of happiness? Can he achieve evil intention in the full sense without real awareness of evil's opposite? I have no final answer to these questions.[110]

---

tial psychopath, "though some doubts remain about the details" (*Logokracja*, p. 56); and that Yuri Andropov (1914–1984) demonstrated "psychopathic traits" (see the Wasilewski interview). Ralph Raico characterized Trotsky as "a champion of thought-control, prison camps, and the firing squad for his opponents, and of forced labor for ordinary, nonbrilliant working people. He openly defended chattel slavery" ("Trotsky: The Ignorance and the Evil" [1979]). —Ed.

[108] I.e., in the form of the "special psychological knowledge" discussed above. —Ed.

[109] See, for example, the case of Ira Einhorn (1940–2020), told in Steven Levy, *The Unicorn's Secret: Murder in the Age of Aquarius* (1988). —Ed.

All researchers into psychopathy underline three qualities primarily with regard to this most typical variety: the absence of a sense of guilt for antisocial actions, the inability to love truly, and the tendency to be garrulous in a way which easily deviates from reality.[111]

A neurotic patient is generally taciturn and has trouble explaining what hurts him most. A psychologist must know how to overcome these obstacles with the help of painless interactions. Neurotics are also prone to excessive guilt about actions which are much more easily forgiven. Such patients are capable of honest and enduring love, although they have difficulty expressing it or achieving their dreams. A psychopath's behavior constitutes the antipode of such phenomena and difficulties.

Our first contact with a psychopath is characterized by a talkative stream which flows with ease and avoids truly important matters with equal ease if they are uncomfortable for the speaker. His train of thought also avoids those abstract matters of human feelings and values whose representation is absent in the psychopathic worldview.[112] We then also feel we are dealing with an imitation of the thought patterns of normal people, in which something else is, in fact, "normal." From the logical point of view, the flow of thought is ostensibly correct, albeit removed from commonly accepted criteria. A more detailed formal analysis, however, evidences the use of many suggestive paralogisms.[113]

---

[110]Hervey Cleckley, *The Mask of Sanity* (1976), p. 386. —Ed.

[111]See the Glossary entry "psychopathy" for additional discussion. The classic works remain Cleckley's book, as well as Robert D. Hare's *Without Conscience: The Disturbing World of Psychopaths Among Us* (1999). —Ed.

[112]While psychopaths may be able to mimic emotions and use associated vocabulary, they cannot grasp abstract concepts or metaphors, including abstract social emotions. See Kiehl, *Psychopath Whisperer*, pp. 164–65, and Oakley, *Evil Genes*, pp. 97–100. —Ed.

[113]Hare writes: "What makes psychopaths different ... is the remarkable ease with which they lie, the pervasiveness of their deception, and the callousness with which they carry it out. But there is something else about the speech of psychopaths that is equally puzzling: their frequent use of contradictory and logically inconsistent statements that usually escape detection. Recent research on the language of psychopaths provides us with some important clues to this puzzle, as well as to the uncanny ability psychopaths have to move words—and people—around so easily" (*Without Conscience*, p. 125). He also describes a study finding that psychopathic offenders "frequently 'derailed,' skipping from one topic to another, and giving contradictory and disjointed answers to simple questions, particularly those concerning emotional events" (Babiak and Hare, *Snakes in Suits*, p. 299). Kiehl writes that psychopaths "often speak

Individuals with the psychopathy referred to herein are virtually unfamiliar with the enduring emotions of love for another person, particularly the marriage partner; it constitutes a fairytale from that "other" human world. For them, love is an ephemeral phenomenon aimed at sexual adventure. However, many psychopathic Don Juans are able to play the lover's role well enough for their partners to accept it in good faith. After the wedding, feelings which really never existed are replaced by egoism, egotism, and hedonism. Religion, which teaches love for one's neighbor, also strikes them as a similar fairytale good only for children and those different "others."

One would expect them to feel guilty as a consequence of their many antisocial acts; however, their lack of guilt is the result of all their deficits, which we have been discussing here.[114] The world of normal people whom they hurt is incomprehensible and hostile to them, and life for them is the pursuit of its immediate attractions, moments of pleasure, and temporary feelings of power. They often meet with failure along this road, along with force and moral condemnation from the society of those other incomprehensible people.[115]

quickly, volubly, and interrupt the flow of the conversation frequently, in an energized speech that observers find difficult to follow and process in real time. ... Then, as observers recall the conversation, their minds interpolate, usually in a very positive sense, the information that was presented. The psychopath often comes off as quick witted, even likable, but the listeners' 'gut' feelings detect that there is something not quite right about the individual. It takes practice to sift through psychopathic speak" (*Psychopath Whisperer*, p. 52). —Ed.

[114]Neuroimaging provides a stark illustration of this. Whereas even nonpsychopathic offenders' brains react emotionally to the sight of unpleasant scenes, for psychopaths, Hare told crime writer Katherine Ramsland in an interview, "there was nothing. No difference. But there was overactivation in the same regions of the brain that were overactive during the presentation of emotional words. It's like they're analyzing emotional material in extra-limbic [e.g., language-processing] regions" (Katherine Ramsland, "Dr. Hare: Expert on the Psychopath"). —Ed.

[115]In private correspondence, Łobaczewski wrote to Laura Knight-Jadczyk (editor of the first edition of this book): "For them you are their worst enemy. You are hurting them very painfully. For a psychopath, revealing his real condition, tearing down his Cleckley mask, brings the end of his self-admiration. You are threatening them with destruction of their secret world, and bring to null their dreams of ruling and introducing [a social system where they can rule and be served]. When his real condition is publicly revealed, a psychopath feels like a wounded animal. You are partly right in finding some similarity of the essential psychopath with the thought [processes] of a crocodile. They are somewhat mechanical. But, are they guilty that they have inherited an

In their book *Psychopathy and Delinquency*, W. and J. McCord say the following about them:

> The psychopath feels little, if any, guilt. He can commit the most appalling acts, yet view them without remorse. The psychopath has a warped capacity for love. His emotional relationships, when they exist, are meager, fleeting, and designed to satisfy his own desires. These last two traits, guiltlessness and lovelessness, conspicuously mark the psychopath as different from other men.[116]

The problem of a psychopath's moral and legal responsibility thus remains open and subject to various solutions, frequently ad hoc or emotional, in various countries and circumstances. It remains a subject of discussion and controversy whose solution does not appear possible within the framework of the presently accepted principles of legal thought.[117] Later in this work, we will understand that much in our world and in our future depends on a mature approach to this issue.

Other psychopathies

The cases of essential psychopathy (and those of schizoidia) seem similar enough to each other to be classified as qualitatively homogeneous. Additionally, there is an indeterminate number of hereditary anomalies whose symptoms are sometimes similar to essential psychopathy—but nevertheless different—which can also be classified as psychopathies. We also meet difficult individuals with a tendency to behave in a manner hurtful to other people, for whom tests do not indicate existing damage to brain tissue and anamnesis does not indicate a very abnormal upbringing which could explain their state. The fact that such cases are repeated within families would suggest a hereditary substratum, but we must also take into account

abnormal gene, and that their instinctive substratum is different from that of the majority of the human population? Such a person is not able to feel like a normal person, or to understand a person bearing a normal instinctive endowment. [It is important] to try to understand the psychopath, and have some pity for them." —Ed.

[116] William and Joan McCord, *Psychopathy and Delinquency* (1956), p. 17. —Ed.

[117] See the two-volume *International Handbook on Psychopathic Disorders and the Law* (2021), edited by Alan Felthous and Henning Saß, for the latest theories and research on the subject, including treatment, preventive detention, education, the death penalty, insanity, and other relevant issues. —Ed.

the possibility that harmful factors participated in the fetal stage.[118] This is an area of medicine and psychology warranting more study, as there is more to learn than we already know concretely. From a ponerological, and therefore practical, point of view, each of those cases have a similar role to play and therefore they can be classified the same way.

Such people also attempt to mask their different world of experience and to play the role of normal people to varying degrees, although this is no longer the characteristic "Cleckley mask." Some find it entertaining to demonstrate their strangeness. These psychopathic and related phenomena may, quantitatively speaking, be summarily estimated at two or three times the number of cases of essential psychopathy, i.e., at less than two per cent of the population. These people participate in the genesis of evil in very different ways and to varying degrees, whether taking part openly, or to a lesser extent when they have managed to adapt to the demands of social life.

This type of person finds it easier to adjust to social life. The lesser cases in particular adapt to the demands of the society of normal people, taking advantage of its understanding for the arts and other areas with similar traditions. Their literary or artistic creativity is often disturbing to the ponerologist or moralist; they insinuate to their readers that their world of concepts and experiences is self-evident, though it is apperceived without awareness of its biopsychological background.[119]

The most frequently indicated and long-known of these is *asthenic psychopathy*, which appears in every conceivable intensity, from barely perceptible to an obvious pathological deficiency.[120] (The qualitative

---

[118]In addition to the risks mentioned in previous notes (e.g., birth complications), and well-known risks such as alcohol consumption during pregnancy, recent research into fetal hormone exposure in the womb (e.g., elevated testosterone) suggests "that the pre-birth period is more important than we have previously thought" (Raine, *Anatomy*, p. 198). —Ed.

[119]See Hervey Cleckley, *The Caricature of Love: A Discussion of Social, Psychiatric, and Literary Manifestations of Pathologic Sexuality* (2011). Commenting on the pathology observable in much literary expression (for example, authors like the Marquis de Sade, Gautier, Baudelaire, Swinburne, and Verlaine), he writes: "Homosexuality, algolagnia [sadomasochism], cynical futility, misogyny, impotence, profound ennui, and a basic disgust of life are often so presented that the reader is led to feel that such reactions are accepted as the mark of special and highly refined esthetic sensibilities. ... A positive relish seems to emanate from the contemplation and artistic portrayal of disfigurement, death, ennui, and profanation" (pp. xi, 211). —Ed.

uniformity of such cases, however, raises a number of objections.) These people, asthenic and hypersensitive, do not indicate the same glaring deficit in moral feeling and ability to sense a psychological situation as do essential psychopaths. They are somewhat idealistic and tend to have superficial pangs of conscience as a result of their faulty behavior. On the average, they are also less intelligent than normal people, and their minds easily avoid consistency and accuracy in logical reasoning. Their psychological worldview is to some extent childishly distorted, so their opinions about people can never be trusted. A kind of mask cloaks the world of their personal aspirations, which is at variance with the official ones required by their position. Their behavior towards people who do not notice their faults is urbane, even friendly; however, the same people manifest hostility and a perfidious, preemptive aggression against persons who have a talent for psychology or demonstrate knowledge in this field.[121]

The asthenic psychopath is relatively less vital sexually and is therefore amenable to accepting celibacy;[122] that is why some Catholic monks and priests often represent lesser or minor cases of this anomaly. Such individuals may very likely have inspired the anti-psychological attitude traditional in Church thinking.

The more severe cases are more brutally anti-psychological and contemptuous of normal people; they tend to be active in the processes of the genesis of evil on a larger scale. Their dreams are composed

---

[120] In Western psychiatry (*DSM-5*, *ICD-10*), the closest analogue is avoidant/anxious personality disorder, closely correlated with dependent personality disorder, both of which fall under the *ICD-11* "negative affectivity" trait domain of personality disorder ("A tendency to experience a broad range of negative emotions with a frequency and intensity out of proportion to the situation," e.g., anxiety and vulnerability), with aspects of low dissociality (e.g., "attention-seeking behaviours to ensure being the center of others' focus; believing that one has many admirable qualities ... that one will achieve greatness, and that others should admire one"), and detachment (e.g., "avoidance of social interactions and intimacy"). (Bach and First, "Application of the ICD-11.") —Ed.

[121] Whereas dependent and avoidant individuals (using the *DSM-5* criteria) tend to be "treatment-seeking," this trait has more in common with Clusters A and B (e.g., paranoid, schizoid, narcissistic, antisocial, etc.), who are typically "treatment-resisting." As Peter Tyrer writes, the latter are "fiercely protective of their personality features" ("New Approaches to the Diagnosis of Psychopathy and Personality Disorder" [2004], p. 371). —Ed.

[122] Cleckley writes: "Anti-sexuality, though it may emerge in ... violent repudiations of the flesh..., seems also to manifest itself in ennui, languor, and a curiously vain artificiality" (*Caricature*, p. 241). —Ed.

of a certain dramatic idealism similar to the ideas of normal people. They would like to reform the world to their liking and combat its errors, but are unable to foresee the more far-reaching implications and results. Spiced by deviance, their visions and doctrines may influence naive rebels and people who have suffered actual injustice. Existing social injustice may then look like a justification for a radicalized worldview and becomes a vehicle for the assimilation of such visions.

The following is an example of the thought-pattern of a person who displays a typical and severe case of asthenic psychopathy:

	Symptoms:
"If I had to start life all over again, I'd do exactly the same: it's organic necessity, not the dictates of duty.	A feeling of being different.
I have one thing which keeps me going and bids me be serene even when things are so very sad. That is an unshakable faith in people.	The shallow nostalgia characteristic of this psychopathy.
Conditions will change and evil will cease to reign, and man will be a brother to man, not a wolf as is the case today.	Vision of a new world.
My forbearance derives not from my fancy, but rather from my clear vision of the causes which give rise to evil."	Different psychological knowledge.

Those words were written in prison on December 15, 1913, by Felix Dzerzhinsky,[123] a descendant of Polish gentry who was soon to originate the *Cherezvichayka*[124] in the Soviet Union and to become the greatest idealist among these most famous murderers. Psychopathies surface in all nations.[125]

[123]Felix Dzerzhinsky (1877–1926), Bolshevik revolutionary and secret police head. Versluis quotes Berdyaev describing the type of "fine man" who becomes an inquisitor like those of old: "I am convinced, that such a 'fine' man, convinced in his faith and unselfish, was also Dzerzhinsky, who in his youth was a passionately believing Catholic and indeed wanted to be a monk. This is an interesting psychological problem" (*New Inquisitions*, p. 138). —Ed.

[124]The Cheka, the first secret police set up under Bolshevik rule. Dzerzhinsky was its first Commissar. Established in 1917, it was "empowered on 22 February 1918 to 'arrest and shoot immediately' all members of 'counter-revolutionary organizations'" (Versluis, *New Inquisitions*, p. 64). —Ed.

[125]*Author's note*: Dzerzhinsky is an interesting case. It is said of him that "His honest and incorruptible character, combined with his complete devotion to the cause, gained him swift recognition and the nickname Iron Felix." His monument in the center of Warsaw in "Dzerzhinsky square," was hated by

If the time ever comes when "conditions will change and evil will no longer rule," it could be because progress in the study of pathological phenomena and their ponerogenic role will make it possible for societies to calmly accept the existence of these phenomena and comprehend them as categories of nature. The pathological vision of a new, "just" structure of society can then be appropriately corrected and partially realized within the framework of a normal human system and under its control. Having reconciled ourselves to the fact that such people are different and have a limited capacity for social adjustment, we should create a system of permanent protection for them within the framework of reason and proper knowledge.

***

For our purposes, we should also draw attention to a type with deviant features which was isolated long ago by E. Brzezicki[126] and accepted by Ernst Kretschmer[127] as characteristic of Eastern and Central Europe in particular. *Skirtoids*[128] are vital, egotistical, and thick-skinned individuals who make good soldiers because of their endurance and psychological resistance. In peacetime, however, they are incapable of understanding life's subtler matters or rearing the next generation prudently. They are happy in primitive surroundings; a comfortable environment easily causes hystericization within

the population of the Polish capital as a symbol of Soviet oppression and was toppled down in 1989. As soon as the PZPR started losing power, the square's name was soon changed to its pre–Second World War name "Plac Bankowy" (Bank Square). According to a popular joke of that late People's Republic of Poland era, "Dzerzhinsky deserved a monument for being the Pole to kill the largest number of communists."

[126] *Author's note*: My professor of psychiatry—Jagiellonian University, Kraków (a friend of Kretschmer). [The reference is to Brzezicki, "O potrzebie rozszerzenia typologii Kretschmera [On the Need to Expand Kretschmer's Typology]" (1946). —Ed.]

[127] German psychiatrist Ernst Kretschmer (1888–1964) developed a classification system based on physical and mental constitution in his book *Physique and Character: An Investigation of the Nature of Constitution and of the Theory of Temperament* (1925). A critic of the Nazis, he studied compulsive criminality and developed new methods of psychotherapy and hypnosis. —Ed.

[128] From the Greek *skirtaô*: to rebel, to jump. Brzezicki distinguished skirtoid psychopathy from skirtothymic temperament (reckless, theatrical, willful, strong and persistent in critical situations). Kępiński (*Psychopatie*, pp. 69, 89) places them on the hysterical spectrum and, contra Łobaczewski, says that they are easily hystericized in *difficult* environments. —Ed.

them. They are rigidly conservative in all areas and supportive of governments that rule with a heavy hand.

Kretschmer was of the opinion that this anomaly was a biodynamic phenomenon caused by the crossing of two widely separated ethnic groups, which is frequent in that area of Europe. If that were the case, North America should be full of skirtoids, a hypothesis not born out by observation. Rather, we may assume that skirtoidism is inherited normally, and not sex-linked. If we wish to understand the history of Russia, as well as Poland to a lesser extent, we should take into consideration a certain mark which this anomaly imprints onto the character of the peoples of this region of the world.

Another interesting question suggests itself: What kind of people are the so-called "jackals," hired as mercenaries and assassins by various mafias and groups who take up arms as a means of political struggle? They offer themselves as "professionals" who perform the duty as accepted; no human feelings will interfere with their nefarious plans. They are most certainly not normal people, but none of the deviations described herein fits this picture.[129] As a rule, though essential psychopaths are capable of murdering a defenseless prisoner, they are talkative and incapable of such carefully planned activity and executing such risky operations. Skirtoids are primitive but emotionally dynamic, and schizoids are too cowardly.

Perhaps we should assume this type to be the product of a cross between lesser burdens of various deviations. If we take the statistical probability of the appearance of such hybrids as a basis for our reasoning, then they should be an extremely rare phenomenon when taking into account the above-mentioned quantitative data. However, mate-selection psychology produces pairings which bilaterally represent various anomalies.[130] Carriers of two or even three lesser deviant factors should thus be more frequent. A jackal could then be imagined as the carrier of schizoidal traits in combination with some other psychopathy, e.g., essential psychopathy or skirtoidism. The many possible combinations of such hybrids fill up the pool of a society's burden of hereditary pathological ponerogenic factors.[131]

[129]For example, Mehmet Ali Ağca (1958–), mercenary for the ultranationalist Turkish Grey Wolves and attempted assassin of Pope John Paul II (*Ponerologia*, p. 40). —Ed.

[130]That is, it is possible that personality-disordered individuals seek out similarly disordered mates. —Ed.

***

The above characterizations are selected examples of pathological factors which participate in ponerogenic processes. The growing body of literature in this area will furnish interested readers with a wider range of data and sometimes colorful descriptions of such phenomena. Specialists, by contrast, can put their own knowledge and experience to good use in this regard. The current state of knowledge in this area is nevertheless still insufficient to produce practical solutions for many problems, particularly those on the scale of the individual and family; it is more satisfactory for the purposes of political ponerology. However, further psychological research and studies on the biological nature of these phenomena, especially, are greatly needed for this purpose.

I would like to warn those readers lacking knowledge and experience of their own in this area not to fall prey to the impression that the world surrounding them is dominated by individuals with pathological deviations, whether described herein or not; it is not. The following graphic representation in circle form approximates the presence of individuals with various psychological anomalies in Poland.

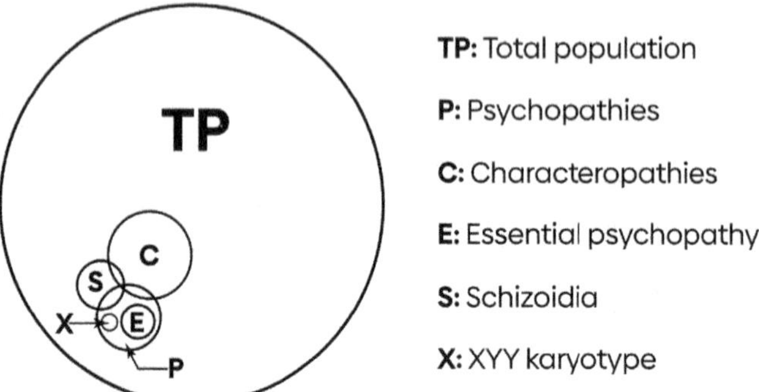

Fig. 1: Pathological phenomena as described in approximate proportion of their appearance.

[131] Łobaczewski suggests Napoleon Bonaparte and Adolf Hitler as examples (*Ponerologia*, p. 40). Since Łobaczewski's understanding of the genetics of personality disorder is out of date by contemporary standards, it may be more fruitful to look at these variations and types in terms of general personality traits, as described above, perhaps with a common underlying personality disorder construct. —Ed.

The fact that deviant individuals are a minority should be emphasized all the more since there have been theories on the exceptionally creative role of abnormal individuals, even an identification of human genius with the psychology of abnormality.[132] Such doctrines have contributed to misfortunes on a large scale, such as the rise of Hitlerism. However, the one-sidedness of these theories appears to be derived from people who were searching for an affirmation of their own personalities by means of such a worldview. Outstanding thinkers, discoverers, and artists have also been specimens of psychological normality, qualitatively speaking. In fact, the psychologically normal person is the richest.

After all, psychologically normal people constitute both the great statistical majority and the natural base of social life in each community. According to natural law, they should thus be the ones to set the pace; moral law as well as the legislation of nations are derived from their nature. Power should be in the hands of normal people. A ponerologist only demands that such authority be endowed with an appropriate understanding of these less-normal people and their ponerogenic role, and that the law be based upon such understanding.

The quantitative and qualitative composition of this biopsychologically deficient fraction of the population certainly varies in time and space on our planet. This may be represented by a single-digit percentage in some nations, in the teens in others.[133] Poland had a relatively low burden, but this share has grown alarmingly; Scandinavian countries, especially Norway, have the lowest burden in Europe; in the U.S., a nation built on the immigration of difficult people,[134] this share is relatively high.[135] Said quantitative and qualitative

[132]See, for example, Sir David Henderson's views on the "creative psychopath" (Thomson, *Understanding*, pp. 19, 108). —Ed.

[133]Current studies estimate the global prevalence of personality disorders to be 7.8%. Prevalence in Western countries is estimated to be between 7.74% when rated by experts and 12.16% when self-rated. See Winsper et al., "The Prevalence of Personality Disorders in the Community: A Global Systematic Review and Meta-analysis" (2019); and Volkert et al., "Prevalence of Personality Disorders in the General Adult Population in Western Countries: Systematic Review and Meta-analysis" (2018). —Ed.

[134]See the descriptions in Woodard's *American Nations*. For an extensive history of pre-revolutionary America, see Murray N. Rothbard, *Conceived in Liberty* (2011, 2019). —Ed.

[135]Some current estimates (keeping in mind that different studies use different methods and may not be directly comparable; they may also include disorders purposefully excluded by Łobaczewski as not significantly ponerogenic in

structure influences the entire psychological and moral climate of the country in question.[136] That is why this problem should be seen clearly and become the subject of conscious concern. However, it seems that the dreams of power so frequently present in these circles did not necessarily come to fruition in those countries where this percentile has been very high. Other historical circumstances were decisive as well in preparing for the emergence of such a macrosocial pathological phenomenon.

In any society in this world, psychopathic individuals and some of the other deviant types create a ponerogenically active network of common collusions, partially estranged from the community of normal people. An inspirational role of essential psychopathy in this network appears to be a common phenomenon. They are aware of being different as they obtain their life-experiences and become familiar with different ways of fighting for their goals. Their world is forever divided into "us and them": their little world with its own laws and customs, and that other foreign world of normal people that they see as full of presumptuous ideas and customs by which they are condemned morally.

Their sense of honor—especially that of the psychopathic inspirers—compels them to cheat and revile that other human world and its values at every opportunity.[137] In contradiction to the customs of normal people, they feel that breaking their promises is appropriate behavior (e.g., offering reassurances, signing documents, and

---

nature): Poland, 8.9%; Norway, 13.4%; USA, 9–21.5%; UK, 4.4%. Different personality disorders predominate in different countries; e.g., avoidant PD in Norway, and obsessive-compulsive PD in many other Western countries (both of which are not particularly ponerogenic). See Gawda, "Cross-cultural Studies on the Prevalence of Personality Disorders" (2018); and Coid et al., "Prevalence and Correlates of Personality Disorder in Great Britain" (2006). —Ed.

[136] For example, the biosocial markers identified by Raine can account for a large proportion of crime in a nation like the United States.Psychopaths in particular are responsible for a disproportionate amount of crime (though making up around 20% of prison populations, they are responsible for more than 50% of serious crimes), and more likely to reoffend upon release from prison (their rate of violent recidivism is three times that of non-psychopathic offenders). See Hare, *Without Conscience*, pp. 87, 96; and Kiehl and Hoffman, "The Criminal Psychopath: History, Neuroscience, Treatment, and Economics" (2011). —Ed.

[137] "The higher the proportion of such individuals, the stronger their pressure on the society to liberalize the moral demands they find uncomfortable" (*Ponerologia*, p. 40). —Ed.

not delivering), because those "others" are so comically naive. They also learn how their personalities can have traumatizing effects on the personalities of those normal people, and how to take advantage of this root of terror for purposes of reaching their goals.[138] This dichotomy of worlds is permanent and does not disappear even if they succeed in realizing their youthful dream of gaining power over the "masses" of normal people. This is dramatic evidence that this peculiar separation is biologically conditioned.

In such people, a dream emerges like some utopia of a "happy" world and a social system which will not reject them or force them to submit to laws and customs whose meaning is incomprehensible to them. They dream of a world in which their simple and radical way of experiencing and perceiving reality would dominate—where they would, of course, be assured safety and prosperity. Those "others," who are different but also more technically skillful than they are, should be put to work to achieve this goal. "We," they say, "after all, will create a new government, one of justice." They are prepared to fight and to suffer for the sake of such a brave new world, and also, of course, to inflict suffering upon others. Such a vision justifies killing people, whose suffering does not move them to compassion because "they" are not quite conspecific. They do not realize that it will be a nightmarish world for "those" people and they will consequently meet with opposition which can last for generations.

Subordinating a normal person to psychologically abnormal individuals has spellbinding, deforming effects on his personality; it engenders trauma and neurosis. This is accomplished in a manner which generally evades the usually sufficient controls of conscious-

[138]Hare writes that psychopaths are "predisposed to take callous but pragmatic advantage of the turmoil and terror experienced by others" (Babiak and Hare, *Snakes in Suits*, p. 164). In Ian Walker's 2009 documentary film *I, Psychopath*, diagnosed psychopath Sam Vaknin described the following to the filmmaker after subjecting him to a series of degrading insults. While Walker was still in shock, Vaknin told him: "Your body was flooded instantly with adrenaline and its relatives like norepinephrine ... Now when these moments pervade the bloodstream, your brain reacts. It shuts down certain centers and activates others. This is called the stress reaction, or stress syndrome, actually. Then when the abuse recedes, the adrenaline levels begin to drop. As they drop, the entire system goes into mayhem. So what bullies usually do, they start and stop, start and stop. That achieves the maximal stress syndrome, and this is the great secret of bullying. Never overdo it. Small doses. The victim will do the rest. Although you are shaking much less [now] ... I must do something about that." —Ed.

ness, so in spite of his resistance, the psychologically altered material penetrates into his personality. Such a situation deprives the person of his natural rights: to practice his own mental hygiene, develop a sufficiently autonomous personality, and utilize his common sense. In the light of natural law, it thus constitutes a kind of crime—which can appear at any social scale—although it is not mentioned in any code of law.

We have already discussed the nature of some pathological personalities, e.g., frontal characteropathy, and how they can deform the personalities of those with whom they interact. Essential psychopathy has exceptionally intense effects in this manner.[139] Something mysterious gnaws into the personality of an individual at the mercy of a psychopath and is then fought as if against a demon haunting him. His emotions become chilled, his sense of psychological reality is stifled. This leads to de-criterialization of thought[140] and a feeling of helplessness, culminating in depressive reactions which can be so severe that psychiatrists sometimes misdiagnose them as a manic-depressive psychosis. However, it is also clear that many such people rebel much earlier than that and start searching for some way of liberating themselves from such an influence.

Many life situations involve far less mysterious effects of other psychological anomalies upon normal people (which are always unpleasant and destructive) and their carriers' unscrupulous drives to use this influence in order to dominate and take advantage of others. Governed by such unpleasant experiences and feelings, as well as egoism and the natural psychological worldview, societies thus have reason to reject such people, helping to push them into marginal positions in social life, including poverty and criminality.[141]

[139]Perhaps the best fictional representation of psychopathy and its interpersonal effects in recent years has been Lionel Shriver's *We Need to Talk about Kevin* (2003, adapted for film in 2011). Cleckley considered Mary Astor's *The Incredible Charlie Carewe* (1962) the best of his time. Two of the most accurate film depictions of psychopathy are the characters Gordon Gekko (Michael Douglas) in *Wall Street* (1987), and Anton Chigurh (Javier Bardem) in *No Country for Old Men* (2007). For an analysis of 126 depictions of psychopathy, see Leistedt and Linkowski, "Psychopathy and the Cinema: Fact or Fiction?" (2014). More recent are Louis Bloom (Jake Gyllenhal) in *Nightcrawler* (2014), Amy Dunne (Rosamund Pike) in *Gone Girl* (2014), and Anna Delvey (Julia Garner) in *Inventing Anna* (2022). —Ed.

[140]Elimination of critical standards. —Ed.

It is unfortunately almost the rule that such behavior is amenable to moralizing justification in our natural worldview categories. Most members of society feel entitled to protect their own persons and property and enact legislation for that purpose. Being based on natural perception of phenomena and on emotional motivations instead of an objective understanding of the problems, such laws will never be able to safeguard the kind of order and safety we would like; psychopaths and other deviants merely perceive such laws as a force which needs to be battled.

To individuals with various psychological deviations, such a social structure dominated by normal people and their conceptual world appears to be a "system of force and oppression."[142] Psychopaths reach such a conclusion as a rule. If, at the same time, a good deal of injustice does in fact exist in a given society, pathological feelings of unfairness and suggestive statements inspired by them can resonate among those who have truly been treated unfairly. Revolutionary doctrines may then be easily propagated among both groups, although each group has completely different reasons for favoring such ideas. The former see them as a means to realize their dreams; the latter unfortunately believe they will bring an improvement in their fate.

***

The presence of pathogenic bacteria in our environment is a common phenomenon; however, it is not the single decisive factor that determines whether an individual or a society becomes ill, since general

[141] Personality disorders—among other mental health problems—are much more prevalent among the homeless (estimated at 23.1%, with individual studies ranging from 2.2% to 71.0%) and in prisons (up to 65%, including 47% antisocial personality disorder). See Fazel et al., "The Prevalence of Mental Disorders among the Homeless in Western Countries: Systematic Review and Meta-Regression Analysis" (2008), and "Serious Mental Disorder in 23,000 Prisoners: A Systematic Review of 62 Surveys" (2002). Poverty, when combined with biological risk factors, also greatly increases the risk of developmental problems and crime, potentially creating a vicious cycle of characteropathy (see Raine, *Anatomy*, pp. 249–250, 263). —Ed.

[142] This attitude is universalized in ideologies such as Marxism and Critical Social Justice, where "oppression" can be defined as "The systemic and pervasive nature of social inequality woven throughout social institutions as well as embedded within individual consciousness. Oppression fuses institutional and systemic discrimination, personal bias, bigotry and social prejudice in a complex web of relationships and structures that saturate most aspects of life in our society" (James Lindsay, "Oppression" [2020]). —Ed.

health, natural and artificial immunity, as well as ease of access to medical care also play a role. Similarly, psychopathological factors alone do not determine the spread of evil. Other circumstances have parallel importance: socioeconomic conditions and moral and intellectual deficits. Those people and nations who are able to endure injustice in the name of moral values can more easily find a way out of such difficulties without resorting to violent means. A rich moral tradition, the experience and reflections of centuries, and Christian social doctrine[143] provide valuable assistance in this regard. Ponerology, on the other hand, opens the way to artificial immunization of people and nations against the etiological causes that cooperate in the genesis of evil.

This book highlights the role of these factors in the genesis of evil, which have been insufficiently understood for centuries; it has been necessary to illuminate them in order to complete the overall picture and permit more effective practical measures to be formulated. At the same time, emphasizing the role of pathological factors in the genesis of evil does not minimize the responsibility of moral failings and intellectual deficits, if they are only of this nature. For it often happens that real moral deficits and a grossly inadequate conception of human reality and psychological and moral situations are frequently caused by some earlier or contemporary distorting influence on the part of pathological factors.[144]

We should consider the presence within every human society of this small minority of individuals who are carriers of qualitatively diverse, but ponerologically active, pathological factors to be an eternal, biologically determined feature of our species. Any discussion on what came first in the process of the genesis of evil—moral failings or the activities of pathological factors—can thus be considered academic speculation. On the other hand, the Bible is worth re-reading through the eyes of a ponerologist.

---

[143] A reference to Catholic social teaching, the Church's doctrine on human dignity and the common good. In *Logokracja*, Łobaczewski cites Pope John Paul II's encyclical *Laborem exercens* [Human Work] (1981). See, for example, Thomas Storck, *An Economics of Justice and Charity: Catholic Social Teaching, Its Development and Contemporary Relevance* (2017) —Ed.

[144] *Author's note (1997):* In fact, biological evil and moral evil are linked by so many psychological interdependencies that a real separation between them is not feasible. Conditions of disjunction in this area do not exist. We can only use analysis and abstraction, and this is important to remember!

Detailed analysis of the personality of the average normal person nearly always reveals certain errors and difficulties caused by the effects upon him of some kind of pathological factor. If the activity was far removed in time or space, or the factor relatively obvious, healthy common sense is better able to correct such effects. If the pathological factor remains incomprehensible, the person has difficulty understanding the cause of his problems; he sometimes appears to remain a lifelong slave of ideas and patterns of behavioral response which originated under the influence of pathological individuals. This is what occurred in the above-mentioned family, where the source of pathological induction[145] was the eldest sister with perinatal damage of the prefrontal fields of her brain cortex. Even when she obviously abused her youngest child, her brothers attempted to interpret this in a paramoralistic manner, a sacrifice in the name of "family honor."

Such matters should be taught to everyone in order to facilitate autopedagogical self-monitoring. Those outstanding psychiatrists who became convinced that developing a sufficiently balanced view of human reality is impossible without factoring in psychopathological findings are therefore correct—a conclusion that is unfortunately difficult to accept by respectable people who believe they have attained a mature worldview without such burdensome studies. The older egotistical defenders of the natural worldview have tradition, *belles-lettres*, even philosophy on their side. They do not realize that during the present difficult times, their manner of comprehending life's questions renders the battle with evil more difficult, especially one of such great political magnitude. However, the younger generation is more familiar with biology and psychology, and is thus more amenable to an objective understanding of the role of pathological phenomena in the processes of the genesis of evil. It would therefore be worthwhile to explain these matters to every individual in order to facilitate his autopedagogical insight into his own personality and his understanding of macrosocial pathological phenomena.

Parallax,[146] often even a wide gap, frequently occurs between human and social reality—which is biological by nature and influenced

[145]Like emotional and hypnotic states, varying degrees of psychopathology can be similarly induced through exposure ("as if participating in someone else's madness," as Łobaczewski puts it further below). Such individuals can have a spellbinding, mind-numbing effect on otherwise normal people, in addition to causing anxiety disorders, posttraumatic stress, etc. —Ed.

[146]The difference in appearance or position of an object when viewed from two different locations. —Ed.

by the above-mentioned psychopathological factors—and the traditional perception of reality present in philosophy, ethics, and secular and canon law. This gap is easily discernible to all those whose psychological worldview was formed in a manner different from the natural way of a normal person. Many of them consciously and subconsciously take advantage of this weakness in order to force themselves into it, along with their myopically determined activities characterized by egoistical concepts of self- or group-interest. Other people—whether pathologically indifferent to other peoples' or nations' hurts, or lacking in knowledge as to what is human and decent—then find an open gate to bulldoze their different way of life through unobliging societies in an attempt to fulfill their grandiose aims, which are in reality insane and unrealistic.

Will we ever be able to overcome this age-old problem of humanity sometime in the yet undetermined future, thanks to progress in the biological and psychological understanding of various pathological factors participating in ponerogenic processes? That will depend on the progress of research and the good will of societies. Scientific and societal awareness of the role played by the above-mentioned factors in the genesis of evil will help public opinion to elaborate a greater repudiation of evil, which will then cease to be so spellbindingly mysterious. If properly modified based on an understanding of the nature of phenomena, the law will permit prophylactic countermeasures to the origin of evil.

At the same time, every society has been subjected to natural eugenic processes[147] over the centuries, which cause individuals with biopsychological deficiencies, including those with the above-mentioned features, to drop out of reproductive competition or reduce their birth rate. These processes are rarely seen in such terms, often conceived instead as a moral evil or obscured by other conditions apparently relegating them to the background.[148] Unfortunately,

[147]Natural eugenics in this context is a synonym for human natural selection, not a reference to eugenic policies such as those developed Sir Francis Galton and others in the late 1800s. For a similar perspective, see Michael McConkey, "The legal system is a eugenics program (for better or for worse)," in *Darwinian Liberalism* (2018), pp. 130–135. —Ed.

[148]"These processes often hide their biological nature under phenomena that the average person finds morally reprehensible" (*Logokracja*, p. 42, machine translation). For example, poverty and crime, as mentioned above. Łobaczewski may also have in mind some or all of the following: sexual selection, shunning and social ostracization, crime-fighting, prison and psychiatric detention, and,

it seems that modern medicine is also interfering with these natural processes. We are now seeing a large-scale increase in hereditary deviations within societies. We will call this the negative balance sheet of eugenic processes. Conscious comprehension of these matters based on proper knowledge and appropriate moral criteria could render these processes less stormy in form, not so full of bitter experience, and more effective.[149]

If human consciousness and conscience are properly formed and good advice in these matters is heeded, the balance of these processes could be tipped markedly in the positive direction. Medicine also has ample opportunity to reduce the number of nonhereditary deviations.[150] After a number of generations, society's burden of inherited pathological factors could be reduced below a certain critical level, their pathological network would begin to break down, and its contribution to ponerogenic processes would fade away.

Ponerogenic Phenomena and Processes

Following a spatio–temporal network of causal links as qualitatively complex as those occurring in ponerogenic processes requires the proper approach and experience. The fact that psychologists daily face multiple cases of dealing with such deviants or their victims means that they become progressively more skilled in understanding and describing the many components of psychological causation. They notice both reciprocal and closed causal systems. However, this skill sometimes proves insufficient in overcoming our human tendency to

on the more extreme side, castration, capital punishment, combat and warfare—though he would probably consider most of these as accompanied by too much of a moralizing interpretation, given his thoughts on retributive justice elsewhere. The Yupik Eskimos described to anthropologist Jane M. Murphy how the group would deal with a psychopath (which they called a *kunlangeta*): "Somebody would have pushed him off the ice when nobody else was looking" (John Seabrook, "Suffering Souls" [2008]). —Ed.

[149] Presumably Łobaczewski means that the evils accompanying things such as poverty and crime can be mitigated, while the incidence of personality disorders can be gradually lessened instead of exacerbated. He expands on this idea in Chapter IX and "Problems of Ponerology," suggesting that practices like mate selection (and perhaps psychiatric and penal reform) can be modified according to moral precepts and ponerology. However, he does not go into detail on how exactly this should be done. —Ed.

[150] For instance, reducing the incidence of infant brain damage, as well as the nutritional interventions suggested by Raine. —Ed.

concentrate upon some facts while ignoring others, provoking an unpleasant sensation that our mind's capacity to understand the reality surrounding us is inefficient. This explains the temptation to use the natural worldview in order to simplify complexity and its implications, a phenomenon as common as the "old sage" known to India's philosophical psychology. Such oversimplification of the causal picture as regards the genesis of evil—often to a single, easily understood cause or perpetrator—itself becomes a cause in this genesis.[151]

So, in deference to the shortcomings of our human reason, let us consciously take the middle road and use the abstraction process, first describing selected phenomena, then the causative sequences characteristic for ponerogenic processes. Such sequences can then be linked into more complex structures ever more sufficient for grasping the full picture of the real causative network. At first the holes in the net will be so large that a school of sprats can swim through undetected, although large fish will be caught. However, this world's evil represents a kind of continuum, where minor species of human evil effectively add up to the genesis of large evil. Making this net denser and filling in the details of the picture already proves to be easier, since ponerogenic laws are analogous regardless of the scale of events. Our common sense commits fewer errors at the level of these minor matters.

In attempting closer observation of these psychological processes and phenomena which lead one man or one nation to hurt another, let us select phenomena as characteristic as possible. We shall again see that the participation of various pathological factors in these processes is the rule; the situation where such participation is not noticeable tends to be the exception.[152]

---

[151] Past and contemporary examples include blaming social problems solely on autocratic rulers, enemy groups (the bourgeoisie, capitalists, communists, fascists, terrorists, Jews, Muslims—or any other racial, political, religious, or social group), or vague abstractions and ideologies (like fascism, socialism/communism, patriarchy, misogyny, Whiteness, social forces, etc.). —Ed.

[152] Łobaczewski elsewhere includes old age as a possible ponerogenic factor, especially in the case of leaders who rule for life in some capacity: "When a man's brain begins to deteriorate, when his memory of past affairs is still intact but his recollection of current ones is failing, when his world begins to shrink to matters that concern only him, then he becomes a focal point of harmful activity. He begins to attract individuals (often carriers of the aforementioned mental anomalies) who are eager to take advantage of the weaknesses of his mind using devious flattery" (*Ponerologia*, p. 42). He includes as examples Henry Ford (1863–1947), Emperor of Ethiopia Haile Selassie I (1892–1975), and Pope Paul VI (1897–1978). —Ed.

Para-appropriate responses

The second chapter sketched the human instinctive substratum's role in our personality development, basic intelligence, the formation of the natural worldview, and societal links and structures. We also indicated that our social, psychological, and moral concepts, as well as our natural instinctual and emotional responses, are not adequate for every situation with which life confronts us. We generally wind up hurting someone if we act according to our natural concepts or responses in situations where they seem to be appropriate, but which are in fact essentially different in nature. As a rule, situations that trigger such para-appropriate emotional responses[153] occur because some pathological factor difficult to understand has entered the picture. Thus, the practical value of our natural worldview generally ends where psychopathology begins.[154]

Familiarity with this common weakness of human nature and the normal person's "naivety" is part of the special knowledge we find

---

[153]That is, inappropriate or maladaptive for the particular situation, even if perhaps appropriate in others resembling it. In *Ponerologia* (p. 44), Łobaczewski writes: "However, when we are faced with a situation that is sufficiently similar, on its surface, to one that has its own coded response, but which is quite different in its essence, then our instinct responds with an emotionally charged sense of certainty, albeit in a completely irrational way." —Ed.

[154]For example, Versluis writes: "A totalitarian leader draws on the ancient instinct to follow the wise man, but the instinct is perverted, so that the society moves inexorably toward the rationalization of monstrosities and horrors" (*New Inquisitions*, p. 144). In addition to obedience to authority, other examples include the tendency to trust or automatically believe in another's honesty, the moralistic pleasure we get when cheaters are punished, etc. A recent study on virtue- and victim-signaling concludes: "The obligation to alleviate others' pain can be found in most of the world's moral systems. It also appears to be built into the structure of the mind by evolution, as evidenced by the human tendency to feel distress at signs of suffering. It is therefore not surprising that many people are motivated to help perceived victims of misfortune or disadvantage. But the downside of this proclivity is that it can also lead people to be easily persuaded that all victim signals are accurate signals, particularly when they perceive the alleged victim as being a 'good person.' When this occurs, well-meaning people might allocate their material and social resources to those who are neither victims nor virtuous, which necessarily diverts resources from those who are legitimately in need. Effective altruism requires the ability to differentiate between false and true victims. Credulous acceptance of all virtuous victim signals as genuine can also enable and reward fraudulent claims, particularly by those with antisocial personality traits" (Ok et al., "Signaling Virtuous Victimhood as Indicators of Dark Triad Personalities" [2020], p. 25). —Ed.

in many psychopathic individuals, as well as some characteropaths. Spellbinders of various schools attempt to provoke such para-appropriate reactions from other people for the sake of their specific goals, or in the service of their fanatical ideologies.[155] In such cases, this hard-to-understand pathological factor is located within the spellbinder himself.

Egotism

We call egotism the attitude—habitual and subconsciously conditioned as a rule—by which we attribute excessive value to our instinctive reflexes, early acquired notions and archetypes, and individual natural worldview. Egotism fosters the dominance of the subconscious life and makes it difficult to accept disintegrative states, which hampers a personality's normal evolution.[156] This in turn favors the appearance of para-appropriate reactions as described above. An egotist measures other people by his own yardstick, treating his concepts and experiential manner as objective criteria. He would like to force other people to feel and think very much the same way he does. Egotist nations have the subconscious goal of teaching or forcing other nations to think in their own categories, which makes them incapable of understanding other people and nations or becoming familiar with the values of their cultures.

When it affects adolescents, it causes distortions in personality development that often prove to be lifelong. Proper rearing and self-rearing thus always aim at de-egotizing a young person or adult, thereby opening the door for his mind and character to develop. Practicing psychologists nevertheless commonly believe that a certain measure of egotism is useful as a factor stabilizing the personality, protecting it from overly facile neurotic disintegration, and thereby

[155]That is, not only are such reactions not appropriate; they are often *deliberately provoked.* For example, a violent reaction can be used to make the target look like the aggressor, and the provoker as the injured party. Ponerogenic groups like antifa also use the tactic of creating a double bind in which either response makes one look bad. For example, see the discussion on the "calibrated level of violence" (designed to make police look weak if they do not respond, or overreactive if they do) in Andy Ngo, *Unmasked: Inside Antifa's Radical Plan to Destroy Democracy* (2021), p. 64. Serial killer Ted Bundy would pretend to be injured or disabled in order to lure women. Dr. George K. Simon describes the different types of manipulation used by psychopaths in his book, *In Sheep's Clothing: Understanding and Dealing with Manipulative People* (2005). —Ed.

[156]See Dąbrowski, *Personality-shaping through Positive Disintegration.* —Ed.

making it possible to overcome life's difficulties. However, rather exceptional people exist whose personality is very well integrated even though they are almost totally devoid of egotism; this allows them to understand others very easily.

The kind of excessive egotism which hampers the development of human values and leads to misjudgment and terrorizing of others well deserves the title "king of human faults." Difficulties, disputes, serious problems, and neurotic reactions sprout up around such an egotist like mushrooms after a rainfall. Egotist nations start wasting money and effort in order to achieve goals derived from their erroneous reasoning and overly emotional reactions. Their inability to acknowledge other nations' values and dissimilarities, derived from other cultural traditions, leads to conflict and war.[157]

We can differentiate between primary and secondary egotism. The former comes from a more natural process, namely the child's natural egotism and child-rearing errors that tend to perpetuate this childish egotism. The secondary type occurs when a personality that has overcome his childish egotism regresses to this state, which leads to an artificial attitude characterized by greater aggression and social noxiousness. Excessive egotism is a constant property of the hysterical personality, whether their hysteria be primary or secondary. That is why the increase in a nation's egotism should be attributed to the above-described hysterical cycle before anything else.

If we analyze the development of excessively egotistical personalities, we often find some non-pathological causes, such as an overly coddled upbringing in a constricted and comfortable environment or being raised by persons less intelligent than the child. However, the main reason for the development of an overly egotistical personality

[157]For a recent case study, see Gordon M. Hahn, *Ukraine over the Edge: Russia, the West and the "New Cold War"* (2018), with general background in chapter 4, "Democracy Promotion: The Dual-Use Technology of Color Revolutions." Regarding the wars in Afghanistan and Iraq, Hahn wrote elsewhere: "When George W. Bush decided to invade Iraq and replace Saddam Hussein's regime with a democratically elected one, he believed that this would, as he said, 'serve as a powerful example of liberty and freedom in a part of the world that is desperate for liberty and freedom.' He and his team held firmly to this conviction, despite numerous warnings that war would fragment the country along tribal, ethnic and religious lines, that any elected government in Baghdad would be Shia-dominated and oppress Sunnis, and that Iran would be the principal beneficiary from a weakened Iraq. Democracy-building is proceeding just as miserably in Afghanistan" ("Dirty-Deal Democratizers, the 'War of Values with Russia,' and Problems of Democracy-Promotion" [2015]). —Ed.

in a normal person is contagion, through psychological induction, by excessively egotistical or hysterical persons who, themselves, developed this characteristic under the influence of various *pathological* causes. Most of the above-described genetic deviations cause the development of pathologically egotistical personalities, among other things.

Many people with various hereditary deviations and acquired defects develop pathological egotism. For such people, forcing others in their environment, whole social groups, and, if possible, entire nations to feel and think like themselves becomes an internal necessity, a ruling concept. A game that a normal person would not take seriously can become a lifelong goal for them, the object of effort, sacrifices, and cunning psychological strategy.

Pathological egotism derives from repressing from one's field of consciousness any objectionable, self-critical associations referring to one's own nature or normality. Dramatic questions such as "who is abnormal here, me or this world of people who feel and think differently?" are answered in the world's disfavor. Such egotism is always linked to a dissimulative attitude,[158] with a Cleckley mask over some pathological quality being hidden from consciousness—both one's own and that of other people. The greatest intensity of such egotism can be found in the prefrontal characteropathy described above (e.g., Stalin).

The importance of the contribution of this kind of egotism to the genesis of evil thus hardly needs elaboration. As a result of its contagiousness, it is primarily a social phenomenon; the mental state of nations is characterized by its average level in society. It must be emphasized that pathological egotism is a constant vehicle for pathological induction, egotizing or traumatizing others, which in turn causes further difficulties. Pathological egotism is a constant component of diverse states wherein someone who appears to be normal (although he is in fact not quite so) is driven by motivations or battles for goals a normal person considers unrealistic or unlikely. The average person might ask: "What could he expect to gain by that?" Public opinion, however, interprets such a situation in accordance with "common sense" and is thus prone to accept a "more likely" version of the situation and events. Such interpretation often results in human tragedy. We should thus always remember that

[158]That is, concealing or disguising one's thoughts, feelings, or character. —Ed.

the principle of law *cui prodest*[159] becomes illusory whenever some pathological factor enters the picture.[160]

Moralizing interpretations

The tendency to impart a moralizing interpretation upon essentially pathological phenomena is an aspect of human nature whose discernible phylogenetic substratum is encoded in our species instinct; that is to say, humans normally fail to differentiate between moral and biological evil. Thus it constitutes an erroneous, para-appropriate—and ponerogenic—response. Our instinct is inclined to judge biological defects, especially hereditary ones, more harshly than moral failings; this is rooted in human nature, which tends towards the elimination of defective individuals. This tendency always surfaces, albeit to varying degrees, within the natural psychological and moral worldview, which is why we should consider it a permanent error of public opinion. We may curb it with increased self-knowledge and self-control, but overcoming it requires knowledge of psychopathology. Young people and less cultured circles always have a greater propensity for such interpretations (although it characterizes traditional aesthetes[161] too), which intensifies whenever our natural reflexes take over control from reason, i.e., in hysterical states, and in direct proportion to the intensity of egotism.

We close the door to a causal comprehension of phenomena and open it to vengeful emotions and psychological error whenever we impose a moralistic interpretation upon faults and errors in human behavior which are in fact largely or wholly derived from the various

---

[159] "Who benefits?" —Ed.

[160] Rectenwald writes: "If the history of the great famine and related offenses are considered, then the notion of individuals acting strictly in accordance [with] their material self-interests must be discounted, at least where totalitarians and ideologues are concerned" (*Google Archipelago*, p. 34). Regarding the unrealistic goals of Islamism, Mozaffari writes: "They are convinced that a reproduction of the Medina model is not only possible, but is necessary in order to restore the lost glory of Muslims. ... Astonishingly, a small group of emigrants, of whom many were young and some were even socially deprived, succeeded in rapidly turning this new model into a vast and powerful empire. They conquered the great empires of the time ... Statements from contemporary Islamists show that they all firmly believe in the feasibility of a similar project, i.e., to make the non-Islamic powers of their time crumble" (*Islamism*, p. 39). —Ed.

[161] Artistic types. —Ed.

influences of pathological factors, whether mentioned above or not, which are often obscured from minds untrained in this area. We thereby also permit these factors to continue their ponerogenic activities, both within ourselves and others. Nothing, however, poisons the human soul and deprives us of our capacity to understand reality more objectively than this very obedience to that common human tendency to take a moralistic view of human behavior.[162]

Practically speaking, to say the least, each instance of behavior that seriously hurts some other person contains within its psychological genesis the influence of some pathological factors, among other things, of course. Therefore, any interpretation of the causes of evil which would limit itself to moral categories is an inappropriate perception of reality, one which generally leads to erroneous behavior, limiting our capacity for counteraction of the causative factors of evil and opening the door to desires for revenge. This frequently starts a new fire in the ponerogenic processes. We shall therefore consider a one-sided moral interpretation of the origins of evil to be wrong and immoral at all times. The idea of overcoming this common human inclination and its results can be considered a moral motive intertwined throughout ponerology.

If we analyze the reasons why some people frequently overuse such emotionally loaded and suggestive interpretations, often indignantly rejecting a more correct interpretation (e.g., Lenin), we shall of course also discover pathological factors acting within them. Intensification of this tendency in such cases is caused by repressing from the field of consciousness any self-critical concepts concerning their own behavior and its internal reasons. The influence of such people causes this tendency to intensify in others.

Paramoralisms

The conviction that moral values exist and that some actions violate moral rules is so common and ancient a phenomenon that it seems not only to be the product of centuries of experience, culture, religion, and socialization, but also to have some foundation at the level of man's phylogenetic instinctive endowment (although it is certainly not totally adequate for moral truth).[163] Thus, any insinuation framed in moral slogans is always suggestive, even if the "moral" criteria used

[162]For a similar view, see Sapolsky, *Behave.* —Ed.

[163]See Haidt, *The Righteous Mind.* —Ed.

are just an *ad hoc* invention. By means of such paramoralisms, one can thus prove any act to be immoral or moral in a manner so actively suggestive that people whose minds will succumb to such reasoning can always be found.[164]

In searching for an example of an evil act whose negative value would not elicit doubt in any social situation, ethics scholars frequently mention child abuse. However, psychologists often meet with paramoral affirmations of such behavior in their practice, such as in the above-mentioned family with the prefrontal field damage in the eldest sister. Her younger brothers emphatically insisted that their sister's sadistic treatment of her son was due to her exceptionally high moral qualifications, and they believed this by auto-suggestion. Paramoralism somehow cunningly evades the control of our common sense, sometimes leading to acceptance or approval of behavior that is openly pathological.[165]

Paramoralistic statements and suggestions so often accompany various kinds of evil that they seem to play an indispensable role.[166]

---

[164]See, for example, Albert Bandura's concept of "moral disengagement" and its related mechanisms (moral justification, euphemistic labeling, advantageous comparison, displacement and diffusion of responsibility, disregarding or misrepresenting injurious consequences, dehumanization, and blaming the victim). Ernest Andrews writes that totalitarian language's "chief defining characteristic was the reduction of all reality, and consequently, of all communication symbols, into a good versus bad representational schema, wherein the *good* equaled all things that were part of the 'socialist/communist' reality, while the *bad* equaled all things that, in some way or to some degree, stood opposed to the things 'socialist/communist.' ... Generally, any lexical item could be turned into a 'politically correct' concept, that is, made 'meaningful,' simply by fitting its referent into the system's basic representational schema" (*Legacies of Totalitarian Language in the Discourse Culture of the Post-Totalitarian Era* [2011], pp. 1–2). Lenin wrote: "We say that morality is entirely subordinated to the interests of the proletariat's class struggle" (Morson, "Leninthink"). —Ed.

[165]This can also take the form of a cultural practice (often with religious justifications), e.g., honor killings, circumcision and female genital mutilation, violent exorcisms often resulting in death, etc. Increasingly common in Western society is "gender-affirming care" for young people with gender dysphoria, i.e., chemical and surgical castration. —Ed.

[166]For example, being classified as a "kulak" ("rich" peasant class) under Stalin—whether or not the accusation was true—was to be considered as "cattle, swine, loathsome, repulsive: they had no souls" (Vasily Grossman, quoted in Hughes, *Disordered Minds*, p. 50). In Romania under Ceaușescu, "Even the term 'intellectual' itself was used as an insult, often regarded as synonymous with 'traitor'" (Moscovici, *Velvet Totalitarianism*, p. 8). Such

Unfortunately, it has become a frequent phenomenon for individuals, lobby groups, or pathopolitical systems to invent ever-new moral criteria for someone's convenience. Therefore, one should not be surprised when an average person gets lost in this nonsense, since such suggestions deprive him of his common sense. In young people this leads to long-lasting psychological difficulties that impact the development of their worldview. Entire "paramoralism factories" have been founded worldwide—especially in pathopolitical totalitarianisms—and a ponerologist finds it hard to believe that they are managed by psychologically normal people.[167]

The conversive features in the genesis of paramoralisms seem to prove they are derived from mostly subconscious rejection (and repression from the field of consciousness) of something completely different, which we call *the voice of conscience.*[168] A ponerologist can nevertheless indicate many observations supporting the opinion that various pathological factors participate in the tendency to use paramoralisms. This was the case in the above-mentioned family. When it occurs with a moralizing interpretation, this tendency intensifies in egotists and hysterics, and its causes are similar. Like all conversive phenomena, the tendency to use paramoralisms is psychologically contagious.

---

paramoralisms acquire their suggestive power at least in part due to the fact that they are inherently vague and indefinable. As Roger Scruton told Rod Dreher, thoughtcrimes, or heresies, "by their very nature make accusation and guilt the same thing" (*Live Not by Lies: A Manual for Christian Dissidents* [2020], p. 57). More generally, such statements are used to justify wars, torture, assassination, and weapons spending in the name of "national security," "democracy promotion," etc. —Ed.

[167] Hitler Youth in Nazi Germany and the communist youth organizations in the USSR (Young Pioneers, Little Octobrists, and the Komsomol) served this purpose by explicitly teaching race and class hatred, as did schools and universities. See Applebaum, *Iron Curtain*, ch. 13 ("*Homo Sovieticus*"). In present times both radical Salafi madrasas and modern Western universities are "paramoralism factories." Janowski writes: "When a society reaches such a high level of social cohesion, universities can play only one role: They are ideological factories, where independent thought must be stopped before it develops" (*Homo Americanus*, p. 135). —Ed.

[168] Morson ("Leninthink") writes: "Lenin worked by a principle of anti-empathy, and this approach was to define Soviet ethics. I know of no other society, except those modeled on the one Lenin created, where schoolchildren were taught that mercy, kindness, and pity are vices. After all, these feelings might lead one to hesitate shooting a class enemy or denouncing one's parents. The word 'conscience' went out of use, replaced by 'consciousness' (in the sense of Marxist-Leninist ideological consciousness)." —Ed.

That explains why we observe it among people raised by individuals in whom it was developed alongside pathological factors. It should be noted here that it is psychopathic individuals, imitating normal people, who develop this characteristic ability to generate paramoralisms. This applies above all to essential psychopathy, and to a lesser extent to schizoidia, as well as other varieties of psychopathy. Similar tendencies occur also in some characteropaths and even in people raised by individuals with pathological traits.

This may be a good place to reflect that true moral law is born and exists independently of our judgments in this regard, and even of our ability to recognize it. It arises from the nature with which man was bestowed. Thus, the attitude required for such understanding is scientific, not creative: we must humbly subordinate our mind to the apprehended reality. That is when we discover the truth about man, both his weaknesses and values, which shows us what is decent and proper with respect to other people and other societies.

Reversive blockades

Emphatically insisting upon something which is the opposite of the truth blocks the average person's mind from perceiving the truth. In accordance with the dictates of healthy common sense, he starts searching for meaning in the "golden mean" between the truth and its opposite, winding up with some satisfactory counterfeit. People who think like this do not realize that this effect is precisely the intent of the person who subjects them to this method.[169] If the counterfeit of the truth is the opposite of a moral truth, it simultaneously represents an extreme paramoralism, and bears its peculiar suggestiveness.

[169]For example, "gaslighting," a form of psychological manipulation that causes the victim to doubt their own perception, memory, or sanity (see Oakley, *Evil Genes*, pp. 146–148). Also, the "big lie," a technique Hitler ascribed to Jews, but which the Nazis themselves were adept at using. Hitler wrote in *Mein Kampf* (vol. I, ch. X): "All this was inspired by the principle—which is quite true within itself—that in the big lie there is always a certain force of credibility; because the broad masses of a nation are always more easily corrupted in the deeper strata of their emotional nature than consciously or voluntarily; and thus in the primitive simplicity of their minds they more readily fall victims to the big lie than the small lie, since they themselves often tell small lies in little matters but would be ashamed to resort to large-scale falsehoods." Political propagandists often use this technique, e.g., Iraq's "weapons of mass destruction" and Russiagate. —Ed.

We rarely see this method being used by normal people; even if raised by pathological people who abused it, they usually only indicate its results in the form of characteristic difficulties in apprehending psychological and social reality properly. Use of this method can be included within the above-mentioned special psychological knowledge developed by psychopaths concerning the weaknesses of human nature and the art of leading others into error. Where the government of a country is inspired by psychopathic personalities, this method is used with virtuosity, and to an extent conterminous[170] with their power.[171]

Conversive thinking

The existence of psychological phenomena known to pre-Freudian philosophical students of the subconscious bears repeating.[172] Unconscious psychological processes outstrip conscious reasoning, both in time and in scope. This makes many psychological phenomena possible that are difficult to understand without realizing the above fact, including those generally described as conversive,[173] such as subconscious blocking out of conclusions, the selection, and, also, substitution of seemingly uncomfortable premises.[174]

---

[170]Sharing the same boundary or area. —Ed.

[171]At this point in *Ponerologia* (pp. 47–48), Łobaczewski includes an additional subsection on "Projection of self-referential associations onto other persons," statements which "suggestively distract from and hinder the perception of reality": "Someone attributes his own qualities, intentions, or deeds to another person, people, or even nations. ... '*He* is vindictive, sadistic, a criminal, an imperialist, etc., not *me*.' Such projection ... can be a nightmare in periods of increased societal hystericization." —Ed.

[172]*Author's note (1997):* These phenomena nowadays seem easier to understand against the background considerations of the holographic nature of memory and association. [See note in Chapter II. —Ed.]

[173]Or dissociative (see Glossary, "Conversive thinking"). —Ed.

[174]Psychologist John Schumaker describes these capacities as dissociative in nature: "the human brain [has] the ability to (a) selectively perceive its environment, (b) selectively process information, (c) selectively store memories, (d) selectively disengage from already stored memories, and (e) selectively replace dissociated data with more 'user-friendly' data" (*The Corruption of Reality: A Unified Theory of Religion, Hypnosis, and Psychopathology* [1995], p. 21). For an introduction to clinical dissociation see Martha Stout's *The Myth of Sanity* (2001). Ross defines dissociation simply as "the opposite of association. ... When two things are dissociated from each other, they are compartmentalized, disconnected, or out of relationship with each other" (*Trauma Model*, p. 46). See also McGilchrist, *The Matter with Things*, pp. 167–180. —Ed.

We speak of *blocking out* conclusions if the inferential process was proper in principle and has almost arrived at a conclusion and final comprehension within the act of internal projection, but becomes stymied by an anticipatory directive from the subconscious, which considers it inconvenient or disturbing. This prevents personality disintegration in a primitive way, which may seem advantageous; however, it also prevents all the advantages which could be derived from a consciously elaborated conclusion and reintegration. A conclusion thus rejected remains in our subconscious and in a more unconscious way causes the next blocking and selection of this kind. This can be extremely harmful, progressively enslaving a person to his own subconscious, and is often accompanied by a feeling of tension and bitterness.

We speak of *selection* of premises whenever the feedback goes deeper into our reasoning and from its database thus deletes and represses into the subconscious just that piece of information which was responsible for arriving at the uncomfortable conclusion. Our subconscious then permits further logical reasoning, except that the outcome will be erroneous in direct proportion to the actual significance of the repressed data. An ever-greater amount of such repressed information is collected in our subconscious memory. Finally, a kind of habit seems to take over: similar material is treated the same way even if reasoning would have reached an outcome quite advantageous to the person.

The most complex process of this type is *substitution* of premises thus eliminated by other data, ensuring an ostensibly more comfortable conclusion. Our associative ability rapidly elaborates a new item to replace the removed one, but it is one leading to a comfortable conclusion.[175] This operation takes the most time, resulting in the characteristic silence of the interlocutor. It is unlikely to be exclusively subconscious. Such substitutions are often effected collectively, in certain groups of people, through the use of verbal

[175] In the words of cartoonist and persuasion expert Scott Adams: "if you think you are smart, but you notice yourself doing something that is clearly dumb, you might spontaneously hallucinate that there was actually a good reason for it ... Your brain will instantly generate a delusion to rationalize the discrepancy" (*Win Bigly: Persuasion in a World Where Facts Don't Matter* [2017], p. 16). Other examples of such rationalizations include: "projecting" one's own unsavory motivations and qualities onto others; "mind-reading" false motives or beliefs on the part of someone you disagree with; "rewriting history" (personal or collective) to be more favorable to one's own preferred position; argument-by-analogy; adjusting the meaning of words; etc. —Ed.

communication. That is why they best qualify for the moralizing epithet "hypocrisy"[176] than either of the above-mentioned processes.

The above examples of conversive phenomena do not exhaust the problem, which is richly illustrated in psychoanalytical works. Our subconscious may carry the roots of human genius within, but its operation is not perfect; sometimes it is reminiscent of a blind computer that foolishly thinks it is smarter than its operator,[177] especially whenever we allow it to be cluttered with anxiously rejected material. This explains why conscious monitoring, even at the price of courageously accepting disintegrative states, is likewise necessary to our nature, not to mention our individual and social good.

There is no such thing as a person whose perfect self-knowledge allows him to eliminate all tendencies toward conversive thinking, but some people are relatively close to this state, while others remain slaves to these processes.[178] There are also societies in which the tendency to conversive thinking is relatively well controlled, and others that indulge in this mania of "wishful thinking." Those people who use conversive operations too often for the purpose of finding convenient conclusions, or constructing some cunning paralogistic or paramoralistic statements, eventually begin to undertake such behavior for ever more trivial reasons, losing the capacity for conscious control over their thought process altogether. This necessarily leads to misguided behavior which must be paid for by others as well as themselves—and whole nations.

---

[176]Or mendacity. In other words, it crosses the border from self-deception to conscious lying. Examples include sophistry, virtue signaling, double standards. Social media arguably compounds the problem, creating political and ideological echo chambers of conversive thinking (see chapter 6 of Lukianoff and Haidt's *Coddling of the American Mind*). Adams provides an example common on Twitter: "when people do not have rational reasons for their views—and you help them achieve that realization—they typically and immediately hallucinate that your argument is some kind of absurd absolute instead of whatever reasonable thing you actually said" (*Win Bigly*, p. 57). To see this in use, watch Channel 4 News presenter Cathy Newman's infamous 2018 interview with Jordan B. Peterson (https://youtu.be/aMcjxSThD54). —Ed.

[177]See Daniel Kahneman, *Thinking, Fast and Slow* (2013), (on system 1, which is fast, involuntary, and emotional, and system 2, which is slower, more effortful, and more logical), and Haidt, *Righteous Mind*, pt. 1 (on the elephant and the rider, i.e., our emotional and rational sides). Though see also McGilchrist, *The Matter with Things*, chs. 17–19. —Ed.

[178]See Wilson, *Strangers to Ourselves*. —Ed.

People who along this road have lost their capacity to think matter-of-factly (and thus their mental hygiene) also lose their natural critical faculties with regard to the statements and behavior of individuals whose abnormal thought processes were formed on a substratum of pathological anomalies, whether inherited or acquired. Conversive thinking arises in such people as a result of constantly pushing self-critical associations out of the field of consciousness. "Hypocrites" thus stop differentiating between what is pathological and what is normal, thus opening an "infection entry" for the ponerologic role of pathological factors.

Generally, each community contains people in whom similar methods of thinking were developed on a large scale, with their various deviations as a backdrop. We find this in both characteropathic and psychopathic personalities. Some have even been influenced by others to grow accustomed to such "reasoning," since conversive thinking is highly contagious and can spread throughout an entire society. In "happy times" especially, the tendency for conversive thinking generally intensifies. It appears accompanied by a rising wave of hysteria in said society, of which it is a symptom.[179] Those who try to maintain common sense and proper reasoning finally wind up in the minority, feeling wronged because their human right to maintain their own mental hygiene is violated by pressure from all sides. This means that unhappy times are not far away.

We should point out that the erroneous thought processes described herein also, as a rule, violate the laws of logic with characteristic treachery. Educating people in the art of proper reasoning can thus serve to counteract such tendencies; it has a hallowed age-old tradition, though for centuries it has proven insufficiently effective. As an example: according to the laws of logic, a question containing an erroneous or unconfirmed suggestion has no answer.[180] Nevertheless, not only does operating with such questions become epidemic among

[179]See Chapter III. Describing "microaggressions" in American culture and universities, Lukianoff and Haidt write: "Teaching people to see *more* aggression in ambiguous interactions, take *more* offense, feel *more* negative emotions, and avoid questioning their initial interpretations strikes us as unwise, to say the least. It is also contrary to the usual goals of good psychotherapy" (*Coddling*, p. 42). —Ed.

[180]Loaded questions, e.g., "Have you stopped beating your wife?" Such questions were routine during Mao's Cultural Revolution to expose "counter-revolutionaries" (see Frank Dikötter, *The Cultural Revolution: A People's History, 1962–1976* [2016], p. 54). —Ed.

people with a tendency to conversive thinking, and a source of terror when used by psychopathic individuals; it also occurs among people who think normally, or even those who have studied logic.[181]

This decreasing tendency in a society's capacity for proper thought should be counteracted, since it also lowers its immunity to ponerogenic processes. An effective measure would be to teach both principles of logic and skillful detection of errors in reasoning—including conversive errors. The broader front of such education should be expanded to include psychology, psychopathology, and the science described herein, for the purpose of raising people who can easily detect any paralogism.

Spellbinders

In order to comprehend ponerogenic pathways of contagion, especially those acting in a wider social context, let us observe the roles and personalities of individuals we shall call "spellbinders," who are highly active in this area in spite of their statistically negligible number.[182]

Spellbinders are generally the carriers of various pathological factors, e.g., paranoid characteropathy and, more often, psychopathy. Individuals with malformations of their personalities frequently play similar roles, although the social scale of influence remains small (family or neighborhood) and does not cross certain boundaries of decency. Spellbinders are characterized by pathological egotism, mostly

[181] Entire worldviews can be constructed on such questions. For example, according to critical race theorist Robin DiAngelo, "the question is not 'did racism take place?' but rather, 'how did racism manifest in this situation?'" (James Lindsay, "Antiracism"). —Ed.

[182] Lasswell refers to this type as "agitators," in contrast to "theorists" and "administrators" (see *Psychopathology*, chs. VI–VII, though his analysis is excessively Freudian). Janowski writes: "The fascist Mussolini, the Nazi Hitler, and the communist Lenin were masters of linguistic and crowd manipulation. Without twisting words and impressing them on people's minds to create a false reality, none of them would have risen to their positions of political power. Totalitarianism is unlikely to succeed if words are not used to create and manipulate reality" (*Homo Americanus*, p. 162). Wolfe writes of Lenin's "inclination to pathos" in contrast to Plekhanov's "analytical logic." In the margins of Plekhanov's draft program for the communist party, Lenin inserted marginal notes suggesting more emotional language and tangible examples, e.g., "indignation" instead of "dissatisfaction," "unemployment and poverty" instead of "worsening of the lot" (Bertram D. Wolfe, *Three Who Made a Revolution: A Biographical History* [1948], p. 224). —Ed.

of the secondary type, i.e., not directly rooted in childhood. Such a person is forced by some internal causes to make an early choice between two possibilities: the first is forcing other people to think and experience things in a manner similar to his own; the second is a feeling of being lonely and different, a pathological misfit in social life. Sometimes the choice is either snake-charming or suicide.

Triumphant repression of deeply disturbing self-critical associations from the field of consciousness gradually gives rise to the phenomena of conversive thinking, paralogistics, paramoralisms, and the use of reversive blockades. These stream so profusely from the mind and mouth of the spellbinder that they flood and enslave the average person's mind. Everything becomes subordinated to the spellbinder's over-compensatory conviction that they are exceptional, sometimes even messianic.[183] This mission requires an ideology which is at least partly true and whose value is supposedly superior. However, if we analyze the exact functions of such an ideology in the spellbinder's personality, we perceive that it is a means of *self*-charming, useful for repressing those tormenting self-critical associations into the subconscious. The ideology's instrumental role in influencing other people serves above all the spellbinder himself.[184]

These spellbinders are not wrong when, extrapolating from past experience, they believe they will always find converts to their ideology. It is only when it turns out that their influence extends to only a limited minority, while most people's attitude to their activities remains critical or painfully disturbed, that they feel shock and disappointment (or even paramoral indignation).[185] The spellbinder is thus confronted with a choice: either withdraw back into his void or strengthen his position by improving the effectiveness of his activities.

[183]Hitler being the pre-eminent example: "Hitler believed he was serving his God by annihilating the allegedly inferior humans and promoting the welfare and prolific reproduction of the supposedly superior Aryans. ... he reveled in Messianism and often portrayed himself as the man chosen by Providence to liberate Germany and lead it to greatness" (Weikart, *Hitler's Religion*, pp. xiii, xvii). —Ed.

[184]See Robins and Post, *Political Paranoia*, pp. 14–17. They write: "The paranoid protects himself against unbearable reality by constructing an alternate reality. The newly constructed reality is a solace for the wounded ego. The paranoid's centrality is a defense against insignificance" (p. 15). —Ed.

[185]See, for example, the communists' recurrent surprise at their own unpopularity and the ineffectiveness of their propaganda in Eastern Europe (Applebaum, *Iron Curtain*, pp. 163, 203–204, 398). —Ed.

The spellbinder places on a high moral plane anyone who has succumbed to his influence and incorporated the experiential manner he imposes. He showers such people with attention and property, if possible. Critics are met with "moral" outrage. It can even be proclaimed that the compliant minority is in fact the moral majority (e.g., the Bolsheviks),[186] since it professes the best ideology and honors a leader whose qualities are above average.

Such activity is always necessarily characterized by the inability to foresee its final results,[187] something obvious from the psychological point of view because its substratum contains pathological phenomena and both spellbinding and self-charming make it impossible to perceive reality accurately enough to foresee results logically. However, spellbinders nurture great optimism and harbor visions of future triumphs similar to those they enjoyed over their own crippled souls. *It is also possible for optimism to be a pathological symptom.*

In a healthy society, the activities of spellbinders meet with criticism tinged with mocking humor and a sense of their pathology effective enough to stifle them quickly. However, when they are preceded by conditions operating destructively upon common sense and social order—such as social injustice, cultural backwardness, the power of privileged but mentally primitive groups, or intellectually limited autocratic rulers sometimes manifesting pathological traits—spellbinders' activities find fertile ground and can lead entire societies into large-scale human tragedy. Such was the genesis of the communist revolutions and, similarly, Hitlerism.[188]

Such an individual fishes an environment or society for people amenable to his influence, deepening their psychological weaknesses until they finally join together in a ponerogenic union. On the other hand, people who have maintained their healthy critical faculties

---

[186]The name came from the Russian word for majority, after Lenin's "hard" Social Democratic Party faction won a majority of votes on several issues over the "soft" faction ("Mensheviks"—minority) at the 2nd Party Congress in 1903. —Ed.

[187]Bertram D. Wolfe, in *Communist Totalitarianism: Keys to the Soviet System* (1961), pp. 314–315, points out that after forty years of communism in Russia, "all of its original promises have turned into their opposites" (e.g., land for the peasants, perpetual peace, consumer goods, "plenty," the withering away of the state, freedom, a worker's paradise, national self-determination, anti-imperialism). —Ed

[188]See Robins and Post, *Political Paranoia*, ch. 4 ("The Need for Enemies: Nationalism, Terrorism, and Paranoid Mass Movements"). —Ed.

intact, based upon their own common sense and moral criteria, attempt to counteract the spellbinders' activities and their results. In the resulting polarization of social attitudes, each side justifies itself by means of moral or paramoral categories.[189] That is why such commonsense resistance is always accompanied by some feeling of helplessness and deficiency of criteria. These criteria can be found in psychopathology—knowledge far too few people are familiar with.

The awareness that a spellbinder is always a pathological individual should protect us from the effects of his influence and from the moralizing interpretation of pathological phenomena, ensuring us an objective criterion for more effective action. Explaining what kind of pathological substratum is hidden behind a given instance of spellbinding activities should enable a modern solution to such situations.

It is a characteristic phenomenon that a high level of talent—especially IQ—causes a man to be more immune to spellbinding activities *only to a moderate degree.* Significant differences in the formation of human attitudes to the influence of such activities should be attributed to other properties of human nature. The most decisive factor in assuming an attitude of critical common sense is good basic intelligence, which conditions our perception of psychological reality.

We can also observe how a spellbinder's activities "husk out" amenable individuals with an astonishing regularity and psychological accuracy. We shall later return to the specific relations that occur between the spellbinder's personality, the ideology he expounds, and the choices made by those who easily succumb. More exhaustive clarification thereof would require separate study within the framework of general ponerology, a work intended for specialists, in order to explain some of those interesting phenomena which are still not properly understood today.

Ponerogenic Associations

We shall give the name "ponerogenic association" to any group of people characterized by ponerogenic processes of above-average social intensity, wherein the carriers of various pathological factors function as inspirers, spellbinders, and leaders, and where a proper pathologi-

[189]See Albert Bandura, *Moral Disengagement: How People Do Harm and Live with Themselves* (2016), esp. ch. 7, on terrorism and counterterrorism. —Ed.

cal social structure is formed. Smaller, less permanent associations may be called "groups" or "unions." Such an association gives birth to evil which hurts other people as well as its own members. We could list various names ascribed to such organizations by linguistic tradition, depending on their social character: gangs, mafias, cliques, and coteries. While seeking to gain their own advantage or to satisfy their ambitions, they come into collision with good conduct and the law but cunningly try to avoid its repression. Such associations frequently aspire to political power on various social scales in order to impose their expedient goals and demands upon societies in the name of a suitably prepared ideology, deriving advantages in the form of disproportionate prosperity and the satisfaction of their craving for power.

The sociological description and classification of such associations in terms of their numbers, goals, officially promulgated ideologies, and internal organizations would of course be scientifically valuable. Such a description, effected by a perceptive observer, could help a ponerologist determine some of the properties of such associations, which cannot be determined by means of natural conceptual language or the language of sociologists.[190]

A description of this kind, however, ought not to cloak the more essential phenomena and psychological interrelationships operating within these associations. Failure to heed this warning can easily cause such a sociological description to indicate properties which are of secondary importance, or even made "for show" to impress the uninitiated, thereby overshadowing the actual phenomena which decide the quality, role, and fate of the association.[191] Particularly if such a description takes a colorful, literary form, it can furnish merely

[190] Eric Hoffer's *The True Believer: Thoughts on the Nature of Mass Movements* (1951) remains the classic account of social movements and their ideologies. It was the first to account for mass movements in terms of individual psychology as opposed to economic forces. The relevant academic fields today include the study of social movements (e.g., antiwar, civil rights, gay rights, feminism, etc.) and "new social movements" (e.g., LGBT, Occupy, antifa, the alt-right, BLM, QAnon, critical race theory, Extinction Rebellion, etc.) in sociology, and terrorism studies in criminology (e.g., Salafi-jihadism). However, these approaches, especially social movement studies, still suffer from all the shortcomings identified by Łobaczewski and more (e.g., "critical" criminology). More useful for ponerology are studies like Gordon M. Hahn's *The Caucasus Emirate Mujahedin: Global Jihadism in Russia's North Caucasus and Beyond* (2014) on the jihadist ponerogenic association which grew out of the Chechen Republic of Ichkeriya nationalist liberation movement. —Ed.

illusory or ersatz knowledge, thus rendering a naturalistic perception and causal comprehension of phenomena more difficult.

One phenomenon all ponerogenic groups and associations have in common is the fact that their members lack the capacity to perceive pathological individuals as such (or lose it under the influence of such a group), interpreting their behavior in a spellbound or melodramatic way—without even a minimal level of criticism—and attributing to them heroic or mentally superior qualities.[192] The opinions, ideas, and judgments of people carrying various psychological deficits are endowed with an importance at least equal to that of outstanding individuals among normal people. The atrophy of natural critical faculties with respect to pathological individuals becomes an opening to their activities, and, at the same time, a criterion for recognizing the association in concern as ponerogenic. Let us call this *the first criterion of ponerogenesis.*[193]

Another phenomenon all ponerogenic groups and associations have in common is their *statistically high concentration* of individuals with various psychological anomalies. Their qualitative composition is crucially important in the formation of the entire association's character, activities, development, or extinction. Unions dominated by various kinds of characteropathic individuals will develop relatively primitive activities, proving rather easy for a society of normal people to break them up via moral and legal means. However, things are quite different when such associations are inspired by psychopathic individuals. Let us adduce the following example illustrating the roles of two different anomalies, selected from among events studied by the author.

---

[191] For an example of this type of description, see Stanislav Vysotsky, *American Antifa: The Tactics, Culture, and Practice of Militant Antifascism* (2021), whose "critical criminological" perspective uncritically justifies the movement's use of violence. —Ed.

[192] For example, see the individuals lionized by BLM and/or antifa in Ngo, *Unmasked*, pp. 23 (Jacob Blake, felony sex crime, domestic abuse), 67 (Blake David Hampe, child pornography), 160 (David Campbell, two counts felony assault), 177ff. (Connor Betts, mass shooter), 183ff. (Michael Reinoehl, murder). White ethnonationalist groups like the Australian National Socialist Network idolize mass murderer Brenton Tarrant and commonly refer to him as "Saint Tarrant" (*60 Minutes Australia*, https://youtu.be/804CxkmnxLY). —Ed.

[193] Oakley writes: "When kindhearted people are unaware that a few leading individuals in 'their group' are likely to be sinister, they are ripe for victimization. Their own kindness, in fact, is turned against them and others" (*Evil Genes*, p. 334). —Ed.

In felonious youth gangs, a specific role is played by boys (and occasionally girls) that carry a characteristic effect sometimes left behind by an inflammation of the parotid glands (the mumps). As already mentioned, this disease entails brain reactions in some cases, leaving behind a discreet but permanent bleaching of feelings and a slight decrease in general mental skills' efficiency and accuracy. Similar results are sometimes left behind after a serious case of diphtheria. As a result, such people easily succumb to the suggestions of more clever individuals. When drawn into a felonious group, they become uncritical helpers and executors of the leader's intentions, tools in the hands of more treacherous, usually psychopathic, leaders.[194] Once arrested, they submit to their leaders' insinuated explanations that the higher (paramoral) group ideal demands that they become scapegoats, taking the majority of blame upon themselves. In court, the same leaders who initiated the delinquencies mercilessly dump all the blame onto their less crafty colleagues. Sometimes a judge actually accepts the insinuations.

Individuals with the above-mentioned post-mumps and post-diphtheria traits constitute less than 1% of the population as a whole, but their share reaches 20% in juvenile delinquent groups. This represents a 20-fold concentration, requiring no further methods of statistical analysis to establish a causal relationship. When studying the contents of ponerogenic associations skillfully enough, we often meet with concentrations of other psychological anomalies which also speak for themselves.[195]

---

[194] This applies as well in the political context; all major political revolutions have used gangs of young people for this purpose (e.g., the Hitler Youth and Mao's Red Guards). Marxist revolutionary Rosa Luxemburg emphasized the need for youth agitation in the early 1900s; despite fellow socialist August Bebel's efforts to tone down her writing, the German Government understood the circumlocution and in April, 1908, passed a law forbidding all persons under twenty years of age to attend political or union meetings. "All youth organizations ... were dissolved, and all youth agitation remained illegal until the revolution of 1918." (Wolfe, *Three Who Made*, p. 600). —Ed.

[195] "Violent men and gang members had higher prevalences of mental disorders and use of psychiatric services than nonviolent men, but a lower prevalence of depression. Violent ruminative thinking, violent victimization, and fear of further victimization accounted for the high levels of psychosis and anxiety disorders in gang members, and with service use in gang members and other violent men. Associations with antisocial personality disorder, substance misuse, and suicide attempts were explained by factors other than violence" (Coid et al., "Gang Membership, Violence, and Psychiatric Morbidity" [2013]). —Ed.

***

Two basic types of the above-mentioned associations should be differentiated: *primary ponerogenic* and *secondary ponerogenic*. Let us describe as primary ponerogenic a group or association whose abnormal members were active from the very beginning, playing the role of crystallizing catalysts as early as the process of creation of the group occurred. We shall call secondary ponerogenic an association which was founded in the name of some idea with an independent social meaning, generally comprehensible within the categories of the natural worldview, but which later succumbed to a certain moral degeneration. This in turn opened the door to infection and activation of the pathological factors within, and later to a ponerization[196] of the group as a whole, or often of a segment.

From the very outset, a primary ponerogenic union is a foreign body within the organism of society, its character colliding with the moral values respected by the majority. The activities of such groups provoke opposition and disgust and are considered immoral. As a rule, therefore, such groups do not grow large, nor do they metastasize into numerous unions; they most often lose their battle with society.[197] Ponerogenic unions of the primary variety are mainly of interest to criminology; our main concern will be associations that succumb to a secondary process of ponerogenic malignancy. This is the process to which we will devote more attention in the following chapters. First, however, let us sketch a few properties of such associations which have already surrendered to this process.

In order to have a chance to develop into a macrosocial ponerogenic association, it suffices that some human organization, characterized by social or political goals and an ideology with some creative value, be accepted by a larger number of normal people *before* it succumbs to a process of ponerogenic malignancy. The primary traditional and ideological values may then, for a long time, protect an association which has succumbed to the ponerization process from the awareness of society, especially its less critical components, providing it with a peculiar "mask of sanity." When the ponerogenic process touches

[196] See Glossary and "The Ponerization Process," below. —Ed.

[197] "The most enduring associations of this kind include mafias, which are primarily concerned with economic gain, though characteristics of a secondary ponerogenic association are also discernible in these organizations" (*Ponerologia*, p. 55). —Ed.

such a human organization which originally emerged and acted in the name of political or social goals, and whose causes were conditioned by history and the social situation, the primary ideology changes its function to become an instrument of propaganda. The original group's primary values will nourish and protect such a secondary ponerogenic association for many years to come, in spite of the fact that those values succumb to characteristic degeneration, because the names and symbols are retained. This will occur despite the fact that the original values will in reality be despised by the new leaders of the association as something good only for "the others." This is where individual and social "common sense" reveals its biggest weaknesses.

This is reminiscent of a situation psychopathologists know well: a person who enjoyed trust and respect in their social circles starts behaving with preposterous arrogance and hurting others, allegedly in the name of his known convictions, which have—in the meantime—succumbed to some invisible psychological process rendering them primitive but emotionally dynamic. However, his old acquaintances—having long known him as the person he was—do not believe the injured parties who complain about his new, or even hidden, behavior, and are prepared to denigrate them morally and consider them liars. This adds insult to their injury and gives encouragement and license to the already unreasonable individual to commit further hurtful acts; as a rule, such a situation lasts until the person's madness becomes obvious.

Within each ponerogenic association, a psychological and organizational structure is created which can be considered a counterpart or caricature of the normal structure of society and its organizations. Individuals with various psychological aberrations complement each other's talents and characteristics. Throughout its ponerogenic evolution, this structure is subjected to characteristic transformations with regard to the character of the association as whole. The earlier phase of an association's activity is usually dominated by characteropathic, particularly paranoid, individuals, who often play an inspirational or spellbinding role in the ponerization process.[198] At this point in time, the association still exhibits certain romantic features and

[198] Hughes writes: "In situations of civil unrest ... individuals with paranoid personality disorder play a central role in fomenting hatred against enemies, real and imagined. In doing so, they have paved the way for some of the worst atrocities in history" (*Disordered Minds*, p. 24). See also Robins and Post, *Political Paranoia*. —Ed.

is not yet characterized by excessively brutal behavior. Soon, however, the more normal members are pushed into fringe functions and are excluded from organizational secrets; some of them thereupon leave such a association and return, not without difficulty, to normal society.[199]

Individuals with inherited deviations then progressively take over the inspirational and leadership positions. The role of essential psychopaths gradually grows, although they like to remain ostensibly in the shadows (e.g., directing small groups), setting the pace and direction for the whole association in the style of an *éminence grise*.[200] In ponerogenic associations on the largest social scales, the leadership role is generally played by a different kind of individual, one more easily digestible and representative to public opinion. Examples include frontal characteropathy, or some more discreet complex of lesser taints.

A spellbinder at first simultaneously plays the role of leader in a ponerogenic group. Later there appears another kind of "leadership talent," a more vital individual who often joined the organization later, once it has already succumbed to ponerization. The spellbinding individual, being weaker, is forced to come to terms with being

---

[199] For example, in 2021 American journalist Bilal Abdul Kareem, who for years was embedded with ex–al Qaeda affiliate Hay'at Tahrir al-Sham in Syria, broke with the group after confirming that they did in fact torture prisoners and after being arrested by the group for speaking out. He expressed his disillusionment with the group and its leader Abu Mohamed al-Jolani in the following words: "They promised to bring Islamic rule. They didn't do it. They promised to bring justice. They didn't do it. I was obligated to report those shortcomings. And that's when they turned hostile to me." At around the same time, Minnesotan BLM leader Rashad Turner quit the group, saying: "I believed the organization stood for exactly what the name implies—black lives do matter. However, after a year on the inside, I learned they had little concern for rebuilding black families and they cared even less about improving the quality of education for students in Minneapolis." American journalist Jack Posobiec quotes former Australian antifa leader Shayne Hunter as saying, "The radical left of Antifa presents itself as being about compassion and empathy; it's a Trojan horse" (Posobiec, *The Antifa*, p. 21). See Hooper and Hashem, "Bilal Abdul Kareem Breaks Silence over HTS Detention in Syria" (2021), and Crane, "Ex-BLM Leader Says He Quit after Learning the 'Ugly Truth' about the Organization" (2021). Historically, the same dynamic played out among the Bolsheviks, among other revolutionary groups. —Ed.

[200] A powerful advisor or decision-maker who operates secretly or otherwise unofficially. Originally referred to the grey-cloaked Capuchin friar François Leclerc du Tremblay, confidant of Cardinal Richelieu. —Ed.

shunted into the shadows and recognizing the new leader's "genius," or accept the threat of total failure. Roles are parceled out. The spellbinder needs support from the primitive but decisive leader, who in turn needs the spellbinder to uphold the association's ideology, so essential in maintaining the proper attitude on the part of those members of the rank and file who betray a tendency to criticism and doubt of the moral variety. The spellbinder must then repackage the ideology appropriately, sliding in new contents under old titles, so that it can continue fulfilling its propaganda function under ever-changing conditions. He also has to uphold the leader's mystique inside and outside the association. Complete trust cannot exist between the two, however, since the leader secretly has contempt for the spellbinder and his ideology, whereas the spellbinder despises the leader for being such a coarse individual. A showdown is always probable; whoever is weaker becomes the loser.

The structure of such an association undergoes further variation and specialization. A chasm opens between the more normal members and the elite initiates who are, as a rule, more pathological. This latter subgroup becomes ever more dominated by hereditary pathological factors, the former by the after-effects of various diseases affecting the brain, less typically psychopathic individuals, and people whose malformed personalities were caused by early deprivation or brutal child-rearing methods on the part of pathological individuals. There is less and less room for normal people in the group. The leaders' secrets and intentions are kept hidden from the association's proletariat; the products of the spellbinders' work must suffice for this segment.

An observer watching such an association's activities and organization from the outside and using natural or sociological concepts will always tend to overestimate the role of the leader and his allegedly autocratic function. The spellbinders and the propaganda apparatus are mobilized to maintain this erroneous outside opinion. The leader, however, is *dependent upon the interests of the association, especially the elite initiates*, to an extent greater than he himself knows. He wages a constant position-jockeying battle; he is an actor subject to control and direction. In macrosocial associations, this position is generally occupied by a more representative individual not deprived of certain critical faculties; initiating him into all those plans and criminal calculations would be counterproductive. In conjunction with part of the elite, a group of psychopathic individuals hiding behind the scenes steers the leader, the way Bormann and his clique steered Hitler,[201] or Beria and his men with Stalin. If the leader does not fulfill his assigned role, he generally knows that the clique representing the elite of the association is in a position to kill or otherwise remove him.

We have sketched the properties of associations in which the ponerogenic process has transformed their original content into a pathological counterpart thereof, their structure and its later transformations, in a manner sufficiently broad to encompass the greatest possible scope of this kind of phenomena, from the smallest to the largest social scale. The general rules governing those phenomena appear to be at least analogous, independent of the quantitative, social, and historical scale of such a phenomenon.

Ideologies

It is a common phenomenon for a ponerogenic association or group to contain a particular ideology which always justifies its activities and furnishes motivational propaganda. Even a small-time gang of hoodlums has its own melodramatic ideology and pathological romanticism. Human nature demands that vile matters be haloed by an over-compensatory mystique in order to silence one's conscience and to deceive consciousness and critical faculties, whether one's own or those of others.[202]

If such a ponerogenic association could be stripped of its ideology, nothing would remain except psychological and moral pathology, naked and unattractive. Such a course of action would of course provoke "moral outrage," and not only among the members of the as-

[201] See, for example, Jochen von Lang, *The Secretary: Martin Bormann – The Man Who Manipulated Hitler* (1979), and Volker Koop, *Martin Bormann: Hitler's Executioner* (2020). —Ed.

[202] Bandura writes: "People do not usually engage in harmful conduct until they have justified to themselves the morality of their actions. Social and moral justifications sanctify harmful practices by investing them with honorable purposes. Righteous and worthy ends are used to justify harmful means. The moral imperative enables people to preserve their sense of self-worth even as they inflict harm on others" (*Moral Disengagement*, p. 49). Social activists, by virtue of being social activists, are permitted to get away with a level of violence and destruction that would otherwise be roundly condemned if not for the use of an ideology (e.g., antifa/BLM riots). Street gangs, mafias, or cartels engaging in similar behavior are universally condemned. —Ed.

sociation. Even normal people, who condemn this kind of association along with its ideologies, would feel hurt and deprived of something constituting part of their own romanticism, their way of perceiving reality, when a widely idealized group is exposed as little more than a gang of criminals. Perhaps even some of the readers of this book will resent the author's stripping evil so unceremoniously of all its literary motifs. The job of effecting such a "strip-tease" may thus turn out to be much more difficult and dangerous than expected.[203]

A primary ponerogenic union is formed at the same time as its ideology, perhaps even somewhat earlier. A normal person perceives such an ideology to be different from the world of human concepts, obviously suggestive, and even cynically comical to a degree. The ideology of a secondary ponerogenic association is formed by gradual adaptation of the primary ideology to functions and goals other than the original formative ones. A certain kind of layering or schizophrenia of ideology takes place during the ponerization process. The outer layer closest to the original content is used for the association's propaganda purposes, especially regarding the outside world, although it can in part also be used inside with regard to disbelieving lower-echelon members. The second layer is initially comprehensible only to the pathological elite of the association: it is more hermetic, generally composed by slipping a different meaning into the same names. Since identical names signify different contents depending on the layer in question, understanding this "doublespeak" requires simultaneous fluency in both languages.[204]

[203]See, for example, the efforts and experiences of dissidents like Aleksandr Solzhenitsyn and others who have dared to observe that the emperor has no clothes, whether in politics, science, or any other field of consequence. —Ed.

[204]From Orwell's "doublethink" and "newspeak" in his novel *1984*. This could be considered a *deliberate*, psychopathic version of conversive thinking, motivated by mendacity and their special psychological knowledge rather than cognitive dissonance. For example, to a pathocratic communist regime, a "counterrevolutionary" is simply anyone who challenges their power, regardless of their actual intentions. Similarly, democracy means one thing in normal language, and another to pathocrats. Agnieszka Kołakowska's note to her translation of Torańska's *"Them"* deserves to be quoted at length: "The people interviewed in this book ... speak in a peculiar dialect of their own. It is an idiom naturally determined by their age, their work, and their ideology: a way of speaking which combines the language of communist propaganda with stilted, archaic expressions and old-fashioned slang. The fact that most of them lack any kind of formal education heightens the general effect. Their sentences are clumsy, their grasp of grammar tenuous; they misuse words, and see language not as

Average people succumb to the first layer's suggestive insinuations for a long time before they learn to understand the second one as well. Anyone with certain psychopathic deviations, especially if he wears the mask of normality with which we are already familiar, immediately perceives the second layer to be attractive and significant; after all, it was built by people like him. Comprehending this doublespeak is therefore a vexatious task for a normal person, provoking quite understandable psychological resistance; this very duality of language, however, is a pathognomonic symptom[205] indicating that the human association in question is touched by the ponerogenic process to an advanced degree.

The ideology of associations affected by such degeneration has certain constant factors regardless of their quality, quantity, or scope of action, namely, *the motivations of an aggrieved group, radical redress of the grievance, and the higher value of the individuals who have joined the organization.*[206] These motivations facilitate sublimation of the feeling of being wronged and different, caused by one's own psychological deficiencies, and appear to liberate their carriers from the need to abide by the insufficiently understood moral demands of "that other" world of normal people.

In a world full of real injustice and humiliation, it is easy for an ideology containing the above elements to form and for a association of its converts to succumb to degradation. When this happens, those people with a tendency to accept the better version of the ideology will tend to justify such ideological duality and the association's activities.[207] The ideology of the proletariat, which aimed at

---

a way of conveying their meaning but as an instrument for distorting and concealing the truth. Years of mendacity and propaganda have made them adept at begging questions, skirting issues, and speaking in hints and allusions; when they feel cornered, they automatically lapse into textbook communist jargon, constructing phrases on such a level of abstraction that they become unintelligible: their words simply fail to refer, and the result is gibberish. ... Inevitably, a lifetime of this has permanently warped their ability to think for themselves" (p. 7). —Ed.

[205]Specifically characteristic or indicative of a disease. —Ed.

[206]*Ponerologia* adds "a contemptuous attitude to the world of normal people and its customs" (p. 53). —Ed.

[207]Bandura writes: "Voltaire put it well when he said, 'Those who can make you believe absurdities can make you commit atrocities.' Over the centuries, much destructive conduct has been perpetrated by ordinary, decent people in the name of righteous ideologies, religious principles, sociopolitical doctrines, and nationalistic imperatives ... True believers sacrifice themselves to their

revolutionary restructuring of the world, was already contaminated by a schizoid deficit in the understanding of, and distrust for, human nature; small wonder, then, that it easily succumbed to a process of typical degeneration in order to nourish and disguise a macrosocial phenomenon whose basic essence is completely different. Common sense fails exceptionally easily in such matters.[208]

For future reference, let us remember: ideologies do not need spellbinders. Spellbinders need ideologies in order to subject them to their own deviant goals.

On the other hand, the fact that some ideology degenerated along with its corollary social movement, later succumbing to this schizophrenia and serving goals which the originators of the ideology would have abhorred, does not prove that it was worthless, totally false, or deceptive from the start. Quite the contrary: it rather appears that under certain historical conditions, the ideology of any social movement, even if it is sacred truth, can yield to the ponerization process.[209]

A given ideology may have contained weak spots from its inception, carrying errors of human thought and emotion within; or, during the

---

principles" (*Moral Disengagement*, p. 50). Martin wrote: "No tyranny was ever for long maintained by force. All tyrannies begin and end in the tyranny of ideas uncritically accepted" (*Behavior of Crowds*, p. 279). —Ed.

[208]Romanian political scientist Vladimir Tismaneanu writes: "The main difficulty with the Marxian project is its lack of sensitivity to the psychological makeup of mankind. This obsession with social classes ... the failure to take into account the infinite diversity of human nature, the eagerness to reduce history to a conflict between polar social categories, that is indeed the substratum of an ideology that, wedded to sectarian and fanatic political movements, has generated many illusions and much grief throughout the twentieth century" (*The Devil in History: Communism, Fascism, and Some Lessons of the Twentieth Century* [2012], p. 164). Marx and Engels dismissed "organizational and scientific skills, discipline, experience, and habits of mutual cooperation"—including specialization, "managerial ability and entrepreneurial innovation"—as unimportant and irrelevant to a functioning society and economy. They saw "exploitation" as the root cause of all economic disparities and projected their concept of "alienation" onto the working class, ignoring workers' *actual* preferences (which don't line up with what Marx and Engels thought they should be). As Sowell writes: "apparently minor intellectual flaws" and faulty assumptions about human nature, economics, and history can have "serious human consequences" (Sowell, *Marxism*, pp. 12, 193–194, 213, 206). —Ed.

[209]See Chapter VIII. Robins and Post write: "Ideologies are seldom without merit. There is generally some, and often a great deal of, truth in their doctrines. Fighting ideologies are not so much incorrect as simplistic or reductionist. It is their simplicity and clarity that make them so appealing and so suitable as an organizing framework for action" (*Political Paranoia*, p. 181). —Ed.

course of its history, it may have been infiltrated by more primitive foreign material containing the effects of ponerogenic factors. Such material destroys an ideology's internal homogeneity. The source of such infection by foreign ideological material may be the prevailing social system with its laws and customs based on a more primitive tradition, or the autocratic imperialism of a mendacious system of rule. It may be, of course, simply another philosophical movement often contaminated by the eccentricities of its founder or leader, who considers the facts to blame for not conforming to his dialectical construct.

The Roman Empire, including its legal system and paucity of psychological concepts, similarly contaminated the primary homogeneous idea of Christianity. Christianity had to adapt to coexistence with a social system wherein "*dura lex sed lex*"[210] decided a person's fate, rather than an understanding of human beings; this then led to a desire to reach the Gospel's goals of the "Kingdom of God" by means of Roman imperial methods. Today we are gradually, but hopefully finally, moving away from this.

The greater and truer the original ideology, the greater the danger concealed for small minds, who can become agents of this preliminary degeneration, which opens the door to infiltration by pathological factors; and the longer it is capable of nourishing and disguising from human criticism that phenomenon which is the product of this peculiar degenerative process.

Thus, if we intend to understand the secondary ponerization process and the kinds of human associations which succumb to it, we must take great care to separate the original ideology from its counterpart, or even caricature, created by the ponerogenic process. Abstracting from any ideology, we must, by analogy, understand the essence of the process itself, which has its own etiological causes which are potentially present in every society, as well as characteristic developmental pathodynamics.

The Ponerization Process

Observation of the ponerization processes of various human associations throughout history easily leads to the conclusion that the initial step is a moral warping of a group's ideological contents. The con-

[210] "The law is harsh, but it is the law." —Ed.

tamination of ideology can be analyzed by means of its infiltration by more earthly foreign contents, or by the impoverishment of its strong foundation in understanding and trust in human nature. This opens the way for invasion by pathological factors and the ponerogenic role of their carriers. Deeper historical and ponerological insight, however, may point us to their presence already in this initial process.

It may seem, then, that such facts could justify the conviction of moralists that maintaining an association's ethical discipline and ideological purity is sufficient protection against derailing and hurtling into an insufficiently comprehended world of error. Such a conviction strikes a ponerologist as a one-sided oversimplification of an eternal reality which is more complex. After all, the loosening of ethical and intellectual controls is sometimes a *consequence* of the direct or indirect insidious influence of these omnipresent pathological factors, along with some other non-pathological human weaknesses.

Sometime during life, every human organism undergoes periods during which physiological and psychological resistance declines, facilitating development of bacteriological infection within. Similarly, every human association or social movement undergoes periods of crisis which weaken its ideological and moral cohesion. This may be caused by pressure on the part of other groups, a general spiritual crisis in the environment, or intensification of its hysterical condition. Just as more stringent sanitary measures are an obvious medical recommendation for a weakened organism, the development of conscious control over the activity of pathological factors is ponerological recommendation—something especially important during a society's periods of moral crisis.[211]

For centuries, individuals exhibiting various psychological anomalies have had the tendency to participate in the activities of human associations. On the one hand, this is made possible by such groups' existing weaknesses; on the other hand, their activities deepen the moral failings and stifle the possibilities of utilizing healthy common sense and understanding matters objectively. In spite of the resulting tragedies and unhappiness, humanity has shown a certain progress, especially in the cognitive area; therefore, a ponerologist may be cautiously optimistic. After all, by detecting and describing these

[211]That is, the phase in a secular cycle when society is weakened and may disintegrate into revolution, civil war, or state collapse, one potential outcome of which is pathocracy. See Chapter III. —Ed.

aspects of the ponerization process of human groups, which could not be understood until recently, we shall be able to counteract such processes earlier and more effectively.

Any human association affected by the process described herein is characterized by a progressive deterioration of natural common sense and the ability to perceive psychological reality, even more so of objective rationality of thought.[212] Someone considering this in terms of traditional categories might consider it an instance of "turning into half-wits" or the development of intellectual deficiencies and moral failings, resulting in criticism. However, a psychological analysis of this process indicates the typical effects of psychological induction, or that the more normal members of the union are being pressured towards an abnormal manner of experiencing by carriers of various pathological anomalies.

Thus, whenever we observe some group member being treated with no critical distance, although he betrays one of the psychological anomalies familiar to us, and his opinions being treated as at least equal to those of normal people, although they are based on a characteristically different view of human matters, we must derive the conclusion that this human group is affected by a ponerogenic process. We shall treat this in accordance with the above-described first criterion of ponerogenesis, which retains its validity regardless of the qualitative and quantitative features of such an association. This is followed by the typical preferential treatment of second-rate individuals and the sidelining of more outstanding ones.[213]

[212]In 1924, Pavlov wrote: "We have a patient in treatment with an extremely relaxed nervous system. When she is shown a red color and told that it is not red but green, she agrees and declares that having looked closely, she was really convinced that it was not red but green ... In a diseased nervous system, in its paradoxical state, sensitivity to reality is lost and only sensitivity to words remains. The word begins to replace reality. The entire Russian population is in such a state now. In general, I must express my sad opinion on the Russian person. The Russian person has such weak brain system that he is not capable to perceive the reality as such. For him there are only words. His conditioned reflexes are coordinated not with reality, but with words" ("Ivan Pavlov," Russian Wikipedia, translated). —Ed.

[213]Łobaczewski refers to this phenomenon—the counterselective condtions of normal members leaving and pathological members joining—as the second criterion of ponerogenesis (*Ponerologia*, p. 52). In a section on Nikolai Bukharin (1888–1938), Orlando Figes writes: "At the age of twenty-nine, he had already established himself as a leading Bolshevik theoretician and squabbled with Lenin on several finer points of party ideology, before leaving Europe with the

Such a state of affairs can simultaneously be a liminal (watershed) situation, whereupon further damage to people's healthy common sense and critical moral faculties becomes ever easier. Once a group has absorbed a sufficient dose of pathological material to give birth to the conviction that these not-quite-normal people are bearers of some sort of special genius, it starts subjecting its more normal members to pressure by means of typical paralogistics and paramoralisms. For many people, such pressure of collective opinion takes on the suggestive force of a moral criterion; for others, it represents a kind of psychological terror ever more difficult to endure. A phenomenon of intense counterselection thus occurs in this phase of ponerization: individuals with a more normal sense of psychological reality leave after entering into conflict with the newly modified group; simultaneously, individuals with various psychological anomalies join the group and easily find a way of life there. The former feel "pushed into counter-revolutionary positions," and the latter can afford to remove their masks of sanity ever more often.

People who have been thus thrown out of a ponerogenic association because they were too normal suffer bitterly; they are unable to understand their specific state. Their ideal, which constituted a part of the meaning of life for them, has now been degraded, although they cannot find a rational basis for this fact. They feel wronged; they "fight against demons" that have penetrated their souls and which they are not in a position to identify. In fact, their personalities have already been modified to a certain extent due to saturation by abnormal psychological material, especially psychopathic material. They easily fall into the opposite extreme in such cases, because unhealthy emotions rule their decisions. What they need is rest, understanding, and good advice in order to find the path of reason. Based on a ponerologic understanding of their condition, psychotherapy could provide rapid positive results. However, if the association they left is sufficiently powerful and succumbing to deep ponerization, a threat looms over them: they may become the objects of revenge, since they have "betrayed" a magnificent ideology.[214] The punishing hand of such leadership may then reach the psychotherapist as well.

claim that 'Lenin cannot tolerate any other person with brains'" (*A People's Tragedy: The Russian Revolution: 1891–1924* [2017], p. 291). —Ed

[214]Conversely, psychopathic members ejected from a normal group will often seek to attack the group that rejected or exposed them. —Ed.

This is the stormy period of a group's ponerization, followed by a certain stabilization in terms of contents, structure, and customs. Rigorous selective measures of a clearly psychological kind are applied to new members. So as to exclude the possibility of becoming sidetracked by defectors, people are observed and tested to eliminate those characterized by excessive mental independence or psychological normality. The new internal function created is something like a "psychologist," and it doubtless takes advantage of the above-described psychological knowledge collected by psychopaths.[215] Spellbinders take care of "ideological purity." The leader's position is relatively secure. Individuals manifesting doubt or criticism are subject to paramoral condemnation.

Maintaining the utmost dignity and style, leadership discusses opinions and intentions which are psychologically and morally pathological. Any mental associations which might expose them as such are eliminated, thanks to the substitution of premises operating in the subconscious process on the basis of prior conditioned reflexes. The association enters a state wherein the whole has donned a mask of ostensible normality. In the next chapter, we shall call such a state the "dissimulative phase" when it pertains to macrosocial ponerogenic phenomena.[216]

Observing the appropriate state corresponding to the first criterion of ponerogenesis requires the skill of a psychologist and specific factual knowledge; the second, more stable phase can be perceived both by a person of average reason and by public opinion in most societies. The interpretation imposed, however, is one-sidedly moralistic or sociological,[217] even demonological, accompanied by a characteristic

[215] Just as inverting a reversive blockade can bring one close to the truth, we can gain an approximation of steps to prevent a group's ponerization by flipping these psychopathic selection methods on their head. Weaknesses in the group's ideology should be identified and *remedied* (not exploited), and psychological criteria should be put in place to exclude the membership or undue influence of individuals with character and personality disorders such as Łobaczewski describes (not vice versa). Contrast with the internal selection dynamics of a group like Scientology (see the note on religious cults in Chapter VIII). —Ed.

[216] Such a reality is very close to that of the inmates taking over the asylum, or as Kretschmer told one of his students before Hitler's rise: "In normal times we diagnose them; in disturbed times they govern us" (quoted in Oakley, *Evil Genes*, p. 332). —Ed.

[217] For instance, a ponerogenic group like ISIS, when not simply dismissed as a gang of morally reprehensible criminals, is often explained in terms of socioeconomic, historical, theological, or geopolitical causes. E.g., Gerges, *ISIS*. —Ed.

feeling of helplessness and deficiency as regards the possibility of both understanding the phenomenon and counteracting the spread of said evil.

However, in this unfortunate phase a significant minority of the population is inclined to consider such a ponerogenic association as comprehensible within the categories of their own worldview, and to consider the outer layer of diffusing ideology as a doctrine containing certain values acceptable to them. The more primitive the society in question, and the further removed from direct contact with the association affected by this pathological state, the more numerous such minorities will be. That is why this very period, during which the customs of the association become somewhat milder, often represents simultaneously its most intensive expansionist activity.

This period may last long, but not forever. Internally, the group is becoming progressively more pathological, finally showing its true qualitative colors again as its activities become ever clumsier. At this point, a society of normal people can easily threaten ponerogenic associations, even at the macrosocial level.[218]

Macrosocial Phenomena

When a ponerogenic process encompasses a society's entire ruling class or nation, or when opposition from the societies of normal people is stifled—as a result of the mass character of the phenomenon, spellbinding methods, and the use of violence and terror—we are dealing with a macrosocial ponerologic phenomenon. In such a case, however, a society's tragedy, often coupled with that of the researcher's own suffering, opens before him an entire volume of ponerologic knowledge, where he can read all about the laws governing such a process if he is only able to familiarize himself in time with its naturalistic language and its different grammar.

Studies on the genesis of evil which are based on observing small groups of people reveal the details of these ponerological laws to us. However, this presents a warped picture that is dependent upon broader environmental circumstances. We then understand these circumstances as the historically conditioned backdrop to the phenomena observed. Nevertheless, such observations may enable us to learn the basic laws of ponerogenesis and hazard a hypothesis to the

[218] *Author's note (1997):* And this is what happened. [The revolutions of 1989. —Ed.]

effect that these laws may be at least analogous, regardless of the quantity and scope of the phenomenon in time and space. They do not, however, permit verification of such a hypothesis.

In studying a macrosocial phenomenon, we can obtain both quantitative and qualitative data, statistical correlation indices, and other observations as accurately as allowed by the state of the art in science, research methodology, and the obviously very difficult situation of the observer. We can then use the classical method, hazarding a hypothesis and then actively searching for facts which could falsify it. The latter approach proved to be the most effective under particularly difficult circumstances. The widespread causal regularity of ponerogenic processes would then be confirmed within the bounds of the above-mentioned possibilities. We are faced with the staggering realization of the precision with which this macrosocial phenomenon is subject to its own peculiar laws. The comprehension of the phenomenon thus acquired can serve as a basis for predicting its future development, to be verified by time. It is then, too, that we become aware that the colossus has an Achilles heel after all.

The study of macrosocial ponerogenic phenomena meets with obvious problems: their period of genesis, duration, and decay is several times longer than the researcher's scientific activity. Simultaneously, there are other transformations in history, customs, economics, and technology.[219] However, the difficulties confronted in abstracting the appropriate symptoms need not be insuperable, since our criteria are based on eternal phenomena subject to relatively limited transformations in time—their characteristic difference from normal reality makes this task easier.

The traditional interpretation of these great historical diseases has already taught historians to distinguish two phases. The first

[219]For example, a modern ponerological approach will need to take into account the massive growth of technology that has not only connected the world to a degree unheard of in history, but also raised the specter of high-tech "social credit" systems of control utilizing mass surveillance and collection of personal data. See Michael Rectenwald, *Google Archipelago*; Yasha Levine, *Surveillance Valley: The Secret Military History of the Internet* (2018); and Dreher, *Live Not by Lies*, ch. 4 ("Capitalism, Woke and Watchful"). Dreher writes (p. 8): "Today's totalitarianism demands allegiance to a set of progressive beliefs, many of which are incompatible with logic—and certainly with Christianity. Compliance is forced less by the state than by elites who form public opinion, and by private corporations that, thanks to technology, control our lives far more than we would like to admit." —Ed.

is represented by a period of spiritual crisis in a society, which historiosophy associates with exhausting of the ideational, moral, and religious values heretofore nourishing the society in question. Egoism among individuals and social groups increases, and the links of moral duty and social networks are felt to be loosening. Trifling matters thereupon dominate human minds to such an extent that there is no room left for thinking about public matters or a feeling of commitment to the future. An atrophy of the hierarchy of values within the perception of personal and social reality is an indication thereof; it has been described both in historical monographs and in psychiatric papers. The country's government is finally paralyzed, helpless in the face of problems which could be solved without great difficulty under other circumstances. Let us associate such periods of crisis with the familiar phase in social hystericization.

The next phase has been marked by bloody tragedies, revolutions, wars, and the fall of empires. The deliberations of historians or moralists regarding these events always leave behind a certain feeling of deficiency with reference to the possibility of perceiving certain psychological factors discerned within the nature of phenomena; the essence of these factors remains outside the scope of their scientific experience.

A historian observing these great historical diseases of associations, nations, and empires is struck first of all by their similarities, easily forgetting that all diseases have many symptoms in common because they are states of ill health. A ponerologist thinking in naturalistic terms therefore tends to doubt that we are dealing with only one kind of societal disease. It seems, however, that despite a certain degree of variation of forms that depend on the times and ethnological and civilizational conditions, these phenomena are related. For it is the secondary characteristics of the phenomena that undergo change, and these are the ones more easily perceived by a researcher not armed with ponerological knowledge. Differentiating the essence of such states is more appropriate to the reasoning patterns we are familiar with from the natural sciences. The complex conditions of social life, however, preclude using the method of differentiation, which is similar to the etiological criterion[220] in medicine; qualitatively speaking, the phenomena become layered in time, conditioning each other and transforming constantly.[221] We should then rather use certain

[220]Determining the precise cause of a disease. —Ed.

abstract patterns, similar to those used in analyzing the neurotic states of human beings.[222]

Governed by this type of reasoning, let us here attempt to differentiate two pathological states of societies; their essence and contents appear different enough, but they can operate sequentially in such a way that the first opens the door to the second. The first such state has already been sketched in the chapter on the hysteroidal cycle; we shall adduce a certain number of other psychological details hereunder. The next chapter shall be dedicated to the second pathological state, for which I have adopted the denomination of "pathocracy."

States of Societal Hystericization

When perusing scientific or literary descriptions of hysterical phenomena, such as those dating from the last great increase in hysteria in Europe encompassing the quarter-century preceding World War I, a non-specialist may gain the impression that this was endemic to individual cases, particularly among women.[223] The contagious nature of hysterical states, however, had already been discovered and described by Jean-Martin Charcot.[224] It is practically impossible for

[221]The above line of reasoning may apply to some of the similarities found by philosophers like Legutko and Janowski between communism and liberalism. The differences (e.g., communism's comparative brutality) may indicate that the negative qualities apparent in liberalism today are symptoms of either an advanced stage of societal hysteria along with various ponerogenic phenomena, or an early stage of pathocracy (or both). —Ed.

[222]I.e., focus on general syndromes (collections of symptoms) and the techniques known to work on them. Cognitive behavioral therapy, for instance, can be effective even in the absence of knowledge of the problem's precise cause. —Ed.

[223]See the classic study from the time period by Sigmund Freud and Josef Breuer, *Studies on Hysteria* (1895). In antiquity, hysteria was believed to be caused by wandering uterus, one cure for which was to turn women upside down. —Ed.

[224]Jean-Martin Charcot (1825–1893), French neurologist. The physical manifestations of hysteria led him to conclude that it was a result of a weak neurological system. Once triggered by traumatic events, hysteria was progressive and irreversible. An early advocate of hypnosis, Charcot saw similarities between hypnotic and hysteric states, and used hypnosis to study his patients' symptoms. Lasswell writes: "By 1883 he had demonstrated the possibility of producing hysterical symptoms by means of ideas (verbal stimuli). Time and again he hypnotized individuals and produced muscular contractures, hypersensitivity, and hyposensitivity, together with allied symptoms of hysteria" (*Psychopathology*, p. 18). In *Corruption of Reality*, John Schumaker highlights the similarities between hypnosis and various "mental illnesses" (e.g., anorexia,

hysteria to manifest itself as a mere individual phenomenon, since it is contagious by means of psychological resonance, identification, and imitation.[225] Each human being has a predisposition for this malformation of the personality, albeit to varying degrees, although it is normally overcome by rearing and self-rearing, which are amenable to correct thinking and emotional self-discipline.

During "happy times" of peace dependent upon social injustice, the child of the privileged classes does not learn to make an effort to understand himself, others, and the situation, and his tendency toward conversive thinking is sometimes tolerated; he learns to repress from his field of consciousness any uncomfortable ideas suggesting that he and his parents benefit from the disadvantage of others. Such young people learn to disqualify and disparage the moral and mental values of anyone whose work they are using to over-advantage. Young minds thus ingest habits of subconscious selection and substitution of data, which leads to a hysterical, conversive economy of reasoning and the dominance of emotionalism.[226] They grow up to be some-

---

paranoia, hysteria), classifying both as dissociative phenomena. F. W. H. Myers also considered hysteria a "self-suggestive malady" (see Kelly et al., *Irreducible Mind*, pp. 97–101, 162–167). —Ed.

[225]See Lee Daniel Kravetz, *Strange Contagion: Inside the Surprising Science of Infectious Behaviors and Viral Emotions and What They Tell Us about Ourselves* (2017), inspired by suicide clusters spread by social contagion, particularly among young students. The effect is amplified by mass media reporting (p. 15), and Facebook has shown that physical proximity is "no longer a restriction for social contagion" (p. 178). Examples of recent social contagions include bulimia (cases spiked after it appeared as a diagnosis in 1980), anorexia, repressed memories, and cutting. Women are more susceptible (p. 159), and adolescent girls are at the center of most of these outbreaks, including the latest: rapid-onset gender dysphoria. Abigail Shrier quotes psychologists Pettit and Joiner on why girls are so susceptible: their tendencies for co-rumination, excessive reassurance seeking, and negative-feedback seeking (*Irreversible Damage: The Transgender Craze Seducing Our Daughters* [2020], p. 36). As for why these hysterias take on different forms in different time periods, she quotes journalist Ethan Watters, who popularized historian of psychiatry Edward Shorter's work: "Patients unconsciously endeavor to produce symptoms that will correspond to the medical diagnostics of the time" (p. 136). For the influence of social media on the rise in depression and anxiety (also affecting mostly girls), see Lukianoff & Haidt, *Coddling of the American Mind*, pp. 144–61. —Ed.

[226]Shrier provides a remarkably explicit example from a guide to chest binding, a method used by young girls to compress their breasts in order to make them look more boyish, published in *Cosmopolitan* magazine: "[Binding] offered me the ability to shove something that was bothering me to the back of my mind and not have to worry about it" (*Irreversible Damage*, p. 145). —Ed.

what hysterical adults who, by means of the ways adduced above, thereupon transmit their hysteria to the next generation, which then develops these characteristics to an even greater degree. The hysterical patterns of experience and behavior grow and spread downwards from the privileged classes until crossing the boundary of the first criterion of ponerology.[227]

When egocentric emotionalism prevails and the habits of subconscious selection and substitution of thought-data spread to the macrosocial level, a society tends to develop contempt for factual criticism and to humiliate anyone sounding an alarm.[228] Contempt is also shown for other nations which have maintained normal thought-patterns and for their opinions. Egotistic thought-terrorization is accomplished by the society itself and its processes of conversive, moralistic thinking. This obviates the need for censorship of the press, theater, or broadcasting, as a pathologically hypersensitive censor lives within the citizens themselves.[229] When three "egos" govern—egoism, egotism, and egocentrism—the feeling of social links and responsibility disappears, and the society in question splinters into groups ever more hostile to each other.[230] When a hysterical

[227]The atrophy of natural critical faculties with respect to pathological individuals. See Glossary. —Ed.

[228]The 2010s saw the rise of "cancel culture" in the English-speaking world, echoing Mao's Cultural Revolution. Its targets have included public figures sounding the alarm about disturbing trends, like psychologist Jordan B. Peterson (compelled speech), NYU professor Michael Rectenwald (political correctness), biologist Bret Weinstein (neoracist segregation), journalist Andy Ngo (antifa), journalist Abigail Shrier (gender dysphoria), professor Mike Adams (riots and COVID authoritarianism; his suicide was later celebrated by his detractors) and private citizens like James Damore ("Google's Ideological Echo Chamber") and Lindsay Shepherd (free speech about pronouns). See https://www.canceledpeople.org. —Ed.

[229]In American culture this self-censorship touches all aspects of life: media, the workplace, universities, and schools. Gibson & Sutherland, in "Keeping Your Mouth Shut: Spiraling Self-Censorship in the United States" (2020), found that "Over the course of the period from the heyday of McCarthyism to the present, the percentage of the American people not feeling free to express their views has tripled. In 2019, fully four in ten Americans engaged in self-censorship." Politically incorrect books are regularly banned from sale by major corporations. See, e.g., Shrier, "Book Banning in an Age of Amazon" (2021). For this phenomenon in the media, see Taibbi, "The Sovietization of the American Press" (2021), and Attkisson, *Slanted: How the News Media Taught Us to Love Censorship and Hate Journalism* (2020), esp. pp. 60–70. —Ed.

[230]For this phenomenon of polarization and the above on increasing generational hysteria, see Lukianoff & Haidt, *Coddling*, chapters 6 ("The Polarization Cy-

environment stops differentiating the opinions of limited, not-quite-normal people from those of normal, reasonable persons, this opens the door for activation of the pathological factors of a various nature to enter in.

In such conditions, individuals who are governed by a pathological view of reality and abnormal goals caused by their different nature develop their activities. If a given society does not manage to overcome the state of hystericization under its ethnological and political circumstances, a huge bloody tragedy can be the result.[231] One variation of such a tragedy can be pathocracy, though its appearance is also conditioned by other long-term causes. Thus, minor setbacks in terms of political failure or military defeat (such as in Vietnam) can be a warning in such a situation and may turn out to be a blessing in disguise if properly understood and allowed to become a factor in the regeneration of a society's normal thought patterns and customs. The most valuable advice a ponerologist can offer under such circumstances is for a society to avail itself of the assistance of modern science, taking particular advantage of data remaining from the last great increase of hysteria in Europe.

A greater resistance to hystericization characterizes those social groups which earn their daily bread by daily effort, and where the practicalities of everyday life force the mind to think soberly and reflect on generalities. As an example: peasants continue to view the hysterical customs of the well-to-do classes through their own earthy perception of psychological reality and their sense of humor.[232] Similar customs on the part of the bourgeoisie incline workers to bitter criticism and revolutionary anger. Whether couched in economic, ideological, or political terms, the criticism and demands of these

cle") and 8 ("Paranoid Parenting"). See also Jean W. Twenge and W. Keith Campbell, *The Narcissism Epidemic: Living in the Age of Entitlement* (2010). —Ed.

[231] In her book *The Paranoia Switch* (2007), psychologist Martha Stout argues that failure to adequately handle cultural states of hystericization can result in tragedy. She analyzes the psychological–neurological effects of terror and the ways leaders manipulate the cultural panic that ensues from events such as the attacks on 9/11. Exploiting the public's fear instills feelings of helplessness and loss of hope, which are contagious. Rather than seeking to calm and heal such trauma, "cowbird politicians" exploit such states for their own ends, leading to cultural regression and a backlash against scapegoats. —Ed.

[232] "Meme culture" is arguably one modern manifestation of this reaction to hysteria among the elite class. —Ed.

social groups always contain a component of psychological, moral, and anti-hysterical motivation. For this reason, it is most appropriate to consider these demands with deliberation and take these classes' feelings into account.[233] On the other hand, tragic results can derive from thoughtless action—especially the use of force—paving the way for spellbinders to make themselves heard.

Ponerology

Ponerology utilizes the scientific progress of the last decades and years, especially in the realms of biology, medicine, psychopathology, and clinical psychology. It clarifies unknown causal links and analyzes the processes of the genesis of evil, acknowledging those factors whose role has been previously ignored or underestimated. In initiating this new discipline, the author has also utilized his professional experience in these areas and the results of his own recent research.

A ponerological approach facilitates an understanding of some of mankind's more dramatic difficulties on both levels, the macrosocial and the individual human. This new discipline will make it possible to achieve first theoretical, and then practical, solutions for problems we have been attempting to solve by ineffective traditional means, problems against which we have felt powerless for centuries. These latter means are based on historical traditions and excessively moralizing attitudes, which makes them overrate force as a means of counteracting evil. Ponerology can help equalize such one-sidedness by means of modern naturalistic thinking, supplementing our comprehension of the causes and genesis of evil with the facts necessary to build a more stable foundation for preventive inhibition of the processes of ponerogenesis and counteraction of their results.

The synergetic activity of several measures aimed at the same valuable goal, such as treating a sick person, usually produces better effects than the mere sum of the factors involved. In building a second wing for the activities of moralistic efforts to date, ponerology will make it possible to achieve results which are also better than the sum of their useful effects. By reinforcing trust in commonly accepted

[233]In the context of American politics, see Codevilla, *Ruling Class*, ch. 4, who calls them "the country class" (as distinct from the ruling class and their minority of supporters); presidential candidate Hillary Clinton called them "the deplorables." —Ed.

moral values, it will make it possible to answer many heretofore unanswerable questions and utilize means not used thus far, especially on a larger social scale.

Societies have a right to defend themselves against any evil harassing or threatening them. National governments are obligated to use effective means for this purpose, but also to use them as skillfully as possible. In order to discharge this essential function, the authorities of nations obviously have utilized such an understanding of the nature and genesis of evil as was available in a given era and civilization, as well as whatever means they can muster. Society's survival must be protected, but abuse of power and sadistic degenerations come about all too easily.

We now have rational and moral doubts about prior generations' comprehension and counteraction of evil. Opinion in free societies demands an end to the possibility of committing abuses of power such as we have witnessed, and continue to witness, in our century. The demand that repressive measures be humanized and limited so as to set boundaries to possible abuse has become characteristic of our times.[234] Morally sensitive individuals wish to protect their personalities and those of their children from the destructive influence conveyed by the awareness that severe punishment, including capital punishment, is being meted out.

And so it is that the methods of counteracting evil are being mitigated in their severity, but at the same time this social opinion is incapable of indicating other effective methods to protect the citizenry against the birth of evil and violence against citizens. This creates an ever-widening gap between the need for counteraction and the means at our disposal; as a result, many kinds of evil can develop at every social scale, whether by individuals, organized crime, or political movements. Under such circumstances, it may be understandable that some voices clamor for a return to the old-fashioned, iron-fisted methods so inimical to the development of human thought. However, this approach not only contradicts the spirit of the times; it threatens a return to tragic abuses.

[234]For example, witness the rise of the human rights movement in the wake of World War II, the UN's Universal Declaration of Human Rights, and various international human rights treaties and organizations. Such developments are at least in part motivated in reaction to the continued practice of torture, war crimes, collective punishment, ethnic cleansing, etc. —Ed.

Ponerology studies the nature of evil and the complex processes of its genesis, thereby opening new ways for counteracting it. It points out that evil has certain weaknesses in its structure and genesis which can be exploited to inhibit its development as well as to quickly eliminate the fruits of such development. If the ponerogenic activity of pathological factors is subjected to conscious controls of a scientific, individual, and societal nature, we can counteract evil as effectively as by means of persistent calls to respect moral values. The ancient method of the moralists and this completely new one can thus combine to produce results more favorable than an arithmetic sum of the two. Ponerology also leads to the possibilities of prophylactic behavior at the levels of individual, societal, and macrosocial evil. This new approach ought to enable societies to feel safe again, both on the level of domestic affairs and on the scale of international threats.

Methods of counteracting evil which are conditioned upon knowledge of its causation, supported by ever-increasing scientific progress, will of course be much more complex, just as the nature and genesis of evil are complex. Any allegedly fair relationship between a person's crime and the punishment meted out, as well as the use of punishment as a panacea for combating evil, will become relics of archaic thinking, something ever more difficult to comprehend for students of history. That is why our times demand that we further develop the discipline initiated herein and undertake detailed research, especially as regards the nature of many pathological factors which take part in ponerogenesis. An appropriately ponerological reading of history is a necessary condition for understanding macrosocial ponerogenic phenomena whose duration exceeds the observational capabilities of a single person or which appear centuries apart. The author utilized this method in the following chapter, reconstructing the phase wherein characteropathic factors dominated in the initial period of the creation of pathocracy, which he could not observe for himself.

In teaching us about the causes and genesis of evil, ponerology says little about human guilt. Thus, it does not solve the perennial problem of human responsibility, although it does shed additional light from the side of psychological causation. We become aware of just how much we have failed to understand in this area, and how much remains to be researched, by attempting to correct our comprehension of the complex causation of evil and by acknowledging greater dependence upon factors that act on the individual from within *and* from without. At that point, any moral judgment about another person or his blameworthiness may strike us as based mostly upon emotional responses and centuries-old tradition.[235]

We have the right and duty to critically judge our own behavior and the moral value of our motivations. This is what we are called upon to do by our *conscience*, a phenomenon as ubiquitous as it is incomprehensible within the boundaries of naturalistic thinking. Even if armed with all the present and future accomplishments of ponerology, will we ever be in a position to abstract and evaluate the individual blame of another person? In terms of theory, this appears ever more doubtful; in terms of practice, ever more unnecessary.

If we consistently abstain from moral judgments of other people, we transfer our attention to tracking the causal processes that condition the behavior of another person or society. This improves our prospects for proper mental hygiene and our capacity to apprehend psychological reality. Such restraint also enables us to avoid an error which poisons minds and souls all too effectively, namely superimposing a moralizing interpretation upon the activity of pathological factors. We also avoid emotional entanglements and better control our own egotism and egocentrism, thus facilitating objective analysis of phenomena.

If such an attitude strikes some readers as being close to moral indifference, we should reiterate that the here-adduced method of analyzing evil and its genesis gives rise to a new type of rational distance from its temptations, as well as activating additional theoretical and practical possibilities for counteracting it. Also, we should give thought to the astonishing and obvious convergence between the conclusions we can derive from this naturalistic analysis of the phenomena described and what is written in the books of the great religions and in the Christian Gospels: "Judge not, that ye be not judged. For with what judgment ye judge, ye shall be judged; and with what measure ye mete, it shall be measured to you again" (Matt. 7:1-2).

These values, unfortunately often overshadowed by a government's immediate needs, as well as the activity of our instinctive and emotional reflexes goading us to revenge and punishment of others, find

[235]Raine writes: "If some individuals have damaged brains, can they be said to be fully in control of their actions and cognitions? Do they have complete freedom of will, or does the brain damage place constraints on such freedom?" (quoted by Oakley, *Evil Genes*, p. 328). —Ed.

at least partial rational justification in this new science. Practicing such rigorous understanding and behavior can only confirm these values with added clarity.

This new discipline will be applicable to many walks of life. The author has utilized these accomplishments and tested their practical value in the course of individual psychotherapy upon his patients; as a result, their personalities and futures were rearranged in a manner more favorable and long-lasting than if it were based on earlier skills.[236] Bearing in mind the exceptional nature of our times, when a comprehensive mobilization of moral and mental values must be effected to counteract the evil threatening the world, in the coming chapters the author shall suggest the adoption of just such an attitude, whose end result ought to be an act of forgiveness heretofore unheard of in history. Keep in mind also that understanding and forgiveness does not exclude correction of conditions and taking prophylactic measures.

Disentangling the Gordian knot of present times—the result of the activity of a large-scale clandestine and ponerogenic organization and the appearance of the macrosocial pathological phenomenon initiated by it, which has inflicted irreparable wounds on humanity and poisoned the minds of millions of people—may appear impossible without the development and utilization of this new discipline. This knot can no longer be cut with a sword. A psychologist cannot afford to be as impatient as Alexander the Great. That is why we have here described it within the necessary scope, adaptation, and selection of data, so as to enable clarification of the problems to be discussed later in the book. Perhaps the future will make it possible to elaborate a general theoretical work.

[236] *Author's note (1997):* Psychologists can familiarize themselves with this approach in the author's work in Polish titled *Chirurgia słowa* [Word Surgery].

CHAPTER V PATHOCRACY

As a youth, I read a book about a naturalist wandering through the Amazon-basin wilderness. At some moment a small animal fell from a tree onto the nape of his neck, clawing his skin painfully and sucking his blood. The biologist cautiously removed it—without anger, since that was its form of feeding—and proceeded to study it carefully. This story stubbornly stuck in my mind during those very difficult times when the Red vampire fell onto our necks, sucking the blood of a hapless nation.

Maintaining the attitude of a naturalist, one who attempts to track the nature of a macrosocial phenomenon in spite of all adversity, insured a certain intellectual distance, protected one's own mental hygiene, and gave a perhaps illusory sense of security. The premonition that this very method may help find a certain creative solution made it easier to exercise strict control over the natural, moralizing reflexes of revulsion and other painful emotions that such an allegedly political system provokes in any normal person when it deprives him of his joy of life and personal safety, ruining his own future and that of his nation. Scientific curiosity becomes a loyal ally during such times.

So, may the reader please imagine a very large hall in an old Gothic university building. Many of us gathered there early in our studies in order to listen to the lectures of Professor of Philosophy Roman Ingarden[1] and other eminent scholars. We were herded back there the year before graduation (1951) in order to listen to the indoctrination lectures which recently had been introduced.[2]

[1]Roman Ingarden (1893–1970), philosopher, the greatest Polish phenomenologist, reputedly Edmund Husserl's favorite student, taught secretly in Lviv during German occupation and began teaching at Jagiellonian University in 1946. He was made "inactive" in 1950 for being an "enemy of materialism," reinstated in 1957 after Stalin's death, although forced to early retirement in 1963. Ingarden was also a member of the Society of Mental Hygiene, and was interested in psychiatric problems, such as perceptual disorders. —Ed.

Someone nobody knew appeared behind the lectern and informed us that he would now be the professor. He spoke with zeal, but there was nothing scientific about it: he failed to distinguish between scientific concepts and popular beliefs. He treated such borderline notions as though they were wisdom that could not be doubted. For ninety minutes each week, he flooded us with naive, presumptuous paralogistics and a pathological view of world and human affairs. We were treated with contempt and poorly concealed hatred. Since scoffing and making jokes could entail dreadful consequences, we had to listen attentively and with the utmost gravity.

The grapevine soon discovered this person's origins. He had come from a Kraków suburb and attended high school, although no one knew if he had graduated. In any case, this was the first time he had crossed university portals—and as a professor, at that!—as a result of his advancement within the Party.

"You can't convince anyone this way!" we whispered to each other. "It's actually propaganda directed against themselves." But after such mind-torture, it took a long time for someone to break the silence. We studied ourselves, since we felt something strange had taken over our minds and something valuable was leaking away irretrievably. The world of psychological reality and moral values seemed suspended as if in a chilly fog. Our feeling of human and student solidarity—a value accepted until then—lost its original meaning, as did patriotism. So we asked each other, "Are you going through this too?" Each of us

[2]See John Connelly, *Captive University: The Sovietization of East German, Czech, and Polish Higher Education 1945–1956* (2000), who writes: "in each place prominent representatives of 'bourgeois' disciplines such as sociology or modern philosophy had been removed, and colleagues that remained behind were made to lecture and teach according to detailed, state-approved study programs" (p. 4). Subjects like history, philosophy, law, and sociology "were transformed into vehicles for the transmission of ideology," but the hard sciences (e.g., STEM fields) were left more or less untouched. For Łobaczewski's university, Jagiellonian, see pp. 84, 102. On the ideological transformation of Russian science, Pavlov said in a 1929 speech: "The introduction into the Statutes of the Academy [of Sciences] of a paragraph that all work should be carried out on the platform of the teachings of Marx and Engels—is this not the greatest violence to scientific thought? How does this differ from the medieval Inquisition? ... We are ordered (!) to elect as members of the Higher Scientific Institution people who we cannot, in good conscience, recognize as scientists. ... The former intelligentsia is partly exterminated, partly corrupted. ... We live in a society where the state is everything, and a man is nothing, and such a society has no future, regardless of any Volkhovstroi and Dnieper hydroelectric power stations" ("Ivan Pavlov," Russian Wikipedia, transl.). —Ed.

experienced this worry about his own personality and future in his own way. Some of us answered the questions with silence. The depth and quality of these experiences turned out to be different for each individual.

We thus wondered how to protect ourselves from the results of this "indoctrination." Teresa D. made the first suggestion: Let's spend a weekend in the mountains. It worked. Pleasant company, a bit of joking, then exhaustion followed by deep sleep in a shelter, and our human personalities returned, albeit with a certain remnant. Time also proved to create a kind of psychological immunity, although not with everyone. Analyzing the psychopathic characteristics of the "professor's" personality proved another excellent way of protecting one's own mental hygiene.

You can just imagine our worry, disappointment, and surprise when some colleagues we knew well suddenly began to change their worldview; their thought-patterns furthermore reminded us of the "professor's" chatter. Their feelings, which had just recently been friendly, became noticeably cooler, although not yet hostile. Benevolent but critical student arguments bounced right off them. They gave the impression of possessing some secret knowledge; in their eyes, we became only their former colleagues, still believing what those "professors of old" had taught us. We had to be careful of what we said to them. These former colleagues soon joined the Party.[3]

Who were they, what social groups did they come from, what kind of students and people were they? How and why did they change so much in less than a year? Why did neither I nor a majority of my fellow students succumb to this phenomenon and process? Many such questions fluttered through our heads then. It was in those times, from those questions, and out of such anxiety that the idea was born that this phenomenon and system of government could be objectively understood; an idea whose greater meaning crystallized with time. Many of us participated in the initial observations and reflections, but most crumbled away in the face of material or academic problems.

[3]The communist Polish United Workers' Party, which established a one-party state in 1948 led by Bolesław Bierut. For an engaging account of the communist takeover of Poland (as well as East Germany and Hungary), including its impact in the universities, see Applebaum, *Iron Curtain*, esp. ch. 13, pp. 310–312. Poland's fate was settled at the Tehran and Yalta Conferences where Roosevelt and Churchill ceded Poland (among other nations) to the Soviets (see pp. 19, 70, 197). —Ed.

Only a few remained; so the author of this book may be the last of the Mohicans.

It was relatively easy to determine the environments and origins of the people who succumbed to this process, which I later called "transpersonification."[4] They came from all social groups, including aristocratic and fervently religious families, and caused a break in our student solidarity to the order of some 6%. The remaining majority suffered varying degrees of personality disintegration which gave rise to individual efforts to search for the criteria and values necessary to find ourselves again; the efforts were varied and often creative.

Even then, we had no doubts as to the pathological nature of this "transpersonification" process, which ran similarly but not identically in all cases. The duration of the results of this phenomenon also varied. Some of these people later became zealots. Others later took advantage of various circumstances to withdraw and re-establish their lost links to the society of normal people. They were replaced. *The only constant value of the new social system was the magic number of 6%.*

We tried to evaluate the talent level of those colleagues who had succumbed to this personality-transformation process, and reached the conclusion that, on average, it was slightly lower than the average of the student population. Their lesser resistance obviously resided in *other* biopsychological features which were most probably qualitatively heterogeneous.

It was therefore necessary to study subjects bordering on psychology and psychopathology in order to answer the questions arising from our observations; scientific neglect in these areas proved an obstacle difficult to overcome. At the same time, someone guided by special knowledge apparently vacated the libraries of anything we could have found on the topic; books were indexed, but not physically present.

Analyzing these events now in hindsight, we could say that the "professor" was dangling bait over our heads, based on the psychopath's above-mentioned special psychological knowledge. He knew in advance that he would fish out amenable individuals—this was the

[4]Compare the descriptions from parents whose children have undergone similar personality transformations associated with gender dysphoria in Shrier, *Irreversible Damage*. More generally, witness the results of postmodernist indoctrination in western academia, which has resulted in "social justice" (see Rectenwald, *Springtime* and *Beyond Woke*). —Ed.

primary aim of such "ideological training"—but the limited numbers must have disappointed him and his superiors.[5] The transpersonification process generally took hold above all in those individuals whose instinctive substratum was marked by pallor or certain deficits. To a lesser extent, it also worked among people who manifested other hereditary deficiencies, in which cases the state provoked was impermanent, being largely the result of psychopathological induction—akin to participating in someone else's madness.

This knowledge about the existence of susceptible individuals and how to influence them will continue being a psychological weapon for world conquest as long as it remains the secret of such "professors." When it becomes skillfully popularized science, it will help nations to develop immunity. But none of us knew this at the time.

Nevertheless, we must admit that in demonstrating his personality (a typical case of essential psychopathy) and the fundamental properties of pathocracy to us in such a way as to force us into in-depth experience, the professor helped us understand the nature of the phenomenon in a larger scope than many a true scientific researcher who later took part in this work. As observed during subsequent training lectures, the facilitators generally had the same mental anomaly.

The Nature and Genesis of the Phenomenon

The time-cycle sketched in Chapter III was referred to as hysteroidal because the intensification or diminution of a society's hysterical condition can be considered its chief measurement. It does not, of course, constitute the only quality subject to change within the framework of a corresponding periodicity. The present chapter shall deal with the phenomenon which can emerge from the phase of maximal intensification of hysteria. Such a sequence, however, does not appear to result from any relatively constant laws of history; quite the contrary,

[5]Such university indoctrination programs included topics like "the essence of Soviet democracy," "Poland in the camp of freedom," "characteristics of imperialism—the decadent phase of capitalism," and "the collaboration and venality of the bourgeoisie as politics of national betrayal." "The effects of the courses seemed questionable, however. In 1949 over 400 of the 1,247 students in Kraków failed examinations ... Perhaps even more troubling, success in the exams did not necessarily reflect acceptance of the new ideology. ... Party functionaries never ceased worrying that students were not taking Marxism-Leninism seriously" (Connelly, *Captive University*, pp. 209, 210). —Ed.

some additional circumstances and factors must participate in such a period of a society's general spiritual crisis and cause its reason and structure to degenerate in such a way as to bring about the spontaneous generation of this mysterious and worst disease of society.[6] As already indicated, let us call this phenomenon "pathocracy"; this is not the first time it has emerged during the history of our planet.

It appears that this phenomenon, whose causes also appear to be potentially present in every society, has its own characteristic process of genesis, only partially conditioned by, and hidden behind, the maximal hysterical intensity of the above-described cycle. As a result of this coincidence, unhappy times become exceptionally cruel and enduring and their causes impossible to understand within the categories of natural human concepts. Let us therefore bring this process of the origin of pathocracy closer, methodically isolating it from other phenomena we can recognize as conditioning or merely accompanying it.

A psychologically normal, highly intelligent person called to high office experiences doubts as to whether he can meet the demands expected of him and seeks the assistance of others whose opinions he values. At the same time, he feels nostalgia for his old life, freer and less burdensome, to which he would like to return after fulfilling his social obligations. In reality, he is able to do so when circumstances require it.

Nevertheless, every society worldwide contains individuals whose dreams of power arise very early, as we have already discussed. They are generally discriminated against in some way by society, which uses a moralizing interpretation with regard to their failings and innate or acquired deficiencies, although these individuals are rarely guilty of them. They would like to change this unfriendly world into something else. Dreams of power also represent an overcompensation for the feeling of inferiority and humiliation, the second angle in Adler's rhombus.[7] A significant and active proportion of this group

[6]Versluis describes some of pre-existing conditions, writing that totalitarianism emerges "as the bastion of certainty after a period of prolonged and intense uncertainty ... It helps ... if there is a preceding socioeconomic disaster, so that people are predisposed..., on the one hand, [to] look for scapegoats, and on the other, to imagine a better future if only the scapegoats were removed. But there also must be a charismatic ideologue to act as the movement's impetus and centre" (*New Inquisitions*, pp. 135, 144). —Ed.

[7]Alfred Adler (1870–1937), author of *The Neurotic Character* (1912), was an Austrian psychiatrist who rejected Freud's emphasis on sexuality and theorized

is composed of individuals with various deviations who imagine this better world in their own way, with which we are already familiar. Once they rise to power, they become incapable of returning to normal life.

In the prior chapter, the readers have become acquainted with examples of these deviances selected in such a way as to permit us now to present the ponerogenesis of pathocracy and to introduce the essential factors of this historical phenomenon which is so difficult to understand. It has certainly appeared many times in history, on various continents and social scales. However, no one has ever managed to identify it objectively because it would hide in one of the ideologies characteristic of the respective culture and era, developing in the very bosom of different social movements, appropriating their language and caricaturizing their ideas. Identification was so difficult because the indispensable naturalistic knowledge needed for proper classification of phenomena in this area did not develop until our contemporary times. Thus, historians, sociologists, and political scientists discern many similarities, but they possess no identifying criteria because the latter belongs to another scientific discipline.[8]

Who plays the first crucial role in this process of the origin of pathocracy, schizoids or characteropaths? It appears to be the former; therefore, let us delineate their role first.

During stable times which are ostensibly happy, albeit marked by injustice to individuals and nations,[9] doctrinaire people believe they have found a simple solution to fix such a world. Such a histori-

---

that neurotic behavior was an overcompensation for feelings of inferiority. He saw the human personality as the result of processes by which inferiority feelings are converted to superiority feelings according to the guidance of an unconscious self-ideal, which is at odds with social demands. This process can lead to an inferiority complex, where the individual becomes egocentric, power-hungry, and aggressive to compensate for feelings of inferiority. Adler believed that personality can be distinguished into four types (the rhombus): getting, avoiding, ruling, and socially useful. —Ed.

[8]Versluis provides a useful summary of common features shared by three exemplars of pathocracy (the Inquisitions, fascism, and communism), noting that "what are often depicted as incommensurable and opposed systems are in fact very nearly identical in how they actually operate. Secret police, secret imprisonments, torture, show trials, insistence on public confessions, public executions, gulags, or concentration camps in which people are held incommunicado and interminably" (*New Inquisitions*, p. viii). —Ed.

[9]For example, pre-revolutionary France and Russia, in which real injustices were prevalent and fostered revolutionary sentiment. —Ed.

cal period is always characterized by an impoverished psychological worldview, so that a schizoidal worldview does not stand out as odd during such times and is accepted as legal tender.[10] These doctrinaire individuals characteristically manifest a certain contempt with regard to moralists then preaching the need to rediscover lost human values and moral discipline, and to develop a richer, more appropriate psychological worldview.[11]

Schizoid characters—proudly asserting the superiority of their rational minds over the minds of "others" who are guided by emotions—aim to impose their own conceptual world upon other people or social groups, using relatively controlled pathological egotism and the exceptional tenacity derived from their persistent nature. They are thus eventually able to overpower another individual's personality, which causes the latter's behavior to turn desperately illogical. They may also exert a similar influence upon the group of people they have joined. They are psychological loners who feel better in some human organization, wherein they attempt to play the role of sages, becoming zealots for some ideology,[12] religious bigots, materialists, or—less often—adherents of an ideology with satanic features. If their activities consist of direct contact on a small social scale, their acquaintances easily perceive them as eccentrics, which limits their ponerogenic role. However, if they manage to hide their own personality behind the written word, their influence may poison the minds of society on a large scale and for a long time.

The conviction that Karl Marx is the best example of this is correct, as he was the best-known figure of that kind, with his characteristic pessimism in his understanding of human nature and deficits

[10]See McGilchrist's characterization of the "schizo-autistic" philosophical style in *The Matter with Things*, pp. 614–620: such philosophers "are more likely to take things out of context, think in disembodied [i.e., detached] schemata, and adopt irrationally rationalistic approaches. They tend towards utilitarianism in ethics" (p. 615). Examples: Descartes, Spinoza, Kant, Bentham, Freud, Russell, Ryle. —Ed.

[11]The contemporary negative reactions to Jordan B. Peterson, especially from activists in media and universities, are typical. —Ed.

[12]Versluis writes: "By embracing a rigid ideology, whatever it is, the ideologue now is able to convince himself that he is the possessor of the truth. He is part of the 'inner circle,' the elite group who are called to take on themselves the burden of policing society, of 'improving' the human world. Ordinary people, they don't understand, and so must be coerced, sometimes even tortured or killed 'for their own good'" (*New Inquisitions*, p. 140). —Ed.

in psychological worldview.[13] J. Frostig,[14] a psychiatrist of the old school, included Engels and others into a category he called "bearded schizoidal fanatics." The infamous writings attributed to the "Learned Elders of Zion" at the turn of the century begin with a typically schizoidal declaration.[15] The nineteenth century, especially

[13] *Author's note (1997)*: Young Marx's upbringing should also be taken into account. He was raised officially in Protestant Christianity, but among his family in the spirit of Judaism, which must have led not only to frustration but also to symptoms of a bimorphic personality. [Sowell, *Marxism*, ch. 9, provides a brief overview of Marx's life and character. Marx lived a parasitic lifestyle, relying on others for money, not paying his debts, and often wasting what money he had. In 1837 his father despaired: "will you ever be capable of truly human, domestic happiness? Will ... you ever be capable of imparting happiness to those immediately around you?" (https://marxists.architexturez.net/archive/marx/letters/papa/1837-fl2.htm). Sowell and Marx's contemporaries describe him as an egomaniac, "domineering, impetuous, passionate, full of boundless self-confidence," arrogant, dogmatic, blaming his own failures on others, "self-centered, if not exploitative," Machiavellian, "provoking and intolerable." A fellow revolutionary, Carl Schurz, wrote: "Everyone who contradicted him he treated with abject contempt; every argument that he did not like he answered either with biting scorn at the unfathomable ignorance that had prompted it, or with opprobrious aspersions upon the motives of him who had advanced it" (pp. 167, 174, 175, 177, 181). See also "The Jewish Question about Marx" (1989) by Dennis Fischman, who writes that Marx's father Heschel's conversion to Lutheranism just prior to Karl's birth was "a matter of economics, not faith: the Prussian government had begun to enforce its requirement that all lawyers be Christians. ... In all probability, Karl Marx's father was one of the many Jews who converted 'without really relinquishing their family and social ties with the Jewish community'" (p. 759). While Heschel was not himself religious, his wife Henriette (Marx's mother) was raised Orthodox and remained closer to her religious roots. Marx's own comments on Jews are notorious, though he supported their political equality (see Sowell, pp. 175–176). On "bimorphic" or "dual personality" see Brian Skea, "A Jungian Perspective on the Dissociability of the Self" (1995). While the term is no longer used in modern psychiatry, Jungian psychology understands it in terms of unintegrated, conflicting "true" and "false" selves (conscious vs. unconscious, outer vs. inner, persona vs. essence). Such symptoms may occur when one diverges too much from the other, or is too dominant. —Ed.]

[14] *Author's note*: Professor of King John Kasimir University in Lviv (now Ukraine). I used his manual *Psychiatria*. Poland was then under pathocratic rule and his works were removed from public libraries as "ideologically improper." [Frostig was one of Poland's most active and prominent psychiatrists. See Ziskind and Somerfield-Ziskind, "In Memoriam: Peter Jacob Frostig, 1896–1959" (1960). —Ed.]

[15] "The Protocols of the Learned Elders of Zion" begin: "men with bad instincts are more in number than the good, and therefore the best results in governing

its latter half, appears to have been a time of exceptional activity on the part of schizoidal individuals, often but not always of Jewish descent—activity which found fertile ground in the materialism of the age.[16] After all we have to remember that 97% of all Jews do not manifest this anomaly, and that it also appears among all European nations, albeit to a markedly lesser extent. Our inheritance from this period includes world-images, scientific traditions, and legal concepts

---

them are attained by violence and terrorism, and not by academic discussions. Every man aims at power, everyone would like to become a dictator if only he could, and rare indeed are the men who would not be willing to sacrifice the welfare of all for the sake of securing their own welfare" (http://www.holocaustresearchproject.org/holoprelude/protocols.html). First published in Russian in 1903, much of the "Protocols" contain material copied or paraphrased from Maurice Joly's satirical *Dialogue in Hell between Machiavelli and Montesquieu* (1864). —Ed.

[16] *Author's note (1997)*: As this anomaly is three times more likely to affect Jews than native Europeans, Jews played a leading role during this time. Schizoids' level of commitment and their historical role in the genesis of pathocracy were determined by ethnic alienation, and an implicit ponerogenic doctrine. [For the status and conditions of Jews in the Russian Empire, see Erich E. Haberer, *Jews and Revolution in Nineteenth-Century Russia* (1995), who writes: "it is fair to say that the collusion of specifically Jewish traits and motifs in radical Jews [e.g., cosmopolitanism and Westernism] strengthened the [Populist] movement in the 1870s, gave it staying power in the 1880s, and pioneered revolutionary developments in the 1890s. ... they proved to be the vanguard—and often the actual leaders—of a new epoch in Russian revolutionary history" (p. 272). Many young, alienated, recently secularized Jews found in socialism a replacement for the religion they'd abandoned, an "ideology of salvation" aimed at eliminating all systems of authority and resulting in "a socialist republic of universal brotherhood devoid of national, religious, and social discrimination or even distinctions" (pp. 267–268, 259). Additional factors—e.g., a trend toward secularization and social mobility caused by the Haskalah Jewish Enlightenment movement and Alexander II's reforms—contributed to the sometimes-remarkable overrepresentation of radicalized Jews among Russian revolutionaries and terrorists in the late 1800s, by which time Russian Jews made up 4–5% of the general population but at least 16% of revolutionary activists (pp. 255–257). Among the Populist movement of the 1870s and 1880s, that proportion peaked at around 30% (in the South as high as 40%). For the twentieth century, including the communist revolutionaries among whom Jews were similarly overrepresented, see Alain Brossat and Sylvie Klingberg, *Revolutionary Yiddishland: A History of Jewish Radicalism* (2017). Both centuries are covered in Aleksandr Solzhenitsyn's *Two Hundred Years Together*, the English translation of which is scheduled to be published in 2024 (see https://www.solzhenitsyncenter.org/his-writings/large-works-and-novels/two-hundred-years-together). For the "implicit ponerogenic doctrine," see the notes in Chapter VIII. —Ed.]

flavored with the shoddy ingredients of a schizoidal apprehension of reality.

Humanists are prepared to understand that era and its legacy within categories characterized by their own traditions. They search for societal, ideological, and moral causes for known phenomena. Such an explanation, while containing many valuable insights, can never constitute the whole truth, since it ignores the biological factors which participated in the genesis of the phenomena. Schizoidia is the most frequent factor, albeit not the only one.

In spite of the fact that the writings of schizoidal authors contain the above-described deficiency, or even an openly formulated schizoidal declaration which constitutes sufficient warning to specialists, the average reader accepts them not as a view of reality warped by this anomaly, but rather as an idea to which he should consider seriously based on his convictions and his reason. That is the first mistake. The oversimplified schema of reality—pessimistic regarding human nature and devoid of psychological color—tends to be suggestive, exerting an intense attracting influence on individuals who are insufficiently critical, frequently frustrated as result of downward social adjustment, culturally neglected, or characterized by some psychological deficiencies of their own.[17] Such writings provoke others to harsh criticism based on their healthy common sense, though they also fail to grasp the essential cause of the error.

Societal interpretation of such writings and doctrinaire declarations breaks down into three main trifurcations, engendering divisiveness and conflict. The first branch is the path of aversion, based on rejection of the contents of the work due to personal motivations, differing convictions, or moral revulsion. These reactions contain a component of the moralistic interpretation of pathological phenomena.

The second and third branches relate to two distinctly different apperception types among those persons who *accept* the contents of such works: the *critically-corrective* and the *pathological.* The critically-corrective approach is taken by people whose feel for psychological reality is normal; they tend to incorporate chiefly the more valuable elements of the work. They trivialize the obvious errors and fill in the schizoid deficiencies by means of their own richer world-view. This gives rise to a more sensible, measured, and thus creative

[17]Thus such writings are particularly attractive to a hystericized society in the disintegrative phase of a secular cycle (see Chapter III). —Ed.

interpretation, but it cannot be completely free from the influence of the error frequently adduced above.

Pathological acceptance is manifested by individuals with diverse psychological deviations of their own, whether inherited or acquired, as well as by many people bearing personality malformations or who have been injured by social injustice. That explains why this scope is wider than the circle drawn by the direct action of pathological factors. This form of apperception often brutalizes the authors' concepts and inspires acceptance of violent methods and revolutionary means.[18]

The passage of time and bitter experience has unfortunately not prevented this characteristic misunderstanding born of schizoid nineteenth-century creativity, with Marx's works at the fore, from affecting people and depriving them of their common sense.[19] If only for purposes of the above-mentioned psychological experiment, let us develop awareness of this pathological factor by searching the works of K. Marx for several statements with these characteristic deficits.

---

[18]For Lenin's brutalization of Marx, see Gary Saul Morson, "Leninthink" (2021), and Sowell, *Marxism*, pp. 207–215. Lenin fully embraced terror and defined the dictatorship as "rule based upon force and unrestricted by any laws" (p. 210). As already noted, while Marx did not *explicitly* endorse violence in his published writings, and his "dictatorship of the proletariat" was ideally democratic, he did not renounce violence or terrorism (Sowell, pp. 147, 149, 152, 159) and in fact fully supported them in private correspondence and elsewhere throughout his career. See also Wolfe, *Marxism: One Hundred Years in the Life of a Doctrine* (1965), pp. 152, 164, 165, 223. —Ed.

[19]*Author's note (1997):* The clandestine, very rich, and influential organizations were inundated with schizoid personalities and material, which contributed to their loss of control and common sense. This marked the beginning of the tragedy of our age. [Łobaczewski writes elsewhere: "The naivety of revolutionaries lay in the fact that they assumed that their goals could be realized by means that violated the laws of social life and thus the basis of their own ideas. They did not realize that in doing so they were already aiming at a different goal. If a revolution was brought about by clandestine organizations and in the name of clandestine intentions, its aims could not be achieved by such a means either. Therefore, no revolution has yet led to the full-fledged realization of the goals in the name of which it broke out" (*Logokracja*, p. 183 [machine translation]). Cynthia and Michael Stohl write: "clandestine organizations are a significant and embedded part of the contemporary organizational landscape; they recruit and socialize members in unique ways, they simultaneously are known and unknown to society, they exert influence on legitimate enterprise, and, although they are hard to see and understand, we ignore them at our peril" ("Clandestine/Hidden Organizations" [2016]). Examples include secret societies, revolutionary and terrorist groups, resistance movements, organized crime networks, etc. —Ed.]

When conducted by several people with diverse worldviews, the experiment will show how a clear picture of reality can be restored, and it becomes easier to find a common language.

Schizoidia has thus played an essential role as one of the factors in the genesis of the evil threatening our contemporary world. Practicing psychotherapy upon the world will therefore demand that the results of such evil be eliminated as skillfully as possible.[20]

The first researchers—the author and his colleagues—attracted by the idea of objectively understanding this phenomenon initially failed to perceive the role of *characteropathic personalities* in the genesis of pathocracy. However, when we attempted to reconstruct the early phase of said genesis, we had to acknowledge that characteropaths played a significant role in this process. We already know from the preceding chapter how their defective experiential and thought patterns take hold in human minds, insidiously destroying their way of reasoning and their ability to utilize healthy common sense. This role has also proved essential because their activities as fanatical leaders or spellbinders in various ideologies open the door to psychopathic individuals and the vision of the world they want to impose.

In the ponerogenic process of the pathocratic phenomenon, characteropathic individuals adopt ideologies created by doctrinaire, often schizoidal people, recast them into an active propaganda form, and disseminate it with their characteristic pathological egotism and paranoid intolerance for any philosophies which may differ from their own. They also inspire further transformation of this ideology into its *pathological counterpart.* Something which had a doctrinaire character and circulated in numerically limited groups is now activated at a societal level, thanks to their zeal.

It also appears that this process tends to intensify with time; initial activities are undertaken by persons with milder characteropathic features, for whom it is easy to hide their aberrations both from themselves and from their social circles. Paranoid individuals then become

[20]That is, the psychological, social, and political effects of said schizoidal ideologies that have shaped the twentieth century. For details on the nature of this "world therapy," with specific reference to ideologies, see Chapter IX. In general, Łobaczewski has in mind a process of presenting objective information to the patient about the pathological nature of the influences on his life and personality development, which in itself begins the healing process. With regard to ideologies, this involves identifying the pathological elements and rejecting ideologies founded upon them. —Ed.

principally active. Toward the end of the process, an individual with frontal characteropathy and the highest degree of pathological egotism can easily take over leadership, as happened in Russia.

As long as the characteropathic individuals play a dominant role within a social movement already affected by the ponerogenic process, the ideology, whether doctrinaire from the outset or later vulgarized and further perverted by these latter people, continues to keep and maintain its connection with the content of the original prototype. The ideology continuously affects the movement's activities and remains an essential justifying motivation for many. In this phase, therefore, such an association does not move in the direction of criminal acts on a mass scale and does not blame the normal person for the condition he is in. To a certain extent, at this stage, one can still justifiably define such a movement or pathopolitical association by the name derived from its original ideology.

In the meantime, however, the carriers of other (mainly hereditary) pathological factors become engaged in this already sick social movement and proceed with the work of final transformation of the contents of such an association in such a way that it becomes a pathological caricature of its original ideology. This is effected under the ever-growing influence of *psychopathic* personalities of various types and through the inspirational role of essential psychopathy in particular.

Such leadership eventually engenders a wholesale showdown: the adherents of the original ideology are shunted aside or terminated. (This group includes many characteropaths, especially of the lesser and paranoidal varieties.) The old ideological motivations and the doublespeak based on them will then serve to hide the actual, new contents of the phenomenon.[21] From this time on, using the ideological name of the movement in order to understand its essence becomes the keystone of mistakes.

[21]Morson writes in "Leninthink": "In his history of Marxism, Kołakowski explains some puzzling aspects of Bolshevik practice ... Everyone understands why Bolsheviks shot liberals, socialist revolutionaries, Mensheviks, and Trotskyites. But what, he asks, was the point of turning the same fury on the Party itself, especially on its most loyal, Stalinists, who accepted Leninist-Stalinist ideology without question? Kołakowski observes that it is precisely the loyalty to the ideology that was the problem. ... 'The [great] purge, therefore, was designed to destroy such ideological links as still existed within the party, to convince its members that they had no ideology or loyalty except to the latest orders from on high. ... Loyalty to Marxist ideology as such is still—[in 1978]—a crime and a source of deviations of all kinds.'" —Ed.

Psychopathic individuals generally stay away from social organizations characterized by reason and ethical discipline. After all, such organizations are created by that other world of normal people so foreign to them. Therefore, they hold various social ideologies in contempt, at the same time easily discerning all their actual shortcomings. However, once the process of poneric degeneration of some human association into its yet undefined cartoon counterpart has begun and advanced sufficiently, they perceive this fact with almost infallible sensitivity: a circle has been created wherein they can hide their deficiencies and psychological otherness, find their own *modus vivendi*, and maybe even realize their youthful utopian dream. So they then begin infiltrating the rank and file of such a movement; pretending to be sincere adherents poses no difficulty, since it is second nature for them to play a role and hide behind a mask of normality.

Psychopaths' interest in such movements is not merely the result of their egoism and lack of moral scruples. These people have in fact been wronged by nature and repelled by society. An ideology liberating a social class or nation from injustice may thus seem to them to be friendly; unfortunately it also gives rise to unrealistic hopes that they themselves will be liberated as well.[22] The pathological motivations which appear in an association at the time it begins to be affected by the ponerogenic process strike them as familiar and hope-inspiring. They therefore insinuate themselves into such a movement preaching revolution and war against that "unfair" world so foreign to them and find their own roles within it.[23]

They initially perform subordinate functions in such a movement and execute the leaders' orders, especially whenever something needs to be done which inspires revulsion in others. Their evident zealotry and cynicism gives rise to criticism on the part of the association's more reasonable members, but it also earns the respect of some of

[22] This is also a hidden motivation for movements to "defund" or abolish the police and prison system. For idealistic believers, this means an end to authoritarian oppression, when in reality it results in the mass release of criminals and a state of lawlessness in which those criminals are free to commit crimes, often in the name of the ideology, as happened during the Russian Revolution (see Figes, *People's Tragedy*, pp. 533–536). —Ed.

[23] A piece of graffiti in CHAZ, the so-called Capitol Hill Autonomous Zone established in Seattle during the protest/riots of 2020, is representative: "No work. No cops. End this stupid f***ing world." A booklet handed out in CHAZ included the following: "Our contempt for the media is inextricable from our hatred of this entire world" (Ngo, *Unmasked*, pp. 40, 41). —Ed.

its more extreme revolutionaries. They thus find protection among those people who earlier played a role in the movement's ponerization, and repay the favor with compliments or by making things easier for them. Thus they climb up the organizational ladder, gain influence, and almost involuntarily bend the contents of the entire group to their own way of experiencing reality and to the goals derived from their deviant nature. A mysterious disease is already raging inside the association. The adherents of the original ideology feel ever more constricted by powers they do not understand; they start fighting with demons that invade their personalities and making mistakes.

If such a movement triumphs by revolutionary means and in the name of slogans of freedom, the welfare of the people, social justice, and internationalism, this only brings about further transformation of the governmental system thus created into a macrosocial pathological phenomenon. Within this system, the common man is blamed for not having been born a psychopath, and is considered good for nothing except hard work, fighting, and dying to protect a system of government he can neither sufficiently comprehend nor ever consider to be his own.

An ever-strengthening network of psychopathic and related individuals gradually starts to dominate, overshadowing the others. Characteropathic individuals who played an essential role in ponerizing the movement and preparing for revolution are also eliminated. Adherents of the revolutionary ideology are unscrupulously "pushed into a counter-revolutionary position." They are now condemned for "moral" reasons in the name of new criteria whose paramoralistic essence they are not in a position to comprehend. Violent *negative selection* of the original group now ensues.[24] The inspirational role of essential psychopathy is now also consolidated; it remains characteristic for the entire future of this macrosocial pathological phenomenon.

In spite of these transformations, the pathological block of the revolutionary movement remains a permanent minority. This biologically conditioned fact cannot be changed even by using propaganda tactics to declare themselves the moral majority—followers of a new, more glorious leader and version of the ideology—as was the case with the Bolsheviks. The rejected majority and the very forces which naively

[24]See, for example, the various waves of violent negative selection during Mao's Great Leap Forward and Cultural Revolution (Dikötter, *Mao's Great Famine: The History of China's Most Devastating Catastrophe, 1958–1962* [2017], pp. 192–193, 299–300, and *Cultural Revolution*, pp. 3, 9). —Ed.

elevated such an association to power start mobilizing against this block. Ruthless confrontation with these forces becomes the only way to safeguard the long-term survival of the pathological authority. We must thus consider the bloody triumph of a pathological minority over the movement's more normal majority to mark the watershed phase during which the movement's new nature starts to be consolidated.[25]

The entire life of a society thus affected becomes subordinated to deviant thought-criteria and permeated by their specific experiential mode, especially the one described in the section on essential psychopathy. At this point, using the name of the original ideology to designate this phenomenon is meaningless and becomes an error rendering it more difficult to comprehend, and thus counter effectively.

I shall accept the denomination of *pathocracy*[26]for a system of government thus created, wherein a small pathological minority takes control over a society of normal people. The name thus selected, above all, emphasizes the basic quality of the macrosocial psychopathological phenomenon, and differentiates it from the many possible social systems dominated by normal people's structure, custom, and law.[27] I tried to find a name which would more clearly designate the psychopathological, even psychopathic quality of such a government, but I gave up because it would leave out some observable phenomena (to be referred to below) and for practical considerations (to avoid lengthening the denomination). Such a name sufficiently indicates the phenomenon's basic quality and also emphasizes that the ideological cloak (or some other ideology which cloaked similar phenomena in the past) *does not constitute its essence.* When I happened to hear that a Hungarian scientist unknown to me had

[25]The "purges" of Stalin in the late 1930s and Mao in the late 1960s are prototypical examples (each took place approximately 20 years after the initial imposition of pathocracy in its initial stages). —Ed.

[26]From the Greek *pathos* (disease, suffering) + *-kratia* (rule, power). —Ed.

[27]For example, democracy, oligarchy, autocracy, theocracy, monarchy, republic, feudalism, etc., though each can be subject to pathological degeneration to greater or lesser degrees. Łobaczewski uses the term pathocracy to capture the essence of the system commonly referred to as "totalitarianism." While totalitarian systems are authoritarian by nature, not all "authoritarian" systems are necessarily pathocratic. For example, while tsarist Russia was an absolute monarchy, Łobaczewski does not argue that it was a pathocracy, with the possible exception of its final years (see the Polish edition, p. 137). —Ed.

already used this term, my decision was finalized. I think this name is consistent with the demands of semantics, since no concise term can adequately characterize such a complex phenomenon. I shall also henceforth designate the social systems wherein the links, structure, and customs of normal people dominate *in any way* as "the systems of normal man."

More on the Contents of the Phenomenon

The achievement of absolute domination by pathocrats in the government of a country cannot be permanent since large sectors of the society become disaffected by such rule and eventually find some way of toppling it. Pathocracy at the highest levels of government also does not represent the entire picture of the consolidated phenomenon. Such a system of government must extend downward. All leadership positions (down to village headman, the managers of workplaces and agricultural cooperatives, not to mention the directors of police units, secret police personnel, and activists and propagandists in the pathocratic party) must be filled by individuals whose sense of connection with such a system of power is conditioned by corresponding psychological deviations, which are usually inherited.[28] However, such people constitute a very small percentage of the population and this makes them more valuable to the pathocrats. Their intellectual level or professional skills cannot be taken into account, since people representing superior abilities—especially in technical fields—are even harder to find. After such a system has lasted several years, one hundred percent of all the cases of essential psychopathy are involved in pathocratic activity; they are considered the most loyal, even though some of them were formerly involved on the other side in some way. As far as other aberrations are concerned, the percentage is no longer so high.

Under such conditions, no area of social life can develop normally, whether in economics, culture, science, technology, administration,

[28]A resident of Lijiang, Yunnan, during the communist revolution in China described this phenomenon: "All the scamps and the village bullies, who had not done a stroke of honest work in their life, suddenly blossomed forth as the accredited members of the Communist Party, and swaggered with special armbands and badges and the peculiar caps ... which seemed to be the hallmark of the Chinese Red" (Frank Dikötter, *The Tragedy of Liberation: A History of the Chinese Revolution 1945–1957* [2017], p. 197). —Ed.

etc. Pathocracy progressively paralyzes everything. Normal people must develop a level of patience beyond the ken of anyone living in a normal man's system just in order to explain what to do and how to do it to some obtuse mediocrity or psychological deviant. This special kind of pedagogy[29] requires a great deal of time and effort, but it would otherwise not be possible to maintain tolerable living conditions and necessary achievements in the economic area or intellectual life of a society.[30] Meanwhile, pathocracy progressively intrudes everywhere and dulls everything, although to varying degrees. Those people who initially found the original ideology attractive eventually come to the realization that they are in fact dealing with something completely different. The disillusionment experienced by such former ideological adherents is bitter in the extreme.

Thus, the pathological minority's attempts to retain power will always be threatened by the society of normal people, whose criticism and practical knowledge keep growing. It is therefore necessary to employ, on the one hand, any and all methods of coercion, terror, and exterminatory policies against individuals known for their patriotic feelings and military training, and on the other hand, the specific psychological "indoctrination" activities such as those we have presented.[31] Individuals lacking a natural feeling of social bonds become irreplaceable in both of these activities. Such efforts are spearheaded by people alienated from the society in question due to their abnormal natures, as well as brought up in the spirit of a pathological vision of domination over other nations, racial doctrines, and with contempt

---

[29] I.e., instructing deviants and incompetents in low- or mid-level positions of power while avoiding their wrath. Łobaczewski is referring to bureaucrats, low-level managers, co-workers, direct supervisors, etc., not to highly placed officials. —Ed.

[30] Since top leadership remained inaccessible for this kind of special pedagogy, Łobaczewski presumably means that such interactions were necessary to maintain even a minimum level of economic productivity and cultural life. (Not that the latter part of the sentence in question is not present in the Polish.) —Ed

[31] Wolfe writes: "In the state's war against its own people, these are the weapons: mass propaganda, terror, isolation, indoctrination, total organization and total regulation. These means are something new in history. In fact they could only exist in an era of advanced technology where the state can reach with loudspeaker, newspaper, telephone, police wagon, tank and plane all the far corners and most secret places of its domain. It is that monster which Herzen and Tolstoy prophetically foretold: 'Someday Genghis Khan will return with the telegraph.'" (*Communist Totalitarianism*, p. 268). —Ed.

for others. Further downstream are cases of essential psychopathy and other aberrations.

The phenomenon of pathocracy matures during this period: an extensive and active indoctrination system is built, with a suitably refurbished ideology constituting the vehicle or Trojan horse for the process of pathologizing the thought processes of individuals and society. The goal—forcing human minds to incorporate pathological experiential methods and thought-patterns, and consequently accepting such rule—is never openly admitted. This goal is conditioned by pathological egotism; thus it strikes the pathocrats as not only obvious and indispensable, but also feasible. Thousands of activists must therefore participate in this work. However, time and experience confirm what a psychologist may have long foreseen: the entire effort produces results so very limited that it is reminiscent of the labors of Sisyphus. It only results in producing a general stifling of intellectual development, neurotic resentment, and deep-rooted protest against affront-mongering "hypocrisy." The authors and executors of this program are incapable of understanding that the decisive factor making their work difficult is the fundamental nature of normal human beings.

The entire system of violence, terror, and forced indoctrination, or, rather, pathologization, thus proves effectively unfeasible, which causes the pathocrats no small measure of surprise. Reality places a question mark on their conviction that such methods can change people in such fundamental ways so that they can eventually recognize this pathocratic kind of government as a normal state.

During the initial shock, the feeling of social links between normal people fades. After that has been survived, however, the overwhelming majority of people begin to manifest their own phenomenon of psychological immunization. Society simultaneously starts collecting practical knowledge on the subject of this new reality and its psychological properties. Normal people slowly learn to perceive the weak spots of such a system and exploit opportunities to safely influence it for a more expedient arrangement of their lives. They begin to give each other advice in these matters, thus slowly regenerating the feelings of social links and reciprocal trust. A characteristic new phenomenon occurs: separation between the pathocrats and the society of normal people. The latter have an advantage of talent, professional skills, and healthy common sense. They therefore hold certain advantageous cards. The pathocracy finally realizes that it must find some *modus vivendi* or relations with the majority of society: "After all, somebody's got to do the work for us. And who would treat us when we're ill?" say the more moderate pathocrats.

There are other imperatives and pressures felt by the pathocrats, especially from outside. The pathological face must be hidden from the world somehow, since recognition of it by world opinion (scientific and social) would be a catastrophe. Ideological propaganda alone would then be an insufficient disguise. Primarily in the interests of the new elite and its expansionary plans, a pathocratic state must maintain political and trade relations with the countries of normal man. Such a state aims to achieve international recognition as a *certain kind* of political structure; and it fears recognition in terms of a clinical diagnosis of its true nature.

All this makes pathocrats tend to limit their measures of terror, subjecting their propaganda and indoctrination methods to a certain cosmetology, and to accord the society they control some margin of autonomous activity, especially regarding cultural life. The more liberal pathocrats would not be averse to giving such a society a certain minimum of economic prosperity in order to reduce the level of irritation, but their own corruption and inability to administer the economy prevents them from doing so, as well as the fear that the people will use some of these resources for activities directed against them.

Thus is born a new phase in the course of this great societal disease of nations: methods of activity become milder, and there is coexistence with countries whose structure is that of normal man.[32] Any psychopathologist studying this phenomenon will be reminded of the dissimulative state or phase of a patient attempting to play the role of a normal person, hiding his pathological reality although he continues to be sick or abnormal. Let us therefore use the term "*the dissimulative phase of pathocracy*" for the state of affairs wherein a pathocratic system ever more skillfully plays the role of a normal sociopolitical system with "different" doctrinal institutions.[33] In this

[32]For example, the post-Stalin "Khrushchev Thaw," followed by the Brezhnev years and Gorbachev's Perestroika; possibly also the Deng Xiaoping (1904–1997, in power 1978–1989) era following Mao in China. —Ed.

[33]In reference to the Soviet Union and the stabilization of its social hierarchies, Gorlizki and Khlevniuk write: "From the 1940s to the 1970s the country moved from being a repressive autocracy to an oligarchy with low to medium levels of repression. ... the composition of regional party and state administrations

phase, normal people within the country affected by this phenomenon become immune and adapt themselves to the situation, regaining to some extent the ability to act rationally. On the outside, however, this phase is marked by outstanding ponerogenic activity. The pathological material of this system can all too easily infiltrate into other societies, particularly if they are more primitive, and all the avenues of pathocratic expansion are facilitated because of the decrease of critical sensitivity of natural common sense on the part of the nations constituting the territory of expansionism.

Meanwhile, in the pathocratic country, the active structure of government rests in the hands of alienated and psychopathic individuals, and essential psychopathy plays a starring role. However, especially during the dissimulative phase, individuals with obvious pathological traits must be removed from certain areas of activity, namely political posts with international exposure, where such personalities could betray the pathological contents of the system. Such individuals would also be limited in their ability to perform diplomatic functions or to comprehend the political and economic landscape of normal countries. Therefore, the persons selected for such positions have thought processes more similar to the world of normal people; in general, they are sufficiently connected to the pathological system to provide a guarantee of loyalty. An expert in various psychological anomalies can nevertheless discern the discreet deviations upon which such links are based. Another factor linking such individuals to the system is the great personal advantages accorded to them by the pathocracy for their faithful service. Small wonder, then, that such loyalty is sometimes deceptive. This applies in particular to the sons of typical pathocrats, who of course enjoy trust because they have been reared to allegiance since infancy; if through some happy genetic coincidence they have not inherited pathological properties, their nature takes precedence over nurture. Like birds of a feather, normal people are drawn to life in the normal world; therefore the shortage of loyal followers will be a major weakness of every pathocracy throughout its existence.

Similar needs apply to other areas as well. The site manager appointed for a new factory is often someone barely connected with the

became more stratified, more status conscious, and more socially conservative" (*Substate Dictatorship*, pp. 4–5, 305). For details on the institutional changes that accompanied and facilitated this process, see their book. —Ed.

pathocratic system but whose skills are essential. Once the plant is operational, administration is taken over by party pathocrats, which often leads to its technical ruin. When such management brings a state farm to ruin, an agricultural engineer—who used to manage his own farm—is hired to restore it to a functional condition. The army similarly needs people endowed with perspicacity and essential qualifications, especially in the area of modern weapons. At crucial moments, healthy common sense can override the results of pathocratic military training.

During the dissimulative phase of the ruling system, many people adapt to the more bearable status quo, accepting it out of necessity, but not without criticism. They fulfill their duties amid doubts and conflicts of conscience, always searching for more sensible paths which they discuss within trusted circles. In effect, they are always hanging in a limbo between pathocracy on the one side, and the world of normal people and their own nature on the other. Unfortunately, these adaptations "get into the blood," becoming a habit, and form a second nature that will prove longer lasting than the pathocracy itself.

The following questions thus suggest themselves: what would happen if the network of like-minded psychopaths achieves power in all leadership positions, including those with international exposure? This can happen, especially during the later phases of the phenomenon. Goaded by their deviant character, such people thirst for just that, even though it ultimately conflicts with their own life interests. They do not take into account that this would lead to economic ruin and exposure of the pathological nature of the system, bringing the pathocracy to a catastrophe. However, they are for some time moderated in their zeal by the less pathological and more critical wing of the ruling apparatus. Germs also are not aware that they will be burned alive or buried deep in the ground along with the human body whose death they are causing.

If the many managerial positions are assumed by individuals deprived of sufficient abilities to feel and understand the majority of other people, and who also exhibit deficiencies in technical imagination and practical skills (faculties indispensable for governing economic and political matters), this then results in an exceptionally serious crisis in all areas, both within the country in question and with regard to international relations. Within, the situation becomes unbearable even for those citizens who were able to feather their nest into a relatively comfortable *modus vivendi.* Outside, other societies start to feel the pathological quality of the phenomenon quite distinctly. Such a state of affairs cannot last long. One must then be prepared for ever more rapid changes, and also behave with great circumspection.

***

Pathocracy is born from parasitizing great social movements, then becoming a disease of entire societies, nations, and empires. In the course of human history, it has affected social, political, and religious movements, distorting the accompanying ideologies, characteristic for the time and ethnological conditions, and turning them into caricatures of themselves. This occurs as a result of the activities of similar etiological factors in this phenomenon, namely the participation of pathological factors in a pathodynamically similar process. That explains why all the pathocracies of the world are and have been so similar in their essential properties. Contemporaneous ones easily find a common language, even if the ideologies nourishing them and protecting their pathological contents from identification differ widely.

Identifying these phenomena through history and properly classifying them according to their true nature and contents—not according to the ideology in question which succumbed to the characteristic process of caricaturization—is a job for historians equipped with the necessary criteria. Only a socially dynamic ideology that contains creative elements can nurture and protect an essentially pathological phenomenon from recognition and criticism for so long; only such an ideology can furnish it with the motivational tools of influence internally and for implementing its expansionist goals externally.

Defining the moment at which an ideological movement has been transformed into something we can call a pathocracy as a result of the ponerogenic process is a matter of convention. The process is temporally cumulative and reaches a point of no return at some particular moment. Eventually, however, internal confrontation with the adherents of the original ideology occurs, thus finally affixing the seal of the pathocratic character of the phenomenon.[34] Nazism most

[34]For example, Stalin's purges in the USSR and Spain of any communists or socialists (whether Marxist, Leninist, Trotskyists, or even Stalinists) who could disagree with him on anything. See, for example, Lynne Viola, *Stalinist*

certainly passed this point of no return, but was prevented from all-out confrontation with the adherents of the original ideology, as well as the downward-extending pathologization of life and the economy, because the Allied armies smashed its entire military might.[35] At that point the countries occupying West Germany began to introduce a system of normal man, and the Soviets introduced a pathocracy in East Germany, though based on a different ideology.[36] The latter found the fertile ground there, as the diversity of ideologies did not turn out to be an obstacle.

Pathocracy and Its Ideology

A great ideology with a mesmerizing vision and values can also easily deprive people of the capacity for self-critical control over their behavior. The adherents of such ideas tend to lose sight of the fact that the means used, not just the end, will be decisive for the result of their activities. Whenever they reach for overly radical methods of action, still convinced that they are serving their idea, they are not aware that their goal has already changed. The principle "the end justifies the means" opens the door to a different kind of person for whom a great idea is useful for purposes of liberating themselves from the uncomfortable chains of normal human custom, respect for mankind, and moral values. Every great ideology thus contains danger, especially for small minds. Therefore, every great social movement and its ideology can become a host upon which some pathocracy initiates its parasitic life.

The ideology in question may have been marked by deficits in truth and moral criteria from the very outset, or by the effects of activities by pathological factors. The original, very high-minded idea may also have succumbed to early contamination under the influence of a particular time and social circumstance. If such an ideology is infiltrated by foreign, local cultural material which, being

Perpetrators on Trial: Scenes from the Great Terror in Soviet Ukraine (2017). —Ed.

[35]While Nazism is often regarded as the epitome of political evil, Łobaczewski here argues that it did not have time to develop into a mature pathocracy. As Janowski writes: "The ultimate expression of totalitarianism was, of course, communism, which, unlike fascism, was its most perfect embodiment" (*Homo Americanus*, p. 228). —Ed.

[36]That is, communism as opposed to Nazism —Ed.

heterogeneous, destroys the original coherent structure of the idea, the actual value may become so enfeebled that it loses some of its attractiveness for reasonable people. Once weakened, however, the sociological structure can succumb to further degeneration, including the activation of pathological factors, until it has become transformed into its caricature: the name is the same, but different contents have been slipped in.

Differentiating the essence of the pathological phenomenon from its contemporary ideological host (both in its original and distorted forms) is thus a basic and necessary task, both for scientific-theoretical purposes and for finding practical solutions for the problems derived from the existence of the above-mentioned macrosocial phenomena. If, in order to designate a pathological phenomenon, we accept the name furnished by the ideology of a social movement which succumbed to degenerative poneric processes, we lose any ability to evaluate that ideology and its original contents, to understand the role of the distorted form, or to effect proper classification of the phenomenon. This error only appears to be semantic in nature; it actually becomes, as has been said, the keystone of all other comprehension errors regarding such phenomena, rendering us intellectually helpless, depriving us of our capacity for purposeful, practical action, and further protecting the pathocracy and its heirs from such a dangerous truth.

This error is based upon compatible propaganda elements of incompatible social systems. It has, unfortunately, become much too common and is reminiscent of the very first clumsy attempts to classify mental diseases according to the systems of delusions manifested by patients. Even today, people who have not received training in this field will consider a sick person who manifests sexual delusions to be crazy in this area, or someone with religious delusions to be afflicted with "religious mania." The author has even encountered a patient who insisted that he had become the object of cold and hot rays (paresthesia) on the basis of a special agreement concluded by the USA and the USSR.

As early as the end of the nineteenth century, famous pioneers of contemporary psychiatry correctly distinguished between the disease and the patient's system of delusions. A disease has its own etiological causes, whether identified or not, and its own pathodynamics and characteristic symptoms. Various delusional systems can become manifest within the same disease, and similar systems can appear in various diseases. The delusions, which have sometimes become so systemic that they convey the impression of an actual story, originate in the patient's nature and intelligence, and in the conditions of the environment in which he grew up and lived. These can also be disease-induced caricaturizations of his former political and social convictions. After all, every mental illness has its particular style of deforming human minds, producing nuanced but characteristic differences known for some time to psychiatrists, and which help them render a diagnosis.

Thus deformed, the world of former fantasies is put to work for a different purpose: concealing the dramatic state of the disease from one's own consciousness and from public opinion for as long as possible. An experienced psychiatrist does not attempt premature disillusionment of such a delusional system, which may otherwise trigger suicidal tendencies in the patient.[37] The doctor's main object of interest remains the disease he is trying to cure. There is usually insufficient time to discuss a patient's delusions with him unless it becomes necessary for reasons of the safety of said patient and other people. Once the disease has been cured, however, psychotherapeutic assistance in reintegrating the patient into the world of normal thought is definitely indicated.

If we effect a sufficiently penetrating analysis of the phenomenon of pathocracy and its relationship to its ideology, we are faced with a clear analogy to the above-described relationship now familiar to all psychiatrists. Some differences will appear later in the form of details and statistical data, which can be interpreted as a function of the above-mentioned characteristic style of caricaturizing an ideology which pathocracy effects, and as a result of the macrosocial character of the phenomenon.

As a counterpart of disease, pathocracy has its own etiological factors which make it potentially present in every society, no matter how healthy. It also has its own pathodynamic processes which are differentiated as a function of whether the pathocracy in question was born in that particular country (primary pathocracy), was artificially infected in the country by some other system of the kind, or was imposed by force. We have already sketched above the ponerogenesis

[37]For a case study, see Robins and Post, *Political Paranoia*, pp. 14–17, 80. They write: "The paranoid belief system is the structure that holds the paranoid together, his protection against psychological disintegration" (p. 82). —Ed.

and course of such a macrosocial phenomenon in its primary form, intentionally refraining from mentioning any particular ideology. We shall soon address the other two courses mentioned above. The ideology of pathocracy is created by caricaturizing the original ideology of a social movement in a manner characteristic of that particular pathological phenomenon. The above-mentioned hysteroidal states of societies also deform the contemporary ideologies of the times in question, using a style characteristic for them.[38]

Just as doctors are interested in disease, the author has become primarily interested in the pathocratic phenomenon and the analysis thereof. In a similar manner, the primary concern of those people who have assumed responsibility for the fate of nations should be curing the world of this heretofore mysterious disease and preventing its reappearance in the future. The proper time will come for critical and analytical attitudes toward ideologies which have become the "delusional systems" of such phenomena in historical and modern times. We should at present focus our attention upon the very essence of the macrosocial pathological phenomena, separate from its ideologies, as well as distinguishing between their original and pathological versions.

A pathocracy's ideology changes its function, just as occurs with a mentally ill person's delusional system. It stops being a human conviction outlining methods of action and takes on other duties which are not openly defined. It becomes a dogma concealing the diseased reality from people's critical consciousness, both inside and outside one's nation. Inside, the original function soon becomes ineffective for two reasons. On the one hand, daily life teaches those who live in such a country too many lessons about reality for them to believe in the ideology for long. On the other hand, the masses of common people notice the contemptuous attitude toward the ideology represented by the pathocrats themselves. For that reason, the main operational theater for the ideology consists of nations remaining outside the immediate ambit of the pathocracy, that naive world still

[38]See, for example, the analyses of early twentieth-century Marxism in Sowell, *Marxism*, ch. 10, and Leszek Kołakowski, *Main Currents of Marxism* (2005), bk. 2; and of contemporary liberal-democratic deformations by Rectenwald, McConkey, Pluckrose and Lindsay. Rectenwald argues that "Woke" social justice ideology weaponizes grievances, transforming them into the means by which to punish others and invert the existing social hierarchy (in *Beyond Woke* [2020], pp. 120–124). —Ed.

prone to being mesmerized by ideologies. The ideology thus becomes the instrument for external action to a degree even greater than in the above-mentioned relationship between the disease and its delusional system.

Understanding the nature of a disease is basic to any search for the proper methods of treatment. The same applies by analogy with regard to this macrosocial pathological phenomenon, especially since, in the latter case, *mere understanding of the nature of the disease starts curing human minds and souls.* Throughout the entire process, reasoning approximated to the style elaborated by medicine and psychology is the proper method which leads to untangling the contemporary Gordian knot.

Psychopaths are conscious of being different from the world of normal people. That is why the "political system" inspired by their nature and its secret ideology also conceal an awareness of being different. When we observe the role of the overt ideology in this macrosocial phenomenon, quite conscious of the existence of this specific awareness, then we will understand why ideology is relegated to an instrumental role—as something useful in dealing with those other naive people and nations. Pathocrats must nevertheless appreciate the function of ideology as being something essential in any ponerogenic group, especially in the semi-political system which is their "homeland." This factor of awareness simultaneously constitutes a certain qualitative difference between the two above-mentioned relationships.[39] Pathocrats are conscious of their secret ideology, which derives from their deviant natures, and therefore they treat the official ideology with barely concealed contempt.

This is also why a well-developed pathocratic system no longer has a clear and direct relationship to its original ideology—or even to its caricature—which it only keeps as its primary, traditional tool of action. For practical purposes of intrigue and pathocratic expansion in environments where one cannot count on a response to the traditional one, other ideologies may be useful, even if they contradict the main one and heap moral denunciation upon it. This was the method used by the Soviet pathocracy in America.[40] Ideologies built around

[39]That is, the relationship between pathocracy and its ideology within its geographical boundaries, and between the ideology and the outside world. —Ed.

[40]For example, from 1928 until 1958, the Soviet Comintern supported black self-determination groups in the U.S. See Braswell, "When the Soviet Union Tried to Woo Black America" (2017). In 1970 KGB Chairman Andropov

local themes are created with the aim of expanding pathocracy in the world. Racial, nationalist, or religious themes, rejected by the main ideology, prove to be useful in different parts of the world. Religious ideology was used in Vietnam, for example.[41] However, these other ideologies must be used with care, refraining from official acknowledgement within environments wherein the original ideology can be made to appear too foreign, discredited, and useless.

The main ideology succumbs to symptomatic deformation, in keeping with the characteristic style of this very disease and with what has already been stated about the matter. The names, slogans, and official contents are kept, but another, different content is insinuated underneath, thus giving rise to the well-known doublespeak phenomenon within which the same names have two meanings: one for initiates, one for everyone else. The latter is derived from the original ideology; the former has a specifically pathocratic meaning, something which is known not only to the pathocrats themselves, but also to those people living under long-term subjection to their rule. It should be noted here that similar doublespeak can also be found in other ideologies created to address ad hoc needs.

Doublespeak is only one of many symptoms. For example, it is necessary to point out the peculiar facility for producing new suggestive names and notions in such a manner as to drive William of Ockham to a nervous breakdown.[42] These suggestions are accepted virtually uncritically, in particular outside the immediate scope of

---

requested authorization to support and assist the Black Panthers in the U.S. in order to "bring definite difficulties to the ruling classes" and to distract the Nixon administration from its foreign policy. The Soviets also supported the 1980s peace movement (in addition to the work done through the World Peace Council). See Vladimir Bukovsky, *Judgment in Moscow: Soviet Crimes and Western Complicity* (2019), pp. 28–29, 406–426. There are also unproven allegations, including from GRU and KGB defectors, that they infiltrated the Vietnam antiwar movement in the 1960s and 1970s. —Ed.

[41]Ho Chi Minh's ideology, while officially rejecting Confucianism, was presented as a kind of "reformed" Confucianism. As Dustin Huddleston writes: "Ho Chi Minh successfully tapped into the Confucian ideology of the people to gain support and faith in the Vietnamese population. Ho also used Confucian doctrine to generate acceptance of socialism among the Vietnamese" (http://web.archive.org/web/20210519204901/www.units.miamioh.edu/vietnamcapstone/projects/DustinsProject.htm). —Ed.

[42]William of Ockham (1287–1347), English philosopher and theologian, whose views on parsimony or simplicity became known as "Occam's Razor," i.e., "entities should not be multiplied beyond necessity." —Ed.

such a system's rule.[43] One should bear in mind that such an ability is characteristic of most psychopathic and paranoid individuals and that these statements are paramoralistic in nature. The action of paralogisms and paramoralisms in this deformed ideology becomes comprehensible to us based on the information presented in Chapter IV. *Anything which threatens pathocratic rule becomes deeply immoral.*[44] This also applies to the concept of forgiving the pathocrats

[43]For example stock phrases (slogans, epithets, Marxist-Leninist quotations), technical vocabulary, countless "isms" (e.g., collaborationism, deviationism, groupism, rightism, utopism, etc.). See John Wesley Young, *Totalitarian Language: Orwell's Newspeak and Its Nazi and Communist Antecedents* (1991), esp. pp. 205–211, 247–248. Young writes: "So large is the number of neologisms in a country like the Soviet Union, and so unusual the style of their construction—many of them are contractions or abbreviations of several larger words—that some observers have claimed that a Communist revolution creates in effect a new language ... It is the combination of lies, Manichaean oversimplifications, perversions of meaning, judgmental definitions, elastic terminology, and other features that account for the inverted character of Communist discourse" (pp. 206, 207). For a case study of such language's pervasiveness in Czechoslovakia, see Věra Schmiedtová, "What Did the Totalitarian Language in the Former Socialistic Czechoslovakia Look Like?" (n.d.), and "A Small Dictionary of Life under Communist Totalitarian Rule (Czechoslovakia 1948–1989)" (2014). See also Victor Klemperer's classic, *The Language of the Third Reich* (2000); Andrews (ed.), *Legacies of Totalitarian Language*; Petre Petrov and Lara Ryazanova-Clarke (eds.), *The Vernaculars of Communism: Language, Ideology, and Power in the Soviet Union and Eastern Europe* (2015); and Ji Fengyuan, *Linguistic Engineering: Language and Politics in Mao's China* (2004).

While new euphemisms entered public discourse during the War on Terror (e.g., "extraordinary rendition," "collateral damage," and "enhanced interrogation techniques"), what sets totalitarian language apart is the sheer number and systematic omnipresence of such terms. In recent years this linguistic facility has exploded in the West. As Michael Rectenwald writes: "The terms proliferate almost as rapidly as the gender identities" (*Springtime for Snowflakes*, p. viii). Legutko provides an incomplete list: "Today one can be accused of racism, sexism, eurocentrism, euroscepticism, homophobia, transphobia, islamophobia, binarism, hate speech, logocentrism, patriarchy, phallocentrism, misogyny, ageism, speciesism, white supremacy, nationalism, illiberalism—and the list tends to grow" ("The Necessity of Opposition" [2021]). See also James Lindsay's *Translations from the Wokish* for an encyclopedia of contemporary social justice doublespeak. —Ed.

[44]In communist doublespeak, for example, words such as "the People," "socialist," "worker," etc., always had positive connotations, but "reactionary," "capitalistic," "bourgeois," "counter-revolutionary," etc., always had extremely negative connotations. See the papers by Schmiedtová cited in the previous note. While American President George W. Bush infamously paramoralized,

themselves; it is disempowering and thus extremely dangerous to the survival of such a system.

We thus have the right to ignore all this new nomenclature and to invent appropriate names which would indicate the nature of the phenomena as accurately as possible, in keeping with our recognition and respect for the laws of scientific methodology and semantics. Such accurate terms will also serve to protect our minds from the suggestive effects of those other deliberately manufactured names and paralogisms, including the pathological material the latter contain. The author exercises this obvious right for his own benefit and for the benefit of his readers.

The Expansion of Pathocracy

The world's tendency to fasten its gaze upon its rulers has a long tradition dating back to the times when sovereigns could virtually ignore their subjects' opinions. However, rulers have always been dependent upon the situation in their country, even long ago, and even more so in pathocratic systems, and the influence of various social groups has reached their thrones by various means.

Much too common is the pattern of error which reasons that purportedly autocratic leaders of countries affected by this pathocracy actually possess decision-making powers in areas where they in fact do not. Millions of people, including ministers and members of parliaments, ponder the dilemma of whether such a ruler could not, under certain circumstances, modify his convictions somewhat, relinquish his dreams of conquering the world, and direct attention and resources towards the welfare of his citizens; they continue to hope that this will be the eventual outcome. People with personal experience in such a system may attempt to persuade such people that their ideas, although decent, lack a foundation in reality, but at the same time they sense a lack of concrete arguments to explain the matter. Such an explanation is in fact impossible within the realm of the natural language of psychological concepts; only an objective comprehension of the pathological phenomenon permits light to be shed upon the

"You are either with us, or with the terrorists," the use of paramoralisms has increased exponentially since then, most often in the service of critical social justice theory, e.g., sexist, racist, transphobic, fascist, white supremacist, domestic terrorist, etc. —Ed.

causes of the perennial imperialism of every pathocracy and by implication the deceitfulness of their leaders' promises of peace.

This macrosocial pathological phenomenon affects an entire society, starting with the leaders and infiltrating every village, small town, factory, or collective farm. The pathological social structure gradually covers the entire country, creating a "new class" within that nation.[45] This privileged class feels permanently threatened by the "others," i.e., by the majority of normal people. Neither do the pathocrats entertain any illusions about their personal fate should there be a return to the system of normal man.[46]

A normal person deprived of his property, privileges, or high position takes a job that will provide an income, and after a while develops some level of prosperity; but pathocrats usually don't possess any solid practical talent, and the time frame of their rule eliminates any residual possibilities of adapting to the demands of normal work. Since they are incapable of this kind of sacrifice, the survival of a system which is the best for them becomes a self-evident moral value. If the laws of normal man were to be reinstated, they and theirs could be subjected to judgment, including a moralizing interpretation of their psychological deviations; they would be threatened by a loss of freedom and life, not merely of position and privilege. Such a threat must be battled by means of psychological and political cunning implemented with a lack of scruples with regard to those other "inferior-quality" people.

---

[45]See Milovan Djilas, *The New Class: An Analysis of the Communist System* (1957), and Michael Voslensky, *Nomenklatura: The Soviet Ruling Class* (1984). For a history of this new class told through the vehicle of the giant Moscow apartment complex which housed many of them, see Yuri Slezkine's *The House of Government: A Saga of the Russian Revolution* (2017). Harold D. Lasswell writes: "A revolution is a shift in the class composition of elites. ... World revolutions have been accompanied by sudden shifts in the ruling vocabulary of the elite. ... From the 'divine right of kings' to the 'rights of man,' from the 'rights of man' to the 'proletarian dictatorship'; these have been the principal vocabulary changes in the political history of the modern world. In each case a language of protest, long a utopian hope, became the language of an established order, an ideology. The ruling elite elicited loyalty, blood, and taxes from the populace with new combinations of vowels and consonants" (*Political Writings*, pp. 392, 393). —Ed.

[46]Witness the fate of former dictator of communist Romania Nicolae Ceaușescu (1918–1989), who was overthrown, sentenced to death after a one-hour show trial, and executed by firing squad along with his wife in December 1989. See Frank Dikötter, *How to Be a Dictator: The Cult of Personality in the Twentieth Century* (2019), pp. 166–185; and Moscovici, *Velvet Totalitarianism*, p. 7. —Ed.

In general, this new class is in the position to purge its leaders should their behavior jeopardize the existence of such a system.[47] This could occur particularly if the leadership wished to go too far in compromising with the society of normal people, since their qualifications make them essential for production. Such compromises pose a more direct threat to the more numerous and influential middle echelons of the pathocratic elite structure than to the leaders,[48] and also threaten an intensification of the bottom-up depathologization of the system. Pathocracy survives thanks to the feeling of being threatened by the society of normal people, as well as by other countries wherein various forms of the system of normal man persist. For the rulers, staying on the top is therefore the classic problem of "to be or not to be."

We can thus formulate a more cautious question: Can such a system ever waive territorial and political expansion abroad and settle for its present possessions?[49] What would happen if such a state of affairs ensured internal peace, corresponding order, and relative prosperity within the nation? The overwhelming majority of the country's population would then make skillful use of all the emerging possibilities, taking advantage of their superior qualifications and increased resources in order to fight for an ever-increasing scope of activities; thanks to their higher birth rate, their power will increase. This majority will be joined by some sons from the privileged class who did not inherit the pathological genes. The pathocracy's dominance will weaken imperceptibly but steadily, finally leading to a situation wherein the society of normal people reaches for power. Every pathocratic heart trembles before such a nightmarish vision.

Thus, the biological, psychological, moral, and economic destruction of this ever-threatening majority becomes a "biological" necessity for the pathocrats. Many means serve this end, starting with the maintenance of extreme poverty and including concentration camps as well as warfare with an obstinate, well-armed foe who will dev-

---

[47] See Gorlizki and Khlevniuk, *Substate Dictatorship*, for a description and analysis of the patronage system of the Soviet Nomenklatura, including the means by which regional leaders were kept in check (e.g., overpromotion, informal and political exclusion, kompromat), and the reasons for their removal (e.g., scandal, amoral behavior, incompetence, natural turnover). —Ed.

[48] Because they are the ones most often inclined to make such compromises, as middlemen between the "new class" and the normal majority. —Ed.

[49] See, for example, Aristotle A. Kallis, *Fascist Ideology: Territory and Expansionism in Italy and Germany, 1922–1945* (2000). —Ed.

astate and debilitate the human power thrown at him—namely the very power jeopardizing pathocrats' rule.[50] Many people will die, many others will lose their strength and health. Once safely dead, the soldiers will then be decreed heroes to be revered in paeans (by poets ordered to do so), useful for raising a new generation faithful to the pathocracy.[51]

Any war waged by a pathocratic nation has two fronts: the internal and the external. The internal front is more important for the leaders and the governing elite, and the internal threat is the deciding factor where unleashing war is concerned. In pondering whether to start a war against the pathocratic country, other nations must therefore give primary consideration to the fact that such a war can be used as an executioner of the common people whose increasing power represents incipient jeopardy for the pathocracy. After all, pathocrats give short shrift to the blood and suffering of people they consider to be not quite conspecific. Kings may have suffered due to the death of their knights, but pathocrats never do: "We have a lot of people here."[52] Should the situation be, or become, ripe in such a country, however, anyone furnishing assistance to the nation will be blessed by it; anyone withholding it will be cursed.

Pathocracy has other internal reasons for pursuing expansionism through the use of all means possible. As long as that "other" world governed by the systems of normal man exists, it induces into the

[50]As Orwell fictionalized in *1984*'s perpetual war between Oceania and Eastasia and Eurasia. If not attacked from without, events can be manipulated, exploited, or manufactured for a *casus belli*. For example, the Nazis used false-flag terrorism as a pretext for invading Poland in 1939 with the Gleiwitz Incident (the Reichstag fire is also widely believed to have been a false flag, though this has never been proven). —Ed.

[51]*Author's note (1997):* By starting the war, Hitler saved the existence of the Soviet pathocracy for at least 40 years. [The USSR suffered around 27 million deaths in WWII. —Ed.]

[52]Mao Zedong's personal physician quotes him as saying, "We have so many people. We can afford to lose a few. What difference does it make?" Another, from Jung and Halliday's biography: "We are prepared to sacrifice 300 million Chinese for the victory of the world revolution." For more, see "Mao and Terror: Mao's Glorification of Political Mass Murder – Documentary Quotations," worldfuturefund.org. On the cult of martyrdom in Islamism, Mozaffari writes: "Death in the path of Allah is celebrated and recognized as the highest degree of felicity that a Muslim can achieve. Worldly life has no value in itself. It becomes valuable only if and when it is spent on Allah's recommended duties. Martyrdom stands as the most glorious duty. ... Therefore, war finds quite new significance in the eyes of Islamists" (*Islamism*, p. 273). —Ed.

strivings of the non-pathological majority a certain sense of direction. The non-pathological majority of the country's population will never stop dreaming of the reinstatement of the normal man's system in any possible form. This majority will never stop watching other countries, waiting for the opportune moment; its attention and power must therefore be distracted from this purpose, and the masses must be "educated" and channeled in the direction of imperialist strivings. This goal must be pursued doggedly so that everyone knows what is being fought for and in whose name harsh discipline and poverty must be endured. The latter factor effectively limits the possibility of "subversive" activities on the part of the society of normal people.

The ideology must, of course, furnish a corresponding justification for this alleged right to conquer the world and must therefore be properly concocted. Expansionism is derived from the very nature of pathocracy, not from ideology, but this fact must be masked by ideology. Whenever this phenomenon has been witnessed in history, imperialism was always its most demonstrative quality.

On the other hand, there are countries with governments of normal man wherein the overwhelming majority of societies shudder to think a similar system could be imposed on them. The governments of such nations try to contain this expansionism using whatever means and understanding of the phenomenon available to them. The citizens of those countries would sigh with relief if some upheaval were to replace this malevolent and incomprehensible system with a more human, more easily understood, governmental system with whom peaceful coexistence would be possible.[53]

Such countries thus undertake various means of action for this purpose, their quality depending on the possibility of understanding that other reality. Such efforts resonate within the country, and the military power of normal man's countries limits the pathocracy's possibilities of armed maneuvers. Weakening these countries, especially by utilizing the response pathocracy awakens in some of their deviant citizens, again becomes a matter of the pathocracy's survival.

[53] *Author's note (1997):* The citizens of these countries breathed a sigh of relief when the process of depathologization began in the former Soviet Union. But the elimination of pathocracy and the formation of a normal human system is a difficult and turbulent process that requires a considerable amount of time. Only skillful action based on an understanding of the nature of the pathological phenomenon could regulate and accelerate this process.

Economic factors constitute a non-negligible part of the motivation for this expansionist tendency. Since the managerial functions have been taken over by individuals with mediocre intelligence and pathological character traits, the pathocracy becomes incapable of properly administering anything at all. The area suffering most severely must always be whichever one requires a person to act independently, not wasting time searching for the proper way to behave. Agriculture is dependent upon changing climate conditions and the appearance of pests and plant diseases, so the farmer must act quickly. Thus, a farmer's personal qualities have been an essential factor of success in this area, as it was for many centuries. Pathocracy therefore invariably brings about food shortages.

However, many countries with normal man's systems abound in sufficiency of industrial products and experience problems with food *surpluses* even though they experience temporary economic recessions and the citizens are by no means overworked. The temptation to dominate such a country and its prosperity, that perennial imperialist motive, thus becomes even stronger.[54] The collected prosperity of the conquered nation can be exploited for a time, the citizens forced to work harder for paltry remuneration. For the moment, no thought is given to the fact that introducing a pathocratic system within such a country will eventually cause similar unproductive conditions; after all, a corresponding self-knowledge in this area is non-existent for pathocrats. Unfortunately, the idea of conquering rich countries also motivates the minds of many poor *non*-pathological fellows who would like to use this opportunity to grab something for themselves and eat their fill of good food.

As has been the case for centuries, military power is of course the primary means for achieving these ends. Throughout the centuries, though, whenever history has registered the appearance of pathocracy (regardless of the ideological cloak covering it), specific measures of influence have also become apparent—something in the order of specific intelligence in the service of international intrigue facilitating conquest. This quality is derived from the above-discussed personality characteristics inspiring the overall phenomenon; it should constitute data for historians to identify this type of phenomenon throughout history.

[54]The Polish is slightly different: "Taking possession of such goods poses a great temptation not only to governments, but also to ordinary citizens who would want to take advantage of it." —Ed.

People exist everywhere in the world whose personalities show a peculiar susceptibility; even a faraway pathocracy evokes a resonating response in them, a feeling flowing from the depths of their natures that "there is a place for people like us there." Uncritical, frustrated, and disadvantaged people also exist everywhere, and they can be reached by appropriately elaborated propaganda.[55] The future of a nation is greatly dependent on how many such people it contains. Thanks to its special psychological knowledge and its conviction that normal people are naive, a pathocracy is able to improve its "anti-psychotherapeutic" techniques and to insinuate its deviant world of concepts to these others, doing so with the usual pathological egotism.

The most frequently used methods include paralogistic and conversive methods such as the projection of one's own qualities and intentions onto other persons, social groups, or nations; paramoral indignation; and reversive blockades. This last method is a pathocratic favorite used on the mass scale, driving the minds of average people into a dead end because, as a result, it causes them to search for the truth in the "golden mean" between the reality and its opposite.

We should thus point out that although various works in the area of psychopathology contain descriptions of most of these methods of deception,[56] an overall summary filling in the gaps is absent and sorely needed. How much better it would be if the people and governments of normal man's countries could take advantage of such a work and behave like an experienced psychologist. One could write down the accusations made against those countries due to the pathocracy projecting its own properties onto them; with a few analytical cosmetic changes we would then obtain a blueprint of the pathocratic empire's intentions for a very low cost. Similarly, one could also invert statements with reversive blockades to arrive at a close approximation of the truth.[57]

---

[55] Susceptibility to indoctrination remains understudied. See *Indoctrinability, Ideology, and Warfare: Evolutionary Perspectives* (1998), edited by Irenäus Eibl-Eibesfeldt and Frank Kemp Salter. —Ed.

[56] For example, Simon, *In Sheep's Clothing* and *Character Disturbance.* —Ed.

[57] In 2004, British columnist John O'Sullivan wrote: "Vladimir Bukovsky, the great anti-Soviet dissident, once reproved me for quoting the old joke about the two main official Soviet newspapers: 'There's no truth in *Pravda* [Truth] and no news in *Izvestia* [News.]' He pointed out that you could learn a great deal of truthful news from both papers if you read them with proper care. In particular, they often denounced 'anti-Soviet lies.' These lies had never previously been reported by them. Nor were they lies. And their exposure as such was the first

Law has become the measure of right conduct within the countries of normal human systems. We often forget how imperfect a creation of human minds it really is, how dependent all laws are on formulations based upon only those premises adequately known and understood by legislators. In legal theory, we accept its regulatory nature as a given and consequently agree that in certain cases its activities may not be quite concurrent with human reality. Law conceived in such a manner furnishes an insufficient foundation for counteracting a phenomenon whose character lies outside of the limits of legislators' knowledge and imagination, so its nature remains beyond the scope of adequate legal qualification. Quite the contrary: pathocracy knows how to take advantage of the weaknesses of such a legalistic manner of thinking.[58]

However, this macrosocial phenomenon's internal actions and external expansion are in fact based upon psychological data, regardless of how these data are deformed within the pathocrats' personalities in line with that special psychological knowledge of theirs. As such, it prevails over the legal systems of normal man due to its vastly superior cunning. This makes pathocracy a caricature of the social system of the future. After all, the future *should* belong to social systems which are based on a continuously improving comprehension of man's nature. Evolution proceeding in this direction can, among other things, ensure greater resistance to the expansionary methods this macrosocial phenomenon uses in its quest to dominate the world

---

that readers had been told of them. By reading the denunciation carefully, however, intelligent readers could decipher what the original story must have been. It was a roundabout way of getting information—but it worked. That is exactly how intelligent readers now have to read the *New York Times* and most of the establishment media" (*National Review*, Sept. 7, 2004). On the continued relevance of this advice, see Taibbi, "Sovietization of the American Press." —Ed.

[58]Even jailed psychopaths are able to game the system: "Porter found that the psychopaths were roughly 2.5 times more likely to be conditionally released than non-psychopaths. ... Porter suggests these results may be because the psychopath is able to use his finely honed skills of deception and manipulation to convince prison officials to release him early. It seems prison mental health experts and parole boards are no less immune than the rest of us to being fooled by the psychopath's mask of sanity" (Kiehl and Hoffman, "The Criminal Psychopath"). Oakley writes: "Altruists who draw up rules and legislation to deter Machiavellian behavior are often surprised to find their policy turned on its head and used by Machiavellians for fruitless investigations" (*Evil Genes*, p. 335). —Ed.

and to the danger of its re-emergence. Psychological methods of conquest must be countered with psychological means of defense. The basis of such a defense, or healing a nation liberating itself from this condition, is always an understanding of the nature of this terrible disease.

Imposed Pathocracies

The genesis of pathocracy in any country is so lengthy a process that it is difficult to pinpoint when it began. The original ideology, whether it was born earlier as an ideology of a social movement, or was conceived and deliberately inspired by external forces, will remain a part of the pathocracy for a long time, nourishing it, hiding the pathological nature of the phenomenon from human consciousness, and succumbing to the previously described process of caricaturization. Such a pathocracy thus bears all the features of a secondary ponerogenic association.

If we take into consideration those historical examples which should be qualified in that regard, we will most frequently observe the figure of an autocratic ruler whose intellectual mediocrity and infantile personality finally opened the door to the ponerogenesis of the phenomenon.[59] Wherever a society's common sense is sufficiently influential, its self-preservation instinct is able to overcome this ponerogenic process rather early. Things are different when an active nucleus of this disease already exists and can dominate by means of infection or the imposition of force.

Whenever a nation experiences a "system crisis" or a hyperactivity of ponerogenic processes within, it becomes the object of a pathocratic penetration whose purpose is to serve up the country as booty. It will then become easy to take advantage of its internal weaknesses and revolutionary movements in order to impose rule on the basis of

[59] See the discussion in Chapter IV under "Acquired Deviations." The Polish edition (pp. 137–138) contains what appears to be an alternate version of some of the ideas in this section. It adds the following idea: "The indifference of the privileged and the lack of social bonds between them and the exploited plebs create division and hostility, increasing the risk of revolution. As a result, a pathological structure, in which abnormal individuals begin to play an increasing role on both sides of the barricades, develops gradually from generation to generation." He gives the examples or pre-revolutionary France and Russia where this was the case. —Ed.

a limited use of force. This will be an artificially infected pathocracy, which bears characteristics that are a fusion of both secondary and primary ponerogenic associations.

Conditions such as a great war or temporary weakness in a country whose system did not exhibit such wide-scope infirmities earlier can sometimes cause it to submit to the violence of a pathocratic neighbor country (against their will). Such a pathocracy will predominantly show characteristics of a primary ponerogenic association. Its system of power will immediately crystallize around deviant personalities, and essential psychopathy will play a leading role from the very beginning. After forcible imposition of such a system the course of pathologization of life becomes different; such a pathocracy will be less stable but more repugnant, its very existence dependent upon the factor of never-ending outside force.

Pathocracy imposed by force

Let us now address the latter situation first.[60] Brute force must first crush the resistance of an exhausted nation. People possessing military or leadership skills must be exterminated, imprisoned, or forced into silence. Anyone appealing to moral values and legal principles like the natural rights of man and nation must also be silenced. The new principles are never explicitly enunciated.[61] People must learn the new unwritten law via painful experience. All this is done in the name of wonderful ideas in which their preachers themselves do not believe.[62] The stultifying influence of this deviant world of concepts finishes the job, killing people's hope, but common sense and self-preservation demand caution and endurance.

This is followed by the shock of something seemingly unthinkable, almost unreal and tragic: some people from every social group, whether disadvantaged paupers, aristocrats, officials, literati, stu-

[60]The primary examples are the nations invaded and occupied by Germany and the USSR during World War II. —Ed.

[61]Janowski writes: "Law is no longer law, but a codex of positive regulations instituted for the *ad hoc* needs of stopping undesirable behavior whenever it surfaces. The collective's understanding of itself does not need to be explicit or consciously articulated (in most cases it is not, but is presumed and fluid), and so ideology does not need to be articulated either" (*Homo Americanus*, p. 136). —Ed.

[62]See, for example, Nicholas O'Shaughnessy, *Selling Hitler: Propaganda and the Nazi Brand* (2016). —Ed.

dents, scientists, priests, atheists, or nobodies known to no one, suddenly start changing their personality and worldview. Decent people and patriots just yesterday, they now espouse the new ideology and behave contemptuously to anyone still adhering to the old values, faith in God, or patriotism. Only later does it become evident that this ostensibly avalanche-like process has its natural limits. With time, the society becomes stratified based on factors entirely different from the old political convictions, wealth, or social status. We already know the causes for this, but they were not understood by anyone at the time.[63]

Through direct contact with the phenomenon, society simultaneously begins to sense that its true content is significantly different from the notions disseminated earlier, while the country was still independent. This divergence is another traumatizing factor, because it calls into question the value of beliefs once accepted with confidence and popularized in a sovereign country, deepening the sense of powerlessness. Years must pass before the mind has adapted to the new concepts and people become familiar with new reality in practical terms. When those of us who have experienced this then travel to Western Europe, or especially to the United States, people who keep to the old system of notions and have an egotistical trust in it strike us as being naïve and arrogant.

Pathocracy imposed by force arrives in a finished form; we could even call it ripe. People observing it close up were unable to distinguish the earlier phases of its development, when the schizoids and characteropaths were in charge. The need for the existence of these phases and their character had to be reconstructed in this work on the basis of historical and theoretical data, which is not the same as direct observation.

In an imposed system, psychopathic material is already dominant; it was perceived as something contrary to human nature, virtually bereft of the mask of ideology rendered ever less necessary in a conquered country, but nevertheless still masked by its incomprehensibility to people still thinking in the categories of the natural psychological worldview. This gave rise to a painful sense of the inadequacy of our old way of thinking for the purposes of comprehending the reality which had overwhelmed us. The objective categories es-

[63] *Author's note (1997):* About six percent of a given population sided with the pathocracy and became active.

sential for this understanding would not be created until many years of effort had passed.

In the meantime, individuals with the above-described deviant characteristics unerringly sensed that the time had come for their dreams of power to come true—the time to exact revenge upon those "others" who had humiliated and condemned them in the name of those moral principles of theirs. This violent formative process of pathocracy lasted barely eight years or so, thereupon making a similarly accelerated transformation into the dissimulative phase.[64]

In a country upon which a quasi-political structure has been imposed, the new system's functions, psychological mechanisms, and mysterious causal links are essentially analogous to those of the country which gave rise to the phenomenon. The system spreads downward until it reaches every village and every human individual. The actual contents and internal causes of this phenomenon also manifest no essential difference, regardless of whether we make our observation in the capital or in some outlying small town. If the entire organism is sick, diagnostic biopsy tissue can be collected wherever this can be performed most expediently. Those living in countries with normal human systems who attempt to understand this other system by penetrating with their imagination the walls of the Kremlin which conceal the intentions of the highest authorities, do not realize that this is a very onerous and unreliable method. In order to perceive the essence of the phenomenon, we can more easily situate ourselves in

[64]For Poland, the period from approximately 1948 to 1956 (the "Polish October" thaw). See Applebaum, *Iron Curtain*, for a history of this time and the tactics used, including "a new wave of arrests; the expansion of labor camps; much tighter control over the media, intellectuals, and the arts. Certain patterns were followed almost everywhere: first the elimination of 'right-wing' or anticommunist parties, then the destruction of the noncommunist left, then the elimination of opposition within the communist party itself" (p. xxxi, chs. 11–18). However, even prior to the imposition of the one-party system—as early as 1945 to 1946—the Soviets had already been using some of the techniques described below ("Artificially Infected Pathocracy"). The features that distinguished the imposition of pathocracy in Eastern Europe from political and revolutionary warfare elsewhere, however, included the creation of a Soviet-dominated secret police force to target political enemies (as well as occupying key government positions); taking total control of radio broadcasts (and significant control of print media); infiltrating, harassing, and banning youth and civic organizations (not even chess clubs were spared); the presence of the Red Army; and (where possible) engaging in mass ethnic cleansing. —Ed.

a small town, where it is much easier to peek backstage and analyze the nature of such a system.

However, some of the differences between the nature of the pathocratic phenomenon in its country of origin and in the country on which it is forcibly imposed turn out to be permanent. In the latter, the system's pathological properties are immediately more obvious. The system will always strike the society that has been taken over as something foreign associated with the other country and its brute force. The society's historical tradition and culture constitute a pillar for those strivings aimed in the direction of normal man's structures. The more mature cultural formations in particular prove to be the most highly resistant to the system's destructive activities. The subjugated nation finds support and inspiration for its psychological and moral resistance in its own historical, cultural, religious, and moral traditions.

These values, elaborated through centuries, cannot easily be destroyed or co-opted by pathocracy; quite the contrary, they even embark upon a more intensive life in the new society. These values progressively cleanse themselves of patriotic buffoonery, and their principal contents become more real in their eternal meaning. If forced by necessity, the culture of the country in question is concealed in private homes or disseminated via conspiracy; however, it continues to survive and develop, creating values which could not have arisen during happier times. As a result, such a society's opposition becomes ever more enduring, ever more skillfully effected. It is reinforced by ever more practical knowledge of the characteristics of such a bizarre system and by specific psychological and moral experience. What it does not acquire is a theoretical foundation for this resistance, of the kind presented in this work.

It turns out that those who believed they could impose such a system, trusting that it would then function on the pathocracy's self-operating mechanisms, were overly optimistic. Imposed pathocracy always remains an alien system to the extent that, if it should fall in the country of its birth, its endurance within the subjugated nation would only be a matter of weeks.[65]

[65] *Author's note (1997):* This is what happened.

Artificially infected pathocracy

If a nucleus of this macrosocial pathological phenomenon already exists in the world, always cloaking its true quality behind an ideological mask of some political system, it irradiates into other nations via coded news difficult for normal people to understand, but easy to read for psychopathic individuals. "That's the place for us, we now have a homeland where our dreams about ruling those 'others' can come true. We can finally live in safety and prosperity." The more powerful this nucleus and the pathocratic nation, the wider the scope of its inductive siren-call, heard by individuals whose nature is correspondingly deviant, as though they were superheterodyne receivers[66] naturally attuned to the same wavelength. Unfortunately, what is being used today are real radio transmitters in the hundreds of kilowatts, as well as loyal covert agents networking our planet.

Whether directly or indirectly—i.e., by means of the above-mentioned agents—this call of pathocracy, once appropriately "decked-out" for the needs of various ethnic groups, reaches a significantly wider circle of people, including both individuals with various psychological deviations and those who are frustrated, deprived of the opportunity to earn an education and make use of their talents, physically or morally injured, or simply primitive. The scope of the response to this call may vary in proportion, but nowhere will it represent the majority. Nonetheless, the home-bred spellbinders who arise never take into account the fact that they are not able to enrapture the majority.[67]

Various nations' different degrees of resistance to this activity depend upon many cultural and economic factors, such as prosperity

[66] Advanced analog radio receiver technology still used today in many radios. —Ed.

[67] The most obvious example of recent years has been the ponerogenic siren call of the Islamic State, sent not over radio but the Internet (social media). Tens of thousands of susceptible individuals from around the world responded to the call to fight and die in Iraq and Syria. On their ideology, see Shiraz Maher, *Salafi-Jihadism: The History of an Idea* (2016), and Haroro J., Ingram et al., *The ISIS Reader: Milestone Texts of the Islamic State Movement* (2020). For a similar though less overtly brutal dynamic on the part of liberal democracy (especially in its current "social justice" form), see Legutko, *Demon in Democracy.* Though written with Soviet revolutionary and political warfare in mind, this subchapter is now directly applicable to the foreign interventionism ("democracy promotion," "color revolution" tactics, "responsibility to protect" military invasions) of the U.S. and its allies. —Ed.

and its equitable distribution, the society's educational level (especially that of the poorer classes), the proportion of participation of individuals who are primitive or have various deviations, and the current phase of the hysteroidal cycle. Some nations have developed immunity as a result of more direct contact with the phenomenon, something we shall discuss in the next chapter.

In countries just emerging from primitive conditions and lacking political experience, an appropriately elaborated revolutionary doctrine reaches the autochthonous soil of the population and into the hands of people who treat it like a certain kind of ideological reality. This also occurs in nations where an over-egoistical ruling class defends its position by means of naively moralizing doctrines,[68] where lawlessness is rampant, or where an intensification of the hysteria level stifles the operation of common sense. People who have become enamored with revolutionary slogans no longer watch to make sure that whoever expounds such an ideology is a truly sincere adherent, and not just someone using the mask of ideology to conceal other motives derived from his deviant personality or from the different foundations of their secret doctrine or "morality."

In addition to these spellbinders, we can find another kind of preacher of revolutionary ideas, one whose status is basically linked to the money he receives for his activities. However, it is unlikely that its ranks include people who could be characterized as psychologically normal with no reservations on the basis of the above-mentioned criteria. Their indifference to the human suffering caused by their own activities is derived from deficiencies in their perceived value of societal links or in their capacity to foresee the results of their activities. In ponerogenic processes, moral deficiencies, intellectual failings, and pathological factors intersect in a spatio-temporal causative network giving rise to individual and national suffering. Any war waged with psychological weapons costs only a fraction as much as classical warfare, but it does have a cost, especially when it is being waged simultaneously in many countries throughout the world.[69]

---

[68]See, for example, McConkey, *Managerial Class*, pp. 37–49; and Legutko, *The Cunning of Freedom: Saving the Self in an Age of False Idols* (2021), ch. 9, where he compares the notion of aristocracy with distortions such as *hereditary* aristocracy, where social status is grounded in birthright, somehow entitling its members a privileged moral position in society. —Ed.

[69]For a concise overview, see Dickey et al., "Russian Political Warfare: Origin, Evolution, and Application," sections II–III: "Operations ranged from

People acting in the name of pathocracy's interests may effect their activities in parallel, under the banner of the official ideology, some other suitably crafted ideology, or even with the assistance of a contradictory ideology battling the official one. In these latter cases, the service must be performed by individuals whose response to the call of the pathocracy is sufficiently vehement so as to prevent the self-suggestive activities of the other ideology they are using from weakening the links with their actual hopes for power.

Whenever a society contains serious social problems, there will also be some group of sensible people striving to improve the social situation by means of energetic reforms, so as to eliminate the cause of social tension. Others consider it their duty to bring about a moral rejuvenation of society. Elimination of social injustice and reconstruction of the country's morals and civilization would deprive a pathocracy of any chance to take over. Such reformers and moral-

---

basic intelligence collection and analysis to subversion, media manipulation, propaganda, forgeries, political repression, political assassinations, agents of influence, the establishment of opposition parties and criminal organizations, antiwar movements and front organizations, and proxy paramilitary operations" (p. 47). While there was no Soviet PW manual, the same methods were used throughout Eastern Europe immediately after WWII (though with the addition of overt Red Army presence and Soviet influence), recreating the phases of ponerogenesis in the target nation, including violent purges (pp. 50–53). See Applebaum's *Iron Curtain* for a narrative account. See also Thomas Rid, *Active Measures: The Secret History of Disinformation and Political Warfare* (2020); Bukovsky, *Judgment in Moscow*, and the Bukovsky Archives online (https://bukovsky-archive.com/). During the Cold War, the CIA engaged in similar operations. Dickey et al. write: "winning the sociopolitical narrative across the globe necessitated discrediting the principles of Soviet communism, especially among Third World nationalist movements fighting Western colonialism. Where socialist and communist ideologies were firmly entrenched or beginning to threaten national interests, the United States adopted more aggressive policies. These often conflicted with 'American principles of Democracy, anti-colonialism and national self-determination,' by directly interfering in the social and political fabric of states, often supporting colonial powers or dictatorial regimes and subverting democratic movements." American political warfare tools included "coercive state diplomacy, public diplomacy and psychological warfare, conventional and nuclear military posturing and paramilitary activity, covert action, and influence through economic statecraft" (pp. 87–88). For correctives to the contemporary political agendas evident in the above authors, see David J. Blake, *Loaded for Guccifer 2.0* (2020); Sandor Fabian, "The Russian Hybrid Warfare Strategy – Neither Russian nor Strategy" (2019); Alex Krainer, *Grand Deception* (2018); Ben Norton, "Behind NATO's 'Cognitive Warfare': Battle for Your Brain Waged by Western Militaries" (2021); Patrick Lawrence, "The Casualties of Empire" (2022). —Ed.

ists must therefore be consistently neutralized by means of liberal or conservative positions—e.g., as defenders of the disadvantaged, civil liberties, liberalism, or hedonism—and appropriately suggestive catchwords and paramoralisms; if necessary, the best among them has to be murdered.

Psychological warfare strategists must decide rather early on which ideology would be most efficient in a particular country because of its adaptability to said nation's conditions and traditions. After all, the appropriately adapted ideology must perform the function of a Trojan horse, transporting pathocracy into the country. Only a few people discover the real ideology of conquest and the true task of this instrumental ideology. Those who do so consider themselves superior because they possess knowledge not available to others. These various ideologies are then gradually conformed to one's own original master plan. Finally, off comes the mask.[70]

At the right time, these people are deployed to form a local revolutionary organization, with recruits picked from disgruntled localities, abnormal individuals, as well as common thugs. Local militias are organized and armed, commanded by trained officer–agents familiar with the secret doctrine as well as the operative ideology concocted for propagation in the country in question. Those agents share a characteristic contempt for those whom they command and whom they deceive. Assistance must then be given so groups of trusted conspirators adhering to the concocted ideology can stage a coup d'état, whereupon an iron-fisted government is installed and so-called justice reigns. Once this has been brought about, the diversionary guerrilla

[70]For example, the KGB supported various socialist and liberationist groups and ideologies in the Third World, often without their members' knowledge. The CIA has also supported contradictory ideologies and groups. The example with the most far-reaching consequences has been the covert program in support of the mujahedeen against the Soviets in Afghanistan. In their fight against communism, the U.S. and its allies in fact supported a rival ponerogenic totalitarian movement, and have continued to do so even after 9/11. For example, former U.S. ambassador James Jeffrey has referred to al-Qaeda in Syria as "an asset" to the U.S. strategy in Syria. See Boghani, "Syrian Militant and Former Al Qaeda Leader Seeks Wider Acceptance" (2021). See also Mozaffari, *Islamism*, pp. 104–105; Max Blumenthal, *The Management of Savagery: How America's National Security State Fueled the Rise of Al Qaeda, ISIS, and Donald Trump* (2020); former U.S. diplomat J. Michael Springmann's *Visas for Al Qaeda: CIA Handouts That Rocked the World: An Insider's View* (2015); and Rubinstein, "Did the CIA Pressure Yemen to Release al-Qaeda Propagandist Anwar al-Awlaki?" (2021). —Ed.

activities are stymied so that the new authorities can take credit for bringing about internal peace. Any of those recently useful thugs who cannot or will not submit to the new decrees is "gently" invited before his former leader and shot in the back of the head.

This is how such governmental systems are born. A network of pathological ponerogenic factors is already active, and the inspirational role of essential psychopathy is developed. However, that does not yet represent a complete picture of pathocracy. Many local leaders and adherents persist in their original convictions which, albeit radical, strike them as serving the good of a much larger proportion of formerly disadvantaged persons, not just a few percent of pathocrats and the interests of a would-be worldwide empire.

Local leaders continue to think along the lines of social revolution, invoking its slogans and appealing to the political goals they believe in. They demand that the "friendly power" furnish them not only the promised assistance, but also a certain measure of autonomy they consider crucial. They are not sufficiently familiar with the mysterious "us-and-them" dichotomy, and they still feel a sense of connection with their own nation. At the same time they are instructed and ordered to submit to the dictates of ambassadors whose meaning and purpose are hard to understand. Frustration and doubts thus grow, followed by "ideological deviations" whose nature is nationalistic or practical.

Conflict progressively increases, especially when wide circles of society begin to doubt whether those people allegedly acting in the name of some great ideology do in fact believe in it. Thanks to everyday experience and contact with the pathocratic nation, similarly wide circles simultaneously increase their practical knowledge about the reality and behavioral methods of that system. Should such a semi-colony thus achieve too much independence or even decide to defect, too much of this knowledge could then reach the consciousness of normal man's countries. This could represent a serious defeat for pathocracy.

An ever more pervasive tightening of control is thus necessary until full pathocracy can be achieved, with the help of those already fully committed to the cause. Those leaders whom the central authorities consider to be effectively transitional can be imprisoned or eliminated unless they indicate a sufficient degree of submission. Geopolitical conditions are generally decisive in this area. That explains why it is easier for such leaders to survive on an outlying island than in countries bordering the empire.[71] Should such leaders manage to maintain a larger degree of autonomy by *concealing* their doubts, they might be able to take advantage of their geopolitical position if the conditions are amenable.

During such a phase of crisis of trust, skillful policy on the part of normal man's countries could still tip the scales in favor of a structure which may be revolutionary and leftist, but not pathocratic. However, such policy lacks not only the necessary prudence, but also objective knowledge about the phenomenon, which are prerequisites that would make implementing it possible. Emotional factors, coupled with a moralizing interpretation of pathological phenomena, frequently play much too great a part in political decision-making and result in inept decisions. This contributes to the perpetuation of pathocracy in a tyrannized country.

No full-fledged pathocracy can develop until the second upheaval and the purging of its transitional leadership, which was insufficiently loyal thereto. This is the counterpart of a showdown with the true adherents of the ideology within the genesis of the original pathocracy, which can then develop, due both to the appropriately imposed leaders and to the activity of this phenomenon's homegrown ponerogenic mechanisms.

After the initial governmental period—brutal, bloody, and psychologically naive—such a pathocracy thereupon begins its transformation into its dissimulative form, which has already been described in discussing the genesis of the phenomenon and the force-imposed pathocracy. During this period not even the most skillful outside policy can possibly undermine the existence of such a system. The period of weakness is still to come—when a mighty network of the society of normal people is formed and its separation from the pathological system has taken place.

The above lapidary description of an infectious imposition of pathocracy indicates that this process repeats all the phases of independent ponerogenesis *condensed in time and content.* Underneath the ruler-

---

[71]Presumably a reference to Cuba, where the original revolutionaries led by Fidel Castro (1926–2016) held on to power for the duration despite ties to the USSR. Both Castro's Cuba and Hugo Chávez's (1954–2013) Venezuela probably qualify as what Łobaczewski describes in the next paragraph as "revolutionary and leftist, but not pathocratic." For a discussion along that line, see *The Duran*'s interview with Robert Barnes, "Understanding the Crisis in Cuba" (Jul. 31, 2021, https://youtu.be/qMhRmlTVk1w). —Ed.

ship of its incompetent administrative predecessors, we can even discern a period of hyperactivity on the part of schizoidal individuals mesmerized by the vision of their own rule based on contempt for human nature, especially if they are numerous within a given country. They do not realize that pathocracy will never make their dreams come true; it will rather shunt them into the shadows, since individuals with whom we are already familiar will become the leaders.

A pathocracy thus generated will be more strongly imprinted upon the subjugated country than one imposed by force. At the same time, however, it maintains certain characteristics of its divergent content, sometimes referred to as "ideological" although it is in fact a derivate of the different ethnological substratum, history, and national way of thinking upon which its scion was grafted. Should conditions such as a nation's social and cultural traditions, the size and spread of its population, or geographic isolation permit independence from the primary pathocratic nation, more measured factors and the society of normal people will thus find some way of influencing the governmental system, taking advantage of the opportunities afforded by the dissimulative phase. In the presence of advantageous conditions and skillful outside assistance, this could lead to progressive depathologization of the system.

General Considerations

The path to comprehending the true contents of the phenomenon and its internal causality can only be opened by overcoming natural reflexes and emotions and the tendency toward moralizing interpretations of pathological phenomena, followed by data collected and elaborated in difficult everyday clinical work and subsequent generalizations in the form of theoretical ponerology. Such comprehension naturally also encompasses those who would create such an inhuman system. The problem of the psychobiological determination of their behavior is thus sketched in all its clarity, showing how their capacity for moral judgments and their field of behavior selection is narrowed well below the levels available to a normal person. Understanding even one's enemies—the flip side of the most difficult teaching of the Gospel: to love them—turns out to be an effort justified by natural knowledge. Moral condemnation alone proves to be an obstacle along the path toward curing the world of this disease.

A result of the character of the phenomenon described in this chapter is that no attempt to understand its nature or to track its internal causal links and transformations in time would be possible if all we had at our disposal were the natural language of psychological, social, and moral concepts even in that partially perfected form used by the social sciences. It would also be impossible to predict subsequent phases in the development of this phenomenon or to distinguish its places and times of weakness, as well as the causes of its decline, for purposes of counteraction.

It was therefore necessary to elaborate an appropriate and sufficiently comprehensive conceptual language; this required more time and effort than studying the phenomenon itself. It has therefore become necessary to bore readers somewhat by introducing this conceptual language in a manner both parsimonious and adequate, which would at the same time be comprehensible to those readers not trained in the area of psychopathology. Anyone who wants to repair television sets instead of making them worse must first familiarize himself with electronics, which is also beyond the ambit of our natural conceptual language. However, upon learning to understand this macrosocial phenomenon in the corresponding reference system, a scientist stands in wonder as though before the open tomb of Tutankhamun for a while before he is able to understand the living laws of the phenomenon with ever greater speed and skill, thereupon complementing this comprehension with a huge array of detailed data.

The first conclusion which suggested itself soon after meeting with the "professor" was that the phenomenon's development is limited by nature in terms of the participation of susceptible individuals within a given society. The initial evaluation of approximately 6% proved realistic; progressively collected detailed statistical data assembled later were unable to refute it. This value varies from country to country in the magnitude of about one percentage point upward or downward. Quantitatively speaking, this number is broken down into 0.6% essential psychopaths, i.e., about 1/10 of this 6%. However, this anomaly plays a disproportionate role compared to its numbers by saturating the phenomenon as a whole with its own quality of thought and experience. Other psychopathies, known as asthenic, schizoidal, anankastic, hysterical, et al.,[72] definitely play second (though necessary) fiddle al-

[72]Anankastic is obsessive-compulsive personality disorder (see Glossary). In *Logokracja*, p. 56, Łobaczewski writes that anankastics are "silent despots"

though, in sum, they are much more numerous. Relatively primitive skirtoidal individuals become fellow-travelers, goaded by their lust for life, but their activities are limited by considerations of their own advantage and they generally try to avoid seriously harming others. In non-Semitic nations, schizoids are somewhat more numerous than essential psychopaths. Although highly active in the early phases of the genesis of the phenomenon, they betray an attraction to pathocracy as well as the rational distance of efficient thinking. Thus they are torn between such a system and the society of normal people.

Persons with less pronounced inclinations in the pathocratic direction include those affected by some states caused by the toxic activities of certain substances such as ether,[73] carbon monoxide,[74] and possibly some endotoxins,[75] under the condition that this brain tissue impairment occurred in childhood. Among individuals carrying other indications of brain tissue damage, only two described types have a similar inclination, namely frontal and paranoidal characteropaths. In the case of frontal characteropathy, this is principally the result of an incapacity for self-critical reflection and for the abandonment of a dead-end path onto which one has thoughtlessly stumbled. Because of their weaknesses, paranoid characteropaths uncritically seek support from such a system. In general, however, the carriers of various kinds of brain tissue damage lean clearly toward the society of normal people, and as a result of their psychological problems, ultimately suffer even more than healthy people in the developed phase of pathocracy. This is why we often find them among political refugees.

It also turned out that the carriers of some *physiological* anomalies known to physicians and sometimes to psychologists, and which are

---

who are difficult to get along with and who become the cause of neurosis in others. Hysterical is histrionic personality disorder. —Ed.

[73]Synthetic ether lipid analogs are both cytostatic and cytotoxic; bioactive ether lipids are involved in neurological disorders. Ether anesthetic has been used for recreational purposes and the perseverance of its use has resulted in serious nervous disorders. —Ed.

[74]Carbon monoxide intoxication (COI) can result in severe neuropsychiatric lesions. Cognitive impairments and other neurological symptoms are frequently present years following COI. Affective disorders are observed in almost three-fourths of patients and personality disorders in more than half. See Borras et al., "Long-term Psychiatric Consequences of Carbon Monoxide Poisoning: A Case Report and Literature Review" (2009). —Ed.

[75]Endotoxins, e.g., lipopolysaccharide (LPS) or lipooligosaccharide (LOS), are found in the outer membrane of various gram-negative bacteria and are an important source of such bacteria's ability to cause disease. —Ed.

primarily hereditary in nature, manifest split tendencies comparable to schizoids.[76] In a similar manner, people whom nature has unfortunately saddled with a short life and an early cancer-related death frequently indicate a characteristic and irrational attraction for this phenomenon. These latter observations were decisive in my agreeing to call the phenomenon by this name, which had originally struck me as semantically overly loose. An individual's decreased resistance to the effects of pathocracy and his attraction to this phenomenon appear to be *a holistic response of his organism*, not merely of his psychological makeup alone.

Approximately 6% of the population constitute the active structure of the new rulership, which carries its own peculiar consciousness of its goals and dominance. Twice as many people constitute a second group: those who have managed to warp their personalities to meet the demands of the new reality, which happens in the dissimulative phase with particular ease. This leads to attitudes which can already be interpreted within the categories of the natural psychological worldview, i.e., the errors we are committing are much smaller.[77] It is of course not possible to draw an exact boundary between these groups—the separation adduced here is merely descriptive in nature—but society commonly distinguishes between these two types of people.

From a clinical point of view, this second group consists of individuals who are, on the average, weaker, more sickly, and less vital. The frequency of known mental diseases in this group is at twice the rate of the national average. We can thus assume that the genesis of their submissive attitude toward the regime, their greater susceptibility to pathological effects, and their skittish opportunism includes various relatively impalpable anomalies. We observe not only physiological anomalies, but also shallow affective responses and the anomalies described above at the lowest intensity, with the exception of essential psychopathy, which as a rule leads to active participation.

The 6% group constitutes the new nobility—"Now we the nobility!" The 12% group gradually forms the new bourgeoisie, whose economic

[76]Raine discusses "minor physical anomalies" (e.g., single palmar crease, gap between first and second toes, tongue fissure, attached earlobes, electrostatic hair, and curved little fingers) thought to be markers for fetal neural maldevelopment, and which, when combined with environmental risk factors, predispose for antisocial behavior (*Anatomy of Violence*, pp. 191–194). —Ed.

[77]That is, moralizing interpretations are more suitable for such attitudes, e.g., accusations of self-interest, greed, cowardice, hypocrisy, etc. —Ed.

situation is quite advantageous. Adapting to the new conditions by means of various doctrines or loose ideas—not without conflicts of conscience—transforms this latter group into both dodgers[78] and, simultaneously, intermediaries between the oppositional society and the active pathological group, whom they can talk to in the appropriate language. They play such a crucial role within this system that both sides must take them into account. Since their talents and skills are better than those of the active group, they assume various managerial positions. Normal people see them as persons they can approach, generally without being subjected to pathological arrogance. So they feel they have a role to play in the system, which gives them some sense of self-justification.

So it is that only 18% of the country's population is in favor of the new system of government; but concerning the layer we have called the bourgeoisie, we may even be doubtful of the sincerity of their attitudes. There are opportunists and there are people forced into this double role.[79] There are also those who have consciously decided to play this double game in order to ensure their own safety while contributing to the survival of the social values they believe in. This is the situation in the author's homeland.[80] This proportion can be variously estimated in other countries, from 15% in Hungary to 21% in Bulgaria, but it is never more than a relatively small minority.[81]

The great majority of the population gradually forms the society of normal people, creating a network rooted in mutual understanding. It behooves us to wonder why these people reject the advantages conformity affords, consciously preferring the opposing role: poverty, harassment, and curtailment of human freedoms. What ideals mo-

[78]Maneuverers skilled at navigating the new system. —Ed.

[79]For examples, see Applebaum, *Iron Curtain*, ch. 16 ("Reluctant Collaborators"). —Ed.

[80]Wayne Cristaudo relates that Polish émigré and author Leopold Tyrmand "reported that at a dinner party in America 'a distinguished Negro writer' asked him what percentage of the population would vote anti-Communist if there were free elections in an Eastern European country. When Tyrmand responded that, if the elections were really free and all positions could be presented, and if there were no fear of persecution, then it would be about 85 percent, the writer responded, 'I don't believe it'—a little later exclaiming more heatedly, when Tyrmand tried to explain how things worked in Poland: 'It's impossible! It's against any logic!'" ("Those Pesky Poles! Forever Defying Totalitarianism" [2021]). —Ed.

[81]The concepts of rightwing and leftwing authoritarianism are probably relevant here. See the Glossary entry "authoritarianism." —Ed.

tivate them? Is this merely a kind of romanticism representing ties to tradition and religion? Still, so many people with a religious upbringing change their worldview very quickly ... The next chapter is dedicated to this question. For the moment, let us limit ourselves to stating that a person with a normal human instinctive substratum, good basic intelligence, and full faculties of critical thought would have a difficult time accepting such a compromise; it would devastate his personality and engender neurosis and a sense of moral degradation. At the same time, such a system easily distinguishes and separates him from "its own" kind, regardless of his sporadic hesitations. No method of propaganda can change the nature of this macrosocial phenomenon or the nature of a normal human being. They remain foreign to each other.

The above-described subdivision into three sections should not be identified with membership in any party which is officially ideological but in fact pathocratic. Such a system contains many normal people forced to join such a party by various circumstances, and who must pretend as best they can to represent said party's more reasonable and moderate adherents. The longer such a system persists, the higher their numbers and the bigger the internal threat they pose to the pathocracy. After a year or two of mindlessly following instructions, they start becoming independent and reestablishing their severed ties to society. Their former friends begin to get the gist of their double game and place some trust in them once again.

Large numbers of the adherents of the former ideology, which for the pathocracy has an official although significantly corrupted function, are in a more complicated and often dramatic situation. They have to maintain their party membership. However, they are the first to notice the changes to the ideology, its content and purpose. They are therefore the first to protest that this political system does not truly represent their old political beliefs.

We must also remember that specially trusted people, whose loyalty to the pathocracy is a foregone conclusion due to their psychological nature and the functions they perform, do not have to belong to the party. So they can pass as non-partisan, which makes it easier for them to penetrate opposition circles. (This is also how they could pass as not a threat and operate abroad.)[82]

[82]Western authorities knew that it was extremely difficult for non-partisan citizens to obtain a travel permit; thus being allowed to visit Western countries signaled

After a typical pathocratic structure has been formed, the population is effectively divided according to completely different lines from what someone raised outside the purview of this phenomenon might imagine, and in a manner whose actual conditions are also impossible to comprehend for someone lacking essential specialized training in psychopathology. However, an intuitive sense for these causes gradually forms among the majority of society in a country affected by the phenomenon. If we treat the former stratification, whose formation was decisively influenced by talent, as horizontal, the new one should be referred to as vertical, because it cuts across all the former social strata, each of which contains people susceptible to transpersonification. It also cuts through levels of talent, because there is little correlation with IQ.

A person raised in a normal man's system is accustomed since childhood to seeing economic problems in the foreground, then ideological ones, and next, possibly also social injustice. Such notions have proved illusory and ineffective in tragic circumstances: the macrosocial phenomenon has its own properties and laws which can only be studied and comprehended within the appropriate categories.

However, in leaving behind our old natural method of comprehension and learning to track the internal causality of the phenomenon, we marvel at the surprising exactness with which the latter turns out to be subjected to its own regular laws. With regard to *individuals*, there is always a greater scope of some individual differences and environmental influences. In statistical analyses these variable factors disappear and the essential characteristics surface. The entirety is thus clearly subject to causative determination to a degree that the researcher could not have anticipated. This explains the relative ease of transition from studying its causation to predicting future changes in the phenomenon. In time, the adequacy of collected knowledge has been confirmed by the accuracy of these predictions.

Let us now take individual cases into consideration. For instance: we meet two people whose behavior makes us suspect they are psychopaths, but their attitudes to the pathocratic system are quite

loyalty to the communist system. Additionally, Western governments kept blacklists of active communists, so Polish authorities allowed or advised those most trusted to get rid of their party membership and be vocal about their "non-party" status. The same applied when infiltrating domestic opposition, which in turn also increased the chances of being welcomed abroad. This was how spies, fake dissidents, and agitators were planted in the West. —Ed.

different; the first is affirmative, the second painfully critical. Studies on the basis of tests detecting brain tissue damage will indicate such pathology in the second person, but not in the first; in the second case we are dealing with behavior which may be strongly reminiscent of psychopathy, but the substratum is different.[83]

If a carrier of an essential psychopathy gene was a member of the decidedly anticommunist government party before the war, he will be treated as an "ideological enemy" during the pathocracy's formative period. However, he soon appears to find a *modus vivendi* with the new authorities and enjoys a certain amount of tolerance, even if he is occasionally critical of them. They nevertheless sense he is one of "their own." The moment when he becomes transformed into an adherent of the new "ideology" and finds the way back to the ruling party is only a matter of time and circumstance.

If the family of a typical zealous pathocrat produces a son who does not inherit the appropriate gene, thanks to a happy genetic coincidence (or he was born from a biopsychologically normal partner), such a son will be raised in the corresponding youth organization, unaware of many matters of history and religion, and faithful to the ideology and the party, which he joins early. By mature manhood, however, he will begin to lean toward the society of normal people. The opposition—that world which feels and thinks normally—becomes ever closer to him psychologically; therein he finds himself and a set of values previously unknown to him. A conflict eventually arises between himself and his family, party, and environment, under conditions which may be more or less dramatic. This starts out with critical statements and the writing of rather naive appeals requesting changes in the party, in the direction of healthy common sense, of course. Such people then finally begin to do battle on society's side, enduring sacrifices and suffering. Others decide to abandon their native country and wander foreign lands, lonely among people who cannot understand them or the problems under which they were raised. Such people's life stories are worthy of both a psychological study and the pen of an outstanding writer.

With regard to the phenomenon as whole, one can predict its primary properties in various ethnological manifestations and processes

[83]I.e., examples of "pseudo-," "secondary," or "acquired" psychopathy, "sociopathy," or antisocial personality disorder (see notes in the section on frontal characteropathy in Chapter IV). In other words, all essential psychopaths will support a pathocratic system, but not all characteropaths will. —Ed.

of transformation and estimate the time at which they will occur. Regardless of its genesis, no pathocratic activation of the population of a country affected by this phenomenon can exceed the above-discussed boundaries set by biological factors. The phenomenon will develop according to the patterns we have already described, gnawing ever deeper into the country's social fabric. The resulting pathocratic monoparty will bifurcate from the very outset: one wing is consistently pathological and earns nicknames such as "doctrinarian," "hardliners," "*beton*,"[84] etc. The second is considered more liberal, and in fact this is where the reverberation of the original ideology remains alive for the longest. The representatives of this second wing try as hard as their shrinking powers permit to bend this strange reality into a direction more amenable to human reason, and they do not lose complete touch with society's links. This wing continuously grows in size, attracting large numbers of people looking for some *modus vivendi* there; they weaken the party's pathocratic unity. The first internal crisis of weakness occurs some ten years after such a system has emerged; the more liberal wing of the party begins to oust the hardliners. As a result, the society of normal people gains a bit more freedom. During this time frame, skillful outside action can already count on internal cooperation.[85]

Pathocracy corrodes the entire social organism, wasting its skills and creative power, destroying its most talented members. The effects of the more ideological wing of the party and its revivifying influence upon the workings of the entire country gradually weaken. Typical pathocrats take over all the managerial functions in an increasingly devastated nation. Such a state must be short-term, since no ideology can vivify it. The time comes when the common masses of people want to live like human beings and the system can no longer resist. There will be no great counter-revolution; a more or less stormy process of regeneration will instead ensue. This will lead to the emergence of a system of normal man years later.

Pathocracy is even less a socioeconomic system than it is a social structure or political system. It is a macrosocial disease process affecting mass social movements and reaching for power over entire nations, running the course of its characteristic pathodynamic prop-

[84]"Concrete." A then-popular term for hardline party leaders in Poland. —Ed.

[85]E.g., color revolutions, coups, and covert action sponsored from the outside. See Dickey et al., "Political Warfare," pp. 122–138, on CIA support for Solidarity in Poland. —Ed.

erties. The phenomenon changes too quickly in time for us to be able to comprehend it in the categories of political systems, which would imply a certain stability—not ruling out the evolutionary processes to which social systems are subject. Any way of comprehending the phenomenon by imputing to it certain enduring ideological properties or normal human notions thus quickly causes us to lose sight of its actual contents. The dynamics of transformation in time are part of the nature of the phenomenon; we cannot possibly achieve comprehension from outside its parameters.

As long as we keep using methods of comprehending this pathological phenomenon which apply certain political or economic doctrines whose contents are heterogeneous with regard to its true nature, we will not be able to identify the causes and properties of the disease. A suitably crafted ideology will be able to cloak behind a Cleckley mask the essential qualities from the minds of scientists, politicians, and common people. It will be able to continue to act as a Trojan horse for the psychological strategy of this pathological phenomenon's expansion. In such a state of affairs, we will never elaborate any causatively active methods which could stifle the phenomenon's pathological self-reproduction or its expansionist external influences. Its inductive call will not be silenced.[86] *Ignoti nulla est curatio morbi*!

However, once we understand a disease's etiological factors and their activities as well as the pathodynamics of its changes, we find that the search for a curative method generally becomes much easier. Something similar applies with regard to the macrosocial pathological phenomenon discussed above.

[86] *Author's note (1997):* In such a situation, it will also not be possible to skillfully and effectively help nations freeing themselves from the rule of pathocracy and assist them on their path towards a spiritual, social, and economic rehabilitation. These nations need this knowledge the most, because it will enable them to understand the causes of their individual and social difficulties.

CHAPTER VI
NORMAL PEOPLE UNDER PATHOCRATIC RULE

As adduced above, the anomaly distinguished as essential psychopathy inspires the overall phenomenon in a well-developed pathocracy and betrays biological analogies to the well-known phenomenon called Daltonism—color-blindness or near-blindness with respect to red and green. For the purpose of an intellectual exercise, let us thus imagine that Daltonists have managed to take over power in some country and have forbidden the citizens from distinguishing these colors, thus eliminating the distinction between green (unripe) and red (ripe) tomatoes. Special vegetable patch inspectors armed with pistols and batons would patrol the areas to make sure the citizens were not selecting only ripe tomatoes to pick, which would indicate that they were distinguishing between red and green. Such inspectors could not, of course, be totally color-blind themselves (otherwise they could not exercise this extremely important function); they could not suffer more than near-blindness as regards these colors. However, they would have to belong to the clan of people made nervous by any discussion about colors.

With such authorities around, the citizens might even be willing to eat a green tomato and affirm quite convincingly that it was ripe. But once the severe inspectors left for some other garden far enough away, there would be a shower of comments it does not behoove me to reproduce in a scientific work. The citizens would then pick nicely vine-ripened tomatoes, make a salad with onions and cream, and add a few drops of rum for flavor.

May I suggest that all normal people whom fate has forced to live under pathocratic rule make the serving of a salad according to the above recipe into a symbolic custom. Any guest recognizing the symbol by its color and aroma will refrain from making any comments. Such a custom might hasten the reinstallation of a normal man's system.

The pathological authorities are convinced that the appropriate pedagogical means, indoctrination, propaganda, and terror can teach a person with a normal instinctive substratum, range of feelings, and basic intelligence to think and feel according to their own different fashion. This conviction is only slightly less unrealistic, psychologically speaking, than the belief that people able to see colors normally can be broken of this habit.[1]

Actually, normal people cannot get rid of the characteristics with which the *Homo sapiens* species was endowed by its phylogenetic past. Such people will thus never stop feeling and perceiving psychological and socio-moral phenomena in much the same way their ancestors have been doing for hundreds of generations. Any attempt to make a society subjugated to the above phenomenon "learn" this different experiential manner imposed by pathological egotism is, in principle, fated for failure regardless of how many generations it might last. It does, however, call forth a series of undesirable psychological results which may give the pathocrats the appearance of success. The mass incidence of such moderate deficiencies in human personality and worldview induced by the above-mentioned behavior, the necessary adaptations,[2] and sadly the degree of saturation with pathological content, will later constitute a challenge for appropriate socio-psychological activity. However, the threat of these effects also provokes society to elaborate pinpointed, well-thought-out self-defense measures based on its cognitive and creative efforts.

Pathocratic leadership believes that it can achieve a state wherein those "other" people's minds become dependent by means of the effects of their personality, perfidious pedagogy, mass-disinformation, and psychological terror; such faith is of fundamental importance for them. In their conceptual world, pathocrats consider it virtually self-evident that the "others" should accept their obvious, realistic,

[1]In chapter 3 of his classic, *The Captive Mind* (1953), Czesław Miłosz writes: "A constant and universal masquerade creates an aura that is hard to bear, yet it grants the performers certain not inconsiderable satisfactions. To say that something is white when one thinks it is black, to smile inwardly when one is outwardly solemn, to hate when one manifests love, to know when one pretends not to know, and thus to play one's adversary for a fool (even as he is playing you for one)—these actions lead one to prize one's own cunning above all else" (p. 53). Miłosz called this hypocritical subterfuge "ketman," from the Persian practice used by religious dissenters to avoid persecution. See also Versluis, *New Inquisitions*, pp. 8–9. —Ed.

[2]Coping mechanisms, compromises, survival strategies. See Sebastian Haffner's 1939 memoir, *Defying Hitler* (2002), for a personal account of such phenomena in the early years of Nazi pathocracy. —Ed.

and simple way of apprehending reality, and thus recognize the superiority of their different personalities. For some mysterious reason, though, the "others" wriggle out, slither away, and tell each other jokes about those in power.[3] Someone must be responsible for this: pre-revolutionary oldsters raised in capitalism, or some radio stations abroad.[4] It thus becomes necessary to encourage the youth to distrust their elders, improve the methods of influence, find better "soul engineers" with a certain literary talent, and isolate society from improper literature and science, foreign and domestic. Those experiences and intuitions whispering that this is a Sisyphean labor must be repressed from the pathocrat's field of consciousness.

This dramatic conflict is thus of essential significance for both sides. The stubborn majority feels insulted in its humanity, restricted in its right to intellectual development, and forced to think in a manner contrary to healthy common sense.[5] The other stifles the premonition

[3]"What is the difference between Stalin and Roosevelt? Roosevelt collects the jokes that people tell about him, and Stalin collects the people who tell jokes about him." For a history of communist jokes, including many examples, see Ben Lewis, *Hammer and Tickle: A Cultural History of Communism* (2009). The joke is from p. 75. Lewis quotes Soviet dissident Vladimir Bukovsky: "Packed to the hilt with information, a Soviet joke is worth volumes of philosophical essays. The simplification of the joke exposes the absurdity of all propaganda tricks" (p. 11). —Ed.

[4]A reference to Radio Free Europe and Voice of America. —Ed.

[5]Versluis writes: "Whether gradually or suddenly, reason and common human decency are no longer possible in such a system: there is only a pervasive atmosphere of terror" (*New Inquisitions*, p. 142). Miłosz describes the "collective atmosphere" during the first stage of imposed pathocracy in Poland: "People who flee from the people's democracies usually give as their chief motive the fact that life in these countries is psychically unbearable. ... 'I felt as if I was turning into a machine.' ... To forestall doubt, the Party fights any tendency to delve into the depths of a human being" (*Captive Mind*, pp. 23, 206). In her book *Stasiland: Stories from behind the Berlin Wall* (2003), Anna Funder tells the stories of both the Stasi agents and the citizens who suffered under them in the German Democratic Republic. The book portrays life under an abusive, psychologically foreign regime and the resulting psychological problems which normal citizens suffer as a result: "Many people withdrew into what they called 'internal emigration.' They sheltered their secret inner lives in an attempt to keep something of themselves from the authorities" (p. 96). They suffered torture, complete lack of privacy, PTSD, depression, and a culture of lies which they had to learn to navigate. For more fictional descriptions of ordinary life under communism, see *Red Plenty* by Francis Spufford (2012), which covers the Khrushchev period in the USSR, and *Velvet Totalitarianism/Reincarnation of Love* by Claudia Moscovici (2009), set during 1980s Romania. —Ed.

that if this goal cannot be reached, sooner or later things will revert to normal man's rule, including their vengeful lack of understanding of the otherness of pathocrats' nature. So if it is not achievable, it is best not to think about the future, just prolong the status quo by means of the above-mentioned efforts. Toward the end of this book, it will behoove us to consider the possibilities for untying this Gordian knot.

However, such a patho-pedagogical system, rife with pathological egotization and limitations, produces serious negative results, poisoning minds especially in those generations unfamiliar with any other conditions of life. Personality development is impoverished, particularly regarding the more subtle values widely accepted in free societies. We observe a characteristic lack of respect for one's own organism, for the voice of nature and instinct, as well as for conscience, accompanied by the brutalization of feelings and customs and the vulgarization of language, justified by a sense of injustice. This internal sense of protest against something difficult to understand has to be suppressed by reason, which creates a characteristic state of over-control of emotions. The youth, however, create for themselves a whole system of collective protection of their personalities, treating the information given at "cattle roundups" with mockery. The tendency to be morally judgmental in interpreting the behavior of those who caused one's suffering sometimes leads to dramatic or demonic doctrines, as well as often-futile dreams of revenge. At the same time, adaptation and resourcefulness within these different conditions become the object of cognition among the young.

It should be noted that all these effects are only to a small extent caused by the influence of official, but in reality despised, doctrine. Above all, they are the result of the pathological nature of the phenomenon and the abnormal personalities active in it. Therefore, despite the mass occurrence of these phenomena, they cannot be considered something completely new for psychologists, which we do not encounter in individual experience.

A person who has been the object of the egotistic behavior of pathological individuals for a long time becomes saturated with their characteristic psychological material to such an extent that we can frequently discern the kind of psychological anomalies which affected him. At the same time he suffers from a dramatic sense of incomprehensibility of his condition and an internal protest against the trauma experienced, which is a normal human reaction. Every psychotherapist should therefore be able to lead such a person towards human normality.

The personalities of former concentration-camp inmates were saturated with generally psychopathic material ingested from camp commanders and tormentors, creating a phenomenon so widespread that it often became the main focus of psychotherapy. Becoming aware of this makes it easier for them to throw off this burden and re-establish contact with the normal human world. In particular, being shown appropriate statistical data concerning the appearance of psychopathy in a given population facilitates their search for understanding of their nightmare years and a rebuilding of trust in their fellow man.

This kind of psychotherapy would be extremely useful for those people who need it most, but it has unfortunately proved too risky for a psychotherapist. Patients easily make connective transfers, unfortunately all too often correct, between the information learned during such therapy (particularly in the area of psychopathy) and the reality surrounding them under the rule of "people's democracy." They tried to share the data thus obtained with others who had experienced similar hardship. Former camp inmates find it difficult to hold their tongues in check, which has occasionally attracted the attention of political authorities to the therapist.

I was once referred a patient who had been an inmate in a Nazi concentration camp. She came back from that hell in such exceptionally good condition that she was able to marry and bear three children. However, her child-rearing methods were so extremely iron-fisted as to be much too reminiscent of the concentration-camp life so stubbornly persevering in former prisoners. The children's reaction was neurotic protest and aggressiveness against other children.

During the mother's psychotherapy, we recalled the figures of male and female SS officers to her mind, pointing out their psychopathic characteristics (such people were primary recruits). In order to help her eliminate their pathological material from her person, I furnished her with the approximate statistical data regarding the appearance of such individuals within the population as a whole. This helped her reach a more objective view of that reality, repress its manifestation within herself, and thus re-establish her bond with society and trust in normal people. Her parenting methods were therefore easier to correct.

During one of her last visits, the patient showed to me a little card on which she had written the names of local pathocratic notables and added her own diagnoses, which were largely correct. So I made a hushing gesture with my finger, tore up the piece of paper, and admonished her with emphasis that we were dealing only with her problems. The patient understood and, I am sure, she did not make her reflections on the matter known in the wrong places.

When American soldiers returned from North Vietnamese prison camps, many of them proved to have been subjected to indoctrination and other methods of influencing by pathological material. A certain degree of transpersonification appeared in many of these, as American personalities with impoverished psychological worldviews proved to have little resilience. In the USA this was called "programming," and outstanding psychotherapists proceeded to effect therapy for the purpose of deprogramming them. It turned out that they met with opposition and critical commentary concerning their skills, among other things. Those therapists did not recognize the need to use the same methods they most likely already used when dealing with people who had been influenced by psychopathic personalities. Unfortunately, they could not attend the ideological training provided by our "professor." When I heard about this, I breathed a deep sigh and thought: Dear God, what interesting work that would make for a psychotherapist who understands such matters in their real context.[6]

The pathocratic world, the world of pathological egotism and terror, is so difficult to understand for people raised outside the scope of this phenomenon that they often manifest a childlike naivety, creating doctrines that become a substitute for knowledge. They believe

[6]The classic account is psychiatrist Robert Jay Lifton's study of American servicemen held captive during the Korean War, *Thought Reform and the Psychology of Totalism: A Study of "Brainwashing" in China* (1961). Psychiatrist Colin A. Ross's *The C.I.A. Doctors: Human Rights Violations by American Psychiatrists* (2006) contains an informative case study of psychopathic induction and transpersonification (i.e., classical thought reform, brainwashing, mind control, or coercive influence) on a highly suggestive individual. Ross describes the case of a Danish man, Palle Hardrup, who, under the influence of a psychopathic criminal, Bjorn Neilson, was coerced through various means (hypnosis, suggestion, social isolation, religious deception) to rob two banks and kill two people. Hardrup was found guilty but not responsible on account of insanity (multiple personality created by Neilson). The techniques used by Neilson are the same used by coercive religions, intelligence agencies, and secret police. According to Zimbardo, these kinds of character transformations (*Lucifer Effect*, pp. 190–194 and ch. 10) can occur without any overt mind control or hypnosis (p. 258). See also Denise Winn's *The Manipulated Mind: Brainwashing, Conditioning and Indoctrination* (2000). —Ed.

in them, even if they have studied psychopathology and are psychologists by profession. There are no real data in their behavior, advice, rebukes, and psychotherapy. That explains why their efforts are tiresome and hurtful and frequently come to naught. Their egotism transforms their good will into bad results.

If someone has personally experienced such a nightmarish reality, he considers people who have not progressed in understanding it within the same time frame to be mediocre and presumptuous, sometimes even malicious.[7] In the course of his experience and contact with this macrosocial phenomenon, he has collected a certain amount of practical knowledge about the phenomenon and its psychology and learned to protect his own personality and help others. This experience, unceremoniously rejected by "people who don't understand anything," becomes a psychological burden for him, forcing him to live within a narrow circle of persons whose experiences have been similar.[8] Such a person should rather be treated as the bearer of valuable scientific data; understanding would constitute at least partial psychotherapy for him, and would simultaneously open the door to a comprehension of reality. How many billions of dollars must this cost, and how much more will be paid in the form of mistakes and suffering?

I would here like to remind psychologists that these kinds of experiences and their destructive effects upon the human personality are not unknown to them. We often meet with patients requiring appropriate assistance: individuals raised under the influence of pathological, especially psychopathic, personalities and who were forced with pathological egotism to accept an abnormal way of thinking. Even an approximate determination of the type of pathological factors which operated on him allows us to pinpoint psychotherapeutic measures. In practice we most frequently meet cases wherein such a pathological situation operated on a patient's personality in early childhood, as a result of which we must utilize long-term measures and work very

[7]See the observations from other Eastern Europeans in Dreher's *Live Not by Lies*, e.g., "they consider Americans to be hopelessly naive on the subject. In talking at length to some of the emigrants who found refuge in America, I discovered that they are genuinely angry that their fellow Americans don't recognize what is happening. ... It is very hard for Americans who have never lived through this kind of ideological fog" (pp. xi, xii). —Ed.

[8]*Author's note (1997):* In a similar manner, scientific knowledge about the phenomenon described herein has been rejected.

carefully, using various techniques, in order to help him develop his true personality.[9] Cases where this phenomenon impacts an adult are less frequent. An analogous situation happens in a pathocracy, but the timing of exposure to the strongest influencing factor differs. The quality of the factors at work, though, can be considered known.

Mental difficulties found in normal people collectively living under a pathocratic regime are not as severe as those found in mentally disturbed individuals or in such cases as those mentioned above, but the fact that they occur on a large scale creates conditions for their social perseverance. Children living under a pathocracy, by contrast, are protected until school age. Then they encounter decent people who, accepting certain risks, attempt to limit the destructive influences as much as possible. The strongest assimilation of pathological material and influence of the above-mentioned ways of behavior occur during adolescence and the ensuing period of mental maturation. Thus the input of decent people rescues the society of normal people from deeper deformations in personality development and widespread neurosis. These periods of life are retained in conscious memory and are therefore more easily accessible to insight, reflection, and disillusionment. Such people's psychotherapy, which will be necessary on a mass scale, would consist almost exclusively of utilizing the correct knowledge of the essence of the phenomenon and its effects. Let us hope that this will happen one day!

Regardless of the social scale within which human individuals were forcibly reared by pathological persons—whether individual, group, societal, or macrosocial—the principles of psychotherapeutic action will thus be similar, and should be based upon data known to us and an understanding of the psychological situation. Making a patient more aware of the kind of pathological factors which affected him, and jointly understanding the results of such effects, is basic to such therapy. In individual cases, we do not utilize this method if we have indications that the patient has *inherited* this factor. However, when what is at stake with regard to macrosocial phenomena is the welfare of entire nations, such limitations should not be considered.

---

[9]Łobaczewski cites Polish-Swiss psychologist and psychoanalyst Alice Miller's 1980 book *For Your Own Good: Hidden Cruelty in Child-Rearing and the Roots of Violence.* See also Lawson, *Borderline Mother*, and Ross, *Trauma Model.* —Ed.

From the Perspective of Time

If a person with a normal instinctive substratum and basic intelligence has already heard and read about such a system of ruthless autocratic rule "based on a fanatical ideology," he believes he has already formed an opinion on the subject. However, direct confrontation with the phenomenon will inevitably produce in him the feeling of intellectual helplessness. All his prior convictions prove to be virtually useless; they explain next to nothing, which aggravates his anxiety. This provokes a nagging sensation that he and the society in which he was educated were quite naive.

Anyone capable of accepting this bitter sensation of void with an awareness of his own ignorance worthy of a philosopher can also find paths to orient and guide him within this deviant world. However, egotistically protecting his habits of worldview from disintegrative disillusionment, and attempting to combine them paramoralistically with observations from this new and highly divergent reality, only reaps mental chaos. The latter has produced unnecessary disappointment and conflicts with the new rulership in some people; others have subordinated their personalities to the pathological reality. One of the differences observed between a normally resistant person and somebody who has undergone a transpersonification is that the former is better able to survive this disintegrating cognitive void, whereas the latter fills the void—in an uncontrolled manner—with the ubiquitous pathological propaganda material.

When the human mind comes into contact with this new reality so different from any experiences encountered by a person raised in a society dominated by normal people, it releases psychophysiological shock symptoms in the human brain with a higher tonus of cortical inhibition and a stifling of feelings, which then sometimes gush forth uncontrollably.[10] The mind then works more slowly and less keenly because the associative mechanisms have become inefficient. Especially when a person has direct contact with psychopathic representatives of the new rule, who use their special knowledge and experience so as to exploit the traumatizing effect of their personal-

[10]Ross writes: "In the DSM-IV-TR criteria for acute stress disorder ... it states that while experiencing the criterion A event, the person may experience numbing, detachment, absence of emotional responsiveness, a reduction in awareness of his or her surroundings, derealization, depersonalization, or dissociative amnesia" (*Trauma Model*, p. 60). —Ed.

ities on the minds of the "others," his mind succumbs to a state of short-term catatonia.[11] Their humiliating and arrogant techniques, brutal paramoralizations, and so forth deaden his thought processes and capacity for self-defense, and their divergent experiential method anchors in his mind. In the presence of this kind of phenomenon, any moralizing evaluation of a person's behavior in such a situation thus becomes inaccurate at best.[12]

Only once these unbelievably unpleasant psychological states have passed, thanks to rest in benevolent company, is it possible to reflect—always a difficult and painful process—or to become aware that one's mind and common sense have been fooled by something which cannot fit into the normal human imagination. Man and society stand at the beginning of a long road of unknown experiences which, after much trial and error, finally leads to a certain hermetic knowledge of what the qualities of the phenomenon are and how best to build up psychological resistance thereto. This makes it possible to adapt to life in this different world and thus arrange more tolerable living conditions, especially during the dissimulative phase and beyond. We shall then be able to observe new psychological phenomena: knowledge, immunization, and adaptation such as could not have been predicted before and which cannot be understood in the world remaining under the rule of normal man's systems. A normal person can never completely adapt to a pathological system, although it is easy to be pessimistic about such a prospect.

Such experiences are exchanged during evening discussions among a circle of friends, thereby creating within people's minds a kind of cognitive aggregation which is initially incoherent due to deficiencies in understanding the phenomenon, but with time intuition fills in

[11]Perhaps related to parasympathetic or dorsal vagal shutdown, associated with immobility and dissociation, the body's response to traumatic situations where fight or flight responses are not options. See Porges, *Polyvagal Theory*. —Ed.

[12]Funder quotes a series of Stasi directives outlining how methodical they were in their psychological operations against normal citizens: "To develop apathy ... to achieve a situation in which [the subject's] conflicts ... are irresolvable ... to give rise to fears ... to develop/create disappointments ... to restrict his talents or capabilities ... to harness dissentions and contradictions around him for that purpose [reducing his capacity to act]." In another document, they outline their "*Zersetzungsmassnahmen*" directive (*zersetzung* involves the annihilation of the inner self), which involved these methods: "targeted spreading of rumours about particular persons ... making compromising situations for them by creating confusion over the facts ... the engendering of hysterical and depressive behaviours in the target persons" (*Stasiland*, p. 286). —Ed.

the blanks.[13] The participation of moral categories in such a comprehension of the macrosocial phenomenon and in the behavior of people active within it is much greater within such a new worldview than the above-adduced natural knowledge would dictate. The ideology officially preached by the pathocracy continues to retain its ever-diminishing suggestive powers until such time as human reason manages to localize it as something subordinate or instrumental which is not descriptive of the essence of the phenomenon.

Moral and religious values, as well as a nation's centuries-old cultural heritage, furnish most societies with support for the long road through the jungle of strange phenomena, as well as for the individual and social search for paths of resistance and a way out.[14] However, this apperceptive capacity possessed by people within the framework of the natural worldview contains a deficiency which hides the nucleus of the phenomenon for many years. Scientists who arrived at the heart of the matter in the past paid for it with their unpublicized deaths, or have been forced into exile. When abroad, they encountered complete lack of understanding and were sometimes harassed by their own countrymen inspired by intelligence agents from their homeland.[15]

Under the conditions created by imposed pathocratic rule in particular, where the described psychological deficiencies are decisive in joining the activities of such a system, our natural human instinctive substratum is an instrumental factor in joining the opposition of the majority. Similarly, the environmental conditions of upbringing, and the economic and ideological motivations which influenced the formation of an individual personality, including those political attitudes which were assumed earlier, play the role of modifying factors, though they are not as enduring in time. The effect of these latter factors, albeit relatively more pronounced in relation to individuals, disappears in statistical terms and diminishes through the years of pathocratic rule. Decisions to choose the difficult path on the side of

[13]See, for example, Dreher's discussion of the Benda family's "parallel polis" in Czechoslovakia—seminars and discussions held in private homes (*Live Not by Lies*, pp. 120–122). —Ed.

[14]Dreher writes: "every single Christian [dissident] I interviewed for this book, in every ex-communist country, conveyed a sense of deep inner peace—a peace that they credit to their faith, which gave them ground on which to stand firm" (*Live Not by Lies*, p. 151). —Ed.

[15]Cf. Moscovici, *Velvet Totalitarianism*, p. 6–7, on the Romanian Securitate's operations (including assassination) targeting dissidents abroad. —Ed.

the society of normal people are once again predominantly determined by factors usually inherited by biological means, and thus are not the product of personal choice. Under such conditions, both healthy instinct and feelings, and the resulting basic intelligence, play instrumental roles, stimulating man to make decisions both consciously and subconsciously.

Man's general intelligence, especially his intellectual level, plays a relatively limited role in this process of selecting a path of action, as expressed by statistically significant but low correlation (-0.16). The higher a person's general level of talent, the harder it usually is for him to reconcile himself with this different reality and to find a *modus vivendi* within it. At the same time, there are gifted and talented people who join the pathocracy,[16] and harsh words of contempt for the system can be heard on the part of simple, uneducated people. Only those people with the highest degree of talent or intelligence—which, as mentioned, does not accompany psychopathies—are unable to find meaning to life within such a system. They are sometimes able to take advantage of their superior mental faculties in order to find exceptional ways in which to be useful to others, or to help depathologize the system. Wasting the best talents spells eventual catastrophe for any social system.[17]

Since those factors subject to the laws of genetics prove decisive, society becomes divided, by means of criteria not known before, into the adherents of the new rule, the new middle class mentioned above, and the majority opposition. Since the properties which cause this new division appear in more or less equal proportions within any old social group or level, this new division cuts right through the traditional layers of society. If intellectual talents played an important

[16]For a literary description of Polish intellectuals who accepted the new system to varying degrees, see Miłosz's *Captive Mind.* See also Julien Benda's *The Treason of the Intellectuals* (1928) and Raymond Aron's *The Opium of the Intellectuals* (1955). —Ed.

[17]Historically, pathocracies target the intelligentsia for elimination. The independence of great minds and artists whose creative work does not conform to the narrow constraints of Party ideology constitutes a grave threat. Those who are not destroyed may be harassed, surveilled, censored, imprisoned (like Solzhenitsyn and Dostoevsky before him), or assassinated, if they are not co-opted. For the elimination of intellectuals during Mao's Cultural Revolution, see Dikötter, *Cultural Revolution*, pp. 27–30, 40–41, 76–77. For Pol Pot, for whom even eyeglasses were seen as a sign of education and forbidden on punishment of death, see Hughes, *Disordered Minds*, pp. 93. —Ed.

role in the formation of the former social stratification, here they play a rather minor one. In this new division, the most instrumental factor is a healthy instinctive substratum and resulting basic intelligence which, as we already know, is widely distributed throughout all social groups.

Even those people who were the object of social injustice in the former system and then bestowed with another system, which allegedly protected them, slowly start criticizing the latter. Again, normal human nature is at work here.[18] Even though they were forced to join the pathocratic party, most of the former prewar communists in the author's homeland later gradually became critical, expressed in the crude language of the workers. They were the first to deny that the ruling system was communist in nature, persuasively pointing out the actual differences between the ideology and reality. They tried to inform their comrades in still independent countries of this by letters. Worried about this "treason," these comrades transmitted such letters to their local party committees, from where these were returned to the security services of the country of origin. The authors of the letters paid with their lives or with years of prison; no other social group was finally subjected to such stringent police surveillance as were they.

Regardless of whatever our evaluation of communist ideology or the parties might be, we are presumably justified in believing that the old communists were quite competent to distinguish what was and what was not in accordance with their ideology and beliefs. Their highly emphatic statements on the subject, quite popular among Poland's old communist circles, are impressive or even persuasive.[19] Because of the operational language used therein, however, we must designate them as overly moralizing interpretations of the role of deviant personalities and not in keeping with the character of this work. At the same time, we must admit that the majority of Poland's prewar communists were not psychopaths; neither did they carry other psychopathologies.[20]

[18] Dąbrowski writes in *Moralność w polityce* [Morality in Politics]: "As we already know, the ease and strength of decisions, their [psychopaths'] readiness and brutal ability to 'lead,' high dynamism—all that in the beginning of their activities gains the recognition of the milieu and—often—of the wider community. Only—generally—failures, unscrupulously manifesting their own interests, brutality, and cruelty correct the opinions, often hitherto positive, about them." (Thanks to Iza Rosca for the reference and translation.) —Ed.

[19] *Author's note*: "A hoard of motherf***ers who climbed up to the feeding trough upon the backs of the working class."

From the point of view of economics and reality, any system wherein most of the property and workplaces are state owned *de jure* and *de facto* is state capitalism. Such a system exhibits the traits of a primitive nineteenth-century capitalist exploiter who has not yet sufficiently grasped his role in society and how his own interests are in many ways linked to his workers' welfare. Workers are very much aware of these traits, especially if they have collected a certain amount of knowledge in connection with their earlier political activities.

A reasonable socialist aiming to replace capitalism with some system in conformity with his social idea, which would be based on worker participation in the administration of the workplace and the profits, should reject such a system as the "worst variety of capitalism." After all, concentrating capital and rulership in one place always leads to degeneration, regardless of its political form. Capital must be subject to the authority of fairness. Eliminating such a degenerate form of capitalism should thus be a priority task for any socialist, thus clearing the path for further cautious transformations. Nonetheless, such reasoning by means of social and economic categories and omitting the pathological core of the issue obviously misses the crux of the matter.

The experience of history teaches us that any attempt to realize the communist idea by way of revolutionary means, whether violent or underhanded, leads to a skewing of this process in the direction of anachronistic and pathological forms whose essence and contents remain inaccessible to minds utilizing the moral, social, and economic concepts of the natural worldview. Evolution constructs and transforms faster than revolution, and without such tragic complications.[21] This means that ideas must reach a necessary level of theoretical maturity based on the most optimal knowledge before they can be implemented on a social scale.

---

[20]Cf. Polish journalist Teresa Torańska's interviews with some of the pre-war communists who held leading roles in the period of High Stalinism, in her bestselling, but now out-of-print, book *"Them"*. —Ed.

[21]See Martin, *Behavior of Crowds*, pp. 166–167. Dąbrowski writes: "some superficially 'attractive' political and social systems may include degenerative elements. This is often due to a one-sided concern for revolutionary changes which may be positive, but are pursued without regard for disastrous consequences resulting from a one-sided approach to the problem of social change. The totalitarian systems represent typical examples of such failures" (*Dynamics of Concepts*, p. 49). —Ed.

One of the first discoveries made by a society of normal people is that it is superior to the new rulers in intelligence and practical skills, no matter what geniuses they appear to be. The knots stultifying reason are gradually loosened, and the fear and fascination with the new rulership's secret knowledge and purposeful action begin to diminish, followed by familiarization with new skills and knowledge about this new deviant reality.

The world of normal people is always superior to the pathocratic one whenever constructive activity is needed, whether it be the reconstruction of a devastated country, the area of technology, the organization of economic life, or scientific and medical work. "They want to build things, but they can't get much done without us." Qualified experts are able to make certain demands ever more frequently; unfortunately, they are just as often only considered qualified until the job has been done. Once the factory has started up, the experts can leave; management will be taken over by someone else, incapable of further progress, under whose leadership much of the effort expended will be wasted.

As we have already pointed out, every psychological anomaly is in fact a kind of deficiency. Although psychopathies are based primarily upon deficiencies in the instinctive substratum, the effect of this on mental development also leads to deficiencies in general intelligence, as discussed above, and this is often accompanied by deficits of technical aptitude. This deficiency is not compensated by the formation of that special psychological knowledge we observe among most psychopaths. Such knowledge loses its mesmerizing power when normal people learn to understand these phenomena as well. The psychopathologist was thus not surprised by the fact that the world of normal people is dominant regarding skill and talent. For that society, however, this represented the first significant discovery that brought a certain degree of hope and psychological relief.

Since our intelligence is superior to theirs, we can recognize them and understand how they think and act. This is what a person learns in such a system on his own initiative, forced by daily necessity. He learns it while working in his office, school, or factory, when he needs to deal with the authorities, and when he is arrested, something only a few people manage to avoid. The author and many others learned a good deal about the psychology of this macrosocial phenomenon during compulsory indoctrination training. The organizers and lecturers (usually psychopathic) cannot have intended such a result. Practical knowledge of this new reality thus grows, thanks to which the society gains a resourcefulness of action which enables it to take ever better advantage of the weak spots of the rulership system. This permits gradual reorganization of the initially almost completely broken societal links, which bears fruit with time.

This new understanding is incalculably rich in casuistic[22] detail; I would nevertheless characterize it as descriptive, even overly literary. It contains practical knowledge of the phenomenon in the categories of the natural moralistic worldview, correspondingly modified or warped in accordance with the need to understand matters which are in fact outside the scope of its applicability. This also opens the door to the creation of certain doctrines which merit separate study because they contain a partial truth, such as the teleological or demonological interpretations of the phenomenon.[23]

The development of familiarity with the phenomenon is accompanied by development of a communicative language, by means of which society can stay informed and issue warnings of danger. A third language thus appears alongside the ideological doublespeak described above; in part, it borrows names used by the official ideology, but with their meanings appropriately modified. In part, this language operates with words borrowed from still more lively circulating jokes, sayings, or events.[24] In spite of its strangeness, this

---

[22]Determining a correct response (e.g., to a moral dilemma) based on analysis of previous cases or paradigms. Casuistry is a method of ethical case analysis. —Ed.

[23]For example, Russian philosopher Nikolai A. Berdyaev's interpretation of the Russian Revolution as demonic in nature and the revolutionaries as demonically possessed in "Spirits of the Russian Revolution" (1918), drawing on Dostoevsky's earlier insights in his novel *The Devils* (1872). The Protestant mystic Jakob Böhme (1575–1624) had similar insights in the early 1600s, arguing that there are two human species: those who humbly serve God and are persecuted like Jesus, and the tyrants who only pretend to be human, who incarnate evil even as they disguise themselves in holy garb. See Versluis, *New Inquisitions*, pp. 136–140 (on Berdyaev), 149–150 (on Böhme). The tendency to see a demonic aspect to Hitler's nature is covered in Ron Rosenbaum's *Explaining Hitler: The Search for the Origins of His Evil* (2014), as well as Norman Mailer's novel *The Castle in the Forest* (2007). —Ed.

[24]For example, Polish leader Gomułka would refer to bricks as "ceramic units" in speeches and quickly became known as "the one of ceramic units." Schmiedtová calls this "'our' language": "language employed by common users where content is denoted directly without involving manipulative tendencies inherent to the language of propaganda. [It involves] irony, play on words, subtle humor, and the overall distance towards the totalitarian language" ("Totali-

language becomes a useful means of communication and plays a part in regenerating societal links.[25] Lo and behold, this language can be translated and communicated in relations with residents of other countries with analogous governmental systems, even if the other country's "official ideology" is different. For this language is common to people living in pathocracies and would be easily understood in all the nations ever plagued by this macrosocial disease throughout history. However, in spite of efforts on the part of literati and journalists, this language remains only communicative inside; it becomes hermetic outside the scope of the phenomenon, uncomprehended by people lacking the appropriate personal experience.[26]

The specific role of certain individuals during such times is worth pointing out; they participate in a more rapid discovery of the nature of this new reality and help others find the right path. They have a normal nature but experienced an unfortunate childhood, being

---

tarian Language," p. 4). Unfortunately, Lewis (*Hammer and Tickle*) makes a point of excluding jokes involving puns or other plays on words, due to the difficulties of translation. Dikötter provides some examples of how Chinese adapted popular propaganda songs to mock the party during the Great Famine: "Without the Communist Party, There Would be No New China" became "Without the Communist Party, There Would be No Dried Yam" (a symbol of the famine), and "The Sky Above the Liberated Areas is Bright and the People are Happy" became "The Sky Above the Liberated Areas is Dark and the People are Unhappy" (*Cultural Revolution*, p. 32). See also Anna Wierzbicka, "Antitotalitarian Language in Poland: Some Mechanisms of Linguistic Self-Defense" (1990). —Ed.

[25] As one Pole described it: "It seems curious how quickly we learned this code, even in primary school, with almost zero knowledge of politics ... we knew exactly what could be said in different settings, at school, among close friends and not so close, at home and on holiday." Another recalls asking his mother if it was right to swear allegiance to "democracy," since it had been brought by the Russians: "She explained to him that there were two kinds of democracy: 'real' democracy and 'Soviet' democracy. He should admire the former and keep his distance from the latter" (Applebaum, *Iron Curtain*, p. 397). Dreher writes of his discussion with Polish historian Paweł Skibiński: "Teaching current generations of college students who grew up in the postcommunist era is challenging because they do not have a natural immunity to the ideological abuse of language. 'For me, it's obvious. I remember this false use of language. But for our students, it's impossible to understand'" (*Live Not by Lies*, pp. 119–120). —Ed.

[26] *Author's note (1997):* Today the cognitive habits associated with using such a language of different concepts are among the root causes of the chaos left in the minds of individuals as well as entire societies emerging from a pathocracy. [See Andrews (ed.), *Legacies of Totalitarian Language.* —Ed.]

subjected very early to the domination of individuals with various psychological deviations, including pathological egotism and methods of terrorizing others. The new rulership system strikes such people as a large-scale societal multiplication of what they knew from personal experience. From the very outset, such individuals saw this reality much more prosaically, immediately treating the ideology in accordance with the paralogistic stories well known to them, whose purpose was to cloak the bitter reality of their youthful experiences from public opinion. They soon reach the truth, since the genesis and nature of evil are analogous irrespective of the social scale in which it appears.

Such people are rarely understood in happy societies, but they were invaluable then; their explanations and advice proved accurate and were transmitted to others joining the network of this apperceptive heritage. However, their own suffering was doubled, since this was too much of a similar kind of abuse for one life to handle. They therefore nursed dreams of escaping into the freedom still existing in the outside world.

Finally, society sees the appearance of individuals who have collected exceptional intuitive perception and practical knowledge in the area of how pathocrats think and how such a system of rule operates. Some of them become so proficient in their deviant language and its idiomatics that they are able to use it, much like a foreign language they have learned well. Since they are able to decipher the rulership's intentions and weaknesses, such people then offer advice to people who are having trouble with the authorities. These usually selfless advocates of the society of normal people play an irreplaceable role in the life of society. The pathocrats, however, can never learn to think in normal human categories. At the same time, the ability to predict the reactions of such an authority also leads to the conclusion that the system is rigidly causative and lacking in natural and rational freedom of choice.

This new understanding, expressed in language derived from a deviant reality, is something foreign to people who wish to understand this macrosocial phenomenon but who think in the categories of the countries of normal man. Attempts to understand this language produce a certain feeling of helplessness which gives rise to the tendency of creating one's own doctrines, built from the concepts of one's own world and a certain amount of appropriately co-opted pathocratic propaganda material. Such a doctrine (e.g., American anticommunism) makes it even more difficult to understand that other reality. Their creators and adherents, however, are ready to treacherously oppose anyone whose more accurate knowledge calls into question their outstanding talents. May the objective description adduced herein enable them to overcome the impasse thus engendered.

In countries subjected to pathocratic rule, this knowledge, language, and especially human experience create a mediating cognitive structure in such a way that most people could assimilate this objective description of the phenomenon without major difficulties and with the help of carefully focused attention. Difficulties will only be encountered by the oldest generation and a certain proportion of young people raised in the system from childhood who have already developed certain archetypes and adaptations; these are psychologically understandable.[27]

Natural Immunization

Parallel to the development of practical knowledge and a language of insider communication, other psychological phenomena take form; they are truly significant in the survival and transformation of social life under pathocratic rule, and consequently for the pathocracy itself. Discerning them is essential if one wishes to understand individuals and nations fated to live under such conditions and to evaluate the situation politically. They include people's psychological immunization and their adaptation to life under such deviant conditions.

[27] *Author's note (1997):* How fortunate that by the will of God a man capable of sensing this different reality, and who also had direct experience of it, was elected Pope. Unfortunately, people acting according to the spirit of his adversary managed to prevent him from making use of his understanding of the nature of this phenomenon. Our nation continues to pay a high price for this. Other nations are also incurring losses. Time will tell what price the Catholic Church will end up paying. [Polish-born Karol Józef Wojtyła (1920–2005), or Pope John Paul II, was elected in 1978. In the bibliography, Łobaczewski cites Gordon Thomas and Max Morgan-Witts, *Pontiff: The Vatican, the KGB, and the Year of the Three Popes* (1984). See also Paul Kengor, *A Pope and a President: John Paul II, Ronald Reagan, and the Extraordinary Untold Story of the 20th Century* (2018). Communist spies were prevalent in the Vatican at the time; JPII's translator during his historic meeting with Gorbachev in 1989, Stanisław Szłowieniec, reported to the Polish Security Service (https://www.rp.pl/historia/art14031561-papiez-nie-poparl-stanu-wojennego). —Ed.]

The methods of psychological terror (that specific pathocratic art), the techniques of pathological arrogance, and the striding roughshod into other people's souls initially have such traumatic effects that people are deprived of their capacity for purposeful reaction; I have already adduced the psychophysiological aspects of such states. Ten or twenty years later, analogous behavior is already recognized as well-known buffoonery and does not deprive the victim of his ability to think and defend himself. His answers are usually well-thought-out strategies, issued from the position of a normal person's superiority and often laced with irony. When man can look suffering and even death in the eye with the required calm, a dangerous weapon falls out of the ruler's hands.

We have to understand that this process of immunization is not merely a result of the above-described increase in practical knowledge of the macrosocial phenomenon. It is the effect of a many-layered, gradual process of growth in knowledge, familiarization with the phenomenon, creation of the appropriate reactive habits, reconstruction of social links, and self-control, with an overall conception and moral principles being worked out in the meantime. After several years, the same stimuli which formerly caused chilly spiritual impotence or mental paralysis now provoke the desire to drink a shot or two of vodka so as to get rid of this filth.

There was a time when many people dreamed of finding some pill which would make it easier to endure dealing with the authorities or attending the forced indoctrination sessions generally chaired by a psychopathic character. Indeed, even though largactil (chlorpromazine) failed in this respect, some antidepressants did in fact prove to have the desired effect. Twenty years later, this had been forgotten entirely. This process of immunization can be illustrated by the experiences of the author himself:

When I was arrested for the first time on May 1, 1951, violence, arrogance, and psychopathic methods of forced confession deprived me almost entirely of my capacity for self-defense. My brain stopped functioning after only a few days' detention without water, to such a point that I couldn't even properly remember the incident which resulted in my sudden arrest. I was not even aware that it had been purposely provoked and that conditions permitting self-defense did in fact exist. They did almost anything they wanted to me. I only managed to gather enough strength to refuse to sign the completely fabricated reports.

When I was arrested for the last time in 1968, I was interrogated by five fierce-looking security functionaries. At one particular moment, after thinking through their predicted reactions, I let my gaze take in each face sequentially with great attentiveness. The most important one asked me, "What's on your mind, buster, staring at us like that?" I answered without any fear of consequences: "I'm just wondering why so many of the gentlemen in your line of work end up in a psychiatric hospital." They were taken aback for a while, whereupon the same man exclaimed, "Because it's such damned horrible work!" "I am of the opinion that it is the other way around," I calmly responded. Then I was taken back to my cell.

Three days later, I had the opportunity to talk to him again, but this time he was much more respectful. Then he ordered me to be taken away—outside, as it turned out. I stood there for a while, not knowing what would happen next. Finally, I rode the streetcar home past a large park, still unable to believe my eyes. Once in my room, I lay down on the bed; the world was not quite real yet, but a man exhausted from nights on the board[28] *falls asleep quickly. When I awoke, I spoke out loud: "Dear God, aren't you supposed to be in charge here in this world?!"*

By this time, not only was my psyche largely immune, but I also knew that up to 1/5 of all secret police officials wind up in psychiatric hospitals.[29] I also knew that their "occupational disease" was the congestive dementia formerly encountered only among old prostitutes. Man cannot violate the natural human feelings inside him with impunity, no matter what kind of profession he performs. From that viewpoint, Comrade Captain was partially right. At the same time, however, my reactions had become resistant, a far cry from what they had been seventeen years earlier.

***

All these transformations of human consciousness and the unconscious result in individual and collective adaptation to living under

[28] A reference to the beds in prison, which were notoriously uncomfortable, some literally just wooden boards with no mattress. —Ed.

[29] For portraits of the personalities of some of the NKVD officers arrested during the Great Terror, and who had been involved in carrying out prior purges, see Alexander Vatlin, *Agents of Terror: Ordinary Men and Extraordinary Violence in Stalin's Secret Police* (2016), and Lynne Viola, *Stalinist Perpetrators on Trial* (2017). —Ed.

such a system. Under altered conditions of both material and moral limitations, an existential resourcefulness emerges which is prepared to overcome many difficulties. A new network of the society of normal people is also created for self-help and mutual assistance.

This society acts in concert and is aware of the true state of affairs; it begins to develop ways of influencing various elements of authority and achieving goals which are socially and economically useful. Patiently instructing and convincing the rulership's mediocre representatives takes considerable time and requires pedagogical skills. Therefore, the most even-tempered people are selected for this job, people with sufficient familiarity with pathocrats' psychology and a specific talent for influencing them. (The representatives of the intermediary social class, referred to as the new bourgeoisie, are sometimes useful or even necessary in this work.) The opinion that society is totally deprived of any influence upon government in such a country is thus inaccurate. In reality, the ever better organized society does co-govern to a certain extent, sometimes succeeding and sometimes failing in its attempt to create more tolerable living conditions, but the successes are much less impressive than they would be in a free society. This, however, occurs in a manner totally different from what happens in democratic countries and is incomprehensible to the people living there.

These cognitive processes—the development of a hermetic knowledge and language of mutual understanding, psychological immunization and adaptation—permit the creation of new interpersonal and societal links, which operate within the scope of the large majority we have already called the "society of normal people." Similar links are also formed with those of the regime's bourgeoisie who can to some extent be trusted, and as time passes it happens more and more frequently. In time, the social links created are significantly *more* effective than those active in societies governed by normal human systems, especially when compared to countries with traditional capitalism. Exchange of information, warnings, and assistance encompass the entire society. Whoever is able to do so offers aid to anyone who finds himself in trouble, often in such a way that the person helped does not even know who rendered the assistance. However, if he caused his misfortune by his own lack of circumspection with regard to the authorities, he meets with reproach, but never the withholding of assistance.

It is possible to create such links because this new division of society gives only limited consideration to factors such as the level of talent, education, or traditions attached to former social layers. Reduced economic disparities make building such links easier. One side of this division contains those of the highest intellectual culture, simple ordinary people, intellectuals, white-collar workers, factory workers, and peasants united by the common protest of their human nature against the domination of para-human experiential and governmental methods. These links engender interpersonal understanding and mutual sympathy among people and social groups formerly divided by economic differences and social traditions. The thought processes serving these links are of a more psychological character, able to comprehend someone else's motivations. At the same time, the ordinary folk retain respect for people who have been educated and represent intellectual values. Certain social and moral values also appear and may prove to outlive pathocracy.

The genesis, however, of this great interpersonal solidarity only becomes comprehensible when we know the nature of the pathological macrosocial phenomenon which brought about the liberation of such attitudes, complete with recognition of one's own humanity and that of others. Another reflection suggests itself, namely how very different these great links are from America's "competitive society," for whom this phenomenon is almost completely incomprehensible even though it is operational to some degree in the world of workers and trade unions there in particular.

One would think that a nation's cultural and intellectual life would quickly degenerate when subjected to the country's isolation from cultural and scientific links with other nations, pathocratic limitations upon the development of one's thought, the system of censorship and the intellectual level of its directors, and all those other attributes of such rule. Reality nevertheless does not validate such pessimistic predictions. The necessity for constant mental effort so crucial for finding some tolerable way of life not totally bereft of moral sense within such a deviant reality causes the development of realistic perception, especially in the area of socio-psychological phenomena. Protecting one's mind from the effects of paralogistic propaganda, as well as one's personality from the influence of paramoralisms and the other techniques already described, sharpens controlled thinking processes and the ability to discern these phenomena. Such training is also a special kind of common man's university.

During such times, social and scientific thought reaches back to ancient values in its search for the historical causes of its misfortunes and for ways to improve its fate in the present and future. Society laboriously reviews its national history in quest of interpretations of the facts which would be more profound from the point of view of psychological and moral realism. We soberly discern what happened years and centuries ago, perceiving the errors of former generations, and the consequences of succumbing to foreign intelligence activities or emotionally prejudiced decision-making. Such a great revision of individual, social, and historical worldviews in this search for the meaning of values, life, and history is a product of unhappy times and will help along the way back to happy ones.[30]

People begin to develop an interest in the values of cultures which were once considered remote, but which developed an equally mature, albeit distinct philosophical and moral thought. Life is viewed through a psychological lens. Moral problems applicable in individual life as well as in history and politics also become objects of consideration. The mind starts reaching ever deeper in this area, achieving ever more subtle understanding of the matter, because it is precisely in this world that the old oversimplifications proved to be unsatisfactory. An understanding of other people, including those who commit errors and crimes, becomes a way of approaching problems, one which was formerly underrated. Forgiveness is only one step beyond understanding. As Mme. de Staël wrote: "*Tout comprendre, c'est tout pardonner.*"[31]

A society's religion is affected by analogous transformations. Anti-religious propaganda, too arrogant and naive to reach far, has often had the opposite effect. It manages to persuade simple-minded and abnormal individuals, but at the same time many formerly indifferent people begin to search for truth in the spiritual realm. For this reason

[30] On this reexamination of history, or "counter-history," Versluis writes: "When one has reached an impasse, it is necessary to return to history and understand what went wrong, what paths had been ignored or suppressed, and hence what alternative avenues were. ... counter-history potentially offers the recovery of what has been lost or ignored" (*Mystical State*, p. 36). —Ed.

[31] *Author's note*: "To understand all is to forgive all." [Germaine de Staël (1766–1817) was a French political theorist, a voice of moderation during the French Revolution, and an early critic of Napoleon. Frequently misquoted, the proverb comes from her 1807 work *Corinne, ou l'Italie* and actually reads: "*Tout comprendre rend très indulgent.*" (To understand all is to be very lenient.) —Ed.]

the proportion of the people maintaining religious beliefs is not significantly affected, particularly in countries wherein the pathocracy was imposed by force. What does change is the content and quality of these beliefs such that religion in time becomes more and more attractive even to people raised indifferent to faith. The old religiosity, dominated by tradition, ritual, and insincere moralizing, now becomes transformed into *faith*, rooted in the necessity of self-study and convictions which determine the criteria of conduct.

Anyone reading the Gospel during such times finds something that is hard to understand for other Christians. So striking is the similarity between the social relations there under the government of ancient pagan—practically already atheistic—Rome, and these under an atheistic pathocracy, that the reader imagines the situations described more easily and senses the reality of events more vividly. Such reading also furnishes him with encouragement and advice which he can use in his own circumstances. This revised appreciation of the Gospel played an increasingly important role in shaping people's beliefs.

Thus, during brutal times of confrontation with evil, human capabilities of discriminating phenomena become subtler; apperceptive and moral sensibility develops, although critical faculties sometimes border on cynicism. This gives rise to values which eventually, having undergone a certain refinement, may turn out to have a creative potential.

***

I once got into a mountain-bound bus[32] *full of young high-school and university students. During the trip, song filled the vehicle and the neighboring hills. Old prewar songs both witty and frivolous, and new ones somewhat sorrowful. Leśmian's*[33] *poems: "Our ancestor Noah was a brave man...," and others. The text, however, had been corrected with humor and literary talent, eliminating the overly bawdy treatment of the divine matters described in the Old Testament, which offended these young people raised during difficult times. Was it an unintended result?*

[32] *Author's note (1997):* To the Polish resort town of Zakopane, at the base of the Tatras Mountains. —Ed.

[33] Bolesław Leśmian (1878–1937), a highly influential poet and member of the Polish Academy of Literature. —Ed.

***

As a result of all these transformations, including the de-egotization of thought and attitude connected thereto, society becomes capable of a mental creativity which goes beyond normal conditions. This effort could be useful in any cultural, scientific, technological, or economic area—even in politics—if the authorities did not oppose and stifle it because they feel threatened by such activity.

Human genius is not born of lazy prosperity and among genteel camaraderie, but rather stands in perpetual confrontation with a recalcitrant reality which is different from ordinary human experience.[34] Under such conditions, broad theoretical approaches are found to have practical and existential values. The old system of thought which remains in use in free countries starts to look backward, somewhat naive, and bereft of a sense for a hierarchy of values under pathocratic rule.

If nations which arrived at such a state were to regain their freedom, many valuable accomplishments of human thought would mature within a short time. No excessive fears would be in order as to whether such a nation would then be capable of elaborating a workable socioeconomic system. Quite the contrary: the absence of egoistical pressure groups, the conciliatory nature of a society which has years of bitter experience behind it, a penetrating and morally profound understanding of human reality, and the capacity of self-sacrifice for the common good would permit the way out to be found relatively rapidly. Danger and difficulty would rather come from outside pressures on the part of nations which do not adequately understand the social and political conditions in such a country. But unfortunately, pathocracy cannot be low-dosed like an otherwise poisonous drug! Meanwhile, it persists and destroys whatever good has been born under its rule.

[34]In *Logokracja*, p. 31, Łobaczewski writes: "exceptional human creativity is most often the product of two coexisting circumstances: 1) when an individual is both highly talented and 2) forced at an early age by life conditions to cooperate in overcoming real difficulties, often under unusual conditions. Such people develop the necessary accuracy of thought, an objective grasp of reality, perseverance, and the ability to take novel paths. A person with similar talents, but brought up in the comfort of an easy life, may be a good scientist or politician, but will not develop the creativity allowing for the paving of new paths. Governing a country requires both a certain stability and novelty. Each of these types of people should therefore find their way into public activity." —Ed.

The older generation, raised in a normal man's country, generally reacts by developing the above-mentioned skills, i.e., by enrichment. The younger generation raised under pathocratic rule to a large extent assimilates pathological psychological material and succumbs to an impoverishment of worldview—despite their elders' best efforts. Their personalities become rigid, traumatized, and dominated by habitual structures; over-control of emotion emerges. These are typical results of the influence of abnormal personalities, though on a mass scale and not of the highest intensity. It is in this mass scale of the effects that the danger lies.

Admittedly, a large majority of young people consciously reject paralogistic propaganda and its corresponding indoctrination; however, this process of self-protection demands time and effort which could better be used for active apperception of more valuable contents. The latter are accessible only with difficulty, due both to limited supply and to apperceptive problems caused by a sense of unreality or even the effects of reversive blockades. There arises the feeling of a certain void which is hard to fill. In spite of human good will, certain paralogisms and paramoralisms, as well as cognitive materialism, anchor and persevere in young minds. The human mind is not able to disprove every single falsity which has been suggested to it.

The emotional life of people raised within such a deviant psychological reality is also fraught with difficulties. The constant efforts to control one's emotions, so as to avoid having some stormy reaction provoke repression on the part of a vindictive and unforgiving regime, cause feelings to be relegated to the role of something rather problematic, something which should not be given a natural outlet. Suppressed emotional reactions surface later, when the person can afford to express them; they are delayed and inappropriate to the situation at hand. This is sometimes the cause of family squabbles. Worries about the future awaken secondary egotism among people too adapted to living in a pathological social structure.

Neurosis is human nature's response if a normal person is subordinated to the domination of psychologically abnormal people. The same applies to the subordination of a society and its members to a pathological system of authority. In a pathocratic state, every person with a normal nature thus exhibits a certain chronic neurotic state, kept under control thanks to the arduous efforts of reason. The severity of these states varies among individuals, depending upon one's traits and external circumstances, usually more serious in direct proportion to the individual's talents. Psychotherapy upon such people is only possible and effective if we can rely on sufficient familiarity with these states and their causes. Western-educated psychologists thus proved to be completely inadequate in treating patients in countries where this problem has always existed, albeit to varying degrees.

A psychologist working in such a country must develop special operational techniques unknown and even unfathomable to specialists practicing in the free world. They have the purpose of partially liberating the voice of instinct and feeling from this abnormal over-control, and of rediscovering the voice of nature's wisdom within, but this must be done in such a way as to avoid exposing the patient to the unfortunate results of excessive freedom of reaction in the conditions under which he must live. A psychotherapist must operate carefully, with the help of allusions, because only rarely may he openly inform the patient of the system's pathological nature. However, even under such conditions, we can achieve a greater freedom of feeling, experiencing, and intuiting psychological situations, more appropriate thought processes, and better decision-making capabilities. As a result of all this, the patient subsequently behaves with greater caution and feels much safer.

If Western radio stations—unhampered by the fears for personal safety experienced by psychologists on the other side—abandoned primitive counterpropaganda in favor of a similar psychotherapeutic technique, they would contribute mightily to the future of countries still under pathocratic rule today. Toward the end of this book, I shall attempt to persuade the reader that psychological matters are as important to the future as high politics, economics, or powerful weapons.

When all this practical knowledge, language, immunization, and adaptation to living in a pathocratic world suddenly become a pointless burden that hampers the process of normalizing human relations, then ensuring widespread comprehension of the nature of the phenomenon, as well as understanding of the impact of its causes and effects on the self, becomes a necessary condition for individuals and societies to achieve full spiritual health and the capacity for self-realization.

Understanding

Understanding those normal people, whether outstanding or average, fated to live under pathocratic rule, their human nature and its responses to this fundamentally deviant reality, their dreams, their methods of comprehending such a reality (including all the difficulties along the way), and their need to adapt and become immune (including the side-effects thereof) is the *sine qua non* precondition for such a course of action that would effectively assist them in their efforts to achieve a normal man's system—to improve conditions and spiritually rehabilitate man and society.

It would be psychologically impossible for a scientist or politician in a free country to incorporate the practical knowledge such people acquired over many years of day-to-day experience. This knowledge cannot be transmitted; no journalistic or literary efforts will ever achieve anything in this area. However, an analogous knowledge formulated in objective naturalistic language becomes transferable across national borders and into different cultures, and can become a lasting legacy of human progress. It can be assimilated by people who have no such specific experiences; it can also be back-transmitted over there, where a great need for this science exists, as do the minds which are already prepared to receive it. Such knowledge would actually act upon their battered personalities in much the same way as the best of medicines. Mere awareness that one was subject to the influence of a mental deviant is in and of itself a crucial part of treatment. It would also act as a vaccine against the emergence of pathocracy. Thus it would enable us to eliminate already-existing ponerogenic phenomena or anticipate and prevent their tragic consequences.

Whoever wants to maintain the freedom of his country and of the world already threatened by this macrosocial pathological phenomenon, whoever would like to heal this sick planet of ours, should not only understand the nature of this great disease, but should also be conscious of potentially regenerative healing powers. Every country within the scope of this macrosocial phenomenon contains a large majority of normal people living and suffering there who will never accept pathocracy; their protest against it derives from the depths of their own souls and their human nature as conditioned by properties transmitted by means of biological heredity. The forms of this protest and the ideologies by which they would like to realize their natural wishes for a system of normal man may nevertheless change.

The organizational or political structures by which they would like to regain their human right to live in freedom are, however, of secondary importance to these people. There are of course differences of opinion in this area, but they are not likely to lead to overly violent conflict among persons who see before them a goal worthy of sacrifice. Those whose attitudes are more penetrating and balanced see the original ideology—as it was before its caricaturization by the ponerization process—as the most practical basis for effecting society's aims. Certain modifications would endow this ideology with a more mature form more in keeping with the demands of present times; it could thereupon serve as the foundation for a process of evolution, or rather transformation, into a socioeconomic system capable of adequate functioning. The author's convictions are somewhat different. Outside pressure based on categories generally accepted in the free world, which aims to impose an economic system that has lost its historically conditioned roots in such a country, or which is intent on exploiting the weaknesses of a nation emerging from the power of a pathocracy, will only hinder its healing process and could result in grave difficulties.[35]

People who have long had to live in this strange world of otherness are therefore hard to understand for someone who has fortunately avoided that fate. What makes this understanding even more difficult

[35]This is what happened. On the Russian transition to a market economy, Hahn writes: "The West provided no economic assistance to Gorbachev as the Soviet economy crashed in 1989 ... Little assistance arrived before 1994, leaving the Russian people to struggle through a depression far worse than the American depression of the 1930s ... Then the West backed a hastily implemented, poorly conceived, disastrous and broadly unpopular privatization and economic reform program that left the general public out and enriched the old 'red' enterprise directors and a young generation of unscrupulous 'new Russian' bandits and oligarchs" (*Ukraine over the Edge*, pp. 50–51). In 1989, the Solidarity movement succeeded in leading a coalition government in Poland (though many communists remained in power). During the early '80s, the movement had hoped to reform Poland's economy based on socialized enterprise, with state-run companies under the control of workers' cooperatives. By 1989, however, it had moved to a more free-market position, at which point the IMF released monetary aid under condition of specific "reforms." Poland's swift transition to a market economy in the '90s was rocky, as Łobaczewski predicted; standard of living dropped and unemployment rose as industry was plundered and taken over for cents on the dollar (often by foreigners). A similar dynamic played out in other ex-communist nations, though Poland performed better than most in some regards. See Rosser, "How Shocking Was Shock Therapy?" (2019). —Ed.

are the aforementioned doctrines, which give this different reality an ideological character that our country has perceived as surreal for a long while. Without being aware of the changes imprinted in human personalities, one cannot offer any meaningful advice.

Let us refrain from imposing categories upon them which are only meaningful within the world of normal man's governments; let us not pigeonhole them into any political or economic doctrines which are often quite unlike the reality they are familiar with. Instead, overcoming our egotism and the extraordinary difficulties described above, let us try to approach these societies with adequate psychological objectivity. In order to improve the chances of solving these most challenging problems of modern times, let us welcome them with feelings of human solidarity, reciprocal respect, and a greater trust in their normal human nature and their reason.

CHAPTER VII
PSYCHOLOGY AND PSYCHIATRY UNDER PATHOCRATIC RULE

If there were ever such a thing as a country with a system like that envisaged by an American believer in the local doctrine of "communism," wherein the working people's leftist ideology would be the basis for government—which, I believe, would be stern, but not bereft of healthy humanistic thought[1]—the contemporary social, biohumanistic, and medical sciences would be considered valuable, appropriately developed, and used for the good of the working people. Psychological advice for youths and for persons with various personal problems would naturally be the concern of the authorities and of society as a whole. Seriously ill patients would have the advantage of correspondingly skillful care. However, quite the opposite is the case within a pathocratic structure.

When I came to the West, I met people—not just those with leftist views—who unquestioningly believed that communist countries existed in more or less the form expounded by American political doctrines. These persons were almost certain that psychology and psychiatry must enjoy freedom in those countries referred to as communist, and that matters were similar to what was mentioned above. When I contradicted them, they refused to believe me and kept asking why, "Why isn't it like that?" *What can politics have to do with psychiatry?* My attempts to explain what that other reality looks like met with the difficulties we are already familiar with, although some

[1] As noted previously, Marx's vision of the dictatorship of the proletariat was ostensibly democratic and non-militaristic in nature, with universal suffrage, an open society, and freedom of religion. However, his and Engels's writings also had "authoritarian and terroristic elements," as well as support for compulsory labor, common dwellings for citizens, and undermining the family. Marx wrote, "When our turn comes, we shall not disguise our terrorism" (Sowell, *Marxism*, pp. 144, 182). In theory, Marx believed that in order to create equality, it is necessary to first impose inequality in the form of a dictatorship of the proletariat. In more practical terms, he despised peasants and the working class. —Ed.

people had previously heard about the abuse of psychiatry. However, such "whys" kept cropping up in conversation, and remained unanswered.

The situation in these scientific areas—of their social and healing roles, and of the people occupied in these matters—can only be comprehended once we have perceived the true nature of pathocracy in the light of the ponerological approach. Let us thus imagine something which is only possible in theory, namely, that a country under pathocratic rule is inadvertently allowed to freely develop these sciences, enabling a normal influx of scientific literature and contacts with scientists in other countries. Psychology, psychopathology, and psychiatry would flourish abundantly and produce outstanding representatives. What would the result be?

This accumulation of proper knowledge would, within a short time, enable the undertaking of investigations whose meaning we already understand. Missing elements and insufficiently investigated questions would be complemented and deepened by means of the appropriate detailed research. A diagnosis of the pathocratic state of affairs would then be elaborated within the first dozen or so years of the formation of the pathocracy, especially if it is imposed by force. The basis of the deductive rationale would be significantly wider than anything the author can present here, and would be illustrated by means of a rich body of analytical and statistical material.

Once transmitted to world scientific opinion and popularized, such a diagnosis would quickly become incorporated into the worldview of reasonable people of various political attitudes, forcing naive political and propaganda doctrines out of societal consciousness. It would reach the nations that were the objects of the pathocratic empire's expansionist intentions. This would render the usefulness of any ideology as a pathocratic Trojan horse doubtful at best, for the critical thinking abilities and reason of a large proportion of humanity would have been sufficiently strengthened. In spite of differences among them, other countries with normal human systems would be united by characteristic solidarity in the defense of an understood danger, similar to the solidarity linking normal people living under pathocratic rule. This consciousness, now popularized in the countries affected by this phenomenon, would simultaneously reinforce psychological resistance on the part of their normal human societies and furnish them with new measures of self-defense. Can any pathocratic empire risk permitting such a possibility?

In times when the above-mentioned disciplines are developing swiftly in many countries, the problem of preventing such a psychiatric threat becomes a matter of "to be or not to be" for pathocracy. Any possibility of such a situation emerging must thus be staved off preemptively and skillfully, both within and without the empire. At the same time, the empire is able to find effective preventive measures—which have tragic consequences for many ordinary people as well as for science—thanks to its consciousness of being different as well as that special psychological knowledge of psychopaths, partially reinforced by academic knowledge.

Both inside and outside the boundaries of countries affected by the above-mentioned phenomenon, a purposeful and conscious system of control, terror, and diversion is thus set to work whose task was to prevent the pathological nature of the system from being revealed. Nowadays, it continues to operate covertly in an attempt to delay this fateful moment.[2] Any scientific papers published under such governments or imported from abroad must be monitored to ascertain that they do not contain any data which could be harmful to the pathocracy. Specialists with superior talent become the objects of surveillance, blackmail, and malicious control. They can forget about a scientific career. This of course causes results to become inferior with reference to these areas of science. The entire operation must of course be managed in such a way as to avoid attracting the attention of public opinion in countries with normal human structures. The effects of such a "bad break" could be too far-reaching. This explains why people caught doing investigative work in this area are murdered "noiselessly" or forced abroad and there, in this incomprehensible world, taken care of by the secret police with their sophisticated system of degrading terror.[3] as objects of appropriately organized harassment campaigns.

Battles are thus being fought on secret fronts which may be reminiscent of World War II. The soldiers and leaders fighting in various theaters were not aware that their fate depended on the outcome of that other war, waged by scientists and other soldiers of underground armies, whose goal was preventing the Germans from producing the atom bomb. The Allies won that battle, and the United States be-

---

[2]That is, at the time of writing. —Ed.

[3]Or as the original English translation put it, "appropriately organized harassment campaigns." —Ed.

came the first to possess this lethal weapon. For the present, however, the West keeps losing scientific and political battles on this new secret front. Lone fighters are looked upon as odd, denied assistance, or forced to work hard for their bread as a result of the efforts of secret police agents and the anticommunist doctrine (a poor excuse for knowledge). Meanwhile, the ideological Trojan horse keeps invading new countries.[4]

An examination of the methodology of such battles, both on the internal and external fronts, points to that specific pathocratic self-knowledge so difficult to comprehend in the light of the natural language of concepts. In order to be able to control people and those relatively non-popularized areas of science, one must know, or be able to sense, what is going on and which fragments of psychopathology are most dangerous and whom to suspect of knowing too much. (Psychopaths' special psychological knowledge must underlie these skills.) The examiner of this methodology thus also becomes aware of the boundaries and imperfections of this self-knowledge and practice, i.e., the other side's weaknesses, errors, and gaffes, and may manage to take advantage of them in order to sneak in some of that knowledge for other people's benefit. Thus, this guerilla warfare is completely incomprehensible to those living in systems ruled by normal people, regardless of whether those systems condemn "communism" or believe in it.

In nations with pathocratic systems, supervision over scientific and cultural organizations is assigned to a special department of especially trusted people, a "nameless office" composed almost entirely of relatively intelligent persons who betray characteristic psychopathic traits. These people must be capable of completing their academic studies, albeit sometimes by forcing examiners to issue generous evaluations. Their talents are usually inferior to those of average students, especially regarding psychological science. In spite of that, they are rewarded for their services by obtaining academic degrees and positions and are allowed to represent their country's scientific community abroad. As especially trusted individuals, they are allowed to *not* participate in local meetings of the party, or even to avoid joining it entirely. In case of need, they might then pass for non-party. In spite

[4]See "Artificially Infected Pathocracy" in Chapter V. Today, the most prominent ideological Trojan horses are Islamism in Muslim-majority nations, and "social justice" among liberal democracies. —Ed.

of that, these scientific and cultural superintendents are well known to the society of normal people, who learn the art of differentiation rather quickly, and easily recognize them by their characteristic way of thinking. They are not always properly distinguished from agents of the political police; although they consider themselves to be in a better class than the latter, they must nevertheless cooperate with them.

We often meet with such people abroad, where various foundations and institutes give them scientific grants with the conviction that they are thereby assisting the development of proper knowledge in countries under "communist" governments.[5] These benefactors do not realize that they are rendering a disservice to such science and to real scientists by allowing these gatekeepers to attain a certain semi-authentic authority, and by allowing them to become more familiar with whatever they shall later eliminate from the scientist's awareness.

After all, those people shall later have the power to permit someone to take a doctorate, embark upon a scientific career, achieve academic tenure, and become promoted. Very mediocre scientists themselves, they attempt to knock down more talented persons, governed not only by secret instructions but also by self-interest and that typical jealousy which characterizes a pathocrat's attitude toward normal people. They will be the ones monitoring scientific papers for their "proper ideology" and attempting to ensure that a good specialist will be denied the scientific literature he needs.

Controls are exceptionally malicious and treacherous in the psychological sciences in particular, for reasons now understandable to us.[6]

---

[5]In an interview with Sott.net, Łobaczewski related the following: "when I finally had some income [in New York], I went to a congress of Polish culture in London. Well, immediately two allegedly famous psychologists sat next to me, one from Canada, the other supposedly from South Africa—some major scholars. But the one from Canada did not know the time difference between Ottawa and London, and I also caught the other on some other contradiction. So finally they stopped pretending and it turned out that these were two Security Service (SB) agents from Kraków. And so I lent my book—I did not give it away—to a local philosopher. Soon after, it turned out that he did not have it in his possession—they did. It occurred under instructions from the Polish government in London ..." —Ed.

[6]Similar but less comprehensive dynamics are discernible in Western academia. For instance, H. Aronson and Francis Terrel's 1999 paper, "On the Nature of Things: The Politics of Scientific Evaluation," examines "an inferred avoidance by clinically oriented psychology journals of innovative findings and studies that are inconsistent with theories currently in vogue. It suggests that manuscripts

Written and unwritten lists are compiled for subjects that may not be taught, and corresponding directives are issued to appropriately distort other subjects. This list is so vast in the area of psychology that nothing remains of this science except a skeleton picked bare of anything that might be subtle or penetrating.

A psychiatrist's required curriculum contains neither the minimal knowledge from the areas of general, developmental, and clinical psychology, nor the basic skills in psychotherapy. Due to such a state of affairs, the most mediocre or privileged of physicians becomes a psychiatrist after a course of study lasting only weeks. This opens the door of psychiatric careers to individuals who are by nature inclined to serving the pathocratic authority, and it has fateful repercussions upon the level of treatment. It later permits psychiatry to be abused for purposes for which it should never be used.[7] Since they are

---

which challenge existing models and approaches to practice have a high probability of rejection [e.g., 'increasing evidence that personality and mental illness may have a basis in biological or genetic factors']." The psychological community "appears to demand that the field avoid those scientific ventures that might correct the faulty theories. Instead, genetic theories were categorized as 'politically incorrect' and ignored. Environmentally based theories were in. And we held them close." This trend has largely reversed and nature-based theories are now common, though biology is currently under assault. See, for example, Debra Soh's *The End of Gender: Debunking the Myths about Sex and Identity in Our Society* (2020). —Ed.

[7]The Wikipedia entry on the subject ("Political abuse of psychiatry in the Soviet Union") is worth reading. In 1950 the Russian Academy of Sciences adopted Moscow professor Andrei Snezhnevsky's theory of "slowly progressing" or "sluggish" schizophrenia, a diagnosis used to institutionalize political dissidents as "paranoids" with "delusions of societal reformation": "most frequently ideas about a 'struggle for truth and justice' are formed by personalities with a paranoid structure ... A characteristic feature ... is the patient's conviction of his own righteousness, an obsession with asserting his trampled rights, and the significance of these feelings for the patient's personality" (Lewis, *Hammer and Tickle*, p. 233). See also Robins and Post, *Political Paranoia*, pp. 30–31. Western literature on psychiatry was forbidden, and psychiatrists who protested risked prison or their own diagnosis as "insidiously schizophrenic." Snezhnevsky's theories were still popular in the 1990s, and while Russian psychiatry still has many problems (most notably underfunding), it has since transitioned to a biopsychosocial model and adopted the use of the WHO's *ICD*. See Savenko and Perekhov, "The State of Psychiatry in Russia" (2014), and Morozov, "The Evolution of Psychiatry in Russia" (2017). For abuse of psychiatry in China, see Robin Munro, "Judicial Psychiatry in China and Its Political Abuses" (2000) and the sources listed in Clarke, "New book: 'China's Psychiatric Inquisition'" (2007), which discuss Munro's 2006 book *China's Psychiatric Inquisition: Dissent, Psychiatry and the Law in Post-1949 China.*

undereducated, these psychologists then prove helpless in the face of many human problems, especially in cases where detailed knowledge is needed. Such knowledge must then be acquired on one's own by searching for it in foreign literature that is difficult to access, a feat not everyone is able to manage.

Such behavior carries in its wake a good deal of damage and human injustice in areas of life and health which have nothing whatsoever to do with politics. Unfortunately, however, such behavior is necessary from the pathocrat's point of view in order to prevent these dangerous sciences from jeopardizing the existence of a system they consider the best of all possible worlds.

Specialists in the areas of psychology and psychopathology would find an analysis of this system of prohibitions and recommendations highly interesting. This makes it possible to realize that this may be one of the roads via which we can reach the crux of the matter, i.e., the nature of this macrosocial phenomenon. The prohibitions engulf depth psychology,[8] the analysis of the human instinctive substratum, dream analysis,[9] the psychology of emotion, and such phenomena as bimorphia and polymorphia of personality.[10] As already pointed out in Chapter II, an understanding of human instinct is a key to understanding man; however, a knowledge of said instinct's anomalies also represents a key to understanding pathocracy. Although used ever more rarely in psychological practice, dream analysis shall always remain the best school of psychological thought; that makes it

For a short account of ideological "Critical Social Justice Therapy" in the U.S., see Satel, "Keep Social-Justice Indoctrination out of the Therapist's Office" (2021). —Ed.

[8]The theories and practices of psychoanalysts like Sigmund Freud, Carl Jung, and Alfred Adler. In Hungary, for example, psychoanalysts were labeled "reactionaries," books by Freud, Jung, and Adler banned, and psychiatrists forced to follow Soviet practice, i.e., electroshock and insulin therapy, "whose primary goal was to persuade people to conform" (Applebaum, *Iron Curtain*, p. 395). (Both treatments were developed in the West to treat schizophrenia, among other illnesses. While insulin shock therapy fell out of favor in the 1960s and is no longer used, ECT is still in use to treat severe depression, catatonia, mania, and schizophrenia.) —Ed.

[9]Dream interpretation in western psychiatry traces back to Freudian psychoanalysis and his 1900 book, *The Interpretation of Dreams.* It is also practiced in Gestalt therapy (Fritz Perls) and Jungian analysis. See, for example, Greg Bogart, *Dreamwork and Self-Healing: Unfolding the Symbols of the Unconscious* (2018). —Ed.

[10]Presumably a reference to split personality and multiple personality, i.e., dissociative identity disorder. —Ed.

dangerous by nature. Consequently, even research on the psychology of mate selection[11] and marital adjustment is frowned upon, at best, since it requires comprehensive and subtle knowledge.

The essence of psychopathy may not, of course, be researched or elucidated. Sufficient darkness is cast upon this matter by means of an intentionally devised definition of psychopathy which includes various kinds of character disorders, together with those caused by completely different and known causes.[12] This definition must be memorized not only by every lecturer in psychopathology, psychiatrist, and psychologist, but also by some political functionaries with no education in that area. To betray advanced knowledge in this field arouses immediate suspicion.

This definition must be used in all public appearances whenever it is for some reason impossible to avoid the subject. However, it is preferable for a lecturer in such areas to be someone who always believes whatever is most convenient in his situation, and whose in-

[11] Psychopathic men cause particular damage to women, whom they manipulate into abusive relationships, often fathering many children (with multiple partners) who potentially carry on psychopathic genes. Sandra Brown, CEO of the Institute for Relational Harm Reduction & Public Pathology Education, has written two important books on the subject: *How to Spot a Dangerous Man before You Get Involved* (2005) and, with Jennifer R. Young, *Women Who Love Psychopaths* (2018). —Ed.

[12] In the preface to the fifth edition of his book *The Mask of Sanity*, Hervey Cleckley noted what he called "an almost universal conspiracy of evasion" on the topic of psychopathy among North American researchers and clinicians. While institutions exist to deal with all sorts of illness and crime, when it comes to psychopathy "no measure is taken at all ... nothing exists specifically designed to meet a major and obvious pathologic situation" (p. viii). In the intervening years, psychopathy research has expanded greatly, thanks in large part to the work of Robert Hare and his Psychopathy Checklist–Revised, widely used in prisons, psychiatric units, courts, and for academic research. However, in the United States, a similar "catch-all" definition continues to be used by the American Psychiatric Association in its *DSM*: "antisocial personality disorder." See, for example, Robert Hare, "Psychopathy and Antisocial Personality Disorder: A Case of Diagnostic Confusion" (1996). As Thomson writes, the two diagnoses are "not interchangeable." While 65% of psychopaths are also ASPD, only 5.5% of ASPDs are psychopaths. See the discussion in Thomson, *Understanding Psychopathy*, pp. 27–28. However, that too is slowly changing: "the *DSM-5* Section III ['trait-based'] diagnostic approach for ASPD is more convergent with the construct of psychopathy" than its Section II approach, or previous iterations of the *DSM* (Few et al., "Comparing the Utility of DSM-5 Section II and III Antisocial Personality Disorder Diagnostic Approaches for Capturing Psychopathic Traits" [2015]). —Ed.

telligence does not predestine him to delve into subtle differentiations of a psychological nature.[13]

It is also worth pointing out here that the chief doctrine of said system reads, "Existence defines consciousness."[14] As such, it belongs to psychology rather than to political science. This doctrine actually contradicts a good deal of empirical data indicating the role of hereditary factors in the development of man's personality and fate.[15] Lecturers may refer to research on identical twins, but only in a brief, cautious, and formal fashion. Considerations on this subject, however, may not be published in print.

We return once more to this system's peculiar psychological "genius" and self-knowledge. One might admire how the definition of psychopathy mentioned above effectively blocks the ability to comprehend phenomena covered therein. We may investigate the relationships between these prohibitions and the essence of the macrosocial phenomenon they in fact mirror. We may also observe the limits of these skills and the errors committed by those who execute this strategy. These shortcomings are skillfully taken advantage of for purposes of smuggling through some proper knowledge on the part of the more talented specialists, or by elderly people no longer fearful for their careers or even their lives.

---

[13] *Author's note (1997):* Such a system selected and shaped people in such a way that it continues to influence them despite the formal restoration of independence. Books continue to be published in this spirit, and people who do not accept this state of affairs are considered a threat to the scientific establishment.

[14] In *A Contribution to the Critique of Political Economy* (1859), Marx wrote: "it is not the consciousness of men that determines their existence, but, on the contrary, their social existence that determines their consciousness." Sowell writes: "If the mechanistic conception of materialism is applied, and human beings viewed as mere raw material to be shaped and moulded, then a totalitarian kind of thought control is implied, based on the inconsistent assumption that there are those who have so transcended bad environmental influences that they can undertake this superhuman task" (*Marxism*, p. 33). Marx, like the eighteenth-century materialists, "found crime to be [solely] a product of social conditions" (p. 38). On Stalin, Applebaum writes: "Stalin's famous suspicion of genetics derived precisely from his conviction that propaganda and communist education could alter the human character, permanently" (*Iron Curtain*, p. 153). —Ed.

[15] In his bibliography, Łobaczewski cites Ferdinand Merz and Ingeborg Stelz, *Einführung in die Erbpsychologie* [Introduction to Hereditary Psychology] (1977). In English, see Pinker, *Blank Slate.* —Ed.

The "ideological" battle is thus waged on territory completely unperceived by scientists living under governments of normal human structures and attempting to imagine this other reality. This applies to all people denouncing "communism," as well as those for whom this ideology has become their faith.

Shortly after arriving in the USA, I was handed a newspaper by a young black man on some street in Queens, NY. I reached for my purse, but he waved me off; the paper was free. The front page showed a picture of a young and handsome Brezhnev decorated with all the medals he did not in fact receive until much later.[16] On the last page, however, I found a quite well worked out summary of investigations performed at the University of Massachusetts on identical twins raised separately. These investigations furnished empirical indications for the important role of heredity, and the description contained a literary illustration of the similarity of the fates of twin pairs. How far "ideologically disorientated" the editors of this paper must have been to publish something which could never have appeared in the area subjected to a supposedly communist system.

In that other reality, the battlefront crosses every study of psychology and psychiatry, every psychiatric hospital, every mental health clinic, and the personality of everyone working in these areas. What takes place there: hidden thrust-and-parry duels, a smuggling through of true scientific information and accomplishments, and daily harassment. Scientific data were acquired in order to serve those in need.

Some people become morally derailed under these conditions, whereas others create a solid foundation for their convictions and are prepared to undertake difficulty and risk in order to obtain reliable, experience-based knowledge that they share with others they can trust. The fact that there are such people is a testament to the quality of their characters, their good will, and professional decency. The initial motivation of this latter group is thus not political in character, since they act mainly out of a need to assist others in their

[16]Leonid Brezhnev (1906–1982), leader of the USSR from 1964 to 1982. By his death, he had acquired some 260 such awards, 110 of which he displayed on his jacket, which became the butt of jokes. "The Brezhnev family is having dinner and suddenly the whole building shakes like an earthquake. 'Oh my God, what's that?' asks his daughter Galina. 'Don't worry,' says her mother, 'that's just your father's jacket falling on the floor'" (Lewis, *Hammer and Tickle*, pp. 214–215). —Ed.

difficulties and health problems, and very rarely for reasons related to the issues discussed in this work. Their consciousness of the political causes of the limitations and the moral meaning of this battle emerge gradually, in conjunction with experience and professional maturity, especially if their experience and skills must be used in order to save someone threatened for political reasons.

In the meantime, however, the necessary scientific data and papers must be obtained somehow, taking difficulties and other people's lack of understanding into account. Students and beginning specialists aware of what was removed from the educational curricula attempt to gain access to the scientific data stolen from them. Science starts to be degraded at a worrisome rate once such awareness is missing. Obtaining the necessary scientific publications was made very difficult due to a complete lack of comprehension of these matters abroad, including among Polish émigrés.

***

We need to understand the nature of the macrosocial phenomenon as well as that basic relationship and controversy between the pathological system and those areas of science which describe psychological and psychopathological phenomena. Otherwise, we cannot become fully conscious of the reasons for such a government's widely known and long-published behavior.

A normal person's actions and reactions, his ideas and moral criteria, all too often strike abnormal individuals as strange, foolish, or abnormal. For if a person with some psychological deviations *considers himself normal*, which is of course significantly easier if he possesses power and wealth, then he would consider a normal person different and therefore *abnormal*, whether in reality or as a result of conversive thinking. That explains why such people's government shall always have the tendency to treat any dissidents as "mentally abnormal."

Conduct such as framing a normal person for mental illness and the use of psychiatric institutions for this purpose take place in many countries in which such institutions exist. Contemporary legislation binding upon normal man's countries is not based upon an adequate understanding of the psychology of such behavior, and thus does not constitute a sufficient preventive measure against it.Within the categories of a normal psychological worldview, the motivations for such behavior can stem from personal and family disputes, property matters, intent to discredit witness testimony, and even political motives.[17]

However, when we gain sufficient experience investigating such matters, another, more essential motivation behind such behavior becomes apparent. Such defamatory suggestions are used particularly often by individuals *who are themselves not entirely normal*, and whose behavior has driven someone to a nervous breakdown or to violent protest. The idea of such conduct usually issues from minds with various psychological defects or aberrations. Only rarely does the component of pathological factors take part in the ponerogenesis of such behavior from outside its agents.[18] Among hysterics, such behavior tends to be a projection onto other people of one's own self-critical associations. By contrast, a normal person strikes a *psychopath* as a naive, smart-alecky believer in barely comprehensible theories; calling him "crazy" is not all that far away.

Well-thought-out and carefully framed legislation should therefore require testing of individuals whose suggestions that someone else is psychologically abnormal are too insistent or too doubtfully founded. Such a law would do more to discourage those prone to using such vile tactics more than current laws do.

On the other hand, any system in which the abuse of psychiatry to persecute political opponents has become a common phenomenon should be examined in the light of similar psychological criteria extrapolated onto the macrosocial scale. Any person rebelling internally against a governmental system which shall always strike him as foreign and difficult to understand, thus betraying a natural human reaction, and who is unable to hide this well enough, shall thus easily be designated by the representatives of said government as "mentally abnormal," someone who should submit to psychiatric treatment. A scientifically and morally degenerate psychiatrist becomes a tool easily used for this purpose.[19] Thus is born the sole

[17]For a brief rundown of wrongful involuntary psychiatric commitment and other abuses in various countries, see the Wikipedia entry for "Political abuse of psychiatry." —Ed.

[18]This sentence does not appear in the Polish edition. Presumably it means that the ponerogenesis of such behaviors usually stems directly from the bearers of pathological factors (i.e., psychopaths and characteropaths), and not indirectly (i.e., through secondary influence on normal people). —Ed.

[19]While psychiatry is a modern institution, the methods by which it can create arbitrary categories of normalcy and deviance have a long history, as argued,

method of terror and human torture unfamiliar even to the secret police of Tsar Alexander II.[20]

The abuse of psychiatry for purposes it should never serve thus derives from the very nature of pathocracy as a macrosocial psychopathological phenomenon and is symptomatic of its late dissimulative period. After all, that very area of knowledge and treatment must first be degraded to prevent it from jeopardizing the system itself by pronouncing a dramatic diagnosis, and must then be used as an expedient tool in the hands of the authorities. In every country, however, one meets with people who notice this and act astutely against it.

The pathocracy feels increasingly threatened by this area whenever the medical and psychological sciences make steady progress. After all, not only can these sciences knock the weapon of psychological conquest right out of its hands; they can even strike at its very nature, and from inside the empire, at that. A specific perception

---

for instance, by Hungarian-American psychiatrist Thomas S. Szasz in *The Manufacture of Madness: A Comparative Study of the Inquisition and the Mental Health Movement* (1970). Szasz was a harsh critic of involuntary psychiatric intervention. For a history of North American abuses of psychiatry in the last seventy years see Ross, *C.I.A. Doctors.* Ross focuses on involuntary human experimentation (including children) in CIA "mind control" experiments (including the administering of drugs, hypnosis, and physical and psychological torture), non-lethal weapons, and psychological warfare research run by top American psychiatrists in prestigious institutions, and other abuses. Some declassified files reveal experiments involving the deliberate creation of dissociative identity disorder, amnesia, anxieties, and trauma. For a report on torture and illegal experimentation conducted by CIA health professionals since 9/11, see the Physicians for Human Rights report, "Experiments in Torture: Evidence of Human Subject Research and Experimentation in the 'Enhanced' Interrogation Program" (2010). Their previous report, "Broken Laws, Broken Lives: Medical Evidence of Torture by US Personnel and Its Impact" (2008), details the use of "sensory deprivation, isolation, sleep deprivation, forced nudity, the use of military working dogs to instill fear, cultural and sexual humiliation, mock executions, and the threat of violence or death toward detainees or their loved ones." Psychologists John Jessen and James Mitchell created the "enhanced interrogation techniques," and top psychologists and officials at the American Psychological Association were involved with the torture program. See also Jonathan D. Moreno's *Mind Wars: Brain Science and the Military in the 21st Century* (2012). —Ed.

[20] Created after an assassination attempt on his life in 1866. After the successful assassination in 1881, his successor Alexander III formed the infamous Okhrana to combat leftist revolutionaries and political terrorism, also active during the reign of Nicholas II. —Ed.

of these matters therefore bids the pathocracy to be "ideologically alert" in this area. This also explains why anyone who is both too knowledgeable in this area and too far outside the immediate reach of such authorities should be accused of anything that can be trumped up, including psychological abnormality.[21]

[21] *Author's note (1997):* It is also important to bear in mind that government-funded entities tasked with corrupting these dangerous sciences existed both inside and outside the empire. They were heavily promoted to expand their influence. Therefore, it has become necessary to cleanse these disciplines of the foreign meddling of the previously discussed genesis.

CHAPTER VIII
PATHOCRACY AND RELIGION

For a contemporary thinker, monotheistic faith is primarily an incomplete induction[1] derived from ontological knowledge about the laws governing microcosmic and macrocosmic material and organic and psychological life.[2] He may also make use of certain encounters accessible by means of introspection. The rest complements this induction by means of items man gains by other ways and accepts either individually or in accordance with the dictates of his religion and creed. A soundless, wordless voice unconsciously awakens our associations, reaches our awareness in the quiet of mind, and either complements or rebukes our cognition; this phenomenon is every bit as true as whatever has become accessible to science thanks to modern investigative methods.

In perfecting our cognition in the psychological field and attaining truths formerly available only to mystics, we render ever narrower the space of ignorance which until recently separated the realm of spiritual perception from naturalistic science. Sometime in the not too distant future, these two cognitions will meet and certain divergences will become self-evident. It would thus be better if we were prepared for it. Almost from the outset of my deliberations on the genesis and nature of evil, I have been conscious of the fact that the investigative results summarized in this work can contribute to filling that space which is so hard for the human mind to enter.

The ponerological approach throws new light upon age-old questions heretofore regulated by the dictates of moral systems and must of necessity bring about a revision in our understanding of these issues. As a Christian, the author was initially apprehensive that this would cause dangerous collisions with ancient tradition. Studying the question in the light of the Scriptures caused these apprehensions

[1] An inference from a set of instances that is not exhaustive. —Ed.

[2] For a contemporary abductive argument (inference to past cause from present evidence), see Stephen C. Meyer, *Return of the God Hypothesis: Three Scientific Discoveries that Reveal the Mind behind the Universe* (2021). —Ed.

gradually to fade away. Rather, this now appears to be the way to bring our superficial and overly speculative way of thinking closer to that original and primeval understanding of moral values. Quite characteristically, reading the Gospels can provide teachings clearly convergent with the method of understanding evil derived from naturalistic investigations on its origin. At the same time, we must foresee that the process of correction and reconciliation will be laborious and time consuming, which ultimately will probably prevent any major tumult.

Religion is an eternal and universal phenomenon. In the beginning, the sometimes overly active human imagination complemented whatever esoteric perception could not handle.[3] Once civilization and its concurrent discipline of thought reaches a certain level of development, a monotheistic idea tends to emerge, generally as a conviction of a certain narrow intellectual elite. Such development in religious thought can be considered a historical law rather than individual discovery by such people like Zarathustra or Socrates. The march of religious thought through history constitutes an indispensable factor of the formation of human cultures.[4]

Acceptance of religion's basic truths opens to man a whole field of possible cognition wherein his mind can search for the truth. At that point, we also free ourselves of certain psychological impediments and gain a certain freedom of cognition in areas accessible to naturalistic perception. Rediscovering the true, ancient, religious values strengthens us, showing us the meaning of life and history.[5] It also facilitates our introspective acceptance of phenomena within ourselves

[3]For example, clothe it or fill it in with secondary, more familiar images and interpretations. —Ed.

[4]*Author's note (1997):* Therefore, those who chose to oppose it, as happened in the last great incarnation of pathocracy, betrayed not only a strategic intent to destroy religion, but also significant educational deficiencies in history.

[5]See the accounts of Christian dissidents in Eastern Europe and the USSR in Rod Dreher's book, *Live Not by Lies*, and how their experiences enabled this process of rediscovery. For example: "Like other political prisoners, Krčméry endured repeated tortures. He had been trained to resist brainwashing. In the end, he relied on faith alone to guide his path. The more he surrendered in his weakness, the greater his spiritual strength. ... In that communist prison, the biblical command to bear one another's burdens became intensely real. ... Solzhenitsyn's audacious claim was that suffering had refined him, taught him to love. It was only there, out of the experience of intense suffering, that the prisoner began to understand the meaning of life and first began to sense the good inside himself" (pp. 192, 194). —Ed.

for which naturalistic perception proves insufficient. Parallel to our self-knowledge, we also develop our ability to understand other people, thanks to the acceptance of the existence of an analogous reality within our neighbor.

These values become priceless whenever man is forced into maximum mental effort and profound deliberations in action so as to avoid stumbling into evil, danger, or exceptional difficulties. If there is no possibility of apprehending a situation fully, but a way out must nevertheless be found for one's self, family, or nation, we are indeed fortunate if we can hear that silent voice within saying, "Don't do this," or, "Trust me, do this."

We could thus say that this cognition and faith simultaneously supporting our mind and multiplying our spiritual strength constitute the sole basis for survival and resistance in situations wherein a person or nation is threatened by the products of ponerogenesis, which cannot be measured in the categories of the natural worldview.[6] That is the opinion of many righteous people. We cannot contradict the basic value of such a conviction, but if it leads to contemptuous treatment of objective science in this area and reinforces the egotism of the natural worldview, people holding this conviction are unaware of the fact that they are no longer acting in good faith.

No major religion indicates the nature of the macrosocial pathological phenomenon; therefore we cannot consider religious dictates as a specific basis for overcoming this great historical disease. Religion is neither a specific serum nor an etiotropically active antibiotic[7] with regard to the phenomenon of pathocracy. Although it constitutes a regenerative factor for the spiritual strength of individuals and societies, religious truth and experience do not contain the specific naturalistic knowledge which is essential for understanding the pathology of the phenomenon, and which is simultaneously a curative and a immunity-generating factor for human personalities. Rather, religious faith and the phenomenon of pathocracy are in fact at different levels of reality, the latter being more earthly. That also explains why there can be no true collision between religion and ponerological knowledge about the macrosocial pathological phenomenon.

If we based our societal defense and treatment with regard to the destructive influences of pathocracy only upon the truest religious

[6]See Dreher, *Live Not by Lies*, ch. 8 ("Religion, the Bedrock of Resistance"). —Ed.
[7]A drug attacking the cause of a disease. —Ed.

values, this would be reminiscent of curing an insufficiently comprehended disease exclusively by measures which strengthen body and soul. Such general therapy may furnish satisfactory results in many cases, but it will prove insufficient in others. This macrosocial disease belongs to the latter category.

The fact that this pathocratic phenomenon, which has spread to the most wide-ranging scale in human history, demonstrates hostility to any and all religion—and has destroyed the best religious values in each of its manifestations—does not imply the conclusion that it is always against religion. This relationship would be structured differently under other historical and contemporary conditions. In the light of historical data, it appears obvious that religious systems have also succumbed to ponerogenic processes and manifested the symptoms of a similar disease.

The specific basis for healing our sick world, which is also a curative factor for restoring full reasoning capabilities to the human personality, must therefore be the kind of science which renders the pathological essence of the phenomenon evident and describes it in sufficiently objective language. Resistance to the acceptance of such knowledge is often justified by religious motivation; yet it is largely caused by the egotism of the natural worldview in its traditional overrating of its values and fear of disintegration resulting from acknowledging one's ignorance, and it must be constructively overcome.

***

The pathocratic phenomenon has doubtless appeared many times in history, feeding parasitically upon various social, political, or religious movements, deforming their structures and ideologies in a characteristic fashion. It must therefore have met with various religious systems and with a variety of historical and cultural backgrounds. Two basic possibilities for a relationship between this phenomenon and a religious body can thus be adduced. The first occurs when the religious association itself succumbs to infection and the ponerogenic process, which leads to development of the above-mentioned phenomena within it. The second possibility emerges if a pathocracy develops as a parasite upon some secular movement whose character is social or political, pushing a religious association toward the side of normal people, which must inevitably lead to collision with religious organizations.

In the first case, the religious association succumbs to destruction from within, its organism becomes subordinated to goals completely different from the original idea, and its theosophic and moral values fall prey to characteristic deformation, thereupon serving as a disguise for domination by pathological individuals.[8] The quasi-religious ideology then becomes both a justification for using force and sadism against nonbelievers, heretics, and sorcerers, and a conscience drug for people who put such inspirations into effect.[9]

---

[8]In her book *Schizophrenic Christianity: How Christian Fundamentalism Attracts and Protects Sociopaths, Abusive Pastors, and Child Molesters* (2014), Jeri Massi describes how psychopaths infiltrate fundamentalist congregations and bible colleges, the weaknesses inherent in fundamentalist Christianity which make it susceptible to ponerization, and the methods by which psychopaths operate in such an environment, eventually turning against their own congregations, punishing displays of conscience, and promoting a counterfeit Christianity. For an evangelical perspective, see Chuck DeGroat, *When Narcissism Comes to Church: Healing Your Community from Emotional and Spiritual Abuse* (2020).

Regarding Judaism, see Holocaust survivor and organic chemistry professor Israel Shahak's treatment of classical Judaism, which he describes as "one of the most totalitarian societies in the whole history of mankind" (*Jewish History, Jewish Religion: The Weight of Three Thousand Years* [2008], p. 19). For a Christian critique, see Irish Protestant Hebraist and missionary to the Jews Alexander McCaul's *The Talmud Tested: A Comparison of the Principles and Doctrines of Modern Judaism with the Religion of Moses and the Prophets* (1846). As an example of how this pathology manifests, see the statements of Sephardi Chief Rabbi of Israel from 1973 to 1983 Ovadia Yosef (1920–2013): "Goyim were born only to serve us. Without that, they have no place in the world—only to serve the People of Israel ... In Israel, death has no dominion over them ... With gentiles, it will be like any person—they need to die, but [God] will give them longevity. Why? Imagine that one's donkey would die, they'd lose their money. This is his servant ... That's why he gets a long life, to work well for this Jew" (*Jerusalem Post*, Oct. 18, 2010). Laurent Guyénot, in *From Yahweh to Zion: Three Thousand Years of Exile* (2018), esp. ch. 11 ("Children of the Mad God"), compares features of Yahweh in the Old Testament with the clinical criteria for psychopathy, e.g., commands to exterminate entire peoples, enslave others, and the notion of the chosen people, a mode of thought "based on the denial of the other's humanity" (p. 458). —Ed.

[9]For example, the Catholic Inquisitions, especially the Spanish Inquisition (see Steven Saxonberg, "Premodern Totalitarianism: The Case of Spain Compared to France" [2018], as well as Szasz, *Manufacture of Madness*). In his *New Inquisitions*, Arthur Versluis argues the Inquisition is an archetypal phenomenon that has found expression not only in Catholicism but also the twentieth-century totalitarianisms ("with much fewer limitations and with far greater virulence" than the Inquisition), which share these features: "The unity or totalizing of secular or religious bureaucracies into a single totalitarian power,

Anyone criticizing such a state of affairs is condemned with paramoral indignation, allegedly in the name of the original idea and faith in God, but actually because he feels and thinks within the categories of normal people. Such a system retains the name of the original religion and many other specific designations, swearing on the prophet's beard while using these motifs in its doublespeak. Something which was originally to be an aid in the comprehension of God's truth now scourges nations with the sword of imperialism.[10]

When such phenomena are long-lasting, those people who have retained their faith in religious values will condemn such a state of affairs, thereby indicating that it diverges widely from the truth. They will unfortunately do so without understanding the nature and causes of the pathological phenomenon, i.e., in moral categories, thus

---

the criminalization of thought, the use of torture and murder, the inculcation of terror in the populace, the use of secret evidence and witnesses, and the use of public infamy, humiliation, or 'show trials' or 'show executions' [*autos-da-fe*]" (p. 18). He also traces a philosophical genealogy from Tertullian, Irenaeus, and the Inquisitions to modern totalitarianism through such figures as Joseph de Maistre (1753–1821), Juan Donoso Cortés (1809–1853), Georges Sorel (1847–1922), and Carl Schmitt (1888–1985), among others, all of whom seem to have espoused a schizoidal worldview (see pp. 22, 33, 36, 51). Both Maistre and Schmitt saw the Inquisition as a good juridical model.

The 2010s saw another religious manifestation of the archetype in the rise of the Islamic State in Iraq and Syria (see Fawaz A. Gerges, *ISIS: A History* [2021]). Mozaffari writes regarding Islamism: "All other interpretations of Islam are either declared misleading or said to be fabricated by foreign powers and the enemies of Islam. ... Religion is reduced to a simple tool with multiple tasks: propaganda, mobilization of the masses, and justification for political decisions and for persecuting opponents" (*Islamism*, p. 274). Ponerized fundamentalism in some varieties of Christianity, Judaism, and Islam can be seen in an apocalyptic trend which prophesies a massive war that must be fought (and thus supported or even provoked) in the Middle East in order to usher in the "end times," the coming of the messiah, and some form of world domination. —Ed.

[10]For Islamic imperialism throughout its history, see Robert Spencer, *The History of Jihad: From Muhammad to ISIS* (2019). Mozaffari defines Islamism as follows: "a religiously inspired ideology based on a totalitarian interpretation of Islam, whose final aim is the conquest of the world by all means" (*Islamism*, pp. 267–268). For case studies of the use of the Bible as a charter document for imperialism, see Michael Prior's *The Bible and Colonialism: A Moral Critique* (1999). Prior focuses on the Spanish and Portuguese colonization of Latin America, the Dutch conquest of southern Africa, and the Zionist conquest and settlement of Palestine (see also Versluis, *Mystical State*, ch. 2, "The Legacy of Monolatry"). See also Ilan Pappé's *The Ethnic Cleansing of Palestine* (2007). —Ed.

committing the malignant error with which we are already familiar. Exposed to repression, they will take advantage of some convenient political situation to protest such a state of affairs, breaking away from the original system and creating various sects and denominations. This kind of breakdown can be considered a characteristic consequence of any movement's infection by this disease, be it religious or secular. Religious conflict thereupon assumes the character of political divisions, giving rise to warfare among various believers in the same God.

As we know, this state evolves into the dissimulative phase once human brutality starts to become exhausted; however, this form will be much more long-lasting than a pathocracy feeding on a secular movement. Human individuals cannot easily contain the entire process within their frame of reference, since such a state spans many generations; their criticism will thus be limited to the questions they are immediately familiar with, making it difficult to correct such a reality. However, this gives rise to a gradual but uncoordinated pressure front of reasonable people, thereby instigating some kind of evolution within any group thus engendered. Such evolution will aim at reactivating the original religious values or at overcoming the deformations.

Whether this process achieves its ultimate goal depends upon two conditions: the original idea must be fully fledged (virtuous), and the final crisis must be survived in a skillful manner. If the original idea was merely a human creation, had political aims, or was contaminated by some pathological factor from the outset, the goal is unattainable. If it *is* attainable (because the original teaching was true), then our asymptomatic approximation of it[11] will place us in a position wherein the definitive elimination of the effects of the surmounted illness requires an objective view of its essence and history. Otherwise it is impossible to eliminate the leftover pathological deformations which would survive as a factor opening the door to reinfection. Psychological expertise teaches us that without this final retrospective it is impossible to achieve full health.

Some less-enduring, primary-ponerogenic religious groups may have been started by persons who were carriers of certain psychological anomalies. Particular attention should be focused upon largely para-

[11]That is, our conception of a religion that still carries the results of ponerogenic contamination, but no longer manifests pathocratic symptoms. —Ed.

noidal characteropathies and their above-discussed role in instigating new phases of ponerogenesis. For such people, the world of normal human experience (including religious experience) succumbs to deformation; spellbinding of self and others easily follows, imposed upon other people as a result of pathological egotism. We can observe marginal Christian sects today whose beginnings were doubtless of this nature.[12] However, sects that crystallize around psychopathic personalities are currently more dangerous. They are responsible for an increasing number of human tragedies.[13]

If a religion which later fell apart into numerous doctrinal factions had such a beginning, the above-mentioned regenerative processes—effected by healthy common sense and centuries of deep reflection—will initially lead to an intense elimination of the negative effects and to a refinement of the said religion, later to the drive to achieve historical objectivity, and as a consequence, to the liberalization of its customs. At this point, the imams of this religion will start

[12]Łobaczewski probably has in mind groups like Jehovah's Witnesses and Seventh-day Adventists. Anabaptist groups (e.g., Amish, Hutterite, Mennonite), with their origins in the Radical Reformation in the sixteenth century, are also candidates. For example, German apocalyptic preacher Thomas Müntzer (c. 1489–1525), who became a leader of the peasant uprising of 1525, was convinced the end of the world was near, and saw himself as playing an integral role in the emergence of a new age of man. He and his followers destroyed monasteries, killed monks and priests, and appropriated others' property (since according to the Book of Acts all is to be held in common): "when anyone needed food or clothing he went to a rich man and demanded it of him in Christ's name ... And what was not given freely was taken by force." In a tirade of paramoralisms reminiscent of Lenin, he wrote to Luther, calling him "a basilisk, a viper, an archpagan, an archdevil, a bashful Whore of Babylon, and finally, in a fit of cannibalistic frenzy, he predicted that the devil would boil Luther in his own juice and devour him. 'I would like to smell your frying carcass.'" See Igor Shafarevich, *The Socialist Phenomenon* (2019), pp. 51–59, 68–79 (the quotations are from pp. 74, 76). —Ed.

[13]See Peter A. Olsson, *Malignant Pied Pipers: A Psychological Study of Destructive Cult Leaders from Rev. Jim Jones to Osama bin Laden* (2017). Olsson also covers Charlie Manson (The Family), Marshall Applewhite (Heaven's Gate), Shoko Asahara, and others. See also Tom O'Neill, *Chaos: Charles Manson, the CIA, and the Secret History of the Sixties* (2020); Jeff Guinn, *The Road to Jonestown: Jim Jones and Peoples Temple* (2018); Lawrence Wright, *Going Clear: Scientology, Hollywood, and the Prison of Belief* (2013); and Robins and Post, *Political Paranoia*, ch. 5, on Jones, Koresh, and Asahara. More recently, see the case of Brazilian "psychic surgeon," serial rapist, and accused pedophile João Teixeira de Faria ("John of God"), currently serving a nineteen-year sentence. —Ed.

to perceive this as a threat to the religion's existence and their own social position. This will push them to resort to ruthless measures against anyone daring to criticize or sow doubt. The pathological process begins anew. Such a religion will only be able to continue to exist under the state's protection, which historically speaking does not bode well for its survival. Such is the state of affairs we may be actually witnessing today.[14]

However, the mere fact that some religious association has succumbed to the ponerization process does not constitute proof that the original gnosis or vision was contaminated from the outset by errors which opened the door to invasion by pathological factors, or that it was an effect of their influence. In order for the doors to be opened to infection by pathological factors, it suffices for such a religious movement to succumb to contamination sometime later in its history, e.g., as a result of excessive influence on the part of initially foreign archetypes of philosophy and secular civilization, or of compromises with the goals of the country's rulers.[15] This may initiate a process of further progressive degeneration.

The above briefly summarizes the data already known to us about the causes and laws of the course of the ponerological process, this time with regard to religious groups. Important differences should be underscored, however. Religious associations are among the most enduring and long-lived social structures, historically speaking. Therefore, the ponerological process in such a group will also run its course over a much longer time frame. Religion is a natural phenomenon and is necessary to man to such an extent that every such group, provided it is numerous enough, will contain a large number of normal people (generally the majority) who do not become discouraged and who

[14]*Author's note (1997):* In the light of this, does Islam have much time left? [See, for example, sociologist Ernest Gellner's *Postmodernism, Reason and Religion* (1992), especially the first section on reform in Islam and its resistance to secularization. With reference to such trends in Islam, Mozaffari points out that even during the Abbasid Golden Age in Baghdad (775–861 A.D.), "tangible signs of the coming crisis and decline are visible already": "The same al-Mamun who founded the House of Wisdom and adopted the 'rational' school of thinking ... turned it into governmental doctrine, imposing an official inquisition (*minha*) and severely punishing those who refused to adhere to it" (*Islamism*, pp. 35–36). For a modern call for reform in Islam, see Mustafa Akyol's *Reopening Muslim Minds: A Return to Reason, Freedom, and Tolerance* (2021). —Ed.]

[15]See the discussion in Chapter II. —Ed.

form a permanent wing inhibiting the process of ponerization. In such an association both these processes, ponerogenic and rehabilitative, proceed on a long time scale. For similar reasons, the tenuous equilibrium of the dissimulative phase would settle to the advantage of those people who have normal feelings and truer religious convictions. Nonetheless, respective generations may have the impression that the observed state represents its permanent and essential characteristics, including its shortcomings. They may reconcile themselves to such errors out of habit, or protest against them.

We must therefore pose the following question: Can the most persistent and sensible action based on the natural worldview and historical, philosophical, theological, and moral reflections ever completely eliminate the effects of a ponerological process which has long been surmounted? Based on experience gleaned from individual patients, a psychotherapist would doubt such a possibility. For in those terms, the process can never be fully understood. (The consequences of the influence of pathological factors can only be definitely liquidated if a person becomes aware that he was the object of their activity.) Such a method of careful correction of detail may sound reminiscent of the work done by an art restorer who decided against removing all later paint-overs and revealing the master's original work *in toto*, but rather retained and conserved a few heavy-handed corrections for posterity.

Even against the backdrop of conditions of the times conducive to the healing process, such efforts at step-by-step untying of knots based on the natural worldview only lead toward a moralizing interpretation of the effects of uncomprehended pathological factors, with the consequence of panic and the tendency to retreat to the side that seems more secure. The organism of the religious group thus will retain some dormant foci of the disease which may become active under certain favorable conditions.

We should therefore realize that following the path of naturalistic apperception of the process of the genesis of evil—attributing the proportionate "fault" to the influence of etiological factors—can ease our minds and hearts of the burden represented by the disturbing results of a moralizing interpretation of their role in ponerogenesis. This also permits more detailed identification of the causes and results of their operation, as well as definitive elimination thereof. Objective language proves to be not only more accurate, efficient, and economical to work with, but also much safer as a tool of action when dealing with difficult situations and delicate matters.

Such a more profound and consistent solution for the problems inherited from centuries of ponerological ignorance is possible whenever a given religion represents a current of gnosis and faith which was originally authentic enough. A courageous approach to remedying conditions caused by presently perceptible poneric processes, or by chronic perseverance of survivals from such states far in the past, thus demands both acceptance of this new science and a mature conviction of the veracity of the original teaching. Doubts—even if they are unrealistic or have been repressed deep into the subconscious—will otherwise block any such intent by means of insufficiently objectified fear.[16] We must be convinced that the Truth can endure such a washing in modern detergent; not only will it not lose its eternal values, but it will actually regain its original freshness and noble colors.

With regard to the second above-mentioned situation, when the ponerogenic process leading to pathocracy has affected some secular and political movement, the situation of religion in such a country will be completely different. The religious organization cannot help but assume a critical attitude, becoming a support for opposition on the part of the society of normal people. This in turn provokes the movement affected by this phenomenon to an ever more intolerant attitude toward religion. The polarization of attitudes proves to be inevitable. In the end, both sides begin to view the destruction of the opponent as a matter of life and death. Such a situation thus places a given society's religion before the specter of physical destruction.

Whenever pathocracy emerges in an autonomous process, this means that the religious systems dominating that country were unable to prevent it in time.[17] Usually, the religious organizations of any given country have sufficient influence upon society to be able to oppose nascent evil if they act with courage and reason. If they cannot, this is the result of either fragmentation and strife among various denominations or of internal corruption within the religious system.[18] As a result, religious organizations have long tolerated

[16]I.e., unarticulated doubts will provoke a vague fear, blocking any action. —Ed.

[17]Janowski writes: "A rapid decline in religiosity among Americans may be one reason why the country is becoming totalitarian. ... One could also add that the weak perception of evil may stem from the fact that Americans have not experienced the atrocities that other nations have; they don't even know about them" (*Homo Americanus*, p. 55). —Ed.

[18]For disturbing trends in American Christianity, see Chris Hedges's *American*

and even uncritically inspired the development of pathocracy. This weakness later becomes the cause of religion's defeats at the hands of pathocratic rulers.

In the case of an artificially infected pathocracy, the religious system's joint liability may be lesser, albeit still generally concrete. It is justified to exonerate a country's religious systems for the state of affairs only if the pathocracy has been imposed by force. Specific conditions emerge in this situation: the religious organizations have the morally stronger defensive position, are able to accept material losses (some people may leave and others may be martyred), and can also undergo their own recuperative process.[19]

Pathocrats may be able to use primitive and brutal means to combat religion, but it is very difficult for them to attack the essence of religious convictions. Their propaganda not only misses the mark but also brings about the familiar phenomena of immunization or resistance on the part of normal people, with the final result being the opposite of the intended moral reaction. Pathocrats can only use brute force to destroy religion if they feel the latter's weakness. The principle of "divide and conquer" can be used if there are various denominations with a long history of enmity, but the effects of such measures are generally ephemeral and can lead to religions uniting under a common threat and in the name of the same God.[20]

The specific practical knowledge collected by the society of nor-

---

Fascists: The Christian Right and the War on America (2006), Jeff Sharlet's *The Family: The Secret Fundamentalism at the Heart of American Power* (2009), and chapter 12 of Versluis, *New Inquisitions.* In recent years, critical race theory and social justice have also made inroads into American churches, Catholic and Protestant. See, for example, Patrick Saint-Jean, "Critical Race Theory and Catholicism Go Hand in Hand" (2021), and the *Christian Century* editors, "Critical Race Theory Is a Gift to Christians" (2021). —Ed.

[19]Legutko writes: "by relying on rural religiosity the Church managed to preserve a large area of social practices and religious traditions that was not accessible to the communist ideology. In countries where this type of folk Christianity did not exist or was considerably weaker, the communist system managed to wreak more havoc and penetrated deeper into the social fabric" (*Demon in Democracy*, p. 149). See also the brief account of Catholicism in Poland during the period of High Stalinism in Applebaum, *Iron Curtain*, pp. 424–30. —Ed.

[20]Speaking of his time in prison, Slovakian physician Silvester Krčméry noted that "nobody recognized any confessional differences." Dreher comments: "It is not a false ecumenism that claims all religions are essentially the same. It is rather a mutual recognition that within the context of persecution, embracing Jan Patočka's 'solidarity of the shattered' becomes vital to spiritual survival" (*Live Not by Lies*, p. 155). —Ed.

mal people under pathocratic rule, together with the phenomenon of psychological immunization, begin to exert their own characteristic effect upon the structure of religious denominations. If some religious system succumbed to ponerogenic infection sometime during its history, the effects and chronic survivals thereof persevere within for centuries. As already adduced, remedying this by means of philosophical and moral reflections meets with specific psychological difficulties. But under pathocratic rule, in spite of the abuse suffered by such a religious organization, the latter organism-specific antibodies are transfused, which cure the ponerogenic survivals.

Such a specific process aims unconsciously at ridding the religious structure of those deformations which were the effect of the operation of the pathological factors familiar to us. Insofar as the appearance of pathocracy in various guises throughout human history always results from human errors which opened the door to the pathological phenomenon, one must also look on the other side of the coin. We should understand this in the light of that underrated law, when the effect of a particular causative structure has a teleological meaning of its own.[21] It would, however, be highly advantageous for this recuperative process to be accompanied by greater awareness of its nature, which also acts similarly in terms of developing critical thinking, psychological immunity, prudence, and healing human souls. Such awareness could also help elaborate safer and more effective plans of action.

If individuals and groups believing in God and his Wisdom are able to accept an objective understanding of macrosocial pathological phenomena, especially this most dangerous one, and develop this science sufficiently, then the natural outcome will thus prove to be a certain separation of religious and ponerological problematics, which qualitatively occupy different levels of reality. Church attention can then revert to questions regarding man's relationship with God, an area for which churches have a calling. On the other hand, resistance to ponerological phenomena and their worldwide spread should be largely assumed by scientific and political institutions whose actions are based on a naturalistic understanding of the nature and genesis of evil. Such a separation of duties should never go too far, since the

[21]In other words, the process initiated by human failings and catalyzed by pathocracy fulfills a separate purpose: revealing the errors that opened the door to evil and refining religion in the process. —Ed.

genesis of evil includes participation of human moral failings, and overcoming these based on religious premises has been the responsibility of religious associations since times immemorial.

Some religions and denominations subjected to pathocratic rule are forced by such circumstance to become overly involved in matters conventionally referred to as political, or even in economic efforts. This is necessary in order to protect the existence of the religious organization itself, in order to help fellow believers or other citizens suffering abuse, and to maintain the necessary order that functions for the benefit of society.[22] It is important, however, to avoid having such a state of affairs become permanent in the shape of habit and tradition, since this could later make it more difficult to revert to normal human government.

In spite of existing differences of conviction and tradition, the basis for cooperative effort on the part of people of good will should contain that characteristic convergence of the conclusions we deduce between the precepts of the Christian Gospels (and other monotheistic religions) and a ponerological view of the genesis of evil. The faithful of various religions and denominations do in fact believe in the same God, and at present they are threatened by the same macrosocial pathological phenomenon. This creates sufficient data to enable a search for cooperation in effecting achievements whose value is so obvious. Time and the growth of knowledge will lead the way forward.

[22]Łobaczewski specifies in the Polish edition that he is referring to the Catholic countries subjected to pathocracy (e.g., Poland, Hungary, Czechoslovakia, Yugoslavia). See the chapter on religion in Legutko, *Demon in Democracy*, especially pp. 145–151, for additional background on the role of the Catholic Church in Poland under communism. —Ed.

CHAPTER IX
THERAPY FOR THE WORLD

For centuries, attempts were made to treat various diseases based on a naive understanding of them and upon experience transmitted from generation to generation. This activity was not ineffective; in many cases it produced advantageous results. Superseding this traditional medicine with the newly generating modern science in Europe caused social health to deteriorate initially. However, it was only with the help of modern science that many diseases were vanquished, ailments against which traditional medicine had been helpless. This occurred because a naturalistic comprehension of disease and its causes created a basis for treatment and prevention.

Regarding the phenomena discussed in this work, our situation is similar to the one engendered by the above-mentioned crisis with reference to the health of European nations. We have abandoned the traditional socio-moral organization, developed via Roman tradition and Christianity, but have not yet elaborated more valuable knowledge, one which would fill in the gap thus created. Instead, this gap has been filled by political ideologues and sectarians guided by motives they have no intention of revealing to us. We therefore need to rediscover and affirm the criteria for what is right and wrong, which will support and give weight to the old values and become a foundation for a healthy social structure. Simultaneously, this new, improved knowledge would fulfill a burning need in today's world—to prevail over those effects of ponerogenesis whose nature we have not sufficiently understood.

According to contemporary understanding, effective treatment of a disease becomes possible once we have apprehended its essence, its etiological factors and their properties, and its pathodynamic course within organisms with dissimilar biological properties. Once such knowledge is available, finding the proper treatment measures generally proves a less difficult and dangerous duty. For doctors, disease represents an interesting, even captivating, biological phenomenon. They often accepted the risk of contact with its contagious pathogenic factors and suffered losses in order to comprehend the ailment so as to be able to heal people. Thanks to this, they achieved the possibility of etiotropic disease treatment and artificial immunization of human organisms to disease. The doctor's own health is thus also better protected today; but he ought never to feel any contempt for the patient or his disease.

When we are faced with a macrosocial pathological phenomenon which requires us to proceed in a manner analogous in principle to that governing contemporary medicine, especially with reference to overcoming diseases which quickly propagate among populations, the law demands necessary rigorous measures which become binding upon healthy people as well. It is also worth pointing out that people and political organizations whose worldview is leftist generally present a more consistent attitude in this matter, demanding such sacrifices in the name of the common good.

We must also be aware that the macrosocial ponerogenic phenomenon facing us is analogous to those diseases against which the old traditional medicine proved inadequate. In order to overcome this state of affairs, we must therefore utilize new means based upon an understanding of the essence and causes of the phenomenon, i.e., according to principles analogous to those governing modern medicine. The road to comprehension of the phenomenon was also much more difficult and dangerous than the one which should lead from such understanding to the finding of naturalistically and morally justified—and properly organized—therapeutic activities. These methods are potentially possible and feasible, since they derive from an understanding of the phenomenon per se and become an extension thereof. For in this "disease," as in many cases treated by psychotherapists, understanding alone already begins to heal human personalities. The author confirmed this in practice in individual cases. Similarly, many already-known psychotherapeutic methods could also be used this way.

The insufficiency of efforts based upon the best moral values has become common knowledge after centuries of rebounding as though from rubber bands. The powerful military weapons that jeopardize all humanity can, on the other hand, be considered as indispensable as a straitjacket, something whose use diminishes in proportion to the improved skills governing the behavior of those persons entrusted with the healing arts. We need measures which can reach all people and all nations and which can operate upon the recognized causes of great diseases.

Such therapeutic measures cannot be limited to the phenomenon of pathocracy. Pathocracy will always find a positive response if some independent country is infected with an advanced state of hystericization, or if a small privileged caste oppresses and exploits other citizens, keeping them backward and in the dark; anyone willing to treat the world can then be hounded, and his moral right to act be questioned. Evil in the world, in fact, constitutes a continuum: one kind opens the door to another, irrespective of its qualitative essence or the ideological slogans cloaking it.

It also becomes impossible to find effective means of therapeutic operation if the minds of people undertaking such tasks are affected by a tendency to conversive thinking like subconscious selection and substitution of data, or if some doctrine preventing an objective perception of reality becomes mandatory. In particular, a political doctrine for which it has become a dogma to call a macrosocial pathological phenomenon by the name of its popular ideology blocks an understanding of its real nature so well that purposeful action becomes impossible. Anyone administering such action should undergo an appropriate prior examination, or even a kind of psychotherapy, in order to eliminate any tendencies toward even slightly sloppy thinking.

Like every well-managed treatment, therapy of the world must contain two basic demands: strengthening the overall defensive powers of the human community and attacking its most dangerous disease, etiotropically if possible. Taking into account all the aspects referred to in the theoretical chapter on ponerology, therapeutic efforts should be directed at subjecting the operations of the known factors of the genesis of evil, as well as the processes of ponerogenesis itself, to the controls of scientific and societal consciousness.

Present attempts at trusting moral data alone, no matter how sincerely perceived, also prove inadequate, as would trying to operate solely on the basis of the data contained within this book, ignoring the essential support of moral values. A ponerologist's attitude underscores primarily the naturalistic aspects of phenomena; nevertheless, this does not mean that the traditional ones have diminished in value. Efforts aimed at endowing the life of nations with the necessary moral order should therefore constitute a second wing, working in parallel and rationally supported by naturalistic principles.

Contemporary societies were pushed into a state of moral recession during the late nineteenth and early twentieth centuries; leading them back out is the general duty of this generation and should remain the overall backdrop to their actions as a whole. The starting point should be the intent to fulfill the commandment of loving one's neighbor, including even those who have committed substantial evil. A great therapeutic endeavor can only be effected once we do this in the name of God and with the honest control of moral consciousness, moderation of words, and thoughtfulness of action. At that point, ponerology will prove its practical usefulness in fulfilling this task. People and values mature in action. Thus, a synthesis of traditional moral teachings and this new naturalistic approach can only occur with reasoned behavior.

Truth Is a Healer

It would be difficult to summarize here what many famous scholars, doctors, and psychologists have said about the psychotherapeutic role of making a person aware of what has crowded his subconscious, stifled within by constant painful effort because he feared to look an unpleasant truth in the eye, lacked objective data to derive correct conclusions, or was too proud to permit the awareness that he had behaved in a preposterous fashion. In addition to being quite well understood by specialists, these matters have also become common knowledge to some extent. In any method or technique of analytical psychotherapy, or autonomous psychotherapy, as T. Szasz called it,[1] the guiding operational motivation is to expose to the light of consciousness whatever material has been suppressed by means of subconscious selection of data, or given up in the face of intellectual problems. This is accompanied by a disillusionment of substitutions and rationalizations, whose creation is usually in proportion to the amount of repressed material.

In many cases, it turns out that the material fearfully eliminated from the field of consciousness, and frequently substituted by ostensibly more comfortable associations, would never have had such dangerous results if we had initially mustered the courage to perceive

[1]Thomas Szasz, *The Ethics of Psychoanalysis: The Theory and Method of Autonomous Psychotherapy* (1965). Szasz (1920–2012) was a controversial Hungarian-American psychiatrist and staunch critic of coercive psychiatry, e.g., civil commitment and involuntary psychiatric treatment, as well as the tendency to see "mental illness" as a disease. In the latter, his views align with Dąbrowski, *Psychoneurosis Is Not an Illness* (1972). —Ed.

it consciously. We would then have been in the position to find an independent and often creative way out of the situation.

In some cases, however, especially when dealing with phenomena which are hard to understand within the categories of our natural worldview, leading the patient out of his problems demands furnishing him with crucial objective data, usually from the areas of biology, psychology, and psychopathology, and indicating specific dependencies which he was unable to comprehend before. Instructional activity begins to dominate in psychotherapeutic work at this point. After all, the patient needs this additional data in order to reconstruct his disintegrated personality and form a new worldview more appropriate to reality. Only then can we go on to the more traditional methods. If our activities are to be for the benefit of the people who remain under the influence of a pathocratic system, the above course of action is the most appropriate; the objective data furnished to the patients must derive from a thorough understanding of the nature of the macrosocial phenomenon.

As already adduced, in those few cases where such a course of action could be afforded, the author has been able to observe the healing effect of such a process—making someone consciously aware of the essence and properties of the macrosocial phenomenon—on individual patients rendered neurotic by the influence of pathocratic social conditions. In countries ruled by such governments, almost every normal person carries within him some neurotic response of varying intensity. After all, *neurosis is human nature's normal response to being subjugated to a pathological system.*

In spite of the anxiety which such courageous psychotherapeutic operations necessarily engendered on both sides, my patients quickly assimilated the objective data they were given, supplemented it with their own experiences, and requested additional information and verification of their own applications of this information. Spontaneous and creative reintegration of their personalities took place soon thereafter, accompanied by a similar reconstruction of their worldview. Subsequent psychotherapy merely continued to assist in this ever more autonomous process and in resolving individual problems, i.e., a more traditional approach. These people lost their chronic tensions; their understanding of this deviant reality became increasingly realistic and laced with humor. Reinforcement of their capacity to maintain their own mental hygiene, self-therapy, and self-education was much better than expected. They became more resourceful in practical life matters and were able to offer others good advice—on such occasions, forgetting to keep their pledge of secrecy. (Unfortunately, the number of persons whom a psychotherapist could trust adequately was very limited.)

A similar effect should be attained on a macrosocial scale, something technically feasible under present conditions.[2] If this understanding is put into practice on a social scale, it will liberate spontaneous interaction among such enlightened individuals and the social multiplication of therapeutic phenomena. The latter will then trigger a qualitatively new and most probably rather stormy social reaction of more difficult and somewhat painful reflections; we should be prepared for this in order to calm it down. However, such hindsight would create a new healing modality. Ultimately, this will bring a sense of the triumph of proper science and truth over this insufficiently understood evil and a certain relaxation similar to what was previously observed in individual patients; this cannot be negated by any verbalistic means, and physical force also becomes meaningless.

Using measures so different from anything utilized before will engender an "end of an era" feeling—an era during which this macrosocial phenomenon was able to emerge and develop, but is now dying. That would be accompanied by a sensation of well-being on the part of normal people.

Within this suggested global psychotherapy, objective data in the form of a naturalistic understanding of the phenomenon constitutes the keystone material; this book has therefore collected the most essential data the author was able to obtain and to present here in a somewhat simplified form. This no doubt does not represent the entirety of the knowledge needed; further supplementation will be necessary. On the other hand, I have devoted less attention to methods, since this would simply constitute a manifold duplication (by means of mass transmission) of those kinds of therapies many specialists already know and use in their practice.

The purpose of this activity will be letting the world regain its capacity to make use of healthy common sense and to reintegrate worldviews based on scientifically objectified and appropriately popularized data. The consciousness thus created would be far more appropriate to the reality which was misunderstood until recently; as

[2] *Author's note (1997)*: This, however, proved unrealistic. Countries governed by normal people have failed to achieve this.

a result, man will become more sensible in practical activity, more independent and resourceful in solving life's problems, and he will feel safer. This task is nothing new; it constitutes a good psychotherapist's daily bread. The problem is technical rather than theoretical, namely how to disseminate such sorely needed influences throughout the globe.

***

Every psychotherapist must be prepared for the appearance of psychological resistance and difficulties derived from persistent attitudes and convictions whose lack of foundation becomes revealed in the course of work. Particularly in the case of a large group of people, these resistances become more demonstratively manifest; however, among the members of such a group we also find allies who help us break down these resistances. In order to visualize this, let us revert once more to the case of the N. family, wherein a dozen or so persons collaborated in abusing a pleasant and intelligent thirteen-year-old scapegoat.

When I explained to the uncles and aunts that they had been under the influence of a psychologically abnormal person for years, accepting her delusional world as real and participating (with ostensible honor) in her vindictiveness to the boy who was allegedly to blame for her failures, including those which occurred years before his birth, the shock temporarily stifled their indignation. There was no subsequent attack, probably because this took place in my office at the public health service and I was protected by the white coat I would usually don whenever I did not feel completely safe. I thus suffered only verbal threats. A week later, however, they started returning one by one, pale and rueful; albeit with difficulty, they did offer their cooperation in helping to repair the family situation and the future of this unfortunate boy.

Many people suffer an inevitable shock and react with opposition, protest, and disintegration of their personality when informed of such a state of affairs, namely that they have been under the spellbinding and traumatizing influence of a macrosocial pathological phenomenon, regardless of whether they were followers or opponents thereof. Many people are awakened to anxious protest by the fact that the ideology they either condemned or somehow accepted, but considered a guiding factor, is now being treated as something secondary in importance.[3]

The noisiest protests will come from those who consider themselves fair because they condemned this macrosocial phenomenon with literary talent and raised voices, utilizing the name derived from its most current ideology, as well as making excessive use of moralizing interpretations with regard to pathological phenomena. Forcing them to an apperception of a correct understanding of the pathocracy will be quite a Sisyphean labor, since they would have to become conscious of the fact that their efforts largely served goals which were the opposite of their intentions. Especially if they engaged in such activities professionally, it is more practical to avoid liberating their aggressions; one could even consider such generally elderly people too old for therapy.

Transforming the worldview of people living in countries with normal man's systems proves a more troublesome task, since they are much more egotistically attached to the notions suggested to them since childhood, making it more difficult for them to reconcile themselves with the fact that there are matters which their natural conceptual system cannot assimilate.[4] They also lack the specific experience available to people who have lived under pathocratic rule for years. We must therefore expect resistance and attack on the part of people protecting their livelihoods and positions as well as defending their personalities from a vexatious disintegration. Refraining from such estrangement, we have to count on the accordant reactions of the majority.

The acceptance of such psychotherapy will be different in countries where societies of normal people have already been created, offering solid resistance to pathocratic rule. Many years of experience, practical familiarity with the phenomenon, and psychological immunization there long ago produced fertile ground for sowing the seeds of objective truth and naturalistic comprehension. An explanation of the essence of the macrosocial phenomenon will be received as delayed

[3] *Author's note (1997)*: That said, today these dangers are far less likely to occur. Rather, it is far more likely that this realization will provoke a longer period of reflection and discussion that will gradually restore order to human beliefs.

[4] *Author's note (1997)*: In the USA, the communist doctrine has become part of people's personalities, both the majority who condemned "communism" and the minority who supported it. Unlike in our case, such a revision of worldview is not a life necessity for them. It would also pose a threat to those scientists and politicians whose positions and wealth were built on these doctrines. However, people who base their choices and actions on the truth can also be found there.

psychotherapy that should regrettably have been served much earlier (which would have enabled the patient to avoid many errors) but is nevertheless useful because it provides order and relaxation and permits subsequent reasoned action. Such therapy would be useful in healing people's minds, ensuring that social reality is perceived with full freedom and from a wide perspective; it would also aid the understanding of very personal matters.

Such data, accepted via a rather painful process there, will be associated with the experience already possessed. There will be no egoistically or egotistically inspired protests in that world. The value of an objective view will be appreciated much more rapidly, since it ensures a basis for reasoned activity. Soon thereafter, the feeling of realism in apprehending the surrounding world, followed by a sense of humor, would begin to compensate these people for the experience they have survived, namely the disintegration of their human personalities caused by such therapy.

This disintegration of the prior worldview structure will create a temporary feeling of an unpleasant void. Therapists well know the consequent responsibility of filling this void as quickly as possible with material more credible and trustworthy than the contents of which they were disabused, thus helping to avoid primitive methods of personality reintegration. In practice, it is best to minimize patient anxiety by making advance promises that appropriately objectified material will be furnished in the form of truthful data. This promise must then be kept, partially anticipating the appearance of disintegrative states. I have successfully tested this technique on individual patients and would advise its implementation on a mass scale as safe and effective.

For the people who have already developed *natural* psychological immunity, their increased resistance to the pathocracy's destructive influence upon their personalities, gained due to a consciousness of pathocracy's essence, may be less considerable, but still not without value, since the ameliorated immunization quality comes at a less burdensome cost in terms of nervous tension. However, for those hesitant people who constitute the segment of well-adjusted members of the new middle class, immunizing activities furnished by an awareness of the pathological nature of the phenomenon may tip their attitudinal scale in the direction of decency.

The second key aspect of such operations that should be considered is the influence of such enlightening behavior upon the personalities of the pathocrats themselves. In the course of individual psychotherapy, we tend to avoid making patients aware of permanent aberrations, especially when we have reason to believe that they are conditioned by hereditary factors. Psychotherapists, however, are guided by the consciousness of these conditions' existence in their decision making. Only in the case of the results of slight brain tissue lesions do we decide to make the patient aware of this, so as to help him elaborate a better tolerance of his difficulties and to abrogate unnecessary fears. Regarding psychopathic individuals, we treat their deviations by means of tactful allusive language, bearing in mind that they have a kind of self-knowledge, and we proceed with the techniques of behavior modification to correct their personalities,[5] keeping the interests of society in mind as well.

As far as operations on the macrosocial scale, it will of course not be feasible to retain these latter cautious tactics of activity. Traumatizing the pathocrats will be unavoidable to a certain extent, and even intentional and morally justified in the interests of peace on earth. Similarly, however, our attitude must be defined by an acceptance of biological and psychological facts, renouncing any morally or emotionally charged interpretation of their psychological deviations. In undertaking such work, we must consider the good of society to be paramount; nevertheless, we must not abandon our psychotherapeutic attitude and so must refrain from punishing those whose guilt we are unable to evaluate. Should we forget this, we would increase the risk of their uncontrolled reaction, which could bring about a world catastrophe.

At the same time, we should not nourish exaggerated fears, for example, that such public enlightenment activities will provoke overly dramatic reactions among pathocrats, such as a wave of cruelty or suicide. No. Those individuals described as essential psychopaths, in addition to many other carriers of related hereditary anomalies, have since childhood elaborated a feeling of being psychologically different

[5]For example, positive reinforcement, which is the hallmark of the "decompression model" discussed in note 11. Łobaczewski cites Dennis M. Doren's *Understanding and Treating the Psychopath* (1987) which takes such an approach: "Psychopaths can learn to act 'as if' they experience ... emotions, but they cannot learn to feel them. ... If the therapy goals are to make the psychopath into an upstanding citizen who will care about others, feel what others feel, and feel guilty when he hurts someone ... the therapy is doomed to failure. ... If the therapy goals are to get the person acting 'as if' ... he is empathic and does not wish to hurt others, this can happen" (p. 168). —Ed.

from others. Revealing this awareness to them is less traumatizing than, for instance, suggesting psychological abnormality to a normal person. The ease with which they repress uncomfortable material from their field of consciousness will protect them from violent reactions. They simultaneously retain the desire to be understood. These same people who are cruel to others develop a reflex respect and even friendly feelings for anyone who can show them that he comprehends them. That's why any such threats will end up being all talk and no action.

Therapeutic procedures could be based upon acceptance of their ideology, going as far as reason will permit. Pathocrats have real cause to fear counteraction based upon their own traditional ideology, after it has been sensibly corrected and reconstructed in its more original form. After all, this so-called "revisionism" knocks their weapons and propaganda instruments out of their hands. We should partially accept their feeling that they are fulfilling an historical mission or even functioning as the scourge of God.

The realistic, rather than tactical, objectives of such therapy should include a vision and assurance of a partial fulfillment of their dreams about a social order, based on a solid comprehension of man,[6] which would include an understanding of individuals with various deviations and psychological difficulties, who would be guaranteed the ability to structure their life with more dignity and without being condemned according to the moral concepts of normal people.[7]

Initially, such behavior stifles their violence, caused by a feeling of helplessness in light of the fact that their former secret has suddenly

[6]Partial in the sense that they would be understood psychologically, not moralistically, and able to function and to find a place in society, but not in the sense that they would be given dominion over others. See also the brief discussion under "Other psychopathies" in Chapter IV. —Ed.

[7]*Author's note (1997)*: Former pathocrats should benefit from a far-reaching forbearance based on a good understanding of pathological phenomena, not from a legally absurd "thick line." [A reference to the "thick line" dividing the communist and postcommunist eras, first suggested by Polish Prime Minister Tadeusz Mazowiecki in 1989, whereby no former communists would be prosecuted, no matter what evidence came to light of their crimes (at least, that was how critics interpreted it). In contrast, other countries like Czechoslovakia passed lustration laws banning all former party officials and secret police from positions in the new system of government. In other countries (e.g., Russia), communist parties were allowed to continue to exist and members were not brought to trial, with some exceptions (e.g., the show trial and execution of the Ceaușescus in Romania). —Ed.]

become common knowledge. What can they do if no ideology can be used as a mask anymore? Once the essence of the phenomenon has been scientifically unmasked, the psychological result is that they then feel their historical role to have reached the end. Their work furthermore takes on some historically creative meaning, if the world of normal people offers them conciliation upon unprecedented advantageous conditions. This will cause overall demobilization of the pathocracy, especially in those countries where, practically speaking, the support of an ideology has already been lost. This internal demobilization they fear so much constitutes the second important goal.

A crucial condition of and a complement to therapeutic work must be forgiveness for the pathocrats as derived from understanding, both of them and of the signs of the times. This must be effected by means of correspondingly amended law based on comprehension both of man and of the processes of the genesis of evil operating within societies, which will counteract such processes in a causative manner and supersede the former "penal" law. It should be emphasized, however, that a law which would provide an adequate qualification for acts committed under a pathocracy does not yet exist in any nation's law code. Forecasting the creation of such a law must not be treated merely as a psychotherapeutic promise; it must be scientifically prepared and thereupon effected.

The important goal should be not only to bring order to countries emerging from pathocratic rule, but also to immunize all of humanity against the emergence of such macrosocial phenomena. Awareness of the nature of the phenomenon and its eternal threat should become an integral part of the knowledge base as well as the moral and political culture of all nations. Thanks to this, a ponerogenic group seeking to seize power in a country would be recognized and exposed as early as possible. This should be verified by experts representing international institutions and lead to the appropriate legal and political consequences. The seizure of power in any country by pathological individuals can lead to the development of a brutal pathocracy that also poses the threat of a similar tragedy to other nations. This happens regardless of what ideology this state of madness hides under.[8]

Forgiveness

The contemporary evolution of legal concepts and democratic social morality is geared toward dismantling the old traditions of maintaining law and order by means of punitive repression. Many countries have abandoned capital punishment, disturbed by its genocidal abuses during the last world war. Other punishments and the methods of their execution have also been mitigated, taking psychological motivations and the circumstances of the crime into account. Severe punishments have only been preserved by totalitarian states, but pathocracies have brought this severity to an insane level that reflects their nature. The conscience of the civilized nations protests against the Roman principle *dura lex, sed lex*, and, at the same time, psychologists discern the possibility that many presently unbalanced people can revert to normal social life thanks to appropriate pedagogical measures; practice confirms it only partially, however.

The reason is that mitigating the law has not been balanced with the corresponding methods of stifling the processes of the genesis of evil as based upon its comprehension. This provokes a crisis in the area of societies' anti-crime protection[9] and makes it easier for pathocratic circles to utilize terrorism in order to realize their expansionist goals or to fight against the world of normal people. Under such conditions, many people feel that returning to the tradition of legal severity is the only way to protect society from an excess of evil. Others believe that such traditional behavior morally cripples us and opens the door to irrevocable abuses. They therefore subsume others' life and health under humanistic values. In order to emerge from this crisis, we must galvanize all our efforts in a search for a *new* road, one which would both be more humanitarian and effectively protect defenseless individuals and societies. Such a possibility exists and can be implemented, based on an objective comprehension of the genesis of evil.[10]

---

[8]The Polish version of this chapter is much shorter. In it, the following section is titled "Understanding" and focuses less on forgiveness and more on understanding and not seeking revenge.

[9]I.e., humanization of criminal law results in an increase in crime, because criminals do not fear the lax punishments (*Ponerologia*, p. 11). —Ed.

[10]Zimbardo writes: "We need to adopt a public health model for prevention of evil, of violence, spouse abuse, bullying, prejudice, and more that identifies vectors of social disease to be inoculated against, not dealt with solely at the individual level. A second paradigmatic shift is directed at legal theory to

The tradition—unrealistic in its essence—of a relationship between a person's "guilt," which no other person is in the position to evaluate objectively, and his "punishment," which is rarely effective in reforming him,[11] should be relegated to history. The science of the causes of evil should strengthen society's moral discipline and have a prophylactic effect. Often merely making a person aware that he was under the influence of a pathological individual breaks the circle of destructiveness. Appropriate psychotherapy should therefore be permanently included in any measures to counteract evil. Unfortunately, if someone is shooting at us, we must shoot back even better. At the same time, however, we should bring back the law of forgiveness, that old law of wise sovereigns. After all, it has profound moral and psychological foundations and is more effective than punishment in some situations.

The criminal law codes provide that the perpetrator of a criminal act who, at the time of his transgression, was limited in his ability to discern the significance of the act or to direct his own behavior as a result of mental illness or some other psychological deficiency receives a lesser sentence to the appropriate degree. If we should therefore consider the responsibility of pathocrats in the light of such regulations and in light of what we have already said about the motivations for their behavior, we must then considerably mitigate the scope of justice within the frame of existing regulations.

The above-mentioned legal regulations, which are more modern in Europe than in the USA, are rather outdated everywhere and insufficiently congruent with biopsychological reality. They are a compromise between traditional legal severity and medical humanism. Furthermore, the legislators were in no position to predict the emergence of macrosocial pathological phenomena that dominate individuals without their will and to various degrees limit their ability

reconsider the extent to which powerful situational and systemic factors must be taken into greater account in sentencing mitigation. ... Individuals and groups who behave immorally or illegally must still be held responsible and legally accountable for their complicity and crimes. However, in determining the severity of their sentence, the situational and systemic factors that caused their behavior must be taken into account" (*Lucifer Effect*, pp. viii, 231). —Ed.

[11]See Kiehl, *Psychopath Whisperer*, pp. 218–223, on the ineffectiveness of punishment on certain groups of people, particularly psychopaths. The "Decompression Model," which aims at developing prosocial bonds, is much more effective among youths with conduct disorder problems. —Ed.

to discern the meaning of their own behavior. Susceptible individuals are sucked in surreptitiously, since they are unaware of the pathological quality of such a phenomenon. The specific properties of such pathopolitical systems cause a person's selection of attitudes to be decisively determined by unconscious factors, followed by pressure from pathocratic rulers, who are none too fastidious as to their methods, not even with regard to their own adherents. How should the degree of penal mitigation then judge them fairly?

For instance, if essential psychopathy is virtually 100% predictive concerning attraction to and inclusion in pathocratic activity, should a judgment recognize similar mitigation of punishment? This should also be applied to other hereditary anomalies to a lesser extent, since they too have proved to be primary factors in the selection of attitudes.

We should not fault anyone for having inherited some psychological anomalies from his parents any more than we fault someone in the case of physical or physiological anomalies such as Daltonism. (However, we deprive Daltonists, for example, of the right to pursue those professions where this deficit could cause an accident.) We should also stop blaming people who have succumbed to traumas and diseases, leaving brain tissue damage behind; those who have been subjected to inhumane methods of upbringing should not be considered sinners without taking the context into account, which is an approach the Catholic Church has been guilty of too frequently. In the name of their good and that of society, we should use force with regard to such people, sometimes including forced psychotherapy, supervision, prevention, and care. However, any concept of blame or guilt would only make it more difficult to behave in a way which is not only humanitarian and purposeful, but more effective as well.

In dealing with a macrosocial phenomenon, particularly one whose duration is longer than an individual's active life, its permanent influence forces even normal people to adapt to a certain degree, distorting their personalities and worldviews. Are we, whose instincts and intelligence are normal, and according to the criteria of our moral worldview, in the position to evaluate the guilt of these others for actions they performed within pathocracy's collective madness?[12]

[12] *Author's note (1997):* This is an open problem for philosophy of law, psychology, and jurisprudence to consider based on the data cited in this book—among other things.

Judging them in accordance with traditional legal regulations would constitute reverting to the imposition of normal man's violence upon psychopathic individuals, i.e., to the initial position which engendered pathocracy to begin with. Is subjecting them to vindictive justice worth prolonging the duration of pathocracy for even a single year, let alone an unspecified time? Would eliminating a certain number of psychopaths significantly diminish these anomalies' burden upon society's gene pool and contribute toward a solution to this problem? Unfortunately, the answer is no.

People with various psychological deviations have always existed in every society on earth. Their way of life is always some form of predation upon society's economic creativity, since their own creative capabilities are generally substandard. Whoever plugs into this system of organized parasitism gradually loses whatever limited capacity for lawful work he might have had when subjected to the discipline of a system of normal man.[13]

This phenomenon and its brutality are actually maintained—and the secret network of its heirs strengthened—by the threat of legal retaliation or, even worse, of retribution on the part of the enraged masses. Dreams of revenge distract a society's attention from understanding the biopsychological essence of the phenomenon and stimulate the moralizing interpretations whose results we are already familiar with. This would make it more difficult to find a solution to the present dangerous situation and would similarly complicate any possibilities of reducing the genetic burden of psychopathic individuals on nations with a view to future generations. These problems, however, both present and future, can be solved if we approach them with an understanding of their naturalistic essence and a comprehension of the nature of those people who commit substantial evil. Such a solution would yield the full harvest of the years of our suffering.

Legal retribution would be a repetition of the Nuremberg error. That judgment upon war criminals could have been a never-to-be-

[13]Dikötter describes the conditions following China's "Great Leap Forward" as follows: "So destructive was radical collectivisation that at every level the population tried to circumvent, undermine or exploit the master plan, covertly giving full scope to the profit motive that the party was trying to eliminate. As the catastrophe unfolded, claiming tens of millions of victims, the very survival of an ordinary person came to depend on the ability to lie, charm, hide, steal, cheat, pilfer, forage, smuggle, trick, manipulate or otherwise outwit the state" (*Cultural Revolution*, p. 20). —Ed.

repeated opportunity to show the world the entire psychopathology of the Hitlerian system, with the person of the "Fuehrer" at the head.[14] That would have led to a faster and deeper disabusing of the Nazi tradition in Germany. Such conscious exposure of the operations of pathological factors on a macrosocial scale would have reinforced the process of psychological rehabilitation for Germans and the world as a whole by means of the naturalistic categories applicable to that state of affairs. That would also have constituted a healthy precedent for illuminating and stifling other pathocracies' operations. This is what the Soviets feared, driven by their well-known self-awareness of the pathology of their own system.

What actually happened is that psychiatrists and psychologists succumbed all too easily to the pressures of their own emotions and political factors, their judgments giving short shrift to the obvious pathological properties of both the majority of the defendants and of Nazism as a whole. Several famous individuals with psychopathic features or other deviations were hanged or sentenced to prison terms. Many facts and data which could have served the purposes adduced in this work were hanged and imprisoned along with these individuals.[15] We can thus easily understand why pathocrats were so eager to achieve this precise result. To repeat such errors would be un-

[14]Dr. Gustave Gilbert, prison psychologist at Nuremberg, wrote a book on the conclusions he reached after the short time he was able to spend studying the Nazi leaders being held for war crimes and crimes against humanity. He concluded: "Psychopathic personalities undoubtedly play an important part in major manifestations of social pathology, particularly when they achieve positions of leadership in social groups and movements. It is all too clear that they played a decisive role in the revolutionary nucleus of the Nazi movement, and thus determined the complexion of the government of Nazi Germany" (*Psychology of Dictatorship*, p. 286). He also analyzed the individual and social psychological functions that facilitate these processes, such as the desensitization of empathy caused by inculcating paranoia and hostility, and persecuting scapegoats. Understandably, Gilbert's book is out of print and hard to come by. His conclusions were largely ignored by academia, aside from his Rorschach protocols, to which Gilbert himself devotes very little discussion. See, for example, Jose Brunner, "'Oh Those Crazy Cards Again': A History of the Debate on the Nazi Rorschachs, 1946–2001" (2001). —Ed.

[15]*Author's note (1997):* Were it not for this error, there would be no resurgence of Nazism in Germany today. [Most notable at present in Ukraine with regard to ponerogenic neo-Nazi groups like Right Sector, who were involved in the shootings of both police and protesters during the Maidan Revolution of 2014. For background on their ideology and actions, see Hahn, *Ukraine over the Edge*, pp. 180–185. —Ed.]

acceptable, since the results make it more difficult to comprehend the essence of macrosocial pathological phenomena, and they thereby limit the possibilities of stifling their internal causation.

In today's actual state of affairs, there is only one scientifically and morally justified solution which could remedy the current plight of nations and also furnish a proper beginning for solving the problem of societies' genetic burden with a view to the future. That would be an appropriate law based upon the best possible understanding of macrosocial pathological phenomena and their causes, which would limit pathocrats' responsibility to those cases alone (usually of a criminal sadistic nature) in which it is hard to accept the inability to discern the significance of such an act. However, the issue would be resolved in the light of scientific and social awareness and within the framework of adequate law, not outside of it. Nothing else could enable the societies of normal people to take over power and liberate the internal talents which could ensure a nation's return to normal life.

Such an act of forgiveness is in fact justified by natural reason, since it is derived from a recognition of the psychological causation governing a person while committing evil, both within the scope of our cognition and outside the area we have been able to understand. This scope accessible to scientific cognition increases along with progress in general knowledge; in a pathocracy, however, the image of the phenomenon is so dominated by psychological causation that there is not much room left for free choice.

We shall in fact never be in the position to evaluate the scope of free choice with which an individual person has been endowed. In forgiving, we subordinate our minds to the laws of nature, to the extent that we are able to cognize psychological causation. When we withhold judgment regarding the scope of the remainder unknown to us, we subject our mind to the discipline of refraining from entering a domain barely accessible to it. Forgiveness thus leads our reason into a state of intellectual discipline and order, thereby permitting us to discern the realities of life and their causal relationships more clearly. This makes it easier for us to control our instinct's vindictive reflexes and protect our minds from the tendency to impose moralizing interpretations upon psychopathological phenomena. This is of course to the advantage of both individuals and of societies.

Simultaneously, and in accordance with the precepts of the great religions, forgiveness helps us enjoy supernatural order and thereby gain the right to self-forgiveness. It makes us better able to perceive the voice within saying "do this" or "don't do that." This improves our capacity for proper decision-making in thorny situations when we are lacking some necessary data. In this extremely difficult battle, we must not renounce this assistance and privilege; it may be decisive in tipping the scales toward victory.

Nations which have long had to endure pathocratic rule are now close to accepting such a proposition as a result of their practical knowledge of that other reality and the characteristic evolution of their worldview. However, their motivations are dominated by practicalities and reasons derived from adaptation to life in that divergent reality. Religious motivations for refraining from judgment also appear; comprehension and affirmation thereof mature under such specific conditions.[16] Their thought process and social ethics also evidence a feel for a certain teleological meaning to phenomena, in the sense of a historical watershed.[17]

Such an act of renunciation of judicial and emotional revenge with regard to people whose behavior was conditioned by psychological causation, especially certain specific hereditary factors, is justified by naturalism to a significant degree.[18] Therefore, such naturalistic and rational principles should permit the definitive decisions to mature. The intellectual effort involved in cutting the restraints to a natural comprehending of the problems of evil and a confrontation thereof with moral precepts shall bear fruit in many products of human thought.

People who have lost their ability to adapt to sensible work for hire will have to be guaranteed tolerable living conditions and assistance in their efforts to readapt. The costs incurred by society with regard thereto will probably be less than those involved with any other

---

[16]See, for example, the accounts of Christian dissidents in Dreher, *Live Not by Lies*, especially chapter 10, "The Gift of Suffering." —Ed.

[17]*Author's note:* If we considered a series of Pope John Paul II's actions, we would discern that he is aiming at a similar goal. He appears to be attempting to prepare nations morally for such a breakthrough of understanding and forgiveness. There is no doubt that he is governed by a feeling for psychological reality similar to that of the above-mentioned nations; above all, however, he is guided by a very fresh understanding of the Gospel precepts against a backdrop of similarity regarding times and conditions. The Pope's motivations as well as those of these societies have left the biological aspects in the shadows.

[18]For a similar perspective, see McConkey, *Managerial Liberalism*, p. 162: "Vengeance is less important than simply removing them from power." —Ed.

solution. All this will require appropriate organizational efforts based on this manner of understanding such matters, which will be far removed from traditional legal practice. The promises should be made to the pathocrats, and then kept with the honesty worthy of a society of normal people. Such an act and its execution should therefore be prepared ahead of time from the moral, legal, and organizational points of view.

Just as the idea adduced herein finds a lively response among people familiar with the above-described macrosocial phenomenon from experience, it insults the vengeful feelings of numerous political émigrés who retain the old experiential methods regarding social and moral problems. We should thus expect more opposition from this quarter, justified by moral indignation. Persuasive efforts should therefore be made in that direction.

It would also be advantageous if the solution to this problem could be prepared with a view to the contemporary heritage of the biohumanistic sciences, a heritage which aims at a similar evolution of law even though it continues to hide in the academic world, too immature for practical realization. The value of scientific studies in this area tends to be underrated by conservative-minded societies. This work may be facilitated by means of using such information with a view toward the need for rapid preparation or updating of the law.[19]

Our civilization's legislation arose first from the tradition of Roman law, then from the rights of sovereigns ruling by "divine right," a system which predictably defended their position, and though they were commanding the law of grace, they proved almost completely soulless and vengeful within today's conception of codified regulations. Such a state of affairs abetted rather than prevented the emergence of pathological systems of force. This explains the actual need to effect an essential breakthrough and formulation of *new* principles derived from an understanding of man, including enemies and evildoers. Having emerged from great suffering and a comprehension of its causes, such legislation will be more modern and humanitarian

[19]Since the emergence of critical race theory in Harvard Law School in the 1980s, the trend in the United States has been in the opposite direction. "Critical legal studies," with a focus on essentializing race, is now ubiquitous in law schools. See also Aaron Sibarium, "American Bar Association Poised to Mandate Diversity Training, Affirmative Action at Law Schools" (2021), which details proposed requirements that seemingly instruct schools to break state or federal law. —Ed.

as well as more effective in the area of protecting societies from the products of ponerogenesis. The great decision to forgive similarly derives from the most credible precepts of eternal moral teachings, something also in accordance with the contemporary evolution in societal thought. It takes into account practical concerns as well as a naturalistic comprehension of the genesis of evil. Only such an act of mercy, unprecedented in history, can break the age-old chain of the ponerogenic cycles and open the door both to new solutions for perennial problems and to a new legislative method based on an understanding of the causes of evil.

Such difficult decisions therefore appear in keeping with the signs of the times. The author believes that this precise kind of breakthrough in the methodology of thought and action is within the Divine Plan for this generation.

Ideologies

Just as a psychiatrist is mainly interested in the disease, paying less attention to the patient's delusional system deforming his individual reality, the object of global therapy should be the world's diseases. The deformed ideological systems which grew from historical conditions and a given civilization's weaknesses should be understood insofar as they are a disguise, operational instrument, or Trojan horse for pathocratic infection.

It would first be necessary for societal consciousness to separate these two qualitatively heterogeneous layers of the phenomenon—the original ideology and its distorted counterpart—by means of analysis and scientific evaluation effected upon them. Such a selective understanding should become part and parcel of all nations' consciousness in some appropriately accessible form. This would correspondingly reinforce the human capacity to orient oneself within today's complicated reality by means of discriminating such phenomena in keeping with their nature. This will bring about a correction in moral and worldview attitudes. Concentrating our efforts upon the pathological phenomenon shall then produce proper understanding and sufficiently complete results.

The absence of this basic differentiation in political operations is an error leading to wasted effort and good will, as well as conceptual chaos. We must not embrace ideologies, since all nineteenth-century political ideologies oversimplified social reality to the point of crippling it, even in their original forms, not to mention their pathologically deformed versions.[20] The foreground should nevertheless be occupied by an identification of their role within the macrosocial phenomenon; analysis, criticism, and even, more particularly, combating them can be placed in the background. Any discussions regarding directions needed to change social structures may be held concurrently as long as they take this basic separation of phenomena into account. Thus corrected, social consciousness can effect a solution to these problems more easily, and social groups which are intransigent today will become more amenable to compromise.

Only after such a separation of phenomena, and the rejection of both the caricature and the doublespeak phenomena, will it become possible to discuss the values and errors of various ideologies and their prospects for development. Marxist ideology will be particularly difficult to deal with in this process, for it seems that it would be easier to create a similar but entirely new ideology than to analyze and correct the deficiencies of an ideology that has been contaminated from its inception by schizoid material and other influences of pathological origin.[21]

Once a mentally ill person has been successfully cured of his illness, we often try to restore the former patient to the world of his more reality-based convictions. The psychotherapist then searches the delusionally caricaturized world for the original and always more sensible contents and tries to arrange them correctly, thereupon building a bridge right over the period of madness to a now healthy reality. Such an operation of course requires the necessary skills in the domain of psychopathology, since every disease has its own style of

[20]Including liberal-democratic ideology, as McConkey, Legutko, and Janowski also argue. See their respective books, *Darwinian Liberalism*, *Demon in Democracy*, and *Homo Americanus*, which focus on the flaws inherent in liberal democracy's original ideals, like blank slate psychology and natural equality. For a focused analysis of the pathologically deformed version, see Helen Pluckrose and James Lindsay's *Cynical Theories*. —Ed.

[21]Kołakowski wrote similarly: "This does not mean that socialism is a dead option. I do not think it is. But I do think that this option was destroyed not only by the experience of socialist states, but because of the self-confidence of its adherents, by their inability to face both the limits of our efforts to change society and the incompatibility of the demands and values which made up their creed. In short, that the meaning of this option has to be revised entirely, from the very roots" (quoted in Cristaudo, "Those Pesky Poles!"). —Ed.

deforming the patient's original world of experiences and convictions. We are now in a similar situation, which likewise requires common sense and skills in psychopathology, as well as knowledge from other fields, especially history. The deformed ideological system created by pathocracy should be subjected to analogous analysis, fishing out the original and certainly more sensible values. This must utilize knowledge of the specific style whereby a pathocracy caricaturizes the ideology of a movement upon which it feeds parasitically.

This great disease of pathocracy accommodates various social ideologies to its own properties and the pathocrats' intentions, thereby depriving them of any possibility of natural development and maturation in the light of man's healthy common sense and scientific reflection. This process also transforms these ideologies into destructive factors, preventing them from participating in the constructive evolution of social structures and condemning their adherents to frustration. Along with its degenerate growth, such an ideology is rejected by all those social groups governed by healthy common sense. The activities of such an ideology thus induce nations to stick to their old tried-and-true basics in terms of structural forms, providing hardline conservatives with the best weapon possible.[22] This causes stagnation of the evolutionary processes, which is contrary to the overall laws of social life, and brings about a polarization of attitudes among various social groups, resulting in revolutionary moods. The operations of the pathologically altered ideology thus facilitate the pathocracy's penetration and expansion.

Only by means of retrospective psychological analysis upon the ideology, reverting to the time which preceded ponerogenic infection, and taking into account the pathological quality and the causes for its deformation, can the original creative values be discovered and bridges built right over the time frame of morbid phenomena ("errors and distortions").

Such skillful unhusking of the original ideology, including some reasonable elements which emerged after the ponerogenic infection appeared, may be enriched by values elaborated in the meantime and become capable of further creative evolution. It will thus be in the position to activate transformations in accordance with the

[22]They can also lead to a right-wing reaction sometimes approaching the same degree of pathology, e.g., the anticommunist regimes of Hitler, Franco, and Pinochet. —Ed.

evolutionary nature of social structures, which will in turn render these societies more resistant to penetration by pathocratic influences.

Such analysis presents us with problems which must be skillfully overcome, namely finding the proper semantic designations. Thanks to characteristic creativity in this area, pathocracy produces a mass of suggestive names prepared in such a way as to divert attention from a phenomenon's essential qualities.[23] Whoever has been ensnared in this semantic trap even once loses not only the capacity for objective analysis of that type of phenomenon; he also partially loses his ability to use his common sense.[24] Producing such effects within human minds is the specific purpose of this patho-semantics; one must first protect one's own person against them and then proceed to protect social consciousness.

The only names we can accept are those with a historical tradition contemporary to the facts and reaching back to pre-infection times. For instance, if we call pre-Marxist socialism "Utopian socialism,"[25] it will be difficult for us to understand that it was much more realistic and socially creative than the later movements already laced with pathological material, which were much complained about and indeed utopian.

---

[23]For example, Legutko writes: "We were surrounded by entities whose reality seemed precarious but whose power of influence was enormous. 'Party,' 'working class,' 'revisionists,' ... 'socialist renewal,' 'leading role of the party,' 'fraternal Parties,' 'domestic export'—all these terms, and many others impossible to translate into English, were supposed to describe real facts, processes, and institutions, but were actually political declarations. It was impossible to conduct any serious debate about the real issues, because the language served to conceal rather than to reveal" (*Demon in Democracy*, p. 127). Janowski adds: "today's American Newspeak is fundamentally totalitarian. By accepting it, using it, we not only get caught in the totalitarian unreality, but we become its accessory cofounders" (*Homo Americanus*, p. 58). See Janowski's discussion of American and communist newspeak in chapter 4 of his book. —Ed.

[24]Janowski provides an example: "Liquidation of multiple political parties by absorbing them into one party (socialist or communist), was called 'democratic centralization.' Since democracy is associated with multiplicity of views, opinions, etc., by preserving the word *democracy* in the term 'democratic centralization,' one could make an entire population believe that democracy became even stronger by being centralized. In fact, it meant that democracy had been destroyed" (*Homo Americanus*, p. 58). —Ed.

[25]For example, the "timeless" (not historically dialectic) and "universal" (not class-based) socialism of Robert Owen, Fourier, and St. Simon (Sowell, *Marxism*, pp. 13–14, 156–157). Marx and Engels were the first to refer to them as "Utopian." —Ed.

However, such caution does not suffice when we are dealing with phenomena which cannot be measured within the natural structure of concepts because they were produced by a macrosocial pathological process. We must thus again underscore that the light of natural healthy common sense or even the philosophical principles of scientific methodologyare insufficient for effecting such retrospective refinement of ideological values later deformed by such a process. Psychological objectivity, adequate knowledge in the area of psychopathology, and the data contained in the prior chapters of this book are indispensable for this purpose.

Thus equipped, we also become qualified to create the necessary names which would elucidate the essential properties of phenomena, providing we pay sufficient attention to precepts of semantics with all the probity and economy as would demand William of Ockham or Karl R. Popper.[26] After all, these names will spread throughout the earth and help many people correct their worldview and social attitude. Such activity, albeit legalistic, actually aims at depriving pathocratic circles of their name-controlling monopoly; their predictable protests will merely prove that we are on the right track.

Ideology thus regenerated regains the natural life and evolutionary capacity which pathologization has stifled. At the same time, however, it loses its ability to fulfill imposed functions such as feeding a pathocracy and cloaking it from both healthy common-sense criticism and something even more dangerous, namely a feel for psychological reality and its humorous aspects.

Condemning an ideology because of its errors, whether contained from the outset or absorbed later, will never deprive it of this imputed function, especially not in the minds of people who failed to condemn it for similar reasons. If we further attempt to analyze such a condemned ideology, we will never achieve the effect which has a curative influence upon the human personality; we will simply miss the truly important factors and be unable to fill a certain space with contents. Our thoughts will then be forced to evade whatever blocks their freedom, thereby erring among ostensible truths. Once something succumbs to psychopathological factors, it cannot be understood unless the proper categories are utilized.

[26]Karl R. Popper (1902–1994), Austrian-British philosopher of science and advocate of the principle of falsifiability in the scientific method. Author of *The Logic of Scientific Discovery* (1934) and *The Open Society and Its Enemies* (1945). —Ed.

Immunization

Many infectious diseases give an organism a natural immunity for a period between a few years and many. Medicine imitates this biological mechanism by introducing vaccines which enable an organism to become immune without passing through the disease. More and more frequently, psychotherapists attempt to immunize a patient's psyche to various traumatizing factors which are too difficult to eliminate from his life. In practice, we use this most often with people subjected to the destructive influence of characteropathic individuals. Immunizing someone against the destructive effects of psychopathic personalities is somewhat more difficult; however, it represents the closest analogy to the task which should be performed with regard to nations succumbing to the influence of pathocratic psychological subversion and those at risk from such methods of expansion. By explaining to a man the pathological character of the influences he was under, and by analyzing how his human nature responded to such influences, we create the necessary intellectual distance as well as improve his resistance and tolerance to such influences.

Societies governed by a pathocratic system for many years develop the above-described natural immunization, along with the characteristic over-adaptation to the phenomenon and sardonic humor. In combination with the growth of practical knowledge, this state should be taken into account every time we wish to evaluate a given country's political situation. We should also underscore that this immunity refers to the pathological phenomenon per se, not its ideology, which explains why it is also effective against any other pathocracy, no matter the ideological mask. The psychological experience gained permits the same phenomenon to be recognized according to its actual properties; the ideology is treated in accordance with its true role.[27]

Psychotherapy properly conducted upon an individual who succumbed to the destructive influence of life conditions under pathocratic rule always brings about a significant improvement in psychological immunization. In making a patient conscious of the patholog-

[27]For examples of this natural immunity, see the subjects of Dreher's book, *Live Not by Lies*, as well as the observations of Legutko (*Demon in Democracy*) and Janowski (*Homo Americanus*). All lived under pathocracy in Eastern Europe or the USSR, and all see the same phenomenon taking shape in "the West," though under the ideology of "liberal democracy." —Ed.

ical qualities of such influences, we facilitate his development of that critical detachment and spiritual serenity which natural immunization could not have produced. We thus do not merely imitate nature; we actually achieve a better-than-natural quality of immunity, which is more effective in protecting a patient from neurotic tensions and reinforcing his practical everyday resourcefulness. An awareness of the biological essence of the phenomenon provides him with an advantage both over the phenomenon and those people who lack such awareness.

This type of psychological immunity also proves more permanent. If natural immunity lasts the life of the generation wherein it was produced, scientifically based immunity can be transmitted further. Similarly, natural immunity plus the practical knowledge upon which it is based may be very difficult to transmit to nations which have not had such direct experience, but the kind which is based on generally accessible scientific data can be transmitted to other nations without superhuman efforts.

We are faced with two related goals. In countries affected by the above-discussed phenomenon, we should attempt to transform the existing natural immunity into that better-quality immunity, thus making it possible to arrange one's life without excessive psychological adaptations and tensions. With regard to those individuals and societies which indicate an obvious immunodeficiency and are threatened by pathocratic expansion, we should facilitate the development of artificial immunity.

This immunity is generated mainly as a natural result of understanding the actual contents of the macrosocial phenomenon and its appropriate popularization. This awareness causes a stormy experiential period not bereft of protest, but this substitute disease process is short-lived. Stripping the naturalistic reality heretofore protected by an ideological mask is an effective and necessary assistance for individuals and societies. Within a short period of time, this begins to protect them from the ponerogenic activities of pathological factors mobilized within the pathocracy's monolithic front, as well as on the interpersonal level. This leads to the very valuable phenomenon of intellectual and moral resilience. Appropriate indications of the practical means for protecting one's own mental hygiene will facilitate and accelerate the creation of such valuable psychological immunity in a manner similar to the results of a vaccination.

Such individual and collective psychological immunity, based on a naturalistically objectified understanding of this other reality, is colored by a sense of proper knowledge, which thus creates a new human network; achieving such immunity appears a necessary precondition for success regarding any efforts and actions of a political nature which would aim at having governments taken over by a society of normal people. Without such consciousness and immunization, it will always be difficult to achieve cooperation between free countries and nations suffering under pathocratic rule. No language of common communication can be guaranteed by any political doctrines based on the natural imagination of people lacking both the practical experience and a naturalistic understanding of the phenomenon.

***

The most modern and expensive weapons threatening humanity with global catastrophe are presently obsolete the very day they are produced. Why? They are the weapons of a war which must never take place, and the nations of the world pray that it never does. The history of mankind has been a history of wars, which makes it lack eternal meaning in our eyes. A new great war would represent the triumph of madness over the nations' will to live.

At the same time, in the face of the pathocratic empire's use of weapons of psychological warfare on a mass scale, we are confronted with a new threat and a new necessity to defend ourselves. These new weapons, no matter who uses them, must be countered by new means of defense. International reason must therefore prevail, reinforced by rediscovered moral values and naturalistic science concerning the causes and genesis of evil. The "new weapon" suggested herein kills no one; it is nevertheless capable of stifling the process of the genesis of evil within a person and activating his own curative powers. If societies are furnished an understanding of the pathological nature of evil—something they were unaware of before—they will be able to effect concerted action based on moral and naturalistic criteria.

This new method of solving eternal problems will be the most humanitarian weapon ever used in human history, as well as the only one which can be used safely and effectively. We may also hope that using such a weapon will help end centuries of warfare among nations.

CHAPTER X
A VISION OF THE FUTURE

If it is to bear ripe fruit, every human activity must take root in the soil of two time frames: past and future. The past provides us knowledge and experience which teach us to solve problems and warn us when we are about to commit errors reminiscent of past mistakes. A realistic apperception of the past and a sometimes painful understanding of its errors and evils thus become necessary preconditions for building a happier future. A similarly realistic vision of the future, complemented by well-thought-out, detailed data, endows our contemporary activities with a direction and renders their goals more concrete. Mental effort aimed at forming such a vision enables us to overcome psychological barriers to free reason and imagination, barriers caused by egotism and the survival of habits from the past. People fixated upon the past gradually lose contact with the present and are thus incapable of doing much good for the future. Let us therefore direct our minds toward the future, beyond the ostensibly insuperable realities of the present age.

There are many advantages to be gained from constructively planning the future, including the more distant time perspective, if we can foresee its shape and facilitate pinpointed solutions. This requires that we properly analyze reality and make correct predictions, i.e., discipline of thought so as to exclude any subconscious data manipulation and any excessive influence from our emotions and preferences. Elaborating such an original vision so as to make it a reified blueprint for a new reality is the best way to educate human minds for other similarly difficult tasks in the concrete future.

This would also permit timely elimination of many differences of opinion which could later lead to violent conflicts; these sometimes result from an insufficiently realistic apperception of the present state of affairs, various pipe-dream attitudes, or propaganda activities. If it is logically developed and avoids collisions with an adequately objective understanding of phenomena which have already been discussed in part, such a constructive vision can come true in future reality.

Such planning should be reminiscent of a well-organized technical project, wherein the designers' work is preceded by an examination of conditions and possibilities. Executing the work also requires time-frame planning in accordance with the appropriate technical data and the factor of human safety. We know from experience that increasing the scope and accuracy of design activities makes their execution and utility more profitable. Similarly, the more modern and inventive constructions generally prove more effective than tradition-bound ones.

The design and construction of a new social system should also be based upon proper distinctions of reality and should receive appropriate elaboration in many details in order to prove effective in execution and action. This will require abandoning some traditional customs of political life which allowed human emotions and egoism to play too great a role. Creative reasoning has become the sole and necessary solution, since it ascertains real data and finds novel solutions without losing the ability to act under real-life conditions.

The absence of such prior constructive effort would lead both to knowledge gaps about the reality to be operated in and to a shortage of people with the crucial preparation needed for creating new systems. Regaining the right to decide one's own fate, particularly for a nation now affected by pathocracy, would be improvisation, which is expensive and dangerous. Violent disputes among the adherents of various structural concepts, which may often be unrealistic, immature, or outdated because they have lost their historical significance in the meantime, may even cause a civil war.

The reconstruction of normal social and state life cannot be an easy task wherever the old socio-psychological structures created by long historical processes have been almost totally destroyed by revolution, war, genocide at the hands of the enemy, the emigration of the old elite, the introduction of state capitalism, and the development of pathocracy. The replacement is a pathological structure reaching into every corner of a country, causing all areas of life to degenerate and become unproductive. The new caste and organizational structure obviously try to maintain their position by all available means, which is what any other privileged class would do in their place. Under such conditions, it proves unfeasible to reconstruct a social system based on outdated traditions and the unrealistic expectations that such a structure already exists. What is needed is a plan of action which will first permit the fastest possible reconstruction of this basic socio-psychological structure and then allow it to participate in social life's autonomization process.

The past has furnished us virtually no pattern for this indispensable activity, which can thus be based only upon the more general kind of data described at the beginning of this work. We are therefore immediately faced with the need to rely upon modern science. At least one generation's worth of time has also been lost, and with it the evolution which should have creatively transformed the old structural forms. Reverting to those forms would be a dangerous error of relapse, which inevitably leads to resurgence of even older nineteenth-century forms, such as primitive exploitative capitalism. We should thus be guided by notions of what *should* have happened if a given society had had the right to free development during this time, rather than by data from the past, presently outdated, albeit historically real.

Since ideology has never been of essential value in a pathocracy, it can easily be replaced with a more convenient one, depending on what the specific circumstances require. However, the pathocratic bond formed due to the natural characteristics of certain people, acquired wealth, and privileges will prove much more durable than many Western ideologues presume.[1]

[1]*Author's note (1997)*: Under these conditions, the reconstruction of a social system rooted in past traditions and old political doctrines—not free from defects and deficiencies—will inevitably be a path of trial and error with little chance of success. Such an endeavor buys the heirs of pathocracy a lot of time to fight for their survival. Such a nation-wide disease will take much longer to heal than those difficulties faced by nations that have regained their independence after years of being governed by a foreign, yet psychologically normal, power, or the problems the Polish nation withstood having regained its independence after the First World War. [As Łobaczewski observed in an interview with Sott.net (http://youtu.be/DU7LKAsjt4k), many Polish communist pathocrats simply integrated into the new system and continued to stay in positions of power, a view shared by Poland's current leadership: "The [PiS] party and its leader, Jarosław Kaczyński, argue that Poland did not become truly independent after 1989. Instead, the communist elites and some elements among the opposition came to an arrangement that allowed 'post-communists' to remain in influential positions in politics, the judiciary, the economy and the media" ("'We Are Still Cleansing Poland of Dirt,' Says President Ahead of Reelection Bid," *Notes from Poland*, Jun. 2, 2020). As Legutko writes: "following some slight touch-ups and finding themselves in new circumstances, the former members of the Communist Party adapted themselves perfectly to liberal democracy, its mechanisms, and the entire ideological interpretation that accompanied these mechanisms" (*Demon*, p. 2).

In the meantime, many formerly understood concepts fell out of use, and many divergent ways of thinking have taken root in those countries. Private capitalism's world of social institutions has become distant and hard to understand.[2] There is no one left who has been brought up in a family environment that would teach them the skills necessary to become creative capitalists who understand their role in society or to act independently within such a system. Democracy has become an imperfectly comprehended slogan for communicating within the society of normal people.[3] The workers cannot imagine the reprivatization of great industrial plants and oppose any efforts in that direction. They believe that rendering the country independent would bring them participation in both management and profits. Those societies have accepted some social institutions, such as a public health service and free education through university level. They want the operation of such institutions reformed by subordinating them to healthy common sense and appropriate scientific criteria as well as tried-and-true elements of valid traditions. What should be restored is the general laws of nature which should govern societies; the structural forms should be reconstructed in a more modern manner, which will facilitate their acceptance.

Some transformations already made are historically irreversible. Regaining the right to shape one's own future would thus create a dangerous and even tragic "system void." The nation faces the task of building a just and sufficiently functional social system, but without following a preconceived plan. Thus, the longed-for independence results in a legal vacuum and social chaos, from which the heirs of the pathocratic elite benefit. A premonition of such a critical situation already worries people in those countries, stifling their will to act; this situation should be prevented immediately. The only way is well-organized effort in analytical and constructive thought directed toward a societal system with highly modern economic and political foundations.

For a similar dynamic in Russia, see Gordon M. Hahn's *Russia's Revolution from Above, 1985–2000: Reform, Transition and Revolution in the Fall of the Soviet Communist Regime* (2001). —Ed.]

[2] *Author's note (1997)*: They are only known to those who operated outside the country on behalf of the pathocratic elite. This gives them an advantage.

[3] The Polish edition includes six paragraphs on democracy at this point. See Appendix II. —Ed.

Nations suffering under pathocratic governments should also participate in such a constructive effort, which would represent excellent input to the above-mentioned general task of treating our sick world. Undeterred in our hope that the time will soon come when such nations will revert to normal human systems, we should build a social system with a view to what will happen after pathocracy. This social system will be different from and better than anything which existed earlier. A realistic vision of a better future and participation in creating it will heal battered human souls and bring order into thought processes. This constructive work trains people to govern themselves under such different conditions and knocks the weapon out of the hands of anyone who serves evil, increasing the latter's feeling of frustration and an awareness that his pathological work is nearing an end.

A careful reading of this book may cause us to discern the outlines of a creative vision of such a future societal system so sorely needed by nations suffering under pathocratic rule; if so, this represents a reward for the author's effort rather than the result of pure chance. Just such a vision accompanied me throughout the period of my work on this book (although the latter nowhere indicates a name nor any more precise details for it), rendering assistance and proving a useful support in the future. In some way, it is thus present on the pages and between the lines of this work.

Such a social system of the future would have to guarantee its citizens wide scope personal freedom and an open door to utilizing their creative potentials in both individual and collective efforts. At the same time, however, it must not indicate the well-known weaknesses manifested by a democracy in its domestic and foreign policy. Not only should individuals' personal interest and the common good be appropriately balanced in such a system; they should be woven right into the overall picture of social life at a level of understanding of its laws where any discrepancy between them disappears. The opinion of the broad mass of the citizenry, dictated primarily by the voices of basic intelligence and dependent upon the natural worldview, should be well heard and properly taken into account. Therefore, it could not be drowned out by the bleating of goats—the uproar of demagogues and psychopaths.

One of the foundations of this political system would be the principle of competence. On this basis, a citizen wishing to obtain the right to vote would have to acquire the necessary popular historical, social, and legal knowledge and pass an examination. Citizens seeking election to parliament or higher offices would first have to acquire the necessary scientific background. The weaknesses of public opinion should be counterbalanced by the skills of those with objective knowledge of the laws of nature and social life, and who possess the appropriate knowledge and training in their specialized fields. Appropriate and well-thought-out system solutions should be used for this purpose.

The foundations for practical solutions within such an improved system would contain criteria such as creating the right conditions for enriched development of human personalities, including the psychological worldview, whose societal role has already been adduced. Individuals' socio-occupational adjustment, self-realization, and creation of an interpersonal network, which serve their own interests as well as those of the wider society, form the socio-psychological structure which is the foundation on which a nation's health and creativity are built, and therefore should be facilitated to the maximum possible extent. Structural, legal, and economic solutions should be considered in such a way that fulfilling these criteria would also open the door for an individual's optimal self-realization within social life, which would simultaneously be for the good of the community. Other traditional criteria such as the dynamics of economic development will thereupon prove secondary to these more general values. The result of this would be the nation's economic development, political skill, and creative role in the international sphere.[4]

The priorities in terms of value criteria would thus shift consistently in the direction of psychological, social, and moral data. This is in keeping with the spirit of the times, but actual execution thereof

[4]In his bibliography, Łobaczewski cites John Clark and Aaron Wildavsky's *The Moral Collapse of Communism: Poland as a Cautionary Tale* (1990), which argues that "all communist political economies comprising ruling parties that tolerate no rivals and central planning without market prices are doomed to failure (that is, to the loss of national product and national leadership) *because they are based on immoral premises and practices*" (p. 1, emphasis added). As Peter Kwasniewski writes in the foreword to Storck, *Economics of Justice and Charity*, in reference to Catholic social teaching: "The popes reiterate that economics cannot be rightly understood or virtuously practiced apart from well-ordered politics, culture, and religion: the economic realm is *not* sufficient unto itself or even intelligible in itself, but rather serves as a subordinate element in a complete vision of human life and society, the whole of which must be grasped and assented to before any of its parts can flourish. The health of the part depends on the coherence of the whole" (p. xiii). —Ed.

demands imaginative effort and constructive thought in order to achieve the above-mentioned practical goals. After all, everything begins and ends within the human psyche.

Such a system would have to be evolutionary by nature, as it would be based upon an acceptance of evolution as a law of nature.[5] Natural evolutionary factors would play an important role therein, such as the course of cognition continually progressing from more primitive and easily accessible data to more actual, intrinsic, and subtle matters. The principle of evolution would have to be imprinted firmly enough upon the basic philosophical foundations of such a system so as to protect it consistently from social tensions and revolutionary tendencies. The factors stimulating this evolution would be: the development of moral culture, the development of scientific knowledge continuously deepening our insight into ourselves and society, as well as technological progress.

Such a social and state system would by its very nature be more resistant to the dangers posed by ponerogenesis on any social scale, and even more so to the emergence of pathocratic tendencies. Its foundations would be an improved development of the psychological worldview and society's structure of links coupled with a scientific and social consciousness of the essence of such phenomena. This should furnish the foundation for sufficiently mature methods of education. Such a system should also have built-in permanent institutions which were heretofore unknown and whose task will be care for the biological, psychological, and moral welfare of society, preventing the development of ponerogenic processes within society, and protection against the entry of mentally abnormal persons into positions of power.[6] The

---

[5]Broadly speaking, in biopsychological terms evolution is the development from lower to higher levels of organization, and from the most automatic to the most voluntary. See Dąbrowski, *Multilevelness*, for an account of personality development from this perspective. See also McConkey, *Darwinian Liberalism*, for a defense of the evolutionary principle in politics, exemplified in such institutions as the common law, the marketplace of ideas, the scientific method, and the goods and services market. —Ed.

[6]The idea of screening for psychopathy in politics has also been raised by Clive R. Boddy in "Psychopathy Screening for Public Leadership" (2016) and "Populism and Political Personality: What Can We Learn from the Dark Triad Personality of Hermann Goering?" (2021). Clinical psychologist Martha Stout writes: "It is interesting to speculate about a perhaps not-too-distant future in which we have at last developed a fully valid and reliable test for conscience-lessness that goes beyond Robert Hare's Psychopathy Checklist, a future in which we are as adamant about seeing political candidates' scores on that test

latter is what has given rise to the greatest tragedies of recent years.

A "Council of Wise Men" would be an institution composed of several people with extremely high general, medical, and psychological qualifications; it would have the right to examine the physical and psychological health of candidates before the latter are elected to the highest government positions. A negative council opinion should be hard to challenge. That same council would serve the head of state, the legislative authorities, and the executives regarding counsel in matters entering its scope of scientific competence. It would also address the public in important matters of biological and psychological life, indicating essential moral aspects. Such a council's duties would also include maintaining contact and discussions with the religious authorities in such matters.

The security system for persons with various psychological deviations would be in charge of making their life easier while skillfully limiting their participation in the processes of the genesis of evil. The thoughtful supervision of people with various mental aberrations should enable them to adapt to the requirements of the society of normal people and induce them to live more agreeably within it. After all, such persons are not impervious to persuasion, provided it is based upon proper knowledge of the matter. Such an approach would also help progressively diminish societies' gene-pool burden of hereditary aberrations. This would require the popularization of psychological education. The Council of Wise Men would furnish the scientific supervision for such activities.

The legal system would be subjected to wide-ranging transformations in virtually every area, progressing from formulae whose establishment was based on a society's natural worldview and ancient tradition to legal solutions based upon an objective apperception of reality, particularly the psychological one. As a result, law studies would have to undergo true modernization, since the law would become a scientific discipline sharing the same epistemological principles as all the other sciences.

What is now called "penal" law would be superseded by another kind of law with a completely modernized foundation based on an understanding of the genesis of evil and of the personalities of people

as we are about the disclosure of their income tax returns. How might society change if there were such a tool?" (*Outsmarting the Sociopath Next Door* [2020], p. 247). —Ed.

who commit evil. Such law would be significantly more humanitarian while furnishing individuals and societies more effective protection from undeserved abuse. Of course, the operational measures would be much more complex and more dependent upon a better understanding of causation than could ever possibly be the case in a punitive system. A trend toward transformations in this direction is evident in the legislation of civilized nations.[7] The social system proposed herein would have to break through traditions in this area in a more effective way.

No government whose system is based on an understanding of the laws of nature, whether concerning physical and biological phenomena or the nature of man, can lay a claim to sovereignty in the meaning we have inherited from the nineteenth century and subsequent nationalistic or totalitarian systems. We share the same air and water throughout our planet. Common cultural values and basic moral criteria are becoming widespread. The world is interlinked in transportation, communication, and trade and has become Our Planet. Under such conditions, interdependence and cooperation with other nations and supranational institutions, as well as moral responsibility for our overall fate, become a law of nature. The national organism becomes autonomous but not independent. This must be regulated by means of the appropriate treaties and incorporated into national constitutions.

A system thus envisaged would be superior to all its predecessors, being based upon an understanding of the laws of nature operating within individuals and societies, with objective knowledge progressively superseding opinions based upon natural responses to phenomena. We should call it a "LOGOCRACY." Due to their properties and conformity to the laws of nature and evolution, logocratic systems could guarantee social and international order on a long-term basis. In keeping with their nature, they would then become transformed into more perfect forms, a vague and faraway vision of which may beckon to us in the present.

---

[7] For example, the Norwegian criminal justice system, which focuses on restorative justice and rehabilitation, accompanied by some of the lowest incarceration and recidivism rates in the world. While most Norwegians prisons are "closed" (high security), "open" prisons are designed to be as similar to the outside world as possible, with open spaces, houses instead of cells, brick instead of concrete, and various types of recreation and classes to teach responsibility and reintegration into normal society. A tiered system would also take into account those who cannot be reintegrated, or who require close and regular supervision if they can be. —Ed.

The author has survived many dangerous situations and become disappointed with many people and institutions. However, the Great Providence has never disappointed him under the most difficult circumstances. This condition suffices to permit him to promise that elaborating a more detailed draft for such a necessary better system will also be possible.[8] And so I pass this book on to my honored readers together with my faith in the practical possibility of creating such a system, one that would not be perfect, but better than any we have known before.

[8]The first draft of *Logokracja* was completed by the time Łobaczewski left the United States in 1990. After developments in Poland in the 1990s, he revised and updated the book, which was eventually published in 2007, shortly before his death. —Ed.

APPENDIX I
Preface to the Polish Edition (1997)

This book was originally written in 1984 in New York and translated into English by Dr. Aleksandra Chciuk-Celt in collaboration with the author as *Political Ponerology*. The book, written mostly at dawn before a day of tedious manual labor necessary to make a living and without access to sufficient scientific tools, was nevertheless produced satisfactorily and still in time to play its intended role. This was accomplished with great difficulty and despite the circumstances in which the author found himself in the USA. This situation could not have been foreseen or easily overcome.

Threatened with arrest for the fourth time in 1977, and hoping that I would be able to pass on these exceptionally valuable research results to Western scientists, I chose the offered passport. After extremely difficult experiences, I arrived in the USA, but as a recognized possessor of dangerous knowledge. There I soon realized that I had not come out from under the surveillance of the Polish Security Service of the time. Their activities were carried out with a deviousness that even an experienced psychologist did not think possible.

As was once also the case with this writer, the people of our country are unaware of the psychological difference between the United States and the rest of the world. The Chinese or Africans think and understand the world and life in a way that is closer to us than the typical American does, and it is easier to find a common language with them. A psychologist from Poland had to learn this difference through suffering, having only limited prior theoretical knowledge.

The people there think and act with previously assimilated patterns. This makes our explanations seem surreal for them, which gives them a sense of powerlessness or evokes feelings of resentment. In no society in the world does the subconscious selection of premises operate with such overpowering effectiveness as in this country of wishful thinking. Their way of thinking proves effective in everyday life, but when applied to more difficult issues, such as those concerning the author and his task, it leads to decision-making based on secondary and tertiary considerations to the exclusion of the crux of the matter. In this way, the author's and other researchers' laborious effort has been perceived as something out of the realm of American surrealism.

In such conditions, the intelligence and subversion agents, adequately trained in the system of the Soviet empire and familiar with these American characteristics, acted with astonishing effectiveness, and they were protected by American law, customs, and the aforementioned way of thinking. The methods of psychological subversion, which our society easily deciphered and which therefore failed them in Poland, turned out to be remarkably effective there. Thanks to this, the once Polish and now Polish-Jewish institutions in New York became a marionette show directed by them. It was therefore impossible to reach out for help and support anywhere. Even a meaningful conversation was repeatedly refused, until the author's strength and health failed. As I laid in the intensive care unit at Bickman Hospital, it seemed that my work was finished.

Polish readers, however, should be given an explanation of the long history of the creation of this research. However, the author's knowledge in this particular matter contains more gaps than reliable data. Time and lived experiences have also erased from memory a few previously familiar names. I could not or did not want to know about the activities of certain people in those years, although I was anonymously informed about the results of their work. This was necessary for reasons of safety and due to the conspiratorial experience gained in the Home Army.

In spite of this, I would like to take this opportunity to pay my humble tribute to all those researchers and specialists who initiated this work or whose research I have been able to benefit from, regardless of whether or not their names were once known to me or have faded from my memory. I also hope that some from the younger generation may still be among the living and that I will be able to shake their hands one day.

At some point in the late fifties, scientists of the past generation from Poland, Hungary, and other countries of "people's democracies" met to discuss common psychiatric matters. After official lectures and discussions were over, pre-war acquaintances would meet and there would be a hushed exchange of opinions on the pathology of the system that had overtaken our countries and which, unfortunately, is still called "communism" today. It turned out that the observations of psychiatrists and psychologists from various countries not only were similar, but also noted important characteristics of the phenomenon. However, these properties were scientifically detectable only to them, not to humanists and politically active people. This was the genesis of this work. I was not present.

As the future author of this study, I worked with the Krakow-based branch of this research group, and I came into contact with the main branch later and only briefly. I never knew who was intended to synthesize our efforts, and I never imagined that this task would fall on me.

Around a year after the work commenced, the author, working far away from larger cities, was given the task of studying certain mental aberrations and classifying them. Guided by my own observations and experience, I immediately realized that these matters were crucial for the understanding of the nature of the whole of the phenomenon in question. So I increased my efforts, the results of which the reader will find in this work. At this point, however, my contact with the scientists ended abruptly. This was undoubtedly a result of an intervention of political factors that discovered a trail of this movement and caused casualties. Thank God, the author remained outside the circle of suspects. Fear was the only negative consequence.

Data of priceless value for science and politics remained in my possession. These were the results of the work of other researchers as well as my own. However, they were so incomplete that it would be pointless to pass them on to foreign scientists who were not prepared to receive them. Opportunities to do so were also lacking. I was forced to work for years in complete solitude in order to fill in the blanks in the data and reassemble them into a comprehensible whole. Two versions were lost and the currently existing American version was therefore already the second reconstruction. The first version was destroyed a few hours before a search was performed by the security services. The second one did not reach its addressee in Rome. Most of the statistical calculations and analyses of individual cases, i.e., data that specialists would find convincing, were irretrievably lost with it. The above-mentioned English version contains only those statistical data that, being the most frequently used, have remained in memory or have been reconstructed with sufficient reliability. At the same time, data from the locally available literature have been added where necessary, primarily to make the work more accessible to non-specialists in psychopathology. The same data are present in this edition.

The English version received positive reviews as "very informative" but was not published. American publishers I approached found the book troublesome because it required international distribution. However, something more significant than just the dollar and the American mindset stood in the way.

Showing some enthusiasm for its value, Professor Zbigniew Brzezinski agreed to publish this work. However, unforeseen difficulties kept delaying the publication. For a long time the reasons for this were not clear to me, until one day, while attending his lecture, I noticed that he omitted any data that could have come from this work and that he certainly had knowledge of. So I understood that he considered the publication to be an obstacle to his personal strategy for success. His thinking was certainly flawed, however.

Over ten years have passed since those events. In preparing the current Polish edition, the time-references needed to be changed. What was a prediction in that study has since become reality. In many places, therefore, it was necessary to change the future tense to the past and to discuss the issues in the context of the new reality. What remained unaltered were the fundamental findings that stood the test of time. In its new form the work should also play a new role.

The original version was written for readers living in free countries and outside the immediate influence of the macrosocial pathological phenomenon. It was therefore necessary to explain what for the inhabitants of "communist" countries was already clear due to years of personal experience. Those parts were omitted in the present edition. Despite these changes and the removal of a few other passages, the original style has been preserved in the background, content, and layout. I hope, however, that this will not prevent Polish readers from assimilating the contents of this work. On the contrary, it should become more accessible to the younger generation, as well as to our compatriots who have been living abroad for a long time. Thanks to such operations the work as a whole has been somewhat shortened.

I am unable to verify whether this work has already played any political role, but the following events took place: I entrusted a copy of the first version of this work to the Polish government-in-exile in London. Following their advice, I lent a similar one to a philosopher there. He was unable to return it to me because he no longer had it. I do not know how many pounds sterling this cost the intelligence service of the time. Following this, agents cornered me while I was resting in Ravenscourt Park and, issuing threats, they tried to force me not to write anything more. I believe, however, that their plunder was passed on to "big brother." For during the conversation between the Pope and Gorbachev the latter clearly made use of the content of my work. He tried to suss out whether John Paul II understood these matters. Unfortunately, he found out that he did not. But did reading this work influence his historical decisions? Maybe some of the readers will be able to shed some light on this subject? *Habent sua fata libelli* [books have their own destinies].[1]

I want to pay special tribute to my former professors at the Jagiellonian University, Stefan Szuman, Roman Ingarden, and others who taught me to think objectively and to seek the truth about man. I thank Professor Boleslaw Wysocki of Harvard University, Massachusetts, who studied this work, approved of the terminology used, and advised me to add the present first chapter, which is of a more literary nature and serves as an introduction for the Reader. I thank Professor Zdzislaw J. Ryn from Krakow for studying this work and expressing his appreciation for it, as well as his encouragement to persevere.

Andrzej Łobaczewski
Rzeszów, October 1997

[1]The historic meeting between Gorbachev and John Paul II took place at the Vatican on December 1, 1989 (two months later the Communist Party of the Soviet Union gave up its monopoly on political power). It is unclear which report Łobaczewski refers to, as the talk was private and a transcript was not released until 2009 (an English translation of the Russian record, which Gorbachev makes use of in his memoirs: https://nsarchive2.gwu.edu/NSAEBB/NSAEBB298/index.htm). Contemporary newspaper reports contain only generalities, and the official Russian transcript does not support Łobaczewski's speculation. According to the transcript, the two spoke alone for several minutes without interpreters. Statements by some Vatican sources contradict this, claiming that interpreters were present for the whole talk. Additionally, in 2011 a document from the Polish Institute of National Remembrance was published (https://www.rp.pl/historia/art14031561-papiez-nie-poparl-stanu-wojennego). This was a summary of the talk prepared by the Pope's translator, Stanisław Szłowieniec, for the Polish Ministry of Public Security, delivered five days after the talk, and suggests that some specific subjects do not appear in the official transcript (e.g., a specific reference to "cessation of production and experiments with chemical weapons, as well as the export of weapons to the Third World countries" by the Pope). While the only existing transcript may be incomplete, it seems likely that Łobaczewski read more into whatever report he had seen than was actually there, perhaps influenced by Gorbachev's

humane presentation and concern for morality and freedom of religion, and appreciation of the risks of democracy. See Kengor, *Pope and President*, pp. 487–491. (Thanks to Iza Rosca for her research on this issue.) —Ed.

APPENDIX II
On Democracy (1997)

(From the Polish version of Chapter X.)

Democracy has become an insufficiently understood slogan uniting the society of normal people. At the same time, a similar, but different ideology of democracy has become a new mask worn by the other side, behind which old, familiar issues are hidden. There are also organized pressure groups in the world that proclaim democracy as the sole standard of social morality and the only acceptable system. In reality, these people know very well that it is a difficult system to implement, one that often leads to volatility and weakness. Thus, imposing democracy on "naive nations" can be economically and politically profitable.

Democracy, in its modern understanding, is one of the political-system doctrines that emerged at the end of the eighteenth century, the time of seemingly rational, emotionally charged thinking, but poor in psychological understanding. From the psychological point of view, democracy contains a defect we are already familiar with. It allows individuals who are too primitive mentally and morally to be able to act in the name of the common good, or even their own, to participate in the process of governing the country. As a rule, they are driven by an excessively short-sighted self-interest, or by the influence of ponerogenic groups that know how to take advantage of them. Thus, the possibility of creating a relatively well-functioning democracy depends on how large this primitive faction is in a given country. As it turned out, the tragedies of the past years have increased their numbers in Poland.

Democracy can develop properly under three conditions: when the nation has a sufficiently established tradition of self-governance that predates democratic times; when respect for moral values and honesty in political affairs is sufficiently widespread; and when the destructive faction is sufficiently small. If these conditions are not met, democracy degenerates into various forms of rule by special interest groups, with hidden ideologies and even totalitarian characteristics.

This danger is an inherent feature of the ideology of democracy.[1] Although democracy is founded on the values of respect for individuals, and those values must be appreciated and maintained, it is not a system rooted in natural law and therefore it cannot provide a moral criterion for nations.

Bearing this in mind the construction of a state system better than democracy is not only a topic worthy of academic reflection, it is also an achievable undertaking, which may become a necessity in modern times. In order for such a system to prove itself in action, its planning and development should be based on a thorough understanding of psychological and social realities. Such an endeavor would have to be built on objective knowledge of the laws of nature, as well as contemporary knowledge, not doctrines of the eighteenth and nineteenth centuries. Ponerology would have to play its necessary role in this.

While living in the USA in late 1980s, in the faint hope that the time of the return of the subjugated nations to systems based on the rule of normal man was approaching, the author created an outline of such a system, entitled *Logocracy: A Conception of the State System*. Hoping that it would trigger a creative discussion on political solutions, he had it published in 1991 in Kraków. Unfortunately, the distribution of the book was blocked by secret orders.

Such an effort of constructive thinking, involving scientists and public opinion, would be the best school of political thought. It would also assist the process of global therapy discussed previously. The experience of our nation, especially the time covering the period of state reconstruction after the First World War, should be carefully utilized.

[1] See, e.g., J. L. Talmon, *The Origins of Totalitarian Democracy* (1960). —Ed.

APPENDIX III
A Response to Father Bogusław (2000)

(From the booklet Ponerologia.*)*

Father Bogusław became acquainted with ponerology, and after a long silence, still deeply troubled, he shared his opinion with me, which stemmed from the eternal teachings of the Church.

"These inquiries into the role of pathological factors in the genesis of evil are very earthly, because they attempt to substitute transcendental truth with biological explanations. For how can one speak about the nature of evil without mentioning the role of its main perpetrator? Have you, my friend, never encountered the work of Satan?"

Subjectively speaking, I think I have indeed experienced it, but it is not something that can be explained in terms of biology. Ponerology is a biological science and its possibilities extend only as far as the reach of a human mind armed with what other scientific disciplines can provide. It is a knowledge that is much-needed in many practical areas of life. I, on the other hand, am not a demonologist, and if I were to speak on matters in which I am a layman, I would be flippantly poaching on someone else's territory. How, then, could I possibly answer the esteemed Father Doctor? I can only do so with the help of a parable:

There was a chemical factory that manufactured complex chemical compounds and sold them at a very high price. Their production method was kept secret. One day, a new worker came to work there claiming to be a car mechanic, but one who was skillful at any job. His grease-stained jeans, unshaven face, and colloquial language matched his self-report quite well, so no one recognized him as a doctor of chemistry.

He worked alongside other laborers, repaired equipment, and turned out to be a really skillful mechanic. In the meantime, he stole samples of semi-finished products used there and sent them to his company's laboratory. He worked out how the apparatus used for the final synthesis operated. Our mechanic knew very well that the factory was managed by a Chief Executive Officer and a technical director, and that there was also a production safety clerk. But he wasn't interested in any acquaintance with them. He was too busy observing the processes the plant's equipment was used for.

And yet, someone began to suspect him and reported him to the clerk. They realized he was a chemist and fired him. He was lucky because he managed to avoid a heavy beating or death at the hands of hired thugs. So he thanked God for that. But the CEO's decisive intervention came too late, for this supposed worker had already discovered the secrets of the syntheses that were taking place in his chemical kitchen.

APPENDIX IV
Problems of Ponerology (2006)

(First published with the first edition of Polical Ponerology.*)*

Since the beginning of modern psychiatry at the end of the nineteenth century, the study of pathological deviations was pursued in Europe. During the first thirty years of the twentieth century, several eminent European psychiatrists were pioneers in these matters. Then followed a time of persecution of not only the science, but the scientists, and it seems, based on a review of what is currently known in the West, that much of this work was irretrievably lost.

As an example, when I was a student, a story reached Poland to the effect that an eminent German professor who had written an analysis of Hitler's psychopathic personality came to an unhappy end. He apparently tried to warn the Germans that such a Fuehrer would lead Germany to a terrible calamity. He was taken to a concentration camp where he died while being beaten. It was said that his last words were, "*Ich habe das deutlich nachgewiesen*!" (I proved it evidently!). I was unable to find out a name, so this must be consigned to anecdotal evidence, but it is interesting nonetheless because it was one of many such stories that were racing through the academic community at the time.

It seems that, at the same time, the Soviets realized the dangers of science. Not only did they bring a halt to the study of genetics,[1] they methodically sought to stamp out independent research in

[1] J. Steven Jones writes: "Genetics came to a stop [in the USSR] for twenty-five years because of ideology. That some qualities are beyond human intervention because they are coded into biology could not be accepted by Marxists ... Marx had insisted that man could be changed by altering society; once the revolution had succeeded a new and better humankind would emerge. ... The process of producing a new man had gone further in the Soviet Union than anywhere else. The masses had fulfilled the first five-year plan in four years, destroying millions of kulaks and intellectuals—wreckers and saboteurs—in the process ... The ideology—and the faked experiments—had disastrous effects. In 1942 Lysenko claimed that if winter wheat (which is cultivated in places with a climate mild enough to sustain it) were planted in Siberia among the

psychology and to take political control of the science to use it for their own nefarious ends. A few years after the end of World War II, all the public libraries in Poland were searched and the "dangerous" books were removed and destroyed. Professors were informed of what subjects were permitted in their lectures, and how they were to teach those subjects. The "authorities" knew best what a psychiatrist or a clinical psychologist was permitted to understand. In this way, much of the valuable research that was underway at the time was strangled and mostly forgotten.

Then, in America, Hervey Cleckley and other researchers undertook the task of discovering anew things that had already been researched in the crucible of the very subject they sought to understand: socially dangerous psychological anomalies. But they did not have access to the older European scientific output; no one in the West did, as it had been thoroughly erased from public view.

For me and for other searchers of the genesis of evil and the nature of macro-social pathological phenomena which engulfed our countries, this older European science, preserved in our minds from lectures given before the political suppression began, created the basis of our understanding. Retrieving this science of those researchers and psychiatrists of this era that was erased by fascism and communism is, I believe, a vital precondition for further progress in the study of macrosocial evil. It is important to note that the developing European terminology for this field was better elaborated and univocal. It seems that, in the West today, that there is great confusion of terminology.

---

stubble of spring wheat (which grows over the summer) it would be able to survive the coldest winter. The 'vernalization of wheat' (which simply did not work) was imposed on farmers and led to famine. ... In 1948, genetics in the USSR stopped ... The inheritance of acquired characters became law ... Much later Khrushchev said to Lysenko: 'You and your experiments can go to the moon' and, by the 1970s, genetics in the Soviet Union had rejoined the world of science. Lysenko was the mirror of the view that held in Germany and elsewhere during the 1930s: that genes did everything. Hitler himself is known to have read a textbook on human genetics and many experts in 'race hygiene' (as the subject was then called) were involved in the extermination movement. Breeding from those with the finest genes and eradicating those with the worst was the only way to improve society. That idea, too, failed the test of history" (*In the Blood: God, Genes and Destiny* [1995]). See also Wolfe, *Communist Totalitarianism*, pp. 95–113 ("Science Joins the Party"). For similarly disastrous policies in China, see Dikötter, *Mao's Great Famine*. —Ed.

As I have learned from the paper of Salekin, Trobst, and Krioukova,[2] a well-developed personality inventory is being used in the U.S. as the main system for discovery and estimation of psychopathies. This way may lead to a valuable degree of probability of diagnosis, but may not provide sufficient certainty due to the variation in types. We are in need of practical actions and further scientific progress. The necessary certainty of diagnosis can sometimes be provided by knowledge of various kinds of mental anomalies elaborated by the suppressed European scientific work now lost.

In accordance with my experience as a clinical psychologist and researcher of the nature of evil in the domains of psychopathology, it appears to me that nearly half of the pathologic factors taking part in the processes of the generation of evil—what I call ponerogenesis—are the results of various kinds of brain tissue lesions. The psychopathies make up a lesser percentage of these types. There are other factors too, such as what are popularly referred to as multiple personalities. The concentration of our attention on psychopathies only can lead to unilateral comprehension of the general problem and to mistakes in praxis, particularly psychotherapy. The situation concerning cases of psychopathy is much more confused. But an exhaustive knowledge of the biological nature and genetic properties of particular kinds of psychopathies may, I hope, permit a way to open for understanding. It is for this reason I offer these remarks based on my training and experience in the crucible of those types of events that we hope to—no, we must—understand.

The aim should be the reduction of the activity of pathology in the genesis of evil in society and its tragic results at all scales from individuals (such as women who fall prey to psychopaths), to families, social groups, social movements, and on to the largest scale of political events. Such an aim requires a firm foundation of profound and detailed knowledge of the nature of all abnormalities. All of the output of the older psychiatrists as well as contemporary achievements must be carefully considered and utilized in further exploration. The actual state of current knowledge may be sufficient for understanding the macrosocial phenomenon, but it is still not adequate for full realization of the task before us, including individual cases.

[2]Salekin et al., "Construct Validity of Psychopathy in a Community Sample: A Nomological Net Approach" (2001). —Ed.

The main task seems to me to be distinguishing of anomalies caused by damage in brain tissue from those transmitted by heredity. It is also the daily bread of the psychologist. Estimation of the location and the kind of damage is not really difficult using standard tests and technology. Those with pathologies that result from such mechanical disorders can be observed to be the most frequent initiators of the macrosocial processes that lead to human suffering on a grand scale; they open the door to the further activity of the genetically transmitted pathological factors. These conditions seem to be easier to take under control via psychotherapy. Since the brain lesions are not hereditary, the therapist is under an obligation to inform the patient and those concerned with the life of the patient that the danger of a hereditary problem does not exist, and so the management plan would be different from a case where heredity is a factor.

The most active cases, in terms of ponerological activity (and here we do no necessarily mean overt criminal behavior, though that can also play a part even if undetected), appeared in my cases to be frontal characteropathy. (I believe that characteropathies are often referred to in the West as "personality disorders.")

The damage of the brain center BA10 is predominantly caused in newborns as a result of neonatal hypoxia or various diseases that are common at that crucial age. The pathological features are not noticeable in pre-school children. However, the problems augment throughout life until, usually, after the age of fifty, there is a severe ponerogenic personality. A good and typical example is Stalin. Comparative considerations should be included in the list of this particular ponerogenic characteropathy, which developed against the backdrop of perinatal damage to his brain's prefrontal fields. Literature and news about him abounds in indications: brutal, charismatic, snake-charming; issuing of irrevocable decisions; inhuman ruthlessness, pathologic revengefulness directed at anyone who got in his way; and egotistical belief in his own genius on the part of a person whose mind was, in fact, only average. This state explains as well his psychological dependence on a psychopath like Beria. Some photographs reveal the typical deformation of his forehead which appears in people who suffered very early damage to the areas mentioned above.

Modern trends in obstetrical and neonatal care have greatly reduced the incidence of this type of characteropathy, but more needs to be done. Nowadays we meet with lighter cases. So it is that improved medical services—particularly for women and children—is among those things that must be included in any plan to deal with evil on the macrosocial scale. Let us hope that another Stalin will never appear.

Let me briefly sketch, once again, the main categories with some additional details not included in the original text.

Paranoid character disorders are another characteropathy that contributes to the genesis of evil. We know today that the psychological mechanism of paranoid phenomena is twofold: one is caused by damage to the brain tissue, the other is functional or behavioral. Certain brain tissue lesions cause a certain slackening of accurate thinking and, as a consequence, loss of control of the personality structure. Most typical are those cases caused by an aggression in the diencephalon by various pathological factors, resulting in its permanently decreased tonal ability, and similarly of the tonus of inhibition in the brain cortex. Particularly during sleepless nights, runaway thoughts give rise to a paranoid view of human reality, as well as to ideas which can be either gently naive or violently revolutionary.

In persons free of brain tissue lesions, such phenomena most frequently occur as a result of being reared by people with paranoid characteropathy, along with the psychological terror of their childhood. Such psychological material is then assimilated, creating the rigid stereotypes of abnormal experiencing. This makes it difficult for thought and worldview to develop normally, and the terror-blocked contents become transformed into permanent, functional, congestive centers.

It is characteristic of paranoid behavior for people to be capable of relatively correct reasoning and discussion as long as the conversation involves minor differences of opinion. This stops abruptly when the partner's arguments begin to undermine their overvalued ideas, crush their long-held stereotypes of reasoning, or force them to accept a conclusion they had subconsciously rejected before. Such a stimulus unleashes upon the partner a torrent of pseudo-logical, largely paramoralistic, suggestive abuse.

Such reactions generally only serve to repel cultivated and logical people, who then tend to avoid the paranoid types. However, the power of the paranoid lies in the fact that they easily enslave less critical minds, e.g., people with other kinds of psychological deficiencies, who have been victims of individuals with character disorders, and, in particular, a large segment of young people.

A member of the labor class may perceive this power to enslave to be a kind of victory over educated people and thus take the paranoid person's side. However, this is not the normal reaction among the common people, where intelligence and perception of psychological reality occurs no less often than among intellectuals.

In sum then, the response of accepting paranoid argumentation is qualitatively more frequent in reverse proportion to the civilization level of the community in question. Nevertheless, paranoid individuals become aware of their enslaving influence through experience and attempt to take advantage of it in a pathologically egotistic manner.

Psychopathies are the hereditarily transmitted anomalies, mainly of the human instinctive substratum. They represent deficiencies of this natural phylogenetic endowment, but are of a diverse nature. We know of a number of distinct kinds of these anomalies which differ both in nature as well as in hereditary transmission. Therefore, it should be understood from the outset that they are biologically different entities.

The most active in terms of ponerogenesis is what the suppressed scientists referred to as "essential psychopathy." Nowadays this type is described by many researchers, though they often use varying nomenclature.

This anomaly is best known due to its often dramatic involvement in life tragedies involving women. Colin Wilson discusses what he calls the "Right Man," which might in other uses also be called the "dominant male" or the "alpha male," though here we are concerned with extremes in behavior, not just ordinary dominance or leadership characteristics. This description, though using different terminology, gives a good picture of the type of the essential psychopath. Most often the essential psychopath is a domestic household tyrant terrorizing his family, but they can be found in all fields of human endeavor. They are recognized early as childhood bullies and torturers of helpless creatures.

Wilson's discussion is based on the work of A.E. Van Vogt, who is the author of a number of psychological studies. Van Vogt's concept of the "Right Man" or "violent man" is important here for its descriptive power of the pathology in question—not necessarily for its interpretation. Wilson writes:

> In 1954, Van Vogt began work on a war novel called *The Violent Man*, which was set in a Chinese prison camp. The commandant of the camp is one

of those savagely authoritarian figures who would instantly, and without hesitation, order the execution of anyone who challenges his authority. Van Vogt was creating the type from observation of men like Hitler and Stalin. And, as he thought about the murderous behavior of the commandant, he found himself wondering: "What could motivate a man like that?" Why is it that some men believe that anyone who contradicts them is either dishonest or downright wicked? Do they really believe, in their heart of hearts, that they are gods who are incapable of being fallible? If so, are they in some sense insane, like a man who thinks he is Julius Caesar?

Looking around for examples, it struck Van Vogt that male authoritarian behavior is far too commonplace to be regarded as insanity. ... [For example, m]arriage seems to bring out the "authoritarian" personality in many males, according to Van Vogt's observation. ...

"[T]he violent man" or the "Right Man" ... is a man driven by a manic need for self-esteem—to feel he is a "somebody". He is obsessed by the question of "losing face", so will never, under any circumstances, admit that he might be in the wrong. ...

Equally interesting is the wild, insane jealousy. Most of us are subject to jealousy, since the notion that someone we care about prefers someone else is an assault on our *amour propre.* But the Right Man, whose self-esteem is like a constantly festering sore spot, flies into a frenzy at the thought, and becomes capable of murder.

... He feels he [is] justified in exploding, like an angry god. ... [H]e feels he is inflicting just punishment. ...

[T]he one thing that becomes obvious in all case histories of Right Men is that their attacks are not somehow "inevitable"; some of their worst misdemeanours are carefully planned and calculated, and determinedly carried out. The Right Man does these things because he thinks they will help him to achieve his own way, which is what interests him.

And this in turn makes it plain that the Right Man problem is a problem of *highly dominant* people. Dominance is a subject of enormous interest to biologists and zoologists because the percentage of dominant animals—or human beings—seems to be amazingly constant. ... [B]iological studies have confirmed ... [that f]or some odd reason, precisely five per cent—one in twenty—of any animal group are dominant—have leadership qualities. ...

... The "average" member of the dominant five per cent sees no reason why he should not be rich and famous too. He experiences anger and frustration at his lack of "primacy", and is willing to consider unorthodox methods of elbowing his way to the fore. This clearly explains a great deal about the rising levels of crime and violence in our society.

We can also see how large numbers of these dominant individuals develop into "Right Men". In every school with five hundred pupils there are about twenty-five dominant ones struggling for primacy. Some of these have natural advantages: they are good athletes, good scholars, good debaters. (And there are, of course, plenty of non-dominant pupils who are gifted enough to carry away some of the prizes.) Inevitably, a percentage of the dominant pupils have no particular talent or gift; some may be downright stupid. How is such a person to satisfy his urge to primacy?

> He will, inevitably, choose to express his dominance in any ways that are possible.[3]

Now, Van Vogt's and Wilson's analysis misses the core of the problem—essential psychopathy—but they have described the type in its external manifestation and have touched on the genetic issues if only tangentially.

In my own researches it became apparent that a profound investigation of this type was necessary when it appeared that it played a chief inspirational role in the macrosocial pathology still called "communism." The frequency of its appearance varies from country to county. My estimation for Poland, my home, is approximately 6 per thousand.

The instinctive substratum of such individuals lacks natural syntonic responses. It is as though there are gaps in the natural endowment, or "missing strings" on the instrument. As a result, such individuals are unable to understand subtle human emotions and even what could be considered moral common sense. They are egoists as well as pathological egotists, trying to force other people to feel and think as they demand.

As a result of my long experience observing this phenomenon and attempts to track it to its source, I share the conviction with other researchers that this anomaly is inherited via the X chromosome and that it is not transferable from father to son. If the mother is normal on both her chromosomes, the son is genotypically free. In some cases, this is essential information so that the punishments for the "sins of the fathers" are not visited upon the sons. The daughters are then the carriers, and they sometimes—more often than not, but not always—demonstrate some pathological characteristics. The question as to why not all of them exhibit pathology is a question that needs to be investigated.

The schizoidal psychopath appears in both sexes and is similar both in presentation and frequency. This suggests that the anomaly is transmitted autosomally. Its average frequency is somewhat higher than essential psychopathy but varies considerably between racial or ethnic groups. Appearing in its highest frequency among Jews, and due to the exceptional tenacity and persistent nature that characterizes this pathology, it marks their whole civilization, worldview, and activity.

---

[3]Colin Wilson's *A Criminal History of Mankind* (1984).

The instinctive substratum of the schizoidal psychopath operates as a whole as upon shifting sand. They lack a natural sense of psychological realities. They have very efficient intellects, but it dangles over dimmed feelings of human nature. Nevertheless, the intellectual aspect persistently strives and endeavors to generate great doctrines and amoral strategies that are cunningly conceived so as to act suggestively upon naive individuals whose intellects are not so well developed. The schizoids and their doctrines have played the initial role in creating the great macrosocial tragedies of our times.

In family relations, the schizoidal psychopath engenders dispirited and depressive states in their partners. The less intellectually developed types seem to be easy tools for more clever intriguers. When their mistakes in judgment or association result in serious troubles, they easily fall into a reactive state closely resembling schizophrenia.

Asthenic psychopathy can be noted to be the most numerically significant classification. There are doubts as to whether all the symptomatically similar cases are sufficiently similar nomologically[4] speaking. It seems that some of the asthenic types have certainly played a role in the genesis of evil, but others seem to be easier able to adjust to the demands of normal social life.

Skirtoidia appears similarly in both sexes. These people are emotionally dynamic, coarse, lacking understanding of subtle issues of morality. The males make very good soldiers, but when their energy is not channeled in such ways, they become overly egotistical, weaker versions of the above-mentioned "right man." They abuse their wives and children, but are sufficiently concerned with their own well-being to not cross the line of the law.

The old psychiatrists of Eastern Europe also included in their taxonomy "debilism" or "*salon debils*."[5] This is a qualitative anomaly understood as hereditary and somewhat similar to schizoidia. Such individuals were generally decent, but marked by flat, coaxing talkativeness and an inability to understand any sort of serious matter.

I have listed above the most often described types of psychopathies with which I am familiar. Various hybrids of these anomalies, and more rare anomalies known or unknown or insufficiently described, comprise the pool lurking within societies. Such a pool exists in all

[4]That is, whether or not they describe the same underlying construct. Nomological validity is a subset of construct validity, the degree to which a test measures what it purports to measure. —Ed.

[5]In French, something akin to "crazy person" or "village idiot." —Ed.

countries of the world (but its composition varies), consisting of from 4% to 9% of the total population.

Detailed knowledge on the nature of all of these anomalies, particularly on their biological properties, is basic to any prospect of realization of practical action in all fields that might help to shield humanity from the actions of such social pathogens. In my own case, the possibilities of one person, working in the most inconvenient and impossible conditions, were quite small; now I can only appeal to other researchers to promote work in this important field for the sake of the survival of humanity.

The understanding of what kinds of mental anomalies are active in any process of ponerogenesis, and in what ways they participate, is basic for any effective action. For instance, such understanding is crucial in the psychotherapy of any individual whose worldview has been malformed by the influences of a pathological personality, increasing the success rate of patient management.

For example, attempting to persuade an individual under the spell of an essential psychopath (usually women, but not always) is generally doomed to failure. However, when we ask the question: why did the victim not notice immediately the psychopath's anomalous ways of "feeling" and thinking, we discover quite often that there are, in the victim, circuits of thought and behavior embedded there by early influence of another abnormal personality, generally one characterized by mental disorders caused by brain tissue damage. This has been noted by me so often that it requires special emphasis and consideration. The important thing is that once this is revealed, the door has been opened to effective psychotherapy.

The psychotherapist may then assist the patient to elaborate full awareness of this detrimental influence as well as the means to overcome or to eliminate these very tendencies from his personality. The result is that the patient can re-learn accurate ways of feeling and understanding not only the self, but other people as well.

And so it is that when a patient presents certain problems for which there seems to be no obvious cause, and the psychotherapist becomes aware of the spellbinding influence of a psychopath in the life of his patient, it is more conducive to successful therapy to approach the problem in this way, and thus the concealed problem—the influence of the psychopath—will be solved as well, because the patient will learn to see the abnormality in the process of identifying it in the self.

It is necessary for psychotherapists to be somewhat artful. The fact is, psychotherapy is the initial realm where ponerology has an immediate application. In my experience, the understanding of the macrosocial elements, moving then to the group and family elements, leads to more concise and effective corrective measures being identified and implemented. These analyses can then bring more durable reordering of the patient's personality and assists in enriching the mind with the ability for lifelong self-management. Some difficulties are encountered with less intelligent patients. Nevertheless, my own experience convinces me that the study of ponerology on all scales should be introduced into the studies of psychology and become a part of the occupation of all psychotherapists.

Various mental anomalies are included in the processes of ponerogenesis on all social scales, from individual to macrosocial phenomena. They are active inside individuals, limiting their possibilities of self-control, or they act as traumatizing or fascinating influences on others, particularly young people, distorting their personalities and worldviews. Searching for and within these diverse processes of ponerogenesis is the task and realm of our science. This science of ponerology meets the requirements of the principle of medicine: "*Ignoti nulla est curatio morbi.*" Do not attempt to cure what you do not understand.

The results of the science of ponerology, generally speaking, often corroborate some convictions of ancient moral philosophers, reinforcing them from the side of naturalistic reasoning. Utilizing data not hitherto taken into consideration, or that which has only been discovered in the past few decades, the science of ponerology permits us to understand and to solve many enigmatic and mysterious problems of life, including those which plague individuals, families, communities, and nations. In the very near future, this science might very well prevent another tragedy such as the historical ones of the last century.

The ponerological approach to psychology and psychotherapy may also bring detailed corrections to ethical sciences. Recognizing the real causality and confused processes of ponerogenesis, ponerology introduces the sorting mechanism of the psychological and psychopathological facets of macrosocial problems which must, at all times, be taken into consideration. Therefore, traditional interpretations of evil, in moral terms only, can be left behind as archaic and old-fashioned relics of the unscientific past. There is good reason for this, because moralizing interpretations do not permit sufficiently effective counteraction and neutralizing of the evil which appears one day under one disguise and under another the next. So we may say as well that pure ethical reasoning, without the scientific input of ponerology, has also been immoral. But so it has been for millennia. To overcome this long tradition we must face the resistance of philosophers; but this is our duty.

The ponerological approach appears to be very promising in many realms of science and praxis. Such reinterpretation of the dramatic events of history, both ancient and recent, can replace the dry narrations of historiographers with a vivid picture of the true dynamics which can teach us about the real reasons and thus provide new possibilities of preventing the genesis of evil, or at least better management of its results. The history of mankind demands a rereading and retelling by historians educated in the science of ponerology.

Ponerology was born in the crucible of attempts to understand, scientifically, a macrosocial phenomenon of what can only be called extreme and excessive evil: fascism and Soviet communism. After a time of intellectual adversity, when the usual language of the social sciences proved to be inadequate to describe what was being lived and experienced, it became obvious that the first necessity was to elaborate a new branch of science and a language so as to have adequate categories and nomenclature to deal with something of this magnitude. This elaboration finally permitted the finding of adequate answers and elaboration of proper scientific descriptions of the real nature of the phenomenon. This macrosocial system had all the characteristics of a pathological individual writ very large, as I describe in my book. I was aware that such similar phenomena have appeared in the history of mankind again and again, in various scales, under various historical conditions, and always carried into society, like a Trojan Horse, enrobed in the ideology of some idealistic heterogeneous social movement. This is still true in the present time.

In many countries, the rule of law has helped society to deal with, to some extent, such pathologies at various scales. But without objective premises and aims based on principles revealed by the science of ponerology, the rule of law proceeds only by chance—trial and error. And so it will be until the rule of law is underpinned by the science of ponerology. But change will not be easy! The utilization of this science and what it reveals will cause an earthquake in the minds of traditional jurists. The elaboration of an ameliorated law will demand a lot of work and in the proper time. New ways and methods of combating evil in society are needed rather than just a scheme of punishments. More effective means of dealing with the genesis of evil must be found!

Where to go from here?

The first thing that must be done is to reconstruct the whole science of psychology and to promote and fund research in all areas where psychology is applicable, which generally means all areas of life in society. Then, to promote the science and its usefulness to society at large. It should be taught in high schools, including the necessary data on pathologies, as well as an overview of the macrosocial implications. The popularization of true psychology would improve the ability of people and communities to make better decisions in their lives and plans. A basic knowledge of the true nature of evil—that it can be scientifically elaborated—would make people more circumspect in their engagements with other people and life in general.

Such a popularized background is necessary for the development of the science and its diverse social applications. Communities that understand its values and ideas will support the implementation of those changes necessary to deal with social pathology. Such popularization may enable a development of what could be called "eugenic morality" which would inspire voluntary efforts to contribute to the reduction, from generation to generation, of the burden of genetically transmitted psychopathological anomalies. The naivety of women due to the serious lack of accurate psychological knowledge is a major cause of the increasing numbers of genetic psychopaths being born in the present day and for the past 50 years or so.

What is of crucial importance is to fully grasp the importance of the science of ponerology and how many applications it may have for a future of peace and a humane humanity. This science permits the human mind to understand things that have been, for millennia, unintelligible: the genesis of evil. This understanding could very well bring about a turning point in the history of civilization which, I should add, is presently on the point of self-destruction.

Therefore, my request to you is: Be not shocked with the immense size of the task! Take it as a work to be gradually performed and hope that many other people will come to help, and thus progress will be assured.

It seems that, in the natural order of things, those persons who have suffered the most from psychopaths or bearers of other mental anomalies, will be those called to do this work, to accept the burden. If you do, accept also, ladies and gentlemen, your fate with an open heart and humility, and always with a sense of humor. Cherish assistance from the Universal Mind and know that Great Values often grow from Great Suffering.

Rzeszów, August 24, 2006

GLOSSARY

anankastic psychopathy: Obsessive-compulsive personality disorder. The *ICD-11* defines the "anankastia" (from the Greek *ananke* for force or necessity) personality-disorder trait domain as "a narrow focus on one's rigid standard of perfection and of right and wrong, and on controlling one's own and others' behaviour and controlling situations to ensure conformity to these standards," with specific features of perfectionism (concern with rules, norms of right and wrong, details, hyper-scheduling, orderliness, and neatness) and emotional and behavioural constraint (rigid control over emotional expression, stubbornness, risk-avoidance, perseveration, and deliberativeness). OCPD is characterized by low disinhibition (i.e., high conscientiousness) and negative affectivity (anxiety, negativistic attitudes, rejecting others' advice). For film representations, see Jack Nicholson's character Melvin Udall in *As Good As It Gets* (1997), and Patrick Bergin as Martin Burney in *Sleeping with the Enemy* (1991).

asthenic psychopathy: Asthenia (from the Greek *a-* without + *sthenos* strength) was generally considered a nervous or mental fatigue or weakness characterized by passivity, low energy, inability to enjoy life, low sensation threshold, irritability, and unstable moods. In Western psychiatry, diagnosis of asthenic personality disorder eventually split into dependent and avoidant (also passive-aggressive) personality disorders, though these bear only a passing resemblance to the disorder Łobaczewski describes. The *ICD-11* equivalent for avoidant personality disorder is a combination of negative affectivity (anxiety, avoidance of situations judged too difficult), detachment (avoidance of social interactions and intimacy, see **schizoidia**), and low dissociality (reversed self-centeredness, low self-esteem). The type described in Cleckley's *Caricature of Love* seems much closer to Łobaczewski's.

authoritarianism: Most attempts since the late 1940s to study authoritarianism have focused exclusively on *right-wing* authoritarianism, some explicitly denying its existence on the left, e.g., critical theorist Theodor W. Adorno and colleagues' "F-scale," an attempt to measure the "fascist" personality now widely recognized as flawed,[1] and the current standard, Robert Alte-

[1]This was further developed in their book, *The Authoritarian Personality* (1950). An early critic of their conception was German émigré psychiatrist Hans Eysenck, who argued in his 1954 book *The Psychology of Politics* that the extreme left and right were mirror images of each other, which scandalized leftwing academics "due to their assumption that socialists are well-intended

meyer's RWA scale, which has also come under criticism. RWA conceptualizes authoritarianism as three correlated attitudes/behaviors (authoritarian submission, authoritarian aggression, and conventionalism) as well as social dominance (SDO), but has been criticized for confounding conservative ideology and authoritarianism. For example, the religiously conservative anticommunist dissidents under communism would seem to be outliers, as would the communist revolutionaries.

Recent studies have argued for the existence of LWA (or "authoritarian political correctness"). One recent study, for example, found that "from a Dark Triad perspective, Authoritarian PC advocates have more in common with extreme right advocates than those holding PC views related to compassion."[2] Another study attempts to develop a measure of LWA, identifying three dimensions: anti-hierarchical aggression, top-down censorship, and anti-conventionalism. The authors write: "By and large, LWA and RWA/SDO seem to reflect a shared constellation of traits that might be considered the 'heart' of authoritarianism. These traits include preference for social uniformity, prejudice towards different others, willingness to wield group authority to coerce behavior, cognitive rigidity, aggression and punitiveness towards perceived enemies, outsized concern for hierarchy, and moral absolutism."[3] In terms of personality traits, RWA seems to capture typical conservative traits (high conscientiousness, low openness); SDO the more aggressive, **psychopathic** ones (low honesty-humility, low agreeableness, low emotionality/neuroticism, psychopathic disinhibition and meanness); and Costello et al.'s LWA a mix of typical liberal and SDO (high openness, low conscientiousness, high neuroticism, low honesty-humility, low agreeableness).

borderline personality disorder: BPD is characterized by emotional dysregulation, impulsivity, and cognitive-perceptual impairment. "Strangely enough, people with damage to the dorsolateral and nearby ventromedial areas can have normal intelligence but have no common sense—they are unable to make reasonable decisions."[4] Subclinical borderlines seem to have greater executive control, possibly facilitating their success in the social sphere. As with paranoid personality disorder, some researchers do not consider borderline a valid personality-disorder construct. Many of its features are symptoms, not personality traits, making diagnosis inconsistent; some diagnosed with BPD have internalizing (neurotic) traits, others externalizing

while the Right is inherently malign" (see Smith and McCrae, "From F Scale to Phobias: The Paradoxical Search for the Authoritarian Personality" [2021]).

[2]Moss and O'Connor, "The Dark Triad Traits Predict Authoritarian Political Correctness and Alt-Right Attitudes" (2020).

[3]Costello et al., "Clarifying the Structure and Nature of Left-wing Authoritarianism" (2021), p. 39. See also Conway et al., "Is the Myth of Left-Wing Authoritarianism Itself a Myth?" (2020).

[4]Oakley, *Evil Genes*, p. 203.

(antisocial); some respond to treatment, others don't; there are too many comorbidities; and its three main components are probably best understood as separate conditions: a genetic component linked to bipolar, and two others linked mainly to childhood abuse: emotional dysregulation syndrome and antisocial behavioral.[5] It is also possible that psychopathy (especially in women) may be (mis)diagnosed as BPD (the two are strongly related in women[6]). Colin Ross argues that BPD is a trauma response and should be grouped with the other Axis I disorders, perhaps as "reactive attachment disorder of adulthood."[7]

characteropathy: Disorder of the central nervous system resulting in character disorder or disturbance, as distinct from **psychopathy**/personality disorder. Łobaczewski distinguishes organic causes (such as early traumatic brain injury, neurotoxins) and functional causes (e.g., characteropathic parenting, emotional abuse) and focuses on two types: paranoid and frontal. He refers to the functional varieties as sociopathies.

conversive thinking: Emotionally motivated thinking in which data have been subconsciously converted (blocked, reversed, or transposed), leading to **paralogical** conclusions. From the psychiatric term *conversion*, i.e., hysterical or dissociative in nature. Examples include commonly known cognitive biases (e.g., cognitive dissonance, motivated reasoning, confirmation bias, Dunning-Kruger, hindsight bias, moral dumbfounding, etc.) and the "defense mechanisms" of psychoanalytic theory (e.g., denial, repression, projection, splitting, rationalization, reaction formation, etc.).

disintegration: A weakening or disordering of personality structure or mental functions, e.g., as in episodes of depression or anxiety. Often associated with intense emotion, inner conflict, life-changing events (such as puberty, menopause, unexpected misfortunes or tragedies, etc.). According to Dąbrowski's theory of positive disintegration, disintegration can be negative (leading to psychosis, suicide, chronic mental illness) or positive (leading to higher-level personality integrations).

egocentrism: Self-centeredness; inability to accurately intuit another's perspective; having an exaggerated sense of entitlement; thinking only of oneself, without regard for feelings, interests, of well-being of others.

egoism: Selfishness; acting out of self-interest.

egotism: Self-importance; arrogance; narcissism; placing an excessive or exaggerated value in one's opinions and judgments; "right man" syndrome.

[5] Peter Tyrer, "Why Borderline Personality Disorder is Neither Borderline Nor a Personality Disorder" (2009).

[6] Thomson, *Understanding Psychopathy*, p. 28.

[7] Ross, *Trauma Model*, ch. 21.

essential psychopathy: See **psychopathy.**

etiology: The cause(s) or manner of causation of a disease or condition.

hysteria: Originally considered by Freud to be a number of symptoms caused by hidden trauma, clinical hysteria today is defined as "symptoms of a neurological nature—paralysis, anaesthesia, aphasia, blindness, amnesia, fits, etc.—for which there is no apparent neurological cause."[8] In modern psychiatry the diagnosis of hysteria has been fragmented into histrionic personality disorder (attention-seeking, melodramatic), dissociative disorders (e.g., dissociative identity, dissociative amnesia), and somatic-symptom or related disorders like illness anxiety (e.g., hypochondria), conversion disorder (where psychological stress is "converted" into physical symptoms, e.g., hysterical blindness), factitious disorder (e.g., Munchausen syndrome). Can also refer to various psychogenic illnesses spread through social/emotional contagion (e.g., mass hysteria, mass psychogenic illness). Key symptom of the **hysteroidal cycle.** See also **conversive thinking.**

hysterical psychopathy: Histrionic personality disorder. Characterized by excessive attention-seeking behaviors, including provocative or seductive behavior, exaggerated and theatrical displays of emotion. Characterized in the *ICD-11* by dissociality (egocentric), disinhibition (impulsive), negative affectivity (overreactive), low detachment (extraverted).

hysteroidal cycle: The cycle during which a society's **hysterical** condition (consisting of individual cases and mass social hysteria) rises and falls, with an average period of around two centuries. The peak of mass hystericization may be followed by a crisis such as societal collapse, war, revolution, and/or pathocracy. In the hysteroidal state before and during a societal crisis, radical ideologies take hold, especially among young people, intellectuals, and other "bourgeois elites." Symptoms of this state include: habitually ignoring actual problems and their real causes, focusing on pseudo-problems and convenient but ineffective solutions, the inability to reason and judge evidence soundly, silencing sound criticism and amplifying radical voices, giving overly charitable interpretations to trendy but unscientific ideas (a weakness of "egotism of the natural worldview"). In these conditions, it is very easy for overly simplistic, unscientific, illogical, and totalitarian ideologies to gain adherents. Such ideologies tend to identify the source of society's problem within some group category, whether based on religion, class, or race, e.g., Jews (in the case of Nazism), property owners (in the case of Bolshevism), or "whiteness" (in the case of critical race theory).

Strauss and Howe's generational theory (SHGT) posits a cycle of four human generations, roughly 80 to 90 years total in duration, or the length

[8] Kelly et al., *Irreducible Mind*, p. 162.

of a long human life: 1) the high following a crisis, when collective mentality is strong and societies rebuild on a new foundation; 2) an awakening, where individualism confronts and outstrips the conformity of the previous generation; 3) the unraveling, where institutions stagnate and lose public trust; 4) a crisis of upheaval that often destroys the old order. Below is a table[9] presenting one possible division for the United States and Russia:

Turning (Generation)	*United States*	*Russia*
High (Baby Boomer)	1946–1964 (American High)	1922–1945 (Soviet Transformation)
Awakening (Gen X)	1964–1984 (Consciousness Revolution)	1945–1964 (Khrushchev Thaw)
Unraveling (Millennial)	1984–2007 (Culture Wars)	1965–1989 (Era of Stagnation)
Crisis (Gen Z)	2007–2028?	1990–2012 (Wild Nineties)
High		2013–2035?

While SHGT has some similarities with Łobaczewski's description of the hysteroidal cycle, it is not a scientific theory.[10] In contrast, Peter Turchin's structural-demographic theory (SDT) attempts to discern general historical principles and develop mathematical models which can be tested against the historical record. It too identifies four stages (expansion, stagflation, crisis, depression), but of much longer duration: 200–300 years in pre-industrial societies. Despite their differences, all three theories suggest the U.S. has entered a period of crisis, one which SHGT and SDT suggest will peak sometime in the 2020s. Whereas cycles in different countries may have similar durations, Turchin argues that societies are nonlinear dynamical systems, and thus durations vary depending on how different components interact. The main drivers of political instability include immiseration (e.g., depressed wages, poor health, and social well-being), intraelite competition/elite overproduction, and state fragility (e.g., fiscal crisis). Labor oversupply depresses wages and is the root of elite overproduction, which leads to growing wealth inequality.

induction (psychological, psychopathological): The transfer of emotions, states, and ways of thinking from one person (or group) to another. Examples

[9]Strauss and Howe, *Fourth Turning*, pp. 3, 36, 138. See also Ted Goertzel, "The World Trade Center Bombing as a Fourth Generational Turning Point" (2002). For the timing of Russian generations, see Karashchuk et al., "The Method for Determining Time-Generation Range" (2020).

[10]Peter Turchin, "The Prophecy of the Fourth Turning" (2017).

include hypnotic induction, persuasion, emotional contagion, and the pathologizing effect on one's feeling, thoughts, and personality by **psychopathic** and **characteropathic** individuals.

instinctive substratum: The biologically based emotional–instinctive foundation of our characteristic ways of thinking, feeling, and behaving, and our personality development. It includes the structure and function of our central nervous system and our common psychology and cognition: our basic emotions, "moral taste buds," range of personality traits (Big Five), capacity for language and symbolic thought, possibilities for personal development, and capacity for social engagement and organization. In a word, human nature.

macrosocial: A society-, nation-, or empire-wide social phenomenon. A macrosocial phenomenon affects the entire social structure and can apply to mass movements, social classes, and government structures. The dynamics of psychopathology on the individual, family, or small-group level scale up to the macrosocial level. Thus an individual or group can have the same effect on an entire nation that they might have on a single family, through psychopathological **induction** and the effects of pathological terror and abuse. **Pathocracy** is a macrosocial disease process cloaked by a popular, idealistic ideology.

paralogic (paralogism, paralogistics): An illogical, false logic. A paralogism is a statement or argument intended to be persuasive that is fundamentally illogical. It can either be the result of conversive thinking or deliberate mendacity. Ideological propaganda is a form of paralogistics. It is ostensibly logical, but contains false premises, leaps of logic, and double standards. Paralogic acquires much of its persuasive force due to the presence of **paramoralisms.** Orwell captured the essence of paralogic in *1984*: "War is peace, freedom is slavery, ignorance is strength." James Lindsay defines ideological paralogic as "an alternative logic—a *paralogic*, an illogical fake logic that operates *beside* logic—that has internally comprehensible rules and structure but that does not produce logical results."[11]

paramorality (paramoralism): An immoral, false morality. Paramoralisms can take the form of slogans or suggestive insults (epithets, terms of abuse) with highly negative connotations. They are the means by which something good or neutral can be deemed evil or immoral, or something evil or neutral deemed good. For example, words with positive, neutral, or negative connotations can be transformed into the words implying the worst form of evil, e.g., traitor, counterrevolutionary, Jew, kulak, racist, sexist, transphobe, etc. Those under the influence of a psychopathological individual will often

[11]Lindsay, "Psychopathy and the Origins of Totalitarianism" (2020).

paramorally defend them and even approve of their behavior. If freedom is slavery according to paralogic, then according to paramorality, evil is good, and conscience is evil. James Lindsay defines ideological paramorality as "an immoral false morality which lies beside (and apart from) anything that deserves to be called 'moral.' The goal of the paramorality is to socially enforce the belief that good people accept the paramorality and attendant pseudo-reality while everyone else is morally deficient and evil. That is, it is an inversion of morality."[12]

pathocracy: A **macrosocial** disease of mass social movements and ideologies (whether social, political, or religious) which infects entire societies, nations, and empires. Pathocracy is the result of **ponerized** secondary **ponerogenic unions** which achieve political domination either through revolution from below (a group not in power that gains power, through violent or democratic means) or from above (in which an existing ruling class is infected from within). Pathocracy can also come about through foreign influence, either imposed by force or through artificial infection (psychological warfare, subversion, infiltration). In its early phases after achieving power it is typically led primarily by characteropathic individuals, inspired by schizoid ideologies. This phase of initial consolidation is the most violent and destructive, as the old social order is destroyed and progressively reordered through successive purges until practically all social positions of influence are occupied by people with a variety of personality disorders and character disturbances. This destructive phase is followed by a dissimulative phase once the new order has stabilized, characterized primarily by psychopathic individuals. During this phase, repressions are less intense—though targeted and ruthless when necessary—and normal people learn to adapt to the new system. The dissimulative phase can last decades or centuries until the society of normal people has a chance to develop and reestablish a normal social and governmental structure. Psychopathy plays an essential role in the **ponerogenesis** of pathocracy; the proportion of a society's essential psychopaths who integrate into the new ruling class approaches 100%. Pathocracy is a pathological inversion of a normal social hierarchy, in which social outcasts, criminals, and other psychological deviants rise to the top.

personality disintegration: See **disintegration**.

ponerization: The process by which **ponerogenic associations** become infected and progressively hijacked by individuals with personality disorders, and social-movement ideologies are transformed into caricatures of themselves. Such a group undergoes negative selection, whereby more normal members either become disaffected and leave, or are pushed out. In the first phase, characteropaths act as spellbinders and leaders, but in the next phase psychopaths push them out of their positions, at which point they become

[12]Ibid.

responsible for upholding ideological purity. Ideology undergoes a similar transformation, with the creation of hermetic "insider" understanding, and an ideology for public consumption and support. While Łobaczewski uses the term exclusively in the context of such groups, a similar dynamic can arguably play itself out in any group (or individual). For example, a family that comes under the influence of pathological members; an individual undergoing the **transpersonification** process; a business; school board; corporation; governmental department or agency, etc.

ponerogenesis (adj. ponerogenic): The origin or mode of emergence of evil, which can appear at any social scale, e.g., in a family, the ponerization of a group or movement, and the development of a **pathocracy**.

ponerogenesis, first criterion of: The inability to recognize pathological individuals as such, which becomes an opening to their activities, and to recognize the association in concern as **ponerogenic**. Noticeable when individuals and groups come to idolize and revere criminals.

ponerogenic association: Any group characterized by **ponerogenic** processes of above-average social intensity, wherein the people with various personality and character disorders function as inspirers, spellbinders, and leaders, and where a genuine pathological social structure is formed. Smaller, less permanent associations may be called "groups" or "unions." Primary ponerogenic groups are created by individuals with various personality disorders, e.g., criminal gangs, mafias, cartels, cabals, etc. Secondary ponerogenic groups are normal human social movements or organizations which undergo the process of **ponerization**. Such unions frequently aspire to political power and influence.

ponerology: The science of evil, its genesis, and the individual, family, social, and **macrosocial** dynamics involved. Ponerology utilizes findings from neuroscience, psychopathology, clinical psychology, sociology, history, philosophy, and political science.

psychological induction: See **induction**.

psychopathy: Łobaczewski, following an older European convention, uses the term to refer to what are now called personality disorders. In modern psychiatry and psychology, psychopathy refers to a specific personality disorder assessed by instruments such as Robert Hare's PCL-R, Scott Lilienfeld et al.'s PPI-R, etc.[13] The PCL–R scores individuals on 20 items, which fall under two factors and four facets. Factor 1 (interpersonal–affective):

[13]For an overview of the various assessment tools, see Thomson, *Understanding Psychopathy*, pp. 21–33. For its relation to the Big Five see pp. 103–105 (primarily low agreeableness and low conscientiousness).

glibness/superficial charm, grandiose sense of self-worth, pathological lying, conning/manipulative, lack of remorse or guilt, shallow affect, callous/lack of empathy, failure to accept responsibility. Factor 2 (impulsive–antisocial): need for stimulation, parasitic lifestyle, no realistic long-term goals, impulsivity, irresponsibility, poor behavioral controls, early behavioral problems, revoke conditional release, criminal versatility. Factor 1 corresponds to the *ICD-11* "dissociality" trait domain: "Disregard for the rights and feelings of others, encompassing both self-centeredness and lack of empathy." Factor 2 corresponds to the *ICD-11*'s "disinhibition": "A tendency to act rashly based on immediate external or internal stimuli (i.e., sensations, emotions, thoughts), without consideration of potential negative consequences."[14] In contrast to the PCL-R, David J. Cooke et al.'s CAPP explicitly assesses fearlessness and lack of trait anxiety, and does not directly measure criminal behaviors, only the personality deficits thought to lead to such behavior, thus potentially making it useful in assessing psychopathy in non-criminal community samples.[15]

Kent Kiehl argues that psychopathy is characterized by abnormalities in the paralimbic system of the brain (a core part of the instinctive substratum containing the amygdala, hippocampus, anterior and posterior cingulate, orbital frontal cortex, insula, temporal pole) that develop from birth.[16] Thomson summarizes: "psychopathy is likely to be explained by a collective system of integrated brain regions that are implicated in the job of emotion regulation, social cognition, threat perception/recognition, attention, decision-making and affective processing."[17]

Alongside the **schizoidal declaration**, a psychopathic declaration could be phrased: "I can do whatever I want because I have been wronged in the past; everyone else is dishonorable, selfish, weak and manipulative; therefore, I am justified to take advantage of them."[18] Psychopathic moral and economic decision-making tends to be utilitarian in nature.[19]

As Thomson argues, psychopathy is unlikely to have a single cause; rather it is likely to be more complex and multi-causal in nature, with biological, psychological, and social factors having contributive and interactive effects. While individuals without the genetic predisposition will not develop the full symptomology, specific social factors are likely to have at least an exacerbatory effect on its development, with others having a protective effect. For example, the following potential social risk factors for the development of psychopathic *traits* have been identified: cortisol and tobacco exposure

[14] Bach and First, "Application of the ICD-11."

[15] For popular treatments on the topic, in addition to the books by Babiak, Hare, and Kiehl, see Martha Stout, *The Sociopath Next Door* (2005) and *Outsmarting the Sociopath Next Door* (2020).

[16] Kiehl, *Psychopath Whisperer*, pp. 168–73.

[17] Thomson, op. cit., p. 84.

[18] Adapted from ibid., pp. 29–30.

[19] Ibid., pp. 80, 115.

in utero, lack of breastfeeding, omega-3 deficiency, and lead exposure.[20] Factors contributing to Factor 2 antisocial *behavioral* features include low family socioeconomic status, poor parenting styles, and childhood abuse.

On the lack of identified genes for psychopathy, Essi Viding writes: "The way that genetic risk for psychopathy operates is likely to be probabilistic, rather than deterministic: genes do not directly code for psychopathy. But genes do code for proteins that influence characteristics such as neurocognitive vulnerabilities that may in turn increase the risk for developing psychopathy, particularly under certain environmental conditions. Psychopathy is not a single gene disorder, unlike, for example, Huntington's."[21] Researchers believe psychopathic traits "are best explained by the combination of additive effects, rare alleles, gene–gene interactions, and gene-by-shared-environment interactions."[22] Based on behavioral genetics, including twin studies, heredity accounts for 40–60% of the variance of psychopathy, the rest by environment; molecular genetics can only account for 10–20% at this time. That said, the study of psychopathy's molecular genetics is still in its infancy. One recent study accounted for 30–92% of symptom variance based on gene expression in five genes.[23]

Psychopaths are often also diagnosed with one or more of the following *DSM-5* personality disorders: antisocial, borderline, histrionic, narcissistic, and paranoid. While not identical to "antisocial personality disorder," the two overlap. Many with antisocial personality disorder are better understood as "secondary" psychopaths, or what Łobaczewski calls frontal **characteropaths** (i.e., the etiology is largely environmental in nature). Closely related to Factor 1 and of importance for ponerology is the "dark personality" or "Dark Tetrad" model: narcissism, Machiavellianism, psychopathy, and sadism, all of which. Sadism, psychopathy, and Machiavellianism are all highly correlated with low agreeableness and conscientiousness (i.e., dissociality and disinhibition), while narcissism is highly correlated with extraversion.[24] Paulhaus and colleagues propose that all four dark traits may fall under the Honesty-Humility factor (i.e., deceitful, greedy, sly) of the HEXACO personality model (essentially a "Big Five Plus One" model.[25]

[20]Ibid., pp. 125–128, 146.

[21]Viding, *Psychopathy: A Very Short Introduction* (2020), p. 64.

[22]Thomson, op. cit., pp. 71–72.

[23]See Tiihonen et al., "Neurobiological Roots of Psychopathy" (2020), and Johanson et al., "A Systematic Literature Review of Neuroimaging of Psychopathic Traits" (2020).

[24]Paulhus et al., "Screening for Dark Personalities: The Short Dark Tetrad (SD4)" (2020).

[25]Paulhus and Klaiber, "HEXACO, Dark Personalities, and Brunswik Symmetry" (2020); Kaufman et al., "The Light vs. Dark Triad of Personality: Contrasting Two Very Different Profiles of Human Nature" (2019).

schizoidal declaration: "Human nature is so bad that order in human society can only be maintained by a strong power created by exceptionally rational minds in the name of some higher idea." That is, it can be characterized as cynical regarding human nature, rationalistic, and politically authoritarian and technocratic. For example, the realpolitik of Machiavelli (1469–1527), who characterized men as "ungrateful, fickle, false, cowardly" and the only effective government absolute monarchy,[26] and Thomas Hobbes (1588–1679), who wrote: "during the time men live without a common power to keep them all in awe, they are in that condition which is called war; and such a war as is of every man against every man. ... In such a condition ... the life of man, solitary, poor, nasty, brutish, and short." Konstantin Pobedonostsev (1827–1907), authoritarian monarchist and adviser to the last three Russian tsars, thought humanity "weak, vicious, worthless, and rebellious." Nazi jurist Carl Schmitt's (1888–1985) views were summarized by Leo Strauss (1899–1973): "because man is by nature evil, he, therefore, needs *dominion.*" Strauss himself was favorable to Plato's political philosophy, whose final dialogue, *Laws*, advocates a kind of social-engineering totalitarianism. While Strauss's supporters insist he was apolitical and thought philosophers should understand politics but not participate, Shadia Drury argues that his ideas had a profound influence on the neoconservative movement (e.g., the *covert* rule of the wise[27]).

The Marxian variation tends to be *anti*-authoritarian on the surface. Human nature, which is explicitly denied, is implicitly thought to be wholly at the mercy of environmental forces: *society* is so bad that all states are characterized by exploitation and are by nature coercive. Thus only a revolution in the name of some higher idea (whether led by the oppressed class or an elite vanguard in their name) can create conditions to "fix" the conditions that inevitably corrupt all human interactions.[28]

schizoidal psychopathy: Originally used to describe the personality of premorbid schizophrenics, schizoidia shares some common symptoms with autism

---

[26]However, Machiavelli was more of an empiricist than an ideologue, and preferred a republican system to absolute monarchy. Machiavelli wrote to Zanobi Buondelmonti: "I come now to the last branch of my charge: that I teach princes villainy, and how to enslave. ... If I have been a little too punctual in describing these Monsters in all their lineaments and colours, I hope mankind will know them, the better to avoid them, my Treatise being both a Satire against them, and a true Character of them" (*History of Florence* [1891], pp. 439–440). See also James Burnham, *The Machiavellians: Defenders of Freedom* (2020), esp. ch. 3; and Michael McConkey, "Pathologizing Politics, Part 2" (2022).

[27]See Versluis, *New Inquisitions*, p. 50.

[28]For another example, see James Lindsay's discussions on Herbert Marcuse's essay "Repressive Tolerance" (1965) at *New Discourses* (https://newdiscourses.com/tag/repressive-tolerance/). Marcuse (1898–1979) was a member of the Frankfurt School and father of the "New Left."

and was the basis for the later "Cluster A" personality disorders: schizoid, schizotypal, and paranoid. The *ICD-11* defines the detachment personality disorder trait domain as a tendency to social detachment (avoidance of social interactions, intimacy, and lack of friendships) and emotional detachment (being reserved, aloofness, limited emotional expression and experience). It is the only personality disorder aside from **psychopathy** that features low negative affectivity (absence of emotional intensity and sensitivity). Some research suggests the existence of two distinct groups falling under schizoidal personality disorder: "an 'affect constricted' group, who might better be subsumed within schizotypal personality disorder, and a 'seclusive' group, who might better be subsumed within avoidant personality disorder [see **asthenic psychopathy**]."[29]

systems of normal man: Łobaczewski uses this phrase to describe any society in which the social structure, bonds, and customs are dominated in any way by normal people (i.e., not the **characteropathies** and **psychopathies** identified in the text). This category thus includes practically all historical types of human government and social structures, from monarchy to democracy, liberal to authoritarian (though the two main totalitarianisms of the twentieth century, Nazism and communism, were pathocratic). Łobaczewski is mostly silent on the role and numbers of personality disorders in such governments, though it can be assumed to be more or less proportional to their numbers in society, depending on the context. Barbara Oakley has written on this question, arguing that all power structures will have a higher concentration of pathological individuals than in the general population.[30] However, as long as these numbers remain a minority, and society and customs are still overall dominated by relatively normal individuals, such a system will not qualify as a pathocracy. Society will still be stratified primarily based on traditional categories (e.g., talent, wealth, though with various

[29] Triebwasser et al., "Schizoid Personality Disorder" (2013).

[30] "[T]he closer you climb toward the nexus of power in any given social structure, the more likely you'll be able to find a person with Machiavellian tendencies. ... the larger the social structure and the bigger the payoff, the more Machiavellians eventually seem to find a way to creep to the top in numbers all out of proportion to their underlying percentage in society. ... Machiavellians can have an incalculably restrictive, demoralizing, and corrupt effect on those in their sphere of influence. ... Opaque organizations, systems, and ideologies that easily allow for underhanded interactions play to Machiavellians' strong suit, allowing them to conceal their deceitful practices more easily. Idealistic systems such as communism and some religious or quasi-religious creeds are perfect for Machiavellians because they often lack checks and balances, or don't use them" (Oakley, *Evil Genes*, pp. 333–334). As McConkey writes, managerial liberalism advantages those most skilled at persuasion techniques, i.e., those with dark triad traits (*Managerial Class*, pp. 140, 186). See also McConkey, "Psychopaths and the Managerial Class."

degrees of nepotism and other forms of corruption). If the **ponerization** process begins in an existing power structure, and the numbers and influence of such a group reach a critical mass, the **ponerogenesis** will proceed according to its characteristic dynamics, potentially leading to a **pathocracy**, which extends through all levels of society, radically reorganizing traditional social divisions along primarily biopsychological categories.

transpersonification: The personality transformation undergone by a small percentage of the population in response to psychopathological indoctrination and **macrosocial** psychopathological phenomena. These individuals became fervent supporters of the new pathocracy, to varying degrees. This process only ever affected up to 6% of individuals in Poland, which Łobaczewski identified as those who either suffered some form of traumatic brain injury that affected their personalities, or who were otherwise personality disordered.

BIBLIOGRAPHY

[The original Polish edition and English manuscript of *Political Ponerology* did not include a bibliography. Sources preceded by an asterisk (*) are either taken from the bibliography in Łobaczewski's *Ponerologia* booklet published in 2000, or alluded to or cited by him in the text. For Polish sources, current editions and English translations have been noted where possible. All other sources are those cited by the editor in the footnotes. —Ed.]

Adams, Scott. *Win Bigly: Persuasion in a World Where Facts Don't Matter.* New York: Portfolio/Penguin, 2017.

Akyol, Mustafa. *Reopening Muslim Minds: A Return to Reason, Freedom, and Tolerance.* New York: St. Martin's Essentials, 2021.

*Alliluyeva, Svetlana. *Twenty Letters to a Friend.* London: Harper & Row, 1967.

Anderson, Peter J., and Lex W. Doyle. "Cognitive and Educational Deficits in Children Born Extremely Preterm." *Seminars in Perinatology* 32, no. 1 (2008): 51–58. https://doi.org/10.1053/j.semperi.2007.12.009.

Andrews, Ernest (ed.). *Legacies of Totalitarian Language in the Discourse Culture of the Post-Totalitarian Era.* Lanham, MD: Lexington Books, 2011.

Applebaum, Anne. *Iron Curtain: The Crushing of Eastern Europe, 1944-1956.* New York: Anchor, 2013.

Aron, Raymond. *The Opium of the Intellectuals.* New York: Routledge, 2001 [1955].

Aronson, H., and Francis Terrell. "On the Nature of Things: The Politics of Scientific Evaluation." *Applied & Preventive Psychology* 8, no. 4 (1999): 265–268. https://doi.org/10.1016/S0962-1849(05)80041-1.

Ashworth, Timothy. *Paul's Necessary Sin: The Experience of Liberation.* New York: Routledge, 2016.

*Assagioli, Roberto. *Dynamic Psychology and Psychosynthesis.* New York Research Foundation, 1959.

Astor, Mary. *The Incredible Charlie Carewe.* Alvin Redman, 1962.

Atari, Mohammad, Jonathan Haidt, Jesse Graham, Sena Koleva, et al. "Morality Beyond the WEIRD: How the Nomological Network of Morality Varies Across Cultures." *PsyArXiv Preprints* (2022). https://doi.org/10.31234/osf.io/q6c9r.

Attkisson, Sharyl. *Slanted: How the News Media Taught Us to Love Censorship and Hate Journalism.* New York: HarperCollins, 2020.

Ayim, Tawnya M. "Personality Patterns of Students Who Make a Threat of Targeted School Violence." *UNLV Theses, Dissertations, Professional Papers, and Capstones* 3468 (2018). https://digitalscholarship.unlv.edu/cgi/viewcontent.cgi?article=4471&context=thesesdissertations.

Azize, Joseph. *Gurdjieff: Mysticism, Contemplation, and Exercises.* New York: Oxford University Press, 2020.

Babiak, Paul, and Robert D. Hare. *Snakes in Suits: Understanding and Surviving the Psychopaths in Your Office.* Revised edition. New York: Harper Business, 2019.

Bach, Bo, and Michael B. First. "Application of the ICD-11 Classification of Personality Disorders." *BMC Psychiatry* 18, no. 351 (2018). https://doi.org/10.3390/ijerph18041376.

Bagus, Phillipp, José Antonio Peña-Ramos, and Antonio Sánchez-Bayón. "COVID-19 and the Political Economy of Mass Hysteria." *Journal of Environmental Research and Public Health* 18, no. 4 (2021): 1376. https://www.mdpi.com/1660-4601/18/4/1376/htm.

Bandura, Albert. *Moral Disengagement: How People Do Harm and Live with Themselves.* New York: Worth Publishers, 2016.

Baskerville, Stephen. *The New Politics of Sex: The Sexual Revolution, Civil Liberties, and the Growth of Governmental Power.* Kettering, OH: Angelico Press, 2017.

*Becker, Ernest. *The Structure of Evil: An Essay on the Unification of the Science of Man.* New York: The Free Press, 1968.

Benke, Th., I. Kurzthaler, Ch. Schmidauer, R. Moncayo, and E. Donnemiller. "Mania Caused by a Diencephalic Lesion." *Neuropsychologia* 40, no. 3 (2002): 245–252. https://doi.org/10.1016/S0028-3932(01)00108-7.

Bennett, J. G. *A Spiritual Psychology.* Santa Fe, NM: Bennett Books, 1999.

Berdyaev, Nikolai A. "Spirits of the Russian Revolution." *Russkaya mysl'* (1918). Translated by Fr. S. Janos (2009). http://www.berdyaev.com/berdiaev/berd_lib/1918_299.html.

*Bilikiewicz, Adam (ed.). *Psychiatria* [Psychiatry]. Warszawa: PZWL, 1998.

Birkeland, Søren Fryd. "Paranoid Personality Disorder and Organic Brain Injury: A Case Report." *Journal of Neuropsychiatry and Clinical Neurosciences* 25, no. 1 (2013): 52. https://doi.org/10.1176/appi.neuropsych.12030055.

Blair, James, David Mitchell, and Karina Blair. *The Psychopath: Emotion and the Brain.* Malden, MA: Blackwell, 2005.

Blais, Julie, and Scott Pruysers. "The Power of the Dark Side: Personality, the Dark Triad, and Political Ambition." *Personality and Individual Differences* 113, no. 15 (2017): 167–172. https://doi.org/10.1016/j.paid.2017.03.029.

Blake, David J. *Loaded for Guccifer 2.0: Following a Trail of Digital Geopolitics.* Self-published, 2020.

Blumenthal, Max. *The Management of Savagery: How America's National Security State Fueled the Rise of Al Qaeda, ISIS, and Donald Trump.* Brooklyn, NY: Verso, 2019.

Boddy, Clive R. "Populism and Political Personality: What Can We Learn from the Dark Triad Personality of Hermann Goering?" *The Journal of Psychohistory* 49, no. 1 (Summer 2021): 12–31.

——. "Psychopathy Screening for Public Leadership." *International Journal of Public Leadership* 12, no. 4 (January 1, 2016): 254–274. http://ecite.utas.edu.au/128011.

Bogart, Greg. *Dreamwork and Self-Healing: Unfolding the Symbols of the Unconscious.* New York: Routledge, 2018.

Boghani, Priyanka. "Syrian Militant and Former Al Qaeda Leader Seeks Wider Acceptance in First Interview with U.S. Journalist." PBS *Frontline* (Apr. 2, 2021). https://www.pbs.org/wgbh/frontline/article/abu-mohammad-al-jolani-interview-hayat-tahrir-al-sham-syria-al-qaeda/.

Borras, L., E. Constant, P. De Timary, P. Hugueleta, and Y. Khazaal. "Long-term Psychiatric Consequences of Carbon Monoxide Poisoning: A Case Report and Literature Review." *La Revue de Médecine Interne* 30, no. 1 (2009): 43–48. https://doi.org/10.1016/j.revmed.2008.04.014.

Braswell, Sean. "When the Soviet Union Tried to Woo Black America." *Ozy* (Feb. 17, 2017). https://www.ozy.com/true-and-stories/when-the-soviet-union-tried-to-woo-black-america/62517/.

Brossat Alain, and Sylvie Klingberg. *Revolutionary Yiddishland: A History of Jewish Radicalism.* Translated by David Fernbach. Brooklyn, NY: Verso, 2017 [1983].

Brown, Sandra. *How to Spot a Dangerous Man Before You Get Involved.* Alameda, CA: Hunger House Inc., 2005.

Brown, Sandra, with Jennifer R. Young. *Women Who Love Psychopaths: Inside the Relationships of Inevitable Harm with Psychopaths, Sociopaths & Narcissists.* 3rd edition. Penrose, NC: Mask Publishing, 2018.

Browning, Christopher R. *Ordinary Men: Reserve Police Battalion 101 and the Final Solution in Poland.* Revised edition. New York: Harper Perennial, 2017.

Brunner, Jose. "'Oh Those Crazy Cards Again': A History of the Debate on the Nazi Rorschachs, 1946–2001." *Political Psychology* 22, no. 2 (2001): 233–61. https://doi.org/10.1111/0162-895X.00237.

*Brzezicki, Eugeniusz. "O potrzebie rozszerzenia typologii Kretschmera [On the Need to Expand Kretschmer's Typology]." *Życie Naukowe* 1.1, no. 5 (1946).

Buchanan, John H., and Christopher M. Aanstoos (eds.). *Rethinking Consciousness: Extraordinary Challenges for Contemporary Science.* Anoka, MN: Process Century Press, 2020.

*Bühler, Charlotte. *Das Seelenleben des Jugendlichen. Versuch einer Analyse und Theorie der psychischen Pubertät* [The Inner Life of the Adolescent: An Attempt at Analysis and Theory of Mental Puberty]. 6th ed. Göttingen: Hogrefe, 1967 [1922].

*Bühler, Charlotte Malachowski, and Fred Massarik. *The Course of Human Life: A Study of Goals in the Humanistic Perspective.* New York: Springer, 1968.

Bukovsky, Vladimir. *Judgment in Moscow: Soviet Crimes and Western Complicity.* California: Ninth of November Press, 2019.

Burnham, James. *The Machiavellians: Defenders of Freedom.* London: Lume Books, 2020 [1943].

Calder, Todd. "The Concept of Evil." *Stanford Encyclopedia of Philosophy* (2018). https://plato.stanford.edu/entries/concept-evil/.

"Can psychopaths recognize other psychopaths?" *Quora.* Accessed on February 9, 2021. https://www.quora.com/Can-psychopaths-recognize-other-psychopaths.

Carpenter, James C. *First Sight: ESP and Parapsychology in Everyday Life.* Lanham, MD: Rowman & Littlefield, 2012.

Chan, Xin Bei V., Shi Min S. Goh, and Ngiap Chuan Tan. "Subjects with Colour Vision Deficiency in the Community: What Do Primary Care Physicians Need to Know?" *Asia Pacific Family Medicine* 13, no. 10 (2014). https://doi.org/10.1186/s12930-014-0010-3.

Chang, Jung, and Jon Halliday. *Mao: The Unknown Story.* New York: Anchor, 2006.

Chen, Philip, Scott Pruysers, and Julie Blais. "The Dark Side of Politics: Participation and the Dark Triad." *Political Studies* 69, no. 3 (2021): 577–601. https://doi.org/10.1177/0032321720911566.

*Chirot, Daniel. *Modern Tyrants: The Power and Prevalence of Evil in Our Age.* Princeton, NJ: Princeton University Press, 1994.

Chung, K.C., S.B. Lee, K.C. Park, T.B. Ahn, S.S. Yoon, and D.I. Chang. "Behavioral Changes Caused by Diencephalic Lesion." *Journal of the Neurological Sciences* 283, no. 1 (2009): 301–302. https://doi.org/10.1016/j.jns.2009.02.234.

*Clark, John, and Aaron B. Wildavsky. *The Moral Collapse of Communism: Poland as a Cautionary Tale.* San Francisco, CA: ICS Press, 1991.

Clarke, Donald. "New book: 'China's Psychiatric Inquisition'." *Chinese Law Prof Blog* (Jan. 4, 2007). https://lawprofessors.typepad.com/china_law_prof_blog/2007/01/new_book_chinas.html.

*Cleckley, Hervey. *The Mask of Sanity.* 4th edition. New York: Plume, 1982. [5th edition: Augusta, GA: Emily S. Cleckley, 1988.]

——. *The Caricature of Love: A Discussion of Social, Psychiatric, and Literary Manifestations of Pathologic Sexuality.* Grande Prairie, AB: Red Pill Press, 2011 [1957].

Codevilla, Angelo M. "The Election to End All Elections." *Claremont Review of Books* (Aug. 31, 2020). https://claremontreviewofbooks.com/the-finger-in-the-dike-election/.

——. "Revolution 2020." *The American Mind* (Sep. 23, 2020). https://americanmind.org/salvo/revolution-2020/.

——. "The Rise of Political Correctness: From Marx to Gramsci to Trump." *Claremont Review of Books* (Fall 2016). https://claremontreviewofbooks.com/the-rise-of-political-correctness/.

——. *The Ruling Class: How They Corrupted America and What We Can Do about It.* New York: Beaufort Books, 2010.

Coid, Jeremy, Simone Ullrich, Robert Keers, Paul Bebbington, Bianca L. DeStavola, et al. "Gang Membership, Violence, and Psychiatric Morbidity." *American Journal of Psychiatry* 170, no. 9 (2013): 985–993. https://doi.org/10.1176/appi.ajp.2013.12091188.

Coid, Jeremy, Min Yang, Peter Tyrer, Amanda Roberts, and Simone Ullrich. "Prevalence and Correlates of Personality Disorder in Great Britain." *British Journal of Psychiatry* 188, no. 5 (2006): 423–431. https://doi.org/10.1192/bjp.188.5.423.

Coid, Jeremy, Min Yang, Simone Ullrich, Amanda Roberts, and Robert D. Hare. "Prevalence and Correlates of Psychopathic Traits in the Household Population of Great Britain." *International Journal of Law and Psychiatry* 32, no. 2 (2009): 65–73. https://doi.org/10.1016/j.ijlp.2009.01.002.

Connelly, John. *Captive University: The Sovietization of East German, Czech, and Polish Higher Education 1945–1956.* Chapel Hill, NC: University of North Carolina Press, 2000.

Conway, Lucian, Alivia Zubrod, Linus Chan, James McFarland, and Evert Van de Vliert. "Is the Myth of Left-Wing Authoritarianism Itself a Myth?" *PsyArXiv Preprints* (2020). https://psyarxiv.com/frcks/.

Corredoira, Martín López, and Carlos Castro Perelman (eds.). *Against the Tide: A Critical Review by Scientists of How Physics and Astronomy Get Done.* Boca Raton, FL: Universal Publishers, 2008.

Costello, Thomas, Shauna Bowes, Sean Stevens, Irwin Waldman, Arber Tasimi, Scott O. Lilienfeld. "Clarifying the Structure and Nature of Left-wing Authoritarianism." *PsyArXiv Preprints* (2021). https://psyarxiv.com/3nprq.

Crane, Emily. "Ex-BLM Leader Says He Quit after Learning the 'Ugly Truth' about the Organization." *Daily Mail* (Jun. 1, 2021). https://www.dailymail.co.uk/news/article-9640927/Ex-BLM-leader-says-quit-learning-ugly-truth.html.

Cristaudo, Wayne. "Those Pesky Poles! Forever Defying Totalitarianism." *The Postil Magazine* (Aug. 1, 2021). https://www.thepostil.com/those-pesky-poles-forever-defying-totalitarianism/.

"Critical Race Theory Is a Gift to Christians." *The Christian Century* (Jun. 28, 2021). https://www.christiancentury.org/article/editors/critical-race-theory-gift-christians.

Dąbrowski, Kazimierz. *Multilevelness of Emotional and Instinctive Functions.* Lublin, Poland: Towarzystwo Naukowe KUL, 1996.

——. *Personality-shaping through Positive Disintegration.* Grande Prairie, AB: Red Pill Press, 2015 [1967].

——. *Positive Disintegration.* Anna Maria, FL: Maurice Bassett, 2017 [1964].

*——. *Psychoneurosis Is Not an Illness.* London: Gryf, 1972.

Dąbrowski, Kazimierz, with Andrzej Kawczak and Michael M. Piechowski. *Mental Growth Through Positive Disintegration.* London: Gryf, 1970.

Dąbrowski, Kazimierz, with Andrzej Kawczak and Janina Sochanska. *The Dynamics of Concepts.* London: Gryf, 1973.

DeGroat, Chuck. *When Narcissism Comes to Church: Healing Your Community from Emotional and Spiritual Abuse.* Downers Grove, IL: IVP, 2020.

Desmet, Matthias. *The Psychology of Totalitarianism.* Chelsea, VT: Chelsea Green, in press.

Deutscher, Isaac. "Marx and Russia." BBC (Nov. 1948). https://www.marxists.org/archive/deutscher/1948/marx-russia.htm.

Dickey, Jeffrey V., Thomas B. Everett, Zane M. Galvach, et al. "Russian Political Warfare: Origin, Evolution, and Application." Masters thesis. Naval Postgraduate School, 2015. https://calhoun.nps.edu/handle/10945/45838.

Dikötter, Frank. *The Cultural Revolution: A People's History, 1962–1976.* New York: Bloomsbury, 2016.

——. *How to Be a Dictator: The Cult of Personality in the Twentieth Century.* New York: Bloomsbury, 2019.

——. *Mao's Great Famine: The History of China's Most Devastating Catastrophe, 1958–1962.* New York: Bloomsbury, 2017 [2010].

——. *The Tragedy of Liberation: A History of the Chinese Revolution 1945–1957.* New York: Bloomsbury, 2017 [2013].

Djilas, Milovan. *The New Class: An Analysis of the Communist System.* Orlando, FL: Harvest/HBJ, 1983 [1957].

Docherty, Gerry, and Jim Macgregor. *Hidden History: The Secret Origins of the First World War.* Edinburgh: Mainstream Publishing, 2014.

Doidge, Norman. "Needle Points: Why So Many Are Hesitant to Get the COVID Vaccines, and What We Can Do about It." *Tablet* (Oct. 27, 2021). https://www.tabletmag.com/sections/science/articles/needle-points-vaccinations-chapter-one.

Donaldson-Pressman, Stephanie, and Robert M. Pressman. *The Narcissistic Family: Diagnosis and Treatment.* San Francisco: Jossey-Bass, 1997.

*Doren, Dennis M. *Understanding and Treating the Psychopath.* New York: J. Wiley & Sons, 1987.

Dreher, Rod. *Live Not by Lies: A Manual for Christian Dissidents.* New York: Sentinel, 2020.

Dreher, Rod, and Mathieu Bock-Côté. "Towards Totalitarianism: An Interview with Rod Dreher and Mathieu Bock-Côté." *The Postil Magazine* (Jul. 1, 2021). https://www.thepostil.com/towards-totalitarianism-an-interview-with-rod-dreher-and-mathieu-bock-cote/.

*Drewa, Gerard (ed.). *Podstawy genetyki* [Fundamentals of Genetics]. Volumed. Wroclaw, 1995.

Dvoskin, Joel A., James L. Knoll, and Mollie Silva. “A Brief History of the Criminalization of Mental Illness.” *CNS Spectrums* 25, no. 5 (2019): 1–13. https://doi.org/10.1017/S1092852920000103.

*Edwards, Paul (ed.). *Encyclopedia of Philosophy.* 8 vols. New York: MacMillan & Free Press, 1972.

*Ehrlich, S. K., and R. P. Keogh. “The Psychopath in a Mental Institution.” *Archives of Neurology and Psychiatry* 76 (1956): 286–295. https://doi.org/10.1001/archneurpsyc.1956.02330270058013.

Eibl-Eibesfeldt, Irenäus, and Frank Kemp Salter (eds.). *Indoctrinability, Ideology, and Warfare: Evolutionary Perspectives.* New York: Berghahn Books, 1998.

Engberg-Pedersen, Troels. *Paul and the Stoics.* Louisville, KY: Westminster John Knox Press, 2000.

Ewald, William B. “The Roman Foundations of European Law.” Faculty Scholarship at Penn Law 1235 (1994). https://scholarship.law.upenn.edu/faculty_scholarship/1235.

Fabian, Sandor. “The Russian Hybrid Warfare Strategy – Neither Russian nor Strategy.” *Defense & Security* Analysis 35, no. 3 (2019). https://www.academia.edu/47775790/The_Russian_hy-brid_warfare_strategy_neither_Russian_nor_strategy.

Fahrenberg, Jochen. “The Influence of Gottfried Wilhelm Leibniz on the Psychology, Philosophy, and Ethics of Wilhelm Wundt.” *PsyDok* (2016). http://psydok.psycharchives.de/jspui/handle/20.500.11780/3772.

Fazel, Seena, Vivek Khosla, Helen Doll, and John Geddes. “The Prevalence of Mental Disorders among the Homeless in Western Countries: Systematic Review and Meta-Regression Analysis.” *PLoS Med* 5, no. 12 (2008): e225. https://doi.org/10.1371/journal.pmed.0050225.

Fazel, Seena, and John Danesh. “Serious Mental Disorder in 23,000 Prisoners: A Systematic Review of 62 Surveys.” *The Lancet* 359, no. 9306 (2002): 545–550. https://doi.org/10.1016/S0140-6736(02)07740-1.

Felthous, Alan, and Henning Saß (eds.). *International Handbook on Psychopathic Disorders and the Law.* 2nd edition. West Sussex: John Wiley & Sons, 2021.

Few, L. R., D. R. Lynam, J. L. Maples, J. MacKillop, and J. D. Miller. “Comparing the Utility of DSM-5 Section II and III Antisocial Personality Disorder Diagnostic Approaches for Capturing Psychopathic Traits.” *Personality Disorders: Theory, Research, and Treatment* 6, no. 1 (2015), 64–74. https://doi.apa.org/doi/10.1037/per0000096.

Figes, Orlando. *A People's Tragedy: The Russian Revolution: 1891–1924.* 100th anniversary edition. London: Bodley Head, 2017.

Fischman, Dennis. “The Jewish Question about Marx.” *Polity* 21, no. 4 (1989): 755–775. https://doi.org/10.2307/3234722.

*Freud, Sigmund. *Basic Writings.* New York: Modern Library, 1995 [1938].

*Freud, Sigmund, and Joseph Breuer. *Studies on Hysteria.* New York: Basic Books, 1957 [1895]. [New translation: *Studies in Hysteria.* New York: Penguin, 2004.]

Funder, Anna. *Stasiland: Stories from behind the Berlin Wall.* London: Granta, 2003.

Galassi, Francesco M., and Hutan Shirafian. *Julius Caesar's Disease: A New Diagnosis.* South Yorkshire: Pen and Sword History, 2017.

Gawda, Barbara. "Cross-cultural Studies on the Prevalence of Personality Disorders." *Current Issues in Personality Psychology* 6, no. 4 (2018). https://doi.org/10.5114/cipp.2018.80200.

Gellner, Ernest. *Postmodernism, Reason and Religion.* New York: Routledge, 1992.

Gerges, Fawaz A. *ISIS: A History.* Princeton, NJ: Princeton University Press, 2021.

Gibson, James L., and Joseph L. Sutherland. "Keeping Your Mouth Shut: Spiraling Self-Censorship in the United States." *SSRN* (June 1, 2020). http://dx.doi.org/10.2139/ssrn.3647099.

Gilbert, Gustave M. *Nuremberg Diary.* Amherst, NY: Da Capo Press, 1995 [1947].

——. *The Psychology of Dictatorship.* New York: Ronald, 1950.

Gmirkin, Russell. *Plato and the Creation of the Hebrew Bible.* New York: Routledge, 2017.

Godson, Roy (ed.). *Menace to Society: Political-criminal Collaboration around the World.* New York: Routledge, 2003.

Goertzel, Ted. "The World Trade Center Bombing as a Fourth Generational Turning Point." 2002. https://crab.rutgers.edu/~goertzel/fourthturning.htm.

Golden, Charles J., Michele L. Jackson, Angela Peterson-Rohne, and Samuel T. Gontkovsky. "Neuropsychological Correlates of Violence and Aggression: A Review of the Clinical Literature." *Aggression and Violent Behavior* 1, no. 1 (1996): 3–25. https://doi.org/10.1016/1359-1789(95)00002-X.

Goldensohn, Leon. *The Nuremberg Interviews: An American Psychiatrist's Conversations with the Defendants and Witnesses.* Edited and with an introduction by Robert Gellately. New York: Vintage, 2004.

*Goleman, Daniel. *Emotional Intelligence: Why It Can Matter More Than IQ.* 10th anniversary edition. New York: Bantam, 2006.

——. *Social Intelligence: The New Science of Human Relationships.* New York: Bantam, 2007.

Gonzalez, Mike. *The Plot to Change America: How Identity Politics is Dividing the Land of the Free.* New York: Encounter Books, 2020.

Goodman, Ann B. "A Family History Study of Schizophrenia Spectrum Disorders Suggests New Candidate Genes in Schizophrenia and Autism." *Psychiatric Quarterly* 65, no. 4 (1994): 287–97. https://doi.org/10.1007/bf02354305.

Gorlizki, Yoram, and Oleg Khlevniuk. *Substate Dictatorship: Networks, Loyalty, and Institutional Change in the Soviet Union.* New Haven, CT: Yale University Press, 2020.

Gottfried, Paul. "The Decay of America: A Conversation with Paul Gottfried." *The Postil Magazine* (Jul. 1, 2021). https://www.thepostil.com/the-decay-of-america-a-conversation-with-paul-gottfried/.

*Gray, K. C., and H. C. Hutchinson. "The Psychopathic Personality: A Survey of Canadian Psychiatrists' Opinions." *Canadian Psychiatric Association* 9 (1964): 452–461. https://journals.sagepub.com/doi/pdf/10.1177/070674376400900602.

*Greenfield, Susan A. (ed.). *The Human Mind Explained: An Owner's Guide to the Mysteries of the Mind.* New York: Henry Holt, 1996.

Greenwald, Glenn. "The New Domestic War on Terror Has Already Begun—Even Without the New Laws Biden Wants." greenwald.substack.com (Jun. 2, 2021). https://greenwald.substack.com/p/the-new-domestic-war-on-terror-has.

——. "The New Domestic War on Terror Is Coming." greenwald.substack.com (Jan. 19, 2021). https://greenwald.substack.com/p/the-new-domestic-war-on-terror-is.

*Grossman, Vasily. *Forever Flowing.* New York: Harper & Row, 1972. [New translation by Robert and Elizabeth Chandler: *Everything Flows.* New York: New York Review Books, 2009.]

Guinn, Jeff. *The Road to Jonestown: Jim Jones and Peoples Temple.* New York: Simon & Schuster, 2018.

Guyénot, Laurent. *From Yahweh to Zion: Three Thousand Years of Exile: Jealous God, Chosen People, Promised Land ... Clash of Civilizations.* Lone Rock, WI: Sifting and Winnowing Books, 2018.

Haberer, Erich E. *Jews and Revolution in Nineteenth-Century Russia.* New York: Cambridge University Press, 1995.

Haffner, Sebastian. *Defying Hitler: A Memoir.* New York: Picador, 2002.

Hahn, Gordon M. *The Caucasus Emirate Mujahedin: Global Jihadism in Russia's North Caucasus and Beyond.* Jefferson, NC: McFarland Books, 2014.

——. "Dirty-Deal Democratizers, the 'War of Values with Russia,' and Problems of Democracy-Promotion." *Russian & Eurasian Politics* (Apr. 29, 2015). https://gordonhahn.com/2015/04/29/dirty-deal-democratizers-the-war-of-values-with-russia-and-problems-of-democracy-promotion/.

——. "Ebony, Ivory, Postmodernism, and the New American Communo-Fascists." *Russian & Eurasian Politics* (Mar. 1, 2021). https://gordonhahn.com/2021/03/01/ebony-ivory-postmodernism-and-the-new-american-communo-fascists/.

——. "The New American Communo-Fascism and Its Postmodernist Roots." *Russian & Eurasian Politics* (Apr. 29, 2021). https://gordonhahn.com

/2021/04/29/the-new-american-communo-fascism-and-its-postmodernist-roots/.

——. "Once More About Home: Color Revolutionism Comes Home to Roost Amidst Democracy's Decay." *Russian & Eurasian Politics* (Jan. 7, 2021). https://gordonhahn.com/2021/01/07/once-more-about-home-color-revolutionism-comes-home-to-roost-amidst-democracys-decay/.

——. *Russia's Revolution from Above, 1985–2000: Reform, Transition and Revolution in the Fall of the Soviet Communist Regime.* New York: Routledge, 2001.

——. *The Russian Dilemma: Security, Vigilance, and Relations with the West from Ivan III to Putin.* Jefferson, NC: McFarland Books, 2021.

——. *Ukraine Over the Edge: Russia, the West and the "New Cold War."* Jefferson, NC: McFarland Books, 2018.

Haidt, Jonathan. *The Righteous Mind: Why Good People Are Divided by Politics and Religion.* New York: Vintage, 2013.

Hare, Robert D. "Psychopathy and Antisocial Personality Disorder: A Case of Diagnostic Confusion." *Psychiatric Times* 8, no. 2 (1996). https://www.psychiatrictimes.com/view/psychopathy-and-antisocial-personality-disorder-case-diagnostic-confusion.

——. *Without Conscience: The Disturbing World of Psychopaths Among Us.* New York: Guilford Press, 1999.

*Hartau, Frederyk. *Wilhelm II.* Lublin: Median s.c., 1992.

Havel, Václav. "The Power of the Powerless." *International Journal of Politics* 15, no. 3/4 (Fall-Winter 1985–86): 23–96. https://www.nonviolent-conflict.org/wp-content/uploads/1979/01/the-power-of-the-powerless.pdf.

Haycock, Dean A. *Tyrannical Minds: Psychological Profiling, Narcissism, and Dictatorship.* New York: Pegasus Books, 2019.

Hedges, Chris. *American Fascists: The Christian Right and the War on America.* New York: Free Press, 2006.

*Herling, Gustaw. *A World Apart: Imprisonment in a Soviet Labor Camp During World War II.* New York: Penguin, 1996 [1951].

Hodel, Amanda S. "Rapid Infant Prefrontal Cortex Development and Sensitivity to Early Environmental Experience." *Developmental Review* 48 (2018): 113–144. https://doi.org/10.1016/j.dr.2018.02.003.

*Hoess, Rudolf. *Commandant of Auschwitz: The Autobiography of Rudolph Hoess.* World Pub. Co., 1960. [New edition: Höss, Rudolf. *Death Dealer: The Memoirs of the SS Kommandant at Auschwitz.* Amherst, NY: Da Capo Press, 1992.]

Hoffer, Eric. *The True Believer: Thoughts on the Nature of Mass Movements.* New York: Harper Perennial, 2010 [1951].

Hooper, Simon, and Mohamed Hashem. "Bilal Abdul Kareem Breaks Silence over HTS Detention in Syria." *Middle East Eye* (Jun. 4, 2021). https://www.middleeasteye.net/news/exclusive-bilal-abdul-kareem-breaks-silence-over-hts-detention-syria.

*Horney, Karen. *Neurosis and Human Growth: The Struggle towards Self-Realization.* New York: W. W. Norton, 1991 [1942].

*——. *The Neurotic Personality of Our Time.* New York: W. W. Norton, 1994 [1937].

Hughes, Ian. *Disordered Minds: How Dangerous Personalities Are Destroying Democracy.* Winchester, UK: Zero Books, 2018.

Hunter, Philip. "The Psycho Gene." *EMBO Reports* 11, no. 9 (2010): 667–669. https://doi.org/10.1038/embor.2010.122.

Hviid, Anders, Steven Rubin, and Kathrin Mühlemann. "Mumps." *Lancet* 371, no. 9616 (2008): 932–44. https://doi.org/10.1016/s0140-6736(08)60419-5.

"In Memoriam: Andrzej M. Lobaczewski." *Signs of the Times* (June 16, 2008). https://www.sott.net/article/159686-In-Memoriam-Andrzej-M-obaczewski.

Ingram, Haroro J., Craig Whiteside, and Charlie Winter. *The ISIS Reader: Milestone Texts of the Islamic State Movement.* New York: Oxford University Press, 2020.

Irvine, William B. *A Guide to the Good Life: The Ancient Art of Stoic Joy.* New York: Oxford University Press, 2009.

Janowski, Zbigniew. "Against Equality of Opportunities." *The Postil Magazine* (Sept. 1, 2020). https://www.thepostil.com/against-equality-of-opportunities/.

——. "Breaking the Monopoly of the Mainstream: An Interview with Ryszard Legutko." *The Postil Magazine* (Aug. 1, 2021). https://www.thepostil.com/breaking-the-monopoly-of-the-mainstream-an-interview-with-ryszard-legutko/.

——. *Homo Americanus: The Rise of Totalitarian Democracy in America.* Afterword by Ryszard Legutko. South Bend, IN: St. Augustine's Press, 2021.

——. "The Legutko Affair." *The Postil Magazine* (Aug. 1, 2021). https://www.thepostil.com/the-legutko-affair/.

Janowski, Zbigniew, and Jacob Duggan (eds.). *John Stuart Mill: On Democracy, Freedom and Government & Other Selected Writings.* South Bend, IN: St. Augustine's Press, 2019.

*Jenkins, Richard. "The Psychopathic or Antisocial Personality." *Journal of Nervous and Mental Disease* 131 (1960): 318–332.

Ji Fengyuan. *Linguistic Engineering: Language and Politics in Mao's China.* Honolulu: University of Hawaii Press, 2004.

Johanson, Mika, Olli Vaurio, Jari Tiihonen, and Markku Lähteenvuo. "A Systematic Literature Review of Neuroimaging of Psychopathic Traits." *Frontiers in Psychiatry* 10 (2020). https://doi.org/10.3389/fpsyt.2019.01027.

Jones, J. Steven. *In the Blood: God, Genes and Destiny.* New York: HarperCollins, 1995.

Kahneman, Daniel. *Thinking, Fast and Slow.* New York: Farrar, Straus and Giroux, 2013.

Kallis, Aristotle A. *Fascist Ideology: Territory and Expansionism in Italy and Germany, 1922–1945.* New York: Routledge, 2000.

Kapfhammer, Hans-Peter. "The Concept of Schizoidia in Psychiatry: From Schizoidia to Schizotypy and Cluster A Personality Disorders." *Neuropsychiatry* 31, no. 4 (2017): 155–171. https://doi.org/10.1007/s40211-017-0237-y.

Karashchuk, Oksana S., Elena A. Mayorova, Alexander F. Nikishin, and Olena V. Kornilova. "The Method for Determining Time-Generation Range." *SAGE Open* (October 2020). https://doi.org/10.1177/2158244020968082.

Kaufman, Scott Barry, David Bryce Yaden, Elizabeth Hyde, and Eli Tsukayama. "The Light vs. Dark Triad of Personality: Contrasting Two Very Different Profiles of Human Nature." *Frontiers in Psychology* 10 (2019). https://doi.org/10.3389/fpsyg.2019.00467.

Kelly, Edward F., Emily Williams Kelly, Adam Crabtree, Alan Gauld, Michael Grosso, and Bruce Greyson. *Irreducible Mind: Toward a Psychology for the 21st Century.* Lanham, MD: Rowman & Littlefield, 2007.

Kengor, Paul. *A Pope and a President: John Paul II, Ronald Reagan, and the Extraordinary Untold Story of the 20th Century.* Wilmington, DE: ISI Books, 2018.

Kennedy, Robert F., Jr. "Pandemic and the Road to Totalitarianism." Ron Paul Institute (Oct. 8, 2021). http://www.ronpaulinstitute.org/archives/featured-articles/2021/october/08/pandemic-and-the-road-to-totalitarianism/.

——. *The Real Anthony Fauci: Bill Gates, Big Pharma, and the Global War on Democracy and Public Health.* New York: Skyhorse, 2021.

*Kępiński, Antoni. *Psychopatie* [Psychopathies]. Warszawa: PZWL, 1977.

Khlevniuk, Oleg V. *The History of the Gulag: From Collectivization to the Great Terror.* New Haven, CT: Yale University Press, 2013.

——. *Stalin: New Biography of a Dictator.* New Haven, CT: Yale University Press, 2017.

Kiehl, Kent. "A Cognitive Neuroscience Perspective on Psychopathy: Evidence for Paralimbic System Dysfunction." *Psychiatry Research* 142, nos. 2–3 (2006): 107–128. https://doi.org/10.1016/j.psychres.2005.09.013.

——. *The Psychopath Whisperer: The Science of Those Without Conscience.* New York: Crown, 2015.

Kiehl, Kent A., and Morris B. Hoffman. "The Criminal Psychopath: History, Neuroscience, Treatment, and Economics." *Jurimetrics* 51 (2011): 355–397. https://www.ncbi.nlm.nih.gov/pmc/articles/PMC4059069/.

Klemperer, Victor. *The Language of the Third Reich: LTI: Lingua Tertii Imperii.* New York: Bloomsbury, 2000 [1957].

Knight, Amy. *Beria: Stalin's First Lieutenant.* Princeton, NJ: Princeton University Press, 1993.

Knight-Jadczyk, Laura. *Almost Human: The Metaphysics of Evil.* The Wave or Adventures with Cassiopaea vol. 7. 2nd edition. Otto, NC: Red Pill Press, 2021.

Knoll, James L. "The Recurrence of an Illusion: The Concept of 'Evil' in Forensic Psychiatry." *The Journal of the American Academy of Psychiatry and the Law* 36, no. 1 (2008): 105–116. http://jaapl.org/content/36/1/105.

*Koestler, Arthur. *Darkness at Noon.* New York: Bantam Books, 1966 [1940]. [New, complete translation by Philip Boehm: New York: Vintage Classics, 2019.]

Kołakowski, Leszek. *Main Currents of Marxism.* New York: W. W. Norton, 2005 [1978].

*Konorski, Jerzy. *Integracyjna działalność mózgu* [Integrative Brain Activity]. Warszawa: PWN, 1969.

Koop, Volker. *Martin Bormann: Hitler's Executioner.* Philadelphia: Frontline Books, 2020.

Krainer, Alex. *Grand Deception: The Truth About Bill Browder, the Magnitsky Act, and Anti-Russian Sanctions.* Otto, NC: Red Pill Press, 2018.

Kravetz, Lee Daniel. *Strange Contagion: Inside the Surprising Science of Infectious Behaviors and Viral Emotions and What They Tell Us about Ourselves.* New York: HarperCollins, 2017.

Lasswell, Harold D. *The Political Writings of Harold D. Lasswell.* Glencoe, IL: The Free Press, 1951. [Includes *Psychopathology and Politics* (1930), *Politics: Who Gets What, When, How* (1936), and *Democratic Character.*]

Lawrence, Patrick. "The Casualties of Empire." *Consortium News* (Mar. 8, 2022). https://consortiumnews.com/2022/03/08/patrick-lawrence-the-casualties-of-empire/.

Lawson, Christine Ann. *Understanding the Borderline Mother: Helping Her Children Transcend the Intense, Unpredictable, and Volatile Relationship.* Lanham, MD: Rowman & Littlefield, 2004.

Legutko, Ryszard. *The Cunning of Freedom: Saving the Self in an Age of False Idols.* New York: Encounter Books, 2021.

——. *The Demon in Democracy: Totalitarian Temptations in Free Societies.* New York: Encounter Books, 2016.

——. "The Necessity of Opposition." *The Postil Magazine* (Sept. 1, 2021). https://www.thepostil.com/the-necessity-of-opposition/.

Leistedt, Samuel J., and Paul L. Linkowski. "Psychopathy and the Cinema: Fact or Fiction?" *Journal of Forensic Psychology* 59 no. 1 (2014): 167–174. https://doi.org/10.1111/1556-4029.12359.

Lencz, Todd, Saurav Guha, Ariel Darvasi, et al. "Genome-wide Association Study Implicates *NDST3* in Schizophrenia and Bipolar Disorder."

Nature Communications 4, no. 2739 (2013). https://www.nature.com/articles/ncomms3739.

Levine, Yasha. *Surveillance Valley: The Secret Military History of the Internet.* New York: PublicAffairs, 2018.

Levy, Steven. *The Unicorn's Secret: Murder in the Age of Aquarius.* New York: Prentice Hall Press, 1988.

Lewis, Ben. *Hammer and Tickle: A Cultural History of Communism.* New York: Pegasus, 2009.

Lifton, Robert Jay. *Reform and the Psychology of Totalism: A Study of "Brainwashing" in China.* Chapel Hill, NC: University of North Carolina Press, 1989 [1961].

Lilienfeld, Scott O. "Microaggressions: Strong Claims, Inadequate Evidence." *Perspectives on Psychological Science* 12, no. 1 (2017): 138–169. https://doi.org/10.1177/1745691616659391.

Lindsay, James. "Antiracism." Translations from the Wokish. *New Discourses* (Jun. 25, 2020). https://newdiscourses.com/tftw-antiracism/.

——. "Bourgeois Overproduction and the Problem of the Fake Elite." *New Discourses* (May 20, 2021). https://newdiscourses.com/2021/05/bourgeois-overproduction-problem-fake-elite/.

——. "Oppression." Translations from the Wokish. *New Discourses* (Feb. 5, 2020). https://newdiscourses.com/tftw-oppression/.

——. "Psychopathy and the Origins of Totalitarianism." *New Discourses* (Dec. 25, 2020). https://newdiscourses.com/2020/12/psychopathy-origins-totalitarianism/.

——. *Race Marxism: The Truth about Critical Race Theory and Praxis.* Orlando, FL: New Discourses, 2022.

——. "The Rise of the Woke Cultural Revolution," *New Discourses* (Apr. 14, 2021). https://newdiscourses.com/2021/04/rise-woke-cultural-revolution/.

——. *Translations from the Wokish: A Plain-Language Encyclopedia of Social Justice Terminology.* https://newdiscourses.com/translations-from-the-wokish/.

*Łobaczewski, Andrzej. *Chirurgia słowa: Wybrane zagadnienia psychoterapii* [Word Surgery: Selected Issues in Psychotherapy]. Rzeszów: Mitel, 1997.

*——. *Logokracja: Koncepcja ustroju państwa* [Logocracy: A Conception of the State System]. Krakow, 1991. [Published edition: Krzeszowice: Dom Wydawniczy "Ostoja," 2007.]

*——. *Ponerologia: Nauka o naturze zła* [Ponerology: A Science on the Nature of Evil]. Rzeszów, 2000.

*——. *Ponerologia polityczna: Nauka o naturze zła w zastosowaniu do zagadnień politycznych* [Political Ponerology: A Science on the Nature of Evil Adjusted for Political Purposes]. Rzeszów, 1997. [Published edition: Krzeszowice: Dom Wydawniczy "Ostoja," 2006.]

Lohmeier, Matthew. *Irresistible Revolution: Marxism's Goal of Conquest & the Unmaking of the American Military.* Matthew L. Lohmeier, 2021.

Lukianoff, Greg, and Jonathan Haidt. *The Coddling of the American Mind: How Good Intentions and Bad Ideas Are Setting Up a Generation for Failure.* New York: Penguin, 2019.

*Łuria, Aleksander. *Zaburzenia wyższych czynności korowych wskutek ogniskowych uszkodzeń mózgu* [Higher Cortical Dysfunction Due to Focal Brain Injury]. Warszawa: PWN, 1967.

Lyons, N. S. "No, the Revolution Isn't Over." theupheaval.substack.com (Jan. 18, 2022). https://theupheaval.substack.com/p/no-the-revolution-isnt-over.

Mac Donald, Heather. *The Diversity Delusion: How Race and Gender Pandering Corrupt the University and Undermine Our Culture.* New York: Griffin, 2018.

Macgregor, Jim, and Gerry Docherty. *Prolonging the Agony: How the Anglo-American Establishment Deliberately Extended WWI by Three-and-a-Half Years.* Waterville, OR: Trine Day, 2018.

Machiavelli, Niccolo. *The History of Florence.* London: Routledge, 1891. https://archive.org/details/historyofflorenc00mach.

*Maher, Brendan (ed.). *Contemporary Abnormal Psychology: Selected Readings.* Harmondsworth: Penguin, 1974.

Maher, Shiraz. *Salafi-Jihadism: The History of an Idea.* New York: Oxford University Press, 2016.

Mann, Michael. "Were the Perpetrators of Genocide 'Ordinary Men' or 'Real Nazis'? Results from Fifteen Hundred Biographies." *Holocaust and Genocide Studies* 14, no. 3 (2000): 331–366. https://www.sscnet.ucla.edu/soc/faculty/mann/Doc3.pdf.

"Mao and Terror: Mao's Glorification of Political Mass Murder – Documentary Quotations." World Future Fund (n.d.). http://www.worldfuturefund.org/wffmaster/Reading/Quotes/maoterror.htm.

Marcuse, Herbert. "Repressive Tolerance." Originally published in 1965. https://www.marcuse.org/herbert/publications/1960s/1965-repressive-tolerance-fulltext.html.

Martin, Everett Dean. *The Behavior of Crowds: A Psychological Study.* New York: Harper & Brothers, 1920. https://www.gutenberg.org/files/40914/40914-h/40914-h.htm.

Massi, Jeri. *Schizophrenic Christianity: How Christian Fundamentalism Attracts and Protects Sociopaths, Abusive Pastors, and Child Molesters.* 2nd edition. Jupiter Rising Books, 2014.

McCaul, Alexander. *The Talmud Tested: A Comparison of the Principles and Doctrines of Modern Judaism with the Religion of Moses and the Prophets.* Coeur d'Alene, ID: Independent History and Research, 2013 [1846].

McConkey, Michael. *Darwinian Liberalism.* Vancouver, BC: Biological Realist Publications, 2018.

——. *The Managerial Class on Trial.* Vancouver, BC: Biological Realist Publications, 2021.

——. "Pathologizing Politics, Part 2." *The Circulation of Elites* (Jan. 19, 2022). https://thecirculationofelites.substack.com/p/pathologizing-politics-part-2.

——. "Politics, Psychopathy, Pathocracy." *The Circulation of Elites* (Oct. 24, 2021). https://thecirculationofelites.substack.com/p/politics-psychopathy-pathocracy.

——. "Psychopaths and the Managerial Class." *The Circulation of Elites* (Nov. 17, 2021). https://thecirculationofelites.substack.com/p/psychopaths-and-the-managerial-class.

——. "The Psychorium." *The Circulation of Elites* (Dec. 8, 2021). https://thecirculationofelites.substack.com/p/the-psychorium.

*McCord, William and Joan. *Psychopathy and Delinquency.* New York: Grune & Stratton, 1956.

McCullough, Glenn. "Jacob Boehme and the Spiritual Roots of Psychodynamic Psychotherapy: Dreams, Ecstasy, and Wisdom." PhD diss. University of St. Michael's College, 2019. https://hdl.handle.net/1807/99728.

McGilchrist, Iain. *The Matter with Things: Our Brains, Our Delusions and the Unmaking of the World.* 2 vols. London: Perspectiva Press, 2021.

McGuire, Thomas G., and Jeanne Miranda. "Racial and Ethnic Disparities in Mental Health Care: Evidence and Policy Implications." *HealthAffairs* 27, no. 2 (2008): 393–403. https://www.ncbi.nlm.nih.gov/pmc/articles/PMC3928067/.

Mendaglio, Sal (ed.). *Dąbrowski's Theory of Positive Disintegration.* Scottsdale, AZ: Great Potential Press, 2008.

*Merz, Ferdinand, and Ingeborg Stelzl. *Einführung in die Erbpsychologie* [Introduction to Hereditary Psychology]. Stuttgard und Berlin: Verlag W. Kohlhammer, 1977.

Meyer, Stephen C. *Return of the God Hypothesis: Three Scientific Discoveries that Reveal the Mind behind the Universe.* New York: HarperCollins, 2021.

Milani, Abbas. *The Shah.* New York: Palgrave Macmillan, 2012.

*Miller, Alice. *For Your Own Good: Hidden Cruelty in Child-Rearing and the Roots of Violence.* New York: Farrar, Straus and Giroux, 1990.

Miłosz, Czesław. *The Captive Mind.* New York: Vintage, 1990 [1953].

Montefiore, Simon. *Stalin: Court of the Red Tsar.* New York: Vintage, 2005.

——. *Young Stalin.* New York: Vintage, 2008.

*Morell, Theodor. *Secret Diaries of Hitler's Doctor.* Edited by David Irving. London: Grafton Books, 1990 [1983].

Moreno, Jonathan D. *Mind Wars: Brain Science and the Military in the 21st Century.* New York: Bellevue Literary Press, 2012.

Morozov, Petr Victorovich. "The Evolution of Psychiatry in Russia." *International Journal of Culture and Mental Health* 11, no. 1 (2017). https://doi.org/10.1080/17542863.2017.1394013.

Morson, Gary Saul. "Leninthink." *The New Criterion* 39, no. 8 (2021). https://newcriterion.com/issues/2019/10/leninthink.

Moscovici, Claudia. *Velvet Totalitarianism: Post-Stalinist Romania.* Lanham, MD: University Press of America, 2009.

Moss, Jordan, and Peter J. O'Connor. "The Dark Triad Traits Predict Authoritarian Political Correctness and Alt-Right Attitudes." *Heliyon* 6, no. 7 (2020). https://doi.org/10.1016/j.heliyon.2020.e04453.

Mozaffari, Mehdi. *Islamism: A New Totalitarianism.* Boulder, CO: Rienner, 2017.

Mueller, Steffen, Eckard Wimmer, and Jeronimo Cello. "Poliovirus and Poliomyelitis: A Tale of Guts, Brains, and an Accidental Event." *Virus Research* 111, no. 2 (2005): 175–193. https://doi.org/10.1016/j.virusres.2005.04.008.

Mulder, Roger T., Giles Newton-Howes, Michael J. Crawford, and Peter J. Tyrer. "The Central Domains of Personality Pathology in Psychiatric Patients," *Journal of Personality Disorders* 25, no. 3 (2011): 364–77. https://doi.org/10.1521/pedi.2011.25.3.364.

Munro, Robin. "Judicial Psychiatry in China and Its Political Abuses." *Columbia Journal of Asian Law* 14, no. 1 (2000). https://perma.cc/P3DD-54ZQ.

Murray, Douglas. *The Madness of Crowds: Gender, Race and Identity.* London: Bloomsbury Continuum, 2021.

*Neumayr, Anton. *Dictators in the Mirror of Medicine: Napoleon, Hitler, Stalin.* Trans. David J. Parent. Bloomington, IL: Medi-Ed Press, 1995.

Newton-Howes, Giles, Roger Mulder, and Peter Tyrer. "Diagnostic Neglect: The Potential Impact of Losing a Separate Axis for Personality Disorder." *British Journal of Psychiatry* 206, no. 5 (2015): 355–56. https://doi.org/10.1192/bjp.bp.114.155259.

Ngo, Andy. *Unmasked: Inside Antifa's Radical Plan to Destroy Democracy.* New York: Center Street, 2021.

Norton, Ben. "Behind NATO's 'Cognitive Warfare': 'Battle for Your Brain Waged by Western Militaries." *The Grayzone* (Oct. 8, 2021). https://thegrayzone.com/2021/10/08/nato-cognitive-warfare-brain/.

O'Neill, Tom, with Dan Piepenbring. *Chaos: Charles Manson, the CIA, and the Secret History of the Sixties.* New York: Back Bay Books, 2020.

O'Shaughnessy, Nicholas. *Selling Hitler: Propaganda and the Nazi Brand.* London: Hurst & Co., 2016.

Oakley, Barbara. *Evil Genes: Why Rome Fell, Hitler Rose, Enron Failed, and My Sister Stole My Mother's Boyfriend.* Amherst, NY: Prometheus Books, 2007.

Ok, Ekin, Yi Qian, Brendan Strejcek, and Karl Aquino. "Signaling Virtuous Victimhood as Indicators of Dark Triad Personalities." *Journal of*

Personality and Social Psychology 120, no. 6 (2021): 1634–1661. https://doi.apa.org/doi/10.1037/pspp0000329.

Olsson, Peter A. *Malignant Pied Pipers: A Psychological Study of Destructive Cult Leaders from Rev. Jim Jones to Osama bin Laden.* SBPRA, 2017.

Panksepp, Jaak. *Affective Neuroscience: The Foundations of Human and Animal Emotions.* New York: Oxford University Press, 2004.

Panksepp, Jaak, and Lucy Biven. *The Archaeology of Mind: Neuroevolutionary Origins of Human Emotions.* New York: W. W. Norton, 2012.

Pappé, Ilan. *The Ethnic Cleansing of Palestine.* Oxford: Oneworld Publications, 2007.

Patrick, Christopher J. (ed.). *Handbook of Psychopathy.* 2nd edition. New York: Guilford Press, 2018.

Pauchard, Olivier. "How Ancient Rome Influenced European Law." SWI swissinfo.ch (Aug. 19, 2013). https://www.swissinfo.ch/eng/legal-roman-eagles_how-ancient-rome-influenced-european-law/36688830.

Paulhus, Delroy. L., Erin E. Buckels, Paul D. Trapnell, Daniel N. Jones. "Screening for Dark Personalities: The Short Dark Tetrad (SD4)." *European Journal of Psychological Assessment.* Advance online publication (2020). http://dx.doi.org/10.1027/1015-5759/a000602.

Paulhus, Delroy L., and Patrick Klaiber. "HEXACO, Dark Personalities, and Brunswik Symmetry." *European Journal of Personality* 34 (2020): 541–542. https://www2.psych.ubc.ca/~dpaulhus/research/DARK_TRAITS/ARTICLES/EJP.2020.Paulhus-Klaiber.pdf.

Peck, M. Scott. *People of the Lie: The Hope for Healing Human Evil.* New York: Touchstone, 1998 [1983].

Peterson, Jordan B. *12 Rules for Life: An Antidote to Chaos.* Toronto: Random House Canada, 2018.

——. *Beyond Order: 12 More Rules for Life.* New York: Penguin, 2021.

——. *Maps of Meaning: The Architecture of Belief.* New York: Routledge, 1999.

Peterson, Rolfe Daus, and Carl L. Palmer. "The Dark Triad and Nascent Political Ambition." *Journal of Elections, Public Opinion and Parties* (2019). https://doi.org/10.1080/17457289.2019.1660354.

Petrov, Petre, and Lara Ryazanova-Clarke (eds.). *The Vernaculars of Communism: Language, Ideology, and Power in the Soviet Union and Eastern Europe.* New York: Routledge, 2015.

Physicians for Human Rights. "Broken Laws, Broken Lives: Medical Evidence of Torture by US Personnel and Its Impact." Cambridge: Physicians for Human Rights, 2008. http://brokenlives.info/?page_id=69.

——. "Experiments in Torture: Evidence of Human Subject Research and Experimentation in the 'Enhanced' Interrogation Program." Cambridge: Physicians for Human Rights, 2010. http://phrtorturepapers.org/?page_id=87.

Pinker, Steven. *The Blank Slate: The Modern Denial of Human Nature.* New York: Viking, 2002.

Pluckrose, Helen, and James Lindsay. *Cynical Theories: How Activist Scholarship Made Everything about Race, Gender, and Identity – and Why This Harms Everybody.* Durham, NC: Pitchstone, 2020.

"Political abuse of psychiatry in the Soviet Union." *Wikipedia.org.* https://en.wikipedia.org/wiki/Political_abuse_of_psychiatry_in_the_Soviet_Union.

*Poradowski, Ks. Michal. *Dziedzictwo rewolucji francuskiej* [Legacy of the French Revolution]. Warszawa: Civitas, 1992.

Porges, Stephen W. *The Polyvagal Theory: Neurophysiological Foundations of Emotions, Attachment, Communication, and Self-regulation.* New York: W. W. Norton, 2011.

Posobiec, Jack. *The Antifa: Stories from Inside the Black Bloc.* Washington, DC: Calamo Press, 2021.

Preparata, Guido Giacomo. *Conjuring Hitler: How Britain and America Made the Third Reich.* New York: Pluto Press, 2005.

*Pribram, Karl. *Brain and Perception: Holonomy and the Structure of Figural Processing.* Hillsdale, NJ: Lawrence Erlbaum Associates, 1991.

——. *The Form Within: My Point of View.* Westport, CT: Prospecta Press, 2013.

Prior, Michael. *The Bible and Colonialism: A Moral Critique.* Sheffield: Sheffield Academic Press, 1999.

**Psychotherapy.* Journal of the Division of Psychotherapy of the American Psychological Association. 1963–.

Pulay, Attila J., Frederick S. Stinson, Deborah A. Dawson, et al. "Prevalence, Correlates, Disability, and Comorbidity of DSM-IV Schizotypal Personality Disorder: Results From the Wave 2 National Epidemiologic Survey on Alcohol and Related Conditions." *Primary Care Companion to the Journal of Clinical Psychiatry* 11, no. 2 (2009): 53–67. https://doi.org/10.4088/pcc.08m00679.

Raico, Ralph. "Trotsky: The Ignorance and the Evil." *Libertarian Review* (March 1979). https://mises.org/library/trotsky-ignorance-and-evil.

Raine, Adrian. *The Anatomy of Violence: The Biological Roots of Crime.* New York: Vintage, 2014.

——. "Psychopathy, Schizoid Personality and Borderline/Schizotypal Personality Disorders." *Personality and Individual Differences* 7, no. 4 (1986).

Ramsland, Katherine. "Dr. Hare: Expert on the Psychopath." crimelibrary.com. https://web.archive.org/web/20150210060546/http://www.crimelibrary.com/criminal_mind/psychology/robert_hare/6.html.

Rectenwald, Michael. *Beyond Woke.* Nashville, TN: New English Review Press, 2020.

——. "Fighting Totalitarianism: Rothbard versus Monasticism." *The Mises Institute* (Mar. 4, 2021). https://mises.org/wire/fighting-totalitarianis

m-rothbard-versus-monasticism.

——. *Google Archipelago: The Digital Gulag and the Simulation of Freedom.* Nashville, TN: New English Review Press, 2019.

——. "Living in the Age of Covid: 'The Power of the Powerless." *The Mises Institute* (Aug. 18, 2021). https://mises.org/wire/living-age-covid-powerless.

——. *Springtime for Snowflakes: "Social Justice" and Its Postmodern Parentage.* Nashville, TN: New English Review Press, 2018.

——. *Thought Criminal.* Nashville, TN: New English Review Press, 2020.

——. "Why Postmodernism Is Incompatible with a Politics of Liberty." *The Mises Institute* (Apr. 5, 2021). https://mises.org/wire/why-postmodernism-incompatible-politics-liberty.

——. "The Woke Hegemony: The ESG Index and The Woke Cartels." *Lotus Eaters* (Feb. 23, 2022). https://lotuseaters.com/the-woke-hegemony-the-esg-index-and-the-woke-cartels-23-02-22.

Richards, Charles M. "Ralph Cudworth (1617–1688)." *Internet Encyclopedia of Philosophy* (n.d.). https://iep.utm.edu/cudworth/.

Rid, Thomas. *Active Measures: The Secret History of Disinformation and Political Warfare.* New York: Farrar, Straus and Giroux, 2020.

Robins, Robert S., and Jerrold M. Post. *Political Paranoia: The Psychopolitics of Hatred.* New Haven, CT: Yale University Press, 1997.

Rosenbaum, Ron. *Explaining Hitler: The Search for the Origins of His Evil.* Boston, MA: Da Capo Press, 2014.

Ross, Colin A. *The C.I.A. Doctors: Human Rights Violations by American Psychiatrists.* Richardson, TX: Manitou Communications, 2006.

——. *The Trauma Model: A Solution to the Problem of Comorbidity in Psychiatry.* Richardson, TX: Manitou Communications, 2007.

Rosser, Barkley. "How Shocking Was Shock Therapy?" *Econospeak* (Jan. 9, 2019). https://econospeak.blogspot.com/2019/01/how-shocking-was-shock-therapy.html.

Rothbard, Murray N. *Conceived in Liberty.* 5 volumes. Auburn, AL: Mises Institute, 2011–2019 [1979]. https://mises.org/library/conceived-liberty-2.

Rubinstein, Alexander. "Did the CIA Pressure Yemen to Release al-Qaeda Propagandist Anwar al-Awlaki?" *The Grayzone* (Mar. 22, 2021). https://thegrayzone.com/2021/03/22/cia-yemen-al-qaeda-anwar-al-awlaki/.

Saint-Jean, Patrick. "Critical Race Theory and Catholicism Go Hand in Hand." *U.S. Catholic* (Jul. 20, 2021). https://uscatholic.org/articles/202107/critical-race-theory-and-catholicism-go-hand-in-hand/.

*Salekin, Randall T., Krista K. Trobst, and Maria Krioukova. "Construct Validity of Psychopathy in a Community Sample: A Nomological Net Approach." *Journal of Personality Disorders* 15, no. 5 (2001): 425–441. https://doi.org/10.1521/pedi.15.5.425.19196.

Sapolsky, Robert. *Behave: The Biology of Humans at Our Best and Worst.* New York: Penguin, 2017.

Satel, Sally. "Keep Social-Justice Indoctrination out of the Therapist's Office." *Quillette* (May 7, 2021). https://quillette.com/2021/05/07/keep-social-justice-indoctrination-out-of-the-therapists-office/.

Savenko, Yu. S., and A. Ya. Perekhov. "The State of Psychiatry in Russia." *Psychiatric Times* 31, no. 2 (2014). https://www.psychiatrictimes.com/view/state-psychiatry-russia.

Saxonberg, Steven. "Premodern Totalitarianism: The Case of Spain Compared to France." *Politics, Religion & Ideology* 20, no. 1 (2018): 21–41. https://doi.org/10.1080/21567689.2018.1554479.

Schmiedtová, Věra. "A Small Dictionary of Life under Communist Totalitarian Rule (Czechoslovakia 1948–1989)." *ResearchGate* (2014). https://www.researchgate.net/publication/277278644_A_small_dictionary_of_life_under_communist_totalitarian_rule_Czechoslovakia_1948-1989.

——. "What Did the Totalitarian Language in the Former Socialistic Czechoslovakia Look Like?" *ResearchGate* (no date). https://www.researchgate.net/publication/228548515_What_did_the_totalitarian_language_in_the_former_socialistic_Czechoslovakia_look_like.

Schreiber, Russell. *Gurdjieff's Transformational Psychology: The Art of Compassionate Self-Study.* Sebastopol, CA: Present Moment Press, 2013.

Schumaker, John F. *The Corruption of Reality: A Unified Theory of Religion, Hypnosis, and Psychopathology.* Amherst, NY: Prometheus Books, 1995.

Seabrook, John. "Suffering Souls: The Search for the Roots of Psychopath." *New Yorker* (Nov. 2, 2008). https://www.newyorker.com/magazine/2008/11/10/suffering-souls.

Sebestyen, Victor. *Lenin: The Man, the Dictator, and the Master of Terror.* New York: Pantheon, 2017.

Shafarevich, Igor. *The Socialist Phenomenon.* Foreword by Aleksandr Solzhenitsyn. Shawnee, KS: Gideon House Books, 2019 [1980].

Shahak, Israel. *Jewish History, Jewish Religion: The Weight of Three Thousand Years.* New edition. London: Pluto Press, 2008 [1994].

Sharlet, Jeff. *The Family: The Secret Fundamentalism at the Heart of American Power.* New York: Harper Perennial, 2009.

Sheldrake, Rupert. *Morphic Resonance: The Nature of Formative Causation.* 4th edition. Rochester, VT: Park Street Press, 2009 [1981].

Shrier, Abigail. "Book Banning in an Age of Amazon." abigailshrier.substack.com (Mar. 3, 2021). https://abigailshrier.substack.com/p/book-banning-in-an-age-of-amazon.

——. *Irreversible Damage: The Transgender Craze Seducing Our Daughters.* Washington, DC: Regnery Publishing, 2020.

Shriver, Lionel. *We Need to Talk About Kevin.* New York: Counterpoint, 2003.

Sibarium, Aaron. "American Bar Association Poised to Mandate Diversity Training, Affirmative Action at Law Schools." *Washington Free Beacon* (Aug. 19, 2021). https://freebeacon.com/campus/american-bar-association-poised-to-mandate-diversity-training-affirmative-action-at-law-schools/.

Simon, George K., Jr. *Character Disturbance: The Phenomenon of Our Age.* Chicago: Parkhurst Brothers, 2011.

——. *In Sheep's Clothing: Understanding and Dealing with Manipulative People.* 2nd edition. Chicago: Parkhurst Brothers, 2010.

Skea, Brian. "A Jungian Perspective on the Dissociability of the Self." *The Jung Page* (Jun. 2020, lecture delivered Feb. 1995). https://jungpage.org/learn/articles/analytical-psychology/802-a-jungian-perspective-on-the-dissociability-of-the-self.

Skuse, David H. "X-linked Genes and Mental Functioning." *Human Molecular Genetics* 14, no. 1 (2005): R27–R32. https://doi.org/10.1093/hmg/ddi112.

Slezkine, Yuri. *The House of Government: A Saga of the Russian Revolution.* Princeton, NJ: Princeton University Press, 2017.

Smith, M. L. R., and Niall McCrae. "From F Scale to Phobias: The Paradoxical Search for the Authoritarian Personality." *The European Conservative* (Aug. 12, 2021). https://europeanconservative.com/articles/essay/from-f-scale-to-phobias/.

Soh, Debra. *The End of Gender: Debunking the Myths about Sex and Identity in Our Society.* New York: Threshold Editions, 2020.

*Solzhenitsyn, Aleksandr. *The Gulag Archipelago: An Experiment in Literary Investigation.* 3 vols. New York: Harper & Row, 1973. [Reissue: New York: Harper Perennial, 2007.]

——. *The Gulag Archipelago.* Abridged edition. Foreword by Jordan B. Peterson. London: Vintage Classics, 2018.

Sowell, Thomas. *Marxism: Philosophy and Economics.* New York: Routledge, 2011.

Spence, Richard B. *Wall Street and the Russian Revolution: 1905–1925.* Waterville, OR: Trine Day, 2017.

Spencer, Robert. *The History of Jihad: From Muhammad to ISIS.* New York: Post Hill Press, 2019.

Springmann, J. Michael. *Visas for Al Qaeda: CIA Handouts That Rocked the World: An Insider's View.* Washington, DC: Daena Publications, 2015.

Spufford, Francis. *Red Plenty.* Minneapolis, MN: Graywolf Press, 2012.

Stohl, Cynthia, and Michael Stohl. "Clandestine/Hidden Organizations." In C.R. Scott et al., *The International Encyclopedia of Organizational Communication* (2016). https://doi.org/10.1002/9781118955567.wbieoc022.

Storck, Thomas. *An Economics of Justice and Charity: Catholic Social Teaching, Its Development and Contemporary Relevance.* Kettering,

OH: Angelico Press, 2017.

Stout, Martha. *The Myth of Sanity: Tales of Multiple Personality in Everyday Life.* New York: Penguin, 2001.

——. *Outsmarting the Sociopath Next Door: How to Protect Yourself against a Ruthless Manipulator.* New York: Harmony Books, 2020.

——. *The Paranoia Switch: How Terror Rewires Our Brains and Reshapes Our Behavior—and How We Can Reclaim Our Courage.* New York: Farrar, Straus and Giroux, 2007.

——. *The Sociopath Next Door: The Ruthless Versus the Rest of Us.* New York: Random House, 2005.

Strauss, William, and Neil Howe. *The Fourth Turning: An American Prophecy – What the Cycles of History Tell Us About America's Next Rendezvous with Destiny.* New York: Crown, 1997.

*Styczeń, Tadeusz SDS. *Wprowadzenie do etyki* [Introduction to Ethics]. Lublin: Towarzystwo Naukowe KUL, 1995.

Suffren, Sabrina, Valérie La Buissonnière-Ariza, Alan Tucholka, et al. "Prefrontal Cortex and Amygdala Anatomy in Youth with Persistent Levels of Harsh Parenting Practices and Subclinical Anxiety Symptoms over Time during Childhood." *Development and Psychopathology* (2021), 1–12. https://doi.org/10.1017/S0954579420001716.

Sutton, Antony C. *Wall Street and the Bolshevik Revolution: The Remarkable True Story of the American Capitalists Who Financed the Russian Communists.* Forest Row, UK: Clairview, 2012 [1974].

*Szasz, Thomas S. *The Ethics of Psychoanalysis: The Theory and Method of Autonomous Psychotherapy.* New York: Basic Books, 1965.

——. *The Manufacture of Madness: A Comparative Study of the Inquisition and the Mental Health Movement.* New York: Harper & Row, 1970.

*Szmaglewska, Seweryna. *Smoke over Birkenau.* Henry Holt, 1947.

Taibbi, Matt. "The Sovietization of the American Press." taibbi.substack.com (Mar. 12, 2021). https://taibbi.substack.com/p/the-sovietization-of-the-american.

Talmon, J. L. *The Origins of Totalitarian Democracy.* New York: Praeger, 1960.

*Taylor, Frederick Kräupl. *Psychopathology: Its Causes and Symptoms.* Baltimore: Johns Hopkins University Press, 1979.

Taylor, Steve. "The Problem of Pathocracy." *The Psychologist* 34 (Nov. 2021): 40–45. https://thepsychologist.bps.org.uk/volume-34/november-2021/problem-pathocracy.

——. "Toward a Utopian Society: From Disconnection and Disorder to Empathy and Harmony." *Journal of Humanistic Psychology* (Jun. 2021). https://doi.org/10.1177/00221678211025341.

*Thomas, Gordon, and Max Morgan-Witts. *Pontiff: The Vatican, the KGB, and the Year of the Three Popes.* New York: New American Library, 1984.

Thomson, Nicholas D. *Understanding Psychopathy: The Biopsychosocial Perspective.* New York: Routledge, 2019.

Tiihonen, Jari, Marja Koskuvi, Markku Lähteenvuo, et al. "Neurobiological Roots of Psychopathy." *Molecular Psychiatry* 25 (2020): 3432–3441. https://www.nature.com/articles/s41380-019-0488-z.

Tillier, William. *Personality Development through Positive Disintegration: The Work of Kazimierz Dąbrowski.* Anna Maria, FL: Maurice Bassett, 2018.

Tismaneanu, Vladimir. *The Devil in History: Communism, Fascism, and Some Lessons of the Twentieth Century.* Berkeley and Los Angeles, CA: University of California Press, 2012

Todes, Daniel P. *Ivan Pavlov: A Russian Life in Science.* New York: Oxford University Press, 2014.

Torańska, Teresa. *"Them": Stalin's Polish Puppets.* Translated by Agnieszka Kołakowska. New York: Harper & Row, 1987.

Triebwasser, Joseph, Eran Chemerinski, Panos Roussos, and Larry J. Siever. "Schizoid Personality Disorder." *Journal of Personality Disorders* 26, no. 6 (2013). https://doi.org/10.1521/pedi.2012.26.6.919.

Turchin, Peter. *Ages of Discord; A Structural-Demographic Analysis of American History.* Chaplin, CT: Beresta Books, 2016.

——. "The Ginkgo Model of Societal Crisis." *Cliodynamica* (Aug. 16, 2018). https://peterturchin.com/cliodynamica/the-ginkgo-model-of-societal-crisis/.

——. "The Prophecy of the Fourth Turning." *Cliodynamica* (Nov. 6, 2017). https://peterturchin.com/cliodynamica/prophecy-fourth-turning/.

——. *War and Peace and War: The Rise and Fall of Empires.* New York: Pi Press, 2006.

Turchin, Peter, and Andrey Korotayev. "The 2010 Structural-demographic Forecast for the 2010–2020 Decade: A Retrospective Assessment." *PLoS One* 15, no. 8 (2020): e0237458. https://doi.org/10.1371/journal.pone.0237458.

Turchin, Peter, and Sergey A. Nefedov. *Secular Cycles.* Princeton, NJ: Princeton University Press, 2009.

Twenge, Jean W., and W. Keith Campbell. *The Narcissism Epidemic: Living in the Age of Entitlement.* New York: Atria, 2013.

Tyrer, Peter. "New Approaches to the Diagnosis of Psychopathy and Personality Disorder." *Journal of the Royal Society of Medicine* 97 (2004): 371–74. https://doi.org/10.1002/pmh.78.

——. "Why Borderline Personality Disorder is Neither Borderline Nor a Personality Disorder." *Personality* 3, no. 2 (2009): 86-95. https://doi.org/10.1002/pmh.78.

Ullrich, Volker. *Hitler: Ascent 1889–1939.* New York: Vintage, 2017.

——. *Hitler: Downfall 1939–1945.* New York: Knopf, 2020.

Valentine, Douglas. *The CIA as Organized Crime: How Illegal Operations Corrupt America and the World.* Atlanta, GA: Clarity Press, 2017.

Vatlin, Alexander. *Agents of Terror: Ordinary Men and Extraordinary Violence in Stalin's Secret Police.* Madison, WI: University of Wisconsin Press, 2016.

Versluis, Arthur. *The Mystical State: Politics, Gnosis, and Emergent Cultures.* Minneapolis, MN: New Cultures Press, 2011.

——. *The New Inquisitions: Heretic-Hunting and the Intellectual Origins of Modern Totalitarianism.* New York: Oxford University Press, 2006.

Viola, Lynne. *Stalinist Perpetrators on Trial: Scenes from the Great Terror in Soviet Ukraine.* New York: Oxford University Press, 2017.

Volkert, Jana, Thorsten-Christian Gablonski, and Sven Rabung. "Prevalence of Personality Disorders in the General Adult Population in Western Countries: Systematic Review and Meta-analysis." *British Journal of Psychiatry* 213, no. 6 (2018): 709–15. https://doi.org/10.1192/bjp.2018.202.

von Lang, Jochen. *The Secretary: Martin Bormann – The Man Who Manipulated Hitler.* New York: Random House, 1979.

Voslensky, Michael. *Nomenklatura: The Soviet Ruling Class.* Preface by Milovan Djilas. New York: Doubleday, 1984.

Vysotsky, Stanislav. *American Antifa: The Tactics, Culture, and Practice of Militant Antifascism.* New York: Routledge, 2021.

Waite, Robert G. L. *The Psychopathic God: Adolf Hitler.* Amherst, NY: Da Capo Press, 1993.

Walker, Ian, dir. *I, Psychopath.* 2009; Film Ideas, Inc.

Wasilewski, Marian (with Andrzej Łobaczewski). "The Ponerology." Interview from 1984. http://web.archive.org/web/20180405230609/http://marian-wasilewski.pl/the-ponorelogy/.

Weikart, Richard. *Hitler's Religion: The Twisted Beliefs that Drove the Third Reich.* Washington, DC: Regnery History, 2016.

Weisberg, Susan Shoshana. "Diphtheria." *Disease-a-Month* 53, no. 9 (2007): 430–434. https://doi.org/10.1016/j.disamonth.2007.09.003.

——. "Mumps." *Disease-a-Month* 53, no. 10 (2007): 484–487. https://doi.org/10.1016/j.disamonth.2007.09.011.

West, John G. "The Rise of Totalitarian Science, 2022 Edition." *Evolution News and Science Today* (Jan. 31, 2022). https://evolutionnews.org/2022/01/the-rise-of-totalitarian-science-2022-edition/.

Widiger, Thomas A., and Paul T. Costa Jr. (eds.). *Personality Disorders and the Five-Factor Model of Personality.* 3rd edition. Washington, DC: American Psychological Association, 2013.

Wierzbicka, Anna. "Antitotalitarian Language in Poland: Some Mechanisms of Linguistic Self-Defense." Language in Society 19, no. 1 (1990): 1-–59. https://doi.org/10.1017/S004740450001410X.

*Wilson, Colin. *A Criminal History of Mankind.* New York: Carroll & Graf, 1984.

Wilson, Timothy D. *Strangers to Ourselves: Discovering the Adaptive Unconscious.* Cambridge, MA: Belknap Press, 2004.

Windholz, George. "Pavlov's Conceptualization of Paranoia Within the Theory of Higher Nervous Activity." *History of Psychiatry* 7, no. 25 (1996): 159–66. https://doi.org/10.1177/0957154x9600702508.

——. "Pavlov's Religious Orientation." *Journal for the Scientific Study of Religion* 25, no. 3 (1986): 320–327. https://doi.org/10.2307/1386296.

Winn, Denise. *The Manipulated Mind: Brainwashing, Conditioning and Indoctrination.* Cambridge, MA: Malor Books, 2000.

Winsper, Catherine, Ayten Bilgin, Andrew Thompson, Steven Marwaha, et al. "The Prevalence of Personality Disorders in the Community: A Global Systematic Review and Meta-analysis." *British Journal of Psychiatry* 216, no. 2 (2019). https://doi.org/10.1192/bjp.2019.166.

Wolf, Naomi. *The End of America: Letter of Warning to a Young Patriot.* White River Junction, VT: Chelsea Green Publishing, 2007.

——. "We've Reached 'Step Ten' of the 10 Steps to Fascism." *The Defender* (Mar. 5, 2021). https://childrenshealthdefense.org/defender/naomi-wolf-steps-to-fascism/.

Wolfe, Bertram D. *Communist Totalitarianism: Keys to the Soviet System.* Boston: Beacon Press, 1961. https://archive.org/details/communisttotalit012301mbp/.

——. *Marxism: One Hundred Years in the Life of a Doctrine.* New York: Doubleday, 1965.

——. *Three Who Made a Revolution: A Biographical History.* New York: Dial Press, 1948. https://archive.org/details/in.ernet.dli.2015.276141.

Wolin, Sheldon S. *Democracy Incorporated: Managed Democracy and the Specter of Inverted Totalitarianism.* Princeton, NJ: Princeton University Press, 2017 [2008].

Woodard, Colin. *American Nations: A History of the Eleven Rival Regional Cultures of North America.* New York: Penguin, 2012.

Wright, Lawrence. *Going Clear: Scientology, Hollywood, and the Prison of Belief.* New York: Vintage, 2013.

Wu Wenyuan. "Mao's Red Guards and America's Justice Warriors." *Minding the Campus* (Oct. 4, 2021). https://www.mindingthecampus.org/2021/10/04/maos-red-guards-and-americas-justice-warriors/.

Xiao Li. "America's Cultural Revolution Is Just Like Mao's." *UnHerd* (Jul. 6, 2020). https://unherd.com/2020/07/americas-cultural-revolution-is-familiar-to-the-chinese/.

Young, John Wesley. *Totalitarian Language: Orwell's Newspeak and its Nazi and Communist Antecedents.* Charlottesville: University Press of Virginia, 1991.

Yuriev, Alexander I. "About Psychology and Psychotherapy of the Times of Globalization." *Journal of Modern Education Review* 3, no. 8 (2013): 618–624. https://www.academia.edu/download/58363034/5___Issue_8_of_2013_State_of_Affairs_of_Higher_Education_in_Costa_Rica.pdf.

Zimbardo, Philip. *The Lucifer Effect: Understanding How Good People Turn Evil.* New York: Random House, 2008.

Ziskind, Eugene, and Esther Somerfield-Ziskind. "In Memoriam: Peter Jacob Frostig, 1896–1959." *American Journal of Psychiatry* 117 (November 1960): 479–480. https://doi.org/10.1176/ajp.117.5.479.

NAME INDEX

GENERAL INDEX

ABOUT THE AUTHOR

Andrew M. Lobaczewski (1921–2007) grew up on a rural estate in the beautiful piedmountain region of Poland. During the Nazi occupation he worked on the farm and as an apiarist, then as a soldier of the Home Army, the underground Polish resistance. After the Soviet invasion, the authorities confiscated the estate and evicted Lobaczewski's family.

While working for a living, he studied psychology at Jagiellonian University in Krakow. Conditions under Communist rule turned his attention to matters of psychopathology, especially to the role of psychopathic persons in such a system. He was not the first such researcher; an underground network of scientists of the older generation began the work, but was soon broken up by the secret police.

Dr. Lobaczewski improved his skills in clinical diagnosis and psychotherapy working in mental and general hospitals, and the open mental health service. He was forced to emigrate in 1977 after the political authorities suspected he knew too much about the pathological nature of their rule. In the USA he became a target of Communist agents of intrigue, foreign and domestic. Despite hardship, he completed his book, *Political Ponerology*, in New York in 1984, but was unable to have it published. During this time he completed a draft of a second book, *Logocracy*.

With broken health, he returned to Poland in 1990 under the care of doctors, his old friends. His condition improved gradually, and he was able to complete another book on psychotherapy and socio-psychology, *Word Surgery*, and see his two previous books published in Polish. He passed away in 2007.

CPSIA information can be obtained
at www.ICGtesting.com
Printed in the USA
BVHW070759231222
654910BV00012B/1361